Systematic Theology
Volume 3 - The Doctrine of Salvation

By Augustus Hopkins Strong, D.D., LL.D.
President and Professor of Biblical Theology in the Rochester Theological Seminary
Edited by Anthony Uyl

Devoted Publishing
Woodstock, Ontario, 2017

Systematic Theology: Volume III - The Doctrine of Salvation

A Compendium and Commonplace-Book
Designed For The Use Of Theological Students

By Augustus Hopkins Strong, D.D., LL.D. (1836-1921)
President and Professor of Biblical Theology in the Rochester Theological Seminary
Edited by Anthony Uyl

Revised and Enlarged

The Griffith & Rowland Press; Philadelphia

Originally Published in 1909

Published in Woodstock, Ontario, Canada 2017.

For bulk educational rates, please contact us at the above email address.

ISBN: 978-1-77356-041-0

Table of Contents

"THE EYE SEES ONLY THAT WHICH IT BRINGS WITH IT THE POWER OF SEEING."—Cicero.

"OPEN THOU MINE EYES, THAT I MAY BEHOLD WONDROUS THINGS OUT OF THY LAW."—Psalm 119:18.

"FOR WITH THEE IS THE FOUNTAIN OF LIFE: IN THY LIGHT SHALL WE SEE LIGHT."—Psalm 36:9.

"FOR WE KNOW IN PART, AND WE PROPHESY IN PART; BUT WHEN THAT WHICH IS PERFECT IS COME, THAT WHICH IS IN PART SHALL BE DONE AWAY."—1 Cor. 13:9, 10.

PART VI - SOTERIOLOGY, OR THE DOCTRINE OF SALVATION THROUGH THE WORK OF CHRIST AND OF THE HOLY SPIRIT

Chapter II - The Reconciliation Of Man To God, Or The Application Of Redemption Through The Work Of The Holy Spirit

Section I —The Application Of Christ's Redemption In Its Preparation

(a) In this Section we treat of Election and Calling; Section Second being devoted to the Application of Christ's Redemption in its Actual Beginning,—namely, in Union with Christ, Regeneration, Conversion, and Justification; while Section Third has for its subject the Application of Christ's Redemption in its Continuation,—namely, in Sanctification and Perseverance.

The arrangement of topics, in the treatment of the reconciliation of man to God, is taken from Julius Müller, Proof-texts, 35. "Revelation to us aims to bring about revelation in us. In any being absolutely perfect, God's intercourse with us by faculty, and by direct teaching, would absolutely coalesce, and the former be just as much God's voice as the latter" (Hutton, Essays).

(b) In treating Election and Calling as applications of Christ's redemption, we imply that they are, in God's decree, logically subsequent to that redemption. In this we hold the Sublapsarian view, as distinguished from the Supralapsarianism of Beza and other hyper- Calvinists, which regarded the decree of individual salvation as preceding, in the order of thought, the decree to permit the Fall. In this latter scheme, the order of decrees is as follows: 1. the decree to save certain, and to reprobate others; 2. the decree to create both those who are to be saved and those who are to be reprobated; 3. the decree to permit both the former and the latter to fall; 4. the decree to provide salvation only for the former, that is, for the elect.

Richards, Theology, 302-307, shows that Calvin, while in his early work, the Institutes, he avoided definite statements of his position with regard to the extent of the atonement, yet in his latter works, the Commentaries, acceded to the theory of universal atonement. Supralapsarianism is therefore hyper-Calvinistic, rather than Calvinistic. Sublapsarianism was adopted by the Synod of Dort (1618, 1619). By Supralapsarian is meant that form of doctrine which holds the decree of individual salvation as preceding the decree to permit the Fall; Sublapsarian designates that form of doctrine which holds that the decree of individual salvation is subsequent to the decree to permit the Fall.

The progress in Calvin's thought may be seen by comparing some of his earlier with his later utterances. Institutes, 2:23:5—"I say, with Augustine, that the Lord created those who, as he certainly foreknew, were to go to destruction, and he did so because he so willed." But even then in the Institutes, 3:23:8, he affirms that "the perdition of the wicked depends upon the divine predestination in such a manner that the cause and matter of it are found in themselves. Man falls by the appointment of divine providence, but he falls by his own fault." God's blinding, hardening, turning the sinner he describes as the consequence of the divine desertion, not the divine causation. The relation of God to the origin of sin is not efficient, but permissive. In later days Calvin wrote in his Commentary on 1 John 2:2—"he is the propitiation for our sins; and not for ours only, but also for the whole world"—as follows: "Christ suffered for the sins of the whole world, and in the goodness of God is offered unto all men without distinction, his blood being shed not for a part of the world only, but for the whole human race; for although in the world nothing is found worthy of the favor of God, yet he holds out the propitiation to the whole world, since without exception he summons all to the faith of Christ, which is nothing else than the door unto hope."

Although other passages, such as Institutes, 3:21:5, and 3:23:1, assert the harsher view, we must give Calvin credit for modifying his doctrine with maturer reflection and advancing years. Much that is called Calvinism would have been repudiated by Calvin himself even at the beginning of his career, and is really the exaggeration of his teaching by more scholastic and less religious successors. Renan calls Calvin "the most Christian man of his generation." Dorner describes him as "equally great in intellect and character, lovely in social life, full of tender sympathy and faithfulness to his friends, yielding and forgiving toward personal offences." The device upon his seal is a flaming heart from which is stretched forth a helping hand.

Calvin's share in the burning of Servetus must be explained by his mistaken zeal for God's truth and by the universal belief of his time that this truth was to be defended by the civil power. The following is the inscription on the expiatory monument which European Calvinists raised to Servetus: "On October 27, 1553, died at the stake at Champel, Michael Servetus, of Villeneuve d'Aragon, born September 29, 1511. Reverent and grateful sons of Calvin, our great Reformer, but condemning an error which was that of his age, and steadfastly adhering to liberty of conscience according to the true principles of the Reformation and of the gospel, we have erected this expiatory monument, on the 27th of October, 1903."

John DeWitt, in Princeton Theol. Rev., Jan. 1904:95—"Take John Calvin. That fruitful conception—more fruitful in church and state than any other conception which has held the English speaking world—of the absolute and universal sovereignty of the holy God, as a revolt from the conception then prevailing of the sovereignty of the human head of an earthly church, was historically the mediator and instaurator of his spiritual career." On Calvin's theological position, see Shedd, Dogm. Theol., 1:409, note.

(c) But the Scriptures teach that men as sinners, and not men irrespective of their sins, are the objects of God's saving grace in Christ (John 15:9; Rom. 11:5, 7; Eph. 1:4-6; 1 Pet. 1:2). Condemnation, moreover, is an act, not of sovereignty, but of justice, and is grounded in the guilt of the condemned (Rom. 2:6-11; 2 Thess. 1:5-10). The true order of the decrees is therefore as follows: 1. the decree to create; 2. the decree to permit the Fall; 3. the decree to provide a salvation in Christ sufficient for the needs of all; 4. the decree to secure the actual acceptance of this salvation on the part of some,—or, in other words, the decree of Election.

That saving grace presupposes the Fall, and that men as sinners are the objects of it, appears from John 15:19—"If ye were of the world, the world would love its own: but because ye are not of the world, but I chose you out of the world, therefore the world hateth you"; Rom. 11:5-7—"Even so then at this present time also there is a remnant according to the election of grace. But if it is by grace, it is no more of works: otherwise grace is no more grace. What then? That which Israel seeketh for, that he obtained not; but the election obtained it, and the rest were hardened." Eph. 1:4-6—"even as he chose us in him before the foundation of the world, that we should be holy and without blemish before him in love: having foreordained us unto adoption as sons through Jesus Christ unto himself, according to the good pleasure of his will, to the praise of the glory of his grace, which he freely bestowed on us in the Beloved"; 1 Pet. 1:2—elect, "according to the foreknowledge of God the Father, in sanctification of the Spirit, unto obedience and sprinkling of the blood of Jesus: Grace to you and peace be multiplied."

That condemnation is not an act of sovereignty, but of justice, appears from Rom. 2:6-9—"who will render to every man according to his works ... wrath and indignation ... upon every soul of man that worketh evil"; 2 Thess. 1:6-9—"a righteous thing with God to recompense affliction to them that afflict you ... rendering vengeance to them that know not God and to them that obey not the gospel of our Lord Jesus: who shall suffer punishment." Particular persons are elected, not to have Christ die for them, but to have special influences of the Spirit bestowed upon them.

(d) Those Sublapsarians who hold to the Anselmic view of a limited Atonement, make the decrees 3. and 4., just mentioned, exchange places,—the decree of election thus preceding the decree to provide redemption. The Scriptural reasons for preferring the order here given have been already indicated in our treatment of the extent of the Atonement (pages 771-773).

When "3" and "4" thus change places, "3" should be made to read: "The decree to provide in Christ a salvation sufficient for the elect"; and "4" should read: "The decree that a certain number should be saved,—or, in other words, the decree of Election." Sublapsarianism of the first sort may be found in Turretin, loc. 4, quæs. 9; Cunningham, Hist. Theol., 416-439. A. J. F. Behrends: "The divine decree is our last word in theology, not our first word. It represents the terminus ad quem, not the terminus a quo. Whatever comes about in the exercise of human freedom and of divine grace—that God has decreed." Yet we must grant that Calvinism needs to be supplemented by a more express statement of God's love for the world. Herrick Johnson: "Across the Westminster Confession could justly be written: 'The Gospel for the elect only.' That Confession was written under the absolute dominion of one idea, the doctrine of predestination. It does not contain one of three truths: God's love for a lost world; Christ's compassion for a lost world, and the gospel universal for a lost world."

I. Election

Election is that eternal act of God, by which in his sovereign pleasure, and on account of no foreseen merit in them, he chooses certain out of the number of sinful men to be the recipients of the special grace of his Spirit, and so to be made voluntary partakers of Christ's salvation.

1. Proof of the Doctrine of Election.

A. From Scripture.

We here adopt the words of Dr. Hovey: "The Scriptures forbid us to find the reasons for election in the moral action of man before the new birth, and refer us merely to the sovereign will and mercy of God; that is, they teach the doctrine of personal election." Before advancing to the proof of the doctrine itself, we may claim Scriptural warrant for three preliminary statements (which we also quote from Dr. Hovey), namely:

First, that "God has a sovereign right to bestow more grace upon one subject than upon another,—grace being unmerited favor to sinners."

Mat. 20:12-15—"These last have spent but one hour, and thou hast made them equal unto us.... Friend, I do thee no wrong.... Is it not lawful for me to do what I will with mine own?" Rom. 9:20, 21—"Shall the thing formed say to him that formed it, Why didst thou make me thus? Or hath not the potter a right over the clay, from the same lump to make one part a vessel unto honor, and another unto dishonor?"

Secondly, that "God has been pleased to exercise this right in dealing with men."

Ps. 147:20—"He hath not dealt so with any nation; And as for his ordinances, they have not known them". Rom. 3:1, 2—"What advantage then hath the Jew? or what is the profit of circumcision? Much every way: first of all, that they were intrusted with the oracles of God"; John 15:16—"Ye did not choose me, but I chose you, and appointed you, that ye should go and bear fruit"; Acts 9:15—"he is a chosen vessel unto me, to bear my name before the Gentiles and kings, and the children of Israel."

Thirdly, that "God has some other reason than that of saving as many as possible for the way in which he distributes his grace." n

Mat. 11:21—Tyre and Sidon "would have repented," if they had had the grace bestowed upon Chorazin and Bethsaida; Rom. 9:22-25—"What if God, willing to show his wrath, and to make his power known, endured with much longsuffering vessels of wrath fitted unto destruction: and that he might make known the riches of his glory upon vessels of mercy, which he afore prepared unto glory?"

The Scripture passages which directly or indirectly support the doctrine of a particular election of individual men to salvation may be arranged as follows:

(a) Direct statements of God's purpose to save certain individuals:

Jesus speaks of God's elect, as for example in Mark 13:27—"then shall he send forth the angels, and shall gather together his elect"; Luke 18:7—"shall not God avenge his elect, that cry to him day and night?"

Acts 13:48—"as many as were ordained (τεταγμένοι) to eternal life believed"—here Whedon translates: "disposed unto eternal life," referring to κατηρτισμένα in verse 23, where "fitted" = "fitted themselves." The only instance, however, where τάσσω is used in a middle sense is in 1 Cor. 16:15—"set themselves"; but there the object, ἑαυτούς, is expressed. Here we must compare Rom. 13:1—"the powers that be are ordained (τεταγμέναι) of God"; see also Acts 10:42—"this is he who is ordained (ὡρισμένος) of God to be the Judge of the living and the dead."

Rom. 9:11-16—"for the children being not yet born, neither having done anything good or bad, that the purpose of God according to election might stand, not of works, but of him that calleth.... I will have mercy upon whom I have mercy.... So then it is not of him that willeth, nor of him that runneth, but of God that hath mercy"; Eph. 1:4, 5, 9, 11—"chose us in him before the foundation of the world, [not because we were, or were to be, holy, but] that we should be holy and without blemish before him in love: having foreordained us unto adoption as sons through Jesus Christ unto himself, according to the good pleasure of his will ... the mystery of his will, according to his good pleasure ... in whom also we were made a heritage, having been foreordained according to the purpose of him who worketh all things after the counsel of his will"; Col. 3:12—"God's elect"; 2 Thess. 2:13—"God chose you from the beginning unto salvation in sanctification of the Spirit and belief of the truth."

(b) In connection with the declaration of God's foreknowledge of these persons, or choice to make them objects of his special attention and care;

Rom. 8:27-30—"called according to his purpose. For whom he foreknew, he also foreordained to be conformed to the image of his Son"; 1 Pet. 1:1, 2—"elect ... according to the foreknowledge of God the Father, in sanctification of the Spirit, unto obedience and sprinkling of the blood of Jesus Christ." On the passage in Romans, Shedd, in his Commentary, remarks that "foreknew," in the Hebraistic use, "is more than simple prescience, and something more also than simply 'to fix the eye upon,' or to 'select.' It is this latter, but with the additional notion of a benignant and kindly feeling toward the object." In Rom. 8:27-30, Paul is emphasizing the divine sovereignty. The Christian life is considered from the side of the divine care and ordering, and not from the side of human choice and volition. Alexander, Theories of the Will, 87, 88—"If Paul is here advocating indeterminism, it is strange that in chapter 9 he should be at pains to answer objections to determinism. The apostle's protest in chapter 9 is not against predestination and determination, but against the man who regards such a theory as impugning the righteousness of God."

That the word "know," in Scripture, frequently means not merely to "apprehend intellectually," but to "regard with favor," to "make an object of care," is evident from Gen. 18:19—"I have known him, to the end that he may command his children and his household after him, that they may keep the way of Jehovah, to do righteousness and justice"; Ex. 2:25—"And God saw the children of Israel, and God took knowledge of them"; cf. verse 24—"God heard their groaning, and God remembered his covenant with Abraham, with Isaac, and with Jacob"; Ps. 1:6—"For Jehovah knoweth the way of the righteous; But the way of the wicked shall perish"; 101:4, marg.—"I will know no evil person"; Hosea 13:5—"I did know thee in the wilderness, in the land of great drought. According to their pasture, so were they filled"; Nahum 1:7—"he knoweth them that take refuge in him"; Amos 3:2—"You only have I known of all the families of the earth"; Mat. 7:23—"then will I profess unto them, I never knew you"; Rom. 7:15—"For that which I do I know not"; 1 Cor. 8:3—"if any man loveth God, the same is known by him"; Gal. 4:9—"now that ye have come to know God, or rather, to be known by God"; 1 Thess. 5:12, 13—"we beseech you, brethren, to know them that labor among you, and are over you in the Lord, and admonish you; and to esteem them exceeding highly in love for their work's sake." So the word "foreknow": Rom. 11:2—"God did not cast off his people whom he foreknew"; 1 Pet. 1:20—Christ, "who was foreknown indeed before the foundation of the world."

Broadus on Mat. 7:23—"I never knew you"—says; "Not in all the passages quoted above, nor elsewhere, is there occasion for the oft-repeated arbitrary notion, derived from the Fathers, that 'know' conveys the additional idea of approve or regard. It denotes acquaintance, with all its pleasures and advantages; 'knew,' i. e., as mine, as my people."

But this last admission seems to grant what Broadus had before denied. See Thayer, Lex. N. T., on γινώσκω: "With acc. of person, to recognize as worthy of intimacy and love; so those whom God has judged worthy of the blessings of the gospel are said ὑπὸ τοῦ θεοῦ γινώσκεσθαι (1 Cor. 8:3; Gal. 4:9); negatively in the sentence of Christ: οὐδέποτε ἔγνων ὑμᾶς, 'I never knew you,' never had any acquaintance with you." On προγινώσκω, Rom. 8:29—οὓς προέγνω, "whom he foreknew," see Denney, in Expositor's Greek Testament, in loco: "Those whom he foreknew—in what sense? as persons who would answer his love with love? This is at least irrelevant, and alien to Paul's general method of thought. That salvation begins with God, and begins in eternity, are fundamental ideas with him, which he here applies to Christians, without raising any of the problems involved in the relation of the human will to the divine. Yet we may be sure that προέγνω has the pregnant sense that γινώσκω often has in Scripture, e. g., in Ps. 1:6; Amos 3:2; hence we may render: 'those of whom God took knowledge from eternity' (Eph. 1:4)."

In Rom. 8:28-30, quoted above, "foreknew" = elected—that is, made certain individuals, in the future, the objects of his love and care; "foreordained" describes God's designation of these same individuals to receive the special gift of salvation. In other words, "foreknowledge" is of persons: "foreordination" is of blessings to be bestowed upon them. Hooker, Eccl. Pol., appendix to book v. (vol. 2:751)—" 'whom he did foreknow' (know before as his own, with determination to be forever merciful to them) 'he also predestinated to be conformed to the image of his Son'—predestinated, not to opportunity of conformation, but to conformation itself." So, for substance, Calvin, Rückert, DeWette, Stuart, Jowett, Vaughan. On 1 Pet. 1:1, 2, see Com. of Plumptre. The Arminian interpretation of "whom he foreknew" (Rom. 8:29) would require the phrase "as conformed to the image of his Son" to be conjoined with it. Paul, however, makes conformity to Christ to be the result, not the foreseen condition, of God's foreordination; see Commentaries of Hodge and Lange.

(c) With assertions that this choice is matter of grace, or unmerited favor, bestowed in eternity past:

Eph. 1:5-8—"foreordained ... according to the good pleasure of his will, to the praise of the glory of his grace, which he freely bestowed on us in the Beloved ... according to the riches of his grace"; 2:8—"by grace have ye been saved through faith; and that not of yourselves, it is the gift of God"—here "and that" (neuter τοῦτο, verse 8) refers, not to "faith" but to "salvation." But faith is elsewhere represented as having its source in God,—see page 782, (k). 2 Tim. 1:9—"his own purpose and grace, which was given us in Christ Jesus before times eternal." Election is not because of our merit. McLaren: "God's own mercy, spontaneous, undeserved, condescending, moved him. God is his own motive. His love is not drawn out by our loveableness, but wells up, like an artesian spring, from the depths of his nature."

(d) That the Father has given certain persons to the Son, to be his peculiar possession:

John 6:37—"All that which the Father giveth me shall come unto me"; 17:2—"that whatsoever thou hast given him, to them he should give eternal life"; 6—"I manifested thy name unto the men whom thou gavest me out of the world: thine they were, and thou gavest them to me"; 9—"I pray not for the world, but for those whom thou hast given me"; Eph. 1:14—"unto the redemption of God's own possession"; 1 Pet. 2:9—"a people for God's own possession."

(e) That the fact of believers being united thus to Christ is due wholly to God:

John 6:44—"No man can come to me, except the Father that sent me draw him"; 10:26—"ye believe not, because ye are not of my sheep"; 1 Cor. 1:30—"of him [God] are ye in Christ Jesus" = your being, as Christians, in union with Christ, is due wholly to God.

(f) That those who are written in the Lamb's book of life, and they only, shall be saved:

Phil. 4:3—"the rest of my fellow-workers, whose names are in the book of life"; Rev. 20:15—"And if any was not found written in the book of life, he was cast into the lake of fire"; 21:27—"there shall in no wise enter into it anything unclean ... but only they that are written in the Lamb's book of life" = God's decrees of electing grace in Christ.

(g) That these are allotted, as disciples, to certain of God's servants:

Acts 17:4—(literally)—"some of them were persuaded, and were allotted [by God] to Paul and Silas"—as disciples (so Meyer and Grimm); 18:9, 10—"Be not afraid, but speak and hold not thy peace: for I am with thee, and no man shall set on thee to harm thee: for I have much people in this city."

(h) Are made the recipients of a special call of God:

Rom. 8:28, 30—"called according to his purpose ... whom he foreordained, them he also called"; 9:23, 24—"vessels of mercy, which he afore prepared unto glory, even us, whom he also called, not from the Jews only, but also from the Gentiles"; 11:29—"for the gifts and the calling of God are not repented of"; 1 Cor. 1:24-29—"unto them that are called ... Christ the power of God, and the wisdom of God.... For behold your calling, brethren, ... the things that are despised, did God choose, yea and the things that are not, that he might bring to naught the things that are: that no flesh should glory before God"; Gal. 1:15, 16—"when it was the good pleasure of God, who separated me, even from my mother's womb, and called me through his grace, to reveal his Son in me"; cf. James 2:23—"and he [Abraham] was called [to be] the friend of God."

(i) Are born into God's kingdom, not by virtue of man's will, but of God's will:

John 1:13—"born, not of blood, nor of the will of the flesh, nor of the will of man, but of God"; James 1:18—"Of his own will he brought us forth by the word of truth"; 1 John 4:10—"Herein is love, not that we loved God, but that he loved us." S. S. Times, Oct. 14, 1899—"The law of love is the expression of God's loving nature, and it is only by our participation of the divine nature that we are enabled to render it obedience. 'Loving God,' says Bushnell, 'is but letting God love us.' So John's great saying may be rendered in the present tense: 'not that we love God, but that he loves us.' Or, as Madame Guyon sings: 'I love my God, but with no love of mine, For I have none to give; I love thee, Lord, but all the love is thine, For by thy life I live'."

(j) Receiving repentance, as the gift of God:

Acts 5:31—"Him did God exalt with his right hand to be a Prince and a Savior, to give repentance to Israel, and remission of sins"; 11:18—"Then to the Gentiles also hath God granted repentance unto life"; 2 Tim. 2:25—"correcting them that oppose themselves; if peradventure God may give them repentance unto the knowledge of the truth." Of course it is true that God might give repentance simply by inducing man to repent by the agency of his word, his providence and his Spirit. But more than this seems to be meant when the Psalmist prays: "Create in me a clean heart, O God; And renew a right spirit within me" (Ps. 51:10).

(k) Faith, as the gift of God:

John 6:65—"no man can come unto me, except it be given unto him of the Father"; Acts 15:8, 9—"God ... giving them the Holy Spirit ... cleansing their hearts by faith"; Rom. 12:3—"according as God hath dealt to each man a measure of faith"; 1 Cor. 12:9—"to another faith, in the same Spirit"; Gal. 5:22—"the fruit of the Spirit is ... faith" (A. V.); Phil. 2:13—In all faith, "it is God who worketh in you both to will and to work, for his good pleasure"; Eph. 6:23—"Peace be to the brethren, and love with faith, from God the Father and the Lord Jesus Christ"; John 3:8—"The Spirit breatheth where he wills, and thou [as a consequence] hearest his voice" (so Bengel); see A. J. Gordon, Ministry of the Spirit, 166; 1 Cor. 12:3—"No man can say, Jesus is Lord, but in the Holy Spirit"—but calling Jesus "Lord" is an essential part of faith,—faith therefore is the work of the Holy Spirit; Tit. 1:1—"the faith of God's elect"—election is not in consequence of faith, but faith is in consequence of election (Ellicott). If they get their faith of themselves, then salvation is not due to grace. If God gave the faith, then it was in his purpose, and this is election.

(l) Holiness and good works, as the gift of God.

Eph. 1:4—"chose us in him before the foundation of the world, that we should be holy"; 2:9, 10—"not of works, that no man should glory. For we are his workmanship, created in Christ Jesus for good works, which God afore prepared that we should walk in them"; 1 Pet. 1:2—elect "unto obedience." On Scripture testimony, see Hovey, Manual of Theol. and Ethics, 258-261; also art. on Predestination, by Warfield, in Hastings' Dictionary of the Bible.

These passages furnish an abundant and conclusive refutation, on the one hand, of the Lutheran view that election is simply God's determination from eternity to provide an objective salvation for universal humanity; and, on the other hand, of the Arminian view that election is God's determination from eternity to save certain individuals upon the ground of their foreseen faith.

Roughly stated, we may say that Schleiermacher elects all men subjectively; Lutherans all men objectively; Arminians all believers; Augustinians all foreknown as God's own. Schleiermacher held that decree logically precedes foreknowledge, and that election is individual, not national. But he made election to include all men, the only difference between them being that of earlier or of later conversion. Thus in his system Calvinism and Restorationism go hand in hand. Murray, in Hastings' Bible Dictionary, seems to take this view.

Lutheranism is the assertion that original grace preceded original sin, and that the Quia Voluit of Tertullian and of Calvin was based on wisdom, in Christ. The Lutheran holds that the believer is simply the non-resistant subject of common grace; while the Arminian holds that the believer is the coöperant subject of common grace. Lutheranism enters more fully than Calvinism into the nature of faith. It thinks more of the human agency, while Calvinism thinks more of the divine purpose. It thinks more of the church, while Calvinism thinks more of Scripture. The Arminian conception is that God has appointed men to salvation, just as he has appointed them to condemnation, in view of their dispositions and acts. As Justification is in view of present faith, so the Arminian regards Election as taking place in view of future faith. Arminianism must reject the doctrine of regeneration as well as that of election, and must in both cases make the act of man precede the act of God.

All varieties of view may be found upon this subject among theologians. John Milton, in his Christian Doctrine, holds that "there is no particular predestination or election, but only general.... There can be no reprobation of individuals from all eternity." Archbishop Sumner: "Election is predestination of communities and nations to external knowledge and to the privileges of the gospel." Archbishop Whately: "Election is the choice of individual men to membership in the external church and the means of grace." Gore, in Lux Mundi, 320—"The elect represent not the special purpose of God for a few, but the universal purpose which under the circumstances can only be realized through a few." R. V. Foster, a Cumberland Presbyterian, opposed to absolute predestination, says in his Systematic Theology that the divine decree "is unconditional in its origin and conditional in its application."

B. From Reason.

(a) What God does, he has eternally purposed to do. Since he bestows special regenerating grace on some, he must have eternally purposed to bestow it,—in other words, must have chosen them to eternal life. Thus the doctrine of election is only a special application of the doctrine of decrees.

The New Haven views are essentially Arminian. See Fitch, on Predestination and Election, in Christian Spectator, 3:622—"God's foreknowledge of what would be the results of his present works of grace preceded in the order of nature the purpose to pursue those works, and presented the grounds of that purpose. Whom he foreknew—as the people who would be guided to his kingdom by his present works of grace, in which result lay the whole objective motive for undertaking those works—he did also, by resolving on those works, predestinate." Here God is very erroneously said to foreknow what is as yet included in a merely possible plan. As we have seen in our discussion of Decrees, there can be no foreknowledge, unless there is something fixed, in the future, to be foreknown; and this fixity can be due only to God's predetermination. So, in the present case, election must precede prescience.

The New Haven views are also given in N. W. Taylor, Revealed Theology, 373-444; for criticism upon them, see Tyler, Letters on New Haven Theology, 172-180. If God desired the salvation of Judas as much as of Peter, how was Peter elected in distinction from Judas? To the question, "Who made thee to differ?" the answer must be, "Not God, but my own will." See Finney, in Bib. Sac., 1877:711—"God must have foreknown whom he could wisely save, prior in the order of nature to his determining to save them. But his knowing who would be saved, must have been, in the order of nature, subsequent to his election or determination to save them, and dependent upon that determination." Foster, Christian Life and Theology, 70—"The doctrine of election is the consistent formulation, sub specie eternitatis, of prevenient grace.... 86—With the doctrine of prevenient grace, the evangelical doctrine stands or falls."

(b) This purpose cannot be conditioned upon any merit or faith of those who are chosen, since there is no such merit,—faith itself being God's gift and foreordained by him. Since man's faith is foreseen only as the result of God's work of grace, election proceeds rather upon foreseen unbelief. Faith, as the effect of election, cannot at the same time be the cause of election.

There is an analogy between prayer and its answer, on the one hand, and faith and salvation on the other. God has decreed answer in connection with prayer, and salvation in connection with faith. But he does not change his mind when men pray, or when they believe. As he fulfils his purpose by inspiring true prayer, so he fulfils his purpose by giving faith. Augustine: "He chooses us, not because we believe, but that we may believe: lest we should say that we first chose him." (John 15:16—"Ye did not choose me, but I chose you"; Rom. 9:21—"from the same lump"; 16—"not of him that willeth".)

Here see the valuable discussion of Wardlaw, Systematic Theol., 2:485-549—"Election and salvation on the ground of works foreseen are not different in principle from election and salvation on the ground of works performed." Cf. Prov. 21:1—"The king's heart is in the hand of Jehovah as the watercourses; He turneth it whithersoever he will"—as easily as the rivulets of the eastern fields are turned by the slightest motion of the hand or the foot of the husbandman; Ps. 110:3—"Thy people offer themselves willingly In the day of thy power."

(c) The depravity of the human will is such that, without this decree to bestow special divine influences upon some, all, without exception, would have rejected Christ's salvation after it was offered to them; and so all, without exception, must have perished. Election, therefore, may be viewed as a necessary consequence of God's decree to provide an objective redemption, if that redemption is to have any subjective result in human salvation.

Before the prodigal son seeks the father, the father must first seek him,—a truth brought out in the preceding parables of the lost money and the lost sheep (Luke 15). Without election, all are lost. Newman Smyth, Orthodox Theology of To-day, 56—"The worst doctrine of election, to-day, is taught by our natural science. The scientific doctrine of natural selection is the doctrine of election, robbed of all hope, and without a single touch of human pity in it."

Hodge, Syst. Theol., 2:335—"Suppose the deistic view be true: God created men and left them; surely no man could complain of the results. But now suppose God, foreseeing these very results of creation, should create. Would it make any difference, if God's purpose, as to the futurition of such a world, should precede it? Augustine supposes that God did purpose such a world as the deist supposes, with two exceptions: (1) he interposes to restrain evil; (2) he intervenes, by providence, by Christ, and by the Holy Spirit, to save some from destruction." Election is simply God's determination that the sufferings of Christ shall not be in vain; that all men shall not be lost; that some shall be led to accept Christ; that to this end special influences of his Spirit shall be given.

At first sight it might appear that God's appointing men to salvation was simply permissive, as was his appointment to condemnation (1 Pet. 2:8), and that this appointment was merely indirect by creating them with foresight of their faith or their disobedience. But the decree of salvation is not simply permissive,—it is efficient also. It is a decree to use special means for the salvation of some. A. A. Hodge, Popular Lectures, 143—"The dead man cannot spontaneously originate his own quickening, nor the creature his own creating, nor the infant his own begetting. Whatever man may do after regeneration, the first quickening of the dead must originate with God."

Hovey, Manual of Theology, 287—"Calvinism, reduced to its lowest terms, is election of believers, not on account of any foreseen conduct of theirs, either before or in the act of conversion, which would be spiritually better than that of others influenced by the same grace, but on account of their foreseen greater usefulness in manifesting the glory of God to moral beings and of their foreseen non-commission of the sin against the Holy Spirit." But even here we must attribute the greater usefulness and the abstention from fatal sin, not to man's unaided powers but to the divine decree: see Eph. 2:10—"For we are his workmanship, created in Christ Jesus for good works, which God afore prepared that we should walk in them."

(d) The doctrine of election becomes more acceptable to reason when we remember: first, that God's decree is eternal, and in a certain sense is contemporaneous with man's belief in Christ; secondly, that God's decree to create involves the decree of all that in the exercise of man's freedom will follow; thirdly, that God's decree is the decree of him who is all in all, so that our willing and doing is at the same time the working of him who decrees our willing and doing. The whole question turns upon the initiative in human salvation: if this belongs to God, then in spite of difficulties we must accept the doctrine of election.

The timeless existence of God may be the source of many of our difficulties with regard to election, and with a proper view of God's eternity these difficulties might be removed. Mason, Faith of the Gospel, 349-351—"Eternity is commonly thought of as if it were a state or series anterior to time and to be resumed again when time comes to an end. This, however, only reduces eternity to time again, and puts the life of God in the same line with our own, only coming from further back.... At present we do not see how time and eternity meet."

Royce, World and Individual, 2:374—"God does not temporally foreknow anything, except so far as he is expressed in us finite beings. The knowledge that exists in time is the knowledge that finite beings possess, in so far as they are finite. And no such foreknowledge can predict the special features of individual deeds precisely so far as they are unique. Foreknowledge in time is possible only of the general, and of the causally predetermined, and not of the unique and free. Hence neither God nor man can foreknow perfectly, at any temporal moment, what a free will agent is yet to do. On the other hand, the Absolute possesses a perfect knowledge at one glance of the whole of the temporal order, past, present and future. This knowledge is ill called foreknowledge. It is eternal knowledge. And as there is an eternal knowledge of all individuality and of all freedom, free acts are known as occurring, like the chords in the musical succession, precisely when and how they actually occur." While we see much truth in the preceding statement, we find in it no bar to our faith that God can translate his eternal knowledge into finite knowledge and can thus put it for special purposes in possession of his creatures.

E. H. Johnson, Theology, 2d ed., 250—"Foreknowing what his creatures would do, God decreed their destiny when he decreed their creation; and this would still be the case, although every man had the partial control over his destiny that Arminians aver, or even the complete control that Pelagians claim. The decree is as absolute as if there were no freedom, but it leaves them as free as if there were no decree." A. H. Strong, Christ in Creation, 40, 42—"As the Logos or divine Reason, Christ dwells in humanity everywhere and constitutes the principle of its being. Humanity shares with Christ in the image of God. That image is never wholly lost. It is completely restored in sinners when the Spirit of Christ secures control of their wills and leads them to merge their life in his.... If Christ be the principle and life of all things, then divine sovereignty and human freedom, if they are not absolutely reconciled, at least lose their ancient antagonism, and we can rationally 'work out our own salvation,' for the very reason that 'it is God that worketh in us, both to will and to work, for his good pleasure' (Phil. 2:12, 13)."

2. Objections to the Doctrine of Election.

(a) It is unjust to those who are not included in this purpose of salvation.—Answer: Election deals, not simply with creatures, but with sinful, guilty, and condemned creatures. That any should be saved, is matter of pure grace, and those who are not included in this purpose of salvation suffer only the due reward of their deeds. There is, therefore, no injustice in God's election. We may better praise God that he saves any, than charge him with injustice because he saves so few.

God can say to all men, saved or unsaved, "Friend, I do thee no wrong.... Is it not lawful for me to do what I will with mine own?" (Mat. 20:13, 15). The question is not whether a father will treat his children alike, but whether a sovereign must treat condemned rebels alike. It is not true that, because the Governor pardons one convict from the penitentiary, he must therefore pardon all. When he pardons one, no injury is done to those who are left. But, in God's government, there is still less reason for objection; for God offers pardon to all. Nothing prevents men from being pardoned but their unwillingness to accept his pardon. Election is simply God's determination to make certain persons willing to accept it. Because justice cannot save all, shall it therefore save none?

Augustine, De Predest. Sanct., 8—"Why does not God teach all? Because it is in mercy that he teaches all whom he does teach, while it is in judgment that he does not teach those whom he does not teach." In his Manual of Theology and Ethics, 260, Hovey remarks that Rom. 9:20—"who art thou that repliest against God?"—teaches, not that might makes right, but that God is morally entitled to glorify either his righteousness or his mercy in disposing of a guilty race. It is not that he chooses to save only a few ship-wrecked and drowning creatures, but that he chooses to save only a part of a great company who are bent on committing suicide. Prov. 8:36—"he that sinneth against me wrongeth his own soul: All they that hate me love death." It is best for the universe at large that some should be permitted to have their own way and show how dreadful a thing is opposition to God. See Shedd, Dogm. Theol., 1:455.

(b) It represents God as partial in his dealings and a respecter of persons.—Answer: Since there is nothing in men that determines God's choice of one rather than another, the objection is invalid. It would equally apply to God's selection of certain nations, as Israel, and certain individuals, as Cyrus, to be recipients of special temporal gifts. If God is not to be regarded as partial in not providing a salvation for fallen angels, he cannot be regarded as partial in not providing regenerating influences of his Spirit for the whole race of fallen men.

Ps. 44:3—"For they gat not the land in possession by their own sword, Neither did their own arm save them; But thy right hand, and thine arm, and the light of thy countenance, Because thou wast favorable unto them"; Is. 45:1, 4, 5—"Thus saith Jehovah to his anointed, to Cyrus, whose right hand I have holden, to subdue nations before him.... For Jacob my servant's sake, and Israel my chosen, I have called thee by thy name: I have surnamed thee, though thou hast not known me"; Luke 4:25-27—"There were many widows in Israel ... and unto none of them was Elijah sent, but only to Zarephath, in the land of Sidon, unto a woman that was a widow. And there were many lepers in Israel ... and none of them was cleansed, but only Naaman the Syrian"; 1 Cor. 4:7—"For who maketh thee to differ? and what hast thou that thou didst not receive? but if thou didst receive it, why dost thou glory, as if thou hadst not received it?" 2 Pet. 2:4—"God spared not angels when they sinned, but cast them down to hell"; Heb. 2:16—"For verily not to angels doth he give help, but he giveth help to the seed of Abraham."

Is God partial, in choosing Israel, Cyrus, Naaman? Is God partial, in bestowing upon some of his servants special ministerial gifts? Is God partial, in not providing a salvation for fallen angels? In God's providence, one man is born in a Christian land, the son of a noble family, is endowed with beauty of person, splendid talents, exalted opportunities, immense wealth. Another is born at the Five Points, or among the Hottentots, amid the degradation and depravity of actual, or practical, heathenism. We feel that it is irreverent to complain of God's dealings in providence. What right have sinners to complain of God's dealings in the distribution of his grace? Hovey: "We have no reason to think that God treats all moral beings alike. We should be glad to hear that other races are treated better than we."

Divine election is only the ethical side and interpretation of natural selection. In the latter God chooses certain forms of the vegetable and animal kingdom without merit of theirs. They are preserved while others die. In the matter of individual health, talent, property, one is taken and the other left. If we call all this the result of system, the reply is that God chose the system, knowing precisely what would come of it. Bruce, Apologetics, 201—"Election to distinction in philosophy or art is not incomprehensible, for these are not matters of vital concern; but election to holiness on the part of some, and to unholiness on the part of others, would be inconsistent with God's own holiness." But there is no such election to unholiness except on the part of man himself. God's election secures only the good. See (c) below.

J. J. Murphy, Natural Selection and Spiritual Freedom, 73—"The world is ordered on a basis of inequality; in the organic world, as Darwin has shown, it is of inequality—of favored races—that all progress comes; history shows the same to be true of the human and spiritual world. All human progress is due to elect human individuals, elect not only to be a blessing to themselves, but still more to be a blessing to multitudes of others. Any superiority, whether in the natural or in the mental and spiritual world, becomes a vantage-ground for gaining a greater superiority.... It is the method of the divine government, acting in the provinces both of nature and of grace, that all benefit should come to the many through the elect few."

(c) It represents God as arbitrary.—Answer: It represents God, not as arbitrary, but as exercising the free choice of a wise and sovereign will, in ways and for reasons which are inscrutable to us. To deny the possibility of such a choice is to deny God's personality. To deny that God has reasons for his choice is to deny his wisdom. The doctrine of election finds these reasons, not in men, but in God.

When a regiment is decimated for insubordination, the fact that every tenth man is chosen for death is for reasons; but the reasons are not in the men. In one case, the reason for God's choice seems revealed: 1 Tim. 1:16—"howbeit for this cause I obtained mercy, that in me as chief might Jesus Christ show forth all his longsuffering, for an ensample of them that should thereafter believe on him unto eternal life"—here Paul indicates that the reason why God chose him was that he was so great a sinner: verse 15—"Christ Jesus came into the world to save sinners; of whom I am chief." Hovey remarks that "the uses to which God can put men, as vessels of grace, may determine his selection of them." But since the naturally weak are saved, as well as the naturally strong, we cannot draw any general conclusion, or discern any general rule, in God's dealings, unless it be this, that in election God seeks to illustrate the greatness and the variety of his grace,—the reasons lying, therefore, not in men, but in God. We must remember that God's sovereignty is the sovereignty of God—the infinitely wise, holy and loving God, in whose hands the destinies of men can be left more safely than in the hands of the wisest, most just, and most kind of his creatures.

We must believe in the grace of sovereignty as well as in the sovereignty of grace. Election and reprobation are not matters of arbitrary will. God saves all whom he can wisely save. He will show benevolence in the salvation of mankind just so far as he can without prejudice to holiness. No man can be saved without God, but it is also true that there is no man whom God is not willing to save. H. B. Smith, System, 511—"It may be that many of the finally impenitent resist more light than many of the saved." Harris, Moral Evolution, 401 (for substance)—"Sovereignty is not lost in Fatherhood, but is recovered as the divine law of righteous love. Doubtless thou art our Father, though Augustine be ignorant of us, and Calvin acknowledge us not." Hooker, Eccl. Polity, 1:2—"They err who think that of God's will there is no reason except his will." T. Erskine, The Brazen Serpent, 259—Sovereignty is "just a name for what is unrevealed of God."

We do not know all of God's reasons for saving particular men, but we do know some of the reasons, for he has revealed them to us. These reasons are not men's merits or works. We have mentioned the first of these reasons: (1) Men's greater sin and need; 1 Tim. 1:16—"that in me as chief might Jesus Christ show forth all his longsuffering." We may add to this: (2) The fact that men have not sinned against the Holy Spirit and made themselves unreceptive to Christ's salvation; 1 Tim. 1:13—"I obtained mercy, because I did it ignorantly in unbelief"—the fact that Paul had not sinned with full knowledge of what he did was a reason why God could choose him. (3) Men's ability by the help of Christ to be witnesses and martyrs for their Lord; Acts 9:15, 16—"he is a chosen vessel unto me, to bear my name before the Gentiles and kings, and the children of Israel: for I will show him how many things he must suffer for my name's sake." As Paul's mission to the Gentiles may have determined God's choice, so Augustine's mission to the sensual and abandoned may have had the same influence. But if Paul's sins, as foreseen, constituted one reason why God chose to save him, why might not his ability to serve the kingdom have constituted another reason? We add therefore: (4) Men's foreseen ability to serve Christ's kingdom in bringing others to the knowledge of the truth; John 15:16—"I chose you and appointed you, that ye should go and bear fruit." Notice however that this is choice to service, and not simply choice on account of service. In all these cases the reasons do not lie in the men themselves, for what these men are and what they possess is due to God's providence and grace.

(d) It tends to immorality, by representing men's salvation as independent of their own obedience.—Answer: The objection ignores the fact that the salvation of believers is ordained only in connection with their regeneration and sanctification, as means; and that the certainty of final triumph is the strongest incentive to strenuous conflict with sin.

Plutarch: "God is the brave man's hope, and not the coward's excuse." The purposes of God are an anchor to the storm-tossed spirit. But a ship needs engine, as well as anchor. God does not elect to save any without repentance and faith. Some hold the doctrine of election, but the doctrine of election does not hold them. Such should ponder 1 Pet. 1:2, in which Christians are said to be elect, "in sanctification of the Spirit, unto obedience and sprinkling of the blood of Jesus Christ."

Augustine: "He loved her [the church] foul, that he might make her fair." Dr. John Watson (Ian McLaren): "The greatest reinforcement religion could have in our time would be a return to the ancient belief in the sovereignty of God." This is because there is lack of a strong conviction of sin, guilt, and helplessness, still remaining pride and unwillingness to submit to God, imperfect faith in God's trustworthiness and goodness. We must not exclude Arminians from our fellowship—there are too many good Methodists for that. But we may maintain that they hold but half the truth, and that absence of the doctrine of election from their creed makes preaching less serious and character less secure.

(e) It inspires pride in those who think themselves elect.—Answer: This is possible only in the case of those who pervert the doctrine. On the contrary, its proper influence is to humble men. Those who exalt themselves above others, upon the ground that they are special favorites of God, have reason to question their election.

In the novel, there was great effectiveness in the lover's plea to the object of his affection, that he had loved since he had first set his eyes upon her in her childhood. But God's love for us is of longer standing than that. It dates back to a time before we were born,—aye, even to eternity past. It is a love which was fastened upon us, although God knew the worst of us. It is unchanging, because founded upon his infinite and eternal love to Christ. Jer. 31:3—"Jehovah appeared of old unto me, saying, Yea, I have loved thee with an everlasting love: therefore with lovingkindness have I drawn thee"; Rom. 8:31-39—"If God is for us, who is against us?... Who shall separate us from the love of Christ?" And the answer is, that nothing "shall be able to separate us from the love of God, which is in Christ Jesus our Lord." This eternal love subdues and humbles: Ps. 115:1—"Not unto us, O Jehovah, not unto us, But unto thy name give glory For thy lovingkindness, and for thy truth's sake."

Of the effect of the doctrine of election, Calvin, in his Institutes, 3:22:1, remarks that "when the human mind hears of it, its irritation breaks all restraint, and it discovers as serious and violent agitation as if alarmed by the sound of a martial trumpet." The cause of this agitation is the apprehension of the fact that one is an enemy of God and yet absolutely dependent upon his mercy. This apprehension leads normally to submission. But the conquered rebel can give no thanks to himself,—all thanks are due to God who has chosen and renewed him. The affections elicited are not those of pride and self-complacency, but of gratitude and love.

Christian hymnology witnesses to these effects. Isaac Watts († 1748): "Why was I made to hear thy voice And enter while there's room, When thousands make a wretched choice, And rather starve than come. 'T was the same love that spread the feast That sweetly forced me in; Else I had still refused to taste, And perished in my sin. Pity the nations, O our God! Constrain the earth to come; Send thy victorious word abroad, And bring the wanderers home." Josiah Conder († 1855): "'Tis not that I did choose thee, For, Lord, that could not be; This heart would still refuse thee; But thou hast chosen me;—Hast, from the sin that stained me, Washed me and set me free, And to this end ordained me That I should live to thee. 'T was sovereign mercy called me, And taught my opening mind; The world had else enthralled me, To heavenly glories blind. My heart owns none above thee: For thy rich grace I thirst; This knowing,—if I love thee, Thou must have loved me first."

(f) It discourages effort for the salvation of the impenitent, whether on their own part or on the part of others.—Answer: Since it is a secret decree, it cannot hinder or discourage such effort. On the other hand, it is a ground of encouragement, and so a stimulus to effort; for, without election, it is certain that all would be lost (cf. Acts 18:10). While it humbles the sinner, so that he is willing to err for mercy, it encourages him also by showing him that some will be saved, and (since election and faith are inseparably connected) that he will be saved, if he will only believe. While it makes the Christian feel entirely dependent on God's power, in his efforts for the impenitent, it leads him to say with Paul that he "endures all things for the elects' sake, that they also may attain the salvation that is in Christ Jesus with eternal glory" (2 Tim. 2:10).

God's decree that Paul's ship's company should be saved (Acts 27:24) did not obviate the necessity of their abiding in the ship (verse 31). In marriage, man's election does not exclude woman's; so God's election does not exclude man's. There is just as much need of effort as if there were no election. Hence the question for the sinner is not, "Am I one of the elect?" but rather, "What shall I do to be saved?" Milton represents the spirits of hell as debating foreknowledge and free will, in wandering mazes lost.

No man is saved until he ceases to debate, and begins to act. And yet no man will thus begin to act, unless God's Spirit moves him. The Lord encouraged Paul by saying to him: "I have much people in this city" (Acts 18:10)—people whom I will bring in through thy word. "Old Adam is too strong for young Melanchthon." If God does not regenerate, there is no hope of success in preaching: "God stands powerless before the majesty of man's lordly will. Sinners have the glory of their own salvation. To pray God to convert a man is absurd. God elects the man, because he foresees that the man will elect himself" (see S. R. Mason, Truth Unfolded, 298-307). The doctrine of election does indeed cut off the hopes of those who place confidence in themselves; but it is best that such hopes should be destroyed, and that in place of them should be put a hope in the sovereign grace of God. The doctrine of election does teach man's absolute dependence upon God, and the impossibility of any disappointment or disarrangement of the divine plans arising from the disobedience of the sinner, and it humbles human pride until it is willing to take the place of a suppliant for mercy.

Rowland Hill was criticized for preaching election and yet exhorting sinners to repent, and was told that he should preach only to the elect. He replied that, if his critic would put a chalk-mark on all the elect, he would preach only to them. But this is not the whole truth. We are not only ignorant who God's elect are, but we are set to preach to both elect and non-elect (Ez. 2:7—"thou shalt speak my words unto them, whether they will hear, or whether they will forbear"), with the certainty that to the former our preaching will make a higher heaven, to the latter a deeper hell (2 Cor. 2:15, 16—"For we are a sweet savor of Christ unto God, in them that are saved, and in them that perish; to the one a savor from death unto death; to the other a savor from life unto life"; cf. Luke 2:34—"this child is set for the falling and the rising of many in Israel"—for the falling of some, and for the rising up of others).

Jesus' own thanksgiving in Mat. 11:25, 26—"I thank thee, O Father, Lord of heaven and earth, that thou didst hide these things from the wise and understanding, and didst reveal them unto babes: yea, Father, for so it was well-pleasing in thy sight"—is immediately followed by his invitation in verse 28—"Come unto me, all ye that labor and are heavy laden, and I will give you rest." There is no contradiction in his mind between sovereign grace and the free invitations of the gospel.

G. W. Northrup, in The Standard, Sept. 19, 1889—"1. God will save every one of the human race whom he can save and remain God; 2. Every member of the race has a full and fair probation, so that all might be saved and would be saved were they to use aright the light which they already have."... (Private letter): "Limitations of God in the bestowment of salvation: 1. In the power of God in relation to free will; 2. In the benevolence of God which requires the greatest good of creation, or the greatest aggregate good of the greatest number; 3. In the purpose of God to make the most perfect self-limitation; 4. In the sovereignty of God, as a prerogative absolutely optional in its exercise; 5. In the holiness of God, which involves immutable limitations on his part in dealing with moral agents. Nothing but some absolute impossibility, metaphysical or moral, could have prevented him 'whose nature and whose name is love' from decreeing and securing the confirmation of all moral agents in holiness and blessedness forever."

(g) The decree of election implies a decree of reprobation.—Answer: The decree of reprobation is not a positive decree, like that of election, but a permissive decree to leave the sinner to his self-chosen rebellion and its natural consequences of punishment.

Election and sovereignty are only sources of good. Election is not a decree to destroy,—it is a decree only to save. When we elect a President, we do not need to hold a second election to determine that the remaining millions shall be non-Presidents. It is needless to apply contrivance or force. Sinners, like water, if simply let alone, will run down hill to ruin. The decree of reprobation is simply a decree to do nothing—a decree to leave the sinner to himself. The natural result of this judicial forsaking, on the part of God, is the hardening and destruction of the sinner. But it must not be forgotten that this hardening and destruction are not due to any positive efficiency of God,—they are a self-hardening and a self-destruction,—and God's judicial forsaking is only the just penalty of the sinner's guilty rejection of offered mercy.

See Hosea 11:8—"How shall I give thee up, Ephraim?... my heart is turned within me, my compassions are kindled together"; 4:17—"Ephraim is joined to idols; let him alone"; Rom. 9:22, 23—"What if God, willing to show his wrath, and to make his power known, endured with much longsuffering vessels of wrath fitted unto destruction: and that he might make known the riches of his glory upon vessels of mercy, which he afore prepared unto glory"—here notice that "which he afore prepared" declares a positive divine efficiency, in the case of the vessels of mercy, while "fitted unto destruction" intimates no such positive agency of God,—the vessels of wrath fitted themselves for destruction; 2 Tim. 2:20—"vessels ... some unto honor, and some unto dishonor"; 1 Pet. 2:8—"they stumble at the word, being disobedient: whereunto also they were appointed"; Jude 4—"who were of old set forth ['written of beforehand'—Am. Rev.] unto this condemnation"; Mat. 25:34, 41—"the kingdom prepared for you ... the eternal fire which is prepared [not for you, nor for men, but] for the devil and his angels" = there is an election to life, but no reprobation to death; a "book of life" (Rev. 21:27), but no book of death.

E. G. Robinson, Christian Theology, 313—"Reprobation, in the sense of absolute predestination to sin and eternal damnation, is neither a sequence of the doctrine of election, nor the teaching of the Scriptures." Men are not "appointed" to disobedience and stumbling in the same way that they are "appointed" to salvation. God uses positive means to save, but not to destroy. Henry Ward Beecher: "The elect are whosoever will; the non-elect are whosoever won't." George A. Gordon, New Epoch for Faith, 44—"Election understood would have been the saving strength of Israel; election misunderstood was its ruin. The nation felt that the election of it meant the rejection of other nations.... The Christian church has repeated Israel's mistake."

The Westminster Confession reads: "By the decree of God, for the manifestation of his glory, some men and angels are predestinated unto everlasting life, and others to everlasting death. These angels and men, thus predestinated and foreordained, are particularly and unchangeably designed; and their number is so certain and definite that it cannot be either increased or diminished. The rest of mankind God was pleased, according to the unsearchable counsel of his own will, whereby he extendeth or withholdeth mercy as he pleaseth, for the glory of his sovereign power over his creatures, to pass by and to ordain them to dishonor and wrath for their sin, to the praise of his glorious justice." This reads as if both the saved and the lost were made originally for their respective final estates without respect to character. It is supralapsarianism. It is certain that the supralapsarians were in the majority in the Westminster Assembly, and that they determined the form of the statement, although there were many sublapsarians who objected that it was only on account of their foreseen wickedness that any were reprobated. In its later short statement of doctrine the Presbyterian body in America has made it plain that God's decree of reprobation is a permissive decree, and that it places no barrier in the way of any man's salvation.

On the general subject of Election, see Mozley, Predestination; Payne, Divine Sovereignty; Ridgeley, Works, 1:261-324, esp. 322; Edwards, Works, 2:527 sq.; Van Oosterzee, Dogmatics, 446-458; Martensen, Dogmatics, 362-382; and especially Wardlaw, Systematic Theology, 485-549; H. B. Smith, Syst. of Christian Theology, 502-514; Maule, Outlines of Christian Doctrine, 36-56; Peck, in Bapt. Quar. Rev., Oct. 1891:689-706. On objections to election, and Spurgeon's answers to them, see Williams, Reminiscences of Spurgeon, 189. On the homiletical uses of the doctrine of election, see Bib. Sac., Jan. 1893:79-92.

II. Calling

Calling is that act of God by which men are invited to accept, by faith, the salvation provided by Christ.—The Scriptures distinguish between:

(a) The general, or external, call to all men through God's providence, word, and Spirit.

Is. 45:22—"Look unto me, and be ye saved, all the ends of the earth; for I am God, and there is none else"; 55:6—"Seek ye Jehovah while he may be found; call ye upon him while he is near"; 65:12—"when I called, ye did not answer; when I spake, ye did not hear; but ye did that which was evil in mine eyes, and chose that wherein I delighted not"; Ez. 33:11—"As I live, saith the Lord Jehovah, I have no pleasure in the death of the wicked; but that the wicked turn from his way and live; turn ye, turn ye from your evil ways; for why will ye die, O house of Israel?" Mat. 11:28—"Come unto me, all ye that labor and are heavy laden, and I will give you rest"; 22:3—"sent forth his servants to call them that were bidden to the marriage feast: and they would not come"; Mark 16:15—"Go ye into all the world, and preach the gospel to the whole creation"; John 12:32—"And I, if I be lifted up from the earth, will draw all men unto myself"—draw, not drag; Rev. 3:20—"Behold, I stand at the door and knock: if any man hear my voice and open the door, I will come in to him, and will sup with him, and he with me."

(b) The special, efficacious call of the Holy Spirit to the elect.

Luke 14:23—"Go out into the highways and hedges, and constrain them to come in, that my house may be filled"; Rom. 1:7—"to all that are in Rome, beloved of God, called to be saints: Grace to you and peace from God our father and the Lord Jesus Christ"; 8:30—"whom he foreordained, them he also called: and whom he called, them he also justified"; 11:29—"For the gifts and the calling of God are not repented of"; 1 Cor. 1:23, 24—"but we preach Christ crucified, unto Jews a stumblingblock, and unto Gentiles foolishness; but unto them that are called, both Jews and Greeks, Christ the power of God, and the wisdom of God"; 26—"For behold your calling, brethren, that not many wise after the flesh, not many mighty, not many noble, are called"; Phil. 3:14—"I press on toward the goal unto the prize of the high [marg. 'upward'] calling of God in Christ Jesus"; Eph. 1:18—"that ye may know what is the hope of his calling, what the riches of the glory of his inheritance in the saints"; 1 Thess. 2:12—"to the end that ye should walk worthily of God, who calleth you into his own kingdom and glory"; 2 Thess. 2:14—"whereunto he called you through our gospel, to the obtaining of the glory of our Lord Jesus Christ"; 2 Tim. 1:9—"who saved us, and called us with a holy calling, not according to our works, but according to his own purpose and grace, which was given us in Christ Jesus before times eternal"; Heb. 3:1—"holy brethren, partakers of a heavenly calling"; 2 Pet. 1:10—"Wherefore, brethren, give the more diligence to make your calling and election sure."

Two questions only need special consideration:

A. Is God's general call sincere?

This is denied, upon the ground that such sincerity is incompatible, first, with the inability of the sinner to obey; and secondly, with the design of God to bestow only upon the elect the special grace without which they will not obey.

(a) To the first objection we reply that, since this inability is not a physical but a moral inability, consisting simply in the settled perversity of an evil will, there can be no insincerity in offering salvation to all, especially when the offer is in itself a proper motive to obedience.

God's call to all men to repent and to believe the gospel is no more insincere than his command to all men to love him with all the heart. There is no obstacle in the way of men's obedience to the gospel, that does not exist to prevent their obedience to the law. If it is proper to publish the commands of the law, it is proper to publish the invitations of the gospel. A human being may be perfectly sincere in giving an invitation which he knows will be refused. He may desire to have the invitation accepted, while yet he may, for certain reasons of justice or personal dignity, be unwilling to put forth special efforts, aside from the invitation itself, to secure the acceptance of it on the part of those to whom it is offered. So God's desires that certain men should be saved may not be accompanied by his will to exert special influences to save them.

These desires were meant by the phrase "revealed will" in the old theologians; his purpose to bestow special grace, by the phrase "secret will." It is of the former that Paul speaks, in 1 Tim, 2:4—"who would have all men to be saved." Here we have, not the active σῶσαι, but the passive σωθῆναι. The meaning is, not that God purposes to save all men, but that he desires all men to be saved through repenting and believing the gospel. Hence God's revealed will, or desire, that all men should be saved, is perfectly consistent with his secret will, or purpose, to bestow special grace only upon a certain number (see, on 1 Tim. 2:4, Fairbairn's Commentary on the Pastoral Epistles).

The sincerity of God's call is shown, not only in the fact that the only obstacle to compliance, on the sinner's part, is the sinner's own evil will, but also in the fact that God has, at infinite cost, made a complete external provision, upon the ground of which "he that will" may "come" and "take the water of life freely" (Rev. 22:17); so that God can truly say: "What could have been done more to my vineyard, that I have not done in it?" (Is. 5:4). Broadus, Com. on Mat. 6:10—"Thy will be done"—distinguishes between God's will of purpose, of desire, and of command. H. B. Smith, Syst. Theol., 521—"Common grace passes over into effectual grace in proportion as the sinner yields to the divine influence. Effectual grace is that which effects what common grace tends to effect." See also Studien und Kritiken, 1887:7 sq.

(b) To the second, we reply that the objection, if true, would equally hold against God's foreknowledge. The sincerity of God's general call is no more inconsistent with his determination that some shall be permitted to reject it, than it is with foreknowledge that some will reject it.

Hodge, Syst. Theol., 2:643—"Predestination concerns only the purpose of God to render effectual, in particular cases, a call addressed to all. A general amnesty, on certain conditions, may be offered by a sovereign to rebellious subjects, although he knows that through pride or malice many will refuse to accept it; and even though, for wise reasons, he should determine not to constrain their assent, supposing that such influence over their minds were within his power. It is evident, from the nature of the call, that it has nothing to do with the secret purpose of God to grant his effectual grace to some, and not to others.... According to the Augustinian scheme, the non-elect have all the advantages and opportunities of securing their salvation, which, according to any other scheme, are granted to mankind indiscriminately.... God designed, in its adoption, to save his own people, but he consistently offers its benefits to all who are willing to receive them." See also H. B. Smith, System of Christian Theology, 515-521.

B. Is God's special call irresistible?

We prefer to say that this special call is efficacious,—that is, that it infallibly accomplishes its purpose of leading the sinner to the acceptance of salvation. This implies two things:

(a) That the operation of God is not an outward constraint upon the human will, but that it accords with the laws of our mental constitution. We reject the term "irresistible," as implying a coercion and compulsion which is foreign to the nature of God's working in the soul.

Ps. 110:3—"Thy people are freewill-offerings in the day of thy power: in holy array, Out of the womb of the morning Thou hast the dew of thy youth"—i. e., youthful recruits to thy standard, as numberless and as bright as the drops of morning dew; Phil. 2:12, 13—"Work out your own salvation with fear and trembling; for it is God who worketh in you both to will and to work, for his good pleasure"—i. e., the result of God's working is our own working. The Lutheran Formula of Concord properly condemns the view that, before, in, and after conversion, the will only resists the Holy Spirit: for this, it declares, is the very nature of conversion, that out of non-willing, God makes willing, persons (F. C. 60, 581, 582, 673).

Hos. 4:16—"Israel hath behaved himself stubbornly, like a stubborn heifer," or "or as a heifer that slideth back" = when the sacrificial offering is brought forward to be slain, it holds back, settling on its haunches so that it has to be pushed and forced before it can be brought to the altar. These are not "the sacrifices of God" which are "a broken spirit, a broken and a contrite heart" (Ps. 51:17). E. H. Johnson, Theology, 2d ed., 250—"The N. T. nowhere declares, or even intimates, ... that the general call of the Holy Spirit is insufficient. And furthermore, it never states that the efficient call is irresistible. Psychologically, to speak of irresistible influence upon the faculty of self-determination in man is express contradiction in terms. No harm can come from acknowledging that we do not know God's unrevealed reasons for electing one individual rather than another to eternal life." Dr. Johnson goes on to argue that if, without disparagement to grace, faith can be a condition of justification, faith might also be a condition of election, and that inasmuch as salvation is received as a gift only on condition of faith exercised, it is in purpose a gift, even if only on condition of faith foreseen. This seems to us to ignore the abundant Scripture testimony that faith itself is God's gift, and therefore the initiative must be wholly with God.

(b) That the operation of God is the originating cause of that new disposition of the affections, and that new activity of the will, by which the sinner accepts Christ. The cause is not in the response of the will to the presentation of motives by God, nor in any mere coöperation of the will of man with the will of God, but is an almighty act of God in the will of man, by which its freedom to choose God as its end is restored and rightly exercised (John 1:12, 13). For further discussion of the subject, see, in the next section, the remarks on Regeneration, with which this efficacious call is identical.

John 1:12, 13—"But as many as received him, to them gave he the right to become children of God, even to them that believe on his name: who were born, not of blood, nor of the will of the flesh, nor of the will of man, but of God." God's saving grace and effectual calling are irresistible, not in the sense that they are never resisted, but in the sense that they are never successfully resisted. See Andrew Fuller, Works, 2:373, 513, and 3:807; Gill, Body of Divinity, 2:121-130; Robert Hall, Works, 3:75.

Matheson, Moments on the Mount, 128, 129—"Thy love to Him is to his love to thee what the sunlight on the sea is to the sunshine in the sky—a reflex, a mirror, a diffusion; thou art giving back the glory that has been cast upon the waters. In the attraction of thy life to him, in the cleaving of thy heart to him, in the soaring of thy spirit to him, thou art told that he is near thee, thou hearest the beating of his pulse for thee."

Upton, Hibbert Lectures, 302—"In regard to our reason and to the essence of our ideals, there is no real dualism between man and God; but in the case of the will which constitutes the essence of each man's individuality, there is a real dualism, and therefore a possible antagonism between the will of the dependent spirit, man, and the will of the absolute and universal spirit, God. Such real duality of will, and not the appearance of duality, as F. H. Bradley put it, is the essential condition of ethics and religion."

Section II —The Application Of Christ's Redemption In Its Actual Beginning

Under this head we treat of Union with Christ, Regeneration, Conversion (embracing Repentance and Faith), and Justification. Much confusion and error have arisen from conceiving these as occurring in chronological order. The order is logical, not chronological. As it is only "in Christ" that man is "a new creature" (2 Cor. 5:17) or is "justified" (Acts 13:39), union with Christ logically precedes both regeneration and justification; and yet, chronologically, the moment of our union with Christ is also the moment when we are regenerated and justified. So, too, regeneration and conversion are but the divine and human sides or aspects of the same fact, although regeneration has logical precedence, and man turns only as God turns him.

Dorner, Glaubenslehre, 3:694 (Syst. Doct., 4:159), gives at this point an account of the work of the Holy Spirit in general. The Holy Spirit's work, he says, presupposes the historical work of Christ, and prepares the way for Christ's return. "As the Holy Spirit is the principle of union between the Father and the Son, so he is the principle of union between God and man. Only through the Holy Spirit does Christ secure for himself those who will love him as distinct and free personalities." Regeneration and conversion are not chronologically separate. Which of the spokes of a wheel starts first? The ray of light and the ray of heat enter at the same moment. Sensation and perception are not separated in time, although the former is the cause of the latter.

"Suppose a non-elastic tube extending across the Atlantic. Suppose that the tube is completely filled with an incompressible fluid. Then there would be no interval of time between the impulse given to the fluid at this end of the tube, and the effect upon the fluid at the other end." See Hazard, Causation and Freedom in Willing, 33-38, who argues that cause and effect are always simultaneous; else, in the intervening time, there would be a cause that had no effect; that is, a cause that caused nothing; that is, a cause that that was not a cause. "A potential cause may exist for an unlimited period without producing any effect, and of course may precede its effect by any length of time. But actual, effective cause being the exercise of a sufficient power, its effect cannot be delayed; for, in that case, there would be the exercise of a sufficient power to produce the effect, without producing it,—involving the absurdity of its being both sufficient and insufficient at the same time.

"A difficulty may here be suggested in regard to the flow or progress of events in time, if they are all simultaneous with their causes. This difficulty cannot arise as to intelligent effort; for, in regard to it, periods of non-action may continually intervene; but if there are series of events and material phenomena, each of which is in turn effect and cause, it may be difficult to see how any time could elapse between the first and the last of the series.... If, however, as I suppose, these series of events, or material changes, are always effected through the medium of motion, it need not trouble us, for there is precisely the same difficulty in regard to our conception of the motion of matter from point to point, there being no space or length between any two consecutive points, and yet the body in motion gets from one end of a long line to the other, and in this case this difficulty just neutralizes the other.... So, even if we cannot conceive how motion involves the idea of time, we may perceive that, if it does so, it may be a means of conveying events, which depend upon it, through time also."

Martineau, Study, 1:148-150—"Simultaneity does not exclude duration,"—since each cause has duration and each effect has duration also. Bowne, Metaphysics, 106—"In the system, the complete ground of an event never lies in any one thing, but only in a complex of things. If a single thing were the sufficient ground of an effect, the effect would coëxist with the thing, and all effects would be instantaneously given. Hence all events in the system must be viewed as the result of the interaction of two or more things."

The first manifestation of life in an infant may be in the lungs or heart or brain, but that which makes any and all of these manifestations possible is the antecedent life. We may not be able to tell which comes first, but having the life we have all the rest. When the wheel goes, all the spokes will go. The soul that is born again will show it in faith and hope and love and holy living. Regeneration will involve repentance and faith and justification and sanctification. But the one life which makes regeneration and all these consequent blessings possible is the life of Christ who joins himself to us in order that we may join ourselves to him. Anne Reeve Aldrich, The Meaning: "I lost my life in losing love. This blurred my spring and killed its dove. Along my path the dying roses Fell, and disclosed the thorns thereof. I found my life in finding God. In ecstasy I kiss the rod; For who that wins the goal, but lightly Thinks of the thorns whereon he trod?"

See A. A. Hodge, on the Ordo Salutis, in Princeton Rev., March, 1888:304-321. Union with Christ, says Dr. Hodge, "is effected by the Holy Ghost in effectual calling. Of this calling the parts are two: (a) the offering of Christ to the sinner, externally by the gospel, and internally by the illumination of the Holy Ghost; (b) the reception of Christ, which on our part is both passive and active. The passive reception is that whereby a spiritual principle is ingenerated into the human will, whence issues the active reception, which is an act of faith with which repentance is always conjoined. The communion of benefits which results from this union involves: (a) a change of state or relation, called justification; and (b) a change of subjective moral character, commenced in regeneration and completed through sanctification." See also Dr. Hodge's Popular Lectures on Theological Themes, 340, and Outlines of Theology, 333-429.

H. B. Smith, however, in his System of Christian Theology, is more clear in the putting of Union with Christ before Regeneration. On page 502, he begins his treatment of the Application of Redemption with the title: "The Union between Christ and the individual believer as effected by the Holy Spirit. This embraces the subjects of Justification, Regeneration, and Sanctification, with the underlying topic which comes first to be considered, Election." He therefore treats Union with Christ (531-539) before Regeneration (553-569). He says Calvin defines regeneration as coming to us by participation in Christ, and apparently agrees with this view (559).

"This union [with Christ] is at the ground of regeneration and justification" (534). "The great difference of theological systems comes out here. Since Christianity is redemption through Christ, our mode of conceiving that will determine the character of our whole theological system" (536). "The union with Christ is mediated by his Spirit, whence we are both renewed and justified. The great fact of objective Christianity is incarnation in order to atonement; the great fact of subjective Christianity is union with Christ, whereby we receive the atonement" (537). We may add that this union with Christ, in view of which God elects and to which God calls the sinner, is begun in regeneration, completed in conversion, declared in justification, and proved in sanctification and perseverance.

I. Union with Christ

The Scriptures declare that, through the operation of God, there is constituted a union of the soul with Christ different in kind from God's natural and providential concursus with all spirits, as well as from all unions of mere association or sympathy, moral likeness, or moral influence,—a union of life, in which the human spirit, while then most truly possessing its own individuality and personal distinctness, is interpenetrated and energized by the Spirit of Christ, is made inscrutably but indissolubly one with him, and so becomes a member and partaker of that regenerated, believing, and justified humanity of which he is the head.

Union with Christ is not union with a system of doctrine, nor with external religious influences, nor with an organized church, nor with an ideal man,—but rather, with a personal, risen, living, omnipresent Lord (J. W. A. Stewart). Dr. J. W. Alexander well calls this doctrine of the Union of the Believer with Christ "the central truth of all theology and of all religion." Yet it receives little of formal recognition, either in dogmatic treatises or in common religious experience. Quenstedt, 886-912, has devoted a section to it; A. A. Hodge gives to it a chapter, in his Outlines of Theology, 369 sq., to which we are indebted for valuable suggestions; H. B. Smith treats of it, not however as a separate topic, but under the head of Justification (System, 531-539).

The majority of printed systems of doctrine, however, contain no chapter or section on Union with Christ, and the majority of Christians much more frequently think of Christ as a Savior outside of them, than as a Savior who dwells within. This comparative neglect of the doctrine is doubtless a reaction from the exaggerations of a false mysticism. But there is great need of rescuing the doctrine from neglect. For this we rely wholly upon Scripture. Doctrines which reason can neither discover nor prove need large support from the Bible. It is a mark of divine wisdom that the doctrine of the Trinity, for example, is so inwoven with the whole fabric of the New Testament, that the rejection of the former is the virtual rejection of the latter. The doctrine of Union with Christ, in like manner, is taught so variously and abundantly, that to deny it is to deny inspiration itself. See Kahnis, Luth. Dogmatik, 3:447-450.

1. Scripture Representations of this Union.

A. Figurative teaching. It is illustrated:

(a) From the union of a building and its foundation.

Eph. 2:20-22—"being built upon the foundation of the apostles and prophets, Christ Jesus himself being the chief corner stone; in whom each several building, fitly framed together, groweth into a holy temple in the Lord; in whom ye also are builded together for a habitation of God in the Spirit"; Col. 2:7—"builded up in him"—grounded in Christ as our foundation; 1 Pet. 2:4, 5—"unto whom coming, a living stone, rejected indeed of men, but with God elect, precious, ye also, as living stones, are built up a spiritual house"—each living stone in the Christian temple is kept in proper relation to every other, and is made to do its part in furnishing a habitation for God, only by being built upon and permanently connected with Christ, the chief corner-stone. Cf. Ps. 118:22—"The stone which the builders rejected Is become the head of the corner"; Is. 28:16—"Behold, I lay in Zion for a foundation a stone, a tried stone, a precious corner-stone of sure foundation: he that believeth shall not be in haste."

(b) From the union between husband and wife.

Rom. 7:4—"ye also were made dead to the law through the body of Christ; that ye should be joined to another, even to him who was raised from the dead, that we might bring forth fruit unto God"—here union with Christ is illustrated by the indissoluble bond that connects husband and wife, and makes them legally and organically one; 2 Cor. 11:2—"I am jealous over you with a godly jealousy: for I espoused you to one husband, that I might present you as a pure virgin to Christ"; Eph. 5:31, 32—"For this cause shall a man leave his father and mother, and shall cleave to his wife; and the two shall become one flesh. This mystery is great: but I speak in regard of Christ and of the church"—Meyer refers verse 31 wholly to Christ, and says that Christ leaves father and mother (the right hand of God) and is joined to the church as his wife, the two constituting thenceforth one moral person. He makes the union future, however,—"For this cause shall a man leave his father and mother"—the consummation is at Christ's second coming. But the Fathers, as Chrysostom, Theodoret, and Jerome, referred it more properly to the incarnation.

Rev. 19:7—"the marriage of the Lamb is come, and his wife hath made herself ready"; 22:17—"And the Spirit and the bride say, Come"; cf. Is. 54:5—"For thy Maker is thine husband"; Jer. 3:20—"Surely as a wife treacherously departeth from her husband, so have ye dealt treacherously with me, O house of Israel, saith Jehovah"; Hos. 2:2-5—"for their mother hath played the harlot"—departure from God is adultery; the Song of Solomon, as Jewish interpreters have always maintained, is an allegorical poem describing, under the figure of marriage, the union between Jehovah and his people: Paul only adopts the Old Testament figure, and applies it more precisely to the union of God with the church in Jesus Christ.

(c) From the union between the vine and its branches.

John 15:1-10—"I am the vine, ye are the branches: He that abideth in me, and I in him, the same beareth much fruit: for apart from me ye can do nothing"—as God's natural life is in the vine, that it may give life to its natural branches, so God's spiritual life is in the vine, Christ, that he may give life to his spiritual branches. The roots of this new vine are planted in heaven, not on earth; and into it the half-withered branches of the old humanity are to be grafted, that they may have life divine. Yet our Lord does not say "I am the root." The branch is not something outside, which has to get nourishment out of the root,—it is rather a part of the vine. Rom. 6:5—"if we have become united with him [σύμφυτοι—'grown together'—used of the man and horse in the Centaur, Xen., Cyrop., 4:3:18], in the likeness of his death, we shall be also in the likeness of his resurrection"; 11:24—"thou wast cut out of that which is by nature a wild olive tree, and wast grafted contrary to nature into a good olive tree"; Col. 2:6, 7—"As therefore ye received Christ Jesus the Lord, so walk in him, rooted and builded up in him"—not only grounded in Christ as our foundation, but thrusting down roots into him as the deep, rich, all-sustaining soil. This union with Christ is consistent with individuality: for the graft brings forth fruit after its kind, though modified by the tree into which it is grafted.

Bishop H. W. Warren, in S. S. Times, Oct. 17, 1891—"The lessons of the vine are intimacy, likeness of nature, continuous impartation of life, fruit. Between friends there is intimacy by means of media, such as food, presents, care, words, soul looking from the eyes. The mother gives her liquid flesh to the babe, but such intimacy soon ceases. The mother is not rich enough in life continuously to feed the ever-enlarging nature of the growing man. Not so with the vine. It continuously feeds. Its rivers crowd all the banks. They burst out in leaf, blossom, clinging tendrils, and fruit, everywhere. In nature a thorn grafted on a pear tree bears only thorn. There is not pear-life enough to compel change of its nature. But a wild olive, typical of depraved nature, grafted on a good olive tree finds, contrary to nature, that there is force enough in the growing stock to change the nature of the wild scion."

(d) From the union between the members and the head of the body.

1 Cor. 6:15, 19—"Know ye not that your bodies are members of Christ?... know ye not that your body is a temple of the Holy Spirit which is in you, which ye have from God?" 12:12—"For as the body is one, and hath many members, and all the members of the body, being many, are one body; so also is Christ"—here Christ is identified with the church of which he is the head; Eph. 1:22, 23—"he put all things in subjection under his feet, and gave him to be head over all things to the church, which is his body, the fulness of him that filleth all in all"—as the members of the human body are united to the head, the source of their activity and the power that controls their movements, so all believers are members of an invisible body whose head is Christ. Shall we tie a string round the finger to keep for it its own blood? No, for all the blood of the body is needed to nourish one finger. So Christ is "head over all things to [for the benefit of] the church" (Tyler, Theol. Greek Poets, preface, ii). "The church is the fulness (πλήρωμα) of Christ; as it was not good for the first man, Adam, to be alone, no more was it good for the second man, Christ" (C. H. M.). Eph. 4:15, 16—"grow up in all things into him, who is the head, even Christ; from whom all the body ... maketh the increase of the body unto the building up of itself in love"; 5:29, 30—"for no man ever hated his own flesh; but nourisheth and cherisheth it, even as Christ also the church; because we are members of his body."

(e) From the union of the race with the source of its life in Adam.

Rom. 5:12, 21—"as through one man sin entered into the world, and death through sin.... that, as sin reigned in death, even so might grace reign through righteousness unto eternal life through Jesus Christ our Lord"; 1 Cor. 15:22, 45, 49—"as in Adam all die, so also in Christ shall all be made alive.... The first man Adam became a living soul. The last Adam became a life-giving Spirit.... as we have borne the image of the earthy, we shall also bear the image of the heavenly"—as the whole race is one with the first man Adam, in whom it fell and from whom it has derived a corrupted and guilty nature, so the whole race of believers constitutes a new and restored humanity, whose justified and purified nature is derived from Christ, the second Adam. Cf. Gen. 2:23—"This is now bone of my bones, and flesh of my flesh: she shall be called Woman, because she was taken out of Man"—here C. H. M. remarks that, as man is first created and then woman is viewed in and formed out of him, so it is with Christ and the church. "We are members of Christ's body, because in Christ we have the principle of our origin; from him our life arose, just as the life of Eve was derived from Adam.... The church is Christ's helpmeet, formed out of Christ in his deep sleep of death, as Eve out of Adam.... The church will be nearest to Christ, as Eve was to Adam." Because Christ is the source of all spiritual life for his people, he is called, in Is. 9:6, "Everlasting Father," and it is said, in Is. 53:10, that "he shall see his seed" (see page 680).

B. Direct statements.

(a) The believer is said to be in Christ.

Lest we should regard the figures mentioned above as merely Oriental metaphors, the fact of the believer's union with Christ is asserted in the most direct and prosaic manner. John 14:20—"ye in me"; Rom. 6:11—"alive unto God in Christ Jesus"; 8:1—"no condemnation to them that are in Christ Jesus"; 2 Cor. 5:17—"if any man is in Christ, he is a new creature"; Eph. 1:4—"chose us in him before the foundation of the world"; 2:13—"now in Christ Jesus ye that once were far off are made nigh in the blood of Christ." Thus the believer is said to be "in Christ," as the element or atmosphere which surrounds him with its perpetual presence and which constitutes his vital breath; in fact, this phrase "in Christ," always meaning "in union with Christ," is the very key to Paul's epistles, and to the whole New Testament. The fact that the believer is in Christ is symbolized in baptism: we are "baptized into Christ" (Gal. 3:27).

(b) Christ is said to be in the believer.

John 14:20—"I in you"; Rom. 8:9—"ye are not in the flesh but in the Spirit, if so be that the Spirit of God dwelleth in you. But if any man hath not the Spirit of Christ, he is none of his"—that this Spirit of Christ is Christ himself, is shown from verse 10—"And if Christ is in you, the body is dead because of sin; but the spirit is life because of righteousness"; Gal. 2:20—"I have been crucified with Christ; and it is no longer I that live, but Christ liveth in me"—here Christ is said to be in the believer, and so to live his life within the believer, that the latter can point to this as the dominating fact of his experience,—it is not so much he that lives, as it is Christ that lives in him. The fact that Christ is in the believer is symbolized in the Lord's supper: "The bread which we break, is it not a participation in the body of Christ?" (1 Cor. 10:16).

(c) The Father and the Son dwell in the believer.

John 14:23—"If a man love me, he will keep my word: and my Father will love him, and we will come unto him, and make our abode with him"; cf. 10—"Believest thou not that I am in the Father, and the Father in me? the words that I say unto you I speak not from myself: but the Father abiding in me doeth his works"—the Father and the Son dwell in the believer; for where the Son is, there always the Father must be also. If the union between the believer and Christ in John 14:23 is to be interpreted as one of mere moral influence, then the union of Christ and the Father in John 14:10 must also be interpreted as a union of mere moral influence. Eph. 3:17—"that Christ may dwell in your hearts through faith"; 1 John 4:16—"he that abideth in love abideth in God, and God abideth in him."

(d) The believer has life by partaking of Christ, as Christ has life by partaking of the Father.

John 6:53, 56, 57—"Except ye eat the flesh of the Son of man and drink his blood, ye have not life in yourselves .... He that eateth my flesh and drinketh my blood abideth in me, and I in him. As the living Father sent me and I live because of the Father, so he that eateth me, he also shall live because of me"—the believer has life by partaking of Christ in a way that may not inappropriately be compared with Christ's having life by partaking of the Father. 1 Cor. 10:16, 17—"the cup of blessing which we bless, is it not a communion of the blood of Christ? The bread which we break, is it not a communion of the body of Christ?"—here it is intimated that the Lord's Supper sets forth, in the language of symbol, the soul's actual participation in the life of Christ; and the margin properly translates the word κοινωνία, not "communion," but "participation." Cf. 1 John 1:3—"our fellowship (κοινωνία) is with the Father, and with his Son Jesus Christ." Foster, Christian Life and Theology, 216—"In John 6, the phrases call to mind the ancient form of sacrifice, and the participation therein by the offerer at the sacrificial meal,—as at the Passover."

(e) All believers are one in Christ.

John 17:21-23—"that they may all be one; even as thou, Father, art in me, and I in thee, that they also may be in us: that the world may believe that thou didst send me. And the glory which thou hast given me I have given unto them; that they may be one, even as we are one; I in them, and thou in me, that they may be perfected into one"—all believers are one in Christ, to whom they are severally and collectively united, as Christ himself is one with God.

(f) The believer is made partaker of the divine nature.

2 Pet. 1:4—"that through these [promises] ye may become partakers of the divine nature"—not by having the essence of your humanity changed into the essence of divinity, but by having Christ the divine Savior continually dwelling within, and indissolubly joined to, your human souls.

(g) The believer is made one spirit with the Lord.

1 Cor. 6:17—"he that is joined unto the Lord is one spirit"—human nature is so interpenetrated and energized by the divine, that the two move and act as one; cf. 19—"know ye not that your body is a temple of the Holy Spirit which is in you, which ye have from God?" Rom. 8:26—"the Spirit also helpeth our infirmity: for we know not how to pray as we ought; but the Spirit himself maketh intercession for us with groanings which cannot be uttered"—the Spirit is so near to us, and so one with us, that our prayer is called his, or rather, his prayer becomes ours. Weiss, in his Life of Jesus, says that, in the view of Scripture, human greatness does not consist in a man's producing everything in a natural way out of himself, but in possessing perfect receptivity for God's greatest gift. Therefore God's Son receives the Spirit without measure; and we may add that the believer in like manner receives Christ.

2. Nature of this Union.

We have here to do not only with a fact of life, but with a unique relation between the finite and the infinite. Our descriptions must therefore be inadequate. Yet in many respects we know what this union is not; in certain respects we can positively characterize it.

It should not surprise us if we find it far more difficult to give a scientific definition of this union, than to determine the fact of its existence. It is a fact of life with which we have to deal; and the secret of life, even in its lowest forms, no philosopher has ever yet discovered. The tiniest flower witnesses to two facts: first, that of its own relative independence, as an individual organism; and secondly, that of its ultimate dependence upon a life and power not its own. So every human soul has its proper powers of intellect, affection, and will; yet it lives, moves, and has its being in God (Acts 17:28).

Starting out from the truth of God's omnipresence, it might seem as if God's indwelling in the granite boulder was the last limit of his union with the finite. But we see the divine intelligence and goodness drawing nearer to us, by successive stages, in vegetable life, in the animal creation, and in the moral nature of man. And yet there are two stages beyond all these: first, in Christ's union with the believer; and secondly, in God's union with Christ. If this union of God with the believer be only one of several approximations of God to his finite creation, the fact that it is, equally with the others, not wholly comprehensible to reason, should not blind us either to its truth or to its importance.

It is easier to-day than at any other previous period of history to believe in the union of the believer with Christ. That God is immanent in the universe, and that there is a divine element in man, is familiar to our generation. All men are naturally one with Christ, the immanent God, and this natural union prepares the way for that spiritual union in which Christ joins himself to our faith. Campbell, The Indwelling Christ, 131—"In the immanence of Christ in nature we find the ground of his immanence in human nature.... A man may be out of Christ, but Christ is never out of him. Those who banish him he does not abandon." John Caird, Fund. Ideas of Christianity, 2:233-256—"God is united with nature, in the atoms, in the trees, in the planets. Science is seeing nature full of the life of God. God is united to man in body and soul. The beating of his heart and the voice of conscience witness to God within. God sleeps in the stone, dreams in the animal, wakes in man."

A. Negatively.—It is not:

(a) A merely natural union, like that of God with all human spirits,—as held by rationalists.

In our physical life we are conscious of another life within us which is not subject to our wills: the heart beats involuntarily, whether we sleep or wake. But in our spiritual life we are still more conscious of a life within our life. Even the heathen said: "Est Deus in nobis; agitante calescimus illo," and the Egyptians held to the identification of the departed with Osiris (Renouf, Hibbert Lectures, 185). But Paul urges us to work out our salvation, upon the very ground that "it is God that worketh" in us, "both to will and to work, for his good pleasure" (Phil. 2:12, 13). This life of God in the soul is the life of Christ.

The movement of the electric car cannot be explained simply from the working of its own motor apparatus. The electric current throbbing through the wire, and the dynamo from which that energy proceeds, are needed to explain the result. In like manner we need a spiritual Christ to explain the spiritual activity of the Christian. A. H. Strong, Sermon before the Baptist World Congress in London, 1905—"We had in America some years ago a steam engine all whose working parts were made of glass. The steam came from without, but, being hot enough to move machinery, this steam was itself invisible, and there was presented the curious spectacle of an engine, transparent, moving, and doing important work, while yet no cause for this activity was perceptible. So the church, humanity, the universe, are all in constant and progressive movement, but the Christ who moves them is invisible. Faith comes to believe where it cannot see. It joins itself to this invisible Christ, and knows him as its very life."

(b) A merely moral union, or union of love and sympathy, like that between teacher and scholar, friend and friend,—as held by Socinians and Arminians.

There is a moral union between different souls: 1 Sam. 18:1—"the soul of Jonathan was knit with the soul of David, and Jonathan loved him as his own soul"—here the Vulgate has: "Anima Jonathæ agglutinata Davidi." Aristotle calls friends "one soul." So in a higher sense, in Acts 4:32, the early believers are said to have been "of one heart and soul." But in John 17:21, 26, Christ's union with his people is distinguished from any mere union of love and sympathy: "that they may all be one; even as thou, Father, art in me, and I in thee, that they also may be in us;... that the love wherewith thou lovedst me may be in them, and I in them." Jesus' aim, in the whole of his last discourse, is to show that no mere union of love and sympathy will be sufficient: "apart from me," he says, "ye can do nothing" (John 15:5). That his disciples may be vitally joined to himself, is therefore the subject of his last prayer.

Dorner says well, that Arminianism (and with this doctrine Roman Catholics and the advocates of New School views substantially agree) makes man a mere tangent to the circle of the divine nature. It has no idea of the interpenetration of the one by the other. But the Lutheran Formula of Concord says much more correctly: "Damnamus sententiam quod non Deus ipse, sed dona Dei duntaxat, in credentibus habitent."

Ritschl presents to us a historical Christ, and Pfleiderer presents to us an ideal Christ, but neither one gives us the living Christ who is the present spiritual life of the believer. Wendt, in his Teaching of Jesus, 2:310, comes equally far short of a serious interpretation of our Lord's promise, when he says: "This union to his person, as to its contents, is nothing else than adherence to the message of the kingdom of God brought by him." It is not enough for me to be merely in touch with Christ. He must come to be "not so far as even to be near." Tennyson, The Higher Pantheism: "Closer is he than breathing, and nearer than hands or feet." William Watson, The Unknown God: "Yea, in my flesh his Spirit doth flow, Too near, too far, for me to know."

(c) A union of essence, which destroys the distinct personality and subsistence of either Christ or the human spirit,—as held by many of the mystics.

Many of the mystics, as Schwenkfeld, Weigel, Sebastian Frank, held to an essential union between Christ and the believer. One of Weigel's followers, therefore, could say to another: "I am Christ Jesus, the living Word of God; I have redeemed thee by my sinless sufferings." We are ever to remember that the indwelling of Christ only puts the believer more completely in possession of himself, and makes him more conscious of his own personality and power. Union with Christ must be taken in connection with the other truth of the personality and activity of the Christian; otherwise it tends to pantheism. Martineau, Study, 2:190—"In nature it is God's immanent life, in morals it is God's transcendent life, with which we commune."

Angelus Silesius, a German philosophical poet (1624-1677), audaciously wrote: "I know God cannot live an instant without me; He must give up the ghost, if I should cease to be." Lowde, a disciple of Malebranche, used the phrase "Godded with God, and Christed with Christ," and Jonathan Edwards, in his Religious Affections, quotes it with disapprobation, saying that "the saints do not become actually partakers of the divine essence, as would be inferred from this abominable and blasphemous language of heretics" (Allen, Jonathan Edwards, 224). "Self is not a mode of the divine: it is a principle of isolation. In order to religion, I must have a will to surrender.... 'Our wills are ours, to make them thine.'... Though the self is, in knowledge, a principle of unification; in existence, or metaphysically, it is a principle of isolation" (Seth).

Inge, Christian Mysticism, 30—"Some of the mystics went astray by teaching a real substitution of the divine for human nature, thus depersonalizing man—a fatal mistake, for without human personality we cannot conceive of divine personality." Lyman Abbott: "In Christ, God and man are united, not as the river is united with the sea, losing its personality therein, but as the child is united with the father, or the wife with the husband, whose personality and individuality are strengthened and increased by the union." Here Dr. Abbott's view comes as far short of the truth as that of the mystics goes beyond the truth. As we shall see, the union of the believer with Christ is a vital union, surpassing in its intimacy any union of souls that we know. The union of child with father, or of wife with husband, is only a pointer which hints very imperfectly at the interpenetrating and energizing of the human spirit by the divine.

(d) A union mediated and conditioned by participation of the sacraments of the church,—as held by Romanists, Lutherans, and High-Church Episcopalians.

Perhaps the most pernicious misinterpretation of the nature of this union is that which conceives of it as a physical and material one, and which rears upon this basis the fabric of a sacramental and external Christianity. It is sufficient here to say that this union cannot be mediated by sacraments, since sacraments presuppose it as already existing; both Baptism and the Lord's Supper are designed only for believers. Only faith receives and retains Christ; and faith is the act of the soul grasping what is purely invisible and supersensible: not the act of the body, submitting to Baptism or partaking of the Supper.

William Lincoln: "The only way for the believer, if he wants to go rightly, is to remember that truth is always two-sided. If there is any truth that the Holy Spirit has specially pressed upon your heart, if you do not want to push it to the extreme, ask what is the counter-truth, and lean a little of your weight upon that; otherwise, if you bear so very much on one side of the truth, there is a danger of pushing it into a heresy. Heresy means selected truth; it does not mean error; heresy and error are very different things. Heresy is truth, but truth pushed into undue importance, to the disparagement of the truth upon the other side." Heresy (αἵρεσις) = an act of choice, the picking and choosing of a part, instead of comprehensively embracing the whole of truth. Sacramentarians substitute the symbol for the thing symbolized.

B. Positively.—It is:

(a) An organic union,—in which we become members of Christ and partakers of his humanity.

Kant defines an organism, as that whose parts are reciprocally means and end. The body is an organism; since the limbs exist for the heart, and the heart for the limbs. So each member of Christ's body lives for him who is the head; and Christ the head equally lives for his members: Eph. 5:29, 30—"no man ever hated his own flesh; but nourisheth and cherisheth it, even as Christ also the church; because we are members of his body." The train- despatcher is a symbol of the concentration of energy; the switchmen and conductors who receive his orders are symbols of the localization of force; but it is all one organic system.

(b) A vital union,—in which Christ's life becomes the dominating principle within us.

This union is a vital one, in distinction from any union of mere juxtaposition or external influence. Christ does not work upon us from without, as one separated from us, but from within, as the very heart from which the life-blood of our spirits flows. See Gal. 2:20—"it is no longer I that live, but Christ liveth in me: and that life which I now live in the flesh I live in faith, the faith which is in the Son of God, who loved me, and gave himself up for me;" Col 3:3, 4—"For ye died, and your life is hid with Christ in God. When Christ, who is our life, shall be manifested, then shall ye also with him be manifested in glory." Christ's life is not corrupted by the corruption of his members, any more than the ray of light is defiled by the filth with which it comes in contact. We may be unconscious of this union with Christ, as we often are of the circulation of the blood, yet it may be the very source and condition of our life.

(c) A spiritual union,—that is, a union whose source and author is the Holy Spirit.

By a spiritual union we mean a union not of body but of spirit,—a union, therefore, which only the Holy Spirit originates and maintains. Rom. 8:9, 10—"ye are not in the flesh but in the Spirit, if so be that the Spirit of God dwelleth in you. But if any man hath not the Spirit of Christ, he is none of his. And if Christ is in you, the body is dead because of sin; but the spirit is life because of righteousness." The indwelling of Christ involves a continual exercise of efficient power. In Eph. 3:16, 17, "strengthened with power through his Spirit in the inward man" is immediately followed by "that Christ may dwell in your hearts through faith."

(d) An indissoluble union,—that is, a union which, consistently with Christ's promise and grace, can never be dissolved.

Mat. 28:20—"lo, I am with you always, even unto the end of the world"; John 10:28—"they shall never perish, and no one shall snatch them out of my hand"; Rom. 8:35, 39—"Who shall separate us from the love of Christ?... nor height, nor depth, nor any other creature, shall be able to separate us from the love of God, which is in Christ Jesus our Lord"; 1 Thess. 4:14, 17—"them also that are fallen asleep in Jesus will God bring with him ... then we that are alive, that are left, shall together with them be caught up in the clouds, to meet the Lord in the air: and so shall we ever be with the Lord."

Christ's omnipresence makes it possible for him to be united to, and to be present in, each believer, as perfectly and fully as if that believer were the only one to receive Christ's fulness. As Christ's omnipresence makes the whole Christ present in every place, each believer has the whole Christ with him, as his source of strength, purity, life; so that each may say: Christ gives all his time and wisdom and care to me. Such a union as this lacks every element of instability. Once formed, the union is indissoluble. Many of the ties of earth are rudely broken,—not so with our union with Christ,—that endures forever.

Since there is now an unchangeable and divine element in us, our salvation depends no longer upon our unstable wills, but upon Christ's purpose and power. By temporary declension from duty, or by our causeless unbelief, we may banish Christ to the barest and most remote room of the soul's house; but he does not suffer us wholly to exclude him; and when we are willing to unbar the doors, he is still there, ready to fill the whole mansion with his light and love.

(e) An inscrutable union,—mystical, however, only in the sense of surpassing in its intimacy and value any other union of souls which we know.

This union is inscrutable, indeed; but it is not mystical, in the sense of being unintelligible to the Christian or beyond the reach of his experience. If we call it mystical at all, it should be only because, in the intimacy of its communion and in the transforming power of its influence, it surpasses any other union of souls that we know, and so cannot be fully described or understood by earthly analogies. Eph. 5:32—"This mystery is great: but I speak in regard of Christ and of the church"; Col. 1:27—"the riches of the glory of this mystery among the Gentiles, which is Christ in you, the hope of glory."

See Diman, Theistic Argument, 380—"As physical science has brought us to the conclusion that back of all the phenomena of the material universe there lies an invisible universe of forces, and that these forces may ultimately be reduced to one all-pervading force in which the unity of the physical universe consists; and as philosophy has advanced the rational conjecture that this ultimate all-pervading force is simply will-force; so the great Teacher holds up to us the spiritual universe as pervaded by one omnipotent life—a life which was revealed in him as its highest manifestation, but which is shared by all who by faith become partakers of his nature. He was Son of God: they too had power to become sons of God. The incarnation is wholly within the natural course and tendency of things. It was prepared for, it came, in the fulness of times. Christ's life is not something sporadic and individual, having its source in the personal conviction of each disciple; it implies a real connection with Christ, the head. Behind all nature there is one force; behind all varieties of Christian life and character there is one spiritual power. All nature is not inert matter,—it is pervaded by a living presence. So all the body of believers live by virtue of the all-working Spirit of Christ, the Holy Ghost." An epitaph at Silton, in Dorsetshire, reads: "Here lies a piece of Christ—a star in dust, A vein of gold, a china dish, that must Be used in heaven when God shall feed the just."

A. H. Strong, in Examiner, 1880: "Such is the nature of union with Christ,—such I mean, is the nature of every believer's union with Christ. For, whether he knows it or not, every Christian has entered into just such a partnership as this. It is this and this only which constitutes him a Christian, and which makes possible a Christian church. We may, indeed, be thus united to Christ, without being fully conscious of the real nature of our relation to him. We may actually possess the kernel, while as yet we have regard only to the shell; we may seem to ourselves to be united to Christ only by an external bond, while after all it is an inward and spiritual bond that makes us his. God often reveals to the Christian the mystery of the gospel, which is Christ in him the hope of glory, at the very time that he is seeking only some nearer access to a Redeemer outside of him. Trying to find a union of coöperation or of sympathy, he is amazed to learn that there is already established a union with Christ more glorious and blessed, namely, a union of life; and so, like the miners in the Rocky Mountains, while he is looking only for silver, he finds gold. Christ and the believer have the same life. They are not separate persons linked together by some temporary bond of friendship,—they are united by a tie as close and indissoluble as if the same blood ran in their veins. Yet the Christian may never have suspected how intimate a union he has with his Savior; and the first understanding of this truth may be the gateway through which he passes into a holier and happier stage of the Christian life."

So the Way leads, through the Truth, to the Life (John 14:6). Apprehension of an external Savior prepares for the reception and experience of the internal Savior. Christ is first the Door of the sheep, but in him, after they have once entered in, they find pasture (John 10:7-9). On the nature of this union, see H. B. Smith, System of Christian Theology, 531-539; Baird, Elohim Revealed, 601; Wilberforce, Incarnation, 208-272, and New Birth of Man's Nature, 1-30. Per contra, see Park, Discourses, 117-136.

3. Consequences of this Union as respects the Believer.

We have seen that Christ's union with humanity, at the incarnation, involved him in all the legal liabilities of the race to which he united himself, and enabled him so to assume the penalty of its sin as to make for all men a full satisfaction to the divine justice, and to remove all external obstacles to man's return to God. An internal obstacle, however, still remains—the evil affections and will, and the consequent guilt, of the individual soul. This last obstacle also Christ removes, in the case of all his people, by uniting himself to them in a closer and more perfect manner than that in which he is united to humanity at large. As Christ's union with the race secures the objective reconciliation of the race to God, so Christ's union with believers secures the subjective reconciliation of believers to God.

In Baird, Elohim Revealed, 607-610, in Owen, on Justification, chap. 8, in Boston, Covenant of Grace, chap. 2, and in Dale, Atonement, 265-440, the union of the believer with Christ is made to explain the bearing of our sins by Christ. As we have seen in our discussion of the Atonement, however (page 759), this explains the cause by the effect, and implies that Christ died only for the elect (see review of Dale, in Brit. Quar. Rev., Apr. 1876:221-225). It is not the union of Christ with the believer, but the union of Christ with humanity at large, that explains his taking upon him human guilt and penalty.

Amnesty offered to a rebellious city may be complete, yet it may avail only for those who surrender. Pardon secured from a Governor, upon the ground of the services of an Advocate, may be effectual only when the convict accepts it,—there is no hope for him when he tears up the pardon. Dr. H. E. Robins: "The judicial declaration of acquittal on the ground of the death of Christ, which comes to all men (Rom. 5:18), and into the benefits of which they are introduced by natural birth, is inchoate justification, and will become perfected justification through the new birth of the Holy Spirit, unless the working of this divine agent is resisted by the personal moral action of those who are lost." What Dr. Robins calls "inchoate justification" we prefer to call "ideal justification" or "attainable justification." Humanity in Christ is justified, and every member of the race who joins himself to Christ by faith participates in Christ's justification. H. E. Dudley: "Adam's sin holds us all down just as gravity holds all, while Christ's righteousness, though secured for all and accessible to all, involves an effort of will in climbing and grasping which not all will make." Justification in Christ is the birthright of humanity; but, in order to possess and enjoy it, each of us must claim and appropriate it by faith.

R. W. Dale, Fellowship with Christ, 7—"When we were created in Christ, the fortunes of the human race for good or evil became his. The Incarnation revealed and fulfilled the relations which already existed between the Son of God and mankind. From the beginning Christ had entered into fellowship with us. When we sinned, he remained in fellowship with us still. Our miseries" [we would add: our guilt] "were his, by his own choice.... His fellowship with us is the foundation of our fellowship with him.... When I have discovered that by the very constitution of my nature I am to achieve perfection in the power of the life of Another—who is yet not Another, but the very ground of my being—it ceases to be incredible to me that Another—who is yet not Another—should be the Atonement for my sin, and that his relation to God should determine mine."

A tract entitled "The Seven Togethers" sums up the Scripture testimony with regard to the Consequences of the believer's Union with Christ: 1. Crucified together with Christ—Gal. 2:20—συνεσταύρωμαι. 2. Died together with Christ—Col. 2:20—ἀπεθάνετε. 3. Buried together with Christ—Rom. 6:4—συνετάφημεν. 4. Quickened together with Christ—Eph. 2:5—συνεζωοποίησεν. 5. Raised together with Christ—Col. 3:1—συνηγέρθητε. 6. Sufferers together with Christ—Rom. 8:17—συμπάσχομεν. 7. Glorified together with Christ—Rom. 8:17—συνδοξασθῶμεν. Union with Christ results in common sonship, relation to God, character, influence, and destiny.

Imperfect apprehension of the believer's union with Christ works to the great injury of Christian doctrine. An experience of union with Christ first enables us to understand the death of sin and separation from God which has befallen the race sprung from the first Adam. The life and liberty of the children of God in Christ Jesus shows us by contrast how far astray we had gone. The vital and organic unity of the new race sprung from the second Adam reveals the depravity and disintegration which we had inherited from our first father. We see that as there is one source of spiritual life in Christ, so there was one source of corrupt life in Adam; and that as we are justified by reason of our oneness with the justified Christ, so we are condemned by reason of our oneness with the condemned Adam.

A. H. Strong, Christ in Creation, 175—"If it is consistent with evolution that the physical and natural life of the race should be derived from a single source, then it is equally consistent with evolution that the moral and spiritual life of the race should be derived from a single source. Scripture is stating only scientific fact when it sets the second Adam, the head of redeemed humanity, over against the first Adam, the head of fallen humanity. We are told that evolution should give us many Christs. We reply that evolution has not given us many Adams. Evolution, as it assigns to the natural head of the race a supreme and unique position, must be consistent with itself, and must assign a supreme and unique position to Jesus Christ, the spiritual head of the race. As there was but one Adam from whom all the natural life of the race was derived, so that there can be but one Christ from whom all the spiritual life of the race is derived."

The consequences of union with Christ may be summarily stated as follows:

(a) Union with Christ involves a change in the dominant affection of the soul. Christ's entrance into the soul makes it a new creature, in the sense that the ruling disposition, which before was sinful, now becomes holy. This change we call Regeneration.

Rom. 8:2—"For the law of the Spirit of life in Christ Jesus made me free from the law of sin and of death"; 2 Cor. 5:17—"if any man is in Christ, he is a new creature" (marg.—"there is a new creation"); Gal. 1:15, 16—"it was the good pleasure of God ... to reveal his Son in me"; Eph. 2:10—"For we are his workmanship, created in Christ Jesus for good works." As we derive our old nature from the first man Adam, by birth, so we derive a new nature from the second man Christ, by the new birth. Union with Christ is the true "transfusion of blood." "The death-struck sinner, like the wan, anæmic, dying invalid, is saved by having poured into his veins the healthier blood of Christ" (Drummond, Nat. Law in the Spir. World). God regenerates the soul by uniting it to Jesus Christ.

In the Johnston Harvester Works at Batavia, when they paint their machinery, they do it by immersing part after part in a great tank of paint,—so the painting is instantaneous and complete. Our baptism into Christ is the outward picture of an inward immersion of the soul not only into his love and fellowship, but into his very life, so that in him we become new creatures (2 Cor. 5:17). As Miss Sullivan surrounded Helen Keller with the influence of her strong personality, by intelligence and sympathy and determination striving to awaken the blind and dumb soul and give it light and love, so Jesus envelops us. But his Spirit is more encompassing and more penetrating than any human influence however powerful, because his life is the very ground and principle of our being.

Tennyson: "O for a man to arise in me, That the man that I am may cease to be!" Emerson: "Himself from God he could not free; He builded better than he knew." Religion is not the adding of a new department of activity as an adjunct to our own life or the grafting of a new method of manifestation upon the old. It is rather the grafting of our souls into Christ, so that his life dominates and manifests itself in all our activities. The magnet which left to itself can lift only a three pound weight, will lift three hundred when it is attached to the electric dynamo. Expositor's Greek Testament on 1 Cor. 15:45, 46—"The action of Jesus in 'breathing' upon his disciples while he said, 'Receive the Holy Spirit' (John 20:22 sq.) symbolized the vitalizing relationship which at this epoch he assumed towards mankind; this act raised to a higher potency the original 'breathing' of God by which 'man became a living soul' (Gen. 2:7)."

(b) Union with Christ involves a new exercise of the soul's powers in repentance and faith; faith, indeed, is the act of the soul by which, under the operation of God, Christ is received. This new exercise of the soul's powers we call Conversion (Repentance and Faith). It is the obverse or human side of Regeneration.

Eph. 3:17—"that Christ may dwell in your hearts through faith"; 2 Tim. 3:15—"the sacred writings which are able to make thee wise unto salvation through faith which is in Christ Jesus." Faith is the soul's laying hold of Christ as its only source of life, pardon, and salvation. And so we see what true religion is. It is not a moral life; it is not a determination to be religious; it is not faith, if by faith we mean an external trust that somehow Christ will save us; it is nothing less than the life of the soul in God, through Christ his Son. To Christ then we are to look for the origin, continuance and increase of our faith (Luke 17:5—"said unto the Lord, Increase our faith"). Our faith is but a part of "his fulness" of which "we all received, and grace for grace" (John 1:16).

A. H. Strong, Sermon before the Baptist World Congress, London, 1905—"Christianity is summed up in the two facts: Christ for us, and Christ in us—Christ for us upon the Cross, revealing the eternal opposition of holiness to sin, and yet, through God's eternal suffering for sin making objective atonement for us; and Christ in us by his Spirit, renewing in us the lost image of God, and abiding in us as the all-sufficient source of purity and power. Here are the two foci of the Christian ellipse: Christ for us, who redeemed us from the curse of the law by being made a curse for us, and Christ in us, the hope of glory, whom the apostle calls the mystery of the gospel.

"We need Christ in us as well as Christ for us. How shall I, how shall society, find healing and purification within? Let me answer by reminding you of what they did at Chicago. In all the world there was no river more stagnant and fetid than was Chicago River. Its sluggish stream received the sweepings of the watercraft and the offal of the city, and there was no current to carry the detritus away. There it settled, and bred miasma and fever. At last it was suggested that, by cutting through the low ridge between the city and the Desplaines River, the current could be set running in the opposite direction, and drainage could be secured into the Illinois River and the great Mississippi. At a cost of fifteen millions of dollars the cut was made, and now all the water of Lake Michigan can be relied upon to cleanse that turbid stream. What Chicago River could never do for itself, the great lake now does for it. So no human soul can purge itself of its sin; and what the individual cannot do, humanity at large is powerless to accomplish. Sin has dominion over us, and we are foul to the very depths of our being, until with the help of God we break through the barrier of our self-will, and let the floods of Christ's purifying life flow into us. Then, in an hour, more is done to renew, than all our efforts for years had effected. Thus humanity is saved, individual by individual, not by philosophy, or philanthropy, or self-development, or self-reformation, but simply by joining itself to Jesus Christ, and by being filled in Him with all the fulness of God."

(c) Union with Christ gives to the believer the legal standing and rights of Christ. As Christ's union with the race involves atonement, so the believer's union with Christ involves Justification. The believer is entitled to take for his own all that Christ is, and all that Christ has done; and this because he has within him that new life of humanity which suffered in Christ's death and rose from the grave in Christ's resurrection,—in other words, because he is virtually one person with the Redeemer. In Christ the believer is prophet, priest, and king.

Acts 13:39—"by him [lit.: 'in him' = in union with him] every one that believeth is justified"; Rom. 6:7, 8—"he that hath died is justified from sin ... we died with Christ"; 7:4—"dead to the law through the body of Christ"; 8:1—"no condemnation to them that are in Christ Jesus"; 17—"heirs of God, and joint-heirs with Christ"; 1 Cor. 1:30—"But of him ye are in Christ Jesus, who was made unto us wisdom from God, and righteousness [justification]"; 3:21, 23—"all things are yours ... and ye are Christ's"; 6:11—"ye were justified in the name of the Lord Jesus Christ, and in the Spirit of our God"; 2 Cor. 5:14—"we thus judge, that one died for all, therefore all died"; 21—"Him who knew no sin he made to be sin on our behalf; that we might become the righteousness [justification] of God in him" = God's justified persons, in union with Christ (see pages 760, 761).

Gal. 2:20—"I have been crucified with Christ; and it is no longer I that live, but Christ liveth in me"; Eph. 1:4, 6—"chose us in him ... to the praise of the glory of his grace, which he freely bestowed on us in the Beloved"; 2:5, 6—"even when we were dead through our trespasses, made us alive together with Christ ... made us to sit with him in the heavenly places, in Christ Jesus"; Phil. 3:8, 9—"that I may gain Christ, and be found in him, not having a righteousness of mine own, even that which is of the law, but that which is through faith in Christ, the righteousness which is from God by faith"; 2 Tim. 2:11—"Faithful is the saying: For if we died with him, we shall also live with him." Prophet: Luke 12:12—"the Holy Spirit shall teach you in that very hour what ye ought to say"; 1 John 2:20—"ye have an anointing from the Holy One, and ye know all things." Priest: 1 Pet. 2:5—"a holy priesthood, to offer up spiritual sacrifices, acceptable to God through Jesus Christ"; Rev. 20:6—"they shall be priests of God and of Christ"; 1 Pet. 2:9—"a royal priesthood." King: Rev. 3:21—"He that overcometh, I will give to him to sit down with me in my throne"; 5:10—"madest them to be unto our God a kingdom and priests." The connection of justification and union with Christ delivers the former from the charge of being a mechanical and arbitrary procedure. As Jonathan Edwards has said: "The justification of the believer is no other than his being admitted to communion in, or participation of, this head and surety of all believers."

(d) Union with Christ secures to the believer the continuously transforming, assimilating power of Christ's life,—first, for the soul; secondly, for the body,—consecrating it in the present, and in the future raising it up in the likeness of Christ's glorified body. This continuous influence, so far as it is exerted in the present life, we call Sanctification, the human side or aspect of which is Perseverance.

For the soul: John 1:16—"of his fulness we all received, and grace for grace"—successive and increasing measures of grace, corresponding to the soul's successive and increasing needs; Rom. 8:10—"if Christ is in you, the body is dead because of sin; but the spirit is life because of righteousness"; 1 Cor. 15:45—"The last Adam became a life-giving spirit"; Phil. 2:5—"Have this mind in you, which was also in Christ Jesus"; 1 John 3:2—"if he shall be manifested, we shall be like him." "Can Christ let the believer fall out of his hands? No, for the believer is his hands."

For the body: 1 Cor. 6:17-20—"he that is joined unto the Lord is one spirit ... know ye not that your body is a temple of the Holy Spirit which is in you ... glorify God therefore in your body"; Thess.

5:23—"And the God of peace himself sanctify you wholly; and may your spirit and soul and body be preserved entire, without blame at the coming of our Lord Jesus Christ"; Rom. 8:11—"shall give life also to your mortal bodies through his Spirit that dwelleth in you"; 1 Cor. 15:49—"as we have borne the image of the earthy [man], we shall also bear the image of the heavenly [man]"; Phil. 3:20, 21—"For our citizenship is in heaven; from whence also we wait for a Savior, the Lord Jesus Christ: who shall fashion anew the body of our humiliation, that it may be conformed to the body of his glory, according to the working whereby he is able even to subject all things unto himself."

Is there a physical miracle wrought for the drunkard in his regeneration? Mr. Moody says, Yes; Mr. Gough says, No. We prefer to say that the change is a spiritual one; but that the "expulsive power of a new affection" indirectly affects the body, so that old appetites sometimes disappear in a moment; and that often, in the course of years, great changes take place even in the believer's body. Tennyson, Idylls: "Have ye looked at Edyrn? Have ye seen how nobly changed? This work of his is great and wonderful; His very face with change of heart is changed." "Christ in the soul fashions the germinal man into his own likeness,—this is the embryology of the new life. The cardinal error in religious life is the attempt to live without proper environment" (see Drummond, Natural Law in Spiritual World, 253-284). Human life from Adam does not stand the test,—only divine-human life in Christ can secure us from falling. This is the work of Christ, now that he has ascended and taken to himself his power, namely, to give his life more and more fully to the church, until it shall grow up in all things into him, the Head, and shall fitly express his glory to the world.

As the accomplished organist discloses unsuspected capabilities of his instrument, so Christ brings into activity all the latent powers of the human soul. "I was five years in the ministry," said an American preacher, "before I realized that my Savior is alive." Dr. R. W. Dale has left on record the almost unutterable feelings that stirred his soul when he first realized this truth; see Walker, The Spirit and the Incarnation, preface, v. Many have struggled in vain against sin until they have admitted Christ to their hearts,—then they could say: "this is the victory that hath overcome the world, even our faith" (1 John 5:4). "Go out, God will go in; Die thou, and let him live; Be not, and he will be; Wait, and he'll all things give." The best way to get air out of a vessel is to pour water in. Only in Christ can we find our pardon, peace, purity, and power. He is "made unto us wisdom from God, and justification and sanctification, and redemption" (1 Cor. 1:30). A medical man says: "The only radical remedy for dipsomania is religiomania" (quoted in William James, Varieties of Religious Experience, 268). It is easy to break into an empty house; the spirit cast out returns, finds the house empty, brings seven others, and "the last state of that man becometh worse than the first" (Mat. 12:45). There is no safety in simply expelling sin; we need also to bring in Christ; in fact only he can enable us to expel not only actual sin but the love of it.

Alexander McLaren: "If we are 'in Christ,' we are like a diver in his crystal bell, and have a solid though invisible wall around us, which keeps all sea-monsters off us, and communicates with the upper air, whence we draw the breath of calm life and can work in security though in the ocean depths." John Caird, Fund. Ideas, 2:98—"How do we know that the life of God has not departed from nature? Because every spring we witness the annual miracle of nature's revival, every summer and autumn the waving corn. How do we know that Christ has not departed from the world? Because he imparts to the soul that trusts him a power, a purity, a peace, which are beyond all that nature can give."

(e) Union with Christ brings about a fellowship of Christ with the believer,—Christ takes part in all the labors, temptations, and sufferings of his people; a fellowship of the believer with Christ,—so that Christ's whole experience on earth is in some measure reproduced in him; a fellowship of all believers with one another,—furnishing a basis for the spiritual unity of Christ's people on earth, and for the eternal communion of heaven. The doctrine of Union with Christ is therefore the indispensable preparation for Ecclesiology, and for Eschatology.

Fellowship of Christ with the believer: Phil. 4:13—"I can do all things in him that strengtheneth me"; Heb. 4:15—"For we have not a high priest that cannot be touched with the feeling of our infirmities"; cf. Is. 63:9—"In all their affliction he was afflicted." Heb. 2:18—"in that he himself hath suffered being tempted, he is able to succor them that are tempted" = are being tempted, are under temptation. Bp. Wordsworth: "By his passion he acquired compassion." 2 Cor. 2:14—"thanks be unto God, who always leadeth us in triumph in Christ" = Christ leads us in triumph, but his triumph is ours, even if it be a triumph over us. One with him, we participate in his joy and in his sovereignty. Rev. 3:21—"He that overcometh, I will give to him to sit down with me in my throne." W. F. Taylor on Rom. 8:9—"The Spirit of God dwelleth in you.... if any man hath not the Spirit of Christ, he is none of his"—"Christ dwells in us, says the apostle. But do we accept him as a resident, or as a ruler? England was first represented at King Thebau's court by her resident. This official could rebuke, and even threaten, but no more,—Thebau was sovereign. Burma knew no peace, till England ruled. So Christ does not consent to be represented by a mere resident. He must himself dwell within the soul, and he must reign." Christina Rossetti, Thee Only: "Lord, we are rivers running to thy sea, Our waves and ripples all derived from thee; A nothing we should have, a nothing be, Except for thee. Sweet are the waters of thy shoreless sea; Make sweet our waters that make haste to thee; Pour in thy sweetness, that ourselves may be Sweetness to thee!"

Of the believer with Christ: Phil. 3:10—"that I may know him, and the power of his resurrection, and the fellowship of his sufferings, becoming conformed unto his death"; Col. 1:24—"fill up on my part that which is lacking of the afflictions of Christ in my flesh for his body's sake, which is the church"; 1 Pet. 4:13—"partakers of Christ's sufferings." The Christian reproduces Christ's life in miniature, and, in a true sense, lives it over again. Only upon the principle of union with Christ can we explain how the Christian instinctively applies to himself the prophecies and promises which originally and primarily were uttered with reference to Christ: "thou wilt not leave my soul to Sheol; Neither wilt thou suffer thy holy one to see corruption" (Ps. 16:10, 11). This fellowship is the ground of the promises made to believing prayer: John 14:13—"whatsoever ye shall ask is my name, that will I do"; Westcott, Bib. Com., in loco: "The meaning of the phrase ['in my name'] is 'as being one with me even as I am revealed to you.' Its two correlatives are 'in me' and the Pauline 'in Christ'." "All things are yours" (1 Cor. 3:21), because Christ is universal King, and all believers are exalted to fellowship with him. After the battle of Sedan, King William asked a wounded Prussian officer whether it were well with him. "All is well where your majesty leads!" was the reply. Phil. 1:21—"For to me to live is Christ, and to die is gain." Paul indeed uses the words "Christ" and "church" as interchangeable terms: 1 Cor. 12:12—"as the body is one, and hath many members, ... so also is Christ." Denney, Studies in Theology, 171—"There is not in the N. T. from beginning to end, in the record of the original and genuine Christian life, a single word of despondency or gloom. It is the most buoyant, exhilarating and joyful book in the world." This is due to the fact that the writers believe in a living and exalted Christ, and know themselves to be one with him. They descend crowned into the arena. In the Soudan, every morning for half an hour before General Gordon's tent there lay a white handkerchief. The most pressing message, even on matters of life and death, waited till that handkerchief was withdrawn. It was the signal that Christ and Gordon were in communion with each other.

Of all believers with one another: John 17:21—"that they may all be one"; 1 Cor. 10:17—"we, who are many, are one bread, one body: for we all partake of the one bread"; Eph. 2:15—"create in himself of the two one new man, so making peace"; 1 John 1:3—"that ye also may have fellowship with us: yea, and our fellowship is with the Father, and with his Son Jesus Christ"—here the word κοινωνία is used. Fellowship with each other is the effect and result of the fellowship of each with God in Christ. Compare John 10:16—"they shall become one flock, one shepherd"; Westcott, Bib. Com., in loco: "The bond of fellowship is shown to lie in the common relation to one Lord.... Nothing is said of one 'fold' under the new dispensation." Here is a unity, not of external organization, but of common life. Of this the visible church is the consequence and expression. But this communion is not limited to earth,—it is perpetuated beyond death: 1 Thess. 4:17—"so shall we ever be with the Lord"; Heb. 12:23—"to the general assembly and church of the firstborn who are enrolled in heaven, and to God the Judge of all, and to the spirits of just men made perfect"; Rev. 21 and 22—the city of God, the new Jerusalem, is the image of perfect society, as well as of intensity and fulness of life in Christ. The ordinances express the essence of Ecclesiology—union with Christ—for Baptism symbolizes the incorporation of the believer in Christ, while the Lord's Supper symbolizes the incorporation of Christ in the believer. Christianity is a social matter, and the true Christian feels the need of being with and among his brethren. The Romans could not understand why "this new sect" must be holding meetings all the time—even daily meetings. Why could they not go singly, or in families, to the temples, and make offerings to their God, and then come away, as the pagans did? It was this meeting together which exposed them to persecution and martyrdom. It was the natural and inevitable expression of their union with Christ and so of their union with one another.

The consciousness of union with Christ gives assurance of salvation. It is a great stimulus to believing prayer and to patient labor. It is a duty to "know what is the hope of his calling, what the riches of the glory of his inheritance in the saints, and what the exceeding greatness of his power to us-ward who believe" (Eph. 1:18, 19). Christ's command, "Abide in me, and I in you" (John 15:4), implies that we are both to realize and to confirm this union, by active exertion of our own wills. We are to abide in him by an entire consecration, and to let him abide in us by an appropriating faith. We are to give ourselves to Christ, and to take in return the Christ who gives himself to us,—in other words, we are to believe Christ's promises and to act upon them. All sin consists in the sundering of man's life from God, and most systems of falsehood in religion are attempts to save man without merging his life in God's once more. The only religion that can save mankind is the religion that fills the whole heart and the whole life with God, and that aims to interpenetrate universal humanity with that same living Christ who has already made himself one with the believer. This consciousness of union with Christ gives "boldness" (παρρησία—Acts 4:13; 1 John 5:14) toward men and toward God. The word belongs to the Greek democracies. Freemen are bold. Demosthenes boasts of his frankness. Christ frees us from the hidebound, introspective, self-conscious spirit. In him we become free, demonstrative, outspoken. So we find, in John's epistles, that boldness in prayer is spoken of as a virtue, and the author of the

Epistle to the Hebrews urges us to "draw near with boldness unto the throne of grace" (Heb. 4:16). An engagement of marriage is not the same as marriage. The parties may be still distant from each other. Many Christians get just near enough to Christ to be engaged to him. This seems to be the experience of Christian in the Pilgrim's Progress. But our privilege is to have a present Christ, and to do our work not only for him, but in him. "Since Christ and we are one, Why should we doubt or fear?" "We two are so joined, He'll not be in heaven, And leave me behind."

We append a few statements with regard to this union and its consequences, from noted names in theology and the church. Luther: "By faith thou art so glued to Christ that of thee and him there becomes as it were one person, so that with confidence thou canst say: 'I am Christ,—that is, Christ's righteousness, victory, etc., are mine'; and Christ in turn can say: 'I am that sinner,—that is, his sins, his death, etc., are mine, because he clings to me and I to him, for we have been joined through faith into one flesh and bone.' " Calvin: "I attribute the highest importance to the connection between the head and the members; to the inhabitation of Christ in our hearts; in a word, to the mystical union by which we enjoy him, so that, being made ours, he makes us partakers of the blessings with which he is furnished." John Bunyan: "The Lord led me into the knowledge of the mystery of union with Christ, that I was joined to him, that I was bone of his bone and flesh of his flesh. By this also my faith in him as my righteousness was the more confirmed; for if he and I were one, then his righteousness was mine, his merits mine, his victory also mine. Now could I see myself in heaven and on earth at once—in heaven by my Christ, my risen head, my righteousness and life, though on earth by my body or person." Edwards: "Faith is the soul's active uniting with Christ. God sees fit that, in order to a union's being established between two intelligent active beings, there should be the mutual act of both, that each should receive the other, as entirely joining themselves to one another." Andrew Fuller: "I have no doubt that the imputation of Christ's righteousness presupposes a union with him; since there is no perceivable fitness in bestowing benefits on one for another's sake, where there is no union or relation between."

See Luther, quoted, with other references, in Thomasius, Christi Person und Werk, 3:325. See also Calvin, Institutes, 1:660; Edwards, Works, 4:66, 69, 70; Andrew Fuller, Works, 2:685; Pascal, Thoughts, Eng. trans., 429; Hooker, Eccl. Polity, book 5, ch. 56; Tillotson, Sermons, 3:307; Trench, Studies in Gospels, 284, and Christ the True Vine, in Hulsean Lectures; Schöberlein, in Studien und Kritiken, 1847:7-69; Caird, on Union with God, in Scotch Sermons, sermon 2; Godet, on the Ultimate Design of Man, in Princeton Rev., Nov. 1880—the design is "God in man, and man in God"; Baird, Elohim Revealed, 590-617; Upham, Divine Union, Interior Life, Life of Madame Guyon and Fénelon; A. J. Gordon, In Christ; McDuff, In Christo; J. Denham Smith, Life-truths, 25-98; A. H. Strong, Philosophy and Religion, 220-225; Bishop Hall's Treatise on The Church Mystical; Andrew Murray, Abide in Christ; Stearns, Evidence of Christian Experience, 145, 174, 179; F. B. Meyer, Christian Living—essay on Appropriation of Christ, vs. mere imitation of Christ; Sanday, Epistle to the Romans, supplementary essay on the Mystic Union; H. B. Smith, System of Theology, 531; J. M. Campbell, The Indwelling Christ.

II. Regeneration

Regeneration is that act of God by which the governing disposition of the soul is made holy, and by which, through the truth as a means, the first holy exercise of this disposition is secured.

Regeneration, or the new birth, is the divine side of that change of heart which, viewed from the human side, we call conversion. It is God's turning the soul to himself,—conversion being the soul's turning itself to God, of which God's turning it is both the accompaniment and cause. It will be observed from the above definition, that there are two aspects of regeneration, in the first of which the soul is passive, in the second of which the soul is active. God changes the governing disposition,—in this change the soul is simply acted upon. God secures the initial exercise of this disposition in view of the truth,—in this change the soul itself acts. Yet these two parts of God's operation are simultaneous. At the same moment that he makes the soul sensitive, he pours in the light of his truth and induces the exercise of the holy disposition he has imparted.

This distinction between the passive and the active aspects of regeneration is necessitated, as we shall see, by the twofold method of representing the change in Scripture. In many passages the change is ascribed wholly to the power of God; the change is a change in the fundamental disposition of the soul; there is no use of means. In other passages we find truth referred to as an agency employed by the Holy Spirit, and the mind acts in view of this truth. The distinction between these two aspects of regeneration seems to be intimated in Eph. 2:5, 6—"made us alive together with Christ," and "raised us up with him." Lazarus must first be made alive, and in this he could not coöperate; but he must also come forth from the tomb, and in this he could be active. In the old photography, the plate was first made sensitive, and in this the plate was passive; then it was exposed to the object, and now the plate actively seized upon the rays of light which the object emitted.

Availing ourselves of the illustration from photography, we may compare God's initial work in the soul to the sensitizing of the plate, his next work to the pouring in of the light and the production of the picture. The soul is first made receptive to the truth; then it is enabled actually to receive the truth. But the illustration fails in one respect,—it represents the two aspects of regeneration as successive. In regeneration there is no chronological succession. At the same instant that God makes the soul sensitive, he also draws out its new sensibility in view of the truth. Let us notice also that, as in photography the picture however perfect needs to be developed, and this development takes time, so regeneration is only the beginning of God's work; not all the dispositions, but only the governing disposition, is made holy; there is still need that sanctification should follow regeneration; and sanctification is a work of God which lasts for a whole lifetime. We may add that "heredity affects regeneration as the quality of the film affects photography, and environment affects regeneration as the focus affects photography" (W. T. Thayer).

Sacramentarianism has so obscured the doctrine of Scripture that many persons who gave no evidence of being regenerate are quite convinced that they are Christians. Uncle John Vassar therefore never asked: "Are you a Christian?" but always: "Have you ever been born again?" E. G. Robinson: "The doctrine of regeneration, aside from sacramentarianism, was not apprehended by Luther or the Reformers, was not indeed wrought out till Wesley taught that God instantaneously renewed the affections and the will." We get the doctrine of regeneration mainly from the apostle John, as we get the doctrine of justification mainly from the apostle Paul. Stevens, Johannine Theology, 366—"Paul's great words are, justification, and righteousness; John's are, birth from God, and life. But, for both Paul and John, faith is life-union with Christ."

Stearns, Evidence of Christian Experience, 134—"The sinful nature is not gone, but its power is broken; sin no longer dominates the life; it has been thrust from the centre to the circumference; it has the sentence of death in itself; the man is freed, at least in potency and promise. 218—An activity may be immediate, yet not unmediated. God's action on the soul may be through the sense, yet still be immediate, as when finite spirits communicate with each other." Dubois, in Century Magazine, Dec. 1894:233—"Man has made his way up from physical conditions to the consciousness of spiritual needs. Heredity and environment fetter him. He needs spiritual help. God provides a spiritual environment in regeneration. As science is the verification of the ideal in nature, so religion is the verification of the spiritual in human life." Last sermon of Seth K. Mitchell on Rev. 21:5—"Behold, I make all things new"—"God first makes a new man, then gives him a new heart, then a new commandment. He also gives a new body, a new name, a new robe, a new song, and a new home."

1. Scripture Representations.

(a) Regeneration is a change indispensable to the salvation of the sinner.

John 3:7—"Ye must be born anew"; Gal. 6:15—"neither is circumcision anything, nor uncircumcision, but a new creature" (marg.—"creation"); cf. Heb. 12:14—"the sanctification without which no man shall see the Lord"—regeneration, therefore, is yet more necessary to salvation; Eph. 2:3—"by nature children of wrath, even as the rest"; Rom. 3:11—"There is none that understandeth, There is none that seeketh after God"; John 6:44, 65—"No man can come to me, except the Father that sent me draw him ... no man can come unto me, except it be given unto him of the Father"; Jer. 13:23—"Can the Ethiopian change his skin, or the leopard his spots? then may ye also do good, that are accustomed to do evil."

(b) It is a change in the inmost principle of life.

John 3:3—"Except one be born anew, he cannot see the kingdom of God"; 5:21—"as the Father raiseth the dead and giveth them life, even so the Son also giveth life to whom he will"; Rom. 6:13—"present yourselves unto God, as alive from the dead"; Eph. 2:1—"And you did he make alive, when ye were dead through your trespasses and sins"; 5:14—"Awake, thou that sleepest, and arise from the dead, and Christ shall shine upon thee." In John 3:3—"born anew" = not, "altered," "influenced," "reinvigorated," "reformed"; but a new beginning, a new stamp or character, a new family likeness to God and to his children. "So is every one that is born of the Spirit" (John 3:8) = 1. secrecy of process; 2. independence of the will of man; 3. evidence given in results of conduct and life. It is a good thing to remove the means of gratifying an evil appetite; but how much better it is to remove the appetite itself! It is a good thing to save men from frequenting dangerous resorts by furnishing safe places of recreation and entertainment; but far better is it to implant within the man such a love for all that is pure and good, that he will instinctively shun the impure and evil. Christianity aims to purify the springs of action.

(c) It is a change in the heart, or governing disposition.

Mat. 12:33, 35—"Either make the tree good, and its fruit good; or make the tree corrupt, and its fruit corrupt: for the tree is known by its fruit.... The good man out of his good treasure bringeth forth good things: and the evil man out of his evil treasure bringeth forth evil things"; 15:19—"For out of the heart come forth evil thoughts, murders, adulteries, fornications, thefts, false witness, railings"; Acts 16:14—"And a certain woman named Lydia ... heard us: whose heart the Lord opened to give heed unto the things which were spoken by Paul"; Rom. 6:17—"But thanks be to God, that, whereas ye were servants of sin, ye became obedient from the heart to that form of teaching whereunto ye were delivered"; 10:10—"with the heart man believeth unto righteousness"; cf. Ps. 51:10—"Create in me a clean heart, O God; And renew a right spirit within me"; Jer. 31:33—"I will put my law in their inward parts, and in their hearts will I write it"; Ez. 11:19—"And I will give them one heart, and I will put a new spirit within you; and I will take the stony heart out of their flesh, and will give them a heart of flesh."

Horace Mann: "One former is worth a hundred reformers." It is often said that the redemption of society is as important as the regeneration of the individual. Yes, we reply; but the regeneration of society can never be accomplished except through the regeneration of the individual. Reformers try in vain to construct a stable and happy community from persons who are selfish, weak, and miserable. The first cry of such reformers is: "Get your circumstances changed!" Christ's first call is: "Get yourselves changed, and then the things around you will be changed." Many college settlements, and temperance societies, and self-reformations begin at the wrong end. They are like kindling a coal-fire by lighting kindlings at the top. The fire soon goes out. We need God's work at the very basis of character and not on the outer edge, at the very beginning, and not simply at the end. Mat. 6:33—"seek ye first his kingdom, and his righteousness; and all these things shall be added unto you."

(d) It is a change in the moral relations of the soul.

Eph. 2:5—"when we were dead through our trespasses, made us alive together with Christ"; 4:23, 24—"that ye be renewed in the spirit of your mind, and put on the new man, that after God hath been created in righteousness and holiness of truth"; Col. 1:13—"who delivered us out of the power of darkness, and translated us into the kingdom of the Son of his love." William James, Varieties of Religious Experience, 508, finds the features belonging to all religions: 1. an uneasiness; and 2. its solution. 1. The uneasiness, reduced to its simplest terms, is a sense that there is something wrong about us, as we naturally stand. 2. The solution is a sense that we are saved from the wrongness by making proper connection with the higher powers.

(e) It is a change wrought in connection with the use of truth as a means.

James 1:18—"Of his own will he brought us forth by the word of truth"—here in connection with the special agency of God (not of mere natural law) the truth is spoken of as a means; 1 Pet. 1:23—"having been begotten again, not of corruptible seed, but of incorruptible, through the word of God, which liveth and abideth"; 2 Pet. 1:4—"his precious and exceeding great promises; that through these ye may become partakers of the divine nature"; cf. Jer. 23:29—"Is not my word like fire? saith Jehovah; and like a hammer that breaketh the rock in pieces?" John 15:3—"Already ye are clean because of the word which I have spoken unto you"; Eph. 6:17—"the sword of the Spirit, which is the word of God"; Heb. 4:12—"For the word of God is living, and active, and sharper than any two-edged sword, and piercing even to the dividing of soul and spirit, of both joints and marrow, and quick to discern the thoughts and intents of the heart"; 1 Pet. 2:9—"called you out of darkness into his marvellous light." An advertising sign reads: "For spaces and ideas, apply to Johnson and Smith." In regeneration, we need both the open mind and the truth to instruct it, and we may apply to God for both.

(f) It is a change instantaneous, secretly wrought, and known only in its results.

John 5:24—"He that heareth my word, and believeth him that sent me, hath eternal life, and cometh not into judgment, but hath passed out of death into life"; cf. Mat. 6:24—"No man can serve two masters: for either he will hate the one, and love the other; or else he will hold to one, and despise the other." John 3:8—"The wind bloweth where it will, and thou hearest the voice thereof, but knowest not whence it cometh, and whither it goeth: so is every one that is born of the Spirit"; cf. Phil. 2:12, 13—"work out your own salvation with fear and trembling; for it is God who worketh in you both to will and to work, for his good pleasure"; 2 Pet. 1:10—"Wherefore, brethren, give the more diligence to make your calling and election sure."

(g) It is a change wrought by God.

John 1:13—"who were born, not of blood, nor of the will of the flesh, nor of the will of man, but of God"; 3:5—"Except one be born of water and the Spirit, he cannot enter into the kingdom of God"; 3:8, marg.—"The Spirit breatheth where it will"; Eph. 1:19, 20—"the exceeding greatness of his power to us-ward who believe, according to that working of the strength of his might which he wrought in Christ, when he raised him from the dead, and made him to sit at his right hand in the heavenly places"; 2:10—"For we are his workmanship, created in Christ Jesus for good works, which God afore prepared that we should walk in them"; 1 Pet. 1:3—"Blessed be the God and Father of our Lord Jesus Christ, who according to his great mercy begat us again unto a living hope by the resurrection of Jesus Christ from the dead"; cf. 1 Cor. 3:6, 7—"I planted, Apollos watered; but God gave the increase. So then neither is he that planteth anything, neither he that watereth; but God that giveth the increase."

We have seen that we are "begotten again ... through the word" (1 Pet. 1:23). In the revealed truth with regard to the person and work of Christ there is a divine adaptation to the work of renewing our hearts. But truth in itself is powerless to regenerate and sanctify, unless the Holy Spirit uses it—"the sword of the Spirit, which is the word of God" (Eph. 6:17). Hence regeneration is ascribed preëminently to the Holy Spirit, and men are said to be "born of the Spirit" (John 3:8). When Robert Morrison started for China, an incredulous American said to him: "Mr. Morrison, do you think you can make any impression on the Chinese?" "No," was the reply; "but I think the Lord can."

(h) It is a change accomplished through the union of the soul with Christ.

Rom. 8:2—"For the law of the Spirit of life in Christ Jesus made me free from the law of sin and death"; 2 Cor. 5:17—"if any man is in Christ, he is a new creature" (marg.—"there is a new creation"); Gal. 1:15, 16—"it was the good pleasure of God ... to reveal his Son in me"; Eph. 2:10—"For we are his workmanship, created in Christ Jesus for good works." On the Scriptural representations, see E. D. Griffin, Divine Efficiency, 117-164; H. B. Smith, System of Theology, 553-569—"Regeneration involves union with Christ, and not a change of heart without relation to him."

Eph. 3:14, 15—"the Father, from whom every fatherhood in heaven and on earth is named." But even here God works through Christ, and Christ himself is called "Everlasting Father" (Is. 9:6). The real basis of our sonship and unity is in Christ, our Creator, and Upholder. Sin is repudiation of this filial relationship. Regeneration by the Spirit restores our sonship by joining us once more, ethically and spiritually, to Christ the Son, and so adopting us again into God's family. Hence the Holy Spirit does not reveal himself, but Christ. The Spirit is light, and light does not reveal itself, but all other things. I may know that the Holy Spirit is working within me whenever I more clearly perceive Christ. Sonship in Christ makes us not only individually children of God, but also members of a commonwealth. Ps. 87:4—"Yea, of Zion it shall be said, This one and that one was born in her" = "the most glorious thing to be said about them is not something pertaining to their separate history, but that they have become members, by adoption, of the city of God" (Perowne). The Psalm speaks of the adoption of nations, but it is equally true of individuals.

2. Necessity of Regeneration.

That all men without exception need to be changed in moral character, is manifest, not only from Scripture passages already cited, but from the following rational considerations:

(a) Holiness, or conformity to the fundamental moral attribute of God, is the indispensable condition of securing the divine favor, of attaining peace of conscience, and of preparing the soul for the associations and employments of the blest.

Phillips Brooks seems to have taught that regeneration is merely a natural forward step in man's development. See his Life, 2:353—"The entrance into this deeper consciousness of sonship to God and into the motive power which it exercises is Regeneration, the new birth, not merely with reference to time, but with reference also to profoundness. Because man has something sinful to cast away in order to enter this higher life, therefore regeneration must begin with repentance. But that is an incident. It is not essential to the idea. A man simply imperfect and not sinful would still have to be born again. The presentation of sin as guilt, of release as forgiveness, of consequence as punishment, have their true meaning as the most personal expressions of man's moral condition as always measured by, and man's moral changes as always dependent upon, God." Here imperfection seems to mean depraved condition as distinguished from conscious transgression; it is not regarded as sinful; it needs not to be repented of. Yet it does require regeneration. In Phillips Brooks's creed there is no article devoted to sin. Baptism he calls "the declaration of the universal fact of the sonship of man to God. The Lord's Supper is the declaration of the universal fact of man's dependence upon God for supply of life. It is associated with the death of Jesus, because in that the truth of God giving himself to man found its completest manifestation."

Others seem to teach regeneration by education. Here too there is no recognition of inborn sin or guilt. Man's imperfection of nature is innocent. He needs training in order to fit him for association with higher intelligences and with God. In the evolution of his powers there comes a natural crisis, like that of graduation of the scholar, and this crisis may be called conversion. This educational theory of regeneration is represented by Starbuck, Psychology of Religion, and by Coe, The Spiritual Life. What human nature needs however is not evolution, but involution and revolution—involution, the communication of a new life, and revolution, change of direction resulting from that life. Human nature, as we have seen in our treatment of sin, is not a green apple to be perfected by mere growth, but an apple with a worm at the core, which left to itself will surely rot and perish.

President G. Stanley Hall, in his essay on The Religious Affirmations of Psychology, says that the total depravity of man is an ascertained fact apart from the teachings of the Bible. There had come into his hands for inspection several thousands of letters written to a medical man who advertised that he would give confidential advice and treatment to all, secretly. On the strength of these letters Dr. Hall was prepared to say that John Calvin had not told the half of what is true. He declared that the necessity of regeneration in order to the development of character was clearly established from psychological investigation.

A. H. Strong, Cleveland Sermon, 1904—"Here is the danger of some modern theories of Christian education. They give us statistics, to show that the age of puberty is the age of strongest religious impressions; and the inference is drawn that conversion is nothing but a natural phenomenon, a regular stage of development. The free will, and the evil bent of that will, are forgotten, and the absolute dependence of perverse human nature upon the regenerating spirit of God. The age of puberty is the age of the strongest religious impressions? Yes, but it is also the age of the strongest artistic and social and sensuous impressions, and only a new birth from above can lead the soul to seek first the kingdom of God."

(b) The condition of universal humanity as by nature depraved, and, when arrived at moral consciousness, as guilty of actual transgression, is precisely the opposite of that holiness without which the soul cannot exist in normal relation to God, to self, or to holy beings.

Plutarch has a parable of a man who tried to make a dead body stand upright, but who finished his labors saying: "Deest aliquid intus"—"There's something lacking inside." Ribot, Diseases of the Will, 53—"In the vicious man the moral elements are lacking. If the idea of amendment arises, it is involuntary.... But if a first element is not given by nature, and with it a potential energy, nothing results. The theological dogma of grace as a free gift appears to us therefore founded upon a much more exact psychology than the contrary opinion." "Thou art chained to the wheel of the foe By links which a world cannot sever: With thy tyrant through storm and through calm thou shall go, And thy sentence is bondage forever."

Martensen, Christian Ethics: "When Kant treats of the radical evil of human nature, he makes the remarkable statement that, if a good will is to appear in us, this cannot happen through a partial improvement, nor through any reform, but only through a revolution, a total overturn within us, that is to be compared to a new creation." Those who hold that man may attain perfection by mere natural growth deny this radical evil of human nature, and assume that our nature is a good seed which needs only favorable external influences of moisture and sunshine to bring forth good fruit. But human nature is a damaged seed, and what comes of it will be aborted and stunted like itself. The doctrine of mere development denies God's holiness, man's sin, the need of Christ, the necessity of atonement, the work of the Holy Spirit, the justice of penalty. Kant's doctrine of the radical evil of human nature, like Aristotle's doctrine that man is born on an inclined plane and subject to a downward gravitation, is not matched by a corresponding doctrine of regeneration. Only the apostle Paul can tell us how we came to be in this dreadful predicament, and where is the power that can deliver us; see Stearns, Evidence of Christian Experience, 274.

Dean Swift's worthy sought many years for a method of extracting sunbeams from cucumbers. We cannot cure the barren tree by giving it new bark or new branches,—it must have new sap. Healing snakebites is not killing the snake. Poetry and music, the uplifting power of culture, the inherent nobility of man, the general mercy of God—no one of these will save the soul. Horace Bushnell: "The soul of all improvement is the improvement of the soul." Frost cannot be removed from a window pane simply by scratching it away,—you must raise the temperature of the room. It is as impossible to get regeneration out of reformation as to get a harvest out of a field by mere plowing. Reformation is plucking bitter apples from a tree, and in their place tying good apples on with a string (Dr. Pentecost). It is regeneration or degradation—the beginning of an upward movement by a power not man's own, or the continuance and increase of a downward movement that can end only in ruin.

Kidd, Social Evolution, shows that in humanity itself there resides no power of progress. The ocean steamship that has burned its last pound of coal may proceed on its course by virtue of its momentum, but it is only a question of the clock how soon it will cease to move, except as tossed about by the wind and the waves. Not only is there power lacking for the good, but apart from God's grace the evil tendencies constantly became more aggravated. The settled states of the affections and will practically dominate the life. Charles H. Spurgeon: "If a thief should get into heaven unchanged, he would begin by picking the angels' pockets." The land is full of examples of the descent of man, not from the brute, but to the brute. The tares are not degenerate wheat, which by cultivation will become good wheat,—they are not only useless but noxious, and they must be rooted out and burned. "Society never will be better than the individuals who compose it. A sound ship can never be made of rotten timber. Individual reformation must precede social reconstruction." Socialism will always be a failure until it becomes Christian. We must be born from above, as truly as we have been begotten by our fathers upon earth, or we cannot see the kingdom of God.

(c) A radical internal change is therefore requisite in every human soul—a change in that which constitutes its character. Holiness cannot be attained, as the pantheist claims, by a merely natural growth or development, since man's natural tendencies are wholly in the direction of selfishness. There must be a reversal of his inmost dispositions and principles of action, if he is to see the kingdom of God.

Men's good deeds and reformation may be illustrated by eddies in a stream whose general current is downward; by walking westward in a railway-car while the train is going east; by Capt. Parry's traveling north, while the ice-floe on which he walked was moving southward at a rate much more rapid than his walking. It is possible to be "ever learning, and never able to come to the knowledge of the truth" (2 Tim. 3:7). Better never have been born, than not be born again. But the necessity of regeneration implies its possibility: John 3:7—"Ye must be born anew" = ye may be born anew,—the text is not merely a warning and a command,—it is also a promise. Every sinner has the chance of making a new start and of beginning a new life.

J. D. Robertson, The Holy Spirit and Christian Service, 57—"Emerson says that the gate of gifts closes at birth. After a man emerges from his mother's womb he can have no new endowments, no fresh increments of strength and wisdom, joy and grace within. The only grace is the grace of creation. But this view is deistic and not Christian." Emerson's saying is true of natural gifts, but not of spiritual gifts. He forgot Pentecost. He forgot the all- encompassing atmosphere of the divine personality and love, and its readiness to enter in at every chink and crevice of our voluntary being. The longing men have to turn over a new leaf in life's book, to break with the past, to assert their better selves, is a preliminary impulse of God's Spirit and an evidence of prevenient grace preparing the way for regeneration. Thus interpreted and yielded to, these impulses warrant unbounded hope for the future. "No star is ever lost we once have seen; We always may be what we might have been; The hopes that lost in some far distance seem May be the truer life, and this the dream."

The greatest minds feel, at least at times, their need of help from above. Although Cicero uses the term "regeneration" to signify what we should call naturalization, yet he recognizes man's dependence upon God: "Nemo vir magnus, sine aliquo divino afflatu, unquam fuit." Seneca: "Bonus vir sine illo nemo est." Aristotle: "Wickedness perverts the judgment and makes men err with respect to practical principles, so that no man can be wise and judicious who is not good." Goethe: "Who ne'er his bread in sorrow ate, Who ne'er the mournful midnight hours Weeping upon his bed has sate, He knows you not, ye heavenly Powers." Shakespeare, King Lear: "Is there a reason in nature for these hard hearts?" Robert Browning, in Halbert and Hob, replies: "O Lear, That a reason out of nature must turn them soft, seems clear."

John Stuart Mill (see Autobiography, 132-142) knew that the feeling of interest in others' welfare would make him happy,—but the knowledge of this fact did not give him the feeling. The "enthusiasm of humanity"—unselfish love, of which we read in "Ecce Homo"—is easy to talk about; but how to produce it,—that is the question. Drummond, Natural Law in the Spiritual World, 61-94—"There is no abiogenesis in the spiritual, more than in the natural, world. Can the stone grow more and more living until it enters the organic world? No, Christianity is a new life,—it is Christ in you." As natural life comes to us mediately, through Adam, so spiritual life comes to us mediately, through Christ. See Bushnell, Nature and the Supernatural, 220-249; Anderson, Regeneration, 51-88; Bennet Tyler, Memoir and Lectures, 340-354.

3. The Efficient Cause of Regeneration.

Three views only need be considered,—all others are modifications of these. The first view puts the efficient cause of regeneration in the human will; the second, in the truth considered as a system of motives; the third, in the immediate agency of the Holy Spirit.

John Stuart Mill regarded cause as embracing all the antecedents to an event. Hazard, Man a Creative First Cause, 12-15, shows that, as at any given instant the whole past is everywhere the same, the effects must, upon this view, at each instant be everywhere one and the same. "The theory that, of every successive event, the real cause is the whole of the antecedents, does not distinguish between the passive conditions acted upon and changed, and the active agencies which act upon and change them; does not distinguish what produces, from what merely precedes, change."

We prefer the definition given by Porter, Human Intellect, 592—Cause is "the most conspicuous and prominent of the agencies, or conditions, that produce a result"; or that of Dr. Mark Hopkins: "Any exertion or manifestation of energy that produces a change is a cause, and nothing else is. We must distinguish cause from occasion, or material. Cause is not to be defined as 'everything without which the effect could not be realized.' " Better still, perhaps, may we say, that efficient cause is the competent producing power by which the effect is secured. James Martineau, Types, 1: preface, xiii—"A cause is that which determines the indeterminate." Not the light, but the photographer, is the cause of the picture; light is but the photographer's servant. So the "word of God" is the "sword of the Spirit" (Eph. 6:17); the Spirit uses the word as his instrument; but the Spirit himself is the cause of regeneration.

A. The human will, as the efficient cause of regeneration.

This view takes two forms, according as the will is regarded as acting apart from, or in conjunction with, special influences of the truth applied by God. Pelagians hold the former; Arminians the latter.

(a) To the Pelagian view, that regeneration is solely the act of man, and is identical with self-reformation, we object that the sinner's depravity, since it consists in a fixed state of the affections which determines the settled character of the volitions, amounts to a moral inability. Without a renewal of the affections from which all moral action springs, man will not choose holiness nor accept salvation.

Man's volitions are practically the shadow of his affections. It is as useless to think of a man's volitions separating themselves from his affections, and drawing him towards God, as it is to think of a man's shadow separating itself from him, and leading him in the opposite direction to that in which he is going. Man's affections, to use Calvin's words, are like horses that have thrown off the charioteer and are running wildly,—they need a new hand to direct them. In disease, we must be helped by a physician. We do not stop a locomotive engine by applying force to the wheels, but by reversing the lever. So the change in man must be, not in the transient volitions, but in the deeper springs of action—the fundamental bent of the affections and will. See Henslow, Evolution, 134. Shakespeare, All's Well that Ends Well, 2:1:149—"It is not so with Him that all things knows, As 'tis with us that square our guess with shows; But most it is presumption in us when The help of heaven we count the act of men."

Henry Clay said that he did not know for himself personally what the change of heart spoken of by Christians meant; but he had seen Kentucky family feuds of long standing healed by religious revivals, and that whatever could heal a Kentucky family feud was more than human.—Mr. Peter Harvey was a lifelong friend of Daniel Webster. He wrote a most interesting volume of reminiscenses of the great man. He tells how one John Colby married the oldest sister of Mr. Webster. Said Mr. Webster of John Colby: "Finally he went up to Andover, New Hampshire, and bought a farm, and the only recollection I have about him is that he was called the wickedest man in the neighborhood, so far as swearing and impiety went. I used to wonder how my sister could marry so profane a man as John Colby." Years afterwards news comes to Mr. Webster that a wonderful change has passed upon John Colby. Mr. Harvey and Mr. Webster take a journey together to visit John Colby. As Mr. Webster enters John Colby's house, he sees open before him a large-print Bible, which he has just been reading. When greetings have been interchanged, the first question John Colby asks of Mr. Webster is, "Are you a Christian?" And then, at John Colby's suggestion, the two men kneel and pray together. When the visit is done, this is what Mr. Webster says to Mr. Harvey as they ride away: "I should like to know what the enemies of religion would say to John Colby's conversion. There was a man as unlikely, humanly speaking, to become a Christian as any man I ever saw. He was reckless, heedless, impious, never attended church, never experienced the good influence of associating with religious people. And here he has been living on in that reckless way until he has got to be an old man, until a period of life when you naturally would not expect his habits to change. And yet he has been brought into the condition in which we have seen him to- day,—a penitent, trusting, humble believer." "Whatever people may say," added Mr. Webster, "nothing can convince me that anything short of the grace of Almighty God could make such a change as I, with my own eyes, have witnessed in the life of John Colby." When they got back to Franklin, New Hampshire, in the evening, they met another lifelong friend of Mr. Webster's, John Taylor, standing at his door. Mr. Webster called out: "Well, John Taylor, miracles happen in these latter days as well as in the days of old." "What now, Squire?" asked John Taylor. "Why," replied Mr. Webster, "John Colby has become a Christian. If that is not a miracle, what is?"

(b) To the Arminian view, that regeneration is the act of man, coöperating with divine influences applied through the truth (synergistic theory), we object that no beginning of holiness is in this way conceivable. For, so long as man's selfish and perverse affections are unchanged, no choosing God is possible but such as proceeds from supreme desire for one's own interest and happiness. But the man thus supremely bent on self-gratification cannot see in God, or his service, anything productive of happiness; or, if he could see in them anything of advantage, his choice of God and his service from such a motive would not be a holy choice, and therefore could not be a beginning of holiness.

Although Melanchthon (1497-1560) preceded Arminius (1560-1609), his view was substantially the same with that of the Dutch theologian. Melanchthon never experienced the throes and travails of a new spiritual life, as Luther did. His external and internal development was peculiarly placid and serene. This Præceptor Germaniæ had the modesty of the genuine scholar. He was not a dogmatist, and he never entered the ranks of the ministry. He never could be persuaded to accept the degree of Doctor of Theology, though he lectured on theological subjects to audiences of thousands. Dorner says of Melanchthon: "He held at first that the Spirit of God is the primary, and the word of God the secondary, or instrumental, agency in conversion, while the human will allows their action and freely yields to it." Later, he held that "conversion is the result of the combined action (copulatio) of three causes, the truth of God, the Holy Spirit, and the will of man." This synergistic view in his last years involved the theologian of the German Reformation in serious trouble. Luthardt: "He made a facultas out of a mere capacitas." Dorner says again: "Man's causality is not to be coördinated with that of God, however small the influence ascribed to it. It is a purely receptive, not a productive, agency. The opposite is the fundamental Romanist error." Self-love will never induce a man to give up self-love. Selfishness will not throttle and cast out selfishness. "Such a choice from a selfish motive would be unholy, when judged by God's standard. It is absurd to make salvation depend upon the exercises of a wholly unspiritual power"; see Dorner, Glaubenslehre, 2:716-720 (Syst. Doct., 4:179-183). Shedd, Dogm. Theol., 2:505—"Sin does not first stop, and then holiness come in place of sin; but holiness positively expels sin. Darkness does not first cease, and then light enter; but light drives out darkness." On the Arminian view, see Bib. Sac., 19:265, 266.

John Wesley's theology was a modified Arminianism, yet it was John Wesley who did most to establish the doctrine of regeneration. He asserted that the Holy Spirit acts through the truth, in distinction from the doctrine that the Holy Spirit works solely through the ministers and sacraments of the church. But in asserting the work of the Holy Spirit in the individual soul, he went too far to the opposite extreme of emphasizing the ability of man to choose God's service, when without love to God there was nothing in God's service to attract. A. H. Bradford, Age of Faith: "It is as if Jesus had said: If a sailor will properly set his rudder the wind will fill his sails. The will is the rudder of the character; if it is turned in the right direction, all the winds of heaven will favor; if it is turned in the wrong direction, they will oppose." The question returns: What shall move the man to set his rudder aright, if he has no desire to reach the proper haven? Here is the need of divine power, not merely to coöperate with man, after man's will is set in the right direction, but to set it in the right direction in the first place. Phil. 2:13—"it is God who worketh in you both to will and to work, for his good pleasure."

Still another modification of Arminian doctrine is found in the Revealed Theology of N. W. Taylor of New Haven, who maintained that, antecedently to regeneration, the selfish principle is suspended in the sinner's heart, and that then, prompted by self- love, he uses the means of regeneration from motives that are neither sinful nor holy. He held that all men, saints and sinners, have their own happiness for their ultimate end. Regeneration involves no change in this principle or motive, but only a change in the governing purpose to seek this happiness in God rather than in the world. Dr. Taylor said that man could turn to God, whatever the Spirit did or did not do. He could turn to God if he would; but he could also turn to God if he wouldn't. In other words, he maintained the power of contrary choice, while yet affirming the certainty that, without the Holy Spirit's influences, man would always choose wrongly. These doctrines caused a division in the Congregational body. Those who opposed Taylor withdrew their support from New Haven, and founded the East Windsor Seminary in 1834. For Taylor's view, see N. W. Taylor, Revealed Theology, 369-406, and in The Christian Spectator for 1829.

The chief opponent of Dr. Taylor was Dr. Bennet Tyler. He replied to Dr. Taylor that moral character has its seat, not in the purpose, but in the affections back of the purpose. Otherwise every Christian must be in a state of sinless perfection, for his governing purpose is to serve God. But we know that there are affections and desires not under control of this purpose—dispositions not in conformity with the predominant disposition. How, Dr. Tyler asked, can a sinner, completely selfish, from a selfish motive, resolve not to be selfish, and so suspend his selfishness? "Antecedently to regeneration, there can be no suspension of the selfish principle. It is said that, in suspending it, the sinner is actuated by self-love. But is it possible that the sinner, while destitute of love to God and every particle of genuine benevolence, should love himself at all and not love himself supremely? He loves nothing more than self. He does not regard God or the universe, except as they tend to promote his ultimate end, his own happiness. No sinner ever suspended this selfishness until subdued by divine grace. We can not become regenerate by preferring God to the world merely from regard to our own interest. There is no necessity of the Holy Spirit to renew the heart, if self-love prompts men to turn from the world to God. On the view thus combated, depravity consists simply in ignorance. All men need is enlightenment as to the best means of securing their own happiness. Regeneration by the Holy Spirit is, therefore, not necessary." See Bennet Tyler, Memoir and Lectures, 316-381, esp. 334, 370, 371; Letters on the New Haven Theology, 21-72, 143-163; review of Taylor and Fitch, by E. D. Griffin, Divine Efficiency, 13-54; Martineau, Study, 2:9—"By making it a man's interest to be disinterested, do you cause him to forget himself and put any love into his heart? or do you only break him in and cause him to turn this way and that by the bit and lash of a driving necessity?" The sinner, apart from the grace of God, cannot see the truth. Wilberforce took Pitt to hear Cecil preach, but Pitt declared that he did not understand a word that Cecil said. Apart from the grace of God, the sinner, even when made to see the truth, resists it the more, the more clearly he sees it. Then the Holy Spirit overcomes his opposition and makes him willing in the day of God's power (Psalm 110:3).

B. The truth, as the efficient cause of regeneration.

According to this view, the truth as a system of motives is the direct and immediate cause of the change from unholiness to holiness. This view is objectionable for two reasons:

(a) It erroneously regards motives as wholly external to the mind that is influenced by them. This is to conceive of them as mechanically constraining the will, and is indistinguishable from necessitarianism. On the contrary, motives are compounded of external presentations and internal dispositions. It is the soul's affections which render certain suggestions attractive and others repugnant to us. In brief, the heart makes the motive.

(b) Only as truth is loved, therefore, can it be a motive to holiness. But we have seen that the aversion of the sinner to God is such that the truth is hated instead of loved, and a thing that is hated, is hated more intensely, the more distinctly it is seen. Hence no mere power of the truth can be regarded as the efficient cause of regeneration. The contrary view implies that it is not the truth which the sinner hates, but rather some element of error which is mingled with it.

Lyman Beecher and Charles G. Finney held this view. The influence of the Holy Spirit differs from that of the preacher only in degree,—both use only moral suasion; both do nothing more than to present the truth; both work upon the soul from without. "Were I as eloquent as the Holy Ghost, I could convert sinners as well as he," said a popular preacher of this school (see Bennet Tyler, Letters on New Haven Theology, 164-171). On this view, it would be absurd to pray to God to regenerate, for that is more than he can do,—regeneration is simply the effect of truth.

Miley, in Meth. Quar., July, 1881:434-462, holds that "the will cannot rationally act without motive, but that it has always power to suspend action, or defer it, for the purpose of rational examination of the motive or end, and to consider the opposite motive or end. Putting the old end or motive out of view will temporarily break its power, and the new truth considered will furnish motive for right action. Thus, by using our faculty of suspending choice, and of fixing attention, we can realize the permanent eligibility of the good and choose it against the evil. This is, however, not the realization of a new spiritual life in regeneration, but the election of its attainment. Power to do this suspending is of grace [grace, however, given equally to all]. Without this power, life would be a spontaneous and irresponsible development of evil."

The view of Miley, thus substantially given, resembles that of Dr. Taylor, upon which we have already commented; but, unlike that, it makes truth itself, apart from the affections, a determining agency in the change from sin to holiness. Our one reply is that, without a change in the affections, the truth can neither be known nor obeyed. Seeing cannot be the means of being born again, for one must first be born again in order to see the kingdom of God (John 3:3). The mind will not choose God, until God appears to be the greatest good.

Edwards, quoted by Griffin, Divine Efficiency, 64—"Let the sinner apply his rational powers to the contemplation of divine things, and let his belief be speculatively correct; still he is in such a state that those objects of contemplation will excite in him no holy affections." The Scriptures declare (Rom. 8:7) that "the mind of the flesh is enmity"—not against some error or mistaken notion of God—but "is enmity against God." It is God's holiness, mandatory and punitive, that is hated. A clearer view of that holiness will only increase the hatred. A woman's hatred of spiders will never be changed to love by bringing them close to her. Magnifying them with a compound oxy-hydrogen microscope will not help the matter. Tyler: "All the light of the last day will not subdue the sinner's heart." The mere presence of God, and seeing God face to face, will be hell to him, if his hatred be not first changed to love. See E. D. Griffin, Divine Efficiency, 105-116, 203-221; and review of Griffin, by S. R. Mason, Truth Unfolded, 383-407.

Bradford, Heredity and Christian Problems, 239—"Christianity puts three motives before men: love, self-love, and fear." True, but the last two are only preliminary motives, not essentially Christian. The soul that is moved only by self-love or by fear has not yet entered into the Christian life at all. And any attention to the truth of God which originates in these motives has no absolute moral value, and cannot be regarded as even a beginning of salvation. Nothing but holiness and love are entitled to be called Christianity, and these the truth of itself cannot summon up. The Spirit of God must go with the truth to impart right desires and to make the truth effective. E. G. Robinson: "The glory of our salvation can no more be attributed to the word of God only, than the glory of a Praxiteles or a Canova can be ascribed to the chisel or the mallet with which he wrought into beauty his immortal creations."

C. The immediate agency of the Holy Spirit, as the efficient cause of regeneration.

In ascribing to the Holy Spirit the authorship of regeneration, we do not affirm that the divine Spirit accomplishes his work without any accompanying instrumentality. We simply assert that the power which regenerates is the power of God, and that although conjoined with the use of means, there is a direct operation of this power upon the sinner's heart which changes its moral character. We add two remarks by way of further explanation:

(a) The Scriptural assertions of the indwelling of the Holy Spirit and of his mighty power in the soul forbid us to regard the divine Spirit in regeneration as coming in contact, not with the soul, but only with the truth. The phrases, "to energize the truth," "to intensify the truth," "to illuminate the truth," have no proper meaning; since even God cannot make the truth more true. If any change is wrought, it must be wrought, not in the truth, but in the soul.

The maxim, "Truth is mighty and will prevail," is very untrue, if God be left out of the account. Truth without God is an abstraction, and not a power. It is a mere instrument, useless without an agent. "The sword of the Spirit, which is the word of God" (Eph. 6:17), must be wielded by the Holy Spirit himself. And the Holy Spirit comes in contact, not simply with the instrument, but with the soul. To all moral, and especially to all religious truth, there is an inward unsusceptibility, arising from the perversity of the affections and the will. This blindness and hardness of heart must be removed, before the soul can perceive or be moved by the truth. Hence the Spirit must deal directly with the soul. Denovan: "Our natural hearts are hearts of stone. The word of God is good seed sown on the hard, trodden, macadamized highway, which the horses of passion, the asses of self-will, the wagons of imaginary treasure, have made impenetrable. Only the Holy Spirit can soften and pulverize this soil."

The Psalmist prays: "Incline my heart unto thy testimonies" (Ps. 119:36), while of Lydia it is said: "whose heart the Lord opened to give heed unto the things which were spoken by Paul" (Acts 16:14).

We may say of the Holy Spirit: "He freezes and then melts the soil, He breaks the hard, cold stone, Kills out the rooted weeds so vile,—All this he does alone; And every virtue we possess, And every victory won, And every thought of holiness, Are his, and his alone." Hence, in Ps. 90:16, 17, the Psalmist says, first: "Let thy work appear unto thy servants"; then "establish thou the work of our hands upon us"—God's work is first to appear,—then man's work, which is God's work carried out by human instruments. At Jericho, the force was not applied to the rams' horns, but to the walls. When Jesus healed the blind man, his power was applied, not to the spittle, but to the eyes. The impression is prepared, not by heating the seal, but by softening the wax. So God's power acts, not upon the truth, but upon the sinner.

Ps. 59:10—"My God with his lovingkindness will meet me"; A. V.—"The God of my mercy shall prevent me," i. e., go before me. Augustine urges this text as proof that the grace of God precedes all merit of man: "What didst thou find in me but only sins? Before I do anything good, his mercy will go before me. What will unhappy Pelagius answer here?" Calvin however says this may be a pious, but it is not a fair, use of the passage. The passage does teach dependence upon God; but God's anticipation of our action, or in other words, the doctrine of prevenient grace, must be derived from other portions of Scripture, such as John 1:13, and Eph. 2:10. "The enthusiasm of humanity" to which J. R. Seeley, the author of Ecce Homo, exhorts us, is doubtless the secret of happiness and usefulness,—unfortunately he does not tell us whence it may come. John Stuart Mill felt the need of it, but he did not get it. Arthur Hugh Clough, Clergyman's First Tale: "Would I could wish my wishes all to rest, And know to wish the wish that were the best." Bradford, Heredity, 228—"God is the environment of the soul, yet man has free will. Light fills the spaces, yet a man from ignorance may remain in a cave, or from choice may dwell in darkness." Man needs therefore a divine influence which will beget in him a disposition to use his opportunities aright.

We may illustrate the philosophy of revivals by the canal boat which lies before the gate of a lock. No power on earth can open the lock. But soon the lock begins to fill, and when the water has reached the proper level, the gate can be opened almost at a touch. Or, a steamer runs into a sandbar. Tugs fail to pull the vessel off. Her own engines cannot accomplish it. But when the tide comes in, she swings free without effort. So what we need in religion is an influx of spiritual influence which will make easy what before is difficult if not impossible. The Superintendent of a New York State Prison tells us that the common schools furnish 83 per cent., and the colleges and academies over 4 per cent., of the inmates of Auburn and Sing Sing. Truth without the Holy Spirit to apply it is like sunshine without the actinic ray which alone can give it vitalizing energy.

(b) Even if truth could be energized, intensified, illuminated, there would still be needed a change in the moral disposition, before the soul could recognize its beauty or be affected by it. No mere increase of light can enable a blind man to see; the disease of the eye must first be cured before external objects are visible. So God's work in regeneration must be performed within the soul itself. Over and above all influence of the truth, there must be a direct influence of the Holy Spirit upon the heart. Although wrought in conjunction with the presentation of truth to the intellect, regeneration differs from moral suasion in being an immediate act of God.

Before regeneration, man's knowledge of God is the blind man's knowledge of color. The Scriptures call such knowledge "ignorance" (Eph. 4:18). The heart does not appreciate God's mercy. Regeneration gives an experimental or heart knowledge; see Shedd, Dogm. Theol., 2:495. Is. 50:4—God "wakeneth mine ear to hear." It is false to say that soul can come in contact with soul only through the influence of truth. In the intercourse of dear friends, or in the discourse of the orator, there is a personal influence, distinct from the word spoken, which persuades the heart and conquers the will. We sometimes call it "magnetism,"—but we mean simply that soul reaches soul, in ways apart from the use of physical intermediaries. Compare the facts, imperfectly known as yet, of second sight, mind-reading, clairvoyance. But whether these be accepted or not, it still is true that God has not made the human soul so that it is inaccessible to himself. The omnipresent Spirit penetrates and pervades all spirits that have been made by him. See Lotze, Outlines of Psychology (Ladd), 142, 143.

In the primary change of disposition, which is the most essential feature of regeneration, the Spirit of God acts directly upon the spirit of man. In the securing of the initial exercise of this new disposition—which constitutes the secondary feature of God's work of regeneration—the truth is used as a means. Hence, perhaps, in James 1:18, we read: "Of his own will he brought us forth by the word of truth" instead of "he begat us by the word of truth,"—the reference being to the secondary, not to the primary, feature of regeneration. The advocates of the opposite view—the view that God works only through the truth as a means, and that his only influence upon the soul is a moral influence—very naturally deny the mystical union of the soul with Christ. Squier, for example, in his Autobiog., 343-378, esp. 360, on the Spirit's influences, quotes John 16:8—he "will convict the world in respect of sin"—to show that God regenerates by applying truth to men's minds, so far as to convince them, by fair and sufficient arguments, that they are sinners.

Christ, opening blind eyes and unstopping deaf ears, illustrates the nature of God's operation in regeneration,—in the case of the blind, there is plenty of light,—what is wanted is sight. The negro convert said that his conversion was due to himself and God: he fought against God with all his might, and God did the rest. So our moral successes are due to ourselves and God,—we have done only the fighting against God, and God has done the rest. The sand of Sahara would not bring forth flowers and fruit, even if you turned into it a hundred rivers like the Nile. Man may hear sermons for a lifetime, and still be barren of all spiritual growths. The soil of the heart needs to be changed, and the good seed of the kingdom needs to be planted there.

For the view that truth is "energized" or "intensified" by the Holy Spirit, see Phelps, New Birth, 61, 121; Walker, Philosophy of Plan of Salvation, chap. 18. Per contra, see Wardlaw, Syst. Theol., 3:24, 25; E. D. Griffin, Divine Efficiency, 73-116; Anderson, Regeneration, 123-168; Edwards, Works, 2:547-597; Chalmers, Lectures on Romans, chap. 1; Payne, Divine Sovereignty, lect. 23:363-367; Hodge, Syst. Theol., 3:3-37, 466-485. On the whole subject of the Efficient Cause of Regeneration, see Hopkins, Works, 1:454; Dwight, Theology, 2:418-429; John Owen, Works, 3:282-297, 366-538; Robert Hall, Sermon on the Cause, Agent, and Purpose of Regeneration.

4. The Instrumentality used in Regeneration.

A. The Roman, English and Lutheran churches hold that regeneration is accomplished through the instrumentality of baptism. The Disciples, or followers of Alexander Campbell, make regeneration include baptism, as well as repentance and faith. To the view that baptism is a means of regeneration we urge the following objections:

(a) The Scriptures represent baptism to be not the means but only the sign of regeneration, and therefore to presuppose and follow regeneration. For this reason only believers—that is, persons giving credible evidence of being regenerated—were baptized (Acts 8:12). Not external baptism, but the conscientious turning of the soul to God which baptism symbolizes, saves us (1 Pet. 3:21—συνειδήσεως ἀγαθῆς ἐπερώτημα). Texts like John 3:5, Acts 2:38, Col. 2:12, Tit. 3:5, are to be explained upon the principle that regeneration, the inward change, and baptism, the outward sign of that change, were regarded as only different sides or aspects of the same fact, and either side or aspect might therefore be described in terms derived from the other.

(b) Upon this view, there is a striking incongruity between the nature of the change to be wrought and the means employed to produce it. The change is a spiritual one, but the means are physical. It is far more rational to suppose that, in changing the character of intelligent beings, God uses means which have relation to their intelligence. The view we are considering is part and parcel of a general scheme of mechanical rather than moral salvation, and is more consistent with a materialistic than with a spiritual philosophy.

Acts 8:12—"when they believed Philip preaching good tidings concerning the kingdom of God and the name of Jesus Christ, they were baptized"; 1 Pet. 3:21—"which also after a true likeness doth now save you, even baptism, not the putting away of the filth of the flesh, but the interrogation [marg.—'inquiry', 'appeal'] of a good conscience toward God" = the inquiry of the soul after God, the conscientious turning of the soul to God.

Plumptre, however, makes ἐπερώτημα a forensic term equivalent to "examination," and including both question and answer. It means, then, the open answer of allegiance to Christ, given by the new convert to the constituted officers of the church. "That which is of the essence of the saving power of baptism is the confession and the profession which precede it. If this comes from a conscience that really renounces sin and believes on Christ, then baptism, as the channel through which the grace of the new birth is conveyed and the convert admitted into the church of Christ, 'saves us,' but not otherwise." We may adopt this statement from Plumptre's Commentary, with the alteration of the word "conveyed" into "symbolized" or "manifested." Plumptre's interpretation is, as he seems to admit, in its obvious meaning inconsistent with infant baptism; to us it seems equally inconsistent with any doctrine of baptismal regeneration.

Scriptural regeneration is God's (1) changing man's disposition, and (2) securing its first exercise. Regeneration, according to the Disciples, is man's (1) repentance and faith, and (2) submission to baptism. Alexander Campbell, Christianity Restored: "We plead that all the converting power of the Holy Spirit is exhibited in the divine Record." Address of Disciples to Ohio Baptist State Convention, 1871: "With us regeneration includes all that is comprehended in faith, repentance, and baptism, and so far as it is expressive of birth, it belongs more properly to the last of these than to either of the former." But if baptism be the instrument of regeneration, it is difficult to see how the patriarchs, or the penitent thief, could have been regenerated. Luke 23:43—"This day shalt thou be with me in Paradise." Bossuet: "This day"—what promptitude! "With me"—what companionship! "In Paradise"—what rest! Bersier: " 'This day'—what then? no flames of Purgatory? no long period of mournful expiation? 'This day'—pardon and heaven!"

Baptism is a condition of being outwardly in the kingdom; it is not a condition of being inwardly in the kingdom. The confounding of these two led many in the early church to dread dying unbaptized, rather than dying unsaved. Even Pascal, in later times, held that participation in outward ceremonies might lead to real conversion. He probably meant that an initial act of holy will would tend to draw others in its train. Similarly we urge unconverted people to take some step that will manifest religious interest. We hope that in taking this step a new decision of the will, inwrought by the Spirit of God, may reveal itself. But a religion which consists only in such outward performances is justly denominated a cutaneous religion, for it is only skin-deep. On John 3:5—"Except one be born of water and the Spirit, he cannot enter into the kingdom of God"; Acts 2:38—"Repent ye, and be baptized every one of you in the name of Jesus Christ unto the remission of your sins"; Col. 2:12—"buried with him in baptism, wherein ye were also raised with him through faith"; Tit. 3:5—"saved us, through the washing of regeneration and renewing of the Holy Spirit"—see further discussion and exposition in our chapter on the Ordinances. Adkins, Disciples and Baptists, a booklet published by the Am. Bap. Pub. Society, is the best statement of the Baptist position, as distinguished from that of the Disciples. It claims that Disciples overrate the externals of Christianity and underrate the work of the Holy Spirit. Per contra, see Gates, Disciples and Baptists.

B. The Scriptural view is that regeneration, so far as it secures an activity of man, is accomplished through the instrumentality of the truth. Although the Holy Spirit does not in any way illuminate the truth, he does illuminate the mind, so that it can perceive the truth. In conjunction with the change of man's inner disposition, there is an appeal to man's rational nature through the truth. Two inferences may be drawn:

(a) Man is not wholly passive at the time of his regeneration. He is passive only with respect to the change of his ruling disposition. With respect to the exercise of this disposition, he is active. Although the efficient power which secures this exercise of the new disposition is the power of God, yet man is not therefore unconscious, nor is he a mere machine worked by God's fingers. On the other hand, his whole moral nature under God's working is alive and active. We reject the "exercise-system," which regards God as the direct author of all man's thoughts, feelings, and volitions, not only in its general tenor, but in its special application to regeneration.

Shedd, Dogm. Theol., 2:503—"A dead man cannot assist in his own resurrection." This is true so far as the giving of life is concerned. But once made alive, man can, like Lazarus, obey Christ's command and "come forth" (John 11:43). In fact, if he does not obey, there is no evidence that there is spiritual life. "In us is God; we burn but as he moves"—"Est deus in nobis; agitante calescimus illo." Wireless telegraphy requires an attuned receiver; regeneration attunes the soul so that it vibrates responsively to God and receives the communications of his truth. When a convert came to Rowland Hill and claimed that she had been converted in a dream, he replied: "We will see how you walk, now that you are awake."

Lord Bacon said he would open every one of Argus's hundred eyes, before he opened one of Briareus's hundred hands. If God did not renew men's hearts in connection with our preaching of the truth, we might well give up our ministry. E. G. Robinson: "The conversion of a soul is just as much according to law as the raising of a crop of turnips." Simon, Reconciliation, 377—"Though the mere preaching of the gospel is not the cause of the conversion and revivification of men, it is a necessary condition—as necessary as the action of light and heat, or other physical agencies, are on a germ, if it is to develop, grow, and bear its proper fruit."

(b) The activity of man's mind in regeneration is activity in view of the truth. God secures the initial exercise of the new disposition which he has wrought in man's heart in connection with the use of truth as a means. Here we perceive the link between the efficiency of God and the activity of man. Only as the sinner's mind is brought into contact with the truth, does God complete his regenerating work. And as the change of inward disposition and the initial exercise of it are never, so far as we know, separated by any interval of time, we can say, in general, that Christian work is successful only as it commends the truth to every man's conscience in the sight of God (2 Cor. 4:2).

In Eph. 1:17, 18, there is recognized the divine illumination of the mind to behold the truth—"may give unto you a spirit of wisdom and revelation in the knowledge of him; having the eyes of your heart enlightened, that ye may know what is the hope of his calling" On truth as a means of regeneration, see Hovey, Outlines, 192, who quotes Cunningham, Historical Theology, 1:617—"Regeneration may be taken in a limited sense as including only the first impartation of spiritual life ... or it may be taken in a wider sense as comprehending the whole of that process by which he is renewed or made over again in the whole man after the image of God,—i. e., as including the production of saving faith and union to Christ. Only in the first sense did the Reformers maintain that man in the process was wholly passive and not active; for they did not dispute that, before the process in the second and more enlarged sense was completed, man was spiritually alive and active, and continued so ever after during the whole process of his sanctification."

Dr. Hovey suggests an apt illustration of these two parts of the Holy Spirit's work and their union in regeneration: At the same time that God makes the photographic plate sensitive, he pours in the light of truth whereby the image of Christ is formed in the soul. Without the "sensitizing" of the plate, it would never fix the rays of light so as to retain the image. In the process of "sensitizing," the plate is passive; under the influence of light, it is active. In both the "sensitizing" and the taking of the picture, the real agent is not the plate nor the light, but the photographer. The photographer cannot perform both operations at the same moment. God can. He gives the new affection, and at the same instant he secures its exercise in view of the truth.

For denial of the instrumentality of truth in regeneration, see Pierce, in Bap. Quar., Jan. 1872:52. Per contra, see Anderson, Regeneration, 89-122. H. B. Smith holds middle ground. He says: "In adults it [regeneration] is wrought most frequently by the word of God as the instrument. Believing that infants may be regenerated, we cannot assert that it is tied to the word of God absolutely." We prefer to say that, if infants are regenerated, they also are regenerated in conjunction with some influence of truth upon the mind, dim as the recognition of it may be. Otherwise we break the Scriptural connection between regeneration and conversion, and open the way for faith in a physical, magical, sacramental salvation. Squier, Autobiog., 368, says well, of the theory of regeneration which makes man purely passive, that it has a benumbing effect upon preaching: "The lack of expectation unnerves the efforts of the preacher; an impression of the fortuitous presence neutralizes his engagedness. This antinomian dependence on the Spirit extracts all vitality from the pulpit and sense of responsibility from the hearer, and makes preaching an opus operatum, like the baptismal regeneration of the formalist." Only of the first element in regeneration are Shedd's words true: "A dead man cannot assist in his own resurrection" (Dogm. Theol., 2:503).

Squier goes to the opposite extreme of regarding the truth alone as the cause of regeneration. His words are none the less a valuable protest against the view that regeneration is so entirely due to God that in no part of it is man active. It was with a better view that Luther cried: "O that we might multiply living books, that is, preachers!" And the preacher is successful only as he possesses and unfolds the truth. John took the little book from the Covenant-angel's hand and ate it (Rev. 10:8-11). So he who is to preach God's truth must feed upon it, until it has become his own. For the Exercise-system, see Emmons, Works, 4:339-411; Hagenbach, Hist. Doct., 2:439.

5. The Nature of the Change wrought in Regeneration.

A. It is a change in which the governing disposition is made holy. This implies that:

(a) It is not a change in the substance of either body or soul. Regeneration is not a physical change. There is no physical seed or germ implanted in man's nature. Regeneration does not add to, or subtract from, the number of man's intellectual, emotional or voluntary faculties. But regeneration is the giving of a new direction or tendency to powers of affection which man possessed before. Man had the faculty of love before, but his love was supremely set on self. In regeneration the direction of that faculty is changed, and his love is now set supremely upon God.

Eph. 2:10—"created in Christ Jesus for good works"—does not imply that the old soul is annihilated, and a new soul created. The "old man" which is "crucified"—(Rom. 6:6) and "put away" (Eph. 4:22) is simply the sinful bent of the affections and will. When this direction of the dispositions is changed, and becomes holy, we can call the change a new birth of the old nature, because the same faculties that acted before are acting now, the only difference being that now these faculties are set toward God and purity. Or, regarding the change from another point of view, we may speak of man as having a "new nature," as "recreated," as being a "new creature," because this direction of the affection and will, which ensures a different life from what was led before, is something totally new, and due wholly to the regenerating act of God. In 1 Pet. 1:23—"begotten again, not of corruptible seed, but of incorruptible"—all materialistic inferences from the word "seed," as if it implied the implantation of a physical germ, are prevented by the following explanatory words: "through the word of God, which liveth and abideth."

So, too, when we describe regeneration as the communication of a new life to the soul, we should not conceive of this new life as a substance imparted or infused into us. The new life is rather a new direction and activity of our own affections and will. There is, indeed a union of the soul with Christ; Christ dwells in the renewed heart; Christ's entrance into the soul is the cause and accompaniment of its regeneration. But this entrance of Christ into the soul is not itself regeneration. We must distinguish the effect from the cause; otherwise we shall be in danger of a pantheistic confounding of our own personality and life with the personality and life of Christ. Christ is indeed our life, in the sense of being the cause and supporter of our life, but he is not our life in the sense that, after our union with him, our individuality ceases. The effect of union with Christ is rather that our individuality is enlarged and exalted (John 10:10—"I came that they may have life, and may have it abundantly." See page 799, (c)).

We must therefore take with a grain of allowance the generally excellent words of A. J. Gordon, Twofold Life, 22—"Regeneration is the communication of the divine nature to man by the operation of the Holy Spirit through the word (2 Pet. 1:4).... As Christ was made partaker of human nature by incarnation, that so he might enter into truest fellowship with us, we are made partakers of the divine nature, by regeneration, that we may enter into truest fellowship with God. Regeneration is not a change of nature, i. e., a natural heart bettered. Eternal life is not natural life prolonged into endless duration. It is the divine life imparted to us, the very life of God communicated to the human soul, and bringing forth there its proper fruit." Dr. Gordon's view that regeneration adds a new substance or faculty to the soul is the result of literalizing the Scripture metaphors of creation and life. This turning of symbol into fact accounts for his tendency toward annihilation doctrine in the case of the unregenerate, toward faith cure and the belief that all physical evils can be removed by prayer. E. H. Johnson, The Holy Spirit: "Regeneration is a change, not in the quantity, but in the quality, of the soul." E. G. Robinson, Christian Theology, 320—"Regeneration consists in a divinely wrought change in the moral affections."

So, too, we would criticize the doctrine of Drummond, Nat. Law in the Spir. World: "People forget the persistence of force. Instead of transforming energy, they try to create it. We must either depend on environment, or be self-sufficient. The 'cannot bear fruit of itself' (John 15:4) is the 'cannot' of natural law. Natural fruit flourishes with air and sunshine. The difference between the Christian and the non-Christian is the difference between the organic and the inorganic. The Christian has all the characteristics of life: assimilation, waste, reproduction, spontaneous action." See criticism of Drummond, by Murphy, in Brit. Quar., 1884:118-125—"As in resurrection there is a physical connection with the old body, so in regeneration there is a natural connection with the old soul." Also, Brit. Quar., July, 1880, art.: Evolution Viewed in Relation to Theology—"The regenerating agency of the Spirit of God is symbolized, not by the vitalization of dead matter, but by the agency of the organizing intelligence which guides the evolution of living beings." Murphy's answer to Drummond is republished. Murphy's Natural Selection and Spiritual Freedom, 1-33—"The will can no more create force, either muscular or mental, than it can create matter. And it is equally true that for our spiritual nourishment and spiritual force we are altogether dependent on our spiritual environment, which is God." In "dead matter" there is no sin.

Drummond would imply that, as matter has no promise or potency of life and is not responsible for being without life (or "dead," to use his misleading word), and if it ever is to live must wait for the life-giving influence to come unsought, so the human soul is not responsible for being spiritually dead, cannot seek for life, must passively wait for the Spirit. Plymouth Brethren generally hold the same view with Drummond, that regeneration adds something—as vitality—to the substance of the soul. Christ is transsubstantiated into the soul's substance; or, the πνεῦμα is added. But we have given over talking of vitality, as if it were a substance or faculty. We regard it as merely a mode of action. Evolution, moreover, uses what already exists, so far as it will go, instead of creating new; as in the miracle of the loaves, and as in the original creation of man, so in his recreation or regeneration. Dr. Charles Hodge also makes the same mistake in calling regeneration an "origination of the principle of the spirit of life, just as literal and real a creation as the origination of the principle of natural life." This, too, literalizes Scripture metaphor, and ignores the fact that the change accomplished in regeneration is an exclusively moral one. There is indeed a new entrance of Christ into the soul, or a new exercise of his spiritual power within the soul. But the effect of Christ's working is not to add any new faculty or substance, but only to give new direction to already existing powers.

(b) Regeneration involves an enlightenment of the understanding and a rectification of the volitions. But it seems most consonant with Scripture and with a correct psychology to regard these changes as immediate and necessary consequences of the change of disposition already mentioned, rather than as the primary and central facts in regeneration. The taste for truth logically precedes perception of the truth, and love for God logically precedes obedience to God; indeed, without love no obedience is possible. Reverse the lever of affection, and this moral locomotive, without further change, will move away from sin, and toward truth and God.

Texts which seem to imply that a right taste, disposition, affection, logically precedes both knowledge of God and obedience to God, are the following: Ps. 34:8—"Oh taste and see that Jehovah is good"; 119:36—"Incline my heart unto thy testimonies"; Jer. 24:7—"I will give them a heart to know me"; Mat. 5:8—"Blessed are the pure in heart: for they shall see God"; John 7:17—"If any man willeth to do his will, he shall know of the teaching, whether it is of God"; Acts 16:14—of Lydia it is said: "whose heart the Lord opened to give heed unto the things which were spoken by Paul"; Eph. 1:18—"having the eyes of your heart enlightened." "Change the centre of a circle and you change the place and direction of all its radii."

The text John 1:12, 13—"But as many as received him, to them gave him the right to become children of God, even to them that believe on his name: who were born, not of blood, nor of the will of the flesh, nor of the will of man, but of God"—seems at first sight to imply that faith is the condition of regeneration, and therefore prior to it. "But if ἐξουσίαν here signifies the 'right' or 'privilege' of sonship, it is a right which may presuppose faith as the work of the Spirit in regeneration—a work apart from which no genuine faith exists in the soul. But it is possible that John means to say that, in the case of all who received Christ, their power to believe was given to them by him. In the original the emphasis is on 'gave,' and this is shown by the order of the words"; see Hovey, Manual of Theology, 345, and Com. on John 1:12, 13—"The meaning would then be this: 'Many did not receive him; but some did; and as to all who received him, he gave them grace by which they were enabled to do this, and so to become God's children.' "

Ruskin: "The first and last and closest trial question to any living creature is, 'What do you like?' Go out into the street and ask the first man you meet what his taste is, and, if he answers candidly, you know him, body and soul. What we like determines what we are, and is the sign of what we are; and to teach taste is inevitably to form character." If the taste here spoken of is moral and spiritual taste, the words of Ruskin are sober truth. Regeneration is essentially a changing of the fundamental taste of the soul. But by taste we mean the direction of man's love, the bent of his affections, the trend of his will. And to alter that taste is not to impart a new faculty, or to create a new substance, but simply to set toward God the affections which hitherto have been set upon self and sin. We may illustrate by the engineer who climbs over the cab into a runaway locomotive and who changes its course, not by adding any new rod or cog to the machine, but simply by reversing the lever. The engine slows up and soon moves in an opposite direction to that in which it has been going. Man needs no new faculty of love; he needs only to have his love set in a new and holy direction; this is virtually to give him a new birth, to make him a new creature, to impart to him a new life. But being born again, created anew, made alive from the dead, are physical metaphors, to be interpreted not literally but spiritually.

(c) It is objected, indeed, that we know only of mental substance and of mental acts, and that the new disposition or state just mentioned, since it is not an act, must be regarded as a new substance, and so lack all moral quality. But we reply that, besides substance and acts, there are habits, tendencies, proclivities, some of them native and some of them acquired. They are voluntary, and have moral character. If we can by repeated acts originate sinful tendencies, God can surely originate in us holy tendencies. Such holy tendencies formed a part of the nature of Adam, as he came from the hand of God. As the result of the Fall, we are born with tendencies toward evil for which we are responsible. Regeneration is a restoration of the original tendencies toward God which were lost by the Fall. Such holy tendencies (tastes, dispositions, affections) are not only not unmoral—they are the only possible springs of right moral action. Only in the restoration of them does man become truly free.

Mat. 12:33—"Make the tree good, and its fruit good"; Eph. 2:10—"created in Christ Jesus for good works." The tree is first made good—the character renewed in its fundamental principle, love to God—in the certainty that when this is done the fruit will be good also. Good works are the necessary result of regeneration by union with Christ. Regeneration introduces a new force into humanity, the force of a new love. The work of the preacher is that of coöperation with God in the impartation of a new life—a work far more radical and more noble than that of moral reform, by as much as the origination of a new force is more radical and more noble than the guidance of that force after it has been originated. Does regeneration cure disease and remove physical ills? Not primarily. Mat. 1:21—"thou shalt call his name Jesus; for it is he that shall save his people from their sins." Salvation from sin is Christ's first and main work. He performed physical healing only to illustrate and further the healing of the soul. Hence in the case of the paralytic, when he was expected to cure the body, he said first: "thy sins are forgiven" (Mat. 9:2); but, that they who stood by might not doubt his power to forgive, he added the raising up of the palsied man. And ultimately in every redeemed man the holy heart will bring in its train the perfected body: Rom. 8:23—"we ourselves groan within ourselves, waiting for our adoption, to wit, the redemption of our body."

On holy affection as the spring of holy action, see especially Edwards, Religious Affections, in Works, 3:1-21. This treatise is Jonathan Edwards's Confessions, as much as if it were directly addressed to the Deity. Allen, his biographer, calls it "a work which will not suffer by comparison with the work of great teachers in theology, whether ancient or modern." President Timothy Dwight regarded it as most worthy of preservation next to the Bible. See also Hodge, Essays and Reviews, 1:48; Owen on the Holy Spirit, in Works, 3:297-336; Charnock on Regeneration; Andrew Fuller, Works, 2:461-471, 512-560, and 3:796; Bellamy, Works, 2:502; Dwight, Works, 2:418; Woods, Works, 3:1-21; Anderson, Regeneration, 21-50.

B. It is an instantaneous change, in a region of the soul below consciousness, and is therefore known only in its results.

(a) It is an instantaneous change.—Regeneration is not a gradual work. Although there may be a gradual work of God's providence and Spirit, preparing the change, and a gradual recognition of it after it has taken place, there must be an instant of time when, under the influence of God's Spirit, the disposition of the soul, just before hostile to God, is changed to love. Any other view assumes an intermediate state of indecision which has no moral character at all, and confounds regeneration either with conviction or with sanctification.

Conviction of sin is an ordinary, if not an invariable, antecedent of regeneration. It results from the contemplation of truth. It is often accompanied by fear, remorse, and cries for mercy. But these desires and fears are not signs of regeneration. They are selfish. They are quite consistent with manifest and dreadful enmity to God. They have a hopeful aspect, simply because they are evidence that the Holy Spirit is striving with the soul. But this work of the Spirit is not yet regeneration; at most, it is preparation for regeneration. So far as the sinner is concerned, he is more of a sinner than ever before; because, under more light than has ever before been given him, he is still rejecting Christ and resisting the Spirit. The word of God and the Holy Spirit appeal to lower as well as to higher motives; most men's concern about religion is determined, at the outset, by hope or fear. See Shedd, Dogm. Theol., 2:512.

All these motives, though they are not the highest, are yet proper motives to influence the soul; it is right to seek God from motives of self-interest, and because we desire heaven. But the seeking which not only begins, but ends, upon this lower plane, is never successful. Until the soul gives itself to God from motives of love, it is never saved. And so long as these preliminary motives rule, regeneration has not yet taken place. Bible-reading, and prayers, and church-attendance, and partial reformations, are certainly better than apathy or outbreaking sin. They may be signs that God is working in the soul. But without complete surrender to God, they may be accompanied with the greatest guilt and the greatest danger; simply because, under such influences, the withholding of submission implies the most active hatred to God, and opposition to his will. Instance cases of outward reformation that preceded regeneration,—like that of John Bunyan, who left off swearing before his conversion. Park: "The soul is a monad, and must turn all at once. If we are standing on the line, we are yet unregenerate. We are regenerate only when we cross it." There is a prevenient grace as well as a regenerating grace. Wendelius indeed distinguished five kinds of grace, namely, prevenient, preparatory, operant, coöperant, and perfecting.

While in some cases God's preparatory work occupies a long time, there are many cases in which he cuts short his work in righteousness (Rom. 9:28). Some persons are regenerated in infancy or childhood, cannot remember a time when they did not love Christ, and yet take long to learn that they are regenerate. Others are convicted and converted suddenly in mature years. The best proof of regeneration is not the memory of a past experience, however vivid and startling, but rather a present inward love for Christ, his holiness, his servants, his work, and his word. Much sympathy should be given to those who have been early converted, but who, from timidity, self-distrust, or the faults of inconsistent church members, have been deterred from joining themselves with Christian people, and so have lost all hope and joy in their religious lives. Instance the man who, though converted in a revival of religion, was injured by a professed Christian, and became a recluse, but cherished the memory of his dead wife and child, kept the playthings of the one and the clothing of the other, and left directions to have them buried with him.

As there is danger of confounding regeneration with preparatory influences of God's Spirit, so there is danger of confounding regeneration with sanctification. Sanctification, as the development of the new affection, is gradual and progressive. But no beginning is progressive or gradual; and regeneration is a beginning of the new affection. We may gradually come to the knowledge that a new affection exists, but the knowledge of a beginning is one thing; the beginning itself is another thing. Luther had experienced a change of heart, long before he knew its meaning or could express his new feelings in scientific form. It is not in the sense of a gradual regeneration, but in the sense of a gradual recognition of the fact of regeneration, and a progressive enjoyment of its results, that "the path of the righteous" is said to be "as the dawning light"—the morning- dawn that begins in faintness, but—"that shineth more and more unto the perfect day" (Prov. 4:18). Cf. 2 Cor. 4:4—"the god of this world hath blinded the minds of the unbelieving, that the light of the gospel of the glory of Christ, who is the image of God, should not dawn upon them." Here the recognition of God's work is described as gradual; that the work itself is instantaneous, appears from the following verse 6—"Seeing it is God, that said, Light shall shine out of darkness, who shined in our hearts, to give the light of the knowledge of the glory of God in the face of Jesus Christ."

Illustrate by the unconscious crossing of the line which separates one State of the Federal Union from another. From this doctrine of instantaneous regeneration, we may infer the duty of reaping as well as of sowing: John 4:38—"I sent you to reap." "It is a mistaken notion that it takes God a long time to give increase to the seed planted in a sinner's heart. This grows out of the idea that regeneration is a matter of training; that a soul must be educated from a lost state into a state of salvation. Let us remember that three thousand, whom in the morning Peter called murderers of Christ, were before night regenerated and baptized members of his church." Drummond, in his Nat. Law in the Spir. World, remarks upon the humaneness of sudden conversion. As self- limitation, self-mortification, suicide of the old nature, it is well to have it at once done and over with, and not to die by degrees.

(b) This change takes place in the region of the soul below consciousness.—It is by no means true that God's work in regeneration is always recognized by the subject of it. On the other hand, it is never directly perceived at all. The working of God in the human soul, since it contravenes no law of man's being, but rather puts him in the full and normal possession of his own powers, is secret and inscrutable. Although man is conscious, he is not conscious of God's regenerating agency.

We know our own natural existence only through the phenomena of thought and sense. So we know our own spiritual existence, as new creatures in Christ, only through the new feelings and experiences of the soul. "The will does not need to act solitarily, in order to act freely." God acts on the will, and the resulting holiness is true freedom. John 8:36—"If therefore the Son shall make you free, ye shall be free indeed." We have the consciousness of freedom; but the act of God in giving us this freedom is beyond or beneath our consciousness.

Both Luther and Calvin used the word regeneration in a loose way, confounding it with sanctification. After the Federalists made a distinct doctrine of it, Calvinists in general came to treat it separately. And John Wesley rescued it from identification with sacraments, by showing its connection with the truth. E. G. Robinson: "Regeneration is in one sense instantaneous, in another sense not. There is necessity of some sort of knowledge in regeneration. The doctrine of Christ crucified is the fit instrument. The object of religion is to produce a sound rather than an emotional experience. Revivals of religion are valuable in just the proportion in which they produce rational conviction and permanently righteous action." But none are left unaffected by them. "An arm of the magnetic needle must be attracted to the magnetic pole of the earth, or it must be repelled,—there is no such thing as indifference. Modern materialism, refusing to say that the fear of God is the beginning of wisdom, is led to declare that the hate of God is the beginning of wisdom" (Diesselhoff, Die klassische Poesie, 8).

(c) This change, however, is recognized indirectly in its results.—At the moment of regeneration, the soul is conscious only of the truth and of its own exercises with reference to it. That God is the author of its new affection is an inference from the new character of the exercises which it prompts. The human side or aspect of regeneration is Conversion. This, and the Sanctification which follows it (including the special gifts of the Holy Spirit), are the sole evidences in any particular case that regeneration is an accomplished fact.

Regeneration, though it is the birth of a perfect child, is still the birth of a child. The child is to grow, and the growth is sanctification; in other words, sanctification, as we shall see, is simply the strengthening and development of the holy affection which begins its existence in regeneration. Hence the subject of the epistle to the Romans—salvation by faith—includes not only justification by faith (chapters 1-7), but sanctification by faith (chapters 8-16). On evidences of regeneration, see Anderson, Regeneration, 169-214, 227-295; Woods, Works, 44-55. The transition from justification by faith to sanctification by faith is in chapter 8 of the epistle to the Romans. That begins by declaring that there is no condemnation in Christ, and ends by declaring that there is no separation from Christ. The work of the Holy Spirit follows upon the work of Christ. See Godet on the epistle.

The doctrine of Alexander Campbell was a protest against laying an unscriptural emphasis on emotional states as evidences of regeneration—a protest which certain mystical and antinomian exaggerations of evangelical teaching very justly provoked. But Campbell went to the opposite extreme of practically excluding emotion from religion, and of confining the work of the Holy Spirit to the conscious influence of the truth. Disciples need to recognize a power of the Holy Spirit exerted below consciousness, in order to explain the conscious acceptance of Christ and of his salvation.

William James, Varieties of Religious Experience, 271—"If we should conceive that the human mind, with its different possibilities of equilibrium, might be like a many sided solid with different surfaces on which it could lie flat, we might liken mental revolutions to the spatial revolutions of such a body. As it is pried up, say by a lever, from a position in which it lies on surface A, for instance, it will linger for a time unstably half way up, and if the lever cease to urge it, it will tumble back or relapse, under the continued pull of gravity. But if at last it rotate far enough for its centre of gravity to pass beyond the surface A altogether, the body will fall over, on surface B, say, and will abide there permanently. The pulls of gravity towards A have vanished, and may now be disregarded. The polyhedron has become immune against further attraction from this direction."

III. Conversion

Conversion is that voluntary change in the mind of the sinner, in which he turns, on the one hand, from sin, and on the other hand, to Christ. The former or negative element in conversion, namely, the turning from sin, we denominate repentance. The latter or positive element in conversion, namely, the turning to Christ, we denominate faith.

For account of repentance and faith as elements of conversion, see Andrew Fuller, Works, 1:666; Luthardt, Compendium der Dogmatik, 3d ed., 201-206. The two elements of conversion seem to be in the mind of Paul, when he writes in Rom. 6:11—"reckon ye also yourselves to be dead unto sin, but alive unto God in Christ Jesus"; Col. 3:3—"ye died, and your life is hid with Christ in God." Cf. ἀποστρέφω, in Acts 3:26—"in turning away every one of you from your iniquities," with ἐπιστρέφω in Acts 11:21—"believed" and "turned unto the Lord." A candidate for ordination was once asked which came first: regeneration or conversion. He replied very correctly: "Regeneration and conversion are like the cannon-ball and the hole—they both go through together." This is true however only as to their chronological relation. Logically the ball is first and causes the hole, not the hole first and causes the ball.

(a) Conversion is the human side or aspect of that fundamental spiritual change which, as viewed from the divine side, we call regeneration. It is simply man's turning. The Scriptures recognize the voluntary activity of the human soul in this change as distinctly as they recognize the causative agency of God. While God turns men to himself (Ps. 85:4; Song 1:4; Jer. 31:18; Lam. 5:21), men are exhorted to turn themselves to God (Prov. 1:23; Is. 31:6; 59:20; Ez. 14:6; 18:32; 33:9, 11; Joel 2:12-14). While God is represented as the author of the new heart and the new spirit (Ps. 51:10; Ez. 11:19; 36:26), men are commanded to make for themselves a new heart and a new spirit (Ez. 18:31; 2 Cor. 7:1; cf. Phil. 2:12, 13; Eph. 5:14).

Ps. 85:4—"Turn us, O God of our salvation"; Song 1:4—"Draw me, we will run after thee"; Jer. 31:18—"turn thou me, and I shall be turned"; Lam. 5:21—"Turn thou us unto thee, O Jehovah, and we shall be turned."

Prov. 1:23—"Turn you at my reproof: Behold, I will pour out my spirit unto you"; Is. 31:6—"Turn ye unto him from whom ye have deeply revolted, O children of Israel"; 59:20—"And a Redeemer will come to Zion, and unto them that turn from transgression in Jacob"; Ez. 14:6—"Return ye, and turn yourselves from your idols"; 18:32—"turn yourselves and live"; 33:9—"if thou warn the wicked of his way to turn from it, and he turn not from his way, he shall die in his iniquity"; 11—"turn ye, turn ye from your evil ways; for why will ye die, O house of Israel?" Joel 2:12-14—"turn ye unto me with all your heart."

Ps. 51:10—"Create in me a clean heart, O God; And renew a right spirit within me"; Ez. 11:19—"And I will give them one heart, and I will put a new spirit within you; and I will take the stony heart out of their flesh, and will give them a heart of flesh"; 36:26—"A new heart also will I give you, and a new spirit will I put within you."

Ez. 18:31—"Cast away from you all your transgressions, wherein ye have transgressed; and make you a new heart and a new spirit: for why will ye die, O house of Israel?" 2 Cor. 7:1—"Having therefore these promises, beloved, let us cleanse ourselves from all defilement of flesh and spirit, perfecting holiness in the fear of God"; cf. Phil. 2:12, 13—"work out your own salvation with fear and trembling; for it is God who worketh in you both to will and to work, for his good pleasure"; Eph. 5:14—"Awake, thou that sleepest, and arise from the dead, and Christ shall shine upon thee."

When asked the way to heaven, Bishop Wilberforce replied: "Take the first turn to the right, and go straight forward." Phillips Brooks's conversion is described by Professor Allen, Life, 1:266, as consisting in the resolve "to be true to himself, to renounce nothing which he knew to be good, and yet bring all things captive to the obedience of God, ... the absolute surrender of his will to God, in accordance with the example of Christ: 'Lo, I am come ... to do thy will, O God' (Heb. 10:7)."

(b) This twofold method of representation can be explained only when we remember that man's powers may be interpenetrated and quickened by the divine, not only without destroying man's freedom, but with the result of making man for the first time truly free. Since the relation between the divine and the human activity is not one of chronological succession, man is never to wait for God's working. If he is ever regenerated, it must be in and through a movement of his own will, in which he turns to God as unconstrainedly and with as little consciousness of God's operation upon him, as if no such operation of God were involved in the change. And in preaching, we are to press upon men the claims of God and their duty of immediate submission to Christ, with the certainty that they who do so submit will subsequently recognize this new and holy activity of their own wills as due to a working within them of divine power.

Ps. 110:3—"Thy people offer themselves willingly in the day of thy power." The act of God is accompanied by an activity of man. Dorner: "God's act initiates action." There is indeed an original changing of man's tastes and affections, and in this man is passive. But this is only the first aspect of regeneration. In the second aspect of it—the rousing of man's powers—God's action is accompanied by man's activity, and regeneration is but the obverse side of conversion. Luther's word: "Man, in conversion, is purely passive," is true only of the first part of the change; and here, by "conversion," Luther means "regeneration." Melanchthon said better: "Non est enim coäctio, ut voluntas non possit repugnare: trahit Deus, sed volentem trahit." See Meyer on Rom. 8:14—"led by the Spirit of God": "The expression," Meyer says, "is passive, though without prejudice to the human will, as verse 13 proves: 'by the Spirit ye put to death the deeds of the body.' "

As, by a well known principle of hydrostatics, the water contained in a little tube can balance the water of a whole ocean, so God's grace can be balanced by man's will. As sunshine on the sand produces nothing unless man sow the seed, and as a fair breeze does not propel the vessel unless man spread the sails, so the influences of God's Spirit require human agencies, and work through them. The Holy Spirit is sovereign,—he bloweth where he listeth. Even though there be uniform human conditions, there will not be uniform spiritual results. Results are often independent of human conditions as such. This is the truth emphasized by Andrew Fuller. But this does not prevent us from saying that, whenever God's Spirit works in regeneration, there is always accompanying it a voluntary change in man, which we call conversion, and that this change is as free, and as really man's own work, as if there were no divine influence upon him.

Jesus told the man with the withered hand to stretch forth his hand; it was the man's duty to stretch it forth, not to wait for strength from God to do it. Jesus told the man sick of the palsy to take up his bed and walk. It was that man's duty to obey the command, not to pray for power to obey. Depend wholly upon God? Yes, as you depend wholly upon wind when you sail, yet need to keep your sails properly set. "Work out your own salvation" comes first in the apostle's exhortation; "for it is God who worketh in you" follows (Phil. 2:12, 13); which means that our first business is to use our wills in obedience; then we shall find that God has gone before us to prepare us to obey.

Mat. 11:12—"the kingdom of heaven suffereth violence, and men of violence take it by force." Conversion is like the invasion of a kingdom. Men are not to wait for God's time, but to act at once. Not bodily exercises are required, but impassioned earnestness of soul. Wendt, Teaching of Jesus, 2:49-56—"Not injustice and violence, but energetic laying hold of a good to which they can make no claim. It is of no avail to wait idly, or to seek laboriously to earn it; but it is of avail to lay hold of it and to retain it. It is ready as a gift of God for men, but men must direct their desire and will toward it.... The man who put on the wedding garment did not earn his share of the feast thereby, yet he did show the disposition without which he was not permitted to partake of it."

James, Varieties of Religious Experience, 12—"The two main phenomena of religion, they will say, are essentially phenomena of adolescence, and therefore synchronous with the development of sexual life. To which the retort is easy: Even were the asserted synchrony unrestrictedly true as a fact (which it is not), it is not only the sexual life, but the entire higher mental life, which awakens during adolescence. One might then as well set up the thesis that the interest in mechanics, physics, chemistry, logic, physiology and sociology, which springs up during adolescent years along with that in poetry and religion, is also a perversion of the sexual instinct, but this would be too absurd. Moreover, if the argument from synchrony is to decide, what is to be done with the fact that the religious age par excellence would seem to be old age, when the uproar of the sexual life is past?"

(c) From the fact that the word "conversion" means simply "a turning," every turning of the Christian from sin, subsequent to the first, may, in a subordinate sense, be denominated a conversion (Luke 22:32). Since regeneration is not complete sanctification, and the change of governing disposition is not identical with complete purification of the nature, such subsequent turnings from sin are necessary consequences and evidences of the first (cf. John 13:10). But they do not, like the first, imply a change in the governing disposition,—they are rather new manifestations of a disposition already changed. For this reason, conversion proper, like the regeneration of which it is the obverse side, can occur but once. The phrase "second conversion," even if it does not imply radical misconception of the nature of conversion, is misleading. We prefer, therefore, to describe these subsequent experiences, not by the term "conversion," but by such phrases as "breaking off, forsaking, returning from, neglects or transgressions," and "coming back to Christ, trusting anew in him." It is with repentance and faith, as elements in that first and radical change by which the soul enters upon a state of salvation, that we have now to do.

Luke 22:31, 32—"Simon, Simon, behold, Satan asked to have you, that he might sift you as wheat: but I made supplication for thee, that thy faith fail not; and do thou, when once thou hast turned again [A. V.: 'art converted'], establish thy brethren"; John 13:10—"He that is bathed [has taken a full bath] needeth not save to wash his feet, but is clean every whit [as a whole]." Notice that Jesus here announces that only one regeneration is needed,—what follows is not conversion but sanctification. Spurgeon said he believed in regeneration, but not in re- regeneration. Second blessing? Yes, and a forty-second. The stages in the Christian life are like ice, water, invisible vapor, steam, all successive and natural results of increasing temperature, seemingly different from one another, yet all forms of the same element.

On the relation between the divine and the human agencies, we quote a different view from another writer: "God decrees to employ means which in every case are sufficient, and which in certain cases it is foreseen will be effectual. Human action converts a sufficient means into an effectual means. The result is not always according to the varying use of means. The power is all of God. Man has power to resist only. There is a universal influence of the Spirit, but the influences of the Spirit vary in different cases, just as external opportunities do. The love of holiness is blunted, but it still lingers. The Holy Spirit quickens it. When this love is wholly lost, sin against the Holy Ghost results. Before regeneration there is a desire for holiness, an apprehension of its beauty, but this is overborne by a greater love for sin. If the man does not quickly grow worse, it is not because of positive action on his part, but only because negatively he does not resist as he might. 'Behold, I stand at the door and knock.' God leads at first by a resistible influence. When man yields, God leads by an irresistible influence. The second influence of the Holy Spirit confirms the Christian's choice. This second influence is called 'sealing.' There is no necessary interval of time between the two. Prevenient grace comes first; conversion comes after."

To this view, we would reply that a partial love for holiness, and an ability to choose it before God works effectually upon the heart, seem to contradict those Scriptures which assert that "the mind of the flesh is enmity against God" (Rom. 8:7), and that all good works are the result of God's new creation (Eph. 2:10). Conversion does not precede regeneration,—it chronologically accompanies regeneration, though it logically follows it.

1. Repentance.

Repentance is that voluntary change in the mind of the sinner in which he turns from sin. Being essentially a change of mind, it involves a change of view, a change of feeling, and a change of purpose. We may therefore analyze repentance into three constituents, each succeeding term of which includes and implies the one preceding:

A. An intellectual element,—change of view—recognition of sin as involving personal guilt, defilement, and helplessness (Ps. 51:3, 7, 11). If unaccompanied by the following elements, this recognition may manifest itself in fear of punishment, although as yet there is no hatred of sin. This element is indicated in the Scripture phrase ἐπίγνωσις ἁμαρτίας (Rom. 3:20; cf. 1:32).

Ps. 51:3, 11—"For I know my transgressions; And my sin is ever before me.... Cast me not away from thy presence, And take not thy Holy Spirit from me"; Rom. 3:20—"through the law cometh the knowledge of sin"; cf. 1:32—"who, knowing the ordinance of God, that they that practise such things are worthy of death, not only do the same, but also consent with them that practise them."

It is well to remember that God requires us to cherish no views or emotions that contradict the truth. He wants of us no false humility. Humility (humus) = groundness—a coming down to the hard-pan of facts—a facing of the truth. Repentance, therefore, is not a calling ourselves by hard names. It is not cringing, or exaggerated self-contempt. It is simple recognition of what we are. The "'umble" Uriah Heep is the arrant hypocrite. If we see ourselves as God sees us, we shall say with Job 42:5, 6—"I had heard of thee by the hearing of the ear; But now mine eye seeth thee: Wherefore I abhor myself, And repent in dust and ashes."

Apart from God's working in the heart there is no proper recognition of sin, either in people of high or low degree. Lady Huntington invited the Duchess of Buckingham to come and hear Whitefield, when the Duchess answered: "It is monstrous to be told that you have a heart as sinful as the common wretches that crawl on the earth,—it is highly offensive and insulting." Mr. Moody, after preaching to the prisoners in the jail at Chicago, visited them in their cells. In the first cell he found two, playing cards. They said false witnesses had testified against them. In the second cell, the convict said that the guilty man had escaped, but that he, a mere accomplice, had been caught. In the last cell only Mr. Moody found a man crying over his sins. Henry Drummond, after hearing the confessions of inquirers, said: "I am sick of the sins of these men,—how can God bear it?"

Experience of sin does not teach us to recognize sin. We do not learn to know chloroform by frequently inhaling it. The drunkard does not understand the degrading effects of drink so well as his miserable wife and children do. Even the natural conscience does not give the recognition of sin that is needed in true repentance. The confession "I have sinned" is made by hardened Pharaoh (Ex. 9:27), double minded Balaam (Num. 22:34), remorseful Achan (Josh. 7:20), insincere King Saul (1 Sam. 15:24), despairing Judas (Mat. 27:4); but in no one of these cases was there true repentance. True repentance takes God's part against ourselves, has sympathy with God, feels how unworthily the Ruler, Father, Friend of men has been treated. It does not ask, "What will my sin bring to me?" but, "What does my sin mean to God?" It involves, in addition to the mere recognition of sin:

B. An emotional element,—change of feeling—sorrow for sin as committed against goodness and justice, and therefore hateful to God, and hateful in itself (Ps. 51:1, 2, 10, 14). This element of repentance is indicated in the Scripture word μεταμέλομαι. If accompanied by the following element, it is a λύπη κατὰ Θεόν. If not so accompanied, it is a λύπη τοῦ κόσμου = remorse and despair (Mat. 27:3; Luke 18:23; 2 Cor. 7:9, 10).

Ps. 51:1, 2, 10, 14—"Have mercy upon me ... blot out my transgressions. Wash me thoroughly from mine iniquity, And cleanse me from my sin.... Create in me a clean heart, O God; ... Deliver me from bloodguiltiness, O God"; Mat. 27:3—"Then Judas, who betrayed him, when he saw that he was condemned, repented himself, and brought back the thirty pieces of silver to the chief priests and elders, saying, I have sinned in that I betrayed innocent blood"; Luke 18:23—"when he heard these things, he became exceeding sorrowful; for he was very rich"; 2 Cor. 7:9, 10—"I now rejoice, not that ye were made sorry, but that ye were made sorry unto repentance; for ye were made sorry after a godly sort.... For godly sorrow worketh repentance unto salvation, a repentance which bringeth no regret: but the sorrow of the world worketh death." We must distinguish sorrow for sin from shame on account of it and fear of its consequences. These last are selfish, while godly sorrow is disinterested. "A man may be angry with himself and may despise himself without any humble prostration before God or confession of his guilt" (Shedd, Dogm. Theol., 2:535, note).

True repentance, as illustrated in Ps. 51, does not think of 1. consequences, 2. other men, 3. heredity, as an excuse; but it sees sin as 1. transgression against God, 2. personal guilt, 3. defiling the inmost being. Perowne on Ps. 51:1—"In all godly sorrow there is hope. Sorrow without hope may be remorse or despair, but it is not repentance." Much so-called repentance is illustrated by the little girl's prayer: "O God, make me good,—not real good, but just good enough so that I won't have to be whipped!" Shakespeare, Measure for Measure, 2:3—"'Tis meet so, daughter; but lest you do repent As that the sin hath brought you to this shame, Which sorrow is always towards ourselves, not heaven, Showing we would not spare heaven as we love it, But as we stand in fear.... I do repent me as it is an evil, And take the shame with joy." Tempest, 3:3—"For which foul deed, the Powers delaying, not forgetting, Have incensed the seas, and shores, yea, all the creatures, Against your peace.... Whose wrath to guard you from ... is nothing but heart's sorrow And a clear life ensuing."

Simon, Reconciliation, 195, 379—"At the very bottom it is God whose claims are advocated, whose part is taken, by that in us which, whilst most truly our own, yea, our very selves, is also most truly his, and of him. The divine energy and idea which constitutes us will not let its own root and source suffer wrong unatoned. God intends us to be givers as well as receivers, givers even to him. We share in his image that we may be creators and givers, not from compulsion, but in love." Such repentance as this is wrought only by the Holy Spirit. Conscience indeed is present in every human heart, but only the Holy Spirit convinces of sin. Why is the Holy Spirit needed? A. J. Gordon, Ministry of the Spirit, 189-201—"Conscience is the witness to the law; the Spirit is the witness to grace. Conscience brings legal conviction; the Spirit brings evangelical conviction. The one begets a conviction unto despair; the other a conviction unto hope. Conscience convinces of sin committed, of righteousness impossible, of judgment impending; the Comforter convinces of sin committed, of righteousness imputed, of judgment accomplished—in Christ. God alone can reveal the divine view of sin, and enable man to understand it." But, however agonizing the sorrow, it will not constitute true repentance, unless it leads to, or is accompanied by:

C. A voluntary element,—change of purpose—inward turning from sin and disposition to seek pardon and cleansing (Ps. 51:5, 7, 10; Jer. 25:5). This includes and implies the two preceding elements, and is therefore the most important aspect of repentance. It is indicated in the Scripture term μετάνοια (Acts 2:38; Rom. 2:4).

Ps. 51:5, 7, 10—"Behold, I was brought forth in iniquity; And in sin did my mother conceive me.... Purge me with hyssop, and I shall be clean: Wash me, and I shall be whiter than snow.... Create in me a clean heart, O God; And renew a right spirit within me"; Jer. 25:5—"Return ye now every one from his evil way, and from the evil of your doings"; Acts 2:38—"And Peter said unto them, Repent ye, and be baptized every one of you in the name of Jesus Christ"; Rom. 2:4—"despisest thou the riches of his goodness and forbearance and longsuffering, not knowing that the goodness of God leadeth thee to repentance?"

Walden, The Great Meaning of Metanoia, brings out well the fact that "repentance" is not the true translation of the word, but rather "change of mind"; indeed, he would give up the word "repentance" altogether in the N. T., except as the translation of μεταμέλεια. The idea of μετάνοια is abandonment of sin rather than sorrow for sin,—an act of the will rather than a state of the sensibility. Repentance is participation in Christ's revulsion from sin and suffering on account of it. It is repentance from sin, not of sin, nor for sin—always ἀπό and ἔκ, never περί or ἐπί. The true illustrations of repentance are found in Job (42:6—"I abhor myself, And repent in dust and ashes"); in David (Ps. 51:10—"Create in me a clean heart; And renew a right spirit within me"); in Peter (John 21:17—"thou knowest that I love thee"); in the penitent thief (Luke 23:42—"Jesus, remember me when thou comest in thy kingdom"); in the prodigal son (Luke 15:18—"I will arise and go to my Father").

Repentance implies free will. Hence Spinoza, who knows nothing of free will, knows nothing of repentance. In book 4 of his Ethics, he says: "Repentance is not a virtue, that is, it does not spring from reason; on the contrary, the man who repents of what he has done is doubly wretched or impotent." Still he urges that for the good of society it is not desirable that vulgar minds should be enlightened as to this matter; see Upton, Hibbert Lectures, 315. Determinism also renders it irrational to feel righteous indignation either at the misconduct of other people or of ourselves. Moral admiration is similarly irrational in the determinist; see Balfour, Foundations of Belief, 24.

In broad distinction from the Scriptural doctrine, we find the Romanist view, which regards the three elements of repentance as the following: (1) contrition; (2) confession; (3) satisfaction. Of these, contrition is the only element properly belonging to repentance; yet from this contrition the Romanist excludes all sorrow for sin of nature. Confession is confession to the priest; and satisfaction is the sinner's own doing of outward penance, as a temporal and symbolic submission and reparation to violated law. This view is false and pernicious, in that it confounds repentance with its outward fruits, conceives of it as exercised rather toward the church than toward God, and regards it as a meritorious ground, instead of a mere condition, of pardon.

On the Romanist doctrine of Penance, Thornwell (Collected Writings, 1:423) remarks: "The culpa may be remitted, they say, while the pœna is to some extent retained." The priest absolves, not declaratively, but judicially. Denying the greatness of the sin, it makes man able to become his own

Savior. Christ's satisfaction, for sins after baptism, is not sufficient; our satisfaction is sufficient. But performance of one duty, we object, cannot make satisfaction for the violation of another.

We are required to confess one to another, and specially to those whom we have wronged: James 5:16—"Confess therefore your sins one to another, and pray one for another, that ye may be healed." This puts the hardest stress upon our natural pride. There are a hundred who will confess to a priest or to God, where there is one who will make frank and full confession to the aggrieved party. Confession to an official religious superior is not penitence nor a test of penitence. In the Confessional women expose their inmost desires to priests who are forbidden to marry. These priests are sometimes, though gradually, corrupted to the core, and at the same time they are taught in the Confessional precisely to what women to apply. In France many noble families will not permit their children to confess, and their women are not permitted to incur the danger.

Lord Salisbury in the House of Lords said of auricular confession: "It has been injurious to the moral independence and virility of the nation to an extent to which probably it has been given to no other institution to affect the character of mankind." See Walsh, Secret History of the Oxford Movement; A. J. Gordon, Ministry of the Spirit, 111—"Asceticism is an absolute inversion of the divine order, since it seeks life through death, instead of finding death through life. No degree of mortification can ever bring us to sanctification." Penance can never effect true repentance, nor be other than a hindrance to the soul's abandonment of sin. Penance is something external to be done, and it diverts attention from the real inward need of the soul. The monk does penance by sleeping on an iron bed and by wearing a hair shirt. When Anselm of Canterbury died, his under garments were found alive with vermin which the saint had cultivated in order to mortify the flesh. Dr. Pusey always sat on a hard chair, traveled as uncomfortably as possible, looked down when he walked, and whenever he saw a coal-fire thought of hell. Thieves do penance by giving a part of their ill-gotten wealth to charity. In all these things there is no transformation of the inner life.

In further explanation of the Scripture representations, we remark:

(a) That repentance, in each and all of its aspects, is wholly an inward act, not to be confounded with the change of life which proceeds from it.

True repentance is indeed manifested and evidenced by confession of sin before God (Luke 18:13), and by reparation for wrongs done to men (Luke 19:8). But these do not constitute repentance; they are rather fruits of repentance. Between "repentance" and "fruit worthy of repentance," Scripture plainly distinguishes (Mat. 3:8).

Luke 18:13—"But the publican, standing afar off, would not lift up so much as his eyes unto heaven, but smote his breast, saying, God, be thou merciful to me a sinner ['be propitiated to me the sinner']"; 19:8—"And Zacchæus stood, and said unto the Lord, Behold, Lord, the half of my goods I give to the poor; and if I have wrongfully exacted aught of any man, I restore fourfold"; Mat. 3:8—"Bring forth therefore fruit worthy of repentance." Fruit worthy of repentance, or fruits meet for repentance, are: 1. Confession of sin; 2. Surrender to Christ; 3. Turning from sin; 4. Reparation for wrong doing; 5. Right moral conduct; 6. Profession of Christian faith.

On Luke 17:3—"if thy brother sin, rebuke him; and if he repent, forgive him"—Dr. B. H. Carroll remarks that the law is uniform which makes repentance indispensable to forgiveness. It applies to man's forgiveness of man, as well as to God's forgiveness of man, or the church's forgiveness of man. But I must be sure that I cherish toward the offender the spirit of love, whether he repents or not. Freedom from all malice toward him, however, and even loving prayerful labor to lead him to repentance, is not forgiveness. This I can grant only when he actually repents. If I do forgive him without repentance, then I impose my rule on God when I pray: "Forgive us our debts, as we also have forgiven our debtors" (Mat. 6:12).

On the question whether the requirement that we forgive without atonement implies that God does, see Brit. and For. Evang. Rev., Oct 1881:678-691—"Answer: 1. The present constitution of things is based upon atonement. Forgiveness on our part is required upon the ground of the Cross, without which the world would be hell. 2. God is Judge. We forgive, as brethren. When he forgives, it is as Judge of all the earth, of whom all earthly judges are representatives. If earthly judges may exact justice, much more God. The argument that would abolish atonement would abolish all civil government. 3. I should forgive my brother on the ground of God's love, and Christ's bearing of his sins. 4. God, who requires atonement, is the same being that provides it. This is 'handsome and generous.' But I can never provide atonement for my brother. I must, therefore, forgive freely, only upon the ground of what Christ has done for him."

(b) That repentance is only a negative condition, and not a positive means of salvation.

This is evident from the fact that repentance is no more than the sinner's present duty, and can furnish no offset to the claims of the law on account of past transgression. The truly penitent man feels that his repentance has no merit. Apart from the positive element of conversion, namely, faith in Christ, it would be only sorrow for guilt unremoved. This very sorrow, moreover, is not the mere product of human will, but is the gift of God.

Acts 5:31—"Him did God exalt with his right hand to be a Prince and a Savior, to give repentance to Israel, and remission of sins"; 11:18—"Then to the Gentiles also hath God granted repentance unto life"; 2 Tim. 2:25—"if peradventure God may give them repentance unto the knowledge of the truth." The truly penitent man recognizes the fact that his sin deserves punishment. He never regards his penitence as offsetting the demands of law, and as making his punishment unjust. Whitefield: "Our repentance needeth to be repented of, and our very tears to be washed in the blood of Christ." Shakespeare, Henry V, 4:1—"More will I do: Though all that I can do is nothing worth, Since that my penitence comes after all, Imploring pardon"—imploring pardon both for the crime and for the imperfect repentance.

(c) That true repentance, however, never exists except in conjunction with faith.

Sorrow for sin, not simply on account of its evil consequences to the transgressor, but on account of its intrinsic hatefulness as opposed to divine holiness and love, is practically impossible without some confidence in God's mercy. It is the Cross which first makes us truly penitent (cf. John 12:32, 33). Hence all true preaching of repentance is implicitly a preaching of faith (Mat. 3:1-12; cf. Acts 19:4), and repentance toward God involves faith in the Lord Jesus Christ (Acts 20:21; Luke 15:10, 24; 19:8, 9; cf. Gal. 3:7).

John 12:32, 33—"And I, if I be lifted up from the earth, will draw all men unto myself. But this he said, signifying by what manner of death he should die." Mat. 3:1-12—John the Baptist's preaching of repentance was also a preaching of faith; as is shown by Acts 19:4—"John baptized with the baptism of repentance, saying unto the people that they should believe on him that should come after him, that is, on Jesus." Repentance involves faith: Acts 20:21—"testifying both to Jews and to Greeks repentance toward God, and faith toward our Lord Jesus Christ"; Luke 15:10, 24—"there is joy in the presence of the angels of God over one sinner that repenteth.... this my son was dead, and is alive again; he was lost, and is found"; 19:8, 9—"the half of my goods I give to the poor; and if I have wrongfully exacted aught of any man, I restore fourfold. And Jesus said unto him, To-day is salvation come to this house, forasmuch as he also is a son of Abraham"—the father of all believers; cf. Gal. 3:6, 7—"Even as Abraham believed God, and it was reckoned unto him for righteousness. Know therefore that they that are of faith, the same are sons of Abraham."

Luke 3:18 says of John the Baptist: "he preached the gospel unto the people," and the gospel message, the glad tidings, is more than the command to repent,—it is also the offer of salvation through Christ; see Prof. Wm. Arnold Stevens, on John the Baptist and his Gospel, in Studies on the Gospel according to John. 2 Chron. 34:19—"And it came to pass, when the king had heard the words of the law, that he rent his clothes." Moberly, Atonement and Personality, 44-46—"Just in proportion as one sins, does he render it impossible for him truly to repent. Repentance must be the work of another in him. Is it not the Spirit of the Crucified which is the reality of the penitence of the truly penitent?" If this be true, then it is plain that there is no true repentance which is not accompanied by the faith that unites us to Christ.

(d) That, conversely, wherever there is true faith, there is true repentance also.

Since repentance and faith are but different sides or aspects of the same act of turning, faith is as inseparable from repentance as repentance is from faith. That must be an unreal faith where there is no repentance, just as that must be an unreal repentance where there is no faith. Yet because the one aspect of his change is more prominent in the mind of the convert than the other, we are not hastily to conclude that the other is absent. Only that degree of conviction of sin is essential to salvation, which carries with it a forsaking of sin and a trustful surrender to Christ.

Bishop Hall: "Never will Christ enter into that soul where the herald of repentance hath not been before him." 2 Cor. 7:10—"repentance unto salvation." In consciousness, sensation and perception are in inverse ratio to each other. Clear vision is hardly conscious of sensation, but inflamed eyes are hardly conscious of anything besides sensation. So repentance and faith are seldom equally prominent in the consciousness of the converted man; but it is important to know that neither can exist without the other. The truly penitent man will, sooner or later, show that he has faith; and the true believer will certainly show, in due season, that he hates and renounces sin.

The question, how much conviction a man needs to insure his salvation, may be answered by asking how much excitement one needs on a burning steamer. As, in the latter case, just enough to prompt persistent effort to escape; so, in the former case, just enough remorseful feeling is needed, to induce the sinner to betake himself believingly to Christ.

On the general subject of Repentance, see Anderson, Regeneration, 279-288; Bp. Ossory, Nature and Effects of Faith, 40-48, 311-318; Woods, Works, 3:68-78; Philippi, Glaubenslehre, 5:1-10, 208-246; Luthardt, Compendium, 3d ed., 206-208; Hodge, Outlines of Theology, 375-381; Alexander, Evidences of Christianity, 47-60; Crawford, Atonement, 413-419.

2. Faith.

Faith is that voluntary change in the mind of the sinner in which he turns to Christ. Being essentially a change of mind, it involves a change of view, a change of feeling, and a change of purpose.

We may therefore analyze faith also into three constituents, each succeeding term of which includes and implies the preceding:

A. An intellectual element (notitia, credere Deum),—recognition of the truth of God's revelation, or of the objective reality of the salvation provided by Christ. This includes not only a historical belief in the facts of the Scripture, but an intellectual belief in the doctrine taught therein as to man's sinfulness and dependence upon Christ.

John 2:23, 24—"How when he was in Jerusalem at the passover, during the feast, many believed on his name, beholding his signs which he did. But Jesus did not trust himself unto them, for that he knew all men"; cf. 3:2—Nicodemus has this external faith: "no one can do these signs that thou doest, except God be with him." James 2:19—"Thou believest that God is one; thou doest well: the demons also believe, and shudder." Even this historical faith is not without its fruits. It is the spring of much philanthropic work. There were no hospitals in ancient Rome. Much of our modern progress is due to the leavening influence of Christianity, even in the case of those who have not personally accepted Christ.

McLaren, S. S. Times, Feb. 22, 1902:107—"Luke does not hesitate to say, in Acts 8:13, that 'Simon Magus also himself believed.' But he expects us to understand that Simon's belief was not faith that saved, but mere credence in the gospel narrative as true history. It had no ethical or spiritual worth. He was 'amazed,' as the Samaritans had been at his juggleries. It did not lead to repentance, or confession, or true trust. He was only 'amazed' at Philip's miracles, and there was no salvation in that." Merely historical faith, such as Disciples and Ritschlians hold to, lacks the element of affection, and besides this lacks the present reality of Christ himself. Faith that does not lay hold of a present Christ is not saving faith.

B. An emotional element (assensus, credere Deo),—assent to the revelation of God's power and grace in Jesus Christ, as applicable to the present needs of the soul. Those in whom this awakening of the sensibilities is unaccompanied by the fundamental decision of the will, which constitutes the next element of faith, may seem to themselves, and for a time may appear to others, to have accepted Christ.

Mat. 13:20, 21—"he that was sown upon the rocky places, this is he that heareth the word, and straightway with joy receiveth it; yet hath he not root in himself, but endureth for a while; and when tribulation or persecution ariseth because of the word, straightway he stumbleth"; cf. Ps. 106:12, 13—"Then believed they his words; they sang his praise. They soon forgat his works; they waited not for his counsel"; Ez. 33:31, 32—"And they come unto thee as the people cometh, and they sit before thee as my people, and they hear thy words, but do them not; for with their mouth they show much love, but their heart goeth after their gain. And, lo, thou art unto them as a very lovely song of one that hath a pleasant voice, and can play well on an instrument; for they hear thy words, but they do them not"; John 5:35—Of John the Baptist: "He was the lamp that burneth and shineth; and ye were willing to rejoice for a season in his light"; 8:30, 31—"As he spake these things, many believed on him (εἰς αὐτόν). Jesus therefore said to those Jews that had believed him (αὐτῷ), If ye abide in my word, then are ye truly my disciples." They believed him, but did not yet believe on him, that is, make him the foundation of their faith and life. Yet Jesus graciously recognizes this first faint foreshadowing of faith. It might lead to full and saving faith.

"Proselytes of the gate" were so called, because they contented themselves with sitting in the gate, as it were, without going into the holy city. "Proselytes of righteousness" were those who did their whole duty, by joining themselves fully to the people of God. Not emotion, but devotion, is the important thing. Temporary faith is as irrational and valueless as temporary repentance. It perhaps gained temporary blessing in the way of healing in the time of Christ, but, if not followed by complete surrender of the will, it might even aggravate one's sin; see John 5:14—"Behold, thou art made whole; sin no more, lest a worse thing befall thee." The special faith of miracles was not a high, but a low, form of faith, and it is not to be sought in our day as indispensable to the progress of the kingdom. Miracles have ceased, not because of decline in faith, but because the Holy Spirit has changed the method of his manifestations, and has led the church to seek more spiritual gifts.

Saving faith, however, includes also:

C. A voluntary element (fiducia, credere in Deum),—trust in Christ as Lord and Savior; or, in other words—to distinguish its two aspects:

(a) Surrender of the soul, as guilty and defiled, to Christ's governance.

Mat. 11:28, 29—"Come unto me all ye that labor and are heavy laden, and I will give you rest. Take my yoke upon you, and learn of me"; John 8:12—"I am the light of the world: he that followeth me shall not walk in the darkness"; 14:1—"Let not your heart be troubled: believe in God, believe also in me"; Acts 16:31—"Believe on the Lord Jesus, and thou shalt be saved." Instances of the use of πιστεύω, in the sense of trustful committance or surrender, are: John 2:24—"But Jesus did not trust himself unto them, for that he knew all men"; Rom. 3:2—"they were intrusted with the oracles of God"; Gal. 2:7—"when they saw that I had been intrusted with the gospel of the uncircumcision." πίστις = "trustful self-surrender to God" (Meyer).

In this surrender of the soul to Christ's governance we have the guarantee that the gospel salvation is not an unmoral trust which permits continuance in sin. Aside from the fact that saving faith is only the obverse side of true repentance, the very nature of faith, as submission to Christ, the embodied law of God and source of spiritual life, makes a life of obedience and virtue to be its natural and necessary result. Faith is not only a declaration of dependence, it is also a vow of allegiance. The sick man's faith in his physician is shown not simply by trusting him, but by obeying him. Doing what the doctor says is the very proof of trust. No physician will long care for a patient who refuses to obey his orders. Faith is self-surrender to the great Physician, and a leaving of our case in his hands. But it is also the taking of his prescriptions, and the active following of his directions.

We need to emphasize this active element in saving faith, lest men get the notion that mere indolent acquiescence in Christ's plan will save them. Faith is not simple receptiveness. It gives itself, as well as receives Christ. It is not mere passivity,—it is also self-committal. As all reception of knowledge is active, and there must be attention if we would learn, so all reception of Christ is active, and there must be intelligent giving as well as taking. The Watchman, April 30, 1896—"Faith is more than belief and trust. It is the action of the soul going out toward its object. It is the exercise of a spiritual faculty akin to that of sight; it establishes a personal relation between the one who exercises faith and the one who is its object. When the intellectual feature predominates, we call it belief; when the emotional element predominates, we call it trust. This faith is at once 'An affirmation and an act Which bids eternal truth be present fact.' "

There are great things received in faith, but nothing is received by the man who does not first give himself to Christ. A conquered general came into the presence of his conqueror and held out to him his hand: "Your sword first, sir!" was the response. But when General Lee offered his sword to General Grant at Appomattox, the latter returned it, saying: "No, keep your sword, and go to your home." Jacobi said that "Faith is the reflection of the divine knowing and willing in the finite spirit of man." G. B. Foster, in Indiana Baptist Outlook, June 19, 1902—"Catholic orthodoxy is wrong in holding that the authority for faith is the church; for that would be an external authority. Protestant orthodoxy is wrong in holding that the authority for faith is the book; for that would be an external authority. Liberalism is wrong in holding that the reason is the authority for faith. The authority for faith is the revelation of God." Faith in this revelation is faith in Christ the Revealer. It puts the soul in connection with the source of all knowledge and power. As the connection of a wire with the reservoir of electric force makes it the channel of vast energies, so the smallest measure of faith, any real connection of the soul with Christ, makes it the recipient of divine resources.

While faith is the act of the whole man, and intellect, affection, and will are involved in it, will is the all-inclusive and most important of its elements. No other exercise of will is such a revelation of our being and so decisive of our destiny. The voluntary element in faith is illustrated in marriage. Here one party pledges the future in permanent self-surrender, commits one's self to another person in confidence that this future, with all its new revelations of character, will only justify the decision made. Yet this is rational; see Holland, in Lux Mundi, 46-48. To put one's hand into molten iron, even though one knows of the "spheroidal state" that gives impunity, requires an exertion of will; and not all workmen in metals are courageous enough to make the venture. The child who leaped into the dark cellar, in confidence that her father's arms would be open to receive her, did not act irrationally, because she had heard her father's command and trusted his promise. Though faith in Christ is a leap in the dark, and requires a mighty exercise of will, it is nevertheless the highest wisdom, because Christ's word is pledged that "him that cometh to me I will in no wise cast out" (John 6:37).

J. W. A. Stewart: "Faith is 1. a bond between persons, trust, confidence; 2. it makes ventures, takes much for granted; 3. its security is the character and power of him in whom we believe,—not our faith, but his fidelity, is the guarantee that our faith is rational." Kant said that nothing in the world is good but the good will which freely obeys the law of the good. Pfleiderer defines faith as the free surrender of the heart to the gracious will of God. Kaftan, Dogmatik, 21, declares that the Christian religion is essentially faith, and that this faith manifests itself as 1. doctrine; 2. worship; 3. morality.

(b) Reception and appropriation of Christ, as the source of pardon and spiritual life.

John 1:12—"as many as received him, to them gave he the right to become children of God, even to them that believe on his name"; 4:14—"whosoever drinketh of the water that I shall give him shall never thirst; but the water that I shall give him shall become in him a well of water springing up unto eternal life"; 6:53—"Except ye eat the flesh of the Son of man and drink his blood, ye have not life in yourselves"; 20:31—"these are written, that ye may believe that Jesus is the Christ, the Son of God; and that believing ye may have life in his name"; Eph. 3:17—"that Christ may dwell in your hearts through faith"; Heb. 11:1—"Now faith is assurance of things hoped for, a conviction of things not seen"; Rev. 3:20—"Behold, I stand at the door and knock: if any man hear my voice and open the door, I will come in to him, and will sup with him, and he with me."

The three constituents of faith may be illustrated from the thought, feeling, and action of a person who stands by a boat, upon a little island which the rising stream threatens to submerge. He first regards the boat from a purely intellectual point of view,—it is merely an actually existing boat. As the stream rises, he looks at it, secondly, with some accession of emotion,—his prospective danger awakens in him the conviction that it is a good boat for a time of need, though he is not yet ready to make use of it. But, thirdly, when he feels that the rushing tide must otherwise sweep him away, a volitional element is added,—he gets into the boat, trusts himself to it, accepts it as his present, and only, means of safety. Only this last faith in the boat is faith that saves, although this last includes both the preceding. It is equally clear that the getting into the boat may actually save a man, while at the same time he may be full of fears that the boat will never bring him to shore. These fears may be removed by the boatman's word. So saving faith is not necessarily assurance of faith; but it becomes assurance of faith when the Holy Spirit "beareth witness with our spirit, that we are children of God" (Rom. 8:16). On the nature of this assurance, and on the distinction between it and saving faith, see pages 844-846.

"Coming to Christ," "looking to Christ," "receiving Christ," are all descriptions of faith, as are also the phrases: "surrender to Christ," "submission to Christ," "closing in with Christ." Paul refers to a confession of faith in Rom. 10:9—"if thou shalt confess with thy mouth Jesus as Lord." Faith, then, is a taking of Christ as both Savior and Lord; and it includes both appropriation of Christ, and consecration to Christ. The voluntary element in faith, however, is a giving as well as a taking. The giving, or surrender, is illustrated in baptism by submergence; the taking, or reception, by emergence. See further on the Symbolism of Baptism. McCosh, Div. Government: "Saving faith is the consent of the will to the assent of the understanding, and commonly accompanied with emotion." Pres. Hopkins, in Princeton Rev., Sept. 1878:511-540—"In its intellectual element, faith is receptive, and believes that God is; in its affectional element, faith is assimilative, and believes that God is a rewarder; in its voluntary element, faith is operative, and actually comes to God (Heb. 11:6)."

Where the element of surrender is emphasized and the element of reception is not understood, the result is a legalistic experience, with little hope or joy. Only as we appropriate Christ, in connection with our consecration, do we realize the full blessing of the gospel. Light requires two things: the sun to shine, and the eye to take in its shining. So we cannot be saved without Christ to save, and faith to take the Savior for ours. Faith is the act by which we receive Christ. The woman who touched the border of Jesus' garment received his healing power. It is better still to keep in touch with Christ so as to receive continually his grace and life. But best of all is taking him into our inmost being, to be the soul of our soul and the life of our life. This is the essence of faith, though many Christians do not yet realize it. Dr. Curry said well that faith can never be defined because it is a fact of life. It is a merging of our life in the life of Christ, and a reception of Christ's life to interpenetrate and energize ours. In faith we must take Christ as well as give ourselves. It is certainly true that surrender without trust will not make us possessors of God's peace. F. L. Anderson: "Faith is submissive reliance on Jesus Christ for salvation: 1. Reliance on Jesus Christ—not mere intellectual belief; 2. Reliance on him for salvation—we can never undo the past or atone for our sins; 3. Submissive reliance on Christ. Trust without surrender will never save."

The passages already referred to refute the view of the Romanist, that saving faith is simply implicit assent to the doctrines of the church; and the view of the Disciple or Campbellite, that faith is merely intellectual belief in the truth, on the presentation of evidence.

The Romanist says that faith can coëxist with mortal sin. The Disciple holds that faith may and must exist before regeneration,—regeneration being completed in baptism. With these erroneous views, compare the noble utterance of Luther, Com. on Galatians, 1:191, 247, quoted in Thomasius, III, 2:183—"True faith," says Luther, "is that assured trust and firm assent of heart, by which Christ is laid hold of,—so that Christ is the object of faith. Yet he is not merely the object of faith; but in the very faith, so to speak, Christ is present. Faith lays hold of Christ, and grasps him as a present possession, just as the ring holds the jewel." Edwards, Works, 4:71-73; 2:601-641—"Faith," says Edwards, "includes the whole act of unition to Christ as a Savior. The entire active uniting of the soul, or the whole of what is called coming to Christ, and receiving of him, is called faith in the Scripture." See also Belief, What Is It? 150-179, 290-298.

Hatch, Hibbert Lectures, 530—"Faith began by being: 1. a simple trust in God; then followed, 2. a simple expansion of that proposition into the assent to the proposition that God is good, and, 3. a simple acceptance of the proposition that Jesus Christ was his Son; then, 4. came in the definition of terms, and each definition of terms involved a new theory; finally, 5. the theories were gathered together into systems, and the martyrs and witnesses of Christ died for their faith, not outside but inside the Christian sphere; and instead of a world of religious belief which resembled the world of actual fact in the sublime unsymmetry of its foliage and the deep harmony of its discords, there prevailed the most fatal assumption of all, that the symmetry of a system is the test of its truth and the proof thereof." We regard this statement of Hatch as erroneous, in that it attributes to the earliest disciples no larger faith than that of their Jewish brethren. We claim that the earliest faith involved an implicit acknowledgement of Jesus as Savior and Lord, and that this faith of simple obedience and trust became explicit recognition of our Lord's deity and atonement just so soon as persecution and the Holy Spirit disclosed to them the real contents of their own consciousness.

An illustration of the simplicity and saving power of faith is furnished by Principal J. R. Andrews, of New London, Conn., Principal of the Bartlett Grammar School. When the steamer Atlantic was wrecked off Fisher's Island, though Mr. Andrews could not swim, he determined to make a desperate effort to save his life. Binding a life-preserver about him, he stood on the edge of the deck waiting his opportunity, and when he saw a wave moving shoreward, he jumped into the rough breakers and was borne safely to land. He was saved by faith. He accepted the conditions of salvation. Forty perished in a scene where he was saved. In one sense he saved himself; in another sense he depended upon God. It was a combination of personal activity and dependence upon God that resulted in his salvation. If he had not used the life- preserver, he would have perished; if he had not cast himself into the sea, he would have perished. So faith in Christ is reliance upon him for salvation; but it is also our own making of a new start in life and the showing of our trust by action. Tract 357, Am. Tract Society—"What is it to believe on Christ? It is: To feel your need of him; To believe that he is able and willing to save you, and to save you now; and To cast yourself unreservedly upon his mercy, and trust in him alone for salvation."

In further explanation of the Scripture representations, we remark:

(a) That faith is an act of the affections and will, as truly as it is an act of the intellect.

It has been claimed that faith and unbelief are purely intellectual states, which are necessarily determined by the facts at any given time presented to the mind; and that they are, for this reason, as destitute of moral quality and as far from being matters of obligation, as are our instinctive feelings of pleasure and pain. But this view unwarrantably isolates the intellect, and ignores the fact that, in all moral subjects, the state of the affections and will affects the judgment of the mind with regard to truth. In the intellectual act the whole moral nature expresses itself. Since the tastes determine the opinions, faith is a moral act, and men are responsible for not believing.

John 3:18-20—"He that believeth on him is not judged: he that believeth not hath been judged already, because he hath not believed on the name of the only begotten Son of God. And this is the judgment, that the light is come into the world, and men loved the darkness rather than the light; for their works were evil. For every one that doeth evil hateth the light, and cometh not to the light, lest his works should be reproved"; 5:40—"ye will not come to me, that ye may have life"; 16:8, 9—"And he, when he is come, will convict the world in respect of sin ... of sin, because they believe not on me"; Rev. 2:21—"she willed not to repent." Notice that the Revised Version very frequently substitutes the voluntary and active terms "disobedience" and "disobedient" for the "unbelief" and "unbelieving" of the Authorized Version,—as in Rom. 15:31; Heb. 3:18; 4:6, 11; 11:31. See Park, Discourses, 45, 46.

Savages do not know that they are responsible for their physical appetites, or that there is any right and wrong in matters of sense, until they come under the influence of Christianity. In like manner, even men of science can declare that the intellectual sphere has no part in man's probation, and that we are no more responsible for our opinions and beliefs than we are for the color of our skin. But faith is not a merely intellectual act,—the affections and will give it quality. There is no moral quality in the belief that 2 + 2 = 4, because we can not help that belief. But in believing on Christ there is moral quality, because there is the element of choice. Indeed it may be questioned, whether, in every judgment upon moral things, there is not an act of will.

Hence on John 7:17—"If any man willeth to do his will, he shall know of the teaching, whether it is of God, or whether I speak from myself"—F. L. Patton calls attention to the two common errors: (1) that obedience will certify doctrine,—which is untrue, because obedience is the result of faith, not vice versa; (2) that personal experience is the ultimate test of faith,—which is untrue, because the Bible is the only rule of faith, and it is one thing to receive truth through the feelings, but quite another to test truth by the feelings. The text really means, that if any man is willing to do God's will, he shall know whether it be of God; and the two lessons to be drawn are: (1) the gospel needs no additional evidence; (2) the Holy Ghost is the hope of the world. On responsibility for opinions and beliefs, see Mozley, on Blanco White, in Essays Philos. and Historical, 2:142; T. T. Smith, Hulsean Lectures for 1839. Wilfrid Ward, The Wish to Believe, quotes Shakespeare: "Thy wish was father, Harry, to that thought"; and Thomas Arnold: "They dared not lightly believe what they so much wished to be true."

Pascal: "Faith is an act of the will." Emerson, Essay on Worship: "A man bears beliefs as a tree bears apples. Man's religious faith is the expression of what he is." Bain: "In its essential character, belief is a phase of our active nature, otherwise called the will." Nash, Ethics and Revelation, 257—"Faith is the creative human answer to the creative divine offer. It is not the passive acceptance of a divine favor.... By faith man, laying hold of the personality of God in Christ, becomes a true person. And by the same faith he becomes, under God, a creator and founder of true society." Inge, Christian Mysticism, 52—"Faith begins with an experiment and ends with an experience. But even the power to make the experiment is given from above. Eternal life is not γνῶσις, but the state of acquiring knowledge—ἵνα γιγνώσκωσιν. It is significant that John, who is so fond of the verb 'to know,' never uses the substantive γνῶσις." Crane, Religion of To-morrow, 148—" 'I will not obey, because I do not yet know'? But this is making the intellectual side the only side of faith, whereas the most important side is the will-side. Let a man follow what he does believe, and he shall be led on to larger faith. Faith is the reception of the personal influence of a living Lord, and a corresponding action."

William James, Will to Believe, 61—"This life is worth living, since it is what we make it, from the moral point of view.... Often enough our faith beforehand in an uncertified result is the only thing that makes the result come true.... If your heart does not want a world of moral reality, your head will assuredly never make you believe in one.... Freedom to believe covers only living options which the intellect cannot by itself resolve.... We are not to put a stopper on our heart, and meantime act as if religion were not true"; Psychology, 2:282, 321—"Belief is consent, willingness, turning of our disposition. It is the mental state or function of cognizing reality. We never disbelieve anything except for the reason that we believe something else which contradicts the first thing. We give higher reality to whatever things we select and emphasize and turn to with a will.... We need only in cold blood act as if the thing in question were real, and keep acting as if it were real, and it will infallibly end by growing into such a connection with our life that it will become real. Those to whom God and duty are mere names, can make them much more than that, if they make a little sacrifice to them every day."

E. G. Robinson: "Campbellism makes intellectual belief to be saving faith. But saving faith is consent of the heart as well as assent of the intellect. On the one hand there is the intellectual element: faith is belief upon the ground of evidence; faith without evidence is credulity. But on the other hand faith has an element of affection; the element of love is always wrapped up in it. So Abraham's faith made Abraham like God; for we always become like that which we trust." Faith therefore is not chronologically subsequent to regeneration, but is its accompaniment. As the soul's appropriation of Christ and his salvation, it is not the result of an accomplished renewal, but rather the medium through which that renewal is effected. Otherwise it would follow that one who had not yet believed (i. e., received Christ) might still be regenerate, whereas the Scripture represents the privilege of sonship as granted only to believers. See John 1:12, 13—"But as many as received him, to them gave he the right to become children of God, even to them that believe on his name: who were born, not of blood, nor of the will of the flesh, nor of the will of man, but of God"; also 3:5, 6, 10-15; Gal. 3:26; 2 Pet. 1:3; cf. 1 John 5:1.

(b) That the object of saving faith is, in general, the whole truth of God, so far as it is objectively revealed or made known to the soul; but, in particular, the person and work of Jesus Christ, which constitutes the centre and substance of God's revelation (Acts 17:18; 1 Cor. 1:23; Col. 1:27; Rev. 19:10).

The patriarchs, though they had no knowledge of a personal Christ, were saved by believing in God so far as God had revealed himself to them; and whoever among the heathen are saved, must in like manner be saved by casting themselves as helpless sinners upon God's plan of mercy, dimly shadowed forth in nature and providence. But such faith, even among the patriarchs and heathen, is implicitly a faith in Christ, and would become explicit and conscious trust and submission, whenever Christ were made known to them (Mat. 8:11, 12; John 10:16; Acts 4:12; 10:31, 34, 35, 44; 16:31).

Acts 17:18—"he preached Jesus and the resurrection"; 1 Cor. 1:23—"we preach Christ crucified"; Col. 1:27—"this mystery among the Gentiles, which is Christ in you, the hope of glory: whom we proclaim"; Rev. 19:10—"the testimony of Jesus is the spirit of prophecy." Saving faith is not belief in a dogma, but personal trust in a personal Christ. It is, therefore, possible to a child. Dorner: "The object of faith is the Christian revelation—God in Christ.... Faith is union with objective Christianity—appropriation of the real contents of Christianity." Dr. Samuel Hopkins, the great uncle, defined faith as "an understanding, cordial receiving of the divine testimony concerning Jesus Christ and the way of salvation by him, in which the heart accords and conforms to the gospel." Dr. Mark Hopkins, the great nephew, defined it as "confidence in a personal being." Horace Bushnell: "Faith rests on a person. Faith is that act by which one person, a sinner, commits himself to another person, a Savior." In John 11:25—"I am the resurrection and the life"—Martha is led to substitute belief in a person for belief in an abstract doctrine. Jesus is "the resurrection," because he is "the life." All doctrine and all miracle is significant and important only because it is the expression of the living Christ, the Revealer of God.

The object of faith is sometimes represented in the N. T., as being God the Father. John 5:24—"He that heareth my word, and believeth him that sent me, hath eternal life"; Rom. 4:5—"to him that worketh not, but believeth on him that justifieth the ungodly, his faith is reckoned for righteousness." We can explain these passages only when we remember that Christ is God "manifested in the flesh" (1 Tim. 3:16), and that "he that hath seen me hath seen the Father" (John 14:9). Man may receive a gift without knowing from whom it comes, or how much it has cost. So the heathen, who casts himself as a sinner upon God's mercy, may receive salvation from the Crucified One, without knowing who is the giver, or that the gift was purchased by agony and blood. Denney, Studies in Theology, 154—"No N. T. writer ever remembered Christ. They never thought of him as belonging to the past. Let us not preach about the historical Christ, but rather, about the living Christ; nay, let us preach him, present and omnipotent. Jesus could say: 'Whither I go, ye know the way' (John 14:4); for they knew him, and he was both the end and the way."

Dr. Charles Hodge unduly restricts the operations of grace to the preaching of the incarnate Christ: Syst. Theol., 2:648—"There is no faith where the gospel is not heard; and where there is no faith, there is no salvation. This is indeed an awful doctrine." And yet, in 2:668, he says most inconsistently: "As God is everywhere present in the material world, guiding its operations according to the laws of nature; so he is everywhere present with the minds of men, as the Spirit of truth and goodness, operating on them according to laws of their free moral agency, inclining them to good and restraining them from evil." This presence and revelation of God we hold to be through Christ, the eternal Word, and so we interpret the prophecy of Caiaphas as referring to the work of the personal Christ: John 11:51, 52—"he prophesied that Jesus should die for the nation; and not for the nation only, but that he might also gather together into one the children of God that are scattered abroad."

Since Christ is the Word of God and the Truth of God, he may be received even by those who have not heard of his manifestation in the flesh. A proud and self-righteous morality is inconsistent with saving faith; but a humble and penitent reliance upon God, as a Savior from sin and a guide of conduct, is an implicit faith in Christ; for such reliance casts itself upon God, so far as God has revealed himself,—and the only Revealer of God is Christ. We have, therefore, the hope that even among the heathen there may be some, like Socrates, who, under the guidance of the Holy Spirit working through the truth of nature and conscience, have found the way of life and salvation.

The number of such is so small as in no degree to weaken the claims of the missionary enterprise upon us. But that there are such seems to be intimated in Scripture: Mat. 8:11, 12—"many shall come from the east and the west, and shall sit down with Abraham, and Isaac, and Jacob, in the kingdom of heaven: but the sons of the kingdom shall be cast forth into the outer darkness"; John 10:16—"And other sheep I have, which are not of this fold: them also I must bring, and they shall hear my voice; and they shall become one flock, one shepherd"; Acts 4:12—"And in none other is there salvation: for neither is there any other name under heaven, that is given among men, wherein we must be saved"; 10:31, 34, 35, 44—"Cornelius, thy prayer is heard, and thine alms are had in remembrance in the sight of God.... Of a truth I perceive that God is no respecter of persons: but in every nation he that feareth him, and worketh righteousness, is acceptable to him.... While Peter yet spake these words, the Holy Spirit fell on all them that heard the word"; 16:31—"Believe on the Lord Jesus, and thou shalt be saved, thou and thy house."

And instances are found of apparently regenerated heathen; see in Godet on John 7:17, note (vol. 2:277), the account of the so- called "Chinese hermit," who accepted Christ, saying: "This is the only Buddha whom men ought to worship!" Edwards, Life of Brainard, 173-175, gives an account "of one who was a devout and zealous reformer, or rather restorer, of what he supposed was the ancient religion of the Indians." After a period of distress, he says that God "comforted his heart and showed him what he should do, and since that time he had known God and tried to serve him; and loved all men, be they who they would, so as he never did before." See art. by Dr. Lucius E. Smith, in Bib. Sac., Oct. 1881:622-645, on the question: "Is salvation possible without a knowledge of the gospel?" H. B. Smith, System, 323, note, rightly bases hope for the heathen, not on morality, but on sacrifice.

A chief of the Camaroons in S. W. Africa, fishing with many of his tribe long before the missionaries came, was overtaken by a storm, and while almost all the rest were drowned, he and a few others escaped. He gathered his people together afterwards and told the story of disaster. He said: "When the canoes upset and I found myself battling with the waves, I thought: To whom shall I cry for help? I knew that the god of the hills could not help me; I knew that the evil spirit would not help me. So I cried to the Great Father, Lord, save me! At that moment my feet touched the sand of the beach, and I was safe. Now let all my people honor the Great Father, and let no man speak a word against him, for he can help us." This chief afterwards used every effort to prevent strife and bloodshed, and was remembered by those who came after as a peace- maker. His son told this story to Alfred Saker, the missionary, saying "Why did you not come sooner? My father longed to know what you have told us; he thirsted for the knowledge of God." Mr. Saker told this in England in 1879.

John Fiske appends to his book, The Idea of God, 168, 169, the following pathetic words of a Kafir, named Sekese, in conversation with a French traveler, M. Arbrouseille, on the subject of the Christian religion: "Your tidings," said this uncultured barbarian, "are what I want, and I was seeking before I knew you, as you shall hear and judge for yourself. Twelve years ago I went to feed my flocks; the weather was hazy. I sat down upon a rock, and asked myself sorrowful questions; yes, sorrowful, because I was unable to answer them. Who has touched the stars with his hands—on what pillars do they rest? I asked myself. The waters never weary, they know no other law than to flow without ceasing from morning till night and from night till morning; but where do they stop, and who makes them flow thus? The clouds also come and go, and burst in water over the earth. Whence come they—who sends them? The diviners certainly do not give us rain; for how could they do it? And why do I not see them with my own eyes, when they go up to heaven to fetch it? I cannot see the wind; but what is it? Who brings it, makes it blow and roar and terrify us? Do I know how the corn sprouts? Yesterday there was not a blade in my field; to-day I returned to my field and found some; who can have given to the earth the wisdom and the power to produce it? Then I buried my head in both hands."

On the question whether men are ever led to faith, without intercourse with living Christians or preachers, see Life of Judson, by his son, 84. The British and Foreign Bible Society publish a statement, made upon the authority of Sir Bartle Frere, that he met with "an instance, which was carefully investigated, in which all the inhabitants of a remote village in the Deccan had abjured idolatry and caste, removed from their temples the idols which had been worshiped there time out of mind, and agreed to profess a form of Christianity which they had deduced from the careful perusal of a single Gospel and a few tracts." Max Müller, Chips, 4:177-189, apparently proves that Buddha is the original of St. Josaphat, who has a day assigned to him in the calendar of both the Greek and the Roman churches. "Sancte Socrates, ora pro nobis."

The Missionary Review of the World, July, 1896:519-523, tells the story of Adiri, afterwards called John King, of Maripastoon in Dutch Guiana. The Holy Spirit wrought in him mightily years before he heard of the missionaries. He was a coal-black negro, a heathen and a fetish worshiper. He was convicted of sin and apparently converted through dreams and visions. Heaven and hell were revealed to him. He was sick unto death, and One appeared to him declaring himself to be the Mediator between God and man, and telling him to go to the missionaries for instruction. He was persecuted, but he won his tribe from heathenism and transformed them into a Christian community.

S. W. Hamblen, missionary to China, tells of a very earnest and consistent believer who lived at rather an obscure town of about 2800 people. The evangelist went to visit him and found that he was a worthy example to those around him. He had become a Christian before he had seen a single believer, by reading a Chinese New Testament. Although till the evangelist went to his house he had never met a Baptist and did not know that there were any Baptist churches in existence, yet by reading the New Testament he had become not only a Christian but a strong Baptist in belief, so strong that he could argue with the missionary on the subject of baptism.

The Rev. K. E. Malm, a pioneer Baptist preacher in Sweden, on a journey to the district as far north as Gestrikland, met a woman from Lapland who was on her way to Upsala in order to visit Dr. Fjellstedt and converse with him as to how she might obtain peace with God and get rid of her anxiety concerning her sins. She said she had traveled 60 (= 240 English) miles, and she had still far to go. Malm improved the opportunity to speak to her concerning the crucified Christ, and she found peace in believing on his atonement. She became so happy that she clapped her hands, and for joy could not sleep that night. She said later: "Now I will return home and tell the people what I have found." This she did, and did not care to continue her journey to Upsala, in order to get comfort from Dr. Fjellstedt.

(c) That the ground of faith is the external word of promise. The ground of assurance, on the other hand, is the inward witness of the Spirit that we fulfil the conditions of the promise (Rom. 4:20, 21; 8:16; Eph. 1:13; 1 John 4:13; 5:10). This witness of the Spirit is not a new revelation from God, but a strengthening of faith so that it becomes conscious and indubitable.

True faith is possible without assurance of salvation. But if Alexander's view were correct, that the object of saving faith is the proposition: "God, for Christ's sake, now looks with reconciling love on me, a sinner," no one could believe, without being at the same time assured that he was a saved person. Upon the true view, that the object of saving faith is not a proposition, but a person, we can perceive not only the simplicity of faith, but the possibility of faith even where the soul is destitute of assurance or of joy. Hence those who already believe are urged to seek for assurance (Heb. 6:11; 2 Peter 1:10).

Rom. 4:20, 21—"looking unto the promise of God, he wavered not through unbelief, but waxed strong through faith, giving glory to God, and being fully assured that what he had promised, he was able also to perform"; 8:16—"The Spirit himself beareth witness with our spirit, that we are children of God"; Eph. 1:13—"in whom, having also believed, ye were sealed with the Holy Spirit of promise"; 1 John 4:13—"hereby we know that we abide in him, and he in us, because he hath given us of his Spirit"; 5:10—"He that believeth on the Son of God hath the witness in him." This assurance is not of the essence of faith, because believers are exhorted to attain to it: Heb. 6:11—"And we desire that each one of you may show the same diligence unto the fulness of hope [marg.—'full assurance'] even to the end"; 2 Pet. 1:10—"Wherefore, brethren, give the more diligence to make your calling and election sure." Cf. Prov. 14:14—"a good man shall be satisfied from himself."

There is need to guard the doctrine of assurance from mysticism. The witness of the Spirit is not a new and direct revelation from God. It is a strengthening of previously existing faith until he who possesses this faith cannot any longer doubt that he possesses it. It is a general rule that all our emotions, when they become exceedingly strong, also become conscious. Instance affection between man and woman.

Edwards, Religious Affections, in Works, 3:83-91, says the witness of the Spirit is not a new word or suggestion from God, but an enlightening and sanctifying influence, so that the heart is drawn forth to embrace the truth already revealed, and to perceive that it embraces it. "Bearing witness" is not in this case to declare and assert a thing to be true, but to hold forth evidence from which a thing may be proved to be true: God "beareth witness ... by signs and wonders" (Heb. 2:4). So the "seal of the Spirit" is not a voice or suggestion, but a work or effect of the Spirit, left as a divine mark upon the soul, to be an evidence by which God's children may be known. Seals had engraved upon them the image or name of the persons to whom they belonged. The "seal of the Spirit," the "earnest of the Spirit," the "witness of the Spirit," are all one thing. The childlike spirit, given by the Holy Spirit, is the Holy Spirit's witness or evidence in us.

See also illustration of faith and assurance, in C. S. Robinson's Short Studies for S. S. Teachers, 179, 180. Faith should be distinguished not only from assurance, but also from feeling or joy. Instance Abraham's faith when he went to sacrifice Isaac; and Madame Guyon's faith, when God's face seemed hid from her. See, on the witness of the Spirit, Short, Bampton Lectures for 1846; British and For. Evan. Rev., 1888:617-631. For the view which confounds faith with assurance, see Alexander, Discourses on Faith, 63-118.

It is important to distinguish saving faith from assurance of faith, for the reason that lack of assurance is taken by so many real Christians as evidence that they know nothing of the grace of God. To use once more a well-worn illustration: It is getting into the boat that saves us, and not our comfortable feelings about the boat. What saves us is faith in Christ, not faith in our faith, or faith in the faith. The astronomer does not turn his telescope to the reflection of the sun or moon in the water, when he can turn it to the sun or moon itself. Why obscure our faith, when we can look to Christ?

The faith in a distant Redeemer was the faith of Christian, in Bunyan's Pilgrim's Progress. Only at the end of his journey does Christian have Christ's presence. This representation rests upon a wrong conception of faith as laying hold of a promise or a doctrine, rather than as laying hold of the living and present Christ. The old Scotch woman's direction to the inquirer to "grip the promise" is not so good as the direction to "grip Christ." Sir Francis Drake, the great English sailor, had for his crest an anchor with a cable running up into the sky. A poor boy, taught in a mission school in Ireland, when asked what was meant by saving faith, replied: "It is grasping God with the heart."

The view of Charles Hodge, like that of Alexander, puts doctrine before Christ, and makes the formal principle, the supremacy of Scripture, superior to the material principle, justification by faith. The Shorter Catechism is better: "Faith in Christ is a saving grace, whereby we receive and rest on him alone for salvation, as he is offered to us in the gospel." If this relation of faith to the personal Christ had been kept in mind, much religious despondency might have been avoided. Murphy, Natural Selection and Spiritual Freedom, 30, 31, tells us that Frances Ridley Havergal could never fix the date of her conversion. From the age of six to that of fourteen she suffered from religious fears, and did not venture to call herself a Christian. It was the result of confounding being at peace with God and being conscious of that peace. So the mother of Frederick Denison Maurice, an admirable and deeply religious woman, endured long and deep mental suffering from doubts as to her personal election.

There is a witness of the Spirit, with some sinners, that they are not children of God, and this witness is through the truth, though the sinner does not know that it is the Spirit who reveals it to him. We call this work of the Spirit conviction of sin. The witness of the Spirit that we are children of God, and the assurance of faith of which Scripture speaks, are one and the same thing, the former designation only emphasizing the source from which the assurance springs. False assurance is destitute of humility, but true assurance is so absorbed in Christ that self is forgotten. Self-consciousness, and desire to display one's faith, are not marks of true assurance. When we say: "That man has a great deal of assurance," we have in mind the false and self- centered assurance of the hypocrite or the self-deceiver.

Allen, Jonathan Edwards, 231—"It has been said that any one who can read Edwards's Religious Affections, and still believe in his own conversion, may well have the highest assurance of its reality. But how few there were in Edwards's time who gained the assurance, may be inferred from the circumstance that Dr. Hopkins and Dr. Emmons, disciples of Edwards and religious leaders in New England, remained to the last uncertain of their conversion." He can attribute this only to the semi-deistic spirit of the time, with its distant God and imperfect apprehension of the omnipresence and omnipotence of Christ. Nothing so clearly marks the practical progress of Christianity as the growing faith in Jesus, the only Revealer of God in nature and history as well as in the heart of the believer. As never before, faith comes directly to Christ, abides in him, and finds his promise true: "Lo, I am with you always, even unto the end of the world" (Mat. 28:20). "Nothing before, nothing behind; The steps of faith Fall on the seeming void and find The Rock beneath."

(d) That faith necessarily leads to good works, since it embraces the whole truth of God so far as made known, and appropriates Christ, not only as an external Savior, but as an internal sanctifying power (Heb. 7:15, 16; Gal. 5:6).

Good works are the proper evidence of faith. The faith which does not lead men to act upon the commands and promises of Christ, or, in other words, does not lead to obedience, is called in Scripture a "dead," that is, an unreal, faith. Such faith is not saving, since it lacks the voluntary element—actual appropriation of Christ (James 2:14-26).

Heb. 7:15, 16—"another priest, who hath been made, not after the law of a carnal commandment, but after the power of an endless life"; Gal. 5:6—"For in Christ Jesus neither circumcision availeth anything, nor uncircumcision; but faith working through love"; James 2:14, 26—"What doth it profit, my brethren, if a man say he hath faith, but have not works? Can that faith save him?... For as the body apart from the spirit is dead, even so faith apart from works is dead."

The best evidence that I believe a man's word is that I act upon it. Instance the bank-cashier's assurance to me that a sum of money is deposited with him to my account. If I am a millionaire, the communication may cause me no special joy. My faith in the cashier's word is tested by my going, or not going, for the money. So my faith in Christ is evidenced by my acting upon his commands and promises. We may illustrate also by the lifting of the trolley to the wire, and the resulting light and heat and motion to the car that before stood dark and cold and motionless upon the track. Salvation by works is like getting to one's destination by pushing the car. True faith depends upon God for energy, but it results in activity of all our powers. Rom. 3:28—"We reckon therefore that a man is justified by faith apart from the works of the law." We are saved only by faith, yet this faith will be sure to bring forth good works; see Gal. 5:6—"faith working through love." Dead faith might be illustrated by Abraham Lincoln's Mississippi steamboat, whose whistle was so big that, when it sounded, the boat stopped. Confession exhausts the energy, so that none is left for action.

A. J. Gordon, The First Thing in the World, or The Primacy of Faith: "David Brainard speaks with a kind of suppressed astonishment of what he observed among the degraded North American Indians; how, preaching to them the good news of salvation through the atonement of Christ and persuading them to accept it by faith, and then hastening on in his rapid missionary tours, he found, on returning upon his track a year or two later, that the fruits of righteousness and sobriety and virtue and brotherly love were everywhere visible, though it had been possible to impart to them only the slightest moral or ethical teaching."

(e) That faith, as characteristically the inward act of reception, is not to be confounded with love or obedience, its fruit.

Faith is, in the Scriptures, called a work, only in the sense that man's active powers are engaged in it. It is a work which God requires, yet which God enables man to perform (John 6:29—ἔργον τοῦ Θεοῦ. Cf. Rom. 1:17—δικαιοσύνη Θεοῦ). As the gift of God and as the mere taking of undeserved mercy, it is expressly excluded from the category of works upon the basis of which man may claim salvation (Rom. 3:28; 4:4, 5, 16). It is not the act of the full soul bestowing, but the act of an empty soul receiving. Although this reception is prompted by a drawing of heart toward God inwrought by the Holy Spirit, this drawing of heart is not yet a conscious and developed love: such love is the result of faith (Gal. 5:6). What precedes faith is an unconscious and undeveloped tendency or disposition toward God. Conscious and developed affection toward God, or love proper, must always follow faith and be the product of faith. So, too, obedience can be rendered only after faith has laid hold of Christ, and with him has obtained the spirit of obedience (Rom. 1:5—ὑπακοὴν πίστεως = "obedience resulting from faith"). Hence faith is not the procuring cause of salvation, but is only the instrumental cause. The procuring cause is the Christ, whom faith embraces.

John 6:29—"This is the work of God, that ye believe on him whom he hath sent"; cf. Rom. 1:17—"For therein is revealed a righteousness of God from faith unto faith: as it is written, But the righteous shall live by faith"; Rom. 3:28—"We reckon therefore that a man is justified by faith apart from the works of the law"; 4:4, 5, 16—"Now to him that worketh, the reward is not reckoned as of grace, but as of debt. But to him that worketh not, but believeth on him that justifieth the ungodly, his faith is reckoned for righteousness.... For this cause it is of faith, that it may be according to grace"; Gal. 5:6—"For in Christ Jesus neither circumcision availeth anything, nor uncircumcision; but faith working through love"; Rom. 1:5—"through whom we received grace and apostleship, unto obedience of faith among all the nations."

Faith stands as an intermediate factor between the unconscious and undeveloped tendency or disposition toward God inwrought in the soul by God's regenerating act, on the one hand, and the conscious and developed affection toward God which is one of the fruits and evidences of conversion, on the other. Illustrate by the motherly instinct shown in a little girl's care for her doll,—a motherly instinct which becomes a developed mother's love, only when a child of her own is born. This new love of the Christian is an activity of his own soul, and yet it is a "fruit of the Spirit" (Gal. 5:22). To attribute it wholly to himself would be like calling the walking and leaping of the lame man (Acts 3:8) merely a healthy activity of his own. For illustration of the priority of faith to love, see Shedd, Dogm. Theol., 2:533, note; on the relation of faith to love, see Julius Müller, Doct. Sin, 1:116, 117.

The logical order is therefore: 1. Unconscious and undeveloped love; 2. Faith in Christ and his truth; 3. Conscious and developed love; 4. Assurance of faith. Faith and love act and react upon one another. Each advance in the one leads to a corresponding advance in the other. But the source of all is in God. God loves, and therefore he gives love to us as well as receives love from us. The unconscious and undeveloped love which he imparts in regeneration is the root of all Christian faith. The Roman

Catholic is right in affirming the priority of love to faith, if he means by love only this unconscious and undeveloped affection. But the Protestant is also right in affirming the priority of faith to love, if he means by love a conscious and developed affection. Stevens, Johannine Theology, 368—"Faith is not a mere passive receptivity. As the acceptance of a divine life, it involves the possession of a new moral energy. Faith works by love. In faith a new life-force is received, and new life-powers stir within the Christian man."

We must not confound repentance with fruits meet for repentance, nor faith with fruits meet for faith. A. J. Gordon, The First Thing in the World: "Love is the greatest thing in the world, but faith is the first. The tree is greater than the root, but let it not boast: 'if thou gloriest, it is not thou that bearest the root, but the root thee' (Rom. 11:18). Love has no power to branch out and bear fruit, except as, through faith, it is rooted in Christ and draws nourishment from him. 1 Pet. 1:5—'who by the power of God are guarded through faith unto a salvation ready to be revealed in the last time'; 1 Cor. 13:13—'now abideth faith, hope, love'; Heb. 10:19-25—'draw near ... in fulness of faith ... hold fast the confession of our hope ... provoke unto love and good works'; Rom. 5:1-5—'justified by faith ... rejoice in hope ... love of God hath been shed abroad in our hearts'; 1 Thess. 1:1, 2—'work of faith and labor of love and patience of hope.' Faith is the actinic ray, hope the luminiferous ray, love the calorific ray. But faith contains the principle of the divine likeness, as the life of the parent given to the child contains the principle of likeness to the father, and will insure moral and physical resemblance in due time."

A. J. Gordon, Ministry of the Spirit, 112—" 'The love of the Spirit' (Rom. 15:30) is the love of the Spirit of Christ, and it is given us for overcoming the world. The divine life is the source of the divine love. Therefore the love of God is 'shed abroad in our hearts by the Holy Spirit who is given unto us' (Rom. 5:5). Because we are by nature so wholly without heavenly affection, God, through the indwelling Spirit, gives us his own love with which to love himself." A. H. Strong, Christ in Creation, 286, 287, points out that in 2 Cor. 5:14—"the love of Christ constraineth us"—the love of Christ is "not our love to Christ, for that is a very weak and uncertain thing; nor even Christ's love to us, for that is still something external to us. Each of these leaves a separation between Christ and us, and fails to act as a moving power within.... Not simply our love to Christ, nor simply Christ's love to us, but rather Christ's love in us, is the love that constrains. This is the thought of the apostle." The first fruit of this love, in its still unconscious and undeveloped state, is faith.

(f) That faith is susceptible of increase.

This is evident, whether we consider it from the human or from the divine side. As an act of man, it has an intellectual, an emotional, and a voluntary element, each of which is capable of growth. As a work of God in the soul of man, it can receive, through the presentation of the truth and the quickening agency of the Holy Spirit, continually new accessions of knowledge, sensibility, and active energy. Such increase of faith, therefore, we are to seek, both by resolute exercise of our own powers, and above all, by direct application to the source of faith in God (Luke 17:5).

Luke 17:5—"And the apostles said unto the Lord, Increase our faith." The adult Christian has more faith than he had when a child,—evidently there has been increase. 1 Cor. 12:8, 9—"For to one is given through the Spirit the word of wisdom ... to another faith, in the same Spirit." In this latter passage, it seems to be intimated that for special exigencies the Holy Spirit gives to his servants special faith, so that they are enabled to lay hold of the general promise of God and make special application of it. Rom. 8:26, 27—"the Spirit also helpeth our infirmity ... maketh intercession for us ... maketh intercession for the saints according to the will of God"; 1 John 5:14, 15—"And this is the boldness which we have toward him, that, if we ask anything according to his will, he heareth us: and if we know that he heareth us whatsoever we ask, we know that we have the petitions which we have asked of him." Only when we begin to believe, do we appreciate our lack of faith, and the great need of its increase. The little beginning of light makes known the greatness of the surrounding darkness. Mark 9:24—"I believe; help thou mine unbelief"—was the utterance of one who recognized both the need of faith and the true source of supply.

On the general subject of Faith, see Köstlin, Die Lehre von dem Glauben, 13-85, 301-341, and in Jahrbuch f. d. Theol., 4:177 sq.; Romaine on Faith, 9-89; Bishop of Ossory, Nature and Effects of Faith, 1-40; Venn, Characteristics of Belief, Introduction; Nitzsch, System of Christ. Doct., 294.

IV. Justification

1. Definition of Justification.

By justification we mean that judicial act of God by which, on account of Christ, to whom the sinner is united by faith, he declares that sinner to be no longer exposed to the penalty of the law, but to be restored to his favor. Or, to give an alternative definition from which all metaphor is excluded: Justification is the reversal of God's attitude toward the sinner, because of the sinner's new relation to Christ. God did condemn; he now acquits. He did repel; he now admits to favor.

Justification, as thus defined, is therefore a declarative act, as distinguished from an efficient act;

an act of God external to the sinner, as distinguished from an act within the sinner's nature and changing that nature; a judicial act, as distinguished from a sovereign act; an act based upon and logically presupposing the sinner's union with Christ, as distinguished from an act which causes and is followed by that union with Christ.

The word "declarative" does not imply a "spoken" word on God's part,—much less that the sinner hears God speak. That justification is sovereign, is held by Arminians, and by those who advocate a governmental theory of the atonement. On any such theory, justification must be sovereign; since Christ bore, not the penalty of the law, but a substituted suffering which God graciously and sovereignly accepts in place of our suffering and obedience.

Anselm, Archbishop of Canterbury, 1100, wrote a tract for the consolation of the dying, who were alarmed on account of sin. The following is an extract from it: "Question. Dost thou believe that the Lord Jesus died for thee? Answer. I believe it. Qu. Dost thou thank him for his passion and death? Ans. I do thank him. Qu. Dost thou believe that thou canst not be saved except by his death? Ans. I believe it." And then Anselm addresses the dying man: "Come then, while life remaineth in thee; in his death alone place thy whole trust; in naught else place any trust; to his death commit thyself wholly; with this alone cover thyself wholly; and if the Lord thy God will to judge thee, say, 'Lord, between thy judgment and me I present the death of our Lord Jesus Christ; no otherwise can I contend with thee.' And if he shall say that thou art a sinner, say thou: 'Lord, I interpose the death of our Lord Jesus Christ between my sins and thee.' If he say that thou hast deserved condemnation, say: 'Lord, I set the death of our Lord Jesus Christ between my evil deserts and thee, and his merits I offer for those which I ought to have and have not.' If he say that he is wroth with thee, say: 'Lord, I oppose the death of our Lord Jesus Christ between thy wrath and me.' And when thou hast completed this, say again: 'Lord, I set the death of our Lord Jesus Christ between thee and me.' " See Anselm, Opera (Migne), 1:686, 687. The above quotation gives us reason to believe that the New Testament doctrine of justification by faith was implicitly, if not explicitly, held by many pious souls through all the ages of papal darkness.

2. Proof of the Doctrine of Justification.

A. Scripture proofs of the doctrine as a whole are the following:

Rom. 1:17—"a righteousness of God from faith unto faith"; 3:24-30—"being justified freely by his grace through the redemption that is in Christ Jesus ... the justifier of him that hath faith in Jesus.... We reckon therefore that a man is justified by faith apart from the works of the law ... justify the circumcision by faith, and the uncircumsion through faith"; Gal. 3:11—"Now that no man is justified by the law before God, is evident: for, The righteous shall live by faith; and the law is not of faith; but, He that doeth them shall live in them"; Eph. 1:7—"in whom we have our redemption through his blood, the forgiveness of our trespasses, according to the riches of his grace"; Heb. 11:4, 7—"By faith Abel offered unto God a more excellent sacrifice than Cain, through which he had witness borne to him that he was righteous.... By faith Noah ... moved with godly fear, prepared an ark ... became heir of the righteousness which is according to faith"; cf. Gen. 15:6—"And he believed in Jehovah; and he reckoned it to him for righteousness"; Is. 7:9—"If ye will not believe, surely ye shall not be established"; 28:16—"he that believeth shall not be in haste"; Hab. 2:4—"the righteous shall live by his faith."

Ps. 85:8—"He will speak peace unto his people." God's great word of pardon includes all else. Peace with him implies all the covenant privileges resulting therefrom. 1 Cor. 3:21-23—"all things are yours," because "ye are Christ's; and Christ is God's." This is not salvation by law, nor by ideals, nor by effort, nor by character; although obedience to law, and a loftier ideal, and unremitting effort, and a pure character, are consequences of justification. Justification is the change in God's attitude toward the sinner which makes all these consequences possible. The only condition of justification is the sinner's faith in Jesus, which merges the life of the sinner in the life of Christ. Paul expresses the truth in Gal. 2:16, 20—"Knowing that a man is not justified by the works of the law but through faith in Jesus Christ, even we believed on Christ Jesus, that we might be justified by faith in Christ, and not by the works of the law ... I have been crucified with Christ; and it is no longer I that live, but Christ liveth in me: and that life which I now live in the flesh I live in faith, the faith which is in the Son of God, who loved me, and gave himself up for me."

With these observations and qualifications we may assent to much that is said by Whiton, Divine Satisfaction, 64, who distinguishes between forgiveness and remission: "Forgiveness is the righting of disturbed personal relations. Remission is removal of the consequences which in the natural order of things have resulted from our fault. God forgives all that is strictly personal, but remits nothing that is strictly natural in sin. He imparts to the sinner the power to bear his burden and work off his debt of consequences. Forgiveness is not remission. It is introductory to remission, just as conversion is not salvation, but introductory to salvation. The prodigal was received by his father, but he could not recover his lost patrimony. He could, however, have been led by penitence to work so hard that he earned more than he had lost.

"Here is an element in justification which Protestantism has ignored, and which Romanism has tried to retain. Debts must be paid to the uttermost farthing. The scars of past sins must remain forever. Forgiveness converts the persistent energy of past sin from a destructive to a constructive power. There is a transformation of energy into a new form. Genuine repentance spurs us up to do what we can to make up for time lost and for wrong done. The sinner is clothed anew with moral power. We are all to be judged by our works. That Paul had been a blasphemer was ever stimulating him to Christian endeavor. The faith which receives Christ is a peculiar spirit, a certain moral activity of love and obedience. It is not mere reliance on what Christ was and did, but active endeavor to become and to do like him. Human justice takes hold of deeds; divine righteousness deals with character. Justification by faith is justification by spirit and inward principle, apart from the merit of works or performances, but never without these. God's charity takes the will for the deed. This is not justification by outward conduct, as the Judaizers thought, but by the godly spirit." If this new spirit be the Spirit of Christ to whom faith has united the soul, we can accept the statement. There is danger however of conceiving this spirit as purely man's own, and justification as not external to the sinner nor as the work of God, but as the mere name for a subjective process by which man justifies himself.

B. Scripture use of the special words translated "justify" and "justification" in the Septuagint and in the New Testament.

(a) δικαιόω—uniformly, or with only a single exception, signifies, not to make righteous, but to declare just, or free from guilt and exposure to punishment. The only O. T. passage where this meaning is questionable is Dan. 12:3. But even here the proper translation is, in all probability, not "they that turn many to righteousness," but "they that justify many," i. e., cause many to be justified. For the Hiphil force of the verb, see Girdlestone, O. T. Syn., 257, 258, and Delitzsch on Is. 53:11; cf. James 5:19, 20.

O. T. texts: Ex. 23:7—"I will not justify the wicked"; Deut. 25:1—"they [the judges] shall justify the righteous, and condemn the wicked"; Job 27:5—"Far be it from me that I should justify you"; Ps. 143:2—"in thy sight no man living is righteous"; Prov. 17:15—"He that justifieth the wicked, and he that condemneth the righteous, Both of them alike are an abomination to Jehovah"; Is. 5:23—"that justify the wicked for a bribe, and take away the righteousness of the righteous from him"; 50:8—"He is near that justifieth me"; 53:11—"by the knowledge of himself shall my righteous servant justify many; and he shall bear their iniquities"; Dan. 12:3—"and they that turn many to righteousness, as the stars for ever and ever" ("they that justify many," i. e., cause many to be justified); cf. James 5:19, 20—"My brethren, if any among you err from the truth, and one convert him; let him know, that he who converteth a sinner from the error of his way shall save a soul from death, and shall cover a multitude of sins."

The Christian minister absolves from sin, only as he marries a couple: he does not join them,—he only declares them joined. So he declares men forgiven, if they have complied with the appointed divine conditions. Marriage may be invalid where these conditions are lacking, but the minister's absolution is of no account where there is no repentance of sin and faith in Christ; see G. D. Boardman, The Church, 178. We are ever to remember that the term justification is a forensic term which presents the change of God's attitude toward the sinner in a pictorial way derived from the procedure of earthly tribunals. The fact is larger and more vital than the figure used to describe it.

McConnell, Evolution of Immortality, 134, 135—"Christ's terms are biological; those of many theologians are legal. It may be ages before we recover from the misfortune of having had the truth of Christ interpreted and fixed by jurists and logicians, instead of by naturalists and men of science. It is much as though the rationale of the circulation of the blood had been wrought out by Sir Matthew Hale, or the germ theory of disease interpreted by Blackstone, or the doctrine of evolution formulated by a legislative council.... The Christ is intimately and vitally concerned with the eternal life of men, but the question involved is of their living or perishing, not of a system of judicial rewards and penalties." We must remember however that even biology gives us only one side of the truth. The forensic conception of justification furnishes its complement and has its rights also. The Scriptures represent both sides of the truth. Paul gives us the judicial aspect, John the vital aspect, of justification.

In Rom. 6:7—ὁ γὰρ ἀποθανὼν δεδικαίωται ἀπὸ τῆς ἁμαρτίας = "he that once died with Christ was acquitted from the service of sin considered as a penality." In 1 Cor. 4:4—οὐδὲν γὰρ ἐμαυτῷ σύνοιδα. ἀλλ' οὐκ ἐν τούτῳ δεδικαίωμαι = "I am conscious of no fault, but that does not in itself make certain God's acquittal as respects this particular charge." The usage of the epistle of James does not contradict this; the doctrine of James is that we are justified only by such faith as makes us faithful and brings forth good works. "He uses the word exclusively in a judicial sense; he combats a mistaken view of πίστις, not a mistaken view of δικαιόω"; see James 2:21, 23, 24, and Cremer, N. T. Lexicon, Eng. trans., 182, 183. The only N. T. passage where this meaning is questionable is Rev. 22:11; but here Alford, with א, A and B, reads δικαιοσύνην ποιησάτω.

N. T. texts: Mat. 12:37—"For by thy words thou shalt be justified, and by thy words thou shalt be condemned"; Luke 7:29—"And all the people ... justified God, being baptized with the baptism of John"; 10:29—"But he, desiring to justify himself, said unto Jesus, And who is my neighbor?" 16:15—

"Ye are they that justify yourselves in the sight of men; but God knoweth your hearts"; 18:14—"This man went down to his house justified rather than the other"; cf. 13 (lit.) "God, be thou propitiated toward me the sinner"; Rom. 4:6-8—"Even as David also pronounceth blessing upon the man, unto whom God reckoneth righteousness apart from works, saying, Blessed are they whose iniquities are forgiven, And whose sins are covered. Blessed is the man to whom the Lord will not reckon sin"; cf. Ps. 32:1, 2,—"Blessed is he whose transgression is forgiven, Whose sin is covered. Blessed is the man unto whom Jehovah imputeth not iniquity, And in whose spirit there is no guile."

Rom. 5:18, 19—"So then as through one trespass the judgment came unto all men to condemnation; even so through one act of righteousness the free gift came unto all men to justification of life. For as through the one man's disobedience the many were made sinners, even so through the obedience of the one shall the many be made righteous"; 8:33, 34—"Who shall lay anything to the charge of God's elect? It is God that justifieth; who is he that condemneth?" 2 Cor. 5:19, 21—"God was in Christ reconciling the world unto himself, not reckoning unto them their trespasses.... Him who knew no sin he made to be sin on our behalf; that we might become the righteousness of God [God's justified persons] in him"; Rom. 6:7—"he that hath died is justified from sin"; 1 Cor. 4:4—"For I know nothing against myself; yet am I not hereby justified: but he that judgeth me is the Lord" (on this last text, see Expositor's Greek Testament, in loco).

James 2:21, 23, 24—"Was not Abraham our father justified by works, in that he offered up Isaac his son upon the altar?... Abraham believed God, and it was reckoned unto him for righteousness.... Ye see that by works a man is justified, and not only by faith." James is denouncing a dead faith, while Paul is speaking of the necessity of a living faith; or, rather, James is describing the nature of faith, while Paul is describing the instrument of justification. "They are like two men beset by a couple of robbers. Back to back each strikes out against the robber opposite him,—each having a different enemy in his eye" (Wm. M. Taylor). Neander on James 2:14-26—"James is denouncing mere adhesion to an external law, trust in intellectual possession of it. With him, law means an inward principle of life. Paul, contrasting law as he does with faith, commonly means by law mere external divine requisition.... James does not deny salvation to him who has faith, but only to him who falsely professes to have. When he says that 'by works a man is justified,' he takes into account the outward manifestation only, speaks from the point of view of human consciousness. In works only does faith show itself as genuine and complete." Rev. 22:11—"he that is righteous, let him do righteousness still"—not, as the A. V. seemed to imply, "he that is just, let him be justified still"—i. e., made subjectively holy.

Christ is the great Physician. The physician says: "If you wish to be cured, you must trust me." The patient replies: "I do trust you fully." But the physician continues: "If you wish to be cured, you must take my medicines and do as I direct." The patient objects: "But I thought I was to be cured by trust in you. Why lay such stress on what I do?" The physician answers: "You must show your trust in me by your action. Trust in me, without action in proof of trust, amounts to nothing" (S. S. Times). Doing without a physician is death; hence Paul says works cannot save. Trust in the physician implies obedience; hence James says faith without works is dead. Crane, Religion of To-morrow, 152-155—"Paul insists on apple-tree righteousness, and warns us against Christmas-tree righteousness." Sagebeer, The Bible in Court, 77,78—"By works, Paul means works of law; James means by works, works of faith." Hovey, in The Watchman, Aug. 27, 1891—"A difference of emphasis, occasioned chiefly by the different religious perils to which readers were at the time exposed."

(b) δικαίωσις—is the act, in process, of declaring a man just,—that is, acquitted from guilt and restored to the divine favor (Rom. 4:25; 5:18).

Rom. 4:25—"who was delivered up for our trespasses, and was raised for our justification"; 5:18—"unto all men to justification of life." Griffith-Jones, Ascent through Christ, 367, 368—"Raised for our justification" = Christ's death made our justification possible, but it did not consummate it. Through his rising from the dead he was able to come into that relationship to the believer which restores the lost or interrupted sonship. In the church the fact of the resurrection is perpetuated, and the idea of the resurrection is realized.

(c) δικαίωμα—is the act, as already accomplished, of declaring a man just,—that is, no longer exposed to penalty, but restored to God's favor (Rom. 5:16, 18; cf. 1 Tim. 3:16). Hence, in other connections, δικαίωμα has the meaning of statute, legal decision, act of justice (Luke 1:6; Rom. 2:26; Heb. 9:1).

Rom. 5:16, 18—"of many trespasses unto justification ... through one act of righteousness"; cf. 1 Tim. 3:16—"justified in the spirit." The distinction between δικαίωσις and δικαίωμα may be illustrated by the distinction between poesy and poem,—the former denoting something in process, an ever-working spirit; the latter denoting something fully accomplished, a completed work. Hence δικαίωμα is used in Luke 1:6—"ordinances of the Lord"; Rom. 2:26—"ordinances of the law"; Heb. 9:1—"ordinances of divine service."

(d) δικαιοσύνη—is the state of one justified, or declared just (Rom. 8:10; 1 Cor. 1:30). In Rom. 10:3, Paul inveighs against τὴν ἰδίαν δικαιοσύνην as insufficient and false, and in its place would put τὴν τοῦ Θεοῦ δικαιοσύνην,—that is, a δικαιοσύνη which God not only requires, but provides; which is not only acceptable to God, but proceeds from God, and is appropriated by faith,—hence called δικαιοσύνη πίστεως or ἐκ πίστεως. "The primary signification of the word, in Paul's writings, is therefore that state of the believer which is called forth by God's act of acquittal,—the state of the believer as justified," that is, freed from punishment and restored to the divine favor.

Rom. 8:10—"the spirit is life because of righteousness"; 1 Cor. 1:30—"Christ Jesus, who was made unto us ... righteousness"; Rom. 10:3—"being ignorant of God's righteousness, and seeking to establish their own, they did not subject themselves to the righteousness of God." Shedd, Dogm. Theol., 2:542—"The 'righteousness of God' is the active and passive obedience of incarnate God." See, on δικαιοσύνη, Cremer, N. T. Lexicon, Eng. trans., 174; Meyer on Romans, trans., 68-70—"δικαιοσύνη Θεοῦ (gen. of origin, emanation from) = rightness which proceeds from God—the relation of being right into which man is put by God (by an act of God declaring him righteous)."

E. G. Robinson, Christian Theology, 304—"When Paul addressed those who trusted in their own righteousness, he presented salvation as attainable only through faith in another; when he addressed Gentiles who were conscious of their need of a helper, the forensic imagery is not employed. Scarce a trace of it appears in his discourses as recorded in the Acts, and it is noticeably absent from all the epistles except the Romans and the Galatians."

Since this state of acquittal is accompanied by changes in the character and conduct, δικαιοσύνη comes to mean, secondarily, the moral condition of the believer as resulting from this acquittal and inseparably connected with it (Rom. 14:17; 2 Cor. 5:21). This righteousness arising from justification becomes a principle of action (Mat. 3:15; Acts 10:35; Rom. 6:13, 18). The term, however, never loses its implication of a justifying act upon which this principle of action is based.

Rom. 14:17—"the kingdom of God is not eating and drinking, but righteousness and peace and joy in the Holy Spirit"; 2 Cor. 5:21—"that we might become the righteousness of God in him"; Mat. 3:15—"Suffer it now: for thus it becometh us to fulfil all righteousness"; Acts 10:35—"in every nation he that feareth him, and worketh righteousness, is acceptable to him"; Rom. 6:13—"present yourselves unto God, as alive from the dead, and your members as instruments of righteousness unto God." Meyer on Rom. 3:23—"Every mode of conception which refers redemption and the forgiveness of sins, not to a real atonement through the death of Christ, but subjectively to the dying and reviving with him guaranteed and produced by that death (Schleiermacher, Nitzsch, Hofmann), is opposed to the N. T.,—a mixing up of justification and sanctification."

On these Scripture terms, see Bp. of Ossory, Nature and Effects of Faith, 436-496; Lange, Com., on Romans 3:24; Buchanan on Justification, 226-249. Versus Moehler, Symbolism, 102—"The forgiveness of sins ... is undoubtedly a remission of the guilt and the punishment which Christ hath taken and borne upon himself; but it is likewise the transfusion of his Spirit into us"; Newman, Lectures on Justification, 68-143; Knox, Remains; N. W. Taylor, Revealed Theology, 310-372.

It is a great mistake in method to derive the meaning of δίκαιος from that of δικαιοσύνη, and not vice versa. Wm. Arnold Stevens, in Am. Jour. Theology, April, 1897—"δικαιοσύνη, righteousness, in all its meanings, whether ethical or forensic, has back of it the idea of law; also the idea of violated law; it derives its forensic sense from the verb δικαιόω and its cognate noun δικαίωσις; δικαιοσύνη therefore is legal acceptableness, the status before the law of a pardoned sinner."

Denney, in Expos. Gk. Test., 2:565—"In truth, 'sin,' 'the law,' 'the curse of the law,' 'death,' are names for something which belongs not to the Jewish but to the human conscience; and it is only because this is so that the gospel of Paul is also a gospel for us. Before Christ came and redeemed the world, all men were at bottom on the same footing: Pharisaism, legalism, moralism, or whatever it is called, is in the last resort the attempt to be good without God, to achieve a righteousness of our own, without an initial all-inclusive immeasurable debt to him; in other words, without submitting, as sinful men must submit, to be justified by faith apart from works of our own, and to find in that justification, and in that only, the spring and impulse of all good."

It is worthy of special observation that, in the passages cited above, the terms "justify" and "justification" are contrasted, not with the process of depraving or corrupting, but with the outward act of condemning; and that the expressions used to explain and illustrate them are all derived, not from the inward operation of purifying the soul or infusing into it righteousness, but from the procedure of courts in their judgments, or of offended persons in their forgiveness of offenders. We conclude that these terms, wherever they have reference to the sinner's relation to God, signify a declarative and judicial act of God, external to the sinner, and not an efficient and sovereign act of God changing the sinner's nature and making him subjectively righteous.

In the Canons and Decrees of the Council of Trent, session 6, chap. 9 is devoted to the refutation of the "inanis hæreticorum fiducia"; and Canon 12 of the session anathematizes those who say: "fidem justificantem nihil aliud esse quam fiduciam divinæ misericordiæ, peccata remittentis propter Christum"; or that "justifying faith is nothing but trust in the divine mercy which pardons sins for Christ's sake." The Roman Catholic doctrine on the contrary maintains that the ground of justification is not simply the faith by which the sinner appropriates Christ and his atoning work, but is also the new love and good works wrought within him by Christ's Spirit. This introduces a subjective element which is foreign to the Scripture doctrine of justification.

Dr. E. G. Robinson taught that justification consists of three elements: 1. Acquittal; 2. Restoration to favor; 3. Infusion of righteousness. In this he accepted a fundamental error of Romanism. He says: "Justification and sanctification are not to be distinguished as chronologically and statically different. Justification and righteousness are the same thing from different points of view. Pardon is not a mere declaration of forgiveness—a merely arbitrary thing. Salvation introduces a new law into our sinful nature which annuls the law of sin and destroys its penal and destructive consequences. Forgiveness of sins must be in itself a gradual process. The final consequences of a man's sins are written indelibly upon his nature and remain forever. When Christ said: 'Thy sins are forgiven thee', it was an objective statement of a subjective fact. The person was already in a state of living relation to Christ. The gospel is damnation to the damnable, and invitation, love and mercy to those who feel their need of it. We are saved through the enforcement of law on every one of us. Forgiveness consists in the removal from consciousness of a sense of ill-desert. Justification, aside from its forensic use, is a transformation and a promotion. Sense of forgiveness is a sense of relief from a hated habit of mind." This seems to us dangerously near to a denial that justification is an act of God, and to an affirmation that it is simply a subjective change in man's condition.

E. H. Johnson: "If Dr. Robinson had been content to say that the divine fiat of justification had the manward effect of regeneration, he would have been correct; for the verdict would be empty without this manward efficacy. But unfortunately, he made the effect a part of the cause, identifying the divine justification with its human fruition, the clearance of the past with the provision for the future." We must grant that the words inward and outward are misleading, for God is not under the law of space, and the soul itself is not in space. Justification takes place just as much in man as outside of him. Justification and regeneration take place at the same moment, but logically God's act of renewing is the cause and God's act of approving is the effect. Or we may say that regeneration and justification are both of them effects of our union with Christ. Luke 1:37—"For no word from God shall be void of power." Regeneration and justification may be different aspects of God's turning—his turning us, and his turning himself. But it still is true that justification is a change in God and not in the creature.

3. Elements of Justification.

These are two:

A. Remission of punishment.

(a) God acquits the ungodly who believe in Christ, and declares them just. This is not to declare them innocent,—that would be a judgment contrary to truth. It declares that the demands of the law have been satisfied with regard to them, and that they are now free from its condemnation.

Rom. 4:5—"But to him that worketh not, but believeth on him that justifieth the ungodly, his faith is reckoned for righteousness"; cf. John 3:16—"gave his only begotten Son, that whosoever believeth on him should not perish"; see page 856, (a), and Shedd, Dogm. Theol., 2:549. Rom. 5:1—"Being therefore justified by faith, we have peace with God"—not subjective peace or quietness of mind, but objective peace or reconciliation, the opposite of the state of war, in which we are subject to the divine wrath. Dale, Ephesians, 67—"Forgiveness may be defined: 1. in personal terms, as a cessation of the anger or moral resentment of God against sin; 2. in ethical terms, as a release from the guilt of sin which oppresses the conscience; 3. in legal terms, as a remission of the punishment of sin, which is eternal death."

(b) This acquittal, in so far as it is the act of God as judge or executive, administering law, may be denominated pardon. In so far as it is the act of God as a father personally injured and grieved by sin, yet showing grace to the sinner, it is denominated forgiveness.

Micah 7:18—"Who is a God like into thee, that pardoneth iniquity, and passeth over the transgression of the remnant of his heritage?" Ps. 130:4—"But there is forgiveness with thee, That thou mayst be feared." It is hard for us to understand God's feeling toward sin. Forgiveness seems easy to us, largely because we are indifferent toward sin. But to the holy One, to whom sin is the abominable thing which he hates, forgiveness involves a fundamental change of relation, and nothing but Christ's taking the penalty of sin upon him can make it possible. B. Fay Mills: "A tender spirited follower of Jesus Christ said to me, not long ago, that it had taken him twelve years to forgive an injury that had been committed against him." How much harder for God to forgive, since he can never become indifferent to the nature of the transgression!

(c) In an earthly tribunal, there is no acquittal for those who are proved to be transgressors,—for such there is only conviction and punishment. But in God's government there is remission of punishment for believers, even though they are confessedly offenders; and, in justification, God declares this remission.

There is no forgiveness in nature. F. W. Robertson preached this. But he ignored the vis medicatrix of the gospel, in which forgiveness is offered to all. The natural conscience says: "I must pay my debt." But the believer finds that "Jesus paid it all." Illustrate by the poor man, who on coming to pay his mortgage finds that the owner at death had ordered it to be burned, so that now there is nothing to pay. Ps. 34:22—"Jehovah redeemeth the soul of his servants, And none of them that take refuge in him shall be condemned."

A child disobeys his father and breaks his arm. His sin involves two penalties, the alienation from his father and the broken arm. The father, on repentance, may forgive his child. The personal relation is re-established, but the broken bone is not therefore at once reknit. The father's forgiveness, however, will assure the father's help toward complete healing. So justification does not ensure the immediate removal of all the natural consequences of our sins. It does ensure present reconciliation and future perfection. Clarke, Christian Theology, 364—"Justification is not equivalent to acquittal, for acquittal declares that the man has not done wrong. Justification is rather the acceptance of a man, on sufficient grounds, although he has done wrong." As the Plymouth Brethren say: "It is not the sin-question, but the Son-question." "Their sins and their iniquities will I remember no more" (Heb. 10:17). The father did not allow the prodigal to complete the confession he had prepared to make, but interrupted him, and dwelt only upon his return home (Luke 15:22).

(d) The declaration that the sinner is no longer exposed to the penalty of law, has its ground, not in any satisfaction of the law's demand on the part of the sinner himself, but solely in the bearing of the penalty by Christ, to whom the sinner is united by faith. Justification, in its first element, is therefore that act by which God, for the sake of Christ, acquits the transgressor and suffers him to go free.

Acts 13:38, 39—"Be it known unto you therefore, brethren, that through this man is proclaimed unto you remission of sins: and by him [lit.: 'in him'] every one that believeth is justified from all things, from which ye could not be justified by the law of Moses"; Rom. 3:24, 26—"being justified freely by his grace through the redemption that is in Christ Jesus ... that he might himself be just, and the justifier of him that hath faith in Jesus"; 1 Cor. 6:11—"but ye were justified in the name of the Lord Jesus"; Eph. 1:7—"in whom we have our redemption through his blood, the forgiveness of our trespasses, according to the riches of his grace."

This acquittal is not to be conceived of as the sovereign act of a Governor, but rather as a judicial procedure. Christ secures a new trial for those already condemned—a trial in which he appears for the guilty, and sets over against their sin his own righteousness, or rather shows them to be righteous in him. C. H. M.: "When Balak seeks to curse the seed of Abraham, it is said of Jehovah: 'He hath not beheld iniquity in Jacob, Neither hath he seen perverseness in Israel' (Num. 23:21). When Satan stands forth to rebuke Joshua, the word is: 'Jehovah rebuke thee, O Satan ... is not this a brand plucked out of the fire?' (Zech. 3:2). Thus he ever puts himself between his people and every tongue that would accuse them. 'Touch not mine anointed ones,' he says, 'and do my prophets no harm' (Ps. 105:15). 'It is God that justifieth; who is he that condemneth?' (Rom. 8:33, 34)." It is not sin, then, that condemns,—it is the failure to ask pardon for sin, through Christ. Illustrate by the ring presented by Queen Elizabeth to the Earl of Essex. Queen Elizabeth did not forgive the penitent Countess of Nottingham for withholding the ring of Essex which would have purchased his pardon. She shook the dying woman and cursed her, even while she was imploring forgiveness. There is no such failure of mercy in God's administration.

Kaftan, in Am. Jour. Theology, 4:698—"The peculiar characteristic of Christian experience is the forgiveness of sins, or reconciliation—a forgiveness which is conceived as an unmerited gift of God, which is bestowed on man independently of his own moral worthiness. Other religions have some measure of revelation, but Christianity alone has the clear revelation of this forgiveness, and this is accepted by faith. And forgiveness leads to a better ethics than any religion of works can show."

B. Restoration to favor.

(a) Justification is more than remission or acquittal. These would leave the sinner simply in the position of a discharged criminal,—law requires a positive righteousness also. Besides deliverance from punishment, justification implies God's treatment of the sinner as if he were, and had been, personally righteous. The justified person receives not only remission of penalty, but the rewards promised to obedience.

Luke 15:22-24—"Bring forth quickly the best robe, and put it on him; and put a ring on his hand, and shoes on his feet: and bring the fatted calf, and kill it, and let us eat, and make merry: for this my son was dead, and is alive again; he was lost, and is found"; John 3:16—"gave his only begotten Son, that whosoever believeth on him should ... have eternal life"; Rom. 5:1, 2—"Being therefore justified by faith, we have peace with God through our Lord Jesus Christ; through whom also we have had our access by faith into this grace wherein we stand; and we rejoice in hope of the glory of God"—"this grace" being a permanent state of divine favor; 1 Cor. 1:30—"But of him are ye in Christ Jesus, who was made unto us wisdom from God, and righteousness and sanctification, and redemption: that, according as it is written, He that glorieth, let him glory in the Lord"; 2 Cor. 5:21—"that we might become the righteousness of God in him."

Gal. 3:6—"Even as Abraham believed God, and it was reckoned unto him for righteousness";

Eph. 2:7—"the exceeding riches of his grace in kindness toward us in Christ Jesus"; 3:12—"in whom we have boldness and access in confidence through our faith in him"; Phil. 3:8, 9—"I count all things to be loss for the excellency of the knowledge of Christ Jesus my Lord ... the righteousness which is from God by faith"; Col. 1:22—"reconciled in the body of his flesh through death, to present you holy and without blemish and unreprovable before him"; Tit. 3:4, 7—"the kindness of God our Savior ... that, being justified by his grace, we might be made heirs according to the hope of eternal life"; Rev. 19:8—"And it was given unto her that she should array herself in fine linen, bright and pure: for the fine linen is the righteous acts of the saints."

Justification is setting one right before law. But law requires not merely freedom from offence negatively, but all manner of obedience and likeness to God positively. Since justification is in Christ and by virtue of the believer's union with Christ, it puts the believer on the same footing before the law that Christ is on, namely, not only acquittal but favor. 1 Tim. 3:16—Christ was himself "justified in the spirit," and the believer partakes of his justification and of the whole of it, i. e., not only acquittal but favor. Acts 13:39—"in him every one that believeth is justified" i. e., in Christ; 1 Cor. 6:11—"justified in the name of the Lord Jesus Christ"; Gal. 4:5—"that we might receive the adoption of sons"—a part of justification; Rom. 5:11—"through whom we have now received the reconciliation"—in justification; 2 Cor. 5:21—"that we might become the righteousness of God in him"; Phil. 3:9—"the righteousness which is from God by faith"; John 1:12—"to them gave he the right to become children of God"—emphasis on "gave"—intimation that the "becoming children" is not subsequent to the justification, but is a part of it.

Ellicott on Tit. 3:7—"δικαιοθέντες, 'justified,' in the usual and more strict theological sense; not however as implying only a mere outward non-imputation of sin, but as involving a 'mutationem status,' an acceptance into new privileges, and an enjoyment of the benefits thereof (Waterland, Justif, vol. vi, p. 5); in the words of the same writer: 'Justification cannot be conceived without some work of the Spirit in conferring a title to salvation.' " The prisoner who has simply served out his term escapes without further punishment and that is all. But the pardoned man receives back in his pardon the full rights of citizenship, can again vote, serve on juries, testify in court, and exercise all his individual liberties, as the discharged convict cannot. The Society of Friends is so called, not because they are friends to one another, but because they regard themselves as friends of God. So, in the Middle Ages, Master Eckart, John Tauler, Henry Suso, called themselves the friends of God, after the pattern of Abraham; 2 Chron. 20:7—"Abraham thy friend"; James 2:23—"Abraham believed God, and it was reckoned unto him for righteousness; and he was called the friend of God", i. e., one not merely acquitted from the charge of sin, but also admitted into favor and intimacy with God.

(b) This restoration to favor, viewed in its aspect as the renewal of a broken friendship, is denominated reconciliation; viewed in its aspect as a renewal of the soul's true relation to God as a father, it is denominated adoption.

John 1:12—"But as many as received him, to them gave he the right to become children of God, even to them that believe on his name"; Rom. 5:11—"and not only so, but we also rejoice in God through our Lord Jesus Christ, through whom we have now received the reconciliation"; Gal. 4:4, 5—"born under the law, that he might redeem them that were under the law, that we might receive the adoption of sons"; Eph. 1:5—"having foreordained us unto adoption as sons through Jesus Christ unto himself"; cf. Rom. 8:23—"even we ourselves groan within ourselves, waiting for our adoption, to wit, the redemption of our body"—that is, this adoption is completed, so far as the body is concerned, at the resurrection.

Luther called Psalms 32, 51, 130, 143, "the Pauline Psalms," because these declare forgiveness to be granted to the believer without law and without works. Ps. 130:3, 4—"If thou, Jehovah, shouldst mark iniquities, O Lord, who could stand? But there is forgiveness with thee, That thou mayest be feared" is followed by verses 7, 8—"O Israel, hope in Jehovah; For with Jehovah there is lovingkindness, And with him is plenteous redemption. And he will redeem Israel From all his iniquities." Whitefield was rebuked for declaring in a discourse that Christ would receive even the devil's castaways; but that very day, while at dinner at Lady Huntington's, he was called out to meet two women who were sinners, and to whose broken hearts and blasted lives that remark gave hope and healing.

(c) In an earthly pardon there are no special helps bestowed upon the pardoned. There are no penalties, but there are also no rewards; law cannot claim anything of the discharged, but then they also can claim nothing of the law. But what, though greatly needed, is left unprovided by human government, God does provide. In justification, there is not only acquittal, but approval; not only pardon, but promotion. Remission is never separated from restoration.

After serving a term in the penitentiary, the convict goes out with a stigma upon him and with no friends. His past conviction and disgrace follow him. He cannot obtain employment. He cannot vote. Want often leads him to commit crime again; and then the old conviction is brought up as proof of bad character, and increases his punishment. Need of Friendly Inns and Refuges for discharged criminals.

But the justified sinner is differently treated. He is not only delivered from God's wrath and eternal death, but he is admitted to God's favor and eternal life. The discovery of this is partly the cause of the convert's joy. Expecting pardon, at most, he is met with unmeasured favor. The prodigal finds the father's house and heart open to him, and more done for him than if he had never wandered. This overwhelms and subdues him. The two elements, acquittal and restoration to favor, are never separated. Like the expulsion of darkness and restoration of light, they always go together. No one can have, even if he would have, an incomplete justification. Christ's justification is ours; and, as Jesus' own seamless tunic could not be divided, so the robe of righteousness which he provides cannot be cut in two.

Failure to apprehend this positive aspect of justification as restoration to favor is the reason why so many Christians have little joy and little enthusiasm in their religious lives. The preaching of the magnanimity and generosity of God makes the gospel "the power of God unto salvation" (Rom. 1:16). Edwin M. Stanton had ridden roughshod over Abraham Lincoln in the conduct of a case at law in which they had been joint counsel. Stanton had become vindictive and even violent when Lincoln was made President. But Lincoln invited Stanton to be Secretary of War, and he sent the invitation by Harding, who knew of all this former trouble. When Stanton heard it, he said with streaming eyes: "Do you tell me, Harding, that Mr. Lincoln sent this message to me? Tell him that such magnanimity will make me work with him as man was never served before!"

(d) The declaration that the sinner is restored to God's favor, has its ground, not in the sinner's personal character or conduct, but solely in the obedience and righteousness of Christ, to whom the sinner is united by faith. Thus Christ's work is the procuring cause of our justification, in both its elements. As we are acquitted on account of Christ's suffering of the penalty of the law, so on account of Christ's obedience we receive the rewards of law.

All this comes to us in Christ. We participate in the rewards promised to his obedience: John 20:31—"that believing ye may have life in his name"; 1 Cor. 3:21-23—"For all things are yours; ... all are yours; and ye are Christ's; and Christ is God's." Denovan, Toronto Baptist, Dec. 1883, maintains that "grace operates in two ways: (1) for the rebel it provides a scheme of justification,—this is judicial, matter of debt; (2) for the child it provides pardon,—fatherly forgiveness on repentance." Heb. 7:19—"the law made nothing perfect ... a bringing in thereupon of a better hope, through which we draw nigh unto God." This "better hope" is offered to us in Christ's death and resurrection. The veil of the temple was the symbol of separation from God. The rending of that veil was the symbol on the one hand that sin had been atoned for, and on the other hand that unrestricted access to God was now permitted us in Christ the great forerunner. Bonar's hymn, "Jesus, whom angel hosts adore," has for its concluding stanza: "'T is finished all: the veil is rent. The welcome sure, the access free:—Now then, we leave our banishment, O Father, to return to thee!" See pages 749 (b), 770 (h).

James Russell Lowell: "At the devil's booth all things are sold. Each ounce of dross costs its ounce of gold; For a cap and bells our lives we pay: Bubbles we buy with a whole soul's tasking; 'T is heaven alone that is given away, 'T is only God may be had for the asking." John G. Whittier: "The hour draws near, howe'er delayed and late, When at the Eternal Gate, We leave the words and works we call our own, And lift void hands alone For love to fill. Our nakedness of soul Brings to that gate no toll; Giftless we come to him who all things gives, And live because he lives."

H. B. Smith, System of Christian Doctrine, 523, 524—"Justification and pardon are not the same in Scripture. We object to the view of Emmons (Works, vol. 5), that 'justification is no more nor less than pardon,' and that 'God rewards men for their own, and not Christ's, obedience,' for the reason that the words, as used in common life, relate to wholly different things. If a man is declared just by a human tribunal, he is not pardoned, he is acquitted; his own inherent righteousness, as respects the charge against him, is recognized and declared. The gospel proclaims both pardon and justification. There is no significance in the use of the word 'justify,' if pardon be all that is intended....

"Justification involves what pardon does not, a righteousness which is the ground of the acquittal and favor; not the mere favor of the sovereign, but the merit of Christ, is at the basis—the righteousness which is of God. The ends of the law are so far satisfied by what Christ has done, that the sinner can be pardoned. The law is not merely set aside, but its great ends are answered by what Christ has done in our behalf. God might pardon as a sovereign, from mere benevolence (as regard to happiness); but in the gospel he does more,—he pardons in consistency with his holiness,—upholding that as the main end of all his dealings and works. Justification involves acquittal from all the penalty of the law, and the inheritance of all the blessings of the redeemed state. The penalty of the law—spiritual, temporal, eternal death—is all taken away; and the opposite blessings are conferred, in and through Christ—the resurrection to blessedness, the gift of the Spirit, and eternal life....

"If justification is forgiveness simply, it applies only to the past. If it is also a title to life, it includes the future condition of the soul. The latter alone is consistent with the plan and decrees of God respecting redemption—his seeing the end from the beginning. The reason why justification has been taken as pardon is two-fold: first, it does involve pardon,—this is its negative side, while it has a positive side also—the title to eternal life; secondly, the tendency to resolve the gospel into an ethical system. Only our acts of choice as meritorious could procure a title to favor, a positive reward. Christ might remove the obstacle, but the title to heaven is derived only from what we ourselves do.

"Justification is, therefore, not a merely governmental provision, as it must be on any scheme that denies that Christ's work has direct respect to the ends of the law. Views of the atonement determine the views on justification, if logical sequence is observed. We have to do here, not with views of natural justice, but with divine methods. If we regard the atonement simply as answering the ends of a governmental scheme, our view must be that justification merely removes an obstacle, and the end of it is only pardon, and not eternal life."

But upon the true view, that the atonement is a complete satisfaction to the holiness of God, justification embraces not merely pardon, or acquittal from the punishments of law, but also restoration to favor, or the rewards promised to actual obedience. See also Quenstedt, 3:524; Philippi, Active Obedience of Christ; Shedd, Dogm. Theol., 2:432, 433.

4. Relation of Justification to God's Law and Holiness.

A. Justification has been shown to be a forensic term. A man may, indeed, be conceived of as just, in either of two senses: (a) as just in moral character,—that is, absolutely holy in nature, disposition, and conduct; (b) as just in relation to law,—or as free from all obligation to suffer penalty, and as entitled to the rewards of obedience.

So, too, a man may be conceived of as justified, in either of two senses: (a) made just in moral character; or, (b) made just in his relation to law. But the Scriptures declare that there does not exist on earth a just man, in the first of these senses (Eccl. 7:20). Even in those who are renewed in moral character and united to Christ, there is a remnant of moral depravity.

If, therefore, there be any such thing as a just man, he must be just, not in the sense of possessing an unspotted holiness, but in the sense of being delivered from the penalty of law, and made partaker of its rewards. If there be any such thing as justification, it must be, not an act of God which renders the sinner absolutely holy, but an act of God which declares the sinner to be free from legal penalties and entitled to legal rewards.

Justus is derived from jus, and suggests the idea of courts and legal procedures. The fact that "justify" is derived from justus and facio, and might therefore seem to imply the making of a man subjectively righteous, should not blind us to its forensic use. The phrases "sanctify the Holy One of Jacob" (Is. 29:23; cf. 1 Pet. 3:15—"sanctify in your hearts Christ as Lord") and "glorify God" (1 Cor. 6:20) do not mean, to make God subjectively holy or glorious, for this he is, whatever we may do; they mean rather, to declare, or show, him to be holy or glorious. So justification is not making a man righteous, or even pronouncing him righteous, for no man is subjectively righteous. It is rather to count him righteous so far as respects his relations to law, to treat him as righteous, or to declare that God will, for reasons assigned, so treat him (Payne). So long as any remnant of sin exists, no justification, in the sense of making holy, can be attributed to man: Eccl. 7:20—"Surely there is not a righteous man upon earth, that doeth good and sinneth not." If no man is just, in this sense, then God cannot pronounce him just, for God cannot lie. Justification, therefore, must signify a deliverance from legal penalties, and an assignment of legal rewards. O. P. Gifford: There is no such thing as "salvation by character"; what men need is salvation from character. The only sense in which salvation by character is rational or Scriptural is that suggested by George Harris, Moral Evolution, 409—"Salvation by character is not self-righteousness, but Christ in us." But even here it must be remembered that Christ in us presupposes Christ for us. The objective atonement for sin must come before the subjective purification of our natures. And justification is upon the ground of that objective atonement, and not upon the ground of the subjective cleansing.

The Jews had a proverb that if only one man could perfectly keep the whole law even for one day, the kingdom of Messiah would at once come upon the earth. This is to state in another form the doctrine of Paul, in Rom. 7:9—"When the commandment came, sin revived, and I died." To recognize the impossibility of being justified by Pharisaic works was a preparation for the gospel; see Bruce, Apologetics, 419. The Germans speak of Werk-, Lehre-, Buchstaben-, Negations-, Parteigerechtigkeit; but all these are forms of self-righteousness. Berridge: "A man may steal some gems from the crown of Jesus and be guilty only of petty larceny, ... but the man who would justify himself by his own works steals the crown itself, puts it on his own head, and proclaims himself by his own conquests a king in Zion."

B. The difficult feature of justification is the declaration, on the part of God, that a sinner whose remaining sinfulness seems to necessitate the vindicative reaction of God's holiness against him, is yet free from such reaction of holiness as is expressed in the penalties of the law.

The fact is to be accepted on the testimony of Scripture. If this testimony be not accepted, there is no deliverance from the condemnation of law. But the difficulty of conceiving of God's declaring the sinner no longer exposed to legal penalty is relieved, if not removed, by the three- fold consideration:

(a) That Christ has endured the penalty of the law in the sinner's stead.

Gal. 3:13—"Christ redeemed us from the curse of the law, having become a curse for us." Denovan: "We are justified by faith, instrumentally, in the same sense as a debt is paid by a good note or a check on a substantial account in a distant bank. It is only the intelligent and honest acceptance of justification already provided." Rom. 8:3—"God, sending his own Son ... condemned sin in the flesh" = the believer's sins were judged and condemned on Calvary. The way of pardon through Christ honors God's justice as well as God's mercy; cf. Rom. 3:26—"that he might himself be just, and the justifier of him that hath faith in Jesus."

(b) That the sinner is so united to Christ, that Christ's life already constitutes the dominating principle within him.

Gal. 2:20—"I have been crucified with Christ; and it is no longer I that live, but Christ liveth in me." God does not justify any man whom he does not foresee that he can and will sanctify. Some prophecies produce their own fulfilment. Tell a man he is brave, and you help him to become so. So declaratory justification, when published in the heart by the Holy Spirit, helps to make men just. Harris, God the Creator, 2:332—"The objection to the doctrine of justification by faith insists that justification must be conditioned, not on faith, but on right character. But justification by faith is itself the doctrine of a justification conditioned on right character, because faith in God is the only possible beginning of right character, either in men or angels." Gould, Bib. Theol. N. T., 67-79, in a similar manner argues that Paul's emphasis is on the spiritual effect of the death of our Lord, rather than on its expiatory effect. The course of thought in the Epistle to the Romans seems to us to contradict this view. Sin and the objective atonement for sin are first treated; only after justification comes the sanctification of the believer. Still it is true that justification is never the sole work of God in the soul. The same Christ in union with whom we are justified does at that same moment a work of regeneration which is followed by sanctification.

(c) That this life of Christ is a power in the soul which will gradually, but infallibly, extirpate all remaining depravity, until the whole physical and moral nature is perfectly conformed to the divine holiness.

Phil. 3:21—"who shall fashion anew the body of our humiliation, that it may be conformed to the body of his glory, according to the working whereby he is able even to subject all things unto himself"; Col. 3:1-4—"If then ye were raised together with Christ, seek the things that are above, where Christ is, seated on the right hand of God. Set your mind on the things that are above, not on the things that are upon the earth. For ye died, and your life is hid with Christ in God. When Christ, who is our life, shall be manifested, then shall ye also with him be manifested in glory."

Truth of fact, and ideal truth, are not opposed to each other. F. W. Robertson, Lectures and Addresses, 256—"When the agriculturist sees a small, white, almond-like thing rising from the ground, he calls that an oak; but this is not a truth of fact, it is an ideal truth. The oak is a large tree, with spreading branches and leaves and acorns; but that is only a thing an inch long, and imperceptible in all its development; yet the agriculturist sees in it the idea of what it shall be, and, if I may borrow a Scriptural phrase, he imputes to it the majesty, and excellence, and glory, that is to be hereafter." This method of representation is effective and unobjectionable, so long as we remember that the force which is to bring about this future development and perfection is not the force of unassisted human nature, but rather the force of Christ and his indwelling Spirit. See Philippi, Glaubenslehre, v, 1:201-208.

Gore, Incarnation, 224—"'Looking at the mother,' wrote George Eliot of Mrs. Garth in The Mill on the Floss, 'you might hope that the daughter would become like her—which is a prospective advantage equal to a dowry—the mother too often standing behind the daughter like a malignant prophecy: Such as I am, she will shortly be.' George Eliot imputes by anticipation to the daughter the merits of the mother, because her life is, so to speak, of the same piece. Now, by new birth and spiritual union, our life is of the same piece with the life of Jesus. Thus he, our elder brother, stands behind us, his people, as a prophecy of all good. Thus God accepts us, deals with us, 'in the Beloved,' rating us at something of his value, imputing to us his merits, because in fact, except we be reprobates, he himself is the most powerful and real force at work in us."

5. Relation of Justification to Union with Christ and the Work of the Spirit.

A. Since the sinner, at the moment of justification, is not yet completely transformed in character, we have seen that God can declare him just, not on account of what he is in himself, but only on account of what Christ is. The ground of justification is therefore not, (a) as the Romanists hold, a new righteousness and love infused into us, and now constituting our moral character; nor, (b) as Osiander taught, the essential righteousness of Christ's divine nature, which has become ours by faith; but (c) the satisfaction and obedience of Christ, as the head of a new humanity, and as embracing in himself all believers as his members.

Ritschl regarded justification as primarily an endowment of the church, in which the individual participated only so far as he belonged to the church; see Pfleiderer, Die Ritschl'sche Theologie, 70. Here Ritschl committed an error like that of the Romanist,—the church is the door to Christ, instead of

Christ being the door to the church. Justification belongs primarily to Christ, then to all who join themselves to Christ by faith, and the church is the natural and voluntary aggregation of those who in Christ are thus justified. Hence the necessity for the resurrection and ascension of the Lord Jesus. "For as the ministry of Enoch was sealed by his reception into heaven, and as the ministry of Elijah was also abundantly proved by his translation, so also the righteousness and innocence of Christ. But it was necessary that the ascension of Christ should be more fully attested, because upon his righteousness, so fully proved by his ascension, we must depend for all our righteousness. For if God had not approved him after his resurrection, and he had not taken his seat at his right hand, we could by no means be accepted of God" (Cartwright).

A. J. Gordon, Ministry of the Spirit, 46, 193, 195, 206—"Christ must be justified in the spirit and received up into glory, before he can be made righteousness to us and we can become the righteousness of God in him. Christ's coronation is the indispensable condition of our justification.... Christ the High Priest has entered the Holy of Holies in heaven for us. Until he comes forth again at the second advent, how can we be assured that his sacrifice for us is accepted? We reply: By the gift of the Holy Spirit. The presence of the Spirit in the church is the proof of the presence of Christ before the throne.... The Holy Spirit convinces of righteousness, 'because I go unto the Father, and ye see me no more' (John 16:10). We can only know that 'we have a Paraclete with the Father, even Jesus Christ the Righteous' (1 John 2:1), by that 'other Paraclete' sent forth from the Father, even the Holy Spirit (John 14:25, 26; 15:26). The church, having the Spirit, reflects Christ to the world. As Christ manifests the Father, so the church through the Spirit manifests Christ. So Christ gives to us his name, 'Christians,' as the husband gives his name to the wife."

As Adam's sin is imputed to us, not because Adam is in us, but because we were in Adam; so Christ's righteousness is imputed to us, not because Christ is in us, but because we are in Christ,—that is, joined by faith to one whose righteousness and life are infinitely greater than our power to appropriate or contain. In this sense, we may say that we are justified through a Christ outside of us, as we are sanctified through a Christ within us. Edwards: "The justification of the believer is no other than his being admitted to communion in, or participation of, this head and surety of all believers."

1 Tim. 1:14—"faith and love which is in Christ Jesus"; 3:16—"He who was manifested in the flesh, Justified in the spirit"; Acts 13:39—"and by him [lit.: 'in him'] every one that believeth is justified from all things, from which ye could not be justified by the law of Moses"; Rom. 4:25—"who was delivered up for our trespasses, and was raised for our justification"; Eph. 1:6—"accepted in the Beloved"—Rev. Vers.: "freely bestowed on us in the Beloved"; 1 Cor. 6:11—"justified in the name of the Lord Jesus Christ." "We in Christ" is the formula of our justification; "Christ in us" is the formula of our sanctification. As the water which the shell contains is little compared with the great ocean which contains the shell, so the actual change wrought within us by God's sanctifying grace is slight compared with the boundless freedom from condemnation and the state of favor with God into which we are introduced by justification; Rom. 5:1, 2—"Being therefore justified by faith, we have peace with God through our Lord Jesus Christ; through whom also we have had our access by faith into this grace wherein we stand; and we rejoice in hope of the glory of God."

Here we have the third instance of imputation. The first was the imputation of Adam's sin to us; and the second was the imputation of our sins to Christ. The third is now the imputation of Christ's righteousness to us. In each of the former cases, we have sought to show that the legal relation presupposes a natural relation. Adam's sin is imputed to us, because we are one with Adam; our sins are imputed to Christ, because Christ is one with humanity. So here, we must hold that Christ's righteousness is imputed to us, because we are one with Christ. Justification is not an arbitrary transfer to us of the merits of another with whom we have no real connection. This would make it merely a legal fiction; and there are no legal fictions in the divine government.

Instead of this external and mechanical method of conception, we should first set before us the fact of Christ's justification, after he had borne our sins and risen from the dead. In him, humanity, for the first time, is acquitted from punishment and restored to the divine favor. But Christ's new humanity is the germinal source of spiritual life for the race. He was justified, not simply as a private person, but as our representative and head. By becoming partakers of the new life in him, we share in all he is and all he has done; and, first of all, we share in his justification. So Luther gives us, for substance, the formula: "We in Christ = justification; Christ in us = sanctification." And in harmony with this formula is the statement quoted in the text above from Edwards, Works, 4:66.

See also H. B. Smith, Presb. Rev., July, 1881—"Union with Adam and with Christ is the ground of imputation. But the parallelism is incomplete. While the sin of Adam is imputed to us because it is ours, the righteousness of Christ is imputed to us simply because of our union with him, not at all because of our personal righteousness. In the one case, character is taken into the account; in the other, it is not. In sin, our demerits are included; in justification, our merits are excluded." For further statements of Dr. Smith, see his System of Christian Theology, 524-552.

C. H. M. on Genesis, page 78—"The question for every believer is not 'What am I?' but 'What is

Christ?' Of Abel it is said: 'God testified of his gifts' (Heb. 11:4, A. V.). So God testifies, not of the believer, but of his gift,—and his gift is Christ. Yet Cain was angry because he was not received in his sins, while Abel was accepted in his gift. This was right, if Abel was justified in himself; it was wrong, because Abel was justified only in Christ." See also Hodge, Outlines of Theology, 384-388, 392; Baird, Elohim Revealed, 448.

B. The relation of justification to regeneration and sanctification, moreover, delivers it from the charges of externality and immorality. God does not justify ungodly men in their ungodliness. He pronounces them just only as they are united to Christ, who is absolutely just, and who, by his Spirit, can make them just, not only in the eye of the law, but in moral character. The very faith by which the sinner receives Christ is an act in which he ratifies all that Christ has done, and accepts God's judgment against sin as his own (John 16:11).

John 16:11—"of judgment, because the prince of this world hath been judged"—the Holy Spirit leads the believer to ratify God's judgment against sin and Satan. Accepting Christ, the believer accepts Christ's death for sin, and resurrection to life for his own. If it were otherwise, the first act of the believer, after his discharge, might be a repetition of his offences. Such a justification would offend against the fundamental principles of justice and the safety of government. It would also fail to satisfy the conscience. This clamors not only for pardon, but for renewal. Union with Christ has one legal fruit—justification; but it has also one moral fruit—sanctification.

A really guilty man, when acquitted by judge and jury, does not cease to be the victim of remorse and fear. Forgiveness of sin is not in itself a deliverance from sin. The outward acquittal needs to be accompanied by an inward change to be really effective. Pardon for sin without power to overcome sin would be a mockery of the criminal. Justification for Christ's sake therefore goes into effect through regeneration by the Holy Spirit; see E. H. Johnson, in Bib. Sac., July, 1892:362.

A Buddhist priest who had studied some years in England printed in Shanghai not long ago a pamphlet entitled "Justification by Faith the only true Basis of Morality." It argues that any other foundation is nothing but pure selfishness, but that morality, to have any merit, must be unselfish. Justification by faith supplies an unselfish motive, because we accept the work done for us by another, and we ourselves work from gratitude, which is not a selfish motive. After laying down this Christian foundation, the writer erects the structure of faith in the Amida incarnation of Buddha. Buddhism opposes to the Christian doctrine of a creative Person, only a creative process; sin has relation only to the man sinning, and has no relation to Amida Buddha or to the eternal law of causation; salvation by faith in Amida Buddha is faith in one who is the product of a process, and a product may perish. Tennyson: "They are but broken lights of Thee, And thou, O Christ, art more than they."

Justification is possible, therefore, because it is always accompanied by regeneration and union with Christ, and is followed by sanctification. But this is a very different thing from the Romanist confounding of justification and sanctification, as different stages of the same process of making the sinner actually holy. It holds fast to the Scripture distinction between justification as a declarative act of God, and regeneration and sanctification as those efficient acts of God by which justification is accompanied and followed.

Both history and our personal observation show that nothing can change the life and make men moral, like the gospel of free pardon in Jesus Christ. Mere preaching of morality will effect nothing of consequence. There never has been more insistence upon morality than in the most immoral times, like those of Seneca, and of the English deists. As to their moral fruits, we can safely compare Protestant with Roman Catholic systems and leaders and countries. We do not become right by doing right, for only those can do right who have become right. The prodigal son is forgiven before he actually confesses and amends (Luke 15:20, 21). Justification is always accompanied by regeneration, and is followed by sanctification; and all three are results of the death of Christ. But the sin-offering must precede the thank-offering. We must first be accepted ourselves before we can offer gifts; Heb. 11:4—"By faith Abel offered unto God a more excellent sacrifice than Cain, through which he had witness borne to him that he was righteous, God bearing witness in respect of his gifts."

Hence we read in Eph. 5:25, 26—"Christ also loved the church, and gave himself up for it; that he might sanctify it, having cleansed = [after he had cleansed] it by the washing of water with the word" [= regeneration]; 1 Pet. 1:1, 2—"elect ... according to the foreknowledge of God the Father, in sanctification of the Spirit [regeneration], unto obedience [conversion] and sprinkling of the blood of Jesus Christ [justification]"; 1 John 1:7—"if we walk in the light, as he is in the light, we have fellowship one with another, and the blood of Jesus his Son cleanseth us from all sin"—here the "cleansing" refers primarily and mainly to justification, not to sanctification; for the apostle himself declares in verse 8—"If we say that we have no sin, we deceive ourselves, and the truth is not in us."

Quenstedt says well, that "justification, since it is an act, outside of man, in God, cannot produce an intrinsic change in us." And yet, he says, "although faith alone justifies, yet faith is not alone." Melanchthon: "Sola fides justificat; sed fides non est sola." With faith go all manner of gifts of the Spirit and internal graces of character. But we should let go all the doctrinal gains of the Reformation if we did not insist that these gifts and graces are accompaniments and consequences of justification, instead of being a part or a ground of justification. See Girdlestone, O. T. Synonyms, 104, note—"Justification is God's declaration that the individual sinner, on account of the faith which unites him to Christ, is taken up into the relation which Christ holds to the Father, and has applied to him personally the objective work accomplished for humanity by Christ."

6. Relation of Justification to Faith.

A. We are justified by faith, rather than by love or by any other grace: (a) not because faith is itself a work of obedience by which we merit justification,—for this would be a doctrine of justification by works; (b) nor because faith is accepted as an equivalent of obedience,—for there is no equivalent except the perfect obedience of Christ; (c) nor because faith is the germ from which obedience may spring hereafter,—for it is not the faith which accepts, but the Christ who is accepted, that renders such obedience possible; but (d) because faith, and not repentance, or love, or hope, is the medium or instrument by which we receive Christ and are united to him. Hence we are never said to be justified διὰ πίστιν, = on account of faith, but only διὰ πίστεως, = through faith, or ἐκ πίστεως, = by faith. Or, to express the same truth in other words, while the grace of God is the efficient cause of justification, and the obedience and sufferings of Christ are the meritorious or procuring cause, faith is the mediate or instrumental cause.

Edwards, Works, 4:69-73—"Faith justifies, because faith includes the whole act of unition to Christ as a Savior. It is not the nature of any other graces or virtues directly to close with Christ as a mediator, any further than they enter into the constitution of justifying faith, and do belong to its nature"; Observations on Trinity, 64-67—"Salvation is not offered to us upon any condition, but freely and for nothing. We are to do nothing for it,—we are only to take it. This taking and receiving is faith." H. B. Smith, System, 524—"An internal change is a sine qua non of justification, but not its meritorious ground." Give a man a gold mine. It is his. He has not to work for it; he has only to work it. Working for life is one thing; working from life is quite another. The marriage of a poor girl to a wealthy proprietor makes her possessor of his riches despite her former poverty. Yet her acceptance has not purchased wealth. It is hers, not because of what she is or has done, but because of what her husband is and has done. So faith is the condition of justification, only because through it Christ becomes ours, and with him his atonement and righteousness. Salvation comes not because our faith saves us, but because it links us to the Christ who saves; and believing is only the link. There is no more merit in it than in the beggar's stretching forth his hand to receive the offered purse, or the drowning man's grasping the rope that is thrown to him.

The Wesleyan scheme is inclined to make faith a work. See Dabney, Theology, 637. This is to make faith the cause and ground, or at least to add it to Christ's work as a joint cause and ground, of justification; as if justification were διὰ πίστιν, instead of διὰ πίστεως or ἐκ πίστεως. Since faith is never perfect, this is to go back to the Roman Catholic uncertainty of salvation. See Dorner, Glaubenslehre, 2:744, 745 (Syst. Doct., 4:206, 207). C. H. M. on Gen. 3:7—"They made themselves aprons of fig-leaves, before God made them coats of skin. Man ever tries to clothe himself in garments of his own righteousness, before he will take the robe of Christ's. But Adam felt himself naked when God visited him, even though he had his fig-leaves on him."

We are justified efficiently by the grace of God, meritoriously by Christ, instrumentally by faith, evidentially by works. Faith justifies, as roots bring plant and soil together. Faith connects man with the source of life in Christ. "When the boatman with his hook grapples the rock, he does not pull the shore to the boat, but the boat to the shore; so, when we by faith lay hold on Christ, we do not pull Christ to us, but ourselves to him." Faith is a coupling; the train is drawn, not by the coupling, but by the locomotive; yet without the coupling it would not be drawn. Faith is the trolley that reaches up to the electric wire; when the connection is sundered, not only does the car cease to move, but the heat dies and the lights go out. Dr. John Duncan: "I have married the Merchant and all his wealth is mine!"

H. C. Trumbull: "If a man wants to cross the ocean, he can either try swimming, or he can trust the captain of a ship to carry him over in his vessel. By or through his faith in that captain, the man is carried safely to the other shore; yet it is the ship's captain, not the passenger's faith, which is to be praised for the carrying." So the sick man trusts his case in the hands of his physician, and his life is saved by the physician,—yet by or through the patient's faith. This faith is indeed an inward act of allegiance, and no mere outward performance. Whiton, Divine Satisfaction, 92—"The Protestant Reformers saw that it was by an inward act, not by penances or sacraments that men were justified. But they halted in the crude notion of a legal court room process, a governmental procedure external to us, whereas it is an educational, inward process, the awakening through Christ of the filial spirit in us, which in the midst of imperfections strives for likeness more and more to the Son of God. Justification by principle apart from performance makes Christianity the religion of the spirit." We would add that such justification excludes education, and is an act rather than a process, an act external to the sinner rather than internal, an act of God rather than an act of man. The justified person can say to Christ, as

Ruth said to Boaz: "Why have I found favor in thy sight, that thou shouldest take knowledge of me, seeing I am a foreigner?" (Ruth 2:10).

B. Since the ground of justification is only Christ, to whom we are united by faith, the justified person has peace. If it were anything in ourselves, our peace must needs be proportioned to our holiness. The practical effect of the Romanist mingling of works with faith, as a joint ground of justification, is to render all assurance of salvation impossible. (Council of Trent, 9th chap.: "Every man, by reason of his own weakness and defects, must be in fear and anxiety about his state of grace. Nor can any one know, with infallible certainty of faith, that he has received forgiveness of God."). But since justification is an instantaneous act of God, complete at the moment of the sinner's first believing, it has no degrees. Weak faith justifies as perfectly as strong faith; although, since justification is a secret act of God, weak faith does not give so strong assurance of salvation.

Foundations of our Faith, 216—"The Catholic doctrine declares that justification is not dependent upon faith and the righteousness of Christ imputed and granted thereto, but on the actual condition of the man himself. But there remain in the man an undeniable amount of fleshly lusts or inclinations to sin, even though the man be regenerate. The Catholic doctrine is therefore constrained to assert that these lusts are not in themselves sinful, or objects of the divine displeasure. They are allowed to remain in the man, that he may struggle against them; and, as they say, Paul designates them as sinful, only because they are derived from sin, and incite to sin; but they only become sin by the positive concurrence of the human will. But is not internal lust displeasing to God? Can we draw the line between lust and will? The Catholic favors self here, and makes many things lust, which are really will. A Protestant is necessarily more earnest in the work of salvation, when he recognizes even the evil desire as sin, according to Christ's precept."

All systems of religion of merely human origin tend to make salvation, in larger or smaller degree, the effect of human works, but only with the result of leaving man in despair. See, in Ecclesiasticus 3:30, an Apocryphal declaration that alms make atonement for sin. So Romanism bids me doubt God's grace and the forgiveness of sins. See Dorner, Gesch. prot. Theol., 228, 229, and his quotations from Luther. "But if the Romanist doctrine is true, that a man is justified only in such measure as he is sanctified, then: 1. Justification must be a matter of degrees, and so the Council of Trent declares it to be. The sacraments which sanctify are therefore essential, that one may be increasingly justified. 2. Since justification is a continuous process, the redeeming death of Christ, on which it depends, must be a continuous process also; hence its prolonged reiteration in the sacrifice by the Mass. 3. Since sanctification is obviously never completed in this life, no man ever dies completely justified; hence the doctrine of Purgatory." For the substance of Romanist doctrine, see Moehler, Symbolism, 79-190; Newman, Lectures on Justification, 253-345; Ritschl, Christian Doctrine of Justification, 121-226.

A better doctrine is that of the Puritan divine: "It is not the quantity of thy faith that shall save thee. A drop of water is as true water as the whole ocean. So a little faith is as true faith as the greatest. It is not the measure of thy faith that saves thee,—it is the blood that it grips to that saves thee. The weak hand of the child, that leads the spoon to the mouth, will feed as well as the strong arm of a man; for it is not the hand that feeds, but the meat. So, if thou canst grip Christ ever so weakly, he will not let thee perish." I am troubled about the money I owe in New York, until I find that a friend has paid my debt there. When I find that the objective account against me is cancelled, then and only then do I have subjective peace.

A child may be heir to a vast estate, even while he does not know it; and a child of God may be an heir of glory, even while, through the weakness of his faith, he is oppressed with painful doubts and fears. No man is lost simply because of the greatness of his sins; however ill-deserving he may be, faith in Christ will save him. Luther's climbing the steps of St. John Lateran, and the voice of thunder: "The just shall live by faith," are not certain as historical facts; but they express the substance of Luther's experience. Not obeying, but receiving, is the substance of the gospel. A man cannot merit salvation; he cannot buy it; but one thing he must do,—he must take it. And the least faith makes salvation ours, because it makes Christ ours.

Augustine conceived of justification as a continuous process, proceeding until love and all Christian virtues fill the heart. There is his chief difference from Paul. Augustine believes in sin and grace. But he has not the freedom of the children of God, as Paul has. The influence of Augustine upon Roman Catholic theology has not been wholly salutary. The Roman Catholic, mixing man's subjective condition with God's grace as a ground of justification, continually wavers between self-righteousness and uncertainty of acceptance with God, each of these being fatal to a healthful and stable religious life. High-church Episcopalians, and Sacramentalists generally, are afflicted with this distemper of the Romanists. Dr. R. W. Dale remarks with regard to Dr. Pusey: "The absence of joy in his religious life was only the inevitable effect of his conception of God's method of saving men; in parting with the Lutheran truth concerning justification, he parted with the springs of gladness." Spurgeon said that a man might get from London to New York provided he took a steamer; but it made much difference in his comfort whether he had a first class or a second class ticket. A new realization of the meaning of justification in our churches would change much of our singing from the minor to the major key; would lead us to pray, not for the presence of Christ, but from the presence of Christ; would abolish the mournful upward inflections at the end of sentences which give such unreality to our preaching; and would replace the pessimistic element in our modern work and worship with the notes of praise and triumph. In the Pilgrim's Progress, the justification of the believer is symbolized by Christian's lodging in the Palace Beautiful whose window opened toward the sunrising.

Even Luther did not fully apprehend and apply his favorite doctrine of justification by faith. Harnack, Wesen des Christenthums, 168 sq., states the fundamental principles of Protestantism as: "1. The Christian religion is wholly given in the word of God and in the inner experience which answers to that word. 2. The assured belief that the Christian has a gracious God. 'Nun weisz und glaub' ich's feste, Ich rühm's auch ohne Scheu, Dasz Gott, der höchst' und beste, Mein Freund und Vater sei; Und dasz in allen Fällen Er mir zur Rechten steh', Und dampfe Sturm und Wellen, Und was mir bringet Weh'.' 3. Restoration of simple and believing worship, both public and private. But Luther took too much dogma into Christianity; insisted too much on the authority of the written word; cared too much for the means of grace, such as the Lord's Supper; identified the church too much with the organized body." Yet Luther talked of beating the heads of the Wittenbergers with the Bible, so as to get the great doctrine of justification by faith into their brains. "Why do you teach your child the same thing twenty times?" he said. "Because I find that nineteen times is not sufficient."

C. Justification is instantaneous, complete, and final: instantaneous, since otherwise there would be an interval during which the soul was neither approved nor condemned by God (Mat. 6:24); complete, since the soul, united to Christ by faith, becomes partaker of his complete satisfaction to the demands of law (Col. 2:9, 10); and final, since the union with Christ is indissoluble (John 10:28, 29). As there are many acts of sin in the life of the Christian, so there are many acts of pardon following them. But all these acts of pardon are virtually implied in that first act by which he was finally and forever justified; as also successive acts of repentance and faith, after such sins, are virtually implied in that first repentance and faith which logically preceded justification.

Mat. 6:24—"No man can serve two masters"; Col. 2:9, 10—"in him dwelleth all the fulness of the Godhead bodily, and in him ye are made full, who is the head of all principality and power"; John 10:28, 29—"they shall never perish, and no one shall snatch them out of my hand. My Father, who hath given them unto me, is greater than all; and no one is able to snatch them out of the Father's hand."

Plymouth Brethren say truly that the Christian has sin in him, but not on him, because Christ had sin on him, but not in him. The Christian has sin but not guilt, because Christ had guilt but not sin. All our sins are buried in the grave with Christ, and Christ's resurrection is our resurrection. Toplady: "From whence this fear and unbelief? Hast thou, O Father, put to grief Thy spotless Son for me? And will the righteous Judge of men Condemn me for that debt of sin, Which, Lord, was laid on thee? If thou hast my discharge procured, And freely in my room endured The whole of wrath divine, Payment God cannot twice demand, First at my bleeding Surety's hand, And then again at mine. Complete atonement thou hast made, And to the utmost farthing paid Whate'er thy people owed; How then can wrath on me take place, If sheltered in thy righteousness And sprinkled with thy blood? Turn, then, my soul, unto thy rest; The merits of thy great High-priest Speak peace and liberty; Trust in his efficacious blood, Nor fear thy banishment from God, Since Jesus died for thee!"

Justification, however, is not eternal in the past. We are to repent unto the remission of our sins (Act 2:38). Remission comes after repentance. Sin is not pardoned before it is committed. In justification God grants us actual pardon for past sin, but virtual pardon for future sin. Edwards, Works, 4:104—"Future sins are respected, in that first justification, no otherwise than as future faith and repentance are respected in it; and future faith and repentance are looked upon by him that justifies as virtually implied in that first repentance and faith, in the same manner that justification from future sins is implied in that first justification."

A man is not justified from his sins before he has committed them, nor is he saved before he is born. A remarkable illustration of the extreme to which hyper-Calvinism may go is found in Tobias Crisp, Sermons, 1:358—"The Lord hath no more to lay to the charge of an elect person, yet in the height of iniquity, and in the excess of riot, and committing all the abomination that can be committed ... than he has to the charge of the saint triumphant in glory." A far better statement is found in Moberly, Atonement and Personality, 61—"As there is upon earth no consummated penitence, so neither is there any forgiveness consummated.... Forgiveness is the recognition, by anticipation, of something which is to be, something toward which it is itself a mighty quickening of possibilities, but something which is not, or at least is not perfectly, yet.... Present forgiveness is inchoate, is educational.... It reaches its final and perfect consummation only when the forgiven penitent has become at last personally and completely righteous. If the consummation is not reached but reversed, then forgiveness is forfeited (Mat. 18:32-35)." This last exception, however, as we shall see in our discussion of Perseverance, is only a hypothetical one. The truly forgiven do not finally fall away.

7. Advice to Inquirers demanded by a Scriptural View of Justification.

(a) Where conviction of sin is yet lacking, our aim should be to show the sinner that he is under God's condemnation for his past sins, and that no future obedience can ever secure his justification, since this obedience, even though perfect, could not atone for the past, and even if it could, he is unable, without God's help, to render it.

With the help of the Holy Spirit, conviction of sin may be roused by presentation of the claims of God's perfect law, and by drawing attention, first to particular overt transgressions, and then to the manifold omissions of duty, the general lack of supreme and all-pervading love to God, and the guilty rejection of Christ's offers and commands. "Even if the next page of the copy book had no blots or erasures, its cleanness would not alter the smudges and misshapen letters on the earlier pages." God takes no notice of the promise "Have patience with me, and I will pay thee" (Mat. 18:29), for he knows it can never be fulfilled.

(b) Where conviction of sin already exists, our aim should be, not, in the first instance, to secure the performance of external religious duties, such as prayer, or Scripture-reading, or uniting with the church, but to induce the sinner, as his first and all-inclusive duty, to accept Christ as his only and sufficient sacrifice and Savior, and, committing himself and the matter of his salvation entirely to the hands of Christ, to manifest this trust and submission by entering at once upon a life of obedience to Christ's commands.

A convicted sinner should be exhorted, not first to prayer and then to faith, but first to faith, and then to the immediate expression of that faith in prayer and Christian activity. He should pray, not for faith, but in faith. It should not be forgotten that the sinner never sins against so much light, and never is in so great danger, as when he is convicted but not converted, when he is moved to turn but yet refuses to turn. No such sinner should be allowed to think that he has the right to do any other thing whatever before accepting Christ. This accepting Christ is not an outward act, but an inward act of mind and heart and will, although believing is naturally evidenced by immediate outward action. To teach the sinner, however apparently well disposed, how to believe on Christ, is beyond the power of man. God is the only giver of faith. But Scripture instances of faith, and illustrations drawn from the child's taking the father at his word and acting upon it, have often been used by the Holy Spirit as means of leading men themselves to put faith in Christ.

Bengel: "Those who are secure Jesus refers to the law; those who are contrite he consoles with the gospel." A man left work and came home. His wife asked why. "Because I am a sinner." "Let me send for the preacher." "I am too far gone for preachers. If the Lord Jesus Christ does not save me I am lost." That man needed only to be pointed to the Cross. There he found reason for believing that there was salvation for him. In surrendering himself to Christ he was justified. On the general subject of Justification, see Edwards, Works, 4:64-132; Buchanan on Justification, 250-411; Owen on Justification, in Works, vol. 5; Bp. of Ossory, Nature and Effects of Faith, 48-152; Hodge, Syst. Theol., 3:114-212; Thomasius, Christi Person und Werk, 3:133-200; Herzog, Encyclopädie, art.: Rechtfertigung; Bushnell, Vicarious Sacrifice, 416-420, 435.

Section III —The Application Of Christ's Redemption In Its Continuation

Under this head we treat of Sanctification and of Perseverance. These two are but the divine and the human sides of the same fact, and they bear to each other a relation similar to that which exists between Regeneration and Conversion.

I. Sanctification

1. Definition of Sanctification.

Sanctification is that continuous operation of the Holy Spirit, by which the holy disposition imparted in regeneration is maintained and strengthened.

Godet: "The work of Jesus in the world is twofold. It is a work accomplished for us, destined to effect reconciliation between God and man; it is a work accomplished in us, with the object of effecting our sanctification. By the one, a right relation is established between God and us; by the other, the fruit of the reëstablished order is secured. By the former, the condemned sinner is received into the state of grace; by the latter, the pardoned sinner is associated with the life of God.... How many express themselves as if, when forgiveness with the peace which it procures has been once obtained, all is finished and the work of salvation is complete! They seem to have no suspicion that salvation consists in the health of the soul, and that the health of the soul consists in holiness. Forgiveness is not the reëstablishment of health; it is the crisis of convalescence. If God thinks fit to declare the sinner righteous, it is in order that he may by that means restore him to holiness." O. P. Gifford: "The steamship whose machinery is broken may be brought into port and made fast to the dock. She is safe, but not sound. Repairs may last a long time. Christ designs to make us both safe and sound. Justification gives the first—safety; sanctification gives the second—soundness."

Bradford, Heredity and Christian Problems, 220—"To be conscious that one is forgiven, and yet that at the same time he is so polluted that he cannot beget a child without handing on to that child a nature which will be as bad as if his father had never been forgiven, is not salvation in any real sense." We would say: Is not salvation in any complete sense. Justification needs sanctification to follow it. Man needs God to continue and preserve his spiritual life, just as much as he needed God to begin it at the first. Creation in the spiritual, as well as in the natural world, needs to be supplemented by preservation; see quotation from Jonathan Edwards, in Allen's biography of him, 371.

Regeneration is instantaneous, but sanctification takes time. The "developing" of the photographer's picture may illustrate God's process of sanctifying the regenerate soul. But it is development by new access of truth or light, while the photographer's picture is usually developed in the dark. This development cannot be accomplished in a moment. "We try in our religious lives to practise instantaneous photography. One minute for prayer will give us a vision of God, and we think that is enough. Our pictures are poor because our negatives are weak. We do not give God a long enough sitting to get a good likeness."

Salvation is something past, something present, and something future; a past fact, justification; a present process, sanctification; a future consummation, redemption and glory. David, in Ps. 51:1, 2, prays not only that God will blot out his transgressions (justification), but that God will wash him thoroughly from his iniquity (sanctification). E. G. Robinson: "Sanctification consists negatively, in the removal of the penal consequences of sin from the moral nature; positively, in the progressive implanting and growth of a new principle of life.... The Christian church is a succession of copies of the character of Christ. Paul never says: 'be ye imitators of me' (1 Cor. 4:16), except when writing to those who had no copies of the New Testament or of the Gospels."

Clarke, Christian Theology, 366—"Sanctification does not mean perfection reached, but the progress of the divine life toward perfection. Sanctification is the Christianizing of the Christian." It is not simply deliverance from the penalty of sin, but the development of a divine life that conquers sin. A. A. Hodge, Popular Lectures, 343—"Any man who thinks he is a Christian, and that he has accepted Christ for justification, when he did not at the same time accept him for sanctification, is miserably deluded in that very experience."

This definition implies:

(a) That, although in regeneration the governing disposition of the soul is made holy, there still remain tendencies to evil which are unsubdued.

John 13:10—"He that is bathed needeth not save to wash his feet, but is clean every whit [i. e., as a whole]"; Rom. 6:12—"Let not sin therefore reign in your mortal body, that ye should obey the lusts thereof"—sin dwells in a believer, but it reigns in an unbeliever (C. H. M.). Subordinate volitions in the Christian are not always determined in character by the fundamental choice; eddies in the stream sometimes run counter to the general course of the current.

This doctrine is the opposite of that expressed in the phrase: "the essential divinity of the human." Not culture, but crucifixion, is what the Holy Spirit prescribes for the natural man. There are two natures in the Christian, as Paul shows in Romans 7. The one flourishes at the other's expense. The vine dresser has to cut the rank shoots from self, that all our force may be thrown into growing fruit. Deadwood must be cut out; living wood must be cut back (John 15:2). Sanctification is not a matter of course, which will go on whatever we do, or do not do. It requires a direct superintendence and surgery on the one hand, and, on the other hand a practical hatred of evil on our part that coöperates with the husbandry of God.

(b) That the existence in the believer of these two opposing principles gives rise to a conflict which lasts through life.

Gal. 5:17—"For the flesh lusteth against the Spirit, and the Spirit against the flesh; for these are contrary the one to the other; that ye may not do the things that ye would"—not, as the A. V. had it, "so that ye cannot do the things that ye would"; the Spirit who dwells in believers is represented as enabling them successfully to resist those tendencies to evil which naturally exist within them; James 4:5 (the marginal and better reading)—"That spirit which he made to dwell in us yearneth for us even unto jealous envy"—i. e., God's love, like all true love, longs to have its objects wholly for its own. The Christian is two men in one; but he is to "put away the old man" and "put on the new man" (Eph. 4:22, 23). Compare Ecclesiasticus 2:1—"My son, if thou dost set out to serve the Lord, prepare thy soul for temptation."

1 Tim. 6:12—"fight the good fight of the faith"—ἀγωνίζου τὸν καλὸν ἀγῶνα τῆς πίστεως = the beautiful, honorable, glorious fight; since it has a noble helper, incentive, and reward. It is the commonest of all struggles, but the issue determines our destiny. An Indian received as a gift some tobacco in which he found a half dollar hidden. He brought it back next day, saying that good Indian had fought all night with bad Indian, one telling him to keep, the other telling him to return.

(c) That in this conflict the Holy Spirit enables the Christian, through increasing faith, more fully and consciously to appropriate Christ, and thus progressively to make conquest of the remaining sinfulness of his nature.

Rom. 8:13, 14—"for if ye live after the flesh, ye must die; but if by the Spirit ye put to death the deeds of the body, ye shall live. For as many as are led by the Spirit of God, these are sons of God"; 1 Cor. 6:11—"but ye were washed, but ye were sanctified, but ye were justified in the name of the Lord Jesus Christ, and in the Spirit of our God"; James 1:26—"If any man thinketh himself to be religious, while he bridleth not his tongue but deceiveth his heart, this man's religion is vain"—see Com. of Neander, in loco—"That religion is merely imaginary, seeming, unreal, which allows the continuance of the moral defects originally predominant in the character." The Christian is "crucified with Christ" (Gal. 2:20); but the crucified man does not die at once. Yet he is as good as dead. Even after the old man is crucified we are still to mortify him, or put him to death (Rom. 8:13; Col. 3:5). We are to cut down the old rosebush and cultivate only the new shoot that is grafted into it. Here is our probation as Christians. So "die Scene wird zum Tribunal"—the play of life becomes God's judgment.

Dr. Hastings: "When Bourdaloue was probing the conscience of Louis XIV, applying to him the words of St. Paul and intending to paraphrase them: 'For the good which I would, I do not, but the evil which I would not, that I do,' 'I find two men in me'—the King interrupted the great preacher with the memorable exclamation: 'Ah, these two men, I know them well!' Bourdaloue answered: 'It is already something to know them, Sire; but it is not enough,—one of the two must perish.' " And, in the genuine believer, the old does little by little die, and the new takes its place, as "David waxed stronger and stronger, but the house of Saul waxed weaker and weaker" (2 Sam. 3:1). As the Welsh minister found himself after awhile thinking and dreaming in English, so the language of Canaan becomes to the Christian his native and only speech.

2. Explanations and Scripture Proof.

(a) Sanctification is the work of God.

1 Thess. 5:23—"And the God of peace himself sanctify you wholly." Much of our modern literature ignores man's dependence upon God, and some of it seems distinctly intended to teach the opposite doctrine. Auerbach's "On the Heights," for example, teaches that man can make his own atonement; and "The Villa on the Rhine," by the same author, teaches that man can sanctify himself. The proper inscription for many modern French novels is: "Entertainment here for man and beast." The Tendenznovelle of Germany has its imitators in the sceptical novels of England. And no doctrine in these novels is so common as the doctrine that man needs no Savior but himself.

(b) It is a continuous process.

Phil. 1:6—"being confident of this very thing, that he who began a good work in you will perfect it until the day of Jesus Christ"; 3:15—"Let us therefore, as many as are perfect, be thus minded: and if in anything ye are otherwise minded, this also shall God reveal unto you"; Col. 3:9, 10—"lie not one to another; seeing that ye have put off the old man with his doings, and have put on the new man, that is being renewed unto knowledge after the image of him that created him"; cf. Acts 2:47—"those that were being saved"; 1 Cor. 1:18—"unto us who are being saved"; 2 Cor. 2:15—"in them that are being saved"; 1 Thess. 2:12—"God, who calleth you into his own kingdom and glory."

C. H. Parkhurst: "The yeast does not strike through the whole lump of dough at a flash. We keep finding unsuspected lumps of meal that the yeast has not yet seized upon. We surrender to God in instalments. We may not mean to do it, but we do it. Conversion has got to be brought down to date." A student asked the President of Oberlin College whether he could not take a shorter course than the one prescribed. "Oh yes," replied the President, "but then it depends on what you want to make of yourself. When God wants to make an oak, he takes a hundred years, but when he wants to make a squash, he takes six months."

(c) It is distinguished from regeneration as growth from birth, or as the strengthening of a holy disposition from the original impartation of it.

Eph. 4:15—"speaking the truth in love, may grow up in all things into him, who is the head, even Christ"; 1 Thess. 3:12—"the Lord make you to increase and abound in love one toward another, and toward all men"; 2 Pet. 3:18—"But grow in the grace and knowledge of our Lord and Savior Jesus Christ"; cf. 1 Pet. 1:23—"begotten again, not of corruptible seed, but of incorruptible, through the word of God, which liveth and abideth"; 1 John 3:9—"Whosoever is begotten of God doeth no sin, because his seed abideth in him: and he cannot sin, because he is begotten of God." Not sin only, but holiness also, is a germ whose nature is to grow. The new love in the believer's heart follows the law of all life, in developing and extending itself under God's husbandry. George Eliot: "The reward of one duty done is the power to do another." J. W. A. Stewart: "When the 21st of March has come, we say 'The back of the winter is broken.' There will still be alternations of frost, but the progress will be towards heat. The coming of summer is sure,—in germ the summer is already here." Regeneration is the crisis of a disease; sanctification is the progress of convalescence.

Yet growth is not a uniform thing in the tree or in the Christian. In some single months there is more growth than in all the year besides. During the rest of the year, however, there is solidification, without which the green timber would be useless. The period of rapid growth, when woody fibre is actually deposited between the bark and the trunk, occupies but four to six weeks in May, June, and July. 2 Pet. 1:5—"adding on your part all diligence, in your faith supply virtue; and in your virtue knowledge"—adding to the central grace all those that are complementary and subordinate, till they attain the harmony of a chorus (ἐπιχορηγήσατε).

(d) The operation of God reveals itself in, and is accompanied by, intelligent and voluntary activity of the believer in the discovery and mortification of sinful desires, and in the bringing of the whole being into obedience to Christ and conformity to the standards of his word.

John 17:17—"Sanctify them in the truth: thy word is truth"; 2 Cor. 10:5—"casting down imaginations, and every high thing that is exalted against the knowledge of God, and bringing every thought into captivity to the obedience of Christ"; Phil. 2:12, 13—"work out your own salvation with fear and trembling; for it is God who worketh in you both to will and to work, for his good pleasure"; 1 Pet. 2:2—"as new-born babes, long for the spiritual milk which is without guile, that ye may grow thereby unto salvation." John 15:3—"Already ye are clean because of the word which I have spoken unto you." Regeneration through the word is followed by sanctification through the word. Eph. 5:1—"Be ye therefore imitators of God, as beloved children." Imitation is at first a painful effort of will, as in learning the piano; afterwards it becomes pleasurable and even unconscious. Children unconsciously imitate the handwriting of their parents. Charles Lamb sees in the mirror, as he is shaving, the apparition of his dead father. So our likeness to God comes out as we advance in years. Col. 3:4—"When Christ who is our life, shall be manifested, then shall ye also with him be manifested in glory."

Horace Bushnell said that, if the stars did not move, they would rot in the sky. The man who rides the bicycle must either go on, or go off. A large part of sanctification consists in the formation of proper habits, such as the habit of Scripture reading, of secret prayer, of church going, of efforts to convert and benefit others. Baxter: "Every man must grow, as trees grow, downward and upward at once. The visible outward growth must be accompanied by an invisible inward growth." Drummond: "The spiritual man having passed from death to life, the natural man must pass from life to death." There must be increasing sense of sin: "My sins gave sharpness to the nails, And pointed every thorn." There must be a bringing of new and yet newer regions of thought, feeling, and action, under the sway of Christ and his truth. There is a grain of truth even in Macaulay's jest about "essentially Christian cookery."

A. J. Gordon, Ministry of the Spirit, 63, 109-111—"The church is Christian no more than as it is the organ of the continuous passion of Christ. We must suffer with sinning and lost humanity, and so 'fill up ... that which is lacking of the afflictions of Christ' (Col. 1:24). Christ's crucifixion must be prolonged side by side with his resurrection. There are three deaths: 1. death in sin, our natural condition; 2. death for sin, our judicial condition; 3. death to sin, our sanctified condition.... As the ascending sap in the tree crowds off the dead leaves which in spite of storm and frost cling to the branches all the winter long, so does the Holy Spirit within us, when allowed full sway, subdue and expel the remnants of our sinful nature."

(e) The agency through which God effects the sanctification of the believer is the indwelling Spirit of Christ.

John 14:17, 18—"the Spirit of truth ... he abideth with you, and shall be in you. I will not leave you desolate; I come unto you"; 15:3-5—"Already ye are clean.... Abide in me ... apart from me ye can do nothing"; Rom. 8:9, 10—"the Spirit of God dwelleth in you. But if any man hath not the Spirit of Christ, he is none of his. And if Christ is in you, the body is dead because of sin; but the spirit is life because of righteousness"; 1 Cor. 1:2, 30—"sanctified in Christ Jesus ... Christ Jesus, who was made unto us ... sanctification"; 6:19—"know ye not that your body is a temple of the Holy Spirit which is in you, which ye have from God?" Gal. 5:16—"Walk by the Spirit, and ye shall not fulfil the lust of the flesh"; Eph. 5:18—"And be not drunken with wine, wherein is riot, but be filled with the Spirit"; Col. 1:27-29—"the riches of the glory of this mystery among the Gentiles, which is Christ in you, the hope of glory: whom we proclaim, admonishing every man and teaching every man in all wisdom, that we may present every man perfect in Christ; whereunto I labor also, striving according to his working, which worketh in me mightily"; 2 Tim. 1:14—"That good thing which was committed unto thee guard through the Holy Spirit which dwelleth in us."

Christianity substitutes for the old sources of excitement the power of the Holy Spirit. Here is a source of comfort, energy, and joy, infinitely superior to any which the sinner knows. God does not leave the soul to fall back upon itself. The higher up we get in the scale of being, the more does the new life need nursing and tending,—compare the sapling and the babe. God gives to the Christian, therefore, an abiding presence and work of the Holy Spirit,—not only regeneration, but sanctification. C. E. Smith, Baptism of Fire: "The soul needs the latter as well as the former rain, the sealing as well as the renewing of the Spirit, the baptism of fire as well as the baptism of water. Sealing gives something additional to the document, an evidence plainer than the writing within, both to one's self and to others."

"Few flowers yield more honey than serves the bee for its daily food." So we must first live ourselves off from our spiritual diet; only what is over can be given to nourish others. Thomas à Kempis, Imitation of Christ: "Have peace in thine own heart; else thou wilt never be able to communicate peace to others." Godet: "Man is a vessel destined to receive God, a vessel which must be enlarged in proportion as it is filled, and filled in proportion as it is enlarged." Matthew Arnold, Morality: "We cannot kindle when we will The fire which in the heart resides; The Spirit bloweth and is still; In mystery our soul abides. But tasks in hours of insight willed Can be in hours of gloom fulfilled. With aching hands and bleeding feet, We dig and heap, lay stone on stone; We bear the burden and the heat Of the long day, and wish 't were done. Not till the hours of light return All we have built do we discern."

(f) The mediate or instrumental cause of sanctification, as of justification, is faith.

Acts 15:9—"cleansing their hearts by faith"; Rom. 1:17—"For therein is revealed a righteousness of God from faith unto faith: as it is written, But the righteous shall live from faith." The righteousness includes sanctification as well as justification; and the subject of the epistle to the Romans is not simply justification by faith, but rather righteousness by faith, or salvation by faith. Justification by faith is the subject of chapters 1-7; sanctification by faith is the subject of chapters 8-16. We are not sanctified by efforts of our own, any more than we are justified by efforts of our own.

God does not share with us the glory of sanctification, any more than he shares with us the glory of justification. He must do all, or nothing. William Law: "A root set in the finest soil, in the best climate, and blessed with all that sun and air and rain can do for it, is not in so sure a way of its growth to perfection, as every man may be whose spirit aspires after all that which God is ready and infinitely desirous to give him. For the sun meets not the springing bud that stretches toward him with half that certainty as God, the source of all good, communicates himself to the soul that longs to partake of him."

(g) The object of this faith is Christ himself, as the head of a new humanity and the source of truth and life to those united to him.

2 Cor. 3:18—"we all, with unveiled face, beholding as in a mirror the glory of the Lord, are transformed into the same image from glory to glory, even as from the Lord the Spirit"; Eph. 4:13—"till we all attain unto the unity of the faith, and of the knowledge of the Son of God, unto a fullgrown man, unto the measure of the stature of the fulness of Christ." Faith here is of course much more than intellectual faith,—it is the reception of Christ himself. As Christianity furnishes a new source of life and energy—in the Holy Spirit: so it gives a new object of attention and regard—the Lord Jesus Christ. As we get air out of a vessel by pouring in water, so we can drive sin out only by bringing Christ in. See Chalmers' Sermon on The Expulsive Power of a New Affection. Drummond, Nat. Law in the Spir. World, 123-140—"Man does not grow by making efforts to grow, but by putting himself into the conditions of growth by living in Christ."

1 John 3:3—"every one that hath this hope set on him (ἐπ' αὐτῷ) purifieth himself, even as he is pure." Sanctification does not begin from within. The objective Savior must come first. The hope based on him must give the motive and the standard of self-purification. Likeness comes from liking. We grow to be like that which we like. Hence we use the phrase "I like," as a synonym for "I love." We cannot remove frost from our window by rubbing the pane; we need to kindle a fire. Growth is not the product of effort, but of life. "Taking thought," or "being anxious" (Mat. 6:27), is not the way to grow. Only take the hindrances out of the way, and we grow without care, as the tree does. The moon makes no effort to shine, nor has it any power of its own to shine. It is only a burnt out cinder in the sky. It shines only as it reflects the light of the sun. So we can shine "as lights in the world" (Phil. 2:15), only as we reflect Christ, who is "the Sun of Righteousness" (Mal. 4:2) and "the Light of the world" (John 8:12).

(h) Though the weakest faith perfectly justifies, the degree of sanctification is measured by the strength of the Christian's faith, and the persistence with which he apprehends Christ in the various relations which the Scriptures declare him to sustain to us.

Mat. 9:29—"According to your faith be it done unto you"; Luke 17:5—"Lord, increase our faith"; Rom. 12:2—"be not fashioned according to this world: but be ye transformed by the renewing of your mind, that ye may prove what is the good and acceptable and perfect will of God"; 13:14—"But put ye on the Lord Jesus Christ, and make not provision for the flesh, to fulfil the lusts thereof"; Eph. 4:24—"put on the new man, that after God hath been created in righteousness and holiness of truth"; 1 Tim. 4:7—"exercise thyself unto godliness." Leighton: "None of the children of God are born dumb." Milton: "Good, the more communicated, the more abundant grows." Faith can neither be stationary nor complete (Westcott, Bible Com. on John 15:8—"so shall ye become my disciples"). Luther: "He who is a Christian is no Christian"; "Christianus non in esse, sed in fieri." In a Bible that belonged to Oliver Cromwell is this inscription: "O. C. 1644. Qui cessat esse melior cessat esse bonus"—"He who ceases to be better ceases to be good." Story, the sculptor, when asked which of his works he valued most, replied: "My next." The greatest work of the Holy Spirit is the perfecting of Christian character.

Col. 1:10—"Increasing by the knowledge of God"—here the instrumental dative represents the knowledge of God as the dew or rain which nurtures the growth of the plant (Lightfoot). Mr. Gladstone had the habit of reading the Bible every Sunday afternoon to old women on his estate. Tholuck: "I have but one passion, and that is Christ." This is an echo of Paul's words: "to me to live is Christ" (Phil. 1:21). But Paul is far from thinking that he has already obtained, or is already made perfect. He prays "that I may gain Christ, ... that I may know him" (Phil. 3:8, 10).

(i) From the lack of persistence in using the means appointed for Christian growth—such as the word of God, prayer, association with other believers, and personal effort for the conversion of the ungodly—sanctification does not always proceed in regular and unbroken course, and it is never completed in this life.

Phil. 3:12—"Not that I have already obtained, or am already made perfect: but I press on, if so be that I may lay hold on that for which also I was laid hold on by Jesus Christ"; 1 John 1:8—"If we say that we have no sin, we deceive ourselves, and the truth is not in us." Carlyle, in his Life of John Sterling, chap. 8, says of Coleridge, that "whenever natural obligation or voluntary undertaking made it his duty to do anything, the fact seemed a sufficient reason for his not doing it." A regular, advancing sanctification is marked, on the other hand, by a growing habit of instant and joyful obedience. The intermittent spring depends upon the reservoir in the mountain cave,—only when the rain fills the latter full, does the spring begin to flow. So to secure unbroken Christian activity, there must be constant reception of the word and Spirit of God.

Galen: "If diseases take hold of the body, there is nothing so certain to drive them out as diligent exercise." Williams, Principles of Medicine: "Want of exercise and sedentary habits not only predispose to, but actually cause, disease." The little girl who fell out of bed at night was asked how it happened. She replied that she went to sleep too near where she got in. Some Christians lose the joy of their religion by ceasing their Christian activities too soon after conversion. Yet others cultivate their spiritual lives from mere selfishness. Selfishness follows the line of least resistance. It is easier to pray in public and to attend meetings for prayer, than it is to go out into the unsympathetic world and engage in the work of winning souls. This is the fault of monasticism. Those grow most who forget themselves in their work for others. The discipline of life is ordained in God's providence to correct tendencies to indolence. Even this discipline is often received in a rebellious spirit. The result is delay in the process of sanctification. Bengel: "Deus habet horas et moras"—"God has his hours and his delays." German proverb: "Gut Ding will Weile haben"—"A good thing requires time."

(j) Sanctification, both of the soul and of the body of the believer, is completed in the life to come,—that of the former at death, that of the latter at the resurrection.

Phil. 3:21—"who shall fashion anew the body of our humiliation, that it may be conformed to the body of his glory, according to the working whereby he is able even to subject all things unto himself"; Col. 3:4—"When Christ, who is our life, shall be manifested, then shall we also with him be manifested in glory"; Heb. 12:14, 23—"Follow after peace with all men, and the sanctification without which no man shall see the Lord ... spirits of just men made perfect"; 1 John 3:2—"Beloved, now are we children of God, and it is not yet made manifest what we shall be. We know that, if he shall be manifested, we shall be like him; for we shall see him even as he is"; Jude 24—"able to guard you from stumbling, and to set you before the presence of his glory without blemish in exceeding joy"; Rev. 14:5—"And in their mouth was found no lie: they are without blemish."

A. J. Gordon, Ministry of the Spirit, 121, puts the completion of our sanctification, not at death, but at the appearing of the Lord "a second time, apart from sin, ... unto salvation" (Heb. 9:28; 1 Thess. 3:13; 5:23). When we shall see him as he is, instantaneous photographing of his image in our souls will take the place of the present slow progress from glory to glory (2 Cor. 3:18; 1 John 3:2). If by sanctification we mean, not a sloughing off of remaining depravity, but an ever increasing purity and perfection, then we may hold that the process of sanctification goes on forever. Our relation to Christ must always be that of the imperfect to the perfect, of the finite to the infinite; and for finite spirits, progress must always be possible. Clarke, Christian Theology, 373—"Not even at death can sanctification end.... The goal lies far beyond deliverance from sin.... There is no such thing as bringing the divine life to such completion that no further progress is possible to it.... Indeed, free and unhampered progress can scarcely begin until sin is left behind." "O snows so pure, O peaks so high! I shall not reach you till I die!"

As Jesus' resurrection was prepared by holiness of life, so the Christian's resurrection is prepared by sanctification. When our souls are freed from the last remains of sin, then it will not be possible for us to be holden by death (cf. Acts 2:24). See Gordon, The Twofold Life, or Christ's Work for us and in us; Brit. and For. Evang. Rev., April, 1884:205-229; Van Oosterzee, Christian Dogmatics, 657-662.

3. Erroneous Views refuted by these Scripture Passages.

A. The Antinomian,—which holds that, since Christ's obedience and sufferings have satisfied the demands of the law, the believer is free from obligation to observe it.

The Antinomian view rests upon a misinterpretation of Rom. 6:14—"Ye are not under law, but under grace." Agricola and Amsdorf (1559) were representatives of this view. Amsdorf said that "good works are hurtful to salvation." But Melanchthon's words furnish the reply: "Sola fides justificat, sed fides non est sola." F. W. Robertson states it: "Faith alone justifies, but not the faith that is alone." And he illustrates: "Lightning alone strikes, but not the lightning which is without thunder; for that is summer lightning and harmless." See Browning's poem, Johannes Agricola in Meditation, in Dramatis Personæ, 300—"I have God's warrant, Could I blend All hideous sins as in a cup, To drink the mingled venoms up, Secure my nature will convert The draught to blossoming gladness." Agricola said that Moses ought to be hanged. This is Sanctification without Perseverance.

Sandeman, the founder of the sect called Sandemanians, asserted as his fundamental principle the deadliness of all doings, the necessity for inactivity to let God do his work in the soul. See his essay, Theron and Aspasia, referred to by Allen, in his Life of Jonathan Edwards, 114. Anne Hutchinson was excommunicated and banished by the Puritans from Massachusetts, in 1637, for holding "two dangerous errors: 1. The Holy Spirit personally dwells in a justified person; 2. No sanctification can evidence to us our justification." Here the latter error almost destroyed the influence of the former truth. There is a little Antinomianism in the popular hymn: "Lay your deadly doings down, Down at Jesus' feet; Doing is a deadly thing; Doing ends in death." The colored preacher's poetry only presented the doctrine in the concrete: "You may rip and te-yar, You may cuss and swe-yar, But you're jess as sure of heaven, 'S if you'd done gone de-yar." Plain Andrew Fuller in England (1754-1815) did excellent service in overthrowing popular Antinomianism.

To this view we urge the following objections:

(a) That since the law is a transcript of the holiness of God, its demands as a moral rule are unchanging. Only as a system of penalty and a method of salvation is the law abolished in Christ's death.

Mat. 5:17-19—"Think not that I came to destroy the law or the prophets: I came not to destroy, but to fulfil. For verily I say unto you, Till heaven and earth pass away, one jot or one tittle shall in no wise pass away from the law, till all things be accomplished. Whosoever therefore shall break one of these least commandments, and shall teach men so, shall be called least in the kingdom of heaven: but whosoever shall do and teach them, he shall be called great in the kingdom of heaven"; 48—"Ye therefore shall be perfect, as your heavenly Father is perfect"; 1 Pet. 1:16—"Ye shall be holy; for I am holy"; Rom. 10:4—"For Christ is the end of the law unto righteousness to every one that believeth"; Gal. 2:20—"I have been crucified with Christ"; 3:13—"Christ redeemed us from the curse of the law, having become a curse for us"; Col. 2:14—"having blotted out the bond written in ordinances that was against us, which was contrary to us: and he hath taken it out of the way, nailing it to the cross"; Heb. 2:15—"deliver all them who through fear of death were all their lifetime subject to bondage."

(b) That the union between Christ and the believer secures not only the bearing of the penalty of the law by Christ, but also the impartation of Christ's spirit of obedience to the believer,—in other words, brings him into communion with Christ's work, and leads him to ratify it in his own experience.

Rom. 8:9, 10, 15—"ye are not in the flesh but in the Spirit, if so be that the Spirit of God dwelleth in you. But if any man hath not the Spirit of Christ, he is none of his. And if Christ is in you, the body is dead because of sin; but

the spirit is life because of righteousness.... For ye received not the spirit of bondage again unto fear: but ye received the spirit of adoption, whereby we cry, Abba, Father"; Gal. 5:22-25—"But the fruit of the Spirit is love, joy, peace, longsuffering, kindness, goodness, faithfulness, meekness, self-control; against such there is no law. And they that are of Christ Jesus have crucified the flesh with the passions and the lusts thereof"; 1 John 1:6—"If we say that we have fellowship with him and walk in the darkness, we lie, and do not the truth"; 3:6—"Whosoever abideth in him sinneth not: whosoever sinneth hath not seen him, neither knoweth him."

(c) That the freedom from the law of which the Scriptures speak, is therefore simply that freedom from the constraint and bondage of the law, which characterizes those who have become one with Christ by faith.

Ps. 119:97—"O how love I thy law! it is my meditation all the day"; Rom. 3:8, 31—"and why not (as we are slanderously reported, and as some affirm that we say), Let us do evil, that good may come? whose condemnation is just.... Do we then make the law of none effect through faith? God forbid: nay, we establish the law"; 6:14, 15, 22—"For sin shall not have dominion over you: for ye are not under law, but under grace. What then? shall we sin, because we are not under law, but under grace? God forbid ... now being made free from sin and become servants to God, ye have your fruit unto sanctification, and the end eternal life"; 7:6—"But now we have been discharged from the law, having died to that wherein we were held; so that we serve in newness of the spirit, and not in oldness of the letter"; 8:4—"that the ordinance of the law might be fulfilled in us, who walk not after the flesh, but after the Spirit"; 1 Cor. 7:22—"he that was called in the Lord being a bondservant, is the Lord's freedman"; Gal. 5:1—"For freedom did Christ set us free: stand fast therefore, and be not entangled again in a yoke of bondage"; 1 Tim. 1:9—"law is not made for a righteous man, but for the lawless and unruly"; James 1:25—"the perfect law, the law of liberty."

To sum up the doctrine of Christian freedom as opposed to Antinomianism, we may say that Christ does not free us, as the Antinomian believes, from the law as a rule of life. But he does free us (1) from the law as a system of curse and penalty; this he does by bearing the curse and penalty himself. Christ frees us (2) from the law with its claims as a method of salvation; this he does by making his obedience and merits ours. Christ frees us (3) from the law as an outward and foreign compulsion; this he does by giving to us the spirit of obedience and sonship, by which the law is progressively realized within.

Christ, then, does not free us, as the Antinomian believes, from the law as a rule of life. But he does free us (1) from the law as a system of curse and penalty. This he does by bearing the curse and penalty himself. Just as law can do nothing with a man after it has executed its death-penalty upon him, so law can do nothing with us, now that its death-penalty has been executed upon Christ. There are some insects that expire in the act of planting their sting; and so, when the law gathered itself up and planted its sting in the heart of Christ, it expended all its power as a judge and avenger over us who believe. In the Cross, the law as a system of curse and penalty exhausted itself; so we were set free.

Christ frees us (2) from the law with its claims as a method of salvation: in other words, he frees us from the necessity of trusting our salvation to an impossible future obedience. As the sufferings of Christ, apart from any sufferings of ours, deliver us from eternal death, so the merits of Christ, apart from any merits of ours, give us a title to eternal life. By faith in what Christ has done and simple acceptance of his work for us, we secure a right to heaven. Obedience on our part is no longer rendered painfully, as if our salvation depended on it, but freely and gladly, in gratitude for what Christ has done for us. Illustrate by the English nobleman's invitation to his park, and the regulations he causes to be posted up.

Christ frees us (3) from the law as an outward and foreign compulsion. In putting an end to legalism, he provides against license. This he does by giving the spirit of obedience and sonship. He puts love in the place of fear; and this secures an obedience more intelligent, more thorough, and more hearty, than could have been secured by mere law. So he frees us from the burden and compulsion of the law, by realizing the law within us by his Spirit. The freedom of the Christian is freedom in the law, such as the musician experiences when the scales and exercises have become easy, and work has turned to play. See John Owen, Works, 3:366-651; 6:1-313; Campbell, The Indwelling Christ, 73-81.

Gould, Bib. Theol. N. T., 195—"The supremacy of those books which contain the words of Jesus himself [i. e., the Synoptic Gospels] is that they incorporate, with the other elements of the religious life, the regulative will. Here for instance [in John] is the gospel of the contemplative life, which, 'beholding as in a mirror the glory of the Lord is changed into the same image from glory to glory, as by the Spirit of the Lord' (2 Cor. 3:18). The belief is that, with this beholding, life will take care of itself. Life will never take care of itself. Among other things, after the most perfect vision, it has to ask what aspirations, principles, affections, belong to life, and then to cultivate the will to embody these things. Here is the common defect of all religions. They fail to marry religion to the common life. Christ did not stop short of this final word; but if we leave him for even the greatest of his disciples, we are in danger of missing it." This utterance of Gould is surprising in several ways. It attributes to John alone the contemplative attitude of mind, which the quotation given shows to belong also to Paul. It ignores the constant appeals in John to the will: "He that hath my commandments and keepeth them, he it is that loveth me" (John 14:21). It also forgets that "life" in John is the whole being, including intellect, affection, and will, and that to have Christ for one's life is absolutely to exclude Antinomianism.

B. The Perfectionist,—which holds that the Christian may, in this life, become perfectly free from sin. This view was held by John Wesley in England, and by Mahan and Finney in America.

Finney, Syst. Theol., 500, declares regeneration to be "an instantaneous change from entire sinfulness to entire holiness." The claims of Perfectionists, however, have been modified from "freedom from all sin," to "freedom from all known sin," then to "entire consecration," and finally to "Christian assurance." H. W. Webb-Peploe, in S. S. Times, June 25, 1898—"The Keswick teaching is that no true Christian need wilfully or knowingly sin. Yet this is not sinless perfection. It is simply according to our faith that we receive, and faith only draws from God according to our present possibilities. These are limited by the presence of indwelling corruption; and, while never needing to sin within the sphere of the light we possess, there are to the last hour of our life upon the earth powers of corruption within every man, which defile his best deeds and give to even his holiest efforts that 'nature of sin' of which the 9th Article in the Church of England Prayerbook speaks so strongly." Yet it is evident that this corruption is not regarded as real sin, and is called "nature of sin" only in some non-natural sense.

Dr. George Peck says: "In the life of the most perfect Christian there is every day renewed occasion for self-abhorrence, for repentance, for renewed application of the blood of Christ, for application of the rekindling of the Holy Spirit." But why call this a state of perfection? F. B. Meyer: "We never say that self is dead; were we to do so, self would be laughing at us round the corner. The teaching of Romans 6 is, not that self is dead, but that the renewed will is dead to self, the man's will saying Yes to Christ, and No to self; through the Spirit's grace it constantly repudiates and mortifies the power of the flesh." For statements of the Perfectionist view, see John Wesley's Christian Theology, edited by Thornley Smith, 265-273; Mahan, Christian Perfection, and art. in Bib. Repos. 2d Series, vol. IV, Oct. 1840:408-428; Finney, Systematic Theology, 586-766; Peck, Christian Perfection; Ritschl, Bib. Sac., Oct. 1878:656; A. T. Pierson, The Keswick Movement.

In reply, it will be sufficient to observe:

(a) That the theory rests upon false conceptions: first, of the law,—as a sliding-scale of requirement graduated to the moral condition of creatures, instead of being the unchangeable reflection of God's holiness; secondly, of sin,—as consisting only in voluntary acts instead of embracing also those dispositions and states of the soul which are not conformed to the divine holiness; thirdly, of the human will,—as able to choose God supremely and persistently at every moment of life, and to fulfil at every moment the obligations resting upon it, instead of being corrupted and enslaved by the Fall.

This view reduces the debt to the debtor's ability to pay,—a short and easy method of discharging obligations. I can leap over a church steeple, if I am only permitted to make the church steeple low enough; and I can touch the stars, if the stars will only come down to my hand. The Philistines are quite equal to Samson, if they may only cut off Samson's locks. So I can obey God's law, if I may only make God's law what I want it to be. The fundamental error of perfectionism is its low view of God's law; the second is its narrow conception of sin. John Wesley: "I believe a person filled with love of God is still liable to involuntary transgressions. Such transgressions you may call sins, if you please; I do not." The third error of perfectionism is its exaggerated estimate of man's power of contrary choice. To say that, whatever may have been the habits of the past and whatever may be the evil affections of the present, a man is perfectly able at any moment to obey the whole law of God, is to deny that there are such things as character and depravity. Finney, Gospel Themes, 383, indeed, disclaimed "all expectations of attaining this state ourselves, and by our own independent, unaided efforts." On the Law of God, see pages 537-544.

Augustine: "Every lesser good has an essential element of sin." Anything less than the perfection that belongs normally to my present stage of development is a coming short of the law's demand. R. W. Dale, Fellowship with Christ, 359—"For us and in this world, the divine is always the impossible. Give me a law for individual conduct which requires a perfection that is within my reach, and I am sure that the law does not represent the divine thought. 'Not that I have already obtained, or am already made perfect: but I press on, if so be that I may lay hold on that for which also I was laid hold on by Christ Jesus' (Phil. 3:12)—this, from the beginning, has been the confession of saints." The Perfectionist is apt to say that we must "take Christ twice, once for justification and once for sanctification." But no one can take Christ for justification without at the same time taking him for sanctification. Dr. A. A. Hodge calls this doctrine "Neonomianism," because it holds not to one unchanging, ideal, and perfect law of God, but to a second law given to human weakness when the first law has failed to secure obedience.

(1) The law of God demands perfection. It is a transcript of God's nature. Its object is to reveal God. Anything less than the demand of perfection would misrepresent God. God could not give a law which a sinner could obey. In the very nature of the case there can be no sinlessness in this life for those who have once sinned. Sin brings incapacity as well as guilt. All men have squandered a part of the talent intrusted to them by God, and therefore no man can come up to the demands of that law which requires all that God gave to humanity at its creation together with interest on the investment. (2) Even the best Christian comes short of perfection. Regeneration makes only the dominant disposition holy. Many affections still remain unholy and require to be cleansed. Only by lowering the demands of the law, making shallow our conceptions of sin, and mistaking temporary volition for permanent bent of the will, can we count ourselves to be perfect. (3) Absolute perfection is attained not in this world but in the world to come. The best Christians count themselves still sinners, strive most earnestly for holiness, have imputed but not inherent sanctification, are saved by hope.

(b) That the theory finds no support in, but rather is distinctly contradicted by, Scripture.

First, the Scriptures never assert or imply that the Christian may in this life live without sin; passages like 1 John 3:6, 9, if interpreted consistently with the context, set forth either the ideal standard of Christian living or the actual state of the believer so far as respects his new nature.

1 John 3:6—"Whosoever abideth in him sinneth not; whosoever sinneth hath not seen him, neither knoweth him"; 9—"Whosoever is begotten of God doeth no sin, because his seed abideth in him: and he cannot sin, because he is begotten of God." Ann. Par. Bible, in loco:—"John is contrasting the states in which sin and grace severally predominate, without reference to degrees in either, showing that all men are in one or the other." Neander: "John recognizes no intermediate state, no gradations. He seizes upon the radical point of difference. He contrasts the two states in their essential nature and

principle. It is either love or hate, light or darkness, truth or a lie. The Christian life in its essential nature is the opposite of all sin. If there be sin, it must be the afterworking of the old nature." Yet all Christians are required in Scripture to advance, to confess sin, to ask forgiveness, to maintain warfare, to assume the attitude of ill desert in prayer, to receive chastisement for the removal of imperfections, to regard full salvation as matter of hope, not of present experience.

John paints only in black and white; there are no intermediate tints or colors. Take the words in 1 John 3:6 literally, and there never was and never can be a regenerate person. The words are hyperbolical, as Paul's words in Rom. 6:2—"We who died to sin, how shall we any longer live therein"—are metaphorical; see E. H. Johnson, in Bib. Sac., 1892:375, note. The Emperor William refused the request for an audience prepared by a German-American, saying that Germans born in Germany but naturalized in America became Americans: "Ich kenne Amerikaner, Ich kenne Deutsche, aber Deutsch-Amerikaner kenne Ich nicht"—"I know Americans, I know Germans, but German-Americans I do not know."

Lowrie, Doctrine of St. John, 110—"St. John uses the noun sin and the verb to sin in two senses: to denote the power or principle of sin, or to denote concrete acts of sin. The latter sense he generally expresses by the plural sins.... The Christian is guilty of particular acts of sin for which confession and forgiveness are required, but as he has been freed from the bondage of sin he cannot habitually practise it nor abide in it, still less can he be guilty of sin in its superlative form, by denial of Christ."

Secondly, the apostolic admonitions to the Christians and Hebrews show that no such state of complete sanctification had been generally attained by the Christians of the first century.

Rom. 8:24—"For in hope were we saved: but hope that is seen is not hope: for who hopeth for that which he seeth?" The party feeling, selfishness, and immorality found among the members of the Corinthian church are evidence that they were far from a state of entire sanctification.

Thirdly, there is express record of sin committed by the most perfect characters of Scripture—as Noah, Abraham, Job, David, Peter.

We are urged by perfectionists "to keep up the standard." We do this, not by calling certain men perfect, but by calling Jesus Christ perfect. In proportion to our sanctification, we are absorbed in Christ, not in ourselves. Self-consciousness and display are a poor evidence of sanctification. The best characters of Scripture put their trust in a standard higher than they have ever realized in their own persons, even in the righteousness of God.

Fourthly, the word τέλειος, as applied to spiritual conditions already attained, can fairly be held to signify only a relative perfection, equivalent to sincere piety or maturity of Christian judgment.

1 Cor. 2:6—"We speak wisdom, however, among the perfect," or, as the Am. Revisers have it, "among them that are fullgrown"; Phil. 3:15—"Let us therefore, as many as are perfect, be thus minded." Men are often called perfect, when free from any fault which strikes the eyes of the world. See Gen. 6:9—"Noah was a righteous man, and perfect"; Job 1:1—"that man was perfect and upright." On τέλειος, see Trench, Syn. N. T., 1:110.

The τέλειοι are described in Heb. 5:14—"Solid food is for the mature (τελείων) who on account of habit have their perceptions disciplined for the discriminating of good and evil" (Dr. Kendrick's translation). The same word "perfect" is used of Jacob in Gen. 25:27—"Jacob was a quiet man, dwelling in tents" = a harmless man, exemplary and well-balanced, as a man of business. Genung, Epic of the Inner Life, 132—"'Perfect' in Job = Horace's 'integer vitæ,' being the adjective of which 'integrity' is the substantive."

Fifthly, the Scriptures distinctly deny that any man on earth lives without sin.

1 K. 8:46—"there is no man that sinneth not"; Eccl. 7:20—"Surely there is not a righteous man upon earth, that doeth good, and sinneth not"; James 3:2—"For in many things we all stumble. If any stumbleth not in word, the same is a perfect man, able to bridle the whole body also"; 1 John 1:8—"If we say that we have no sin, we deceive ourselves, and the truth is not in us."

T. T. Eaton, Sanctification: "1. Some mistake regeneration for sanctification. They have been unconverted church members. When led to faith in Christ, and finding peace and joy, they think they are sanctified, when they are simply converted. 2. Some mistake assurance of faith for sanctification. But joy is not sanctification. 3. Some mistake the baptism of the Holy Spirit for sanctification. But Peter sinned grievously at Antioch, after he had received that baptism. 4. Some think that doing the best one can is sanctification. But he who measures by inches, for feet, can measure up well. Some regard sin as only a voluntary act, whereas the sinful nature is the fountain. Stripping off the leaves of the Upas tree does not answer. 6. Some mistake the power of the human will, and fancy that an act of will can free a man from sin. They ignore the settled bent of the will, which the act of will does not change."

Sixthly, the declaration: "ye were sanctified" (1 Cor. 6:11), and the designation: "saints" (1 Cor. 1:2), applied to early believers, are, as the whole epistle shows, expressive of a holiness existing in germ and anticipation; the expressions deriving their meaning not so much from what these early believers were, as from what Christ was, to whom they were united by faith.

When N. T. believers are said to be "sanctified," we must remember the O. T. use of the word.

"Sanctify" may have either the meaning "to make holy outwardly," or "to make holy inwardly." The people of Israel and the vessels of the tabernacle were made holy in the former sense; their sanctification was a setting apart to the sacred use. Num. 8:17—"all the firstborn among the children of Israel are mine.... I sanctified them for myself"; Deut. 33:3—"Yea, he loveth the people; all his saints are in thy hand"; 2 Chron. 29:19—"all the vessels ... have we prepared and sanctified." The vessels mentioned were first immersed, and then sprinkled from day to day according to need. So the Christian by his regeneration is set apart for God's service, and in this sense is a "saint" and "sanctified." More than this, he has in him the beginnings of purity,—he is "clean as a whole," though he yet needs "to wash his feet" (John 13:10)—that is, to be cleansed from the recurring defilements of his daily life. Shedd, Dogm. Theol., 2:551—"The error of the Perfectionist is that of confounding imputed sanctification with inherent sanctification. It is the latter which is mentioned in 1 Cor. 1:30—'Christ Jesus, who was made unto us ... sanctification.' "

Water from the Jordan is turbid, but it settles in the bottle and seems pure—until it is shaken. Some Christians seem very free from sin, until you shake them,—then they get "riled." Clarke, Christian Theology, 871—"Is there not a higher Christian life? Yes, and a higher life beyond it, and a higher still beyond. The Christian life is ever higher and higher. It must pass through all stages between its beginning and its perfection." C. D. Case: "The great objection to [this theory of] complete sanctification is that, if possessed at all, it is not a development of our own character."

(c) That the theory is disapproved by the testimony of Christian experience.—In exact proportion to the soul's advance in holiness does it shrink from claiming that holiness has been already attained, and humble itself before God for its remaining apathy, ingratitude, and unbelief.

Phil. 3:12-14—"Not that I have already obtained, or am already made perfect: but I press on, if so be that I may lay hold on that for which also I was laid hold on by Christ Jesus." Some of the greatest advocates of perfectionism have been furthest from claiming any such perfection; although many of their less instructed followers claimed it for them, and even professed to have attained it themselves.

In Luke 7:1-10, the centurion does not think himself worthy to go to Jesus, or to have him come under his roof, yet the elders of the Jews say: "He is worthy that thou shouldest do this"; and Jesus himself says of him: "I have not found so great faith, no, not in Israel." "Holy to Jehovah" was inscribed upon the mitre of the high priest (Ex. 28:36). Others saw it, but he saw it not. Moses knew not that his face shone (Ex. 34:29). The truest holiness is that of which the possessor is least conscious; yet it is his real diadem and beauty (A. J. Gordon). "The nearer men are to being sinless, the less they talk about it" (Dwight L. Moody). "Always strive for perfection: never believe you have reached it" (Arnold of Rugby). Compare with this, Ernest Renan's declaration that he had nothing to alter in his life. "I have not sinned for some time," said a woman to Mr. Spurgeon. "Then you must be very proud of it," he replied. "Indeed I am!" said she. A pastor says: "No one can attain the 'Higher Life,' and escape making mischief." John Wesley lamented that not one in thirty retained the blessing.

Perfectionism is best met by proper statements of the nature of the law and of sin (Ps. 119:96). While we thus rebuke spiritual pride, however, we should be equally careful to point out the inseparable connection between justification and sanctification, and their equal importance as together making up the Biblical idea of salvation. While we show no favor to those who would make sanctification a sudden and paroxysmal act of the human will, we should hold forth the holiness of God as the standard of attainment, and the faith in a Christ of infinite fulness as the medium through which that standard is to be gradually but certainly realized in us (2 Cor. 3:18).

We should imitate Lyman Beecher's method of opposing perfectionism—by searching expositions of God's law. When men know what the law is, they will say with the Psalmist: "I have seen an end of all perfection; thy commandment is exceeding broad" (Ps. 119:96). And yet we are earnestly and hopefully to seek in Christ for a continually increasing measure of sanctification: 1 Cor. 1:30—"Christ Jesus, who was made unto us ... sanctification"; 2 Cor. 3:18—"But we all, with unveiled face beholding as in a mirror the glory of the Lord, are transformed into the same image from glory to glory, even as from the Lord the Spirit." Arnold of Rugby: "Always expect to succeed, and never think you have succeeded."

Mr. Finney meant by entire sanctification only that it is possible for Christians in this life by the grace of God to consecrate themselves so unreservedly to his service as to live without conscious and wilful disobedience to the divine commands. He did not claim himself to have reached this point; he made at times very impressive confessions of his own sinfulness; he did not encourage others to make for themselves the claim to have lived without conscious fault. He held however that such a state is attainable, and therefore that its pursuit is rational. He also admitted that such a state is one, not of absolute, but only of relative, sinlessness. His error was in calling it a state of entire sanctification. See A. H. Strong, Christ in Creation, 377-384.

A. J. Gordon, Ministry of the Spirit, 116—"It is possible that one may experience a great crisis in his spiritual life, in which there is such a total surrender of self to God and such an infilling of the Holy Spirit, that he is freed from the bondage of sinful appetites and habits, and enabled to have constant victory over self instead of suffering constant defeat.... If the doctrine of sinless perfection is a heresy, the doctrine of contentment with sinful imperfection is a greater heresy.... It is not an edifying spectacle to see a Christian worldling throwing stones at a Christian perfectionist." Caird, Evolution of Religion, 1:138—"If, according to the German proverb, it is provided that the trees shall not grow into the sky, it is equally provided that they shall always grow toward it; and the sinking of the roots into the soil is inevitably accompanied by a further expansion of the branches."

See Hovey, Doctrine of the Higher Christian Life, Compared with Scripture, also Hovey, Higher Christian Life Examined, in Studies in Ethics and Theology, 344-427; Snodgrass, Scriptural Doctrine of Sanctification; Princeton Essays, 1:335-365; Hodge, Syst. Theol., 3:213-258; Calvin, Institutes, III, 11:6; Bib. Repos., 2d Series, 1:44-58; 2:143-166; Woods, Works, 4:465-523; H. A. Boardman, The "Higher Life" Doctrine of Sanctification; William Law, Practical Treatise on Christian Perfection; E. H. Johnson, The Highest Life.

II. Perseverance

The Scriptures declare that, in virtue of the original purpose and continuous operation of God, all who are united to Christ by faith will infallibly continue in a state of grace and will finally attain to everlasting life. This voluntary continuance, on the part of the Christian, in faith and well-doing we call perseverance. Perseverance is, therefore, the human side or aspect of that spiritual process which, as viewed from the divine side, we call sanctification. It is not a mere natural consequence of conversion, but involves a constant activity of the human will from the moment of conversion to the end of life.

Adam's holiness was mutable; God did not determine to keep him. It is otherwise with believers in Christ; God has determined to give them the kingdom (Luke 12:32). Yet this keeping by God, which we call sanctification, is accompanied and followed by a keeping of himself on the part of the believer, which we call perseverance. The former is alluded to in John 17:11, 12—"keep them in thy name.... I kept them in thy name.... I guarded them, and not one of them perished, but the son of perdition"; the latter is alluded to in 1 John 5:18—"he that was

begotten of God keepeth himself." Both are expressed in Jude 21, 24—"Keep yourselves in the love of God.... Now unto him that is able to guard you from stumbling..."

A German treatise on Pastoral Theology is entitled: "Keep What Thou Hast"—an allusion to 2 Tim. 1:14—"That good thing which was committed unto thee guard through the Holy Spirit which dwelleth in us." Not only the pastor, but every believer, has a charge to keep; and the keeping of ourselves is as important a point of Christian doctrine as is the keeping of God. Both are expressed in the motto: Teneo, Teneor—the motto on the front of the Y. M. C. A. building in Boston, underneath a stone cross, firmly clasped by two hands. The colored preacher said that "Perseverance means: 1. Take hold; 2. Hold on; 3. Never let go."

Physically, intellectually, morally, spiritually, there is need that we persevere. Paul, in 1 Cor. 9:27, declares that he smites his body under the eye and makes a slave of it, lest after having preached to others he himself should be rejected; and in 2 Tim. 4:7, at the end of his career, he rejoices that he has "kept the faith." A. J. Gordon, Ministry of the Spirit, 115—"The Christian is as 'a tree planted by the streams of water, that bringeth forth its fruit in its season' (Ps. 1:3), but to conclude that his growth will be as irresistible as that of the tree, coming as a matter of course simply because he has by regeneration been planted in Christ, is a grave mistake. The disciple is required to be consciously and intelligently active in his own growth, as the tree is not, 'to give all diligence to make his calling and election sure' (2 Pet. 1:10) by surrendering himself to the divine action." Clarke, Christian Theology, 379—"Man is able to fall, and God is able to keep him from falling; and through the various experiences of life God will so save his child out of all evil that he will be morally incapable of falling."

1. Proof of the Doctrine of Perseverance.

A. From Scripture.

John 10:28, 29—"they shall never perish, and no one shall snatch them out of my hand. My Father, who hath given them unto me, is greater than all; and no one is able to snatch them out of the Father's hand"; Rom. 11:29—"For the gifts and the calling of God are without repentance"; 1 Cor. 13:7—"endureth all things"; cf. 13—"But now abideth faith, hope, love"; Phil. 1:6—"being confident of this very thing, that he who began a good work in you will perfect it until the day of Jesus Christ"; 2 Thess. 3:3—"But the Lord is faithful, who shall establish you, and guard you from the evil one"; 2 Tim. 1:12—"I know him whom I have believed, and I am persuaded that he is able to guard that which I have committed unto him against that day"; 1 Pet. 1:5—"who by the power of God are guarded through faith unto a salvation ready to be revealed in the last time"; Rev. 3:10—"Because thou didst keep the word of my patience, I also will keep thee from the hour of trial, that hour which is to come upon the whole world, to try them that dwell upon the earth."

2 Tim. 1:12—τὴν παραθήκην μου—Ellicott translates: "the trust committed to me," or "my deposit" = the office of preaching the gospel, the stewardship entrusted to the apostle; cf. 1 Tim. 6:20—

"O Timothy, keep thy deposit"—τὴν παραθήκην; and 2 Tim. 1:14—"Keep the good deposit"—where the deposit seems to be the faith or doctrine delivered to him to preach. Nicoll, The Church's One Foundation, 211—"Some Christians waken each morning with a creed of fewer articles, and those that remain they are ready to surrender to a process of argument that convinces them. But it is a duty to keep. 'Ye have an anointing from the Holy One, and ye know' (1 John 2:20).... Ezra gave to his men a treasure of gold and silver and sacrificial vessels, and he charged them: 'Watch ye, and keep them, until ye weigh them ... in thy chambers of the house of Jehovah' (Ezra 8:29)." See in the Autobiography of C. H. Spurgeon, 1:225, 256, the outline of a sermon on John 6:37—"All that which the Father giveth me shall come unto me; and him that cometh to me I will in no wise cast out." Mr. Spurgeon remarks that this text can give us no comfort unless we see: 1. that God has given us his Holy Spirit; 2. that we have given ourselves to him. Christ will not cast us out because of our great sins, our long delays, our trying other saviors, our hardness of heart, our little faith, our poor dull prayers, our unbelief, our inveterate corruptions, our frequent backslidings, nor finally because every one else passes us by.

B. From Reason.

(a) It is a necessary inference from other doctrines,—such as election, union with Christ, regeneration, justification, sanctification.

Election of certain individuals to salvation is election to bestow upon them such influences of the Spirit as will lead them not only to accept Christ, but to persevere and be saved. Union with Christ is indissoluble; regeneration is the beginning of a work of new creation, which is declared in justification, and completed in sanctification. All these doctrines are parts of a general scheme, which would come to naught if any single Christian were permitted to fall away.

(b) It accords with analogy,—God's preserving care being needed by, and being granted to, his spiritual, as well as his natural, creation.

As natural life cannot uphold itself, but we "live, and move, and have our being" in God (Acts 17:28), so spiritual life cannot uphold itself, and God maintains the faith, love, and holy activity which he has originated. If he preserves our natural life, much more may we expect him to preserve the spiritual. 1 Tim. 6:13—"I charge thee before God who preserveth all things alive" (R. V. marg.)—ζωογονοῦντος τὰ πάντα = the great Preserver of all enables us to persist in our Christian course.

(c) It is implied in all assurance of salvation,—since this assurance is given by the Holy Spirit, and is based not upon the known strength of human resolution, but upon the purpose and operation of God.

S. R. Mason: "If Satan and Adam both fell away from perfect holiness, it is a million to one that, in a world full of temptations and with all appetites and habits against me, I shall fall away from imperfect holiness, unless God by his almighty power keep me." It is in the power and purpose of God, then, that the believer puts his trust. But since this trust is awakened by the Holy Spirit, it must be that there is a divine fact corresponding to it; namely, God's purpose to exert his power in such a way that the Christian shall persevere. See Wardlaw, Syst. Theol., 2:550-578; N. W. Taylor, Revealed Theology, 445-460.

Job 6:11—"What is my strength, that I should wait? And what is mine end, that I should be patient?" "Here is a note of self- distrust. To be patient without any outlook, to endure without divine support—Job does not promise it, and he trembles at the prospect; but none the less he sets his feet on the toilsome way" (Genung). Dr. Lyman Beecher was asked whether he believed in the perseverance of the saints. He replied: "I do, except when the wind is from the East." But the value of the doctrine is that we can believe it even when the wind is from the East. It is well to hold on to God's hand, but it is better to have God's hand hold on to us. When we are weak, and forgetful and asleep, we need to be sure of God's care. Like the child who thought he was driving, but who found, after the trouble was over, that his father after all had been holding the reins, we too find when danger comes that behind our hands are the hands of God. The Perseverance of the Saints, looked at from the divine side, is the Preservation of the Saints, and the hymn that expresses the Christian's faith is the hymn: "How firm a foundation, ye saints of the Lord, Is laid for your faith in his excellent word!"

2. Objections to the Doctrine of Perseverance.

These objections are urged chiefly by Arminians and by Romanists.

A. That it is inconsistent with human freedom.—Answer: It is no more so than is the doctrine of Election or the doctrine of Decrees.

The doctrine is simply this, that God will bring to bear such influences upon all true believers, that they will freely persevere. Moule, Outlines of Christian Doctrine, 47—"Is grace, in any sense of the word, ever finally withdrawn? Yes, if by grace is meant any free gift of God tending to salvation; or, more specially, any action of the Holy Spirit tending in its nature thither.... But if by grace be meant the dwelling and working of Christ in the truly regenerate, there is no indication in Scripture of the withdrawal of it."

B. That it tends to immorality.—Answer: This cannot be, since the doctrine declares that God will save men by securing their perseverance in holiness.

2 Tim. 2:19—"Howbeit the firm foundation of God standeth, having this seal, The Lord knoweth them that are his: and, Let every one that nameth the name of the Lord depart from unrighteousness"; that is, the temple of Christian character has upon its foundation two significant inscriptions, the one declaring God's power, wisdom, and purpose of salvation; the other declaring the purity and holy activity, on the part of the believer, through which God's purpose is to be fulfilled; 1 Pet. 1:1, 2—"elect ... according to the foreknowledge of God the Father, in sanctification of the Spirit, unto obedience and sprinkling of the blood of Jesus Christ"; 2 Pet. 1:10, 11—"Wherefore, brethren, give the more diligence to make your calling and election sure: for if ye do these things, ye shall never stumble: for thus shall be richly supplied unto you the entrance into the eternal kingdom of our Lord and Savior Jesus Christ."

C. That it leads to indolence.—Answer: This is a perversion of the doctrine, continuously possible only to the unregenerate; since, to the regenerate, certainty of success is the strongest incentive to activity in the conflict with sin.

1 John 5:4—"For whatsoever is begotten of God overcometh the world; and this is the victory that hath overcome the world, even our faith." It is notoriously untrue that confidence of success inspires timidity or indolence. Thomas Fuller: "Your salvation is his business; his service your business." The only prayers God will answer are those we ourselves cannot answer. For the very reason that "it is God who worketh in you both to will and to work, for his good pleasure," the apostle exhorts: "work out your own salvation with fear and trembling" (Phil. 2:12, 13).

D. That the Scripture commands to persevere and warnings against apostasy show that certain, even of the regenerate, will fall away.—Answer:

(a) They show that some, who are apparently regenerate, will fall away.

Mat. 18:7—"Woe unto the world because of occasions of stumbling! for it must needs be that the occasions come; but woe to that man through whom the occasion cometh"; 1 Cor. 11:19—"For there must be also factions [lit. 'heresies'] among you, that they that are approved may be made manifest among you"; 1 John 2:19—"They went out from us, but they were not of us; for if they had been of us, they would have continued with us: but they went out, that they might be made manifest that they all are not of us." Judas probably experienced strong emotions, and received strong impulses toward good, under the influence of Christ. The only falling from grace which is recognized in Scripture is not the falling of the regenerate, but the falling of the unregenerate, from influences tending to lead them to Christ. The Rabbins said that a drop of water will suffice to purify a man who has accidentally touched a creeping thing, but an ocean will not suffice for his cleansing so long as he purposely keeps the creeping thing in his hand.

(b) They show that the truly regenerate, and those who are only apparently so, are not certainly distinguishable in this life.

Mal. 3:18—"Then shall ye return and discern between the righteous and the wicked, between him that serveth God and him that serveth him not"; Mat. 13:25, 47—"while men slept, his enemy came and sowed tares also among the wheat, and went away.... Again, the kingdom of heaven is like unto a net, that was cast into the sea, and gathered of every kind"; Rom. 9:6, 7—"For they are not all Israel, that are of Israel: neither, because they are Abraham's seed, are they all children"; Rev. 3:1—"I know thy works, that thou hast a name that thou livest, and thou art dead." The tares were never wheat, and the bad fish never were good, in spite of the fact that their true nature was not for a while recognized.

(c) They show the fearful consequences of rejecting Christ, to those who have enjoyed special divine influences, but who are only apparently regenerate.

Heb. 10:26-29—"For if we sin wilfully after that we have received the knowledge of the truth, there remaineth no more a sacrifice for sins, but a certain fearful expectation of judgment, and a fierceness of fire which shall devour the adversaries. A man that hath set at nought Moses' law dieth without compassion on the word of two or three witnesses: of how much sorer punishment, think ye, shall he be judged worthy, who hath trodden under foot the Son of God, and hath counted the blood of the covenant wherewith he was sanctified an unholy thing, and hath done despite unto the Spirit of grace?" Here "sanctified" = external sanctification, like that of the ancient Israelites, by outward connection with God's people; cf. 1 Cor. 7:14—"the unbelieving husband is sanctified in the wife."

In considering these and the following Scripture passages, much will depend upon our view of inspiration. If we hold that Christ's promise was fulfilled and that his apostles were led into all the truth, we shall assume that there is unity in their teaching, and shall recognize in their variations only aspects and applications of the teaching of our Lord; in other words, Christ's doctrine in John 10:28, 29 will be the norm for the interpretation of seemingly diverse and at first sight inconsistent passages. There was a "faith which was once for all delivered unto the saints," and for this primitive faith we are exhorted "to contend earnestly" (Jude 3).

(d) They show what the fate of the truly regenerate would be, in case they should not persevere.

Heb. 6:4-6—"For as touching those who were once enlightened and tasted of the heavenly gift, and were made partakers of the Holy Spirit, and tasted the good word of God, and the powers of the world to come, and then fell away, it is impossible to renew them again unto repentance; seeing they crucify to themselves the Son of God afresh, and put him to an open shame." This is to be understood as a hypothetical case,—as is clear from verse 9 which follows: "But, beloved, we are persuaded better things of you, and things which accompany salvation, though we thus speak." Dr. A. C. Kendrick, Com. in loco: "In the phrase 'once enlightened,' the 'once' is ἅπαξ = once for all. The text describes a condition subjectively possible, and therefore needing to be held up in earnest warning to the believer, while objectively and in the absolute purpose of God, it never occurs.... If passages like this teach the possibility of falling from grace, they teach also the impossibility of restoration to it. The saint who once apostatizes has apostatized forever." So Ez. 18:24—"when the righteous turneth away from his righteousness, and committeth iniquity ... in them shall he die"; 2 Pet. 2:20—"For if, after they have escaped the defilements of the world through the knowledge of the Lord and Savior Jesus Christ, they are again entangled therein and overcome, the last state is become worse with them than the first." So, in Mat. 5:13—"if the salt have lost its savor, wherewith shall it be salted?"—if this teaches that the regenerate may lose their religion, it also teaches that they can never recover it. It really shows only that Christians who do not perform their proper functions as Christians become harmful and contemptible (Broadus, in loco).

(e) They show that the perseverance of the truly regenerate may be secured by these very commands and warnings.

1 Cor. 9:27—"I buffet my body, and bring it into bondage: lest by any means, after that I have preached to others, I myself should be rejected"—or, to bring out the meaning more fully: "I beat my body blue [or, 'strike it under the eye'], and make it a slave, lest after having been a herald to others, I myself should be rejected" ("unapproved," "counted unworthy of the prize"); 10:12—"Wherefore let him that thinketh he standeth take heed lest he fall." Quarles, Emblems: "The way to be safe is never to be secure." Wrightnour: "Warning a traveler to keep a certain path, and by this means keeping him in that path, is no evidence that he will ever fall into a pit by the side of the path simply because he is warned of it."

(f) They do not show that it is certain, or possible, that any truly regenerate person will fall away.

The Christian is like a man making his way up-hill, who occasionally slips back, yet always has his face set toward the summit. The unregenerate man has his face turned downwards, and he is slipping all the way. C. H. Spurgeon: "The believer, like a man on shipboard, may fall again and again on the deck, but he will never fall overboard."

E. That we have actual examples of such apostasy.—We answer:

(a) Such are either men once outwardly reformed, like Judas and Ananias, but never renewed in heart;

But, per contra, instance the experience of a man in typhoid fever, who apparently repented, but who never remembered it when he was restored to health. Sick-bed and death-bed conversions are not the best. There was one penitent thief, that none might despair; there was but one penitent thief, that none might presume. The hypocrite is like the wire that gets a second-hand electricity from the live wire running parallel with it. This second-hand electricity is effective only within narrow limits, and its efficacy is soon exhausted. The live wire has connection with the source of power in the dynamo.

(b) Or they are regenerate men, who, like David and Peter, have fallen into temporary sin, from which they will, before death, be reclaimed by God's discipline.

Instance the young profligate who, in a moment of apparent drowning, repented, was then rescued, and afterward lived a long life as a Christian. If he had not been rescued, his repentance would never have been known, nor the answer to his mother's prayers. So, in the moment of a backslider's death, God can renew repentance and faith. Cromwell on his death-bed questioned his Chaplain as to the doctrine of final perseverance, and, on being assured that it was a certain truth, said: "Then I am happy, for I am sure that I was once in a state of grace." But reliance upon a past experience is like trusting in the value of a policy of life insurance upon which several years' premiums have been unpaid. If the policy has not lapsed, it is because of extreme grace. The only conclusive evidence of perseverance is a present experience of Christ's presence and indwelling, corroborated by active service and purity of life.

On the general subject, see Edwards, Works, 3:509-532, and 4:104; Ridgeley, Body of Divinity, 2:164-194; John Owen, Works, vol. 11; Woods, Works, 3:221-246; Van Oosterzee, Christian Dogmatics, 662-666.

PART VII - ECCLESIOLOGY, OR THE DOCTRINE OF THE CHURCH

Chapter I - The Constitution Of The Church. Or Church Polity

I. Definition of the Church

(a) The church of Christ, in its largest signification, is the whole company of regenerate persons in all times and ages, in heaven and on earth (Mat. 16:18; Eph. 1:22, 23; 3:10; 5:24, 25; Col. 1:18; Heb. 12:23). In this sense, the church is identical with the spiritual kingdom of God; both signify that redeemed humanity in which God in Christ exercises actual spiritual dominion (John 3:3, 5).

Mat. 16:18—"thou art Peter, and upon this rock I will build my church; and the gates of Hades shall not prevail against it"; Eph. 1:22, 23—"and he put all things in subjection under his feet, and gave him to be head over all things to the church, which is his body, the fulness of him that filleth all in all"; 3:10—"to the intent that now unto the principalities and the powers in the heavenly places might be made known through the church the manifold wisdom of God"; 5:24, 25—"But as the church is subject to Christ, so let the wives also be to their husbands in everything. Husbands, love your wives, even as Christ also loved the church, and gave himself up for it"; Col. 1:18—"And he is the head of the body, the church: who is the beginning, the firstborn from the dead; that in all things he might have the preeminence"; Heb. 12:23—"the general assembly and church of the firstborn who are enrolled in heaven"; John 3:3, 5—"Except one be born anew, he cannot see the kingdom of God. ... Except one be born of water and the Spirit, he cannot enter into the kingdom of God."

Cicero's words apply here: "Una navis est jam bonorum omnium"—all good men are in one boat. Cicero speaks of the state, but it is still more true of the church invisible. Andrews, in Bib. Sac., Jan. 1883:14, mentions the following differences between the church and kingdom, or, as we prefer to say, between the visible church and the invisible church: (1) the church began with Christ,—the kingdom began earlier; (2) the church is confined to believers in the historic Christ,—the kingdom includes all God's children; (3) the church belongs wholly to this world—not so the kingdom; (4) the church is visible,—not so the kingdom; (5) the church has quasi organic character, and leads out into local churches,—this is not so with the kingdom. On the universal or invisible church, see Cremer, Lexicon N. T., transl., 113, 114, 331; Jacob, Eccl. Polity of N. T., 12.

H. C. Vedder: "The church is a spiritual body, consisting only of those regenerated by the Spirit of God." Yet the Westminster Confession affirms that the church "consists of all those throughout the world that profess the true religion, together with their children." This definition includes in the church a multitude who not only give no evidence of regeneration, but who plainly show themselves to be unregenerate. In many lands it practically identifies the church with the world. Augustine indeed thought that "the field," in Mat. 13:38, is the church, whereas Jesus says very distinctly that it "is the world." Augustine held that good and bad alike were to be permitted to dwell together in the church, without attempt to separate them; see Broadus, Com. in loco. But the parable gives a reason, not why we should not try to put the wicked out of the church, but why God does not immediately put them out of the world, the tares being separated from the wheat only at the final judgment of mankind.

Yet the universal church includes all true believers. It fulfils the promise of God to Abraham in Gen. 15:5—"Look now toward heaven, and number the stars, if thou be able to number them: and he said into him, So shall thy seed be." The church shall be immortal, since it draws its life from Christ: Is. 65:22—"as the days of a tree shall be the days of my people"; Zech. 4:2, 3—"a candlestick all of gold ... and two olive-trees by it." Dean Stanley, Life and Letters, 2:242, 243—"A Spanish Roman Catholic, Cervantes, said: 'Many are the roads by which God carries his own to heaven.' Döllinger: 'Theology must become a science not, as heretofore, for making war, but for making peace, and thus bringing about that reconciliation of churches for which the whole civilized world is longing.' In their loftiest moods of inspiration, the Catholic Thomas à Kempis, the Puritan Milton, the Anglican Keble, rose above their peculiar tenets, and above the limits that divide denominations, into the higher regions of a common Christianity. It was the Baptist Bunyan who taught the world that there was 'a common ground of communion which no difference of external rites could efface.' It was the Moravian Gambold who wrote: 'The man That could surround the sum of things, and spy The heart of God and secrets of his empire, Would speak but love. With love, the bright result Would change the hue of intermediate things, And make one thing of all theology.' "

(b) The church, in this large sense, is nothing less than the body of Christ—the organism to which he gives spiritual life, and through which he manifests the fulness of his power and grace. The church therefore cannot be defined in merely human terms, as an aggregate of individuals associated for social, benevolent, or even spiritual purposes. There is a transcendent element in the church. It is the great company of persons whom Christ has saved, in whom he dwells, to whom and through whom he reveals God (Eph. 1:22, 23).

Eph. 1:22, 23—"the church, which is his body, the fulness of him that filleth all in all." He who is the life of nature and of humanity reveals himself most fully in the great company of those who have joined themselves to him by faith. Union with Christ is the presupposition of the church. This alone transforms the sinner into a Christian, and this alone makes possible that vital and spiritual fellowship between individuals which constitutes the organizing principle of the church. The same divine life which ensures the pardon and the perseverance of the believer unites him to all other believers. The indwelling Christ makes the church superior to and more permanent than all humanitarian organizations; they die, but because Christ lives, the church lives also. Without a proper conception of this sublime relation of the church to Christ, we cannot properly appreciate our dignity as church members, or our high calling as shepherds of the flock. Not "ubi ecclesia, ibi Christus," but "ubi Christus, ibi ecclesia," should be our motto. Because Christ is omnipresent and omnipotent, "the same yesterday, and to-day, yea and forever" (Heb. 13:8), what Burke said of the nation is true of the church: It is "indeed a partnership, but a partnership not only between those who are living, but between those who are living, those who are dead, and those who are yet to be born."

McGiffert, Apostolic Church, 501—"Paul's conception of the church as the body of Christ was first emphasized and developed by Ignatius. He reproduces in his writings the substance of all the Paulinism that the church at large made permanently its own: the preëxistence and deity of Christ, the union of the believer with Christ without which the Christian life is impossible, the importance of Christ's death, the church the body of Christ. Rome never fully recognized Paul's teachings, but her system rests upon his doctrine of the church the body of Christ. The modern doctrine however makes the kingdom to be not spiritual or future, but a reality of this world." The redemption of the body, the redemption of institutions, the redemption of nations, are indeed all purposed by Christ. Christians should not only strive to rescue individual men from the slough of vice, but they should devise measures for draining that slough and making that vice impossible; in other words, they should labor for the coming of the kingdom of God in society. But this is not to identify the church with politics, prohibition, libraries, athletics. The spiritual fellowship is to be the fountain from which all these activities spring, while at the same time Christ's "kingdom is not of this world" (John 18:36).

A. J. Gordon, Ministry of the Spirit, 24, 25, 207—"As Christ is the temple of God, so the church is the temple of the Holy Spirit. As God could be seen only through Christ, so the Holy Spirit can be seen only through the church. As Christ was the image of the invisible God, so the church is appointed to be the image of the invisible Christ, and the members of Christ, when they are glorified with him, shall be the express image of his person.... The church and the kingdom are not identical terms, if we mean by the kingdom the visible reign and government of Jesus Christ on earth. In another sense they are identical. As is the king, so is the kingdom. The king is present now in the world, only invisibly and by the Holy Spirit; so the kingdom is now present invisibly and spiritually in the hearts of believers. The king is to come again visibly and gloriously; so shall the kingdom appear visibly and gloriously. In other words, the kingdom is already here in mystery: it is to be here to manifestation. Now the spiritual kingdom is administered by the Holy Spirit, and it extends from Pentecost to Parousia. At the Parousia—the appearing of the Son of man in glory—when he shall take unto himself his great power and reign (Rev. 11:17), when he who has now gone into a far country to be invested with a kingdom shall return and enter upon his government (Luke 19:15), then the invisible shall give way to the visible, the kingdom in mystery shall emerge into the kingdom in manifestation, and the Holy Spirit's administration shall yield to that of Christ."

(c) The Scriptures, however, distinguish between this invisible or universal church, and the individual church, in which the universal church takes local and temporal form, and in which the idea of the church as a whole is concretely exhibited.

Mat. 10:32—"Every one therefore, who shall confess me before men, him will I also confess before my Father who is in heaven"; 12:34, 35—"out of the abundance of the heart the mouth speaketh. The good man out of his good treasure bringeth forth good things"; Rom. 10:9, 10—"if thou shalt confess with thy month Jesus as Lord, and shalt believe in thy heart that God raised him from the dead, thou shalt be saved: for with the heart man believeth unto righteousness; and with the mouth confession is made unto salvation"; James 1:18—"Of his own will he brought us forth by the word of truth, that we should be a kind of firstfruits of his creatures"—we were saved, not for ourselves only, but as parts and beginnings of an organic kingdom of God; believers are called "firstfruits," because from them the blessing shall spread, until the whole world shall be pervaded with the new life; Pentecost, as the feast of first-fruits, was but the beginning of a stream that shall continue to flow until the whole race of man is gathered in.

R. S. Storrs: "When any truth becomes central and vital, there comes the desire to utter it,"—and we may add, not only in words, but in organization. So beliefs crystallize into institutions. But Christian faith is something more vital than the common beliefs of the world. Linking the soul to Christ, it brings Christians into living fellowship with one another before any bonds of outward organization exist; outward organization, indeed, only expresses and symbolizes this inward union of spirit to Christ and to one another. Horatius Bonar: "Thou must be true thyself, If thou the truth wouldst teach; Thy soul must overflow, if thou Another's soul wouldst reach; It needs the overflow of heart To give the lips full speech. Think truly, and thy thoughts Shall the world's famine feed; Speak truly, and each word of thine Shall be a fruitful seed; Live truly, and thy life shall be A great and noble creed."

Contentio Veritatis, 128, 129—"The kingdom of God is first a state of the individual soul, and then, secondly, a society made up of those who enjoy that state." Dr. F. L. Patton: "The best way for a man to serve the church at large is to serve the church to which he belongs." Herbert Stead: "The kingdom is not to be narrowed down to the church, nor the church evaporated into the kingdom." To do the first is to set up a monstrous ecclesiasticism; to do the second is to destroy the organism through which the kingdom manifests itself and does its work in the world (W. R. Taylor). Prof. Dalman, in his work on The Words of Jesus in the Light of Postbiblical Writing and the Aramaic Language, contends that the Greek phrase translated "kingdom of God" should be rendered "the sovereignty of God." He thinks that it points to the reign of God, rather than to the realm over which he reigns. This rendering, if accepted, takes away entirely the support from the Ritschlian conception of the kingdom of God as an earthly and outward organization.

(d) The individual church may be defined as that smaller company of regenerate persons, who, in any given community, unite themselves voluntarily together, in accordance with Christ's laws, for the purpose of securing the complete establishment of his kingdom in themselves and in the world.

Mat. 18:17—"And if he refuse to hear them, tell it unto the church: and if he refuse to hear the church also, let him be unto thee as the Gentile and the publican"; Acts 14:23—"appointed for them elders in every church"; Rom. 16:5—"salute the church that is in their house"; 1 Cor. 1:2—"the church of God which is at Corinth"; 4:17—"even as I teach everywhere in every church"; 1 Thess. 2:14—"the churches of God which are in Judæa in Christ Jesus."

We do not define the church as a body of "baptized believers," because baptism is but one of "Christ's laws," in accordance with which believers unite themselves. Since these laws are the laws of church-organization contained in the New Testament, no Sunday School, Temperance Society, or Young Men's Christian Association, is properly a church. These organizations 1. lack the transcendent element—they are instituted and managed by man only; 2. they are not confined to the regenerate, or to those alone who give credible evidence of regeneration; 3. they presuppose and require no particular form of doctrine; 4. they observe no ordinances; 5. they are at best mere adjuncts and instruments of the church, but are not themselves churches; 6. their decisions therefore are devoid of the divine authority and obligation which belong to the decisions of the church.

The laws of Christ, in accordance with which believers unite themselves into churches, may be summarized as follows: 1. the sufficiency and sole authority of Scripture as the rule both of doctrine and polity; (2) credible evidence of regeneration and conversion as prerequisite to church-membership; (3) immersion only, as answering to Christ's command of baptism, and to the symbolic meaning of the ordinance; (4) the order of the ordinance, Baptism, and the Lord's Supper, as of divine appointment, as well as the ordinances themselves; (5) the right of each member of the church to a voice in its government and discipline; (6) each church, while holding fellowship with other churches, solely responsible to Christ; (7) the freedom of the individual conscience, and the total independence of church and state. Hovey in his Restatement of Denominational Principles (Am. Bap. Pub. Society) gives these principles as follows: 1. the supreme authority of the Scriptures in matters of religion; 2. personal accountability to God in religion; 3. union with Christ essential to salvation; 4. a new life the only evidence of that union; 5. the new life one of unqualified obedience to Christ. The most concise statement of Baptist doctrine and history is that of Vedder, in Jackson's Dictionary of Religious Knowledge, 1:74-85.

With the lax views of Scripture which are becoming common among us there is a tendency in our day to lose sight of the transcendent element in the church. Let us remember that the church is not a humanitarian organization resting upon common human brotherhood, but a supernatural body, which traces its descent from the second, not the first, Adam, and which manifests the power of the divine Christ. Mazzini in Italy claimed Jesus, but repudiated his church. So modern socialists cry: "Liberty,

Equality, Fraternity," and deny that there is need of anything more than human unity, development, and culture. But God has made the church to sit with Christ "in the heavenly places" (Eph. 2:6). It is the regeneration which comes about through union with Christ which constitutes the primary and most essential element in ecclesiology. "We do not stand, first of all, for restricted communion, nor for immersion as the only valid form of baptism, nor for any particular theory of Scripture, but rather for a regenerate church membership. The essence of the gospel is a new life in Christ, of which Christian experience is the outworking and Christian consciousness is the witness. Christian life is as important as conversion. Faith must show itself by works. We must seek the temporal as well as spiritual salvation of men, and the salvation of society also" (Leighton Williams).

E. G. Robinson: "Christ founded a church only proleptically. In Mat. 18:17, ἐκκλησία is not used technically. The church is an outgrowth of the Jewish synagogue, though its method and economy are different. There was little or no organization at first. Christ himself did not organize the church. This was the work of the apostles after Pentecost. The germ however existed before. Three persons may constitute a church, and may administer the ordinances. Councils have only advisory authority. Diocesan episcopacy is antiscriptural and antichristian."

The principles mentioned above are the essential principles of Baptist churches, although other bodies of Christians have come to recognise a portion of them. Bodies of Christians which refuse to accept these principles we may, in a somewhat loose and modified sense, call churches; but we cannot regard them as churches organized in all respects according to Christ's laws, or as completely answering to the New Testament model of church organization. We follow common usage when we address a Lieutenant Colonel as "Colonel," and a Lieutenant Governor as "Governor." It is only courtesy to speak of pedobaptist organizations as "churches," although we do not regard these churches as organized in full accordance with Christ's laws as they are indicated to us in the New Testament. To refuse thus to recognize them would be a discourtesy like that of the British Commander in Chief, when he addressed General Washington as "Mr. Washington."

As Luther, having found the doctrine of justification by faith, could not recognize that doctrine as Christian which taught justification by works, but denounced the church which held it as Antichrist, saying, "Here I stand; I cannot do otherwise, God help me," so we, in matters not indifferent, as feet-washing, but vitally affecting the existence of the church, as regenerate church-membership, must stand by the New Testament, and refuse to call any other body of Christians a regular church, that is not organized according to Christ's laws. The English word "church" like the Scotch "kirk" and the German "Kirche," is derived from the Greek κυριακή, and means "belonging to the Lord." The term itself should teach us to regard only Christ's laws as our rule of organization.

(e) Besides these two significations of the term "church," there are properly in the New Testament no others. The word ἐκκλησία is indeed used in Acts 7:38; 19:32, 39; Heb. 2:12, to designate a popular assembly; but since this is a secular use of the term, it does not here concern us. In certain passages, as for example Acts 9:31 (ἐκκλησία, sing., ℵ A B C), 1 Cor. 12:28, Phil. 3:6, and 1 Tim. 3:15, ἐκκλησία appears to be used either as a generic or as a collective term, to denote simply the body of independent local churches existing in a given region or at a given epoch. But since there is no evidence that these churches were bound together in any outward organization, this use of the term ἐκκλησία cannot be regarded as adding any new sense to those of "the universal church" and "the local church" already mentioned.

Acts 7:38—"the church [marg. 'congregation'] in the wilderness" = the whole body of the people of Israel; 19:32—"the assembly was in confusion"—the tumultuous mob in the theatre at Ephesus; 39—"the regular assembly"; 9:31—"So the church throughout all Judæa and Galilee and Samaria had peace, being edified"; 1 Cor. 12:28—"And God hath set some in the church, first apostles, secondly prophets, thirdly teachers"; Phil. 3:6—"as touching zeal, persecuting the church"; 1 Tim. 3:15—"that thou mayest know how men ought to behave themselves in the house of God, which is the church of the living God, the pillar and ground of the truth."

In the original use of the word ἐκκλησία, as a popular assembly, there was doubtless an allusion to the derivation from ἐκ and καλέω, to call out by herald. Some have held that the N. T. term contains an allusion to the fact that the members of Christ's church are called, chosen, elected by God. This, however, is more than doubtful. In common use, the term had lost its etymological meaning, and signified merely an assembly, however gathered or summoned. The church was never so large that it could not assemble. The church of Jerusalem gathered for the choice of deacons (Acts 6:2, 5), and the church of Antioch gathered to hear Paul's account of his missionary journey (Acts 14:27).

It is only by a common figure of rhetoric that many churches are spoken of together in the singular number, in such passages as Acts 9:31. We speak generically of "man," meaning the whole race of men; and of "the horse," meaning all horses. Gibbon, speaking of the successive tribes that swept down upon the Roman Empire, uses a noun in the singular number, and describes them as "the several detachments of that immense army of northern barbarians,"—yet he does not mean to intimate that these tribes had any common government. So we may speak of "the American college" or "the American theological seminary," but we do not thereby mean that the colleges or the seminaries are bound together by any tie of outward organization.

So Paul says that God has set in the church apostles, prophets, and teachers (1 Cor. 12:28), but the word "church" is only a collective term for the many independent churches. In this same sense, we may speak of "the Baptist church" of New York, or of America; but it must be remembered that we use the term without any such implication of common government as is involved in the phrases "the Presbyterian church," or "the Protestant Episcopal church," or "the Roman Catholic church"; with us, in this connection, the term "church" means simply "churches."

Broadus, in his Com. on Mat., page 359, suggests that the word ἐκκλησία in Acts 9:31, "denotes the original church at Jerusalem, whose members were by the persecution widely scattered throughout Judea and Galilee and Samaria, and held meetings wherever they were, but still belonged to the one original organization.... When Paul wrote to the Galatians, nearly twenty years later, these separate meetings had been organized into distinct churches, and so he speaks (Gal. 1:22) in reference to that same period, of 'the churches of Judæa which were in Christ.' " On the meaning of ἐκκλησία, see Cremer, Lex. N. T., 329; Trench, Syn. N. T., 1:18; Girdlestone, Syn. O. T., 367; Curtis, Progress of Baptist Principles, 301; Dexter, Congregationalism, 25; Dagg, Church Order, 100-120; Robinson, N. T. Lex., sub voce.

The prevailing usage of the N. T. gives to the term ἐκκλησία the second of these two significations. It is this local church only which has definite and temporal existence, and of this alone we henceforth treat. Our definition of the individual church implies the two following particulars:

A. The church, like the family and the state, is an institution of divine appointment.

This is plain: (a) from its relation to the church universal, as its concrete embodiment; (b) from the fact that its necessity is grounded in the social and religious nature of man; (c) from the Scripture,—as for example, Christ's command in Mat. 18:17, and the designation "church of God," applied to individual churches (1 Cor. 1:2).

President Wayland: "The universal church comes before the particular church. The society which Christ has established is the foundation of every particular association calling itself a church of Christ." Andrews, in Bib. Sac., Jan. 1883:35-58, on the conception ἐκκλησία in the N. T., says that "the 'church' is the prius of all local 'churches.' ἐκκλησία in Acts 9:31 = the church, so far as represented in those provinces. It is ecumenical-local, as in 1 Cor. 10:33. The local church is a microcosm, a specialized localization of the universal body. קהל, in the O. T. and in the Targums, means the whole congregation of Israel, and then secondarily those local bodies which were parts and representations of the whole. Christ, using Aramaic, probably used קהל in Mat. 18:17. He took his idea of the church from it, not from the heathen use of the word ἐκκλησία, which expresses the notion of locality and state much more than קהל. The larger sense of ἐκκλησία is the primary. Local churches are points of consciousness and activity for the great all-inclusive unit, and they are not themselves the units for an ecclesiastical aggregate. They are faces, not parts of the one church."

Christ, in Mat. 18:17, delegates authority to the whole congregation of believers, and at the same time limits authority to the local church. The local church is not an end in itself, but exists for the sake of the kingdom. Unity is not to be that of merely local churches, but that of the kingdom, and that kingdom is internal, "cometh not with observation" (Luke 17:20), but consists in "righteousness and peace and joy in the Holy Spirit" (Rom. 14:17). The word "church," in the universal sense, is not employed by any other N. T. writer before Paul. Paul was interested, not simply in individual conversions, but in the growth of the church of God, as the body of Christ. He held to the unity of all local churches with the mother church at Jerusalem. The church in a city or in a house is merely a local manifestation of the one universal church and derived its dignity therefrom. Teaching of the Twelve Apostles: "As this broken bread was scattered upon the mountains, and being gathered became one, so may thy church be gathered together from the ends of the earth into thy kingdom."

Sabatier, Philos. Religion, 92—"The social action of religion springs from its very essence. Men of the same religion have no more imperious need than that of praying and worshiping together. State police have always failed to confine growing religious sects within the sanctuary or the home ... God, it is said, is the place where spirits blend. In rising toward him, man necessarily passes beyond the limits of his own individuality. He feels instinctively that the principle of his being is the principle of the life of his brethren also, that that which gives him safety must give it to all." Rothe held that, as men reach the full development of their nature and appropriate the perfection of the Savior, the separation between the religious and the moral life will vanish, and the Christian state, as the highest sphere of human life representing all human functions, will displace the church. "In proportion as the Savior Christianizes the state by means of the church, must the progressive completion of the structure of the church prove the cause of its abolition. The decline of the church is not therefore to be deplored, but is to be recognized as the consequence of the independence and completeness of the religious life" (Encyc. Brit., 21:2). But it might equally be maintained that the state, as well as the church, will pass away, when the kingdom of God is fully come; see John 4:21—"the hour cometh, when neither in this mountain, nor in Jerusalem, shall ye worship the Father"; 1 Cor. 15:24—"Then cometh the end, when he shall deliver up the kingdom to God, even the Father; when he shall have abolished all rule and all authority and power"; Rev. 21:22—"And I saw no temple therein: for the Lord God the Almighty, and the Lamb, are the temple thereof."

B. The church, unlike the family and the state, is a voluntary society.

(a) This results from the fact that the local church is the outward expression of that rational and free life in Christ which characterizes the church as a whole. In this it differs from those other organizations of divine appointment, entrance into which is not optional. Membership in the church is not hereditary or compulsory. (b) The doctrine of the church, as thus defined, is a necessary outgrowth of the doctrine of regeneration. As this fundamental spiritual change is mediated not by outward appliances, but by inward and conscious reception of Christ and his truth, union with the church logically follows, not precedes, the soul's spiritual union with Christ.

We have seen that the church is the body of Christ. We now perceive that the church is, by the impartation to it of Christ's life, made a living body, with duties and powers of its own. A. J. Gordon, Ministry of the Spirit, 53, emphasizes the preliminary truth. He shows that the definition: The church a voluntary association of believers, united together for the purposes of worship and edification, is most inadequate, not to say incorrect. It is no more true than that hands and feet are voluntarily united in the human body for the purposes of locomotion and work. The church is formed from within. Christ, present by the Holy Ghost, regenerating men by the sovereign action of the Spirit, and organizing them into himself as the living centre, is the only principle that can explain the existence of the church. The Head and the body are therefore one—one in fact, and one in name. He whom God anointed and filled with the Holy Ghost is called "the Christ" (1 John 5:1—"Whosoever believeth that Jesus is the Christ is begotten of God"); and the church which is his body and fulness is also called "the Christ" (1 Cor. 12:12—"all the members of the body, being many, are one body; so also is the Christ").

Dorner includes under his doctrine of the church: (1) the genesis of the church, through the new birth of the Spirit, or Regeneration; (2) the growth and persistence of the church through the continuous operation of the Spirit in the means of grace, or Ecclesiology proper, as others call it; (3) the completion of the church, or Eschatology. While this scheme seems designed to favor a theory of baptismal regeneration, we must commend its recognition of the fact that the doctrine of the church grows out of the doctrine of regeneration and is determined in its nature by it. If regeneration has always conversion for its obverse side, and if conversion always includes faith in Christ, it is vain to speak of regeneration without faith. And if union with the church is but the outward expression of a preceding union with Christ which involves regeneration and conversion, then involuntary church-membership is an absurdity, and a misrepresentation of the whole method of salvation.

The value of compulsory religion may be illustrated from David Hume's experience. A godly matron of the Canongate, so runs the story, when Hume sank in the mud in her vicinity, and on account of his obesity could not get out, compelled the sceptic to say the Lord's Prayer before she would help him. Amos Kendall, on the other hand, concluded in his old age that he had not been acting on Christ's plan for saving the world, and so, of his own accord, connected himself with the church. Martineau, Study, 1:319—"Till we come to the State and the Church, we do not reach the highest organism of human life, into the perfect working of which all the disinterested affections and moral enthusiasms and noble ambitions flow."

Socialism abolishes freedom, which the church cultivates and insists upon as the principle of its life. Tertullian: "Nec religionis est cogere religionem"—"It is not the business of religion to compel religion." Vedder, History of the Baptists: "The community of goods in the church at Jerusalem was a purely voluntary matter; see Acts 5:4—'While it remained, did it not remain thine own? and after it was sold, was it not in thy power?' The community of goods does not seem to have continued in the church at Jerusalem after the temporary stress had been relieved, and there is no reason to believe that any other church in the apostolic age practised anything of the kind." By abolishing freedom, socialism destroys all possibility of economical progress. The economical principle of socialism is that, relatively to the enjoyment of commodities, the individual shall be taken care of by the community, to the effect of his being relieved of the care of himself. The communism in the Acts was: 1. not for the community of mankind in general, but only for the church within itself; 2. not obligatory, but left to the discretion of individuals; 3. not permanent, but devised for a temporary crisis. On socialism, see James MacGregor, in Presb. and Ref. Rev., Jan. 1892:35-68.

Schurman, Agnosticism, 166—"Few things are of more practical consequence for the future of religion in America than the duty of all good men to become identified with the visible church. Liberal thinkers have, as a rule, underestimated the value of the church. Their point of view is individualistic, 'as though a man were author of himself, and knew no other kin.' 'The old is for slaves' they declare. But it is also true that the old is for freedmen who know its true uses. It is the bane of the religion of dogma that it has driven many of the choicest religious souls out of the churches. In its purification of the temple, it has lost sight of the object of the temple. The church, as an institution, is an organism and embodiment such as the religion of spirit necessarily creates. Spiritual religion is not the enemy, it is the essence, of institutional religion."

II. Organization of the Church

1. The fact of organization.

Organization may exist without knowledge of writing, without written records, lists of members, or formal choice of officers. These last are the proofs, reminders, and helps of organization, but they are not essential to it. It is however not merely informal, but formal, organization in the church, to which the New Testament bears witness.

That there was such organization is abundantly shown from (a) its stated meetings, (b) elections, and (c) officers; (d) from the designations of its ministers, together with (e) the recognized authority of the minister and of the church; (f) from its discipline, (g) contributions, (h) letters of commendation, (i) registers of widows, (j) uniform customs, and (k) ordinances; (l) from the order enjoined and observed, (m) the qualifications for membership, and (n) the common work of the whole body.

(a) Acts 20:7—"upon the first day of the week, when we were gathered together to break bread, Paul discoursed with them"; Heb. 10:25—"not forsaking our own assembling together, as the custom of some is, but exhorting one another."

(b) Acts 1:23-26—the election of Matthias; 6:5, 6—the election of deacons.

(c) Phil. 1:1—"the saints in Christ Jesus that are at Philippi, with the bishops and deacons."

(d) Acts 20:17, 28—"the elders of the church ... the flock, in which the Holy Spirit hath made you bishops [marg.: 'overseers']."

(e) Mat. 18:17—"And if he refuse to hear them, tell it unto the church: and if he refuse to hear the church also, let him be unto thee as the Gentile and the publican"; 1 Pet. 5:2—"Tend the flock of God which is among you, exercising the oversight, not of constraint, but willingly, according to the will of God."

(f) 1 Cor. 5:4, 5, 13—"in the name of our Lord Jesus, ye being gathered together, and my spirit, with the power of our Lord Jesus, to deliver such a one unto Satan for the destruction of the flesh, that the spirit may be saved in the day of the Lord Jesus.... Put away the wicked man from among yourselves."

(g) Rom. 15:26—"For it hath been the good pleasure of Macedonia and Achaia to make a certain contribution for the poor among the saints that are at Jerusalem"; 1 Cor. 16:1, 2—"Now concerning the collection for the saints, as I gave order to the churches of Galatia, so also do ye. Upon the first day of the week let each one of you lay by him in store, as he may prosper, that no collection be made when I come."

(h) Acts 18:27—"And when he was minded to pass over into Achaia, the brethren encouraged him, and wrote to the disciples to receive him"; 2 Cor. 3:1—"Are we beginning again to commend ourselves? or need we, as do some, epistles of commendation to you or from you?"

(i) 1 Tim. 5:9—"Let none be enrolled as a widow under threescore years old"; cf. Acts 6:1—"there arose a murmuring of the Grecian Jews against the Hebrews, because their widows were neglected in the daily ministration."

(j) 1 Cor. 11:16—"But if any man seemeth to be contentious, we have no such custom, neither the churches of God."

(k) Acts 2:41—"They then that received his word were baptized"; 1 Cor. 11:23-26—"For I received of the Lord that which also I delivered unto you"—the institution of the Lord's Supper.

(l) 1 Cor. 14:40—"let all things be done decently and in order"; Col. 2:5—"For though I am absent in the flesh, yet am I with you in the spirit, joying and beholding your order, and the stedfastness of your faith in Christ."

(m) Mat. 28:19—"Go ye therefore, and make disciples of all the nations, baptizing them into the name of the Father and of the Son and of the Holy Spirit"; Acts 2:47—"And the Lord added to them day by day those that were being saved."

(n) Phil. 2:30—"because for the work of Christ he came nigh unto death, hazarding his life to supply that which was lacking in your service toward me."

As indicative of a developed organization in the N. T. church, of which only the germ existed before Christ's death, it is important to notice the progress in names from the Gospels to the Epistles. In the Gospels, the word "disciples" is the common designation of Christ's followers, but it is not once found in the Epistles. In the Epistles, there are only "saints," "brethren," "churches." A consideration of the facts here referred to is sufficient to evince the unscriptural nature of two modern theories of the church:

A. The theory that the church is an exclusively spiritual body, destitute of all formal organization, and bound together only by the mutual relation of each believer to his indwelling Lord.

The church, upon this view, so far as outward bonds are concerned, is only an aggregation of isolated units. Those believers who chance to gather at a particular place, or to live at a particular time, constitute the church of that place or time. This view is held by the Friends and by the Plymouth Brethren. It ignores the tendencies to organization inherent in human nature; confounds the visible with the invisible church; and is directly opposed to the Scripture representations of the visible church as comprehending some who are not true believers.

Acts 5:1-11—Ananias and Sapphira show that the visible church comprehended some who were not true believers; 1 Cor. 14:23—"If therefore the whole church be assembled together and all speak with tongues, and there come in men unlearned or unbelieving, will they not say that ye are mad?"—here, if the church had been an unorganized assembly, the unlearned visitors who came in would have formed a part of it; Phil. 3:18—"For many walk, of whom I told you often, and now tell you even weeping, that they are the enemies of the cross of Christ."

Some years ago a book was placed upon the Index, at Rome, entitled: "The Priesthood a Chronic Disorder of the Human Race." The Plymouth Brethren dislike church organizations, for fear they will become machines; they dislike ordained ministers, for fear they will become bishops. They object to praying for the Holy Spirit, because he was given on Pentecost, ignoring the fact that the church after Pentecost so prayed: see Acts 4:31—"And when they had prayed, the place was shaken wherein they were gathered together; and they were all filled with the Holy Spirit, and they spake the word of God with boldness." What we call a giving or descent of the Holy Spirit is, since the Holy Spirit is omnipresent, only a manifestation of the power of the Holy Spirit, and this certainly may be prayed for; see Luke 11:13—"If ye then, being evil, know how to give good gifts unto your children, how much more shall your heavenly Father give the Holy Spirit to them that ask him?"

The Plymouth Brethren would "unite Christendom by its dismemberment, and do away with all sects by the creation of a new sect, more narrow and bitter in its hostility to existing sects than any other." Yet the tendency to organize is so strong in human nature, that even Plymouth Brethren, when they meet regularly together, fall into an informal, if not a formal, organization; certain teachers and leaders are tacitly recognized as officers of the body; committees and rules are unconsciously used for facilitating business. Even one of their own writers, C. H. M., speaks of the "natural tendency to association without God,—as in the Shinar Association or Babel Confederacy of Gen. 11, which aimed at building up a name upon the earth. The Christian church is God's appointed association to take the place of all these. Hence God confounds the tongues in Gen. 11 (judgment); gives tongues in Acts 2 (grace); but only one tongue is spoken in Rev. 7 (glory)."

The Nation, Oct. 16, 1890:303—"Every body of men must have one or more leaders. If these are not provided, they will make them for themselves. You cannot get fifty men together, at least of the Anglo-Saxon race, without their choosing a presiding officer and giving him power to enforce rules and order." Even socialists and anarchists have their leaders, who often exercise arbitrary power and oppress their followers. Lyman Abbott says nobly of the community of true believers: "The grandest river in the world has no banks; it rises in the Gulf of Mexico; it sweeps up through the Atlantic Ocean along our coast; it crosses the Atlantic, and spreads out in great broad fanlike form along the coast of Europe; and whatever land it kisses blooms and blossoms with the fruit of its love. The apricot and the fig are the witness of its fertilizing power. It is bound together by the warmth of its own particles, and by nothing else." This is a good illustration of the invisible church, and of its course through the world. But the visible church is bound to be distinguishable from unregenerate humanity, and its inner principle of association inevitably leads to organization.

Dr. Wm. Reid, Plymouth Brethrenism Unveiled, 79-143, attributes to the sect the following Church-principles: (1) the church did not exist before Pentecost; (2) the visible and the invisible church identical; (3) the one assembly of God; (4) the presidency of the Holy Spirit; (5) rejection of a one-man and man-made ministry; (6) the church is without government. Also the following heresies: (1) Christ's heavenly humanity; (2) denial of Christ's righteousness, as being obedience to law; (3) denial that Christ's righteousness is imputed; (4) justification in the risen Christ; (5) Christ's non-atoning sufferings; (6) denial of moral law as rule of life; (7) the Lord's day is not the Sabbath; (8) perfectionism; (9) secret rapture of the saints,—caught up to be with Christ. To these we may add; (10) premillennial advent of Christ.

On the Plymouth Brethren and their doctrine, see British Quar., Oct. 1873:202; Princeton Rev., 1872:48-77; H. M. King, in Baptist Review, 1881:438-465; Fish, Ecclesiology, 314-316; Dagg, Church Order, 80-83; R. H. Carson, The Brethren, 8-14; J. C. L. Carson, The Heresies of the Plymouth Brethren; Croskery, Plymouth Brethrenism; Teulon, Hist. and Teachings of Plymouth Brethren.

B. The theory that the form of church organization is not definitely prescribed in the New Testament, but is a matter of expediency, each body of believers being permitted to adopt that method of organization which best suits its circumstances and condition.

The view under consideration seems in some respects to be favored by Neander, and is often regarded as incidental to his larger conception of church history as a progressive development. But a proper theory of development does not exclude the idea of a church organization already complete in all essential particulars before the close of the inspired canon, so that the record of it may constitute a providential example of binding authority upon all subsequent ages. The view mentioned exaggerates the differences of practice among the N. T. churches; underestimates the need of divine direction as to methods of church union; and admits a principle of 'church powers,' which may be historically shown to be subversive of the very existence of the church as a spiritual body.

Dr. Galusha Anderson finds the theory of optional church government in Hooker's Ecclesiastical Polity, and says that not until Bishop Bancroft was there claimed a divine right of Episcopacy. Hunt, also, in his Religious Thought in England, 1:57, says that Hooker gives up the divine origin of Episcopacy. So Jacob, Eccl. Polity of the N. T., and Hatch, Organization of Early Christian Churches,—both Jacob and Hatch belonging to the Church of England. Hooker identified the church with the nation; see Eccl. Polity, book viii, chap. 1:7; 4:6; 8:9. He held that the state has committed itself to the church, and that therefore the church has no right to commit itself to the state. The assumption, however, that the state has committed itself to the church is entirely unwarranted; see Gore, Incarnation, 209, 210. Hooker declares that, even if the Episcopalian order were laid down in Scripture, which he denies, it would still not be unalterable, since neither "God's being the author of laws for the government of his church, nor his committing them unto Scripture, is any reason sufficient wherefore all churches should forever be bound to keep them without change."

T. M. Lindsay, in Contemp. Rev., Oct. 1895:548-563, asserts that there were at least five different forms of church government in apostolic times: 1. derived from the seven wise men of the Hebrew village community, representing the political side of the synagogue system; 2. derived from the ἐπισκόπος, the director of the religious or social club among the heathen Greeks; 3. derived from the patronate (προστάτης, προϊστάμενος) known among the Romans, the churches of Rome, Corinth, Thessalonica, being of this sort; 4. derived from the personal preëminence of one man, nearest in family to our Lord, James being president of the church at Jerusalem; 5. derived from temporary superintendents (ἡγούμενοι), or leaders of the band of missionaries, as in Crete and Ephesus. Between all these churches of different polities, there was intercommunication and fellowship. Lindsay holds that the unity was wholly spiritual. It seems to us that he has succeeded merely in proving five different varieties of one generic type—the generic type being only democratic, with two orders of officials, and two ordinances—in other words, in showing that the simple N. T. model adopts itself to many changing conditions, while the main outlines do not change. Upon any other theory, church polity is a matter of individual taste or of temporary fashion. Shall missionaries conform church order to the degraded ideas of the nations among which they labor? Shall church government be despotic in Turkey, a limited monarchy in England, a democracy in the United States of America, and two-headed in Japan? For the development theory of Neander, see his Church History, 1:179-190. On the general subject, see Hitchcock, in Am. Theol. Rev., 1860:28-54; Davidson, Eccl. Polity, 1-42; Harvey, The Church.

2. The nature of this organization.

The nature of any organization may be determined by asking, first: who constitute its members? secondly: for what object has it been formed? and, thirdly: what are the laws which regulate its operations?

The three questions with which our treatment of the nature of this organization begins are furnished us by Pres. Wayland, in his Principles and Practices of Baptists.

A. They only can properly be members of the local church, who have previously become members of the church universal,—or, in other words, have become regenerate persons.

Only those who have been previously united to Christ are, in the New Testament, permitted to unite with his church. See Acts 2:47—"And the Lord added to them day by day those that were being saved [Am. Rev.: 'those that were saved']"; 5:14—"and believers were the more added to the Lord"; 1 Cor. 1:2—"the church of God which is at Corinth, even them that are sanctified in Christ Jesus, called to be saints, with all that call upon the name of our Lord Jesus Christ in every place, their Lord and ours."

From this limitation of membership to regenerate persons, certain results follow:

(a) Since each member bears supreme allegiance to Christ, the church as a body must recognize Christ as the only lawgiver. The relation of the individual Christian to the church does not supersede, but furthers and expresses, his relation to Christ.

1 John 2:20—"And ye have an anointing from the Holy One, and ye know all things"—see Neander, Com., in loco—"No believer is at liberty to forego this maturity and personal independence, bestowed in that inward anointing [of the Holy Spirit], or to place himself in a dependent relation, inconsistent with this birthright, to any teacher whatever among men..... This inward anointing furnishes an element of resistance to such arrogated authority." Here we have reproved the tendency on the part of ministers to take the place of the church, in Christian work and worship, instead of leading it forward in work and worship of its own. The missionary who keeps his converts in prolonged and unnecessary tutelage is also untrue to the church organization of the New Testament and untrue to Christ whose aim

in church training is to educate his followers to the bearing of responsibility and the use of liberty. Macaulay: "The only remedy for the evils of liberty is liberty." "Malo periculosam libertatem"—"Liberty is to be preferred with all its dangers." Edwin Burritt Smith: "There is one thing better than good government, and that is self-government." By their own mistakes, a self-governing people and a self-governing church will finally secure good government, whereas the "good government" which keeps them in perpetual tutelage will make good government forever impossible.

Ps. 144:12—"our sons shall be as plants grown up in their youth." Archdeacon Hare: "If a gentleman is to grow up, it must be like a tree: there must be nothing between him and heaven." What is true of the gentleman is true of the Christian. There need to be encouraged and cultivated in him an independence of human authority and a sole dependence upon Christ. The most sacred duty of the minister is to make his church self-governing and self- supporting, and the best test of his success is the ability of the church to live and prosper after he has left it or after he is dead. Such ministerial work requires self-sacrifice and self- effacement. The natural tendency of every minister is to usurp authority and to become a bishop. He has in him an undeveloped pope. Dependence on his people for support curbs this arrogant spirit. A church establishment fosters it. The remedy both for slavishness and for arrogance lies in constant recognition of Christ as the only Lord.

(b) Since each regenerate man recognizes in every other a brother in Christ, the several members are upon a footing of absolute equality (Mat. 23:8-10).

Mat. 23:8-10—"But be not ye called Rabbi: for one is your teacher, and all ye are brethren. And call no man your father on the earth: for one is your Father, even he who is in heaven"; John 15:5—"I am the vine, ye are the branches"—no one branch of the vine outranks another; one may be more advantageously situated, more ample in size, more fruitful; but all are alike in kind, draw vitality from one source. Among the planets "one star differeth from another star in glory" (1 Cor. 15:41), yet all shine in the same heaven, and draw their light from the same sun. "The serving-man may know more of the mind of God than the scholar." Christianity has therefore been the foe to heathen castes. The Japanese noble objected to it, "because the brotherhood of man was incompatible with proper reverence for rank". There can be no rightful human lordship over God's heritage (1 Pet. 5:3—"neither as lording it over the charge allotted to you, but making yourselves ensamples to the flock").

Constantine thought more highly of his position as member of Christ's church than of his position as head of the Roman Empire. Neither the church nor its pastor should be dependent upon the unregenerate members of the congregation. Many a pastor is in the position of a lion tamer with his head in the lion's mouth. So long as he strokes the fur the right way, all goes well; but, if by accident he strokes the wrong way, off goes his head. Dependence upon the spiritual body which he instructs is compatible with the pastor's dignity and faithfulness. But dependence upon those who are not Christians and who seek to manage the church with worldly motives and in a worldly way, may utterly destroy the spiritual effect of his ministry. The pastor is bound to be the impartial preacher of the truth, and to treat each member of his church as of equal importance with every other.

(c) Since each local church is directly subject to Christ, there is no jurisdiction of one church over another, but all are on an equal footing, and all are independent of interference or control by the civil power.

Mat. 22:21—"Render therefore unto Cæsar the things that are Cæsar's; and unto God the things that are God's"; Acts 5:29—"We must obey God rather than men." As each believer has personal dealings with Christ and for even the pastor to come between him and his Lord is treachery to Christ and harmful to his soul, so much more does the New Testament condemn any attempt to bring the church into subjection to any other church or combination of churches, or to make the church the creature of the state. Absolute liberty of conscience under Christ has always been a distinguishing tenet of Baptists, as it is of the New Testament (cf. Rom. 14:4—"Who art thou that judgest the servant of another? to his own lord he standeth or falleth. Yea, he shall be made to stand; for the Lord hath power to make him stand"). John Locke, 100 years before American independence: "The Baptists were the first and only propounders of absolute liberty, just and true liberty, equal and impartial liberty." George Bancroft says of Roger Williams: "He was the first person in modern Christendom to assert the doctrine of liberty of conscience in religion.... Freedom of conscience was from the first a trophy of the Baptists.... Their history is written in blood."

On Roger Williams, see John Fiske, The Beginnings of New England: "Such views are to-day quite generally adopted by the more civilized portions of the Protestant world; but it is needless to say that they were not the views of the sixteenth century, in Massachusetts or elsewhere." Cotton Mather said that Roger Williams "carried a windmill in his head," and even John Quincy Adams called him "conscientiously contentious." Cotton Mather's windmill was one that he remembered or had heard of in Holland. It had run so fast in a gale as to set itself and a whole town on fire. Leonard Bacon, Genesis of the New England Churches, vii, says of Baptist churches: "It has been claimed for these churches that from the age of the Reformation onward they have been always foremost and always consistent in maintaining the doctrine of religious liberty. Let me not be understood as calling in question their right to so great an honor."

Baptists hold that the province of the state is purely secular and civil,—religious matters are beyond its jurisdiction. Yet for economic reasons and to ensure its own preservation, it may guarantee to its citizens their religious rights, and may exempt all churches equally from burdens of taxation, in the same way in which it exempts schools and hospitals. The state has holidays, but no holy days. Hall Caine, in The Christian, calls the state, not the pillar of the church, but the caterpillar, that eats the vitals out of it. It is this, when it transcends its sphere and compels or forbids any particular form of religious teaching. On the charge that Roman Catholics were deprived of equal rights in Rhode Island, see Am. Cath. Quar. Rev., Jan. 1894:169-177. This restriction was not in the original law, but was a note added by revisers, to bring the state law into conformity with the law of the mother country. Ezra 8:22—"I was ashamed to ask of the king a band of soldiers and horsemen ... because ... The hand of our God is upon all them that seek him, for good"—is a model for the churches of every age. The church as an organized body should be ashamed to depend for revenue upon the state, although its members as citizens may justly demand that the state protect them in their rights of worship. On State and Church in 1492 and 1892, see A. H. Strong, Christ in Creation, 209-246, esp. 239-241. On taxation of church property, and opposing it, see H. C. Vedder, in Magazine of Christian Literature, Feb. 1890: 265-272.

B. The sole object of the local church is the glory of God, in the complete establishment of his kingdom, both in the hearts of believers and in the world. This object is to be promoted:

(a) By united worship,—including prayer and religious instruction; (b) by mutual watchcare and exhortation; (c) by common labors for the reclamation of the impenitent world.

(a) Heb. 10:25—"not forsaking our own assembling together, as the custom of some is, but exhorting one another." One burning coal by itself will soon grow dull and go out, but a hundred together will give a fury of flame that will set fire to others. Notice the value of "the crowd" in politics and in religion. One may get an education without going to school or college, and may cultivate religion apart from the church; but the number of such people will be small, and they do not choose the best way to become intelligent or religious.

(b) 1 Thess. 5:11—"Wherefore exhort one another, and build each other up, even as also ye do"; Heb. 3:13—"Exhort one another day by day, so long as it is called To-day; lest any one of you be hardened by the deceitfulness of sin." Churches exist in order to: 1. create ideals; 2. supply motives; 3. direct energies. They are the leaven hidden in the three measures of meal. But there must be life in the leaven, or no good will come of it. There is no use of taking to China a lamp that will not burn in America. The light that shines the furthest shines brightest nearest home.

(c) Mat. 28:19—"Go ye therefore, and make disciples of all the nations"; Acts 8:4—"They therefore that were scattered abroad went about preaching the word"; 2 Cor. 8:5—"and this, not as we had hoped, but first they gave their own selves to the Lord, and to us through the will of God"; Jude 23—"And on some have mercy, who are in doubt; and some save, snatching them out of the fire." Inscribed upon a mural tablet of a Christian church, in Aneityum in the South Seas, to the memory of Dr. John Geddie, the pioneer missionary in that field, are the words: "When he came here, there were no Christians; when he went away, there were no heathen." Inscription over the grave of David Livingstone in Westminster Abbey: "For thirty years his life was spent in an unwearied effort to evangelize the native races, to explore the undiscovered secrets, to abolish the desolating slave trade of Central Africa, where with his last words he wrote: 'All I can add in my solitude is, May Heaven's richest blessing come down on everyone, American, English or Turk, who will help to heal this open sore of the world.'"

C. The law of the church is simply the will of Christ, as expressed in the Scriptures and interpreted by the Holy Spirit. This law respects:

(a) The qualifications for membership.—These are regeneration and baptism, i. e., spiritual new birth and ritual new birth; the surrender of the inward and of the outward life to Christ; the spiritual entrance into communion with Christ's death and resurrection, and the formal profession of this to the world by being buried with Christ and rising with him in baptism.

(b) The duties imposed on members.—In discovering the will of Christ from the Scriptures, each member has the right of private judgment, being directly responsible to Christ for his use of the means of knowledge, and for his obedience to Christ's commands when these are known.

How far does the authority of the church extend? It certainly has no right to say what its members shall eat and drink; to what societies they shall belong; what alliances in marriage or in business they shall contract. It has no right, as an organized body, to suppress vice in the community, or to regenerate society by taking sides in a political canvass. The members of the church, as citizens, have duties in all these lines of activity. The function of the church is to give them religious preparation and stimulus for their work. In this sense, however, the church is to influence all human relations. It follows the model of the Jewish commonwealth rather than that of the Greek state. The Greek πόλις was limited, because it was the affirmation of only personal rights. The Jewish commonwealth was universal, because it was the embodiment of the one divine will. The Jewish state was the most comprehensive of the ancient world, admitting freely the incorporation of new members, and looking forward to a worldwide religious communion in one faith. So the Romans gave to conquered lands the protection and the rights of Rome. But the Christian church is the best example of incorporation in conquest. See Westcott, Hebrews, 386, 387; John Fiske, Beginnings of New England, 1-20; Dagg, Church Order, 74-99; Curtis on Communion, 1-61.

Abraham Lincoln: "This country cannot be half slave and half free" = the one part will pull the other over; there is an irrepressible conflict between them. So with the forces of Christ and of Antichrist in the world at large. Alexander Duff: "The church that ceases to be evangelistic will soon cease to be evangelical." We may add that the church that ceases to be evangelical will soon cease to exist. The Fathers of New England proposed "to advance the gospel in these remote parts of the world, even if they should be but as stepping-stones to those who were to follow them." They little foresaw how their faith and learning would give character to the great West. Church and school went together. Christ alone is the Savior of the world, but Christ alone cannot save the world. Zinzendorf called his society "The Mustard-seed Society" because it should remove mountains (Mat. 17:20). Hermann, Faith and Morals, 91, 238—"It is not by means of things that pretend to be imperishable that Christianity continues to live on; but by the fact that there are always persons to be found who, by their contact with the Bible traditions, become witnesses to the personality of Jesus and follow him as their guide, and therefore acquire sufficient courage to sacrifice themselves for others."

3. The genesis of this organization.

(a) The church existed in germ before the day of Pentecost,—otherwise there would have been nothing to which those converted upon that day could have been "added" (Acts 2:47). Among the apostles, regenerate as they were, united to Christ by faith and in that faith baptized (Acts 19:4), under Christ's instruction and engaged in common work for him, there were already the beginnings of organization. There was a treasurer of the body (John 13:29), and as a body they celebrated for the first time the Lord's Supper (Mat. 26:26-29). To all intents and purposes they constituted a church, although the church was not yet fully equipped for its work by the outpouring of the Spirit (Acts 2), and by the appointment of pastors and deacons. The church existed without officers, as in the first days succeeding Pentecost.

Acts 2:47—"And the Lord added to them [marg.: 'together'] day by day those that were being saved"; 19:4—"And Paul said, John baptized with the baptism of repentance, saying unto the people that they should believe on him that should come after him, that is, on Jesus"; John 13:29—"For some thought, because Judas had the bag, that Jesus said unto him, Buy what things we have need of for the feast; or, that he should give something to the poor"; Mat. 26:26-29—"And as they were eating, Jesus took bread ... and he gave to the disciples, and said, Take, eat.... And he took a cup, and gave thanks, and gave to them, saying, Drink ye all of it"; Acts 2—the Holy Spirit is poured out. It is to be remembered that Christ himself is the embodied union between God and man, the true temple of God's indwelling. So soon as the first believer joined himself to Christ, the church existed in miniature and germ.

A. J. Gordon, Ministry of the Spirit, 55, quotes Acts 2:41—"and there were added," not to them, or to the church, but, as in Acts 5:14, and 11:24—"to the Lord." This, Dr. Gordon declares, means not a mutual union of believers, but their divine coüniting with Christ; not voluntary association of Christians, but their sovereign incorporation into the Head, and this incorporation effected by the Head, through the Holy Spirit. The old proverb, "Tres faciunt ecclesiam," is always true when one of the three is Jesus (Dr. Deems). Cyprian was wrong when he said that "he who has not the church for his mother, has not God for his Father"; for this could not account for the conversion of the first Christian, and it makes salvation dependent upon the church rather than upon Christ. The Cambridge Platform, 1648, chapter 6, makes officers essential, not to the being, but only to the well being, of churches, and declares that elders and deacons are the only ordinary officers; see Dexter, Congregationalism, 439.

Fish, Ecclesiology, 14-11, by a striking analogy, distinguishes three periods of the church's life: (1) the pre-natal period, in which the church is not separated from Christ's bodily presence; (2) the period of childhood, in which the church is under tutelage, preparing for an independent life; (3) the period of maturity, in which the church, equipped with doctrines and officers, is ready for self-government. The three periods may be likened to bud, blossom, and fruit. Before Christ's death, the church existed in bud only.

(b) That provision for these offices was made gradually as exigencies arose, is natural when we consider that the church immediately after Christ's ascension was under the tutelage of inspired apostles, and was to be prepared, by a process of education, for independence and self- government. As doctrine was communicated gradually yet infallibly, through the oral and written teaching of the apostles, so we are warranted in believing that the church was gradually but infallibly guided to the adoption of Christ's own plan of church organization and of Christian work. The same promise of the Spirit which renders the New Testament an unerring and sufficient rule of faith, renders it also an unerring and sufficient rule of practice, for the church in all places and times.

John 16:12-26 is to be interpreted as a promise of gradual leading by the Spirit into all the truth; 1 Cor. 14:37—"the things which I write unto you ... they are the commandments of the Lord." An examination of Paul's epistles in their chronological order shows a progress in definiteness of teaching with regard to church polity, as well as with regard to doctrine in general. In this matter, as in other matters, apostolic instruction was given as providential exigencies demanded it. In the earliest days of the church, attention was paid to preaching rather than to organization. Like Luther, Paul thought more of church order in his later days than at the beginning of his work. Yet even in his first epistle we find the germ which is afterwards continuously developed. See:

(1) 1 Thess. 5:12, 13 (A. D. 52)—"But we beseech you, brethren, to know them that labor among you, and are over you (προϊσταμένους) in the Lord, and admonish you; and to esteem them exceeding highly in love for their work's sake."

(2) 1 Cor. 12:28 (A. D. 57)—"And God hath set some in the church, first apostles, secondly prophets, thirdly teachers, then miracles, then gifts of healings, helps [ἀντιλήψεις = gifts needed by deacons], governments [κυβερνήσεις = gifts needed by pastors], divers kinds of tongues."

(3) Rom. 12:6-8 (A. D. 58)—"And having gifts differing according to the grace that is given to us, whether prophecy, let us prophesy according to the proportion of our faith; or ministry [διακονίαν], let us give ourselves to our ministry; or he that teacheth, to his teaching; or he that exhorteth, to his exhorting: he that giveth, let him do it with liberality; he that ruleth [ὁ προϊσταμένος], with diligence; he that showeth mercy, with cheerfulness."

(4) Phil. 1:1 (A. D. 62)—"Paul and Timothy, servants of Jesus Christ, to all the saints in Christ Jesus that are at Philippi, with the bishops [ἐπισκόποις, marg.: 'overseers'] and deacons [διακόνοις]."

(5) Eph. 4:11 (A. D. 63)—"And he gave some to be apostles; and some, prophets; and some, evangelists; and some, pastors and teachers [ποιμένας καὶ διδασκάλους]."

(6) 1 Tim. 3:1, 2 (A. D. 66)—"If a man seeketh the office of a bishop, he desireth a good work. The bishop [τὸν ἐπίσκοπον] therefore must be without reproach." On this last passage, Huther in Meyer's Com. remarks: "Paul in the beginning looked at the church in its unity,—only gradually does he make prominent its leaders. We must not infer that the churches in earlier time were without leadership, but only that in the later time circumstances were such as to require him to lay emphasis upon the pastor's office and work." See also Schaff, Teaching of the Twelve Apostles, 62-75.

McGiffert, in his Apostolic Church, puts the dates of Paul's Epistles considerably earlier, as for example: 1 Thess., circ. 48; 1 Cor., c. 51, 52; Rom., 52, 53; Phil., 56-58; Eph., 52, 53, or 56-58; 1 Tim., 56-58. But even before the earliest Epistles of Paul comes James 5:14—"Is any among you sick? let him call for the elders of the church"—written about 48 A. D., and showing that within twenty years after the death of our Lord there had grown up a very definite form of church organization.

On the question how far our Lord and his apostles, in the organization of the church, availed themselves of the synagogue as a model, see Neander, Planting and Training, 28-34. The ministry of the church is without doubt an outgrowth and adaptation of the eldership of the synagogue. In the synagogue, there were elders who gave themselves to the study and expounding of the Scriptures. The synagogues held united prayer, and exercised discipline. They were democratic in government, and independent of each other. It has sometimes been said that election of officers by the membership of the church came from the Greek ἐκκλησία, or popular assembly. But Edersheim, Life and Times of Jesus the Messiah, 1:438, says of the elders of the synagogue that "their election depended on the choice of the congregation." Talmud, Berachob, 55 a: "No ruler is appointed over a congregation, unless the congregation is consulted."

(c) Any number of believers, therefore, may constitute themselves into a Christian church, by adopting for their rule of faith and practice Christ's law as laid down in the New Testament, and by associating themselves together, in accordance with it, for his worship and service. It is important, where practicable, that a council of churches be previously called, to advise the brethren proposing this union as to the desirableness of constituting a new and distinct local body; and, if it be found desirable, to recognize them, after its formation, as being a church of Christ. But such action of a council, however valuable as affording ground for the fellowship of other churches, is not constitutive, but is simply declaratory; and, without such action, the body of believers alluded to, if formed after the N. T. example, may notwithstanding be a true church of Christ. Still further, a band of converts, among the heathen or providentially precluded from access to existing churches, might rightfully appoint one of their number to baptize the rest, and then might organize, de novo, a New Testament church.

The church at Antioch was apparently self-created and self- directed. There is no evidence that any human authority, outside of the converts there, was invoked to constitute or to organize the church. As John Spillsbury put it about 1640: "Where there is a beginning, some must be first." The initiative lies in the individual convert, and in his duty to obey the commands of Christ. No body of Christians can excuse itself for disobedience upon the plea that it has no officers. It can elect its own officers. Councils have no authority to constitute churches. Their work is simply that of recognizing the already existing organization and of pledging the fellowship of the churches which they represent. If God can of the stones raise up children unto Abraham, he can also raise up pastors and teachers from within the company of believers whom he has converted and saved.

Hagenbach, Hist. Doct., 2:294, quotes from Luther, as follows: "If a company of pious Christian laymen were captured and sent to a desert place, and had not among them an ordained priest, and were all agreed in the matter, and elected one and told him to baptize, administer the Mass, absolve, and preach, such a one would be as true a priest as if all the bishops and popes had ordained him." Dexter, Congregationalism, 51—"Luther came near discovering and reproducing Congregationalism. Three things checked him: 1. he undervalued polity as compared with doctrine; 2. he reacted from Anabaptist fanaticisms; 3. he thought Providence indicated that princes should lead and people should follow. So, while he and Zwingle alike held the Bible to teach that all ecclesiastical power inheres under Christ in the congregation of believers, the matter ended in an organization of superintendents and consistories, which gradually became fatally mixed up with the state."

III. Government of the Church

1. Nature of this government in general.

It is evident from the direct relation of each member of the church, and so of the church as a whole, to Christ as sovereign and lawgiver, that the government of the church, so far as regards the source of authority, is an absolute monarchy.

In ascertaining the will of Christ, however, and in applying his commands to providential exigencies, the Holy Spirit enlightens one member through the counsel of another, and as the result of combined deliberation, guides the whole body to right conclusions. This work of the Spirit is the foundation of the Scripture injunctions to unity. This unity, since it is a unity of the Spirit, is not an enforced, but an intelligent and willing, unity. While Christ is sole king, therefore, the government of the church, so far as regards the interpretation and execution of his will by the body, is an absolute democracy, in which the whole body of members is intrusted with the duty and responsibility of carrying out the laws of Christ as expressed in his word.

The seceders from the established church of Scotland, on the memorable 18th of May, 1843, embodied in their protest the following words: We go out "from an establishment which we loved and prized, through interference with conscience, the dishonor done to Christ's crown, and the rejection of his sole and supreme authority as King in his church." The church should be rightly ordered, since it is the representative and guardian of God's truth—its "pillar and ground" (1 Tim. 3:15)—the Holy Spirit working in and through it.

But it is this very relation of the church to Christ and his truth which renders it needful to insist upon the right of each member of the church to his private judgment as to the meaning of Scripture; in other words, absolute monarchy, in this case, requires for its complement an absolute democracy. President Wayland: "No individual Christian or number of individual Christians, no individual church or number of individual churches, has original authority, or has power over the whole. None can add to or subtract from the laws of Christ, or interfere with his direct and absolute sovereignty over the hearts and lives of his subjects." Each member, as equal to every other, has right to a voice in the decisions of the whole body; and no action of the majority can bind him against his conviction of duty to Christ.

John Cotton of Massachusetts Bay, 1643, Questions and Answers: "The royal government of the churches is in Christ, the stewardly or ministerial in the churches themselves." Cambridge Platform, 1648, 10th chapter—"So far as Christ is concerned, church government is a monarchy; so far as the brotherhood of the church is concerned, it resembles a democracy." Unfortunately the Platform goes further and declares that, in respect of the Presbytery and the Elders' power, it is also an aristocracy.

Herbert Spencer and John Stuart Mill, who held diverse views in philosophy, were once engaged in controversy. While the discussion was running through the press, Mr. Spencer, forced by lack of funds, announced that he would be obliged to discontinue the publication of his promised books on science and philosophy. Mr. Mill wrote him at once, saying that, while he could not agree with him in some things, he realized that Mr. Spencer's investigations on the whole made for the advance of truth, and so he himself would be glad to bear the expense of the remaining volumes. Here in the philosophical world is an example which may well be taken to heart by theologians. All Christians indeed are bound to respect in others the right of private judgment while stedfastly adhering themselves to the truth as Christ has made it known to them.

Loyola, founder of the Society of Jesus, dug for each neophyte a grave, and buried him all but the head, asking him: "Art thou dead?" When he said: "Yes!" the General added: "Rise then, and begin to serve, for I want only dead men to serve me." Jesus, on the other hand, wants only living men to serve him, for he gives life and gives it abundantly (John 10:10). The Salvation Army, in like manner, violates the principle of sole allegiance to Christ, and like the Jesuits puts the individual conscience and will under bonds to a human master. Good intentions may at first prevent evil results; but, since no man can be trusted with absolute power, the ultimate consequence, as in the case of the Jesuits, will be the enslavement of the subordinate members. Such autocracy does not find congenial soil in America,—hence the rebellion of Mr. and Mrs. Ballington Booth.

A. Proof that the government of the church is democratic or congregational.

(a) From the duty of the whole church to preserve unity in its action.

Rom. 12:16—"Be of the same mind one toward another"; 1 Cor. 1:10—"Now I beseech you ... that ye all speak the same thing, and that there be no divisions among you; but that ye be perfected together in the same mind and in the same judgment"; 2 Cor. 13:11—"be of the same mind"; Eph. 4:3—"giving diligence to keep the unity of the Spirit in the bond of peace"; Phil. 1:27—"that ye stand fast in one spirit, with one soul striving for the faith of the gospel"; 1 Pet. 3:8—"be ye all likeminded."

These exhortations to unity are not mere counsels to passive submission, such as might be given under a hierarchy, or to the members of a society of Jesuits; they are counsels to coöperation and to harmonious judgment. Each member, while forming his own opinions under the guidance of the Spirit, is to remember that the other members have the Spirit also, and that a final conclusion as to the will of God is to be reached only through comparison of views. The exhortation to unity is therefore an exhortation to be open-minded, docile, ready to subject our opinions to discussion, to welcome new light with regard to them, and to give up any opinion when we find it to be in the wrong. The church is in general to secure unanimity by moral suasion only; though, in case of wilful and perverse opposition to its decisions, it may be necessary to secure unity by excluding an obstructive member, for schism.

A quiet and peaceful unity is the result of the Holy Spirit's work in the hearts of Christians. New Testament church government proceeds upon the supposition that Christ dwells in all believers. Baptist polity is the best possible polity for good people. Christ has made no provision for an unregenerate church-membership, and for Satanic possession of Christians. It is best that a church in which Christ does not dwell should by dissension reveal its weakness, and fall to pieces; and any outward organization that conceals inward disintegration, and compels a merely formal union after the Holy Spirit has departed, is a hindrance instead of a help to true religion.

Congregationalism is not a strong government to look at. Neither is the solar system. Its enemies call it a rope of sand. It is rather a rope of iron filings held together by a magnetic current. Wordsworth: "Mightier far Than strength of nerve or sinew, or the sway Of magic portent over sun and star, Is love." President Wayland: "We do not need any hoops of iron or steel to hold us together." At high tide all the little pools along the sea shore are fused together. The unity produced by the inflowing of the Spirit of Christ is better than any mere external unity, whether of organization or of creed, whether of Romanism or of Protestantism. The times of the greatest external unity, as under Hildebrand, were times of the church's deepest moral corruption. A revival of religion is a better cure for church quarrels than any change in church organization could effect. In the early church, though there was no common government, unity was promoted by active intercourse. Hospitality, regular delegates, itinerant apostles and prophets, apostolic and other epistles, still later the gospels, persecution, and even heresy, promoted unity—heresy compelling the exclusion of the unworthy and factious elements in the Christian community.

Dr. F. J. A. Hort, The Christian Ecclesia: "Not a word in the Epistle to the Ephesians exhibits the one ecclesia as made up of many ecclesiæ.... The members which make up the one ecclesia are not communities, but individual men.... The unity of the universal ecclesia ... is a truth of theology and religion, not a fact of what we call ecclesiastical politics.... The ecclesia itself, i. e., the sum of all its male members, is the primary body, and, it would seem, even the primary authority.... Of officers higher than elders we find nothing that points to an institution or system, nothing like the Episcopal system of later times.... The monarchical principle receives practical though limited recognition in the position ultimately held by St. James at Jerusalem, and in the temporary functions entrusted by St. Paul to Timothy and Titus." On this last statement Bartlett, in Contemp. Rev., July, 1897, says that James held an unique position as brother of our Lord, while Paul left the communities organized by Timothy and Titus to govern themselves, when once their organization was set agoing. There was no permanent diocesan episcopate, in which one man presided over many churches. The ecclesiæ had for their officers only bishops and deacons.

Should not the majority rule in a Baptist church? No, not a bare majority, when there are opposing convictions on the part of a large minority. What should rule is the mind of the Spirit. What indicates his mind is the gradual unification of conviction and opinion on the part of the whole body in support of some definite plan, so that the whole church moves together. The large church has the advantage over the small church in that the single crotchety member cannot do so much harm. One man in a small boat can easily upset it, but not so in the great ship. Patient waiting, persuasion, and prayer, will ordinarily win over the recalcitrant. It is not to be denied, however, that patience may have its limits, and that unity may sometimes need to be purchased by secession and the forming of a new local church whose members can work harmoniously together.

(b) From the responsibility of the whole church for maintaining pure doctrine and practice.

1 Tim. 3:15—"the church of the living God, the pillar and ground of the truth"; Jude 3—"exhorting you to contend earnestly for the faith which was once for all delivered unto the saints"; Rev. 2 and 3—exhortations to the seven churches of Asia to maintain pure doctrine and practice. In all these passages, pastoral charges are given, not by a so-called bishop to his subordinate priests, but by an apostle to the whole church and to all its members.

In 1 Tim. 3:15, Dr. Hort would translate "a pillar and ground of the truth"—apparently referring to the local church as one of many. Eph. 3:18—"strong to apprehend with all saints what is the breadth and length and height and depth." Edith Wharton, Vesalius in Zante, in N. A. Rev., Nov. 1892—"Truth is many- tongued. What one man failed to speak, another finds Another word for. May not all converge, In some vast utterance of which you and I, Fallopius, were but the halting syllables?" Bruce, Training of the Twelve, shows that the Twelve probably knew the whole O. T. by heart. Pandita Ramabai, at Oxford, when visiting Max Müller, recited from the Rig Veda passim, and showed that she knew more of it by heart than the whole contents of the O. T.

(c) From the committing of the ordinances to the charge of the whole church to observe and guard. As the church expresses truth in her teaching, so she is to express it in symbol through the ordinances.

Mat. 28:19, 20—"Go ye therefore, and make disciples of all the nations, baptizing them ... teaching them"; cf. Luke 24:33—"And they rose up that very hour ... found the eleven gathered together, and them that were with them"; Acts 1:15—"And in these days Peter stood up in the midst of the brethren, and said (and there was a multitude of persons gathered together, about a hundred and twenty)"; 1 Cor. 15:6—"then he appeared to above five hundred brethren at once"—these passages show that it was not to the eleven apostles alone that Jesus committed the ordinances.

1 Cor. 11:2—"Now I praise you that ye remember me in all things, and hold fast the traditions, even as I delivered them to you"; cf. 23, 24—"for I received of the Lord that which also I delivered unto you, that the Lord Jesus in the night in which he was betrayed took bread; and when he had given thanks, he brake it, and said, This is my body, which is for you: this do in remembrance of me"—here Paul commits the Lord's Supper into the charge, not of the body of officials, but of the whole church. Baptism and the Lord's Supper, therefore, are not to be administered at the discretion of the individual minister. He is simply the organ of the church; and pocket baptismal and communion services are without warrant. See Curtis, Progress of Baptist Principles, 299; Robinson, Harmony of Gospels, notes, § 170.

(d) From the election by the whole church, of its own officers and delegates. In Acts 14:23, the literal interpretation of χειροτονήσαντες is not to be pressed. In Titus 1:5, "when Paul empowers Titus to set presiding officers over the communities, this circumstance decides nothing as to the mode of choice, nor is a choice by the community itself thereby necessarily excluded."

Acts 1:23, 26—"And they put forward two ... and they gave lots for them; and the lot fell upon Matthias; and he was numbered with the eleven apostles"; 6:3, 5—"Look ye out therefore, brethren, from among you seven men of good report ... And the saying pleased the whole multitude: and they chose Stephen, ... and Philip, and Prochorus, and Nicanor, and Timon, and Parmenas, and Nicolaus"—as deacons; Acts 13:2, 3—"And as they ministered to the Lord, and fasted, the Holy Spirit said, Separate me Barnabas and Saul for the work whereunto I have called them. Then, when they had fasted and prayed and laid their hands on them, they sent them away."

On this passage, see Meyer's comment: " 'Ministered' here expresses the act of celebrating divine service on the part of the whole church. To refer αὐτῶν to the 'prophets and teachers' is forbidden by the ἀφορίσατε—and by verse 3. This interpretation would confine this most important mission-act to five persons, of whom two were the missionaries sent; and the church would have had no part in it, even through its presbyters. This agrees, neither with the common possession of the Spirit in the apostolic church, nor with the concrete cases of the choice of an apostle (ch. 1) and of deacons (ch. 6). Compare 14:27, where the returned missionaries report to the church. The imposition of hands (verse 3) is by the presbyters, as representatives of the whole church. The subject in verses 2 and 3 is 'the church'—(represented by the presbyters in this case). The church sends the missionaries to the heathen, and consecrates them through its elders."

Acts 15:2, 4, 22, 30—"the brethren appointed that Paul and Barnabas, and certain other of them, should go up to Jerusalem.... And when they were come to Jerusalem, they were received of the church and the apostles and the elders.... Then it seemed good to the apostles and the elders, with the whole church, to choose men out of their company, and send them to Antioch with Paul and Barnabas.... So they ... came down to Antioch; and having gathered the multitude together, they delivered the epistle"; 2 Cor. 8:19—"who was also appointed by the churches to travel with us in the matter of this grace"—the contribution for the poor in Jerusalem; Acts 14:23—"And when they had appointed (χειροτονήσαντες) for them elders in every church"—the apostles announced the election of the church, as a College President confers degrees, i. e., by announcing degrees conferred by the Board of Trustees. To this same effect witnesses the newly discovered Teaching of the Twelve Apostles, chapter 15: "Appoint therefore for yourselves bishops and deacons."

The derivation of χειροτονήσαντες, holding up of hands, as in a popular vote, is not to be pressed, any more than is the derivation of ἐκκλησία from καλέω. The former had come to mean simply "to appoint," without reference to the manner of appointment, as the latter had come to mean an "assembly," without reference to the calling of its members by God. That the church at Antioch "separated" Paul and Barnabas, and that this was not done simply by the five persons mentioned, is shown by the fact that, when Paul and Barnabas returned from the missionary journey, they reported not to these five, but to the whole church. So when the church at Antioch sent delegates to Jerusalem, the letter of the Jerusalem church is thus addressed: "The apostles and the elders, brethren, unto the brethren who are of the Gentiles in Antioch and Syria and Cilicia" (Acts 15:23). The Twelve had only spiritual authority. They could advise, but they did not command. Hence they could not transmit government, since they had it not. They could demand obedience, only as they convinced their hearers that their word was truth. It was not they who commanded, but their Master.

Hackett, Com. on Acts—"χειροτονησαντες is not to be pressed, since Paul and Barnabas constitute the persons ordaining. It may possibly indicate a concurrent appointment, in accordance with the usual practice of universal suffrage; but the burden of proof lies on those who would so modify the meaning of the verb. The word is frequently used in the sense of choosing, appointing, with reference to the formality of raising the hand." Per contra, see Meyer, in loco: "The church officers were elective. As appears from analogy of 6:2-6 (election of deacons), the word χειροτονήσαντες retains its etymological sense, and does not mean 'constituted' or 'created.' Their choice was a recognition of a gift already bestowed,—not the ground of the office and source of authority, but merely the means by which the gift becomes [known, recognized, and] an actual office in the church."

Baumgarten, Apostolic History, 1:456—"They—the two apostles—allow presbyters to be chosen for the community by voting." Alexander, Com. on Acts—"The method of election here, as the expression χειροτονήσαντες indicates, was the same as that in Acts 6:5, 6, where the people chose the seven, and the twelve ordained them." Barnes, Com. on Acts: "The apostles presided in the assembly where the choice was made,—appointed them in the usual way by the suffrage of the people." Dexter, Congregationalism, 138—" 'Ordained' means here 'prompted and secured the election' of elders in every church." So in Titus 1:5—"appoint elders in every city." Compare the Latin: "dictator consules creavit" = prompted and secured the election of consuls by the people. See Neander, Church History, 1:189; Guericke, Church History, 1:110; Meyer, on Acts 13:2.

The Watchman, Nov. 7, 1901—"The root-difficulty with many schemes of statecraft is to be found in deep-seated distrust of the capacities and possibilities of men. Wendell Phillips once said that nothing so impressed him with the power of the gospel to solve our problems as the sight of a prince and a peasant kneeling side by side in a European Cathedral." Dr. W. R. Huntington makes the strong points of Congregationalism to be: 1. a lofty estimate of the value of trained intelligence in the Christian ministry; 2. a clear recognition of the duty of every lay member of a church to take an active interest in its affairs, temporal as well as spiritual. He regards the weaknesses of Congregationalism to be: 1. a certain incapacity for expansion beyond the territorial limits within which it is indigenous; 2. an undervaluation of the mystical or sacramental, as contrasted with the doctrinal and practical sides of religion. He argues for the object-symbolism as well as the verbal-symbolism of the real presence and grace of our Lord Jesus Christ. Dread of idolatry, he thinks, should not make us indifferent to the value of sacraments. Baptists, we reply, may fairly claim that they escape both of these charges against ordinary Congregationalism, in that they have shown unlimited capacity of expansion, and in that they make very much of the symbolism of the ordinances.

(e) From the power of the whole church to exercise discipline. Passages which show the right of the whole body to exclude, show also the right of the whole body to admit, members.

Mat. 18:17—"And if he refuse to hear them, tell it unto the church: and if he refuse to hear the church also, let him be unto thee as the Gentile and the publican. Verily I say unto you, What things soever ye shall bind on earth shall be bound in heaven; and what things soever ye shall loose on earth shall be loosed in heaven"—words often inscribed over Roman Catholic confessionals, but improperly, since they refer not to the decisions of a single priest, but to the decisions of the whole body of believers guided by the Holy Spirit. In Mat. 18:17, quoted above, we see that the church has authority, that it is bound to take cognizance of offences, and that its action is final. If there had been in the mind of our Lord any other than a democratic form of government, he would have referred the aggrieved party to pastor, priest, or presbytery, and, in case of a wrong decision by the church, would have mentioned some synod or assembly to which the aggrieved person might appeal. But he throws all the responsibility upon the whole body of believers. Cf. Num. 15:35—"all the congregation shall stone him with stones"—the man who gathered sticks on the Sabbath day. Every Israelite was to have part in the execution of the penalty.

1 Cor. 5:4, 5, 13—"ye being gathered together ... to deliver such a one unto Satan.... Put away the wicked man from among yourselves"; 2 Cor. 2:6, 7—"Sufficient to such a one is this punishment which

was inflicted by the many; so that contrariwise ye should rather forgive him and comfort him"; 7:11—"For behold, this selfsame thing ... what earnest care it wrought in you, yea, what clearing of yourselves.... In every thing ye approved yourselves to be pure in the matter"; 2 Thess. 3:6, 14, 15—"withdraw yourselves from every brother that walketh disorderly ... if any man obeyeth not our word by this epistle, note that man, that ye have no company with him, to the end that he may be ashamed. And yet count him not as an enemy, but admonish him as a brother." The evils in the church at Corinth were such as could exist only in a democratic body, and Paul does not enjoin upon the church a change of government, but a change of heart. Paul does not himself excommunicate the incestuous man, but he urges the church to excommunicate him.

The educational influence upon the whole church of this election of pastors and deacons, choosing of delegates, admission and exclusion of members, management of church finance and general conduct of business, carrying on of missionary operations and raising of contributions, together with responsibility for correct doctrine and practice, cannot be overestimated. The whole body can know those who apply for admission, better than pastors or elders can. To put the whole government of the church into the hands of a few is to deprive the membership of one great means of Christian training and progress. Hence the pastor's duty is to develop the self-government of the church. The missionary should not command, but advise. That minister is most successful who gets the whole body to move, and who renders the church independent of himself. The test of his work is not while he is with them, but after he leaves them. Then it can be seen whether he has taught them to follow him, or to follow Christ; whether he has led them to the formation of habits of independent Christian activity, or whether he has made them passively dependent upon himself.

It should be the ambition of the pastor not "to run the church," but to teach the church intelligently and Scripturally to manage its own affairs. The word "minister" means, not master, but servant. The true pastor inspires, but he does not drive. He is like the trusty mountain guide, who carries a load thrice as heavy as that of the man he serves, who leads in safe paths and points out dangers, but who neither shouts nor compels obedience. The individual Christian should be taught: 1. to realize the privilege of church membership; 2. to fit himself to use his privilege; 3. to exercise his rights as a church member; 4. to glory in the New Testament system of church government, and to defend and propagate it.

A Christian pastor can either rule, or he can have the reputation of ruling; but he can not do both. Real ruling involves a sinking of self, a working through others, a doing of nothing that some one else can be got to do. The reputation of ruling leads sooner or later to the loss of real influence, and to the decline of the activities of the church itself. See Coleman, Manual of Prelacy and Ritualism, 87-125; and on the advantages of Congregationalism over every other form of church-polity, see Dexter, Congregationalism, 236-296. Dexter, 290, note, quotes from Belcher's Religious Denominations of the U. S., 184, as follows: "Jefferson said that he considered Baptist church government the only form of pure democracy which then existed in the world, and had concluded that it would be the best plan of government for the American Colonies. This was eight or ten years before the American Revolution." On Baptist democracy, see Thomas Armitage, in N. Amer. Rev., March, 1887:232-243.

John Fiske, Beginnings of New England: "In a church based upon such a theology [that of Calvin], there was no room for prelacy. Each single church tended to become an independent congregation of worshipers, constituting one of the most effective schools that has ever existed for training men in local self-government." Schurman, Agnosticism, 160—"The Baptists, who are nominally Calvinists, are now, as they were at the beginning of the century, second in numerical rank [in America]; but their fundamental principle—the Bible, the Bible only—taken in connection with their polity, has enabled them silently to drop the old theology and unconsciously to adjust themselves to the new spiritual environment." We prefer to say that Baptists have not dropped the old theology, but have given it new interpretation and application; see A. H. Strong, Our Denominational Outlook, Sermon in Cleveland, 1904.

B. Erroneous views as to church government refuted by the foregoing passages.

(a) The world-church theory, or the Romanist view.—This holds that all local churches are subject to the supreme authority of the bishop of Rome, as the successor of Peter and the infallible vicegerent of Christ, and, as thus united, constitute the one and only church of Christ on earth. We reply:

First,—Christ gave no such supreme authority to Peter. Mat. 16:18, 19, simply refers to the personal position of Peter as first confessor of Christ and preacher of his name to Jews and Gentiles. Hence other apostles also constituted the foundation (Eph. 2:20; Rev. 21:14). On one occasion, the counsel of James was regarded as of equal weight with that of Peter (Acts 15:7-30), while on another occasion Peter was rebuked by Paul (Gal. 2:11), and Peter calls himself only a fellow-elder (1 Pet. 5:1).

Mat. 16:18, 19—"And I also say unto thee, that thou art Peter, and upon this rock I will build my church; and the gates of Hades shall not prevail against it. I will give unto thee the keys of the kingdom of heaven: and whatsoever thou shalt bind on earth shall be bound in heaven; and whatsoever thou shall loose on earth shall be loosed in heaven." Peter exercised this power of the keys for both Jews and

Gentiles, by being the first to preach Christ to them, and so admit them to the kingdom of heaven. The "rock" is a confessing heart. The confession of Christ makes Peter a rock upon which the church can be built. Plumptre on Epistles of Peter, Introd., 14—"He was a stone—one with that rock with which he was now joined by an indissoluble union." But others come to be associated with him: Eph. 2:20—"built upon the foundation of the apostles and prophets, Christ Jesus himself being the chief corner stone"; Rev. 21:14—"And the wall of the city had twelve foundations, and on them twelve names of the twelve apostles of the Lamb." Acts 15:7-30—the Council of Jerusalem. Gal. 2:11—"But when Cephas came to Antioch, I resisted him to the face, because he stood condemned"; 1 Pet. 5:1—"The elders therefore among you I exhort, who am a fellow- elder."

Here it should be remembered that three things were necessary to constitute an apostle: (1) he must have seen Christ after his resurrection, so as to be a witness to the fact that Christ had risen from the dead; (2) he must be a worker of miracles, to certify that he was Christ's messenger; (3) he must be an inspired teacher of Christ's truth, so that his final utterances are the very word of God. In Rom. 16:7—"Salute Andronicus and Junias, my kinsmen, and my fellow-prisoners, who are of note among the apostles" means simply: "who are highly esteemed among, or by, the apostles." Barnabas is called an apostle, in the etymological sense of a messenger: Acts 13:2, 3—"Separate me Barnabas and Saul for the work whereunto I have called them. Then, when they had fasted and prayed and laid their hands on them, they sent them away"; Heb. 3:1—"consider the Apostle and High Priest of our confession, even Jesus." In this latter sense, the number of the apostles was not limited to twelve.

Protestants err in denying the reference in Mat. 16:18 to Peter; Christ recognizes Peter's personality in the founding of his kingdom. But Romanists equally err in ignoring Peter's confession as constituting him the "rock." Creeds and confessions alone will never convert the world; they need to be embodied in living personalities in order to save; this is the grain of correct doctrine in Romanism. On the other hand, men without a faith, which they are willing to confess at every cost, will never convert the world; there must be a substance of doctrine with regard to sin, and with regard to Christ as the divine Savior from sin; this is the just contention of Protestantism. Baptist doctrine combines the merits of both systems. It has both personality and confession. It is not hierarchical, but experiential. It insists, not upon abstractions, but upon life. Truth without a body is as powerless as a body without truth. A flag without an army is even worse than an army without a flag. Phillips Brooks: "The truth of God working through the personality of man has been the salvation of the world." Pascal: "Catholicism is a church without a religion; Protestantism is a religion without a church." Yes, we reply, if church means hierarchy.

Secondly,—If Peter had such authority given him, there is no evidence that he had power to transmit it to others.

Fisher, Hist. Christian Church, 247—"William of Occam (1280-1347) composed a treatise on the power of the pope. He went beyond his predecessors in arguing that the church, since it has its unity in Christ, is not under the necessity of being subject to a single primate. He placed the Emperor and the General Council above the pope, as his judges. In matters of faith he would not allow infallibility even to the General Councils. 'Only Holy Scripture and the beliefs of the universal church are of absolute validity.' " W. Rauschenbusch, in The Examiner, July 28, 1892—"The age of an ecclesiastical organization, instead of being an argument in its favor, is presumptive evidence against it, because all bodies organized for moral or religious ends manifest such a frightful inclination to become corrupt.... Marks of the true church are: present spiritual power, loyalty to Jesus, an unworldly morality, seeking and saving the lost, self-sacrifice and self-crucifixion."

Romanism holds to a transmitted infallibility. The pope is infallible: 1. when he speaks as pope; 2. when he speaks for the whole church; 3. when he defines doctrine, or passes a final judgment; 4. when the doctrine thus defined is within the sphere of faith or morality; see Brandis, in N. A. Rev., Dec. 1892: 654. Schurman, Belief in God, 114—"Like the Christian pope, Zeus is conceived in the Homeric poems to be fallible as an individual, but infallible as head of the sacred convocation. The other gods are only his representatives and executives." But, even if the primacy of the Roman pontiff were acknowledged, there would still be abundant proof that he is not infallible. The condemnation of the letters of Pope Honorius, acknowledging monothelism and ordering it to be preached, by Pope Martin I and the first Council of Lateran in 649, shows that both could not be right. Yet both were ex cathedra utterances, one denying what the other affirmed. Perrone concedes that only one error committed by a pope in an ex cathedra announcement would be fatal to the doctrine of papal infallibility.

Martineau, Seat of Authority, 139, 140, gives instances of papal inconsistencies and contradictions, and shows that Roman Catholicism does not answer to either one of its four notes or marks of a true church, viz.: 1. unity; 2. sanctity; 3. universality; 4. apostolicity. Dean Stanley had an interview with Pope Pius IX, and came away saying that the infallible man had made more blunders in a twenty minutes' conversation than any person he had ever met. Dr. Fairbairn facetiously defines infallibility, as "inability to detect errors even where they are most manifest." He speaks of "the folly of the men who think they hold God in their custody, and distribute him to whomsoever they will." The

Pope of Rome can no more trace his official descent from Peter than Alexander the Great could trace his personal descent from Jupiter.

Thirdly,—There is no conclusive evidence that Peter ever was at Rome, much less that he was bishop of Rome.

Clement of Rome refers to Peter as a martyr, but he makes no claim for Rome as the place of his martyrdom. The tradition that Peter preached at Rome and founded a church there dates back only to Dionysius of Corinth and Irenæus of Lyons, who did not write earlier than the eighth decade of the second century, or more than a hundred years after Peter's death. Professor Lepsius of Jena submitted the Roman tradition to a searching examination, and came to the conclusion that Peter was never in Italy.

A. A. Hodge, in Princetoniana, 129—"Three unproved assumptions: 1. that Peter was primate; 2. that Peter was bishop of Rome; 3. that Peter was primate and bishop of Rome. The last is not unimportant; because Clement, for instance, might have succeeded to the bishopric of Rome without the primacy; as Queen Victoria came to the crown of England, but not to that of Hanover. Or, to come nearer home, Ulysses S. Grant was president of the United States and husband of Mrs. Grant. Mr. Hayes succeeded him, but not in both capacities!"

On the question whether Peter founded the Roman Church, see Meyer, Com. on Romans, transl., vol. 1:23—"Paul followed the principle of not interfering with another apostle's field of labor. Hence Peter could not have been laboring at Rome, at the time when Paul wrote his epistle to the Romans from Ephesus; cf. Acts 19:21; Rom. 15:20; 2 Cor. 10:16." Meyer thinks Peter was martyred at Rome, but that he did not found the Roman church, the origin of which is unknown. "The Epistle to the Romans," he says, "since Peter cannot have labored at Rome before it was written, is a fact destructive of the historical basis of the Papacy" (p. 28). See also Elliott, Horæ Apocalypticæ, 3:560.

Fourthly,—There is no evidence that he really did so appoint the bishops of Rome as his successors.

Denney, Studies in Theology, 191—"The church was first the company of those united to Christ and living in Christ; then it became a society based on creed; finally a society based on clergy." A. J. Gordon, Ministry of the Spirit, 130—"The Holy Spirit is the real 'Vicar of Christ.' Would any one desire to find the clue to the great apostasy whose dark eclipse now covers two thirds of nominal Christendom, here it is: The rule and authority of the Holy Spirit ignored in the church; the servants of the house assuming mastery and encroaching more and more on the prerogatives of the Head, till at last one man sets himself up as the administrator of the church, and daringly usurps the name of the Vicar of Christ." See also R. V. Littledale, The Petrine Claims.

The secret of Baptist success and progress is in putting truth before unity. James 3:17—"the wisdom that is from above is first pure, then peaceable." The substitution of external for internal unity, of which the apostolic succession, so called, is a sign and symbol, is of a piece with the whole sacramental scheme of salvation. Men cannot be brought into the kingdom of heaven, nor can they be made good ministers of Jesus Christ, by priestly manipulation. The Frankish wholesale conversion of races, the Jesuitical putting of obedience instead of life, the identification of the church with the nation, are all false methods of diffusing Christianity. The claims of Rome need irrefragible proof, if they are to be accepted. But they have no warrant in Scripture or in history. Methodist Review: "As long as the Bible is recognized to be authoritative, the church will face Romeward as little as Leo X will visit America to attend a Methodist campmeeting, or Justin D. Fulton be elected as his successor in the Papal chair." See Gore, Incarnation, 208, 209.

Fifthly,—If Peter did so appoint the bishops of Rome, the evidence of continuous succession since that time is lacking.

On the weakness of the argument for apostolic succession, see remarks with regard to the national church theory, below. Dexter, Congregationalism, 715—"To spiritualize and evangelize Romanism, or High Churchism, will be to Congregationalize it." If all the Roman Catholics who have come to America had remained Roman Catholics, there would be sixteen millions of them, whereas there are actually only eight millions. If it be said that the remainder have no religion, we reply that they have just as much religion as they had before. American democracy has freed them from the domination of the priest, but it has not deprived them of anything but external connection with a corrupt church. It has given them opportunity for the first time to come in contact with the church of the New Testament, and to accept the offer of salvation through simple faith in Jesus Christ.

"Romanism," says Dorner, "identifies the church and the kingdom of God. The professedly perfect hierarchy is itself the church, or its essence." Yet Moehler, the greatest modern advocate of the Romanist system, himself acknowledges that there were popes before the Reformation "whom hell has swallowed up"; see Dorner, Hist. Prot. Theol., Introd., ad finem. If the Romanist asks: "Where was your church before Luther?" the Protestant may reply: "Where was your face this morning before it was washed?" Disciples of Christ have sometimes kissed the feet of Antichrist, but it recalls an ancient story. When an Athenian noble thus, in old times, debased himself to the King of Persia, his fellow-citizens at Athens doomed him to death. See Coleman, Manual on Prelacy and Ritualism, 265-274; Park, in Bib. Sac., 2:451; Princeton Rev., Apr., 1876:265.

Sixthly,—There is abundant evidence that a hierarchical form of church government is corrupting to the church and dishonoring to Christ.

A. J. Gordon, Ministry of the Spirit, 131-140—"Catholic writers claim that the Pope, as the Vicar of Christ, is the only mouthpiece of the Holy Ghost. But the Spirit has been given to the church as a whole, that is, to the body of regenerated believers, and to every member of that body according to his measure. The sin of sacerdotalism is, that it arrogates for a usurping few that which belongs to every member of Christ's mystical body. It is a suggestive fact that the name κλῆρος, 'the charge allotted to you,' which Peter gives to the church as 'the flock of God' (1 Pet. 5:2), when warning the elders against being lords over God's heritage, now appears in ecclesiastical usage as 'the clergy,' with its orders of pontiff and prelates and lord bishops, whose appointed function it is to exercise lordship over Christ's flock.... But committees and majorities may take the place of the Spirit, just as perfectly as a pope or a bishop.... This is the reason why the light has been extinguished in many a candlestick.... The body remains, but the breath is withdrawn. The Holy Spirit is the only Administrator."

Canon Melville: "Make peace if you will with Popery, receive it into your Senate, enshrine it in your chambers, plant it in your hearts. But be ye certain, as certain as there is a heaven above you and a God over you, that the Popery thus honored and embraced is the Popery that was loathed and degraded by the holiest of your fathers; and the same in haughtiness, the same in intolerance, which lorded it over kings, assumed the prerogative of Deity, crushed human liberty, and slew the saints of God." On the strength and weakness of Romanism, see Harnack, What is Christianity? 246-263.

(b) The national-church theory, or the theory of provincial or national churches.—This holds that all members of the church in any province or nation are bound together in provincial or national organization, and that this organization has jurisdiction over the local churches. We reply:

First,—the theory has no support in the Scriptures. There is no evidence that the word ἐκκλησία in the New Testament ever means a national church organization. 1 Cor. 12:28, Phil. 3:6, and 1 Tim. 3:15, may be more naturally interpreted as referring to the generic church. In Acts 9:31, ἐκκλησία is a mere generalization for the local churches then and there existing, and implies no sort of organization among them.

1 Cor. 12:28—"And God hath set some in the church, first apostles, secondly prophets, thirdly teachers, then miracles, then gifts of healings, helps, governments, divers kinds of tongues"; Phil. 3:6—"as touching zeal, persecuting the church"; 1 Tim. 3:15—"that thou mayest know how men ought to behave themselves in the house of God, which is the church of the living God, the pillar and ground of the truth"; Acts 9:31—"So the church throughout all Judæa and Galilee and Samaria had peace, being edified." For advocacy of the Presbyterian system, see Cunningham, Historical Theology, 2:514-556; McPherson, Presbyterianism. Per contra, see Jacob, Eccl. Polity of N. T., 9—"There is no example of a national church in the New Testament."

Secondly,—It is contradicted by the intercourse which the New Testament churches held with each other as independent bodies,—for example at the Council of Jerusalem (Acts. 15:1-35).

Acts 15:2, 6, 13, 19, 22—"the brethren appointed that Paul and Barnabas, and certain other of them, should go up to Jerusalem unto the apostles and elders about this question.... And the apostles and the elders were gathered together to consider of this matter.... James answered ... my judgment is, that we trouble not them that from among the Gentiles turn to God ... it seemed good to the apostles and the elders, with the whole church, to choose men out of their company, and send them to Antioch with Paul and Barnabas."

McGiffert, Apostolic Church, 645—"The steps of developing organization were: 1. Recognition of the teaching of the apostles as exclusive standard and norm of Christian truth; 2. Confinement to a specific office, the Catholic office of bishop, of the power to determine what is the teaching of the apostles; 3. Designation of a specific institution, the Catholic church, as the sole channel of divine grace. The Twelve, in the church of Jerusalem, had only a purely spiritual authority. They could advise, but they did not command. Hence they were not qualified to transmit authority to others. They had no absolute authority themselves."

Thirdly,—It has no practical advantages over the Congregational polity, but rather tends to formality, division, and the extinction of the principles of self-government and direct responsibility to Christ.

E. G. Robinson: "The Anglican schism is the most sectarian of all the sects." Principal Rainey thus describes the position of the Episcopal Church: "They will not recognize the church standing of those who recognize them; and they only recognize the church standing of those, Greeks and Latins, who do not recognize them. Is not that an odd sort of Catholicity?" "Every priestling hides a popeling." The elephant going through the jungle saw a brood of young partridges that had just lost their mother. Touched with sympathy he said: "I will be a mother to you," and so he sat down upon them, as he had seen their mother do. Hence we speak of the "incumbent" of such and such a parish.

There were no councils that claimed authority till the second century, and the independence of the churches was not given up until the third or fourth century. In Bp. Lightfoot's essay on the Christian Ministry, in the appendix to his Com. on Philippians, progress to episcopacy is thus described: "In the time of Ignatius, the bishop, then primus inter pares, was regarded only as a centre of unity; in the time of Irenæus, as a depositary of primitive truth; in the time of Cyprian, as absolute vicegerent of Christ in things spiritual." Nothing is plainer than the steady degeneration of church polity in the hands of the Fathers. Archibald Alexander: "A better name than Church Fathers for these men would be church babies. Their theology was infantile." Luther: "Never mind the Scribes,—what saith the Scripture?"

Fourthly,—It is inconsistent with itself, in binding a professedly spiritual church by formal and geographical lines.

Instance the evils of Presbyterianism in practice. Dr. Park says that "the split between the Old and the New School was due to an attempt on the part of the majority to impose their will on the minority.... The Unitarian defection in New England would have ruined Presbyterian churches, but it did not ruin Congregational churches. A Presbyterian church may be deprived of the minister it has chosen, by the votes of neighboring churches, or by the few leading men who control them, or by one single vote in a close contest." We may illustrate by the advantage of the adjustable card-catalogue over the old method of keeping track of books in a library.

A. J. Gordon, Ministry of the Spirit, 137, note—"By the candlesticks in the Revelation being seven, instead of one as in the tabernacle, we are taught that whereas, in the Jewish dispensation, God's visible church was one, in the Gentile dispensation there are many visible churches, and that Christ himself recognizes them alike" (quoted from Garratt, Com. on Rev., 32). Bishop Moule, Veni Creator, 131, after speaking of the unity of the Spirit, goes on to say: "Blessed will it be for the church and for the world when these principles shall so vastly prevail as to find expression from within in a harmonious counterpart of order; a far different thing from what is, I cannot but think, an illusory prospect—the attainment of such internal unity by a previous exaction of exterior governmental uniformity."

Fifthly,—It logically leads to the theory of Romanism. If two churches need a superior authority to control them and settle their differences, then two countries and two hemispheres need a common ecclesiastical government,—and a world-church, under one visible head, is Romanism.

Hatch, in his Bampton Lectures on Organization of Early Christian Churches, without discussing the evidence from the New Testament, proceeds to treat of the post-apostolic development of organization, as if the existence of a germinal Episcopacy very soon after the apostles proved such a system to be legitimate or obligatory. In reply, we would ask whether we are under moral obligation to conform to whatever succeeds in developing itself. If so, then the priests of Baal, as well as the priests of Rome, had just claims to human belief and obedience. Prof. Black: "We have no objection to antiquity, if they will only go back far enough. We wish to listen, not only to the fathers of the church, but also to the grandfathers."

Phillips Brooks speaks of "the fantastic absurdity of apostolic succession." And with reason, for in the Episcopal system, bishops qualified to ordain must be: (1) baptized persons; (2) not scandalously immoral; (3) not having obtained office by bribery; (4) must not have been deposed. In view of these qualifications, Archbishop Whately pronounces the doctrine of apostolic succession untenable, and declares that "there is no Christian minister existing now, who can trace up with complete certainty his own ordination, through perfectly regular steps, to the time of the apostles." See Macaulay's Review of Gladstone on Church and State, in his Essays, 4:166-178. There are breaks in the line, and a chain is only as strong as its weakest part. See Presb. Rev., 1886:89-126. Mr. Flanders called Phillips Brooks "an Episcopalian with leanings toward Christianity." Bishop Brooks replied that he could not be angry with "such a dear old moth-eaten angel." On apostolic succession, see C. Anderson Scott, Evangelical Doctrine, 37-48, 267-288.

Apostolic succession has been called the pipe-line conception of divine grace. To change the figure, it may be compared to the monopoly of communication with Europe by the submarine cable. But we are not confined to the pipe-line or to the cable. There are wells of salvation in our private grounds, and wireless telegraphy practicable to every human soul, apart from any control of corporations.

We see leanings toward the world-church idea in Pananglican and Panpresbyterian Councils. Human nature ever tends to substitute the unity of external organization for the spiritual unity which belongs to all believers in Christ. There is no necessity for common government, whether Presbyterian or Episcopal; since Christ's truth and Spirit are competent to govern all as easily as one. It is a remarkable fact, that the Baptist denomination, without external bonds, has maintained a greater unity in doctrine, and a closer general conformity to New Testament standards, than the churches which adopt the principle of episcopacy, or of provincial organization. With Abp. Whately, we find the true symbol of Christian unity in "the tree of life, bearing twelve manner of

fruits" (Rev. 22:2). Cf. John 10:16—γενήσονται μία ποίμνη, εἷς ποιμήν—"they shall become one flock, one shepherd" = not one fold, not external unity, but one flock in many folds. See Jacob, Eccl.

Polity of N. T., 130; Dexter, Congregationalism, 236; Coleman, Manual on Prelacy and Ritualism, 128-264; Albert Barnes, Apostolic Church.

As testimonies to the adequacy of Baptist polity to maintain sound doctrine, we quote from the Congregationalist, Dr. J. L. Withrow: "There is not a denomination of evangelical Christians that is throughout as sound theologically as the Baptist denomination. There is not an evangelical denomination in America to-day that is as true to the simple plain gospel of God, as it is recorded in the word, as the Baptist denomination." And the Presbyterian, Dr. W. G. T. Shedd, in a private letter dated Oct. 1, 1886, writes as follows: "Among the denominations, we all look to the Baptists for steady and firm adherence to sound doctrine. You have never had any internal doctrinal conflicts, and from year to year you present an undivided front in defense of the Calvinistic faith. Having no judicatures and regarding the local church as the unit, it is remarkable that you maintain such a unity and solidarity of belief. If you could impart your secret to our Congregational brethren, I think that some of them at least would thank you."

A. H. Strong, Sermon in London before the Baptist World Congress, July, 1905—"Coöperation with Christ involves the spiritual unity not only of all Baptists with one another, but of all Baptists with the whole company of true believers of every name. We cannot, indeed, be true to our convictions without organizing into one body those who agree with us in our interpretation of the Scriptures. Our denominational divisions are at present necessities of nature. But we regret these divisions, and, as we grow in grace and in the knowledge of the truth, we strive, at least in spirit, to rise above them. In America our farms are separated from one another by fences, and in the springtime, when the wheat and barley are just emerging from the earth, these fences are very distinguishable and unpleasing features of the landscape. But later in the season, when the corn has grown and the time of harvest is near, the grain is so tall that the fences are entirely hidden, and for miles together you seem to see only a single field. It is surely our duty to confess everywhere and always that we are first Christians and only secondly Baptists. The tie which binds us to Christ is more important in our eyes than that which binds us to those of the same faith and order. We live in hope that the Spirit of Christ in us, and in all other Christian bodies, may induce such growth of mind and heart that the sense of unity may not only overtop and hide the fences of division, but may ultimately do away with these fences altogether."

2. Officers of the Church.

A. The number of offices in the church is two:—first, the office of bishop, presbyter, or pastor; and, secondly, the office of deacon.

(a) That the appellations "bishop," "presbyter," and "pastor" designate the same office and order of persons, may be shown from Acts 20:28—ἐπισκόπους ποιμαίνειν (cf. 17—πρεσβυτέρους); Phil. 1:1; 1 Tim. 3:1, 8; Titus 1:5, 7; 1 Pet. 5:1, 2—πρεσβυτέρους ... παρακαλῶ ὁ συμπρεσβύτερος ... ποιμάνατε ποίμνιον ... ἐπισκοποῦντες. Conybeare and Howson: "The terms 'bishop' and 'elder' are used in the New Testament as equivalent,—the former denoting (as its meaning of overseer implies) the duties, the latter the rank, of the office." See passages quoted in Gieseler, Church History, 1:90, note 1—as, for example, Jerome: "Apud veteres iidem episcopi et presbyteri, quia illud nomen dignitatis est, hoc ætatis. Idem est ergo presbyter qui episcopus."

Acts 20:28—"Take heed unto yourselves, and to all the flock, in which the Holy Spirit hath made you bishops [marg. 'overseers'], to feed [lit. 'to shepherd,' 'be pastors of'] the church of the Lord which he purchased with his own blood"; cf. 17—"the elders of the church" are those whom Paul addresses as bishops or overseers, and whom he exhorts to be good pastors. Phil. 1:1—"bishops and deacons"; 1 Tim. 3:1, 8—"If a man seeketh the office of a bishop, he desireth a good work.... Deacons in like manner must be grave"; Tit. 1:5, 7—"appoint elders in every city.... For the bishop must be blameless"; 1 Pet. 5:1, 2—"The elders therefore among you I exhort, who am a fellow-elder.... Tend [lit. 'shepherd,' 'be pastors of'] the flock of God which is among you, exercising the oversight [acting as bishops], not of constraint, but willingly, according to the will of God." In this last passage, Westcott and Hort, with Tischendorf's 8th edition, follow ℵ and B in omitting ἐπισκοποῦντες. Tregelles and our Revised Version follow A and ℵc in retaining it. Rightly, we think; since it is easy to see how, in a growing ecclesiasticism, it should have been omitted, from the feeling that too much was here ascribed to a mere presbyter.

Lightfoot, Com. on Philippians, 95-99—"It is a fact now generally recognized by theologians of all shades of opinion that in the language of the N. T. the same officer in the church is called indifferently 'bishop' (ἐπίσκοπος) and 'elder' or 'presbyter' (πρεσβύτερος).... To these special officers the priestly functions and privileges of the Christian people are never regarded as transferred or delegated. They are called stewards or messengers of God, servants or ministers of the church, and the like, but the sacerdotal is never once conferred upon them. The only priests under the gospel, designated as such in the N. T., are the saints, the members of the Christian brotherhood." On Titus 1:5, 7—"appoint elders.... For the bishop must be blameless"—Gould, Bib. Theol. N. T., 150, remarks: "Here the word 'for' is quite out of place unless bishops and elders are identical. All these officers, bishops as well as deacons, are confined to the local church in their jurisdiction. The charge of a bishop is not a diocese, but a church. The functions are mostly administrative, the teaching office being subordinate, and a distinction is made between teaching elders and others, implying that the teaching function is not common to them all."

Dexter, Congregationalism, 114, shows that bishop, elder, pastor are names for the same office: (1) from the significance of the words; (2) from the fact that the same qualifications are demanded from all; (3) from the fact that the same duties are assigned to all; (4) from the fact that the texts held to prove higher rank of the bishop do not support that claim. Plumptre, in Pop. Com., Pauline Epistles, 555, 556—"There cannot be a shadow of doubt that the two titles of Bishop and Presbyter were in the Apostolic Age interchangeable."

(b) The only plausible objection to the identity of the presbyter and the bishop is that first suggested by Calvin, on the ground of 1 Tim. 5:17. But this text only shows that the one office of presbyter or bishop involved two kinds of labor, and that certain presbyters or bishops were more successful in one kind than in the other. That gifts of teaching and ruling belonged to the same individual, is clear from Acts 20:28-31; Eph. 4:11; Heb. 13:7; 1 Tim. 3:2—ἐπίσκοπον διδακτικόν.

1 Tim. 5:17—"Let the elders that rule well be counted worthy of double honor, especially those who labor in the word and in teaching"; Wilson, Primitive Government of Christian Churches, concedes that this last text "expresses a diversity in the exercise of the Presbyterial office, but not in the office itself"; and although he was a Presbyterian, he very consistently refused to have any ruling elders in his church.

Acts 20:28, 31—"bishops, to feed the church of the Lord ... wherefore watch ye"; Eph. 4:11—"and some, pastors and teachers"—here Meyer remarks that the single article binds the two words together, and prevents us from supposing that separate offices are intended. Jerome: "Nemo ... pastoris sibi nomen assumere debet, nisi possit docere quos pascit." Heb. 13:7—"Remember them that had the rule over you, men that spake unto you the word of God"; 1 Tim. 3:2—"The bishop must be ... apt to teach." The great temptation to ambition in the Christian ministry is provided against by having no gradation of ranks. The pastor is a priest, only as every Christian is. See Jacob, Eccl. Polity of N. T., 56; Olshausen, on 1 Tim. 5:17; Hackett on Acts 14:23; Presb. Rev., 1886:89-126.

Dexter, Congregationalism, 52—"Calvin was a natural aristocrat, not a man of the people like Luther. Taken out of his own family to be educated in a family of the nobility, he received an early bent toward exclusiveness. He believed in authority and loved to exercise it. He could easily have been a despot. He assumed all citizens to be Christians until proof to the contrary. He resolved church discipline into police control. He confessed that the eldership was an expedient to which he was driven by circumstances, though after creating it he naturally enough endeavored to procure Scriptural proof in its favor." On the question, The Christian Ministry, is it a Priesthood? see C. Anderson Scott, Evangelical Doctrine, 205-224.

(c) In certain of the N. T. churches there appears to have been a plurality of elders (Acts 20:17; Phil. 1:1; Tit. 1:5). There is, however, no evidence that the number of elders was uniform, or that the plurality which frequently existed was due to any other cause than the size of the churches for which these elders cared. The N. T. example, while it permits the multiplication of assistant pastors according to need, does not require a plural eldership in every case; nor does it render this eldership, where it exists, of coördinate authority with the church. There are indications, moreover, that, at least in certain churches, the pastor was one, while the deacons were more than one, in number.

Acts 20:17—"And from Miletus he sent to Ephesus, and called to him the elders of the church"; Phil. 1:1—"Paul and Timothy, servants of Christ Jesus, to all the saints in Christ Jesus that are at Philippi, with the bishops and deacons"; Tit. 1:5—"For this cause I left thee in Crete, that thou shouldest set in order the things that were wanting, and appoint elders in every city, as I gave thee charge." See, however, Acts 12:17—"Tell these things unto James, and to the brethren"; 15:13—"And after they had held their peace, James answered, saying, Brethren, hearken unto me"; 21:18—"And the day following Paul went in with us unto James; and all the elders were present"; Gal. 1:19—"But other of the apostles saw I none, save James the Lord's brother"; 2:12—"certain came from James." These passages seem to indicate that James was the pastor or president of the church at Jerusalem, an intimation which tradition corroborates.

1 Tim. 3:2—"The bishop therefore must be without reproach"; Tit. 1:7—"For the bishop must be blameless, as God's steward"; cf. 1 Tim. 3:8, 10, 12—"Deacons in like manner must be grave.... And let these also first be proved; then let them serve as deacons, if they be blameless.... Let deacons be husbands of one wife, ruling their children and their own houses well"—in all these passages the bishop is spoken of in the singular number, the deacons in the plural. So, too, in Rev. 2:1, 8, 12, 18 and 3:1, 7, 14, "the angel of the church" is best interpreted as meaning the pastor of the church; and, if this be correct, it is clear that each church had, not many pastors, but one.

It would, moreover, seem antecedently improbable that every church of Christ, however small, should be required to have a plural eldership, particularly since churches exist that have only a single male member. A plural eldership is natural and advantageous, only where the church is very numerous and the pastor needs assistants in his work: and only in such cases can we say that New Testament example favors it. For advocacy of the theory of plural eldership, see Fish, Ecclesiology, 229-249; Ladd, Principles of Church Polity, 22-29. On the whole subject of offices in the church, see Dexter, Congregationalism, 77-98; Dagg, Church Order, 241-266; Lightfoot on the Christian Ministry, appended to his Commentary on Philippians, and published in his Dissertations on the Apostolic Age.

B. The duties belonging to these offices.

(a) The pastor, bishop, or elder is:

First,—a spiritual teacher, in public and private;

Acts 20:20, 21, 35—"how I shrank not from declaring unto you anything that was profitable, and teaching you publicly, and from house to house, testifying both to Jews and to Greeks repentance toward God, and faith toward our Lord Jesus Christ.... In all things I gave you an example, that so laboring ye ought to help the weak, and to remember the words of the Lord Jesus, that he himself said, It is more blessed to give than to receive"; 1 Thess. 5:12—"But we beseech you, brethren, to know them that labor among you, and are over you in the Lord, and admonish you"; Heb. 13:7, 17—"Remember them that had the rule over you, men that spake unto you the word of God; and considering the issue of their life, imitate their faith.... Obey them that have the rule over you, and submit to them: for they watch in behalf of your souls, as they that shall give account."

Here we should remember that the pastor's private work of religious conversation and prayer is equally important with his public ministrations; in this respect he is to be an example to his flock, and they are to learn from him the art of winning the unconverted and of caring for those who are already saved. A Jewish Rabbi once said: "God could not be every where,—therefore he made mothers." We may substitute, for the word 'mothers,' the word 'pastors.' Bishop Ken is said to have made a vow every morning, as he rose, that he would not be married that day. His own lines best express his mind: "A virgin priest the altar best attends; our Lord that state commands not, but commends."

Secondly,—administrator of the ordinances;

Mat. 28:19, 20—"Go ye therefore and make disciples of all the nations, baptizing them into the name of the Father and of the Son and of the Holy Spirit: teaching them to observe all things whatsoever I commanded"; 1 Cor. 1:16, 17—"And

I baptized also the household of Stephanas: besides, I know not whether I baptized any other. For Christ sent me not to baptize, but to preach the gospel." Here it is evident that, although the pastor administers the ordinances, this is not his main work, nor is the church absolutely dependent upon him in the matter. He is not set, like an O. T. priest, to minister at the altar, but to preach the gospel. In an emergency any other member appointed by the church may administer them with equal propriety, the church always determining who are fit subjects of the ordinances, and constituting him their organ in administering them. Any other view is based on sacramental notions, and on ideas of apostolic succession. All Christians are "priests unto ... God" (Rev. 1:6). "This universal priesthood is a priesthood, not of expiation, but of worship, and is bound to no ritual, or order of times and places" (P. S. Moxom).

Thirdly,—superintendent of the discipline, as well as presiding officer at the meetings, of the church.

Superintendent of discipline: 1 Tim. 5:17—"Let the elders that rule well be counted worthy of double honor, especially those who labor in the word and in teaching"; 3:5—"if a man knoweth not how to rule his own house, how shall he take care of the church of God?" Presiding officer at meetings of the church: 1 Cor. 12:28—"governments"—here κυβερνήσεις, or "governments," indicating the duties of the pastor, are the counterpart of ἀντιλήψεις, or "helps," which designate the duties of the deacons; 1 Pet. 5:2, 3—"Tend the flock of God which is among you, exercising the oversight, not of constraint, but willingly, according to the will of God; nor yet for filthy lucre, but of a ready mind; neither as lording it over the charge allotted to you, but making yourselves ensamples to the flock."

In the old Congregational churches of New England, an authority was accorded to the pastor which exceeded the New Testament standard. "Dr. Bellamy could break in upon a festival which he deemed improper, and order the members of his parish to their homes." The congregation rose as the minister entered the church, and stood uncovered as he passed out of the porch. We must not hope or desire to restore the New England régime. The pastor is to take responsibility, to put himself forward when there is need, but he is to rule only by moral suasion, and that only by guiding, teaching, and carrying into effect the rules imposed by Christ and the decisions of the church in accordance with those rules.

Dexter, Congregationalism, 115, 155, 157—"The Governor of New York suggests to the Legislature such and such enactments, and then executes such laws as they please to pass. He is chief ruler of the State, while the Legislature adopts or rejects what he proposes." So the pastor's functions are not legislative, but executive. Christ is the only lawgiver. In fulfilling this office, the manner and spirit of the pastor's work are of as great importance as are correctness of judgment and faithfulness to

Christ's law. "The young man who cannot distinguish the wolves from the dogs should not think of becoming a shepherd." Gregory Nazianzen: "Either teach none, or let your life teach too." See Harvey, The Pastor; Wayland, Apostolic Ministry; Jacob, Eccl. Polity of N. T., 99; Samson, in Madison Avenue Lectures, 261-288.

(b) The deacon is helper to the pastor and the church, in both spiritual and temporal things.

First,—relieving the pastor of external labors, informing him of the condition and wants of the church, and forming a bond of union between pastor and people.

Acts 6:1-6—"Now in these days, when the number of the disciples was multiplying, there arose a murmuring of the Grecian Jews against the Hebrews, because their widows were neglected in the daily ministration. And the twelve called the multitude of the disciples unto them, and said, It is not fit that we should forsake the word of God, and serve tables. Look ye out therefore, brethren, from among you seven men of good report, full of the Spirit and of wisdom, whom we may appoint over this business. But we will continue stedfastly in prayer, and in the ministry of the word. And the saying pleased the whole multitude: and they chose Stephen, a man full of faith and of the Holy Spirit, and Philip, and Prochorus, and Nicanor, and Timon, and Parmenas, and Nicolaus a proselyte of Antioch; whom they set before the apostles: and when they had prayed, they laid their hands upon them"; cf. 8-20—where Stephen shows power in disputation; Rom. 12:7—"or ministry διακονίαν, let us give ourselves to our ministry"; 1 Cor. 12:28—"helps"—here ἀντιλήψεις, "helps," indicating the duties of deacons, are the counterpart of κυβερνήσεις, "governments," which designate the duties of the pastor; Phil. 1:1—"bishops and deacons."

Dr. E. G. Robinson did not regard the election of the seven, in Acts 6:1-4, as marking the origin of the diaconate, though he thought the diaconate grew out of this election. The Autobiography of C. H. Spurgeon, 3:22, gives an account of the election of "elders" at the Metropolitan Tabernacle in London. These "elders" were to attend to the spiritual affairs of the church, as the deacons were to attend to the temporal affairs. These "elders" were chosen year by year, while the office of deacon was permanent.

Secondly,—helping the church, by relieving the poor and sick and ministering in an informal way to the church's spiritual needs, and by performing certain external duties connected with the service of the sanctuary.

Since deacons are to be helpers, it is not necessary in all cases that they should be old or rich; in fact, it is better that among the number of deacons the various differences in station, age, wealth, and opinion in the church should be represented. The qualifications for the diaconate mentioned in Acts 6:1-4 and 1 Tim. 3:8-13, are, in substance: wisdom, sympathy, and spirituality. There are advantages in electing deacons, not for life, but for a term of years. While there is no New Testament prescription in this matter, and each church may exercise its option, service for a term of years, with re-election where the office has been well discharged, would at least seem favored by 1 Tim. 3:10—"Let these also first be proved; then let them serve as deacons, if they be blameless"; 13—"For they that have served well as deacons gain to themselves a good standing, and great boldness in the faith which is in Christ Jesus."

Expositor's Greek Testament, on Acts 5:6, remarks that those who carried out and buried Ananias are called οἱ νεώτεροι—"the young men"—and in the case of Sapphira they were οἱ νεανίσκοι—meaning the same thing. "Upon the natural distinction between πρεσβύτεροι and νεώτεροι—elders and young men—it may well have been that official duties in the church were afterward based." Dr. Leonard Bacon thought that the apostles included the whole membership in the "we," when they said: "It is not fit that we should forsake the word of God, and serve tables." The deacons, on this interpretation, were chosen to help the whole church in temporal matters.

In Rom. 16:1, 2, we have apparent mention of a deaconess—"I commend unto you Phœbe our sister, who is a servant [marg.: 'deaconess'] of the church that is at Cenchreæ ... for she herself also hath been a helper of many, and of mine own self." See also 1 Tim. 3:11—"Women in like manner must be grave, not slanderers, temperate, faithful in all things"—here Ellicott and Alford claim that the word "women" refers, not to deacons' wives, as our Auth. Vers. had it, but to deaconesses. Dexter, Congregationalism, 69, 132, maintains that the office of deaconess, though it once existed, has passed away, as belonging to a time when men could not, without suspicion, minister to women.

This view that there are temporary offices in the church does not, however, commend itself to us. It is more correct to say that there is yet doubt whether there was such an office as deaconess, even in the early church. Each church has a right in this matter to interpret Scripture for itself, and to act accordingly. An article in the Bap. Quar., 1869:40, denies the existence of any diaconal rank or office, for male or female. Fish, in his Ecclesiology, holds that Stephen was a deacon, but an elder also, and preached as elder, not as deacon,—Acts 6:1-4 being called the institution, not of the diaconate, but of the Christian ministry. The use of the phrase διακονεῖν τραπέζαις, and the distinction between the diaconate and the pastorate subsequently made in the Epistles, seem to refute this interpretation. On the fitness of women for the ministry of religion, see F. P. Cobbe, Peak of Darien, 199-262; F. E. Willard, Women in the Pulpit; B. T. Roberts, Ordaining Women. On the general subject, see Howell, The Deaconship; Williams, The Deaconship; Robinson, N. T. Lexicon, ἀντιλήψις. On the Claims of the

Christian Ministry, and on Education for the Ministry, see A. H. Strong, Philosophy and Religion, 269-318, and Christ in Creation, 314-331.

C. Ordination of officers.

(a) What is ordination?

Ordination is the setting apart of a person divinely called to a work of special ministration in the church. It does not involve the communication of power,—it is simply a recognition of powers previously conferred by God, and a consequent formal authorization, on the part of the church, to exercise the gifts already bestowed. This recognition and authorization should not only be expressed by the vote in which the candidate is approved by the church or the council which represents it, but should also be accompanied by a special service of admonition, prayer, and the laying- on of hands (Acts 6:5, 6; 13:2, 3; 14:23; 1 Tim. 4:14; 5:22).

Licensure simply commends a man to the churches as fitted to preach. Ordination recognizes him as set apart to the work of preaching and administering ordinances, in some particular church or in some designated field of labor, as representative of the church.

Of his call to the ministry, the candidate himself is to be first persuaded (1 Cor. 9:16; 1 Tim. 1:12); but, secondly, the church must be persuaded also, before he can have authority to minister among them (1 Tim. 3:2-7; 4:14; Titus 1:6-9).

The word "ordain" has come to have a technical signification not found in the New Testament. There it means simply to choose, appoint, set apart. In 1 Tim. 2:7—"whereunto I was appointed [ἐτέθην] a preacher and an apostle ... a teacher of the Gentiles in faith and truth"—it apparently denotes ordination of God. In the following passages we read of an ordination by the church: Acts 6:5, 6—"And the saying pleased the whole multitude: and they chose Stephen ... and Philip, and Prochorus, and Nicanor, and Timon, and Parmenas, and Nicolaus ... whom they set before the apostles: and when they had prayed, they laid their hands upon them"—the ordination of deacons; 13:2, 3—"And as they ministered to the Lord, and fasted, the Holy Spirit said, Separate me Barnabas and Saul for the work whereunto I have called them. Then, when they had fasted and prayed and laid their hands on them, they sent them away"; 14:23—"And when they had appointed for them elders in every church, and had prayed with fasting, they commended them to the Lord, on whom they had believed"; 1 Tim. 4:14—"Neglect not the gift that is in thee, which was given thee by prophecy, with the laying on of the hands of the presbytery"; 5:22—"Lay hands hastily on no man, neither be partaker of other men's sins."

Cambridge Platform, 1648, chapter 9—"Ordination is nothing else but the solemn putting of a man into his place and office in the church whereunto he had right before by election, being like the installing of a Magistrate in the Commonwealth." Ordination confers no authority—it only recognizes authority already conferred by God. Since it is only recognition, it can be repeated as often as a man changes his denominational relations. Leonard Bacon: "The action of a Council has no more authority than the reason on which it is based. The church calling the Council is a competent court of appeal from any decision of the Council."

Since ordination is simply choosing, appointing, setting apart, it seems plain that in the case of deacons, who sustain official relations only to the church that constitutes them, ordination requires no consultation with other churches. But in the ordination of a pastor, there are three natural stages: (1) the call of the church; (2) the decision of a council (the council being virtually only the church advised by its brethren); (3) the publication of this decision by a public service of prayer and the laying-on of hands. The prior call to be pastor may be said, in the case of a man yet unordained, to be given by the church conditionally, and in anticipation of a ratification of its action by the subsequent judgment of the council. In a well-instructed church, the calling of a council is a regular method of appeal from the church unadvised to the church advised by its brethren; and the vote of the council approving the candidate is only the essential completing of an ordination, of which the vote of the church calling the candidate to the pastorate was the preliminary stage.

This setting apart by the church, with the advice and assistance of the council, is all that is necessarily implied in the New Testament words which are translated "ordain"; and such ordination, by simple vote of church and council, could not be counted invalid. But it would be irregular. New Testament precedent makes certain accompaniments not only appropriate, but obligatory. A formal publication of the decree of the council, by laying-on of hands, in connection with prayer, is the last of the duties of this advisory body, which serves as the organ and assistant of the church. The laying-on of hands is appointed to be the regular accompaniment of ordination, as baptism is appointed to be the regular accompaniment of regeneration; while yet the laying-on of hands is no more the substance of ordination, than baptism is the substance of regeneration.

The imposition of hands is the natural symbol of the communication, not of grace, but of authority. It does not make a man a minister of the gospel, any more than coronation makes Victoria a queen. What it does signify and publish, is formal recognition and authorization. Viewed in this light, there not only can be no objection to the imposition of hands upon the ground that it favors sacramentalism, but insistence upon it is the bounden duty of every council of ordination.

Mr. Spurgeon was never ordained. He began and ended his remarkable ministry as a lay preacher. He revolted from the sacramentalism of the Church of England, which seemed to hold that in the imposition of hands in ordination divine grace trickled down through a bishop's finger ends, and he felt moved to protest against it. In our judgment it would have been better to follow New Testament precedent, and at the same time to instruct the churches as to the real meaning of the laying-on of hands. The Lord's Supper had in a similar manner been interpreted as a physical communication of grace, but Mr. Spurgeon still continued to observe the Lord's Supper. His gifts enabled him to carry his people with him, when a man of smaller powers might by peculiar views have ruined his ministry. He was thankful that he was pastor of a large church, because he felt that he had not enough talent to be pastor of a small one. He said that when he wished to make a peculiar impression on his people he put himself into his cannon and fired himself at them. He refused the degree of Doctor of Divinity, and said that "D. D." often meant "Doubly Destitute." Dr. P. S. Henson suggests that the letters mean only "Fiddle Dee Dee." For Spurgeon's views on ordination, see his Autobiography, 1:355 sq.

John Wesley's three tests of a call to preach: "Inquire of applicants," he says, "1. Do they know God as a pardoning God? Have they the love of God abiding in them? Do they desire and see nothing but God? And are they holy, in all manner of conversation? 2. Have they gifts, as well as grace, for the work? Have they a clear sound understanding? Have they a right judgment in the things of God? Have they a just conception of salvation by faith? And has God given them any degree of utterance? Do they speak justly, readily, clearly? 3. Have they fruit? Are any truly convinced of sin, and converted to God, by their preaching?" The second of these qualifications seems to have been in the mind of the little girl who said that the bishop, in laying hands on the candidate, was feeling of his head to see whether he had brains enough to preach. There is some need of the preaching of a "trial sermon" by the candidate, as proof to the Council that he has the gifts requisite for a successful ministry. In this respect the Presbyteries of Scotland are in advance of us.

(b) Who are to ordain?

Ordination is the act of the church, not the act of a privileged class in the church, as the eldership has sometimes wrongly been regarded, nor yet the act of other churches, assembled by their representatives in council. No ecclesiastical authority higher than that of the local church is recognized in the New Testament. This authority, however, has its limits; and since the church has no authority outside of its own body, the candidate for ordination should be a member of the ordaining church.

Since each church is bound to recognize the presence of the Spirit in other rightly constituted churches, and its own decisions, in like manner, are to be recognized by others, it is desirable in ordination, as in all important steps affecting other churches, that advice be taken before the candidate is inducted into office, and that other churches be called to sit with it in council, and if thought best, assist in setting the candidate apart for the ministry.

Hands were laid on Paul and Barnabas at Antioch, not by their ecclesiastical superiors, as High Church doctrine would require, but by their equals or inferiors, as simple representatives of the church. Ordination was nothing more than the recognition of a divine appointment and the commending to God's care and blessing of those so appointed. The council of ordination is only the church advised by its brethren, or a committee with power, to act for the church after deliberation.

The council of ordination is not to be composed simply of ministers who have been themselves ordained. As the whole church is to preserve the ordinances and to maintain sound doctrine, and as the unordained church member is often a more sagacious judge of a candidate's Christian experience than his own pastor would be, there seems no warrant, either in Scripture or in reason, for the exclusion of lay delegates from ordaining councils. It was not merely the apostles and elders, but the whole church at Jerusalem, that passed upon the matters submitted to them at the council, and others than ministers appear to have been delegates. The theory that only ministers can ordain has in it the beginnings of a hierarchy. To make the ministry a close corporation is to recognize the principle of apostolic succession, to deny the validity of all our past ordinations, and to sell to an ecclesiastical caste the liberties of the church of God. Very great importance attaches to decorum and settled usage in matters of ordination. To secure these, the following suggestions are made with regard to

I. PRELIMINARY ARRANGEMENTS to be attended to by the candidate: 1. His letter of dismission should be received and acted upon by the church before the Council convenes. Since the church has no jurisdiction outside of its own membership, the candidate should be a member of the church which proposes to ordain him. 2. The church should vote to call the Council. 3. It should invite all the churches of its Association. 4. It should send printed invitations, asking written responses. 5. Should have printed copies of an Order of Procedure, subject to adoption by the Council. 6. The candidate may select one or two persons to officiate at the public service, subject to approval of the Council. 7. The clerk of the church should be instructed to be present with the records of the church and the minutes of the Association, so that he may call to order and ask responses from delegates. 8. Ushers should be appointed to ensure reserved seats for the Council. 9. Another room should be provided for the private session of the Council. 10. The choir should be instructed that one anthem, one hymn, and one doxology will suffice for the public service. 11. Entertainment of the delegates should be provided for. 12. A member of the church should be chosen to present the candidate to the Council. 13. The church should be urged on the previous Sunday to attend the examination of the candidate as well as the public service.

II. THE CANDIDATE AT THE COUNCIL: 1. His demeanor should be that of an applicant. Since he asks the favorable judgment of his brethren, a modest bearing and great patience in answering their questions, are becoming to his position. 2. Let him stand during his narration, and during questions, unless for reasons of ill health or fatigue he is specially excused. 3. It will be well to divide his narration into 15 minutes for his Christian experience, 10 minutes for his call to the ministry, and 35 minutes for his views of doctrine. 4. A viva voce statement of all these three is greatly preferable to an elaborate written account. 5. In the relation of his views of doctrine: (a) the more fully he states them, the less need there will be for questioning; (b) his statement should be positive, not negative—not what he does not believe, but what he does believe; (c) he is not required to tell the reasons for his belief, unless he is specially questioned with regard to these; (d) he should elaborate the later and practical, not the earlier and theoretical, portions of his theological system; (e) he may well conclude each point of his statement with a single text of Scripture proof.

III. THE DUTY OF THE COUNCIL: 1. It should not proceed to examine the candidate until proper credentials have been presented. 2. It should in every case give to the candidate a searching examination, in order that this may not seem invidious in other cases. 3. Its vote of approval should read: "We do now set apart," and "We will hold a public service expressive of this fact." 4. Strict decorum should be observed in every stage of the proceedings, remembering that the Council is acting for Christ the great head of the church and is transacting business for eternity. 5. The Council should do no other business than that for which the church has summoned it, and when that business is done, the Council should adjourn sine die.

It is always to be remembered, however, that the power to ordain rests with the church, and that the church may proceed without a Council, or even against the decision of the Council. Such ordination, of course, would give authority only within the bounds of the individual church. Where no immediate exception is taken to the decision of the Council, that decision is to be regarded as virtually the decision of the church by which it was called. The same rule applies to a Council's decision to depose from the ministry. In the absence of immediate protest from the church, the decision of the Council is rightly taken as virtually the decision of the church.

In so far as ordination is an act performed by the local church with the advice and assistance of other rightly constituted churches, it is justly regarded as giving formal permission to exercise gifts and administer ordinances within the bounds of such churches. Ordination is not, therefore, to be repeated upon the transfer of the minister's pastoral relation from one church to another. In every case, however, where a minister from a body of Christians not Scripturally constituted assumes the pastoral relation in a rightly organized church, there is peculiar propriety, not only in the examination, by a Council, of his Christian experience, call to the ministry, and views of doctrine, but also in that act of formal recognition and authorization which is called ordination.

The Council should be numerous and impartially constituted. The church calling the Council should be represented in it by a fair number of delegates. Neither the church, nor the Council, should permit a prejudgment of the case by the previous announcement of an ordination service. While the examination of the candidate should be public, all danger that the Council be unduly influenced by pressure from without should be obviated by its conducting its deliberations, and arriving at its decision, in private session. We subjoin the form of a letter missive, calling a Council of ordination; an order of procedure after the Council has assembled; and a programme of exercises for the public service.

LETTER MISSIVE.—The —— church of —— to the —— church of ——: Dear Brethren: By vote of this church, you are requested to send your pastor and two delegates to meet with us in accordance with the following resolutions, passed by us on the —— ——, 19—: Whereas, brother —— , a member of this church, has offered himself to the work of the gospel ministry, and has been chosen by us as our pastor, therefore, Resolved, 1. That such neighboring churches, in fellowship with us, as shall be herein designated, be requested to send their pastor and two delegates each, to meet and counsel with this church, at — o'clock —. M., on ——, 19——, and if, after examination, he be approved, that brother —— be set apart, by vote of the Council, to the gospel ministry, and that a public service be held, expressive of this fact. Resolved, 2. That the Council, if it do so ordain, be requested to appoint two of its number to act with the candidate, in arranging the public services. Resolved, 3. That printed letters of invitation, embodying these resolutions, and signed by the clerk of this church, be sent to the following churches, —— —— —— —— ——, and that these churches be requested to furnish to their delegates an officially signed certificate of their appointment, to be presented at the organization of the Council. Resolved, 4. That Rev. ——, and brethren —— ——, be also invited by the clerk of the church to be present as members of the Council. Resolved, 5. That brethren ——, ——, and ——, be appointed as our delegates, to represent this church in the deliberations of the Council; and that brother

—— be requested to present the candidate to the Council, with an expression of the high respect and warm attachment with which we have welcomed him and his labors among us. In behalf of the church, —— ——, Clerk. ——, 19—.

ORDER OF PROCEDURE.—1. Reading, by the clerk of the church, of the letter-missive, followed by a call, in their order, upon all churches and individuals invited, to present responses and names in writing; each delegate, as he presents his credentials, taking his seat in a portion of the house reserved for the Council. 2. Announcement, by the clerk of the church, that a Council has convened, and call for the nomination of a moderator,—the motion to be put by the clerk,—after which the moderator takes the chair. 3. Organization completed by election of a clerk of the Council, the offering of prayer, and an invitation to visiting brethren to sit with the Council, but not to vote. 4. Reading, on behalf of the church, by its clerk, of the records of the church concerning the call extended to the candidate, and his acceptance, together with documentary evidence of his licensure, of his present church membership, and of his standing in other respects, if coming from another denomination. 5. Vote, by the Council, that the proceedings of the church, and the standing of the candidate, warrant an examination of his claim to ordination. 6. Introduction of the candidate to the Council, by some representative of the church, with an expression of the church's feeling respecting him and his labors. 7. Vote to hear his Christian experience. Narration on the part of the candidate, followed by questions as to any features of it still needing elucidation. 8. Vote to hear the candidate's reasons for believing himself called to the ministry. Narration and questions. 9. Vote to hear the candidate's views of Christian doctrine. Narration and questions. 10. Vote to conclude the public examination, and to withdraw for private session. 11. In private session, after prayer, the Council determines, by three separate votes, in order to secure separate consideration of each question, whether it is satisfied with the candidate's Christian experience, call to the ministry, and views of Christian doctrine. 12. Vote that the candidate be hereby set apart to the gospel ministry, and that a public service be held, expressive of this fact; that for this purpose, a committee of two be appointed, to act with the candidate, in arranging such service of ordination, and to report before adjournment. 13. Reading of minutes, by clerk of Council, and correction of them, to prepare for presentation at the ordination service, and for preservation in the archives of the church. 14. Vote to give the candidate a certificate of ordination, signed by the moderator and clerk of the Council, and to publish an account of the proceedings in the journals of the denomination. 15. Adjourn to meet at the service of ordination.

PROGRAMME OF PUBLIC SERVICE (two hours in length).—1. Voluntary—five minutes. 2. Anthem—five. 3. Reading minutes of the Council, by the clerk of the Council—ten. 4. Prayer of invocation—five. 5. Reading of Scripture—five. 6. Sermon—twenty- five. 7. Prayer of ordination, with laying-on of hands—fifteen. 8. Hymn—ten. 9. Right hand of fellowship—five. 10. Charge to the candidate—fifteen. 11. Charge to the church—fifteen. 12. Doxology—five. 13. Benediction by the newly ordained pastor.

The tenor of the N. T. would seem to indicate that deacons should be ordained with prayer and the laying-on of hands, though not by council or public service. Evangelists, missionaries, ministers serving as secretaries of benevolent societies, should also be ordained, since they are organs of the church, set apart for special religious work on behalf of the churches. The same rule applies to those who are set to be teachers of the teachers, the professors of theological seminaries. Philip, baptizing the eunuch, is to be regarded as an organ of the church at Jerusalem. Both home missionaries and foreign missionaries are evangelists; and both, as organs of the home churches to which they belong, are not under obligation to take letters of dismission to the churches they gather. George Adam Smith, in his Life of Henry Drummond, 265, says that Drummond was ordained to his professorship by the laying-on of the hands of the Presbytery: "The rite is the same in the case whether of a minister or of a professor, for the church of Scotland recognizes no difference between her teachers and her pastors, but lays them under the same vows, and ordains them all as ministers of Christ's gospel and of his sacraments."

Rome teaches that ordination is a sacrament, and "once a priest, always a priest," but only when Rome confers the ordination. It is going a great deal further than Rome to maintain the indelibility of all orders—at least, of all orders conferred by an evangelical church. At Dover in England, a medical gentleman declined to pay his doctor's bill upon the ground that it was not the custom of his calling to pay one another for their services. It appeared however that he was a retired practitioner, and upon that ground he lost his case. Ordination, like vaccination, may run out. Retirement from the office of public teacher should work a forfeiture of the official character. The authorization granted by the Council was based upon a previous recognition of a divine call. When by reason of permanent withdrawal from the ministry, and devotion to wholly secular pursuits, there remains no longer any divine call to be recognized, all authority and standing as a Christian minister should cease also. We therefore repudiate the doctrine of the "indelibility of sacred orders," and the corresponding maxim: "Once ordained, always ordained"; although we do not, with the Cambridge Platform, confine the ministerial function to the pastoral relation. That Platform held that "the pastoral relation ceasing, the ministerial function ceases, and the pastor becomes a layman again, to be restored to the ministry only by a second ordination, called installation. This theory of the ministry proved so inadequate, that it was held scarcely more than a single generation. It was rejected by the Congregational churches of England ten years after it was formulated in New England."

"The National Council of Congregational Churches, in 1880, resolved that any man serving a church as minister can be dealt with and disciplined by any church, no matter what his relations may be in church membership, or ecclesiastical affiliations. If the church choosing him will not call a council, then any church can call one for that purpose"; see New Englander, July, 1883:461-491. This latter course, however, presupposes that the steps of fraternal labor and admonition, provided for in our next section on the Relation of Local Churches to one another, have been taken, and have been insufficient to induce proper action on the part of the church to which such minister belongs.

The authority of a Presbyterian church is limited to the bounds of its own denomination. It cannot ordain ministers for Baptist churches, any more than it can ordain them for Methodist churches or for Episcopal churches. When a Presbyterian minister becomes a Baptist, his motives for making the change and the conformity of his views to the New Testament standard need to be scrutinized by Baptists, before they can admit him to their Christian and church fellowship; in other words, he needs to be ordained by a Baptist church. Ordination is no more a discourtesy to the other denomination than Baptism is. Those who oppose reördination in such cases virtually hold to the Romish view of the sacredness of orders.

The Watchman, April 17, 1902—"The Christian ministry is not a priestly class which the laity is bound to support. If the minister cannot find a church ready to support him, there is nothing to prevent his entering another calling. Only ten per cent. of the men who start in independent business avoid failure, and a much smaller proportion achieve substantial success. They are not failures, for they do useful and valuable work. But they do not secure the prizes. It is not wonderful that the proportion of ministers securing prominent pulpits is small. Many men fail in the ministry. There is no sacred character imparted by ordination. They should go into some other avocation. 'Once a minister, always a minister' is a piece of Popery that Protestant churches should get rid of." See essay on Councils of Ordination, their Powers and Duties, by A. H. Strong, in Philosophy and Religion, 259-268; Wayland, Principles and Practices of Baptists, 114; Dexter, Congregationalism, 136, 145, 146, 150, 151. Per contra, see Fish, Ecclesiology, 365-399; Presb. Rev., 1886:89-126.

3. Discipline of the Church.

A. Kinds of discipline.—Discipline is of two sorts, according as offences are private or public. (a) Private offences are to be dealt with according to the rule in Mat. 5:23, 24; 18:15-17.

Mat. 5:23, 24—"If therefore thou art offering thy gift at the altar, and there rememberest that thy brother hath aught against thee, leave there thy gift before the altar, and go thy way, first be reconciled to thy brother, and then come and offer thy gift"—here is provision for self-discipline on the part of each offender; 18:15-17—"And if thy brother sin against thee, go, show him his fault between thee and him alone: if he hear thee, thou hast gained thy brother. But if he hear thee not, take with thee one or two more, that at the mouth of two witnesses or three every word may be established. And if he refuse to hear them, tell it unto the church: and if he refuse to hear the church also, let him be unto thee as the Gentile and the publican"—here is, first, private discipline, one of another; and then, only as a last resort, discipline by the church. Westcott and Hort, however omit the εἰς σέ—"against thee"—in Mat. 18:15, and so make each Christian responsible for bringing to repentance every brother whose sin he becomes cognizant of. This would abolish the distinction between private and public offences.

When a brother wrongs me, I am not to speak of the offence to others, nor to write to him a letter, but to go to him. If the brother is already penitent, he will start from his house to see me at the same time that I start from my house to see him, and we will meet just half way between the two. There would be little appeal to the church, and little cherishing of ancient grudges, if Christ's disciples would observe his simple rules. These rules impose a duty upon both the offending and the offended party. When a brother brings a personal matter before the church, he should always be asked whether he has obeyed Christ's command to labor privately with the offender. If he has not, he should be bidden to keep silence.

(b) Public offences are to be dealt with according to the rule in 1 Cor. 5:3-5, 13, and 2 Thess. 3:6.

1 Cor. 5:3-5, 13—"For I verily, being absent in body but present in spirit, have already as though I were present judged him that hath so wrought this thing, in the name of the Lord Jesus, ye being gathered together, and my spirit, with the power of our Lord Jesus, to deliver such a one unto Satan for the destruction of the flesh, that the spirit may be saved in the day of the Lord Jesus.... Put away the wicked man from among yourselves."

Notice here that Paul gave the incestuous person no opportunity to repent, confess, or avert sentence. The church can have no valid evidence of repentance immediately upon discovery and arraignment. At such a time the natural conscience always reacts in remorse and self-accusation, but whether the sin is hated because of its inherent wickedness, or only because of its unfortunate consequences, cannot be known at once. Only fruits meet for repentance can prove repentance real. But such fruits take time, And the church has no time to wait. Its good repute in the community, and its influence over its own members, are at stake. These therefore demand the instant exclusion of the wrong-doer, as evidence that the church clears its skirts from all complicity with the wrong. In the case of gross public offences, labor with the offender is to come, not before, but after, his excommunication; cf. 2 Cor. 2:6-8—"Sufficient to such a one is this punishment which was inflicted by the many;... forgive him and comfort him;... confirm your love toward him."

The church is not a Mutual Insurance Company, whose object is to protect and shield its individual members. It is a society whose end is to represent Christ in the world, and to establish his truth and righteousness. Christ commits his honor to its keeping. The offender who is only anxious to escape judgment, and who pleads to be forgiven without delay, often shows that he cares nothing for the cause of Christ which he has injured, but that he has at heart only his own selfish comfort and reputation. The truly penitent man will rather beg the church to exclude him, in order that it may free itself from the charge of harboring iniquity. He will accept exclusion with humility, will love the church that excludes him, will continue to attend its worship, will in due time seek and receive restoration. There is always a way back into the church for those who repent. But the Scriptural method of ensuring repentance is the method of immediate exclusion.

In 2 Cor. 2:6-8—"inflicted by the many" might at first sight seem to imply that, although the offender was excommunicated, it was only by a majority vote, some members of the church dissenting. Some interpreters think he had not been excommunicated at all, but that only ordinary association with him had ceased. But, if Paul's command in the first epistle to "put away the wicked man from among yourselves" (1 Cor. 5:13) had been thus disobeyed, the apostle would certainly have mentioned and rebuked the disobedience. On the contrary he praises them that they had done as he had advised. The action of the church at Corinth was blessed by God to the quickening of conscience and the purification of life. In many a modern church the exclusion of unworthy members has in like manner given to Christians a new sense of their responsibility, while at the same time it has convinced worldly people that the church was in thorough earnest. The decisions of the church, indeed, when guided by the Holy Spirit, are nothing less than an anticipation of the judgments of the last day; see Mat. 18:18—"What things soever ye shall bind on earth shall be bound in heaven; and what things soever ye shall loose on earth shall be loosed in heaven." In John 8:7, Jesus recognizes the sin and urges repentance, while he challenges the right of the mob to execute judgment, and does away with the traditional stoning. His gracious treatment of the sinning woman gave no hint as to the proper treatment of her case by the regular synagogue authorities.

2 Thess. 3:6—"Now we command you, brethren, in the name of our Lord Jesus Christ, that ye withdraw yourselves from every brother that walketh disorderly, and not after the tradition which they received of us." The mere "dropping" of names from the list of members seems altogether contrary to the spirit of the N. T. polity. That recognizes only three methods of exit from the local church: (1) exclusion; (2) dismission; (3) death. To provide for the case of members whose residence has long been unknown, it is well for the church to have a standing rule that all members residing at a distance shall report each year by letter or by contribution, and, in case of failure to report for two successive years, shall be subject to discipline. The action of the church, in such cases, should take the form of an adoption of preamble and resolution: "Whereas A. B. has been absent from the church for more than two years, and has failed to comply with the standing rule requiring a yearly report or contribution, therefore, Resolved, that the church withdraw from A. B. the hand of fellowship."

In all cases of exclusion, the resolution may uniformly read as above; the preamble may indefinitely vary, and should always cite the exact nature of the offence. In this way, neglect of the church or breach of covenant obligations may be distinguished from offences against common morality, so that exclusion upon the former ground shall not be mistaken for exclusion upon the latter. As the persons excluded are not commonly present at the meeting of the church when they are excluded, a written copy of the preamble and resolution, signed by the Clerk of the Church, should always be immediately sent to them.

B. Relation of the pastor to discipline.—(a) He has no original authority; (b) but is the organ of the church, and (c) superintendent of its labors for its own purification and for the reclamation of offenders; and therefore (d) may best do the work of discipline, not directly, by constituting himself a special policeman or detective, but indirectly, by securing proper labor on the part of the deacons or brethren of the church.

The pastor should regard himself as a judge, rather than as a prosecuting attorney. He should press upon the officers of his church their duty to investigate cases of immorality and to deal with them. But if he himself makes charges, he loses dignity, and puts it out of his power to help the offender. It is not well for him to be, or to have the reputation of being, a ferreter-out of misdemeanors among his church members. It is best for him in general to serve only as presiding officer in cases of discipline, instead of being a partisan or a counsel for the prosecution. For this reason it is well for him to secure the appointment by his church of a Prudential Committee, or Committee on Discipline, whose duty it shall be at a fixed time each year to look over the list of members, initiate labor in the case of delinquents, and, after the proper steps have been taken, present proper preambles and resolutions in cases where the church needs to take action. This regular yearly process renders discipline easy; whereas the neglect of it for several successive years results in an accumulation of cases, in each of which the person exposed to discipline has friends, and these are tempted to obstruct the church's dealing with others from fear that the taking up of any other case may lead to the taking up of that one in which they are most nearly interested. The church which pays no regular attention to its discipline is like the farmer who milked his cow only once a year, in order to avoid too great a drain; or like the small boy who did not see how any one could bear to comb his hair every day,—he combed his own only once in six weeks, and then it nearly killed him.

As the Prudential Committee, or Committee on Discipline, is simply the church itself preparing its own business, the church may well require all complaints to be made to it through the committee. In this way it may be made certain that the preliminary steps of labor have been taken, and the disquieting of the church by premature charges may be avoided. Where the committee, after proper representations made to it, fails to do its duty, the individual member may appeal directly to the assembled church; and the difference between the New Testament order and that of a hierarchy is this, that according to the former all final action and responsibility is taken by the church itself in its collective capacity, whereas on the latter the minister, the session, or the bishop, so far as the individual church is concerned, determines the result. See Savage, Church Discipline, Formative and Corrective; Dagg, Church Order, 268-274. On church discipline in cases of remarriage after divorce, see A. H. Strong, Philosophy and Religion, 431-442.

IV. Relation of Local Churches to one another

1. The general nature of this relation is that of fellowship between equals.

Notice here:

(a) The absolute equality of the churches.—No church or council of churches, no association or convention or society, can relieve any single church of its direct responsibility to Christ, or assume control of its action.

(b) The fraternal fellowship and coöperation of the churches.—No church can properly ignore, or disregard, the existence or work of other churches around it. Every other church is presumptively possessed of the Spirit, in equal measure with itself. There must therefore be sympathy and mutual furtherance of each other's welfare among churches, as among individual Christians. Upon this principle are based letters of dismission, recognition of the pastors of other churches, and all associational unions, or unions for common Christian work.

H. O. Rowlands, in Bap. Quar. Rev., Oct. 1891:669-677, urges the giving up of special Councils, and the turning of the Association into a Permanent Council, not to take original cognizance of what cases it pleases, but to consider and judge such questions as may be referred to it by the individual churches. It could then revise and rescind its action, whereas the present Council when once adjourned can never be called together again. This method would prevent the packing of a Council, and the Council when once constituted would have greater influence. We feel slow to sanction such a plan, not only for the reason that it seems destitute of New Testament authority and example, but because it tends toward a Presbyterian form of church government. All permanent bodies of this sort gradually arrogate to themselves power; indirectly if not directly they can assume original jurisdiction; their decisions have altogether too great influence, if they go further than personal persuasion. The independence of the individual church is a primary element of polity which must not be sacrificed or endangered for the mere sake of inter-ecclesiastical harmony. Permanent Councils of any sort are of doubtful validity. They need to be kept under constant watch and criticism, lest they undermine our Baptist church government, a fundamental principle of which is that there is no authority on earth above that of the local church.

2. This fellowship involves the duty of special consultation with regard to matters affecting the common interest.

(a) The duty of seeking advice.—Since the order and good repute of each is valuable to all the others, cases of grave importance and difficulty in internal discipline, as well as the question of ordaining members to the ministry, should be submitted to a council of churches called for the purpose.

(b) The duty of taking advice.—For the same reason, each church should show readiness to receive admonition from others. So long as this is in the nature of friendly reminder that the church is guilty of defects from the doctrine or practice enjoined by Christ, the mutual acceptance of whose commands is the basis of all church fellowship, no church can justly refuse to have such defects pointed out, or to consider the Scripturalness of its own proceeding. Such admonition or advice, however, whether coming from a single church or from a council of churches, is not itself of binding authority. It is simply in the nature of moral suasion. The church receiving it has still to compare it with Christ's laws. The ultimate decision rests entirely with the church so advised or asking advice.

Churches should observe comity, and should not draw away one another's members. Ministers should bring churches together, and should teach their members the larger unity of the whole church of God. The pastor should not confine his interest to his own church or even to his own Association. The State Convention, the Education Society, the National Anniversaries, should all claim his attention and that of his people. He should welcome new laborers and helpers, instead of regarding the ministry as a close corporation whose numbers are to be kept forever small. E. G. Robinson: "The spirit of sectarianism is devilish. It raises the church above Christ. Christ did not say: 'Blessed is the man who accepts the Westminster Confession or the Thirty-Nine Articles.' There is not the least shadow of churchism in Christ. Churchism is a revamped and whitewashed Judaism. It keeps up the middle wall of partition which Christ has broken down."

Dr. P. H. Mell, in his Manual of Parliamentary Practice, calls Church Councils "Committees of Help." President James C. Welling held that "We Baptists are not true to our democratic polity in the conduct of our collective evangelical operations. In these matters we are simply a bureaucracy, tempered by individual munificence." A. J. Gordon, Ministry of the Spirit, 149, 150, remarks on Mat. 18:19—"If two of you shall agree"—συμφωνήσωσιν, from which our word "symphony" comes: "If two shall 'accord,' or 'symphonize' in what they ask, they have the promise of being heard. But, as in tuning an organ, all the notes must be keyed to the standard pitch, else harmony were impossible, so in prayer. It is not enough that two disciples agree with each other,—they must agree with a Third—the righteous and holy Lord, before they can agree in intercession. There may be agreement which is in most sinful conflict with the divine will: 'How is it that ye have agreed together'—συνεφωνήθη—the same word—'to try the Spirit of the Lord?' says Peter (Acts 5:9). Here is mutual accord, but guilty discord with the Holy Spirit."

3. This fellowship may be broken by manifest departures from the faith or practice of the Scriptures, on the part of any church.

In such case, duty to Christ requires the churches, whose labors to reclaim a sister church from error have proved unavailing, to withdraw their fellowship from it, until such time as the erring church shall return to the path of duty. In this regard, the law which applies to individuals applies to churches, and the polity of the New Testament is congregational rather than independent.

Independence is qualified by interdependence. While each church is, in the last resort thrown upon its own responsibility in ascertaining doctrine and duty, it is to acknowledge the indwelling of the Holy Spirit in other churches as well as in itself, and the value of the public opinion of the churches as an indication of the mind of the Spirit. The church in Antioch asked advice of the church in Jerusalem, although Paul himself was at Antioch. Although no church or union of churches has rightful jurisdiction over the single local body, yet the Council, when rightly called and constituted, has the power of moral influence. Its decision is an index to truth, which only the gravest reasons will justify the church in ignoring or refusing to follow.

Dexter, Congregationalism, 695—"Barrowism gave all power into the hands of the elders, and it would have no Councils. Congregationalism is Brownism. It has two foci: Independence and Interdependence." Charles S. Scott, on Baptist Polity and the Pastorate, in Bap. Quar. Rev., July, 1890:291-297—"The difference between the polity of Baptist and of Congregational churches is in the relative authority of the Ecclesiastical Council. Congregationalism is Councilism. Not only the ordination and first settlement of the minister must be with the advice and consent of a Council, but every subsequent unsettlement and settlement." Baptist churches have regarded this dependence upon Councils after the minister's ordination as extreme and unwarranted.

The fact that the church has always the right, for just cause, of going behind the decision of the Council, and of determining for itself whether it will ratify or reject that decision, shows conclusively that the church has parted with no particle of its original independence or authority. Yet, though the Council is simply a counsellor—an organ and helper of the church,—the neglect of its advice may involve such ecclesiastical or moral wrong as to justify the churches represented in it, as well as other churches, in withdrawing, from the church that called it, their denominational fellowship. The relation of churches to one another is analogous to the relation of private Christians to one another. No meddlesome spirit is to be allowed; but in matters of grave moment, a church, as well as an individual, may be justified in giving advice unasked.

Lightfoot, in his new edition of Clemens Romanus, shows that the Epistle, instead of emanating from Clement as Bishop of Rome, is a letter of the church at Rome to the Corinthians, urging them to peace. No pope and no bishop existed, but the whole church congregationally addressed its counsels to its sister body of believers at Corinth. Congregationalism, in A. D. 95, considered it a duty to labor with a sister church that had in its judgment gone astray, or that was in danger of going astray. The only primacy was the primacy of the church, not of the bishop; and this primacy was a primacy of goodness, backed up by metropolitan advantages. All this fraternal fellowship follows from the fundamental conception of the local church as the concrete embodiment of the universal church. Park: "Congregationalism recognizes a voluntary coöperation and communion of the churches, which Independency does not do. Independent churches ordain and depose pastors without asking advice from other churches."

In accordance with this general principle, in a case of serious disagreement between different portions of the same church, the council called to advise should be, if possible, a mutual, not an ex parte, council; see Dexter, Congregationalism, 2, 3, 61-64. It is a more general application of the same principle, to say that the pastor should not shut himself in to his own church, but should cultivate friendly relations with other pastors and with other churches, should be present and active at the meetings of Associations and State Conventions, and at the Anniversaries of the National Societies of the denomination. His example of friendly interest in the welfare of others will affect his church. The strong should be taught to help the weak, after the example of Paul in raising contributions for the poor churches of Judea.

The principle of church independence is not only consistent with, but it absolutely requires under Christ, all manner of Christian coöperation with other churches; and Social and Mission Unions to unify the work of the denomination, to secure the starting of new enterprises, to prevent one church from trenching upon the territory or appropriating the members of another, are only natural outgrowths of the principle. President Wayland's remark, "He who is displeased with everybody and everything gives the best evidence that his own temper is defective and that he is a bad associate," applies to churches as well as to individuals. Each church is to remember that, though it is honored by the indwelling of the Lord, it constitutes only a part of that great body of which Christ is the head.

See Davidson, Eccl. Polity of the N. T.; Ladd, Principles of Church Polity; and on the general subject of the Church, Hodge, Essays, 201; Flint, Christ's Kingdom on Earth, 53-82; Hooker, Ecclesiastical Polity; The Church,—a collection of essays by Luthardt, Kahnis, etc.; Hiscox, Baptist Church Directory; Ripley, Church Polity; Harvey, The Church; Crowell, Church Members' Manual; R. W. Dale, Manual of Congregational Principles; Lightfoot, Com. on Philippians, excursus on the Christian Ministry; Ross, The Church-Kingdom—Lectures on Congregationalism; Dexter, Congregationalism, 681-716, as seen in its Literature; Allison, Baptist Councils in America. For a denial that there is any real apostolic authority for modern church polity, see O. J. Thatcher, Sketch of the History of the Apostolic Church.

Chapter II - The Ordinances Of The Church

By the ordinances, we mean those outward rites which Christ has appointed to be administered in his church as visible signs of the saving truth of the gospel. They are signs, in that they vividly express this truth and confirm it to the believer.

In contrast with this characteristically Protestant view, the Romanist regards the ordinances as actually conferring grace and producing holiness. Instead of being the external manifestation of a preceding union with Christ, they are the physical means of constituting and maintaining this union. With the Romanist, in this particular, sacramentalists of every name substantially agree. The Papal Church holds to seven sacraments or ordinances:—ordination, confirmation, matrimony, extreme unction, penance, baptism, and the eucharist. The ordinances prescribed in the N. T., however, are two and only two, viz.:—Baptism and the Lord's Supper.

It will be well to distinguish from one another the three words: symbol, rite, and ordinance. 1. A symbol is the sign, or visible representation, of an invisible truth or idea; as for example, the lion is the symbol of strength and courage, the lamb is the symbol of gentleness, the olive branch of peace, the sceptre of dominion, the wedding ring of marriage, and the flag of country. Symbols may teach great lessons; as Jesus' cursing the barren fig tree taught the doom of unfruitful Judaism, and Jesus' washing of the disciples' feet taught his own coming down from heaven to purify and save, and the humble service required of his followers. 2. A rite is a symbol which is employed with regularity and sacred intent. Symbols became rites when thus used. Examples of authorized rites in the Christian Church are the laying on of hands in ordination, and the giving of the right hand of fellowship. 3. An ordinance is a symbolic rite which sets forth the central truths of the Christian faith, and which is of universal and perpetual obligation. Baptism and the Lord's Supper are rites which have become ordinances by the specific command of Christ and by their inner relation to the essential truths of his kingdom. No ordinance is a sacrament in the Romanist sense of conferring grace; but, as the sacramentum was the oath taken by the Roman soldier to obey his commander even unto death, so Baptism and the Lord's Supper are sacraments, in the sense of vows of allegiance to Christ our Master.

President H. G. Weston has recorded his objections to the observance of the so-called "Christian Year," in words that we quote, as showing the danger attending the Romanist multiplication of ordinances. "1. The 'Christian Year' is not Christian. It makes everything of actions, and nothing of relations. Make a day holy that God has not made holy, and you thereby make all other days unholy. 2. It limits the Christian's view of Christ to the scenes and events of his earthly life. Salvation comes through spiritual relations to a living Lord. The 'Christian Year' makes Christ only a memory, and not a living, present, personal power. Life, not death, is the typical word of the N. T. Paul craved, not a knowledge of the fact of the resurrection, but of the power of it. The New Testament records busy themselves most of all with what Christ is doing now. 3. The appointments of the 'Christian Year' are not in accord with the N. T. These appointments lack the reality of spiritual life, and are contrary to the essential spirit of Christianity." We may add that where the "Christian Year" is most generally and rigidly observed, there popular religion is most formal and destitute of spiritual power.

I. Baptism

Christian Baptism is the immersion of a believer in water, in token of his previous entrance into the communion of Christ's death and resurrection,—or, in other words, in token of his regeneration through union with Christ.

1. Baptism an Ordinance of Christ.

A. Proof that Christ instituted an external rite called baptism.

(a) From the words of the great commission; (b) from the injunctions of the apostles; (c) from the fact that the members of the New Testament churches were baptized believers; (d) from the universal practice of such a rite in Christian churches of subsequent times.

(a) Mat. 28:19—"Go ye therefore, and make disciples of all the nations, baptizing them into the name of the Father and of the Son and of the Holy Spirit"; Mark 16:16—"He that believeth and is baptized shall be saved"—we hold, with Westcott and Hort, that Mark 16:9-20 is of canonical authority, though probably not written by Mark himself. (b) Acts 2:38—"And Peter said unto them, Repent ye, and be baptized every one of you in the name of Jesus Christ unto the remission of your sins"; (c) Rom.

6:3-5—"Or are ye ignorant that all we who were baptized into Christ Jesus were baptized into his death? We were buried therefore with him through baptism into death: that like as Christ was raised from the dead through the glory of the Father, so we also might walk in newness of life. For if we have become united with him in the likeness of his death, we shall be also in the likeness of his resurrection"; Col. 2:11, 12—"in whom ye were also circumcised with a circumcision not made with hands, in the putting off of the body of the flesh, in the circumcision of Christ; having been buried with him in baptism, wherein ye were also raised with him through faith in the working of God, who raised him from the dead." (d) The only marked exceptions to the universal requisition of baptism are found in the Society of Friends, and in the Salvation Army. The Salvation Army does not regard the ordinance as having any more permanent obligation than feet-washing. General Booth: "We teach our soldiers that every time they break bread, they are to remember the broken body of the Lord, and every time they wash the body, they are to remind themselves of the cleansing power of the blood of Christ and of the indwelling Spirit." The Society of Friends regard Christ's commands as fulfilled, not by any outward baptism of water, but only by the inward baptism of the Spirit.

B. This external rite intended by Christ to be of universal and perpetual obligation.

(a) Christ recognized John the Baptist's commission to baptize as derived immediately from heaven.

Mat. 21:25—"The baptism of John, whence was it? from heaven or from men?"—here Jesus clearly intimates that John's commission to baptize was derived directly from God; cf. John 1:25—the delegates sent to the Baptist by the Sanhedrin ask him: "Why then baptizest thou, if thou art not the Christ, neither Elijah, neither the prophet?" thus indicating that John's baptism, either in its form or its application, was a new ordinance that required special divine authorization.

Broadus in his American Com. on Mat. 3:6, claims that John's baptism was no modification of an existing rite. Proselyte baptism is not mentioned in the Mishna (A. D. 200); the first distinct account of it is in the Babylonian Talmud (Gemara) written in the fifth century; it was not adopted from the Christians, but was one of the Jewish purifications which came to be regarded, after the destruction of the Temple, as a peculiar initiatory rite. There is no mention of it, as a Jewish rite, in the O. T., N. T., Apocrypha, Philo, or Josephus.

For the view that proselyte-baptism did not exist among the Jews before the time of John, see Schneckenburger, Ueber das Alter der jüdischen Proselytentaufe; Stuart, in Bib. Repos., 1833:338-355; Toy, In Baptist Quarterly, 1872:301-332. Dr. Toy, however, in a private note to the author (1884), says: "I am disposed now to regard the Christian rite as borrowed from the Jewish, contrary to my view in 1872." So holds Edersheim, Life and Times of Jesus, 2:742-744—"We have positive testimony that the baptism of proselytes existed in the times of Hillel and Shammai. For, whereas the school of Shammai is said to have allowed a proselyte who was circumcised on the eve of the Passover, to partake, after baptism, of the Passover, the school of Hillel forbade it. This controversy must be regarded as proving that at that time [previous to Christ] the baptism of proselytes was customary."

Porter, on Proselyte Baptism, Hastings' Bible Dict., 4:132—"If circumcision was the decisive step in the case of all male converts, there seems no longer room for serious question that a bath of purification must have followed, even though early mention of such proselyte baptism is not found. The law (Lev. 11-15; Num. 19) prescribed such baths in all cases of impurity, and one who came with the deep impurity of a heathen life behind him could not have entered the Jewish community without such cleansing." Plummer, on Baptism, Hastings' Bible Dict., 1:239—"What is wanted is direct evidence that, before John the Baptist made so remarkable a use of the rite, it was the custom to make all proselytes submit to baptism; and such evidence is not forthcoming. Nevertheless the fact is not really doubtful. It is not credible that the baptizing of proselytes was instituted and made essential for their admission to Judaism at a period subsequent to the institution of Christian baptism; and the supposition that it was borrowed from the rite enjoined by Christ is monstrous."

Although the O. T. and the Apocrypha, Josephus and Philo, are silent with regard to proselyte baptism, it is certain that it existed among the Jews in the early Christian centuries; and it is almost equally certain that the Jews could not have adopted it from the Christians. It is probable, therefore, that the baptism of John was an application to Jews of an immersion which, before that time, was administered to proselytes from among the Gentiles; and that it was this adaptation of the rite to a new class of subjects and with a new meaning, which excited the inquiry and criticism of the Sanhedrin. We must remember, however, that the Lord's Supper was likewise an adaptation of certain portions of the old Passover service to a new use and meaning. See also Kitto, Bib. Cyclop., 3:593.

(b) In his own submission to John's baptism, Christ gave testimony to the binding obligation of the ordinance (Mat. 3:13-17). John's baptism was essentially Christian baptism (Acts 19:4), although the full significance of it was not understood until after Jesus' death and resurrection (Mat. 20:17-23; Luke 12:50; Rom. 6:3-6).

Mat. 3:13-17—"Suffer it now: for thus it becometh us to fulfill all righteousness"; Acts 19:4—"John baptized with the baptism of repentance, saying unto the people that they should believe on him that should come after him, that is, on Jesus"; Mat. 20:18, 19, 22—"the Son of man shall be delivered unto the chief priests and scribes; and they shall condemn him to death, and shall deliver him unto the Gentiles to mock, and to scourge, and to crucify.... Are ye able to drink the cup that I am about to drink?" Luke 12:50—"But I have a baptism to be baptized with; and how am I straitened till it be accomplished!" Rom. 6:3, 4—"Or are ye ignorant that all we who were baptized into Christ Jesus were baptized into his death? We were buried therefore with him through baptism into death: that like as Christ was raised from the dead through the glory of the Father, so we also might walk is newness of life."

Robert Hall, Works, 1:367-399, denies that John's baptism was Christian baptism, and holds that there is not sufficient evidence that all the apostles were baptized. The fact that John's baptism was a baptism of faith in the coming Messiah, as well as a baptism of repentance for past and present sin, refutes this theory. The only difference between John's baptism, and the baptism of our time, is that John baptized upon profession of faith in a Savior yet to come; baptism is now administered upon profession of faith in a Savior who has actually and already come. On John's baptism as presupposing faith in those who received it, see treatment of the Subjects of Baptism, page 950.

(c) In continuing the practice of baptism through his disciples (John 4:1, 2), and in enjoining it upon them as part of a work which was to last to the end of the world (Mat. 28:19, 20), Christ manifestly adopted and appointed baptism as the invariable law of his church.

John 4:1, 2—"When therefore the Lord knew that the Pharisees had heard that Jesus was making and baptizing more disciples than John (although Jesus himself baptized not, but his disciples)"; Mat. 28:19, 20—"Go ye therefore, and make disciples of all the nations, baptizing them into the name of the Father and of the Son and of the Holy Spirit: teaching them to observe all things whatsoever I commanded you: and lo, I am with you always, even unto the end of the world."

(d) The analogy of the ordinance of the Lord's Supper also leads to the conclusion that baptism is to be observed as an authoritative memorial of Christ and his truth, until his second coming.

1 Cor. 11:26—"For as often as ye eat this bread, and drink the cup, ye proclaim the Lord's death till he come." Baptism, like the Lord's Supper, is a teaching ordinance, and the two ordinances together furnish an indispensable witness to Christ's death and resurrection.

(e) There is no intimation whatever that the command of baptism is limited, or to be limited, in its application,—that it has been or ever is to be repealed; and, until some evidence of such limitation or repeal is produced, the statute must be regarded as universally binding.

On the proof that baptism is an ordinance of Christ, see Pepper, in Madison Avenue Lectures, 85-114; Dagg, Church Order, 9-21.

2. The Mode of Baptism.

This is immersion, and immersion only. This appears from the following considerations:

A. The command to baptize is a command to immerse.

We show this:

(a) From the meaning of the original word βαπτίζω. That this is to immerse, appears:

First,—from the usage of Greek writers—including the church Fathers, when they do not speak of the Christian rite, and the authors of the Greek version of the Old Testament.

Liddell and Scott, Greek Lexicon: "βαπτίζω, to dip in or under water; Lat. immergere." Sophocles, Lexicon of Greek Usage in the Roman and Byzantine Periods, 140 B. C. to 1000 A. D.—"βαπτίζω, to dip, to immerse, to sink ... There is no evidence that Luke and Paul and the other writers of the N. T. put upon this verb meanings not recognized by the Greeks." Thayer, N. T. Lexicon: "βαπτίζω, literally to dip, to dip repeatedly, to immerse, to submerge, ... metaphorically, to overwhelm.... βάπτισμα, immersion, submersion ... a rite of sacred immersion commanded by Christ." Prof. Goodwin of Harvard University, Feb. 13, 1895, says: "The classical meaning of βαπτίζω, which seldom occurs, and of the more common βάπτω, is dip (literally or metaphorically), and I never heard of its having any other meaning anywhere. Certainly I never saw a lexicon which gives either sprinkle or pour, as meanings of either. I must be allowed to ask why I am so often asked this question, which seems to me to have but one perfectly plain answer."

In the International Critical Commentary, see Plummer on Luke, p. 86—"It is only when baptism is administered by immersion that its full significance is seen"; Abbott on Colossians, p. 251—"The figure was naturally suggested by the immersion in baptism"; see also Gould on Mark, p. 127; Sanday on Romans, p. 154-157. No one of these four Commentaries was written by a Baptist. The two latest English Bible Dictionaries agree upon this point. Hastings, Bib. Dict., art.: Baptism, p. 243 a—"The mode of using was commonly immersion. The symbolism of the ordinance required this"; Cheyne, Encyc. Biblica, 1:473, while arguing from the Didache that from a very early date "a triple pouring was admitted where a sufficiency of water could not be had," agrees that "such a method [as immersion] is presupposed as the ideal, at any rate, in Paul's words about death, burial and resurrection in baptism (Rom. 6:3-5)."

Conant, Appendix to Bible Union Version of Matthew, 1-64, has examples "drawn from writers in almost every department of literature and science; from poets, rhetoricians, philosophers, critics, historians, geographers; from writers on husbandry, on medicine, on natural history, on grammar, on theology; from almost every form and style of composition, romances, epistles, orations, fables, odes, epigrams, sermons, narratives: from writers of various nations and religions, Pagan, Jew, and Christian, belonging to many countries and through a long succession of ages. In all, the word has retained its ground-meaning without change. From the earliest age of Greek literature down to its close, a period of nearly two thousand years, not an example has been found in which the word has any other meaning. There is no instance in which it signifies to make a partial application of water by affusion or sprinkling, or to cleanse, to purify, apart from the literal act of immersion as the means of cleansing or purifying." See Stuart, in Bib. Repos., 1833:313; Broadus on Immersion, 57, note.

Dale, in his Classic, Judaic, Christic, and Patristic Baptism, maintains that βάπτω alone means "to dip," and that βαπτίζω never means "to dip," but only "to put within," giving no intimation that the object is to be taken out again. But see Review of Dale, by A. C. Kendrick, in Bap. Quarterly, 1869:129, and by Harvey, in Bap. Review, 1879:141-163. "Plutarch used the word βαπτίζω, when he describes the soldiers of Alexander on a riotous march as by the roadside dipping (lit.: baptizing) with cups from huge wine jars and mixing bowls, and drinking to one another. Here we have βαπτίζω used where Dr. Dale's theory would call for βάπτω. The truth is that βαπτίζω, the stronger word, came to be used in the same sense with the weaker; and the attempt to prove a broad and invariable difference of meaning between them breaks down. Of Dr. Dale's three meanings of βαπτίζω—(1) intusposition without influence (stone in water), (2) intusposition with influence (man drowned in water), (3) influence without intusposition,—the last is a figment of Dr. Dale's imagination. It would allow me to say that when I burned a piece of paper, I baptized it. The grand result is this: Beginning with the position that baptize means immerse, Dr. Dale ends by maintaining that immersion is not baptism. Because Christ speaks of drinking a cup, Dr. Dale infers that this is baptism." For a complete reply to Dale, see Ford, Studies on Baptism.

Secondly,—every passage where the word occurs in the New Testament either requires or allows the meaning "immerse."

Mat. 3:6, 11—"I indeed baptize you in water unto repentance ... he shall baptize you in the holy Spirit and in fire"; cf. 2 Kings 5:14—"Then went he [Naaman] down, and dipped himself ἐβαπτίσατο seven times in the Jordan"; Mark 1:5, 9—"they were baptized of him in the river Jordan, confessing their sins.... Jesus came from Nazareth of Galilee, and was baptized of John into the Jordan"; 7:4—"and when they come from the market-place, except they bathe [lit.: 'baptize'] themselves, they eat not: and many other things there are, which they have received to hold, washings [lit.: 'baptizings'] of cups, and pots, and brasen vessels"—in this verse, Westcott and Hort, with א and B, read ῥαντίσωνται, instead of βαπτίσωνται; but it is easy to see how subsequent ignorance of Pharisaic scrupulousness might have changed βαπτίσωνται into ῥαντίσωνται; but not easy to see how ῥαντίσωνται should have been changed into βαπτίσωνται. On Mat. 15:2 (and the parallel passage Mark 7:4), see Broadus, Com. on Mat., pages 332, 333. Herodotus, 2:47, says that if any Egyptian touches a swine in passing, with his clothes, he goes to the river and dips himself from it.

Meyer, Com. in loco—"ἐὰν μὴ βαπτίσωνται is not to be understood of washing the hands (Lightfoot, Wetstein), but of immersion, which the word in classic Greek and in the N. T. everywhere means; here, according to the context, to take a bath." The Revised Version omits the words "and couches," although Maimonides speaks of a Jewish immersion of couches; see quotation from Maimonides in Ingham, Handbook of Baptism, 373—"Whenever in the law washing of the flesh or of the clothes is mentioned, it means nothing else than the dipping of the whole body in a laver; for if any man dip himself all over except the tip of his little finger, he is still in his uncleanness.... A bed that is wholly defiled, if a man dip it part by part, it is pure." Watson, in Annotated Par. Bible, 1126.

Luke 11:38—"And when the Pharisee saw it, he marvelled that he had not first bathed [lit.: 'baptized'] himself before dinner"; cf. Ecclesiasticus 31:25—"He that washeth himself after the touching of a dead body" (βαπτιζόμενος ἀπὸ νεκροῦ); Judith 12:7—"washed herself ἐβαπτίζετο in a fountain of water by the camp"; Lev. 22:4-6—"Whoso toucheth anything that is unclean by the dead ... unclean until the even ... bathe his flesh in water." Acts 2:41—"They then that received his word were baptized: and there were added unto them in that day about three thousand souls." Although the water supply of Jerusalem is naturally poor, the artificial provision of aqueducts, cisterns, and tanks, made water abundant. During the siege of Titus, though thousands died of famine, we read of no suffering from lack of water. The following are the dimensions of pools in modern Jerusalem: King's Pool, 15 feet x 16 x 3; Siloam, 53 x 18 x 19; Hezekiah, 240 x 140 x 10; Bethesda (so-called), 360 x 130 x 75; Upper Gihon, 316 x 218 x 19; Lower Gihon, 592 x 260 x 18; see Robinson, Biblical Researches, 1:323-348, and Samson, Water-supply of Jerusalem, pub. by Am. Bap. Pub. Soc. There was no difficulty in baptizing three thousand in one day; for, in the time of Chrysostom, when all candidates of the year were baptized in a single day, three thousand were once baptized; and, on July 3, 1878, 2222 Telugu

Christians were baptized by two administrators in nine hours. These Telugu baptisms took place at Velumpilly, ten miles north of Ongole. The same two men did not baptize all the time. There were six men engaged in baptizing, but never more than two men at the same time.

Acts 16:33—"And he took them the same hour of the night, and washed their stripes; and was baptized, he and all his, immediately"—the prison was doubtless, as are most large edifices in the East, whether public or private, provided with tank and fountain. See Cremer, Lexicon of N. T. Greek, sub voce—"βαπτίζω, immersion or submersion for a religious purpose." Grimm's ed. of Wilke—"βαπτίζω, 1. Immerse, submerge; 2. Wash or bathe, by immersing or submerging (Mark 7:4, also Naaman and Judith); 3. Figuratively, to overwhelm, as with debts, misfortunes, etc." In the N. T. rite, he says it denotes "an immersion in water, intended as a sign of sins washed away, and received by those who wished to be admitted to the benefits of Messiah's reign."

Döllinger, Kirche und Kirchen, 337—"The Baptists are, however, from the Protestant point of view, unassailable, since for their demand of baptism by submersion they have the clear Bible text; and the authority of the church and of her testimony is not regarded by either party"—i. e., by either Baptists or Protestants, generally. Prof. Harnack, of Giessen, writes in the Independent, Feb. 19, 1885—"1. Baptizein undoubtedly signifies immersion (eintauchen). 2. No proof can be found that it signifies anything else in the N. T. and in the most ancient Christian literature. The suggestion regarding a 'sacred sense' is out of the question. 3. There is no passage in the N. T. which suggests the supposition that any New Testament author attached to the word baptizein any other sense than eintauchen = untertauchen (immerse, submerge)." See Com. of Meyer, and Cunningham, Croall lectures.

Thirdly,—the absence of any use of the word in the passive voice with "water" as its subject confirms our conclusion that its meaning is "to immerse." Water is never said to be baptized upon a man.

(b) From the use of the verb βαπτίζω with prepositions:

First,—with εἰς (Mark 1:9—where Ἰορδάνην is the element into which the person passes in the act of being baptized).

Mark 1:9, marg.—"And it came to pass in those days, that Jesus came from Nazareth of Galilee, and was baptized of John into the Jordan."

Secondly,—with ἐν (Mark 1:5, 8; cf. Mat. 3:11. John 1:26, 31, 33; cf. Acts 2:2, 4). In these texts, ἐν is to be taken, not instrumentally, but as indicating the element in which the immersion takes place.

Mark 1:5, 8—"they were baptized of him in the river Jordan, confessing their sins.... I baptized you in water; but he shall baptize you in the Holy Spirit"—here see Meyer's Com. on Mat. 3:11—"ἐν is in accordance with the meaning of βαπτίζω (immerse), not to be understood instrumentally, but on the contrary, in the sense of the element in which the immersion takes place." Those who pray for a "baptism of the Holy Spirit" pray for such a pouring out of the Spirit as shall fill the place and permit them to be flooded or immersed in his abundant presence and power; see C. E. Smith, Baptism of Fire, 1881:305-311. Plumptre: "The baptism with the Holy Ghost would imply that the souls thus baptized would be plunged, as it were, in that creative and informing Spirit, which was the source of light and holiness and wisdom."

A. J. Gordon, Ministry of the Spirit, 67—"The upper room became the Spirit's baptistery. His presence 'filled all the house where they were sitting' (Acts 2:2).... Baptism in the Holy Spirit was given once for all on the day of Pentecost, when the Paraclete came in person to make his abode in the church. It does not follow that every believer has received this baptism. God's gift is one thing,—our appropriation of that gift is quite another thing. Our relation to the second and to the third persons of the Godhead is exactly parallel in this respect. 'God so loved the world, that he gave his only begotten Son' (John 3:16). 'But as many as received him, to them gave he the right to become children of God, even to them that believe on his name' (John 1:12). We are required to appropriate the Spirit as sons, in the same way that we are required to appropriate Christ as sinners.... 'He breathed on them, and saith unto them, Receive ye'—take ye, actively—'the Holy Spirit' (John 20:22)."

(c) From circumstances attending the administration of the ordinance (Mark 1:10—ἀναβαίνων ἐκ τοῦ ὕδατος; John 3:23—ὕδατα πολλά; Acts 8:38, 39—κατέβησαν εἰς τὸ ὕδωρ ... ἀνέβησαν ἐκ τοῦ ὕδατος).

Mark 1:10—"coming up out of the water"; John 3:23—"And John also was baptizing in Ænon near to Salim, because there was much water there"—a sufficient depth of water for baptizing; see Prof. W. A. Stevens, on Ænon near to Salim, in Journ. Soc. of Bib. Lit. and Exegesis, Dec. 1883. Acts 8:38, 39—"and they both went down into the water, both Philip and the eunuch; and he baptized him. And when they came up out of the water...." In the case of Philip and the eunuch, President Timothy Dwight, in S. S. Times, Aug. 27, 1892, says: "The baptism was apparently by immersion." The Editor adds that "practically scholars are agreed that the primitive meaning of the word 'baptize' was to immerse."

(d) From figurative allusions to the ordinance.

Mark 10:38—"Are ye able to drink the cup that I drink? or to be baptized with the baptism that I am baptized with?"—here the cup is the cup of suffering in Gethsemane; cf. Luke 22:42—"Father, if thou be willing, remove this cup from me"; and the baptism is the baptism of death on Calvary, and of the grave that was to follow; cf. Luke 12:50—"I have a baptism to be baptized with; and how am I straitened till it be accomplished!" Death presented itself to the Savior's mind as a baptism, because it was a sinking under the floods of suffering. Rom. 6:4—"We were buried therefore with him through baptism into death: that like as Christ was raised from the dead through the glory of the Father, so we also might walk in newness of life"—Conybeare and Howson, Life and Epistles of St. Paul, say, on this passage, that "it cannot be understood without remembering that the primitive method of baptism was by immersion." On Luke 12:49, marg.—"I came to cast fire upon the earth, and how would I that it were already kindled!"—see Wendt, Teaching of Jesus, 2:225—"He knew that he was called to bring a new energy and movement into the world, which mightily seizes and draws everything towards it, as a hurled firebrand, which whereever it falls kindles a flame which expands into a vast sea of fire"—the baptism of fire, the baptism in the Holy Spirit?

1 Cor. 10:1, 2—"our fathers were all under the cloud, and all passed through the sea; and were all baptized unto Moses in the cloud and in the sea"; Col. 2:12—"having been buried with him in baptism, wherein ye were also raised with him"; Heb. 10:22—"having our hearts sprinkled from an evil conscience, and having our body washed [λελουμένοι] with pure water"—here Trench, N. T. Synonyms, 216, 217, says that "λούω implies always, not the bathing of a part of the body, but of the whole." 1 Pet 3:20, 21—"saved through water: which also after a true likeness doth now save you, even baptism, not the putting away of the filth of the flesh, but the interrogation of a good conscience toward God, through the resurrection of Jesus Christ"—as the ark whose sides were immersed in water saved Noah, so the immersion of believers typically saves them; that is, the answer of a good conscience, the turning of the soul to God, which baptism symbolizes. "In the ritual of Moses and Aaron, three things were used: oil, blood, and water. The oil was poured, the blood was sprinkled, the water was used for complete ablution first of all, and subsequently for partial ablution to those to whom complete ablution had been previously administered" (Wm. Ashmore).

(e) From the testimony of church history as to the practice of the early church.

Tertullian, De Baptismo, chap. 12—"Others make the suggestion (forced enough, clearly) that the apostles then served the turn of baptism when in their little ship they were sprinkled and covered with the waves; that Peter himself also was immersed enough when he walked on the sea. It is however, as I think, one thing to be sprinkled or intercepted by the violence of the sea; another thing to be baptized in obedience to the discipline of religion." Fisher, Beginnings of Christianity, 565—"Baptism, it is now generally agreed among scholars, was commonly administered by immersion." Schaff, History of the Apostolic Church, 570—"Respecting the form of baptism, the impartial historian is compelled by exegesis and history substantially to yield the point to the Baptists." Elsewhere Dr. Schaff says: "The baptism of Christ in the Jordan, and the illustrations of baptism used in the N. T., are all in favor of immersion, rather than of sprinkling, as is freely admitted by the best exegetes, Catholic and Protestant, English and German. Nothing can be gained by unnatural exegesis. The persistency and aggressiveness of Baptists have driven pedobaptists to opposite extremes."

Dean Stanley, in his address at Eton College, March, 1879, on Historical Aspects of American Churches, speaks of immersion as "the primitive, apostolical, and, till the 13th century, the universal, mode of baptism, which is still retained throughout the Eastern churches, and which is still in our own church as positively enjoined in theory as it is universally neglected in practice." The same writer, in the Nineteenth Century, Oct. 1879, says that "the change from immersion to sprinkling has set aside the larger part of the apostolic language regarding baptism, and has altered the very meaning of the word." Neander, Church Hist., 1:310—"In respect to the form of baptism, it was, in conformity with the original institution and the original import of the symbol, performed by immersion, as a sign of entire baptism into the Holy Spirit, of being entirely penetrated by the same.... It was only with the sick, where exigency required it, that any exception was made. Then it was administered by sprinkling; but many superstitious persons imagined such sprinkling to be not fully valid, and stigmatized those thus baptized as clinics."

Until recently, there has been no evidence that clinic baptism, i. e., the baptism of a sick or dying person in bed by pouring water copiously around him, was practised earlier than the time of Novatian, in the third century; and in these cases there is good reason to believe that a regenerating efficacy was ascribed to the ordinance. We are now, however, compelled to recognize a departure from N. T. precedent somewhat further back. Important testimony is that of Prof. Harnack, of Giessen, in the Independent of Feb. 19, 1885—"Up to the present moment we possess no certain proof from the period of the second century, in favor of the fact that baptism by aspersion was then even facultatively administered; for Tertullian (De Pœnit., 6, and De Baptismo, 12) is uncertain; and the age of those pictures upon which is represented a baptism by aspersion is not certain. The 'Teaching of the Twelve Apostles,' however, has now instructed us that already, in very early times, people in the church took no offence when aspersion was put in place of immersion, when any kind of outward circumstances might render immersion impossible or impracticable.... But the rule was also certainly maintained that immersion was obligatory if the outward conditions of such a performance were at hand." This seems to show that, while the corruption of the N. T. rite began soon after the death of the apostles, baptism by any other form than immersion was even then a rare exception, which those who introduced the change sought to justify upon the plea of necessity. See Schaff, Teaching of the Twelve Apostles, 29-57, and other testimony in Coleman, Christian Antiquities, 275; Stuart, in Bib. Repos., 1883:355-363.

The "Teaching of the Twelve Apostles," section 7, reads as follows: "Baptize ... in living water. And if thou have no living water, baptize in other water; and if thou canst not in cold, then in warm. And if thou have neither, pour water upon the head thrice." Here it is evident that "baptize" means only "immerse," but if water be scarce pouring may be substituted for baptism. Dr. A. H. Newman, Antipedobaptism, 5, says that "The Teaching of the Twelve Apostles" may possibly belong to the second half of the second century, but in its present form is probably much later. It does not explicitly teach baptismal regeneration, but this view seems to be implied in the requirement, in case of an absolute lack of a sufficiency of water of any kind for baptism proper, that pouring water on the head three times be resorted to as a substitute. Catechetical instruction, repentance, fasting, and prayer, must precede the baptismal rite.

Dexter, in his True Story of John Smyth and Sebaptism, maintains that immersion was a new thing in England in 1641. But if so, it was new, as Congregationalism was new—a newly restored practice and ordinance of apostolic times. For reply to Dexter, see Long, in Bap. Rev., Jan. 1883:12, 13, who tells us, on the authority of Blunt's Ann. Book of Com. Prayer, that from 1085 to 1549, the "Salisbury Use" was the accepted mode, and this provided for the child's trine immersion. "The Prayerbook of Edward VI succeeded to the Salisbury Use in 1549; but in this too immersion has the place of honor—affusion is only for the weak. The English church has never sanctioned sprinkling (Blunt, 226). In 1664, the Westminster Assembly said 'sprinkle or pour,' thus annulling what Christ commanded 1600 years before. Queen Elizabeth was immersed in 1533. If in 1641 immersion had been so generally and so long disused that men saw it with wonder and regarded it as a novelty, then the more distinct, emphatic, and peculiarly their own was the work of the Baptists. They come before the world, with no partners, or rivals, or abettors, or sympathizers, as the restorers and preservers of Christian baptism."

(f) From the doctrine and practice of the Greek church.

DeStourdza, the greatest modern theologian of the Greek church, writes; "βαπτίζω signifies literally and always 'to plunge.' Baptism and immersion are therefore identical, and to say 'baptism by aspersion' is as if one should say 'immersion by aspersion,' or any other absurdity of the same nature. The Greek church maintain that the Latin church, instead of a βαπτισμός, practice a mere ῥαντισμός,—instead of baptism, a mere sprinkling"—quoted in Conant on Mat., appendix, 99. See also Broadus on Immersion, 18.

The evidence that immersion is the original mode of baptism is well summed up by Dr. Marcus Dods, in his article on Baptism in Hastings' Dictionary of Christ and the Apostles. Dr. Dods defines baptism as "a rite wherein by immersion in water the participant symbolizes and signalizes his transition from an impure to a pure life, his death to a past he abandons, and his birth to a future he desires." As regards the "mode of baptism," he remarks: "That the normal mode was by immersion of the whole body may be inferred (a) from the meaning of baptizo, which is the intensive or frequentative form of bapto, 'I dip,' and denotes to immerse or submerge—the point is, that 'dip' or 'immerse' is the primary, 'wash' the secondary meaning of bapto or baptizo. (b) The same inference may be drawn from the law laid down regarding the baptism of proselytes: 'As soon as he grows whole of the wound of circumcision, they bring him to baptism, and being placed in the water, they again instruct him in some weightier and in some lighter commands of the Law, which being heard, he plunges himself and comes up, and behold, he is an Israelite in all things' (Lightfoot's Horæ Hebraicæ). To use Pauline language, his old man is dead and buried in water, and he rises from this cleansing grave a new man. The full significance of the rite would have been lost had immersion not been practised. Again, it was required in proselyte baptism that 'every person baptized must dip his whole body, now stripped and made naked, at one dipping. And wheresoever in the Law washing of the body or garments is mentioned, it means nothing else than the washing of the whole body.' (c) That immersion was the mode of baptism adopted by John is the natural conclusion from his choosing the neighborhood of the Jordan as the scene of his labors; and from the statement of John 3:23 that he was baptizing in Enon 'because there was much water there.' (d) That this form was continued in the Christian Church appears from the expression Loutron palingenesias (bath of regeneration, Titus 3:5), and from the use made by St. Paul in Romans 6 of the symbolism. This is well put by Bingham (Antiquities xi.2)." The author quotes Bingham to the effect that "total immersion under water" was the universal practice during the early Christian centuries "except in some particular cases of exigence, wherein they allow of sprinkling, as in the case of a clinic baptism, or where there is a scarcity of water." Dr. Dods continues: "This statement exactly reflects the ideas of the Pauline Epistles and the 'Didache'" (Teaching of the Twelve Apostles).

The prevailing usage of any word determines the sense it bears, when found in a command of Christ. We have seen, not only that the prevailing usage of the Greek language determines the meaning of the word "baptize" to be "immerse," but that this is its fundamental, constant, and only meaning. The original command to baptize is therefore a command to immerse.

As evidence that quite diverse sections of the Christian world are coming to recognize the original form of baptism to be immersion, we may cite the fact that a memorial to the late Archbishop of Canterbury has recently been erected in the parish church of Lambeth, and that it is in the shape of a "font-grave," in which a believer can be buried with Christ in baptism; and also that the Rev. G. Campbell Morgan has had a baptistery constructed in the newly renovated Westminster Congregational Church in London.

Pfleiderer, Philos. Religion, 2:211—"As in the case of the Lord's Supper, so did Baptism also first receive its sacramental significance through Paul. As he saw in the immersing under water the symbolical repetition of the death and resurrection of Christ, baptism appeared to him as the act of spiritual dying and renovation, or regeneration, of incorporation into the mystical body of Christ, that 'new creation.' As for Paul the baptism of adults only was in question, faith in Christ is already of course presupposed by it, and baptism is just the act in which faith realizes the decisive resolution of giving one's self up actually as belonging to Christ and his community. Yet the outward act is not on that account a mere semblance of what is already present in faith, but according to the mysticism common to Paul with the whole ancient world, the symbolical act effectuates what it typifies, and therefore in this case the mortification of the carnal man and the animation of the spiritual man." For the view that sprinkling or pouring constitutes valid baptism, see Hall, Mode of Baptism. Per contra, see Hovey, in Baptist Quarterly, April, 1875; Wayland, Principles and Practices of Baptists, 85; Carson, Noel, Judson, and Pengilly, on Baptism; especially recent and valuable is Burrage, Act of Baptism.

B. No church has the right to modify or dispense with this command of Christ.

This is plain:

(a) From the nature of the church. Notice:

First,—that, besides the local church, no other visible church of Christ is known to the New Testament. Secondly,—that the local church is not a legislative, but is simply an executive, body. Only the authority which originally imposed its laws can amend or abrogate them. Thirdly,—that the local church cannot delegate to any organization or council of churches any power which it does not itself rightfully possess. Fourthly,—that the opposite principle puts the church above the Scriptures and above Christ, and would sanction all the usurpations of Rome.

Mat. 5:19—"Whosoever therefore shall break one of these least commandments, and shall teach men so, shall be called least in the kingdom of heaven: but whosoever shall do and teach them, he shall be called great in the kingdom of heaven"; cf. 2 Sam. 6:7—"And the anger of Jehovah was kindled against Uzzah; and God smote him there for his error; and there he died by the ark of God." Shakespeare, Henry VI, Part I, 2:4—"Faith, I have been a truant in the law, And never yet could frame my will to it, And therefore frame the law unto my will." As at the Reformation believers rejoiced to restore communion in both kinds, so we should rejoice to restore baptism as to its subjects and as to its meaning. To administer it to a wailing and resisting infant, or to administer it in any other form than that prescribed by Jesus' command and example, is to desecrate and destroy the ordinance.

(b) From the nature of God's command:

First,—as forming a part, not only of the law, but of the fundamental law, of the church of Christ. The power claimed for a church to change it is not only legislative but constitutional. Secondly,—as expressing the wisdom of the Lawgiver. Power to change the command can be claimed for the church, only on the ground that Christ has failed to adapt the ordinance to changing circumstances, and has made obedience to it unnecessarily difficult and humiliating. Thirdly,—as providing in immersion the only adequate symbol of those saving truths of the gospel which both of the ordinances have it for their office to set forth, and without which they become empty ceremonies and forms. In other words, the church has no right to change the method of administering the ordinance, because such a change vacates the ordinance of its essential meaning. As this argument, however, is of such vital importance, we present it more fully in a special discussion of the Symbolism of Baptism.

Abraham Lincoln, in his debates with Douglas, ridiculed the idea that there could be any constitutional way of violating the Constitution. F. L. Anderson: "In human governments we change the constitution to conform to the will of the people; in the divine government we change the will of the people to conform to the Constitution." For advocacy of the church's right to modify the form of an ordinance, see Coleridge, Aids to Reflection, in Works, 1:333-348—"Where a ceremony answered, and was intended to answer, several purposes which at its first institution were blended in respect of the time, but which afterward, by change of circumstances, were necessarily disunited, then either the church hath no power or authority delegated to her, or she must be authorized to choose and determine to which of the several purposes the ceremony should be attached." Baptism, for example, at the first symbolized not only entrance into the church of Christ, but personal faith in him as Savior and Lord. It is assumed that entrance into the church and personal faith are now necessarily disunited. Since baptism is in charge of the church, she can attach baptism to the former, and not to the latter.

We of course deny that the separation of baptism from faith is ever necessary. We maintain, on the contrary, that thus to separate the two is to pervert the ordinance, and to make it teach the doctrine of hereditary church membership and salvation by outward manipulation apart from faith. We say with Dean Stanley (on Baptism, in the Nineteenth Century, Oct. 1879), though not, as he does, with approval, that the change in the method of administering the ordinance shows "how the spirit that lives and moves in human society can override the most sacred ordinances." We cannot with him call this spirit "the free spirit of Christianity,"—we regard it rather as an evil spirit of disobedience and unbelief. "Baptists are therefore pledged to prosecute the work of the Reformation until the church shall return to the simple forms it possessed under the apostles" (G. M. Stone). See Curtis, Progress of Baptist Principles, 234-245.

Objections: 1. Immersion is often impracticable.—We reply that, when really impracticable, it is no longer a duty. Where the will to obey is present, but providential circumstances render outward obedience impossible, Christ takes the will for the deed.

2. It is often dangerous to health and life.—We reply that, when it is really dangerous, it is no longer a duty. But then, we have no warrant for substituting another act for that which Christ has commanded. Duty demands simple delay until it can be administered with safety. It must be remembered that ardent feeling nerves even the body. "Brethren, if your hearts be warm, Ice and snow can do no harm." The cold climate of Russia does not prevent the universal practice of immersion by the Greek church of that country.

3. It is indecent.—We reply, that there is need of care to prevent exposure, but that with this care there is no indecency, more than in fashionable sea-bathing. The argument is valid only against a careless administration of the ordinance, not against immersion itself.

4. It is inconvenient.—We reply that, in a matter of obedience to Christ, we are not to consult convenience. The ordinance which symbolizes his sacrificial death, and our spiritual death with him, may naturally involve something of inconvenience, but joy in submitting to that inconvenience will be a test of the spirit of obedience. When the act is performed, it should be performed as Christ enjoined.

5. Other methods of administration have been blessed to those who submitted to them.—We reply that God has often condescended to human ignorance, and has given his Spirit to those who honestly sought to serve him, even by erroneous forms, such as the Mass. This, however, is not to be taken as a divine sanction of the error, much less as a warrant for the perpetuation of a false system on the part of those who know that it is a violation of Christ's commands. It is, in great part, the position of its advocates, as representatives of Christ and his church, that gives to this false system its power for evil.

3. The Symbolism of Baptism.

Baptism symbolizes the previous entrance of the believer into the communion of Christ's death and resurrection,—or, in other words, regeneration through union with Christ.

A. Expansion of this statement as to the symbolism of baptism.

Baptism, more particularly, is a symbol:

(a) Of the death and resurrection of Christ.

Rom. 6:3—"Or are ye ignorant that all we who were baptized into Christ Jesus were baptized into his death?" cf. Mat 3:13—"Then cometh Jesus from Galilee to the Jordan unto John, to be baptized of him"; Mark 10:38—"Are ye able to drink the cup that I drink? or to be baptized with the baptism that I am baptized with?"; Luke 12:50—"But I have a baptism to be baptized with; and how am I straitened till it be accomplished!" Col. 2:12—"buried with him in baptism, wherein ye were also raised with him through faith in the working of God, who raised him from the dead." For the meaning of these passages, see note on the baptism of Jesus, under B. (a), pages 942, 943.

Denney, in Expositor's Greek Testament, on Rom. 6:3-5—"The argumentative requirements of the passage ... demand the idea of an actual union to, or incorporation in Christ.... We were buried with him [in the act of immersion] through that baptism into his death.... If the baptism, which is a similitude of Christ's death, has had a reality answering to its obvious import, so that we have really died in it as Christ died, then we shall have a corresponding experience of resurrection. Baptism, inasmuch as one emerges from the water after being immersed, is a similitude of resurrection as well as of death."

(b) Of the purpose of that death and resurrection,—namely, to atone for sin, and to deliver sinners from its penalty and power.

Rom. 6:4—"We were buried therefore with him through baptism into death: that like as Christ was raised from the dead through the glory of the Father, so we also might walk in newness of life"; cf. 7, 10, 11—"for he that hath died is justified from sin.... For the death that he died, he died unto sin once: but the life that he liveth, he liveth unto God. Even so reckon ye also yourselves to be dead unto sin, but alive unto God in Christ Jesus"; 2 Cor. 5:14—"we thus judge, that one died for all, therefore all died." Baptism is therefore a confession of evangelical faith both as to sin, and as to the deity and atonement of Christ. No one is properly a Baptist who does not acknowledge these truths which baptism signifies.

T. W. Chambers, in Presb. and Ref. Rev., Jan. 1890:113-118, objects that this view of the symbolism of baptism is based on two texts, Rom. 6:4 and Col. 2:12, which are illustrative and not explanatory, while the great majority of passages make baptism only an act of purification. Yet Dr. Chambers concedes: "It is to be admitted that nearly all modern critical expositors (Meyer, Godet, Alford, Conybeare, Lightfoot, Beet) consider that there is a reference here [in Rom. 6:4] to the act of baptism, which, as the Bishop of Durham says, 'is the grave of the old man and the birth of the new—an image of the believer's participation both in the death and in the resurrection of Christ.... As he sinks beneath the baptismal waters, the believer buries there all his corrupt affections and past sins; as he emerges thence, he rises regenerate, quickened to new hopes and a new life.' "

(c) Of the accomplishment of that purpose in the person baptized,—who thus professes his death to sin and resurrection to spiritual life.

Gal. 3:27—"For as many of you as were baptized into Christ did put on Christ"; 1 Pet. 3:21—"which [water] also after a true likeness doth now save you, even baptism, not the putting away of the filth of the flesh, but the interrogation of a good conscience toward God, through the resurrection of Jesus Christ"; cf. Gal. 2:19, 20—"For I through the law died unto the law, that I might live unto God. I have been crucified with Christ; and it is no longer I that live, but Christ liveth in me: and that life which I now live in the flesh I live in faith, the faith which is in the Son of God, who loved me, and gave himself up for me"; Col. 3:3—"For ye died, and your life is hid with Christ in God."

C. H. M.: "A truly baptized person is one who has passed from the old world into the new.... The water rolls over his person, signifying that his place in nature is ignored, that his old nature is entirely set aside, in short, that he is a dead man, that the flesh with all that pertained thereto—its sins and its liabilities—is buried in the grave of Christ and can never come into God's sight again.... When the believer rises up from the water, expression is given to the truth that he comes up as the possessor of a new life, even the resurrection life of Christ, to which divine righteousness inseparably attaches."

(d) Of the method in which that purpose is accomplished,—by union with Christ, receiving him and giving one's self to him by faith.

Rom. 6:5—"For if we have become united [σύμφυτοι] with him in the likeness of his death, we shall be also in the likeness of his resurrection"—σύμφυτοι, or συμπεφυκώς, is used of the man and the horse as grown together in the Centaur, by Lucian, Dial. Mort., 16:4, and by Xenophon, Cyrop., 4:3:18. Col. 2:12—"having been buried with him in baptism, wherein ye were also raised with him through faith in the working of God, who raised him from the dead." Dr. N. S. Burton: "The oneness of the believer and Christ is expressed by the fact that the one act of immersion sets forth the death and resurrection of both Christ and the believer." As the voluntary element in faith has two parts, a giving and a taking, so baptism illustrates both. Submergence = surrender to Christ; emergence = reception of Christ; see page 839, (b). "Putting on Christ" (Gal. 3:27) is the burying of the old life and the rising to a new. Cf. the active and the passive obedience of Christ (pages 749, 770), the two elements of justification (pages 854-859), the two aspects of formal worship (page 23), the two divisions of the Lord's Prayer.

William Ashmore holds that incorporation into Christ is the root idea of baptism, union with Christ's death and resurrection being only a part of it. We are "baptized into Christ" (Rom. 6:3), as the Israelites were "baptized into Moses" (1 Cor. 10:2). As baptism symbolizes the incorporation of the believer into Christ, so the Lord's Supper symbolizes the incorporation of Christ into the believer. We go down into the water, but the bread goes down into us. We are "in Christ," and Christ is "in us." The candidate does not baptize himself, but puts himself wholly into the hands of the administrator. This seems symbolic of his committing himself entirely to Christ, of whom the administrator is the representative. Similarly in the Lord's Supper, it is Christ who through his representative distributes the emblems of his death and life.

E. G. Robinson regarded baptism as implying: 1. death to sin; 2. resurrection to new life in Christ; 3. entire surrender of ourselves to the authority of the triune God. Baptism "into the name of the Father and of the Son and of the Holy Spirit" (Mat 28:19) cannot imply supreme allegiance to the Father, and only subordinate allegiance to the Son. Baptism therefore is an assumption of supreme allegiance to Jesus Christ. N. E. Wood, in The Watchman, Dec. 3, 1896, 15—"Calvinism has its five points; but Baptists have also their own five points: the Trinity, the Atonement, Regeneration, Baptism, and an inspired Bible. All other doctrines gather round these."

(e) Of the consequent union of all believers in Christ.

Eph. 4:5—"one Lord, one faith, one baptism"; 1 Cor. 12:13—"For in one Spirit were we all baptized into one body, whether Jews or Greeks, whether bond or free; and were all made to drink of one Spirit"; cf. 10:3, 4—"and did all eat the same spiritual food; and did all drink the same spiritual drink: for they drank of a spiritual rock that followed them: and the rock was Christ."

In Eph. 4:5, it is noticeable that, not the Lord's Supper, but baptism, is referred to as the symbol of Christian unity. A. H. Strong, Cleveland Sermon, 1904—"Our fathers lived in a day when simple faith was subject to serious disabilities. The establishments frowned upon dissent and visited it with pains and penalties. It is no wonder that believers in the New Testament doctrine and polity felt that they must come out from what they regarded as an apostate church. They could have no sympathy with those who held back the truth in unrighteousness and persecuted the saints of God. But our doctrine has leavened all Christendom. Scholarship is on the side of immersion. Infant baptism is on the decline. The churches that once opposed us now compliment us on our stedfastness in the faith and on our missionary zeal. There is a growing spirituality in these churches, which prompts them to extend to us hands of fellowship. And there is a growing sense among us that the kingdom of Christ is wider than our own membership, and that loyalty to our Lord requires us to recognize his presence and blessing even in bodies which we do not regard as organized in complete accordance with the New Testament model. Faith in the larger Christ is bringing us out from our denominational isolation into an inspiring recognition of our oneness with the universal church of God throughout the world."

(f) Of the death and resurrection of the body,—which will complete the work of Christ in us, and which Christ's death and resurrection assure to all his members.

1 Cor. 15:12, 22—"Now if Christ is preached that he hath been raised from the dead, how say some among you that there is no resurrection of the dead?... For as in Adam all die, so also in Christ shall all be made alive." In the Scripture passages quoted above, we add to the argument from the meaning of the word βαπτίζω the argument from the meaning of the ordinance. Luther wrote, in his Babylonish Captivity of the Church, section 103 (English translation in Wace and Buchheim, First Principles of the Reformation, 192): "Baptism is a sign both of death and resurrection. Being moved by this reason, I would have those that are baptized to be altogether dipped into the water, as the word means and the mystery signifies." See Calvin on Acts 8:38; Conybeare and Howson on Rom. 6:4; Boardman, in Madison Avenue Lectures, 115-135.

B. Inferences from the passages referred to.

(a) The central truth set forth by baptism is the death and resurrection of Christ,—and our own death and resurrection only as connected with that.

The baptism of Jesus in Jordan, equally with the subsequent baptism of his followers, was a symbol of his death. It was his death which he had in mind, when he said: "Are ye able to drink the cup that I drink? or to be baptized with the baptism that I am baptized with?" (Mark 10:38); "But I have a baptism to be baptized with; and how am I straitened till it be accomplished!" (Luke 12:50). The being immersed and overwhelmed in waters is a frequent metaphor in all languages to express the rush of successive troubles; compare Ps. 69:2—"I am come into deep waters, where the floods overflow me"; 42:7—"All thy waves and thy billows are gone over me"; 124:4, 5—"Then the waters had overwhelmed us, The stream had gone over our soul; Then the proud waters had gone over our soul."

So the suffering, death, and burial, which were before our Lord, presented themselves to his mind as a baptism, because the very idea of baptism was that of a complete submersion under the floods of waters. Death was not to be poured upon Christ,—it was no mere sprinkling of suffering which he was to endure, but a sinking into the mighty waters, and a being overwhelmed by them. It was the giving of himself to this, which he symbolized by his baptism in Jordan. That act was not arbitrary, or formal, or ritual. It was a public consecration, a consecration to death, to death for the sins of the world. It expressed the essential nature and meaning of his earthly work: the baptism of water at the beginning of his ministry consciously and designedly prefigured the baptism of death with which that ministry was to close.

Jesus' submission to John's baptism of repentance, the rite that belonged only to sinners, can be explained only upon the ground that he was "made to be sin on our behalf" (2 Cor. 5:21). He had taken our nature upon him, without its hereditary corruption indeed, but with all its hereditary guilt, that he might redeem that nature and reunite it to God. As one with humanity, he had in his unconscious childhood submitted to the rites of circumcision, purification, and legal redemption (Luke 2:21-24; cf. Ex. 13:2, 13; see Lange, Alford, Webster and Wilkinson on Luke 2:24)—all of them rites appointed for sinners. "Made in the likeness of men" (Phil. 2:7), "the likeness of sinful flesh" (Rom. 8:3), he was "to put away sin by the sacrifice of himself" (Heb. 9:26).

In his baptism, therefore, he could say, "Thus it becometh us to fulfil all righteousness" (Mat. 3:15) because only through the final baptism of suffering and death, which this baptism in water foreshadowed, could he "make an end of sins" and "bring in everlasting righteousness" (Dan. 9:24) to the condemned and ruined world. He could not be "the Lord our Righteousness" (Jer. 23:6) except by first suffering the death due to the nature he had assumed, thereby delivering it from its guilt and perfecting it forever. All this was indicated in that act by which he was first "made manifest to Israel" (John 1:31). In his baptism in Jordan, he was buried in the likeness of his coming death, and raised in the likeness of his coming resurrection. 1 John 5:6—"This is he that came by water and blood, even Jesus Christ; not in the water only, but in the water and in the blood" = in the baptism of water at the beginning of his ministry, and in the baptism of blood with which that ministry was to close.

As that baptism pointed forward to Jesus' death, so our baptism points backward to the same, as the centre and substance of his redeeming work, the one death by which we live. We who are "baptized into Christ" are "baptized into his death" (Rom. 6:3), that is, into spiritual communion and participation in that death which he died for our salvation; in short, in baptism we declare in symbol that his death has become ours. On the Baptism of Jesus, see A. H. Strong, Philosophy and Religion, 226-237.

(b) The correlative truth of the believer's death and resurrection, set forth in baptism, implies, first,—confession of sin and humiliation on account of it, as deserving of death; secondly,—declaration of Christ's death for sin, and of the believer's acceptance of Christ's substitutionary work; thirdly,—acknowledgment that the soul has become partaker of Christ's life, and now lives only in and for him.

A false mode of administering the ordinance has so obscured the meaning of baptism that it has to multitudes lost all reference to the death of Christ, and the Lord's Supper is assumed to be the only ordinance which is intended to remind us of the atoning sacrifice to which we owe our salvation. For evidence of this, see the remarks of President Woolsey in the Sunday School Times: "Baptism it [the Christian religion] could share in with the doctrine of John the Baptist, and if a similar rite had existed under the Jewish law, it would have been regarded as appropriate to a religion which inculcated renunciation of sin and purity of heart and life. But [in the Lord's Supper] we go beyond the province of baptism to the very penetrale of the gospel, to the efficacy and meaning of Christ's death."

Baptism should be a public act. We cannot afford to relegate it to a corner, or to celebrate it in private, as some professedly Baptist churches of England are said to do. Like marriage, the essence of it is the joining of ourselves to another before the world. In baptism we merge ourselves in Christ, before God and angels and men. The Mohammedan stands five times a day, and prays with his face toward Mecca, caring not who sees him. Luke 12:8—"Every one who shall confess me before men, him shall the Son of man also confess before the angels of God."

(c) Baptism symbolizes purification, but purification in a peculiar and divine way,—namely, through the death of Christ and the entrance of the soul into communion with that death. The radical defect of sprinkling or pouring as a mode of administering the ordinance, is that it does not point to Christ's death as the procuring cause of our purification.

It is a grievous thing to say by symbol, as those do say who practice sprinkling in place of immersion, that a man may regenerate himself, or, if not this, yet that his regeneration may take place without connection with Christ's death. Edward Beecher's chief argument against Baptist views is drawn from John 3:22-25—"a questioning on the part of John's disciples with a Jew about purifying." Purification is made to be the essential meaning of baptism, and the conclusion is drawn that any form expressive of purification will answer the design of the ordinance. But if Christ's death is the procuring cause of our purification, we may expect it to be symbolized in the ordinance which declares that purification; if Christ's death is the central fact of Christianity, we may expect it to be symbolized in the initiatory rite of Christianity.

(d) In baptism we show forth the Lord's death as the original source of holiness and life in our souls, just as in the Lord's Supper we show forth the Lord's death as the source of all nourishment and strength after this life of holiness has been once begun. As the Lord's Supper symbolizes the sanctifying power of Jesus' death, so baptism symbolizes its regenerating power.

The truth of Christ's death and resurrection is a precious jewel, and it is given us in these outward ordinances as in a casket. Let us care for the casket lest we lose the gem. As a scarlet thread runs through every rope and cord of the British navy, testifying that it is the property of the Crown, so through every doctrine and ordinance of Christianity runs the red line of Jesus' blood. It is their common reference to the death of Christ that binds the two ordinances together.

(e) There are two reasons, therefore, why nothing but immersion will satisfy the design of the ordinance: first,—because nothing else can symbolize the radical nature of the change effected in regeneration—a change from spiritual death to spiritual life; secondly,—because nothing else can set forth the fact that this change is due to the entrance of the soul into communion with the death and resurrection of Christ.

Christian truth is an organism. Part is bound to part, and all together constitute one vitalized whole. To give up any single portion of that truth is like maiming the human body. Life may remain, but one manifestation of life has ceased. The whole body of Christian truth has lost its symmetry and a part of its power to save.

Pfleiderer, Philos. Religion, 2:212—"In the Eleusinian mysteries, the act of reception was represented as a regeneration, and the hierophant appointed to the temple service had to take a sacramental bath, out of which he proceeded as a 'new man' with a new name, which signifies that, as they were wont to say, 'the first one was forgotten,'—that is, the old man was put off at the same time with the old name. The parallel of this Eleusinian rite with the thoughts which Paul has written about Baptism in the Epistle to the Romans, and therefore from Corinth, is so striking that a connection between the two may well be conjectured; and all the more that even in the case of the Lord's Supper, Paul has brought in the comparison with the heathen festivals, in order to give a basis for his mystical theory."

(f) To substitute for baptism anything which excludes all symbolic reference to the death of Christ, is to destroy the ordinance, just as substituting for the broken bread and poured out wine of the communion some form of administration which leaves out all reference to the death of Christ would be to destroy the Lord's Supper, and to celebrate an ordinance of human invention.

Baptism, like the Fourth of July, the Passover, the Lord's Supper, is a historical monument. It witnesses to the world that Jesus died and rose again. In celebrating it, we show forth the Lord's death as truly as in the celebration of the Supper. But it is more than a historical monument. It is also a pictorial expression of doctrine. Into it are woven all the essential truths of the Christian scheme. It tells of the nature and penalty of sin, of human nature delivered from sin in the person of a crucified and risen Savior, of salvation secured for each human soul that is united to Christ, of obedience to Christ as the way to life and glory. Thus baptism stands from age to age as a witness for God—a witness both to the facts and to the doctrine of Christianity. To change the form of administering the ordinance is therefore to strike a blow at Christianity and at Christ, and to defraud the world of a part of God's means of salvation. See Ebrard's view of Baptism, in Baptist Quarterly, 1869:257, and in Olshausen's Com. on N. T., 1:270, and 3:594. Also Lightfoot, Com. on Colossians 2:20, and 3:1.

Ebrard: "Baptism = Death." So Sanday, Com. on Rom. 6—"Immersion = Death; Submersion = Burial (the ratification of death); Emergence = Resurrection (the ratification of life)." William Ashmore: "Solomon's Temple had two monumental pillars: Jachin, 'he shall establish,' and Boaz, 'in it is strength.' In Zechariah's vision were two olive trees on either side of the golden candlestick. In like manner, Christ has left two monumental witnesses to testify concerning himself—Baptism and the Lord's Supper." The lady in the street car, who had inadvertently stuck her parasol into a man's eye, very naturally begged his pardon. But he replied: "It is of no consequence, madame; I have still one eye left." Our friends who sprinkle or pour put out one eye of the gospel witness, break down one appointed monument of Christ's saving truth,—shall we be content to say that we have still one ordinance left? At the Rappahannock one of the Federal regiments, just because its standard was shot away, was mistaken by our own men for a regiment of Confederates, and was subjected to a murderous enfilading fire that decimated its ranks. Baptism and the Lord's Supper are the two flags of Christ's army,—we cannot afford to lose either one of them.

4. The Subjects of Baptism.

The proper subjects of baptism are those only who give credible evidence that they have been regenerated by the Holy Spirit,—or, in other words, have entered by faith into the communion of Christ's death and resurrection.

A. Proof that only persons giving evidence of being regenerated are proper subjects of baptism.

(a) From the command and example of Christ and his apostles, which show:

First, that those only are to be baptized who have previously been made disciples.

Mat. 28:19—"Go ye therefore, and make disciples of all the nations, baptizing them into the name of the Father and of the Son and of the Holy Spirit"; Acts 2:41—"They then that received his word were baptized."

Secondly, that those only are to be baptized who have previously repented and believed.

Mat. 3:2, 3, 6—"Repent ye ... make ye ready the way of the Lord ... and they were baptized of him in the river Jordan, confessing their sins"; Acts 2:37, 38—"Now when they heard this, they were pricked in their heart, and said unto Peter and the rest of the apostles, Brethren, what shall we do? And Peter said unto them, Repent ye, and be baptized every one of you"; 8:12—"But when they believed Philip preaching good tidings concerning the kingdom of God and the name of Jesus Christ, they were baptized, both men and women"; 18:8—"And Crispus, the ruler of the synagogue, believed in the Lord with all his house; and many of the Corinthians hearing believed, and were baptized"; 19:4—"John baptized with the baptism of repentance, saying unto the people that they should believe on him that should come after him, that is, on Jesus."

(b) From the nature of the church—as a company of regenerate persons.

John 3:5—"Except one be born of water and the Spirit, he cannot enter into the kingdom of God"; Rom. 6:13—"neither present your members unto sin as instruments of unrighteousness; but present yourselves unto God, as alive from the dead, and your members as instruments of righteousness unto God."

(c) From the symbolism of the ordinance,—as declaring a previous spiritual change in him who submits to it.

Acts 10:47—"Can any man forbid the water, that these should not be baptized, who have received the Holy Spirit as well as we?" Rom. 6:2-5—"We who died to sin, how shall we any longer live therein? Or are ye ignorant that all we who were baptized into Christ Jesus were baptized into his death? We were buried therefore with him through baptism into death: that like as Christ was raised from the dead through the glory of the Father, so we also might walk in newness of life. For if we have become united with him in the likeness of his death, we shall be also in the likeness of his resurrection"; Gal. 3:26, 27—"For ye are all sons of God, through faith, in Christ Jesus. For as many of you as were baptized into Christ did put on Christ."

As marriage should never be solemnized except between persons who are already joined in heart and with whom the outward ceremony is only the sign of an existing love, so baptism should never be administered except in the case of those who are already joined to Christ and who signify in the ordinance their union with him in his death and resurrection. See Dean Stanley on Baptism, 24—"In the apostolic age and in the three centuries which followed, it is evident that, as a general rule, those who came to baptism came in full age, of their own deliberate choice. The liturgical service of baptism was framed for full-grown converts, and is only by considerable adaptation applied to the case of infants"; Wayland, Principles and Practices of Baptists, 93; Robins, in Madison Avenue Lectures, 136-159.

B. Inferences from the fact that only persons giving evidence of being regenerate are proper subjects of baptism.

(a) Since only those who give credible evidence of regeneration are proper subjects of baptism, baptism cannot be the means of regeneration. It is the appointed sign, but is never the condition, of the forgiveness of sins.

Passages like Mat. 3:11; Mark 1:4; 16:16; John 3:5; Acts 2:38; 22:16; Eph. 5:26; Titus 3:5; and Heb. 10:22, are to be explained as particular instances "of the general fact that, in Scripture language, a single part of a complex action, and even that part of it which is most obvious to the senses, is often mentioned for the whole of it, and thus, in this case, the whole of the solemn transaction is designated by the external symbol." In other words, the entire change, internal and external, spiritual and ritual, is referred to in language belonging strictly only to the outward aspect of it. So the other ordinance is referred to by simply naming the visible "breaking of bread," and the whole transaction of the ordination of ministers is termed the "imposition of hands" (cf. Acts 2:42; 1 Tim. 4:14).

Mat. 3:11—"I indeed baptize you in water unto repentance"; Mark 1:4—"the baptism of repentance unto remission of sins"; 16:16—"He that believeth and is baptized shall be saved"; John 3:5—"Except one be born of water and the Spirit, he cannot enter into the kingdom of God"—here Nicodemus, who was familiar with John's baptism, and with the refusal of the Sanhedrin to recognize its claims, is told that the baptism of water, which he suspects may be obligatory, is indeed necessary to that complete change by which one enters outwardly, as well as inwardly, into the kingdom of God; but he is taught also, that to "be born of water" is worthless unless it is the accompaniment and sign of a new birth of "the Spirit"; and therefore, in the further statements of Christ, baptism is not alluded to; see verses 6, 8—"that which is born of the Spirit is spirit ... so is every one that is born of the Spirit."

Acts 2:38—"Repent ye, and be baptized ... unto the remission of your sins"—on this passage see Hackett: "The phrase 'in order to the forgiveness of sins' we connect naturally with both the preceding verbs ('repent' and 'be baptized'). The clause states the motive or object which should induce them to repent and be baptized. It enforces the entire exhortation, not one part to the exclusion of the other"—i. e., they were to repent for the remission of sins, quite as much as they were to be baptized for the remission of sins. Acts 22:16—"arise, and be baptized, and wash away thy sins, calling on his name"; Eph. 5:26—"that he might sanctify it [the church], having cleansed it by the washing of water with the word"; Tit. 3:5—"according

to his mercy he saved as, through the washing of regeneration [baptism] and renewing of the Holy Spirit [the new birth]"; Heb. 10:22—"having our hearts sprinkled from an evil conscience [regeneration]: and having our body washed with pure water [baptism]"; cf. Acts 2:42—"the breaking of bread"; 1 Tim. 4:14—"the laying on of the hands of the presbytery."

Dr. A. C. Kendrick: "Considering how inseparable they were in the Christian profession—believe and be baptized, and how imperative and absolute was the requisition upon the believer to testify his allegiance by baptism, it could not be deemed singular that the two should be thus united, as it were, in one complex conception.... We have no more right to assume that the birth from water involves the birth from the Spirit and thus do away with the one, than to assume that the birth from the Spirit involves the birth from water, and thus do away with the other. We have got to have them both, each in its distinctness, in order to fulfil the conditions of membership in the kingdom of God." Without baptism, faith is like the works of a clock that has no dial or hands by which one can tell the time; or like the political belief of a man who refuses to go to the polls and vote. Without baptism, discipleship is ineffective and incomplete. The inward change—regeneration by the Spirit—may have occurred, but the outward change—Christian profession—is yet lacking.

Campbellism, however, holds that instead of regeneration preceding baptism and expressing itself in baptism, it is completed only in baptism, so that baptism is a means of regeneration. Alexander Campbell: "I am bold to affirm that every one of them, who in the belief of what the apostle spoke was immersed, did, in the very instant in which he was put under water, receive the forgiveness of his sins and the gift of the Holy Spirit." But Peter commanded that men should be baptized because they had already received the Holy Spirit: Acts 10:47—"Can any man forbid the water, that these should not be baptized, who have received the Holy Spirit as well as we?" Baptists baptize Christians; Disciples baptize sinners, and in baptism think to make them Christians. With this form of sacramentalism, Baptists are necessarily less in sympathy than with pedobaptism or with sprinkling. The view of the

Disciples confines the divine efficiency to the word (see quotation from Campbell on page 821). It was anticipated by Claude Pajon, the Reformed theologian, in 1673: see Dorner, Gesch. prot. Theologie, 448-450. That this was not the doctrine of John the Baptist would appear from Josephus, Ant., 18:5:2, who in speaking of John's baptism says: "Baptism appears acceptable to God, not in order that those who were baptized might get free from certain sins, but in order that the body might be sanctified, because the soul beforehand had already been purified through righteousness."

Disciples acknowledge no formal creed, and they differ so greatly among themselves that we append the following statements of their founder and of later representatives. Alexander Campbell, Christianity Restored, 138 (in The Christian Baptist, 5:100): "In and by the act of immersion, as soon as our bodies are put under water, at that very instant our former or old sins are washed away.... Immersion and regeneration are Bible names for the same act.... It is not our faith in God's promise of remission, but our going down into the water, that obtains the remission of sins." W. E. Garrison, Alexander Campbell's Theology, 247-299—"Baptism, like naturalization, is the formal oath of allegiance by which an alien becomes a citizen. In neither case does the form in itself effect any magical change in the subject's disposition. In both cases a change of opinion and of affections is presupposed, and the form is the culmination of a process.... It is as easy for God to forgive our sins in the act of immersion as in any other way." All work of the Spirit is through the word, only through sensible means, emotions being no criterion. God is transcendent; all authority is external, enforced only by appeal to happiness—a thoroughly utilitarian system.

Isaac Erret is perhaps the most able of recent Disciples. In his tract entitled "Our Position," published by the Christian Publishing Company, St. Louis, he says: "As to the design of baptism, we part company with Baptists, and find ourselves more at home on the other side of the house; yet we cannot say that our position is just the same with that of any of them. Baptists say they baptize believers because they are forgiven, and they insist that they shall have the evidence of pardon before they are baptized. But the language used in the Scriptures declaring what baptism is for, is so plain and unequivocal that the great majority of Protestants as well as the Roman Catholics admit it in their creeds to be, in some sense, for the remission of sins. The latter, however, and many of the former, attach to it the idea of regeneration, and insist that in baptism regeneration by the Holy Spirit is actually conferred. Even the Westminster Confession squints strongly in this direction, albeit its professed adherents of the present time attempt to explain away its meaning. We are as far from this ritualistic extreme as from the anti-ritualism into which the Baptists have been driven. With us, regeneration must be so far accomplished before baptism that the subject is changed in heart, and in faith and penitence must have yielded up his heart to Christ—otherwise baptism is nothing but an empty form. But forgiveness is something distinct from regeneration. Forgiveness is an act of the Sovereign—not a change of the sinner's heart; and while it is extended in view of the sinner's faith and repentance, it needs to be offered in a sensible and tangible form, such that the sinner can seize it and appropriate it with unmistakable definiteness. In baptism he appropriates God's promise of forgiveness, relying on the divine testimonies: 'He that believeth and is baptized shall be saved'; 'Repent and be baptized, every one of you, in the name of Jesus Christ, for the remission of sins, and you shall receive the gift of the Holy Spirit.' He thus lays hold of the promise of Christ and appropriates it as his own. He does not merit it, nor procure it, nor earn it, in being baptized; but he appropriates what the mercy of God has provided and offered in the gospel. We therefore teach all who are baptized that, if they bring to their baptism a heart that renounces sin and implicitly trusts the power of Christ to save, they should rely on the Savior's own promise—'He that believeth and is baptized shall be saved.'"

All these utterances agree in making forgiveness chronologically distinct from regeneration, as the concluding point is distinct from the whole. Regeneration is not entirely the work of God,—it must be completed by man. It is not wholly a change of heart, it is also a change in outward action. We see in this system of thought the beginnings of sacramentalism, and we regard it as containing the same germs of error which are more fully developed in pedobaptist doctrine. Shakespeare represents this view in Henry V, 1:2—"What you speak is in your conscience washed As pure as sin with baptism"; Othello, 2:3—Desdemona could "Win the Moor—were't to renounce his baptism—All seals and symbols of redeemed sin."

Dr. G. W. Lasher, in the Journal and Messenger, holds that Mat. 3:11—"I indeed baptize you in water unto (εἰς) repentance"—does not imply that baptism effects the repentance; the baptism was because of the repentance, for John refused to baptize those who did not give evidence of repentance before baptism. Mat. 10:42—"whosoever shall give ... a cup of cold water only, in (εἰς) the name of a disciple"—the cup of cold water does not put one into the name of a disciple, or make him a disciple. Mat. 12:41—"The men of Nineveh ... repented at (εἰς) the preaching of Jonah" = because of. Dr. Lasher argues that, in all these cases, the meaning of εἰς is "in respect to," "with reference to." So he would translate Acts 2:38—"Repent ye, and be baptized ... with respect to, in reference to, the remission of sins." This is also the view of Meyer. He maintains that βαπτίζειν εἰς always means "baptize with reference to" (cf. Mat. 28:19; 1 Cor. 10:12; Gal. 3:27; Acts 2:38; 8:16; 19:5). We are brought through baptism, he would say, into fellowship with his death, so that we have a share ethically in his death, through the cessation of our life to sin.

The better parallel, however, in our judgment, is found in Rom. 10:10—"with the heart man believeth unto (εἰς) righteousness; and with the mouth confession is made unto (εἰς) salvation,"—where evidently salvation is the end to which works the whole change and process, including both faith and confession. So Broadus makes John's "baptism unto repentance" mean baptism in order to repentance, repentance including both the purpose of the heart and the outward expression of it, or baptism in order to complete and thorough repentance. Expositor's Greek Testament, on Acts 2:38—"unto the remission of your sins": "εἰς, unto, signifying the aim." For the High Church view, see Sadler, Church Doctrine, 41-124. On F. W. Robertson's view of Baptismal Regeneration, see Gordon, in Bap. Quar., 1869:405. On the whole matter of baptism for the remission of sins, see Gates, Baptists and Disciples (advocating the Disciple view); Willmarth, in Bap. Quar., 1877:1-26 (verging toward the Disciple view); and per contra, Adkins, Disciples and Baptists, booklet pub. by Am. Bap. Pub. Society (the best brief statement of the Baptist position); Bap. Quar., 1877:476-489; 1872:214; Jacob, Eccl. Pol. of N. T., 255, 256.

(b) As the profession of a spiritual change already wrought, baptism is primarily the act, not of the administrator, but of the person baptized.

Upon the person newly regenerate the command of Christ first terminates; only upon his giving evidence of the change within him does it become the duty of the church to see that he has opportunity to follow Christ in baptism. Since baptism is primarily the act of the convert, no lack of qualification on the part of the administrator invalidates the baptism, so long as the proper outward act is performed, with intent on the part of the person baptized to express the fact of a preceding spiritual renewal (Acts 2:37, 38).

Acts 2:37, 38—"Brethren, what shall we do?... Repent ye and be baptized." If baptism be primarily the act of the administrator or of the church, then invalidity in the administrator or the church renders the ordinance itself invalid. But if baptism be primarily the act of the person baptized—an act which it is the church's business simply to scrutinize and further, then nothing but the absence of immersion, or of an intent to profess faith in Christ, can invalidate the ordinance. It is the erroneous view that baptism is the act of the administrator which causes the anxiety of High Church Baptists to deduce their Baptist lineage from regularly baptized ministers all the way back to John the Baptist, and which induces many modern endeavors of pedobaptists to prove that the earliest Baptists of England and the Continent did not immerse. All these solicitudes are unnecessary. We have no need to prove a Baptist apostolic succession. If we can derive our doctrine and practice from the New Testament, it is all we require.

The Council of Trent was right in its Canon: "If any one saith that the baptism which is even given by heretics in the name of the Father and of the Son and of the Holy Ghost, with the intention of doing what the church doeth, is not true baptism, let him be anathema." Dr. Norman Fox: "It is no more important who baptizes a man than who leads him to Christ." John Spilsbury, first pastor of the church of Particular Baptists, holding to a limited atonement, in London, was newly baptized in 1633, on the ground that "baptizedness is not essential to the administrator," and he repudiated the demand for apostolic succession, as leading logically to the "popedom of Rome." In 1641, immersion followed, though two or three years before this, or in March, 1639, Roger Williams was baptized by Ezekiel Holliman in Rhode Island. Williams afterwards doubted its validity, thus clinging still to the notion of apostolic succession.

(c) As intrusted with the administration of the ordinances, however, the church is, on its part, to require of all candidates for baptism credible evidence of regeneration.

This follows from the nature of the church and its duty to maintain its own existence as an institution of Christ. The church which cannot restrict admission into its membership to such as are like itself in character and aims must soon cease to be a church by becoming indistinguishable from the world. The duty of the church to gain credible evidence of regeneration in the case of every person admitted into the body involves its right to require of candidates, in addition to a profession of faith with the lips, some satisfactory proof that this profession is accompanied by change in the conduct. The kind and amount of evidence which would have justified the reception of a candidate in times of persecution may not now constitute a sufficient proof of change of heart.

If an Odd Fellows' Lodge, in order to preserve its distinct existence, must have its own rules for admission to membership, much more is this true of the church. The church may make its own regulations with a view to secure credible evidence of regeneration. Yet it is bound to demand of the candidate no more than reasonable proof of his repentance and faith. Since the church is to be convinced of the candidate's fitness before it votes to receive him to its membership, it is generally best that the experience of the candidate should be related before the church. Yet in extreme cases, as of sickness, the church may hear this relation of experience through certain appointed representatives.

Baptism is sometimes figuratively described as "the door into the church." The phrase is unfortunate, since if by the church is meant the spiritual kingdom of God, then Christ is its only door; if the local body of believers is meant, then the faith of the candidate, the credible evidence of regeneration which he gives, the vote of the church itself, are all, equally with baptism, the door through which he enters. The door, in this sense, is a double door, one part of which is his confession of faith, and the other his baptism.

(d) As the outward expression of the inward change by which the believer enters into the kingdom of God, baptism is the first, in point of time, of all outward duties.

Regeneration and baptism, although not holding to each other the relation of effect and cause, are both regarded in the New Testament as essential to the restoration of man's right relations to God and to his people. They properly constitute parts of one whole, and are not to be unnecessarily separated. Baptism should follow regeneration with the least possible delay, after the candidate and the church have gained evidence that a spiritual change has been accomplished within him. No other duty and no other ordinance can properly precede it.

Neither the pastor nor the church should encourage the convert to wait for others' company before being baptized. We should aim continually to deepen the sense of individual responsibility to Christ, and of personal duty to obey his command of baptism just so soon as a proper opportunity is afforded. That participation in the Lord's Supper cannot properly precede Baptism, will be shown hereafter.

(e) Since regeneration is a work accomplished once for all, the baptism which symbolizes this regeneration is not to be repeated.

Even where the persuasion exists, on the part of the candidate, that at the time of baptism he was mistaken in thinking himself regenerated, the ordinance is not to be administered again, so long as it has once been submitted to, with honest intent, as a profession of faith in Christ. We argue this from the absence of any reference to second baptisms in the New Testament, and from the grave practical difficulties attending the opposite view. In Acts 19:1-5, we have an instance, not of rebaptism, but of the baptism for the first time of certain persons who had been wrongly taught with regard to the nature of John the Baptist's doctrine, and so had ignorantly submitted to an outward rite which had in it no reference to Jesus Christ and expressed no faith in him as a Savior. This was not John's baptism, nor was it in any sense true baptism. For this reason Paul commanded them to be "baptized in the name of the Lord Jesus."

In the respect of not being repeated, Baptism is unlike the Lord's Supper, which symbolizes the continuous sustaining power of Christ's death, while baptism symbolizes its power to begin a new life within the soul. In Acts 19:1-5, Paul instructs the new disciples that the real baptism of John, to which they erroneously supposed they had submitted, was not only a baptism of repentance, but a baptism of faith in the coming Savior. "And when they heard this, they were baptized in the name of the Lord Jesus"—as they had not been before. Here there was no rebaptism, for the mere outward submersion in water to which they had previously submitted, with no thought of professing faith in Christ, was no baptism at all—whether Johannine or Christian. See Brooks, in Baptist Quarterly, April, 1867, art.: Rebaptism.

Whenever it is clear, as in many cases of Campbellite immersion, that the candidate has gone down into the water, not with intent to profess a previously existing faith, but in order to be regenerated, baptism is still to be administered if the person subsequently believes on Christ. But wherever it appears that there was intent to profess an already existing faith and regeneration, there should be no repetition of the immersion, even though the ordinance has been administered by the Campbellites.

To rebaptize whenever a Christian's faith and joy are rekindled so that he begins to doubt the reality of his early experiences, would, in the case of many fickle believers, require many repetitions of the ordinance. The presumption is that, when the profession of faith was made by baptism, there was an actual faith which needed to be professed, and therefore that the baptism, though followed by much unbelief and many wanderings, was a valid one. Rebaptism, in the case of unstable Christians, tends to bring reproach upon the ordinance itself.

(f) So long as the mode and the subjects are such as Christ has enjoined, mere accessories are matters of individual judgment.

The use of natural rather than of artificial baptisteries is not to be elevated into an essential. The formula of baptism prescribed by Christ is "into the name of the Father and of the Son and of the Holy Spirit."

Mat. 28:19—"baptizing them into the name of the Father and of the Son and of the Holy Spirit"; cf. Acts 8:16—"they had been baptized into the name of the Lord Jesus"; Rom. 6:3—"Or are ye ignorant that all we who were baptized into Christ Jesus were baptized into his death?" Gal. 3:27—"For as many of you as were baptized into Christ did put on Christ." Baptism is immersion into God, into the presence, communion, life of the Trinity; see Com. of Clark, and of Lange, on Mat. 28:19; also C. E. Smith, in Bap. Rev., 1881:305-311. President Wayland and the Revised Version read, "into the name." Per contra, see Meyer (transl., 1:281, note) on Rom. 6:3; cf. Mat. 10:41; 18:20; in all which passages, as well as in Mat. 28:19, he claims that εἰς τὸ ὄνομα signifies "with reference to the name." In Acts 2:38, and 10:48, we have "in the name." For the latter translation of Mat. 28:19, see Conant, Notes on Mat.,

171. On the whole subject of this section, see Dagg, Church Order, 13-73; Ingham, Subjects of Baptism.

C. Infant Baptism.

This we reject and reprehend, for the following reasons:

(a) Infant baptism is without warrant, either express or implied, in the Scripture.

First,—there is no express command that infants should be baptized. Secondly,—there is no clear example of the baptism of infants. Thirdly,—the passages held to imply infant baptism contain, when fairly interpreted, no reference to such a practice. In Mat. 19:14, none would have "forbidden," if Jesus and his disciples had been in the habit of baptizing infants. From Acts 16:15, cf. 40, and Acts 16:33, cf. 34, Neander says that we cannot infer infant baptism. For 1 Cor. 16:15 shows that the whole family of Stephanas, baptized by Paul, were adults (1 Cor. 1:16). It is impossible to suppose a whole heathen household baptized upon the faith of its head. As to 1 Cor. 7:14, Jacobi calls this text "a sure testimony against infant baptism, since Paul would certainly have referred to the baptism of children as a proof of their holiness, if infant baptism had been practised." Moreover, this passage would in that case equally teach the baptism of the unconverted husband of a believing wife. It plainly proves that the children of Christian parents were no more baptized and had no closer connection with the Christian church, than the unbelieving partners of Christians.

Mat. 19:14—"Suffer the little children, and forbid them not, to come unto me: for to such belongeth the kingdom of heaven"; Acts 16:15—"And when she [Lydia] was baptized, and her household"; cf. 40—"And they went out of the prison, and entered into the house of Lydia: and when they had seen the brethren, they comforted them, and departed." Acts 16:33—The jailor "was baptized, he and all his, immediately"; cf. 34—"And he brought them up into his house, and set food before them, and rejoiced greatly, with all his house, having believed in God"; 1 Cor. 16:15—"ye know the house of Stephanas, that it is the firstfruits of Achaia, and that they have set themselves to minister unto the saints"; 1:16—"And I baptized also the household of Stephanas"; 7:14—"For the unbelieving husband is sanctified in the wife, and the unbelieving wife is sanctified in the brother: else were your children unclean; but now are they holy"—here the sanctity or holiness attributed to unbelieving members of the household is evidently that of external connection and privilege, like that of the O. T. Israel.

Broadus, Am. Com., on Mat. 19:14—"No Greek Commentator mentions infant baptism in connection with this passage, though they all practised that rite." Schleiermacher, Glaubenslehre, 2:383—"All the traces of infant baptism which it has been desired to find in the New Testament must first be put into it." Pfleiderer, Grundriss, 184-187—"Infant baptism cannot be proved from the N. T., and according to 1 Cor. 7:14 it is antecedently improbable; yet it was the logical consequence of the command, Mat. 28:19 sq., in which the church consciousness of the 2d century prophetically expressed Christ's appointment that it should be the universal church of the nations.... Infant baptism represents one side of the Biblical sacrament, the side of the divine grace; but it needs to have the other side, appropriation of that grace by personal freedom, added in confirmation."

Dr. A. S. Crapsey, formerly an Episcopal rector in Rochester, made the following statement in the introduction to a sermon in defence of infant baptism: "Now in support of this custom of the church, we can bring no express command of the word of God, no certain warrant of holy Scripture, nor can we be at all sure that this usage prevailed during the apostolic age. From a few obscure hints we may conjecture that it did, but it is only conjecture after all. It is true St. Paul baptized the household of Stephanas, of Lydia, and of the jailor at Philippi, and in these households there may have been little children; but we do not know that there were, and these inferences form but a poor foundation upon which to base any doctrine. Better say at once, and boldly, that infant baptism is not expressly taught in holy Scripture. Not only is the word of God silent on this subject, but those who have studied the subject tell us that Christian writers of the very first age say nothing about it. It is by no means sure that this custom obtained in the church earlier than in the middle of the second or the beginning of the third century." Dr. C. M. Mead, in a private letter, dated May 27, 1895—"Though a Congregationalist, I cannot find any Scriptural authorization of pedobaptism, and I admit also that immersion seems to have been the prevalent, if not the universal, form of baptism at the first."

A review of the passages held by pedobaptists to support their views leads us to the conclusion expressed in the North British Review, Aug. 1852:211, that infant baptism is utterly unknown to Scripture. Jacob, Eccl. Polity of N. T., 270-275—"Infant baptism is not mentioned in the N. T. No instance of it is recorded there; no allusion is made to its effects; no directions are given for its administration.... It is not an apostolic ordinance." See also Neander's view, in Kitto, Bib. Cyclop., art.: Baptism; Kendrick, in Christian Rev., April, 1863; Curtis, Progress of Baptist Principles, 96; Wayland, Principles and Practices of Baptists, 125; Cunningham, lect. on Baptism, in Croall Lectures for 1886.

(b) Infant baptism is expressly contradicted.

First,—by the Scriptural prerequisites of faith and repentance, as signs of regeneration. In the great commission, Matthew speaks of baptizing disciples, and Mark of baptizing believers; but infants are neither of these. Secondly,—by the Scriptural symbolism of the ordinance. As we should not bury a person before his death, so we should not symbolically bury a person by baptism until he has in spirit died to sin. Thirdly,—by the Scriptural constitution of the church. The church is a company of persons whose union with one another presupposes and expresses a previous conscious and voluntary union of each with Jesus Christ. But of this conscious and voluntary union with Christ infants are not capable. Fourthly,—by the Scriptural prerequisites for participation in the Lord's Supper. Participation in the Lord's Supper is the right only of those who can discern the Lord's body (1 Cor. 11:29). No reason can be assigned for restricting to intelligent communicants the ordinance of the Supper, which would not equally restrict to intelligent believers the ordinance of Baptism.

Infant baptism has accordingly led in the Greek church to infant communion. This course seems logically consistent. If baptism is administered to unconscious babes, they should participate in the Lord's Supper also. But if confirmation or any intelligent profession of faith is thought necessary before communion, why should not such confirmation or profession be thought necessary before baptism? On Jonathan Edwards and the Halfway Covenant, see New Englander, Sept. 1884:601-614; G. L. Walker, Aspects of Religious Life of New England, 61-82; Dexter, Congregationalism, 487, note—"It has been often intimated that President Edwards opposed and destroyed the Halfway Covenant. He did oppose Stoddardism, or the doctrine that the Lord's Supper is a converting ordinance, and that unconverted men, because they are such, should be encouraged to partake of it." The tendency of his system was adverse to it; but, for all that appears in his published writings, he could have approved and administered that form of the Halfway Covenant then current among the churches. John Fiske says of Jonathan Edwards's preaching: "The prominence he gave to spiritual conversion, or what was called 'change of heart,' brought about the overthrow of the doctrine of the Halfway Covenant. It also weakened the logical basis of infant baptism, and led to the winning of hosts of converts by the Baptists."

Other pedobaptist bodies than the Greek Church save part of the truth, at the expense of consistency, by denying participation in the Lord's Supper to those baptized in infancy until they have reached years of understanding and have made a public profession of faith. Dr. Charles E. Jefferson, at the International Congregational Council of Boston, September, 1899, urged that the children of believers are already church members, and that as such they are entitled, not only to baptism, but also to the Lord's Supper—"an assertion that started much thought"! Baptists may well commend Congregationalists to the teaching of their own Increase Mather, The Order of the Gospel (1700), 11—"The Congregational Church discipline is not suited for a worldly interest or for a formal generation of professors. It will stand or fall as godliness in the power of it does prevail, or otherwise.... If the begun Apostacy should proceed as fast the next thirty years as it has done these last, surely it will come that in New England (except the gospel itself depart with the order of it) that the most conscientious people therein will think themselves concerned to gather churches out of churches."

How much of Judaistic externalism may linger among nominal Christians is shown by the fact that in the Armenian Church animal sacrifices survived, or were permitted to converted heathen priests, in order they might not lose their livelihood. These sacrifices continued in other regions of Christendom, particularly in the Greek church, and Pope Gregory the Great permitted them; see Conybeare, in Am. Jour. Theology, Jan. 1893:62-90. In The Key of Truth, a manual of the Paulician Church of Armenia, whose date in its present form is between the seventh and the ninth centuries, we have the Adoptianist view of Christ's person, and of the subjects and the mode of baptism: "Thus also the Lord, having learned from the Father, proceeded to teach us to perform baptism and all other commandments at the age of full growth and at no other time.... For some have broken and destroyed the holy and precious canons which by the Father Almighty were delivered to our Lord Jesus Christ, and have trodden them underfoot with their devilish teaching, ... baptizing those who are irrational, and communicating the unbelieving."

Minority is legally divided into three septennates: 1. From the first to the seventh year, the age of complete irresponsibility, in which the child cannot commit a crime; 2. from the seventh to the fourteenth year, the age of partial responsibility, in which intelligent consciousness of the consequences of actions is not assumed to exist, but may be proved in individual instances; 3. from the fourteenth to the twenty-first year, the age of discretion, in which the person is responsible for criminal action, may choose a guardian, make a will, marry with consent of parents, make business contracts not wholly void, but is not yet permitted fully to assume the free man's position in the State. The church however is not bound by these hard and fast rules. Wherever it has evidence of conversion and of Christian character, it may admit to baptism and church membership, even at a very tender age.

(c) The rise of infant baptism in the history of the church.

The rise of infant baptism in the history of the church is due to sacramental conceptions of Christianity, so that all arguments in its favor from the writings of the first three centuries are equally arguments for baptismal regeneration.

Neander's view may be found in Kitto, Cyclopædia, 1:287—"Infant baptism was established neither by Christ nor by his apostles. Even in later times Tertullian opposed it, the North African church holding to the old practice." The newly discovered Teaching of the Apostles, which Bryennios puts at

140-160 A.D., and Lightfoot at 80-110 A. D., seems to know nothing of infant baptism.

Professor A. H. Newman, in Bap. Rev., Jan. 1884—"Infant baptism has always gone hand in hand with State churches. It is difficult to conceive how an ecclesiastical establishment could be maintained without infant baptism or its equivalent. We should think, if the facts did not show us so plainly the contrary, that the doctrine of justification by faith alone would displace infant baptism. But no. The establishment must be maintained. The rejection of infant baptism implies insistence upon a baptism of believers. Only the baptized are properly members of the church. Even adults would not all receive baptism on professed faith, unless they were actually compelled to do so. Infant baptism must therefore be retained as the necessary concomitant of a State church.

"But what becomes of the justification by faith? Baptism, if it symbolizes anything, symbolizes regeneration. It would be ridiculous to make the symbol to forerun the fact by a series of years. Luther saw the difficulty; but he was sufficient for the emergency. 'Yes,' said he, 'justification is by faith alone. No outward rite, apart from faith, has any efficacy.' Why, it was against opera operata that he was laying out all his strength. Yet baptism is the symbol of regeneration, and baptism must be administered to infants, or the State church falls. With an audacity truly sublime, the great reformer declares that infants are regenerated in connection with baptism, and that they are simultaneously justified by personal faith. An infant eight days old believe? 'Prove the contrary if you can!' triumphantly ejaculates Luther, and his point is gained. If this kind of personal faith is said to justify infants, is it wonderful that those of maturer years learned to take a somewhat superficial view of the faith that justifies?"

Yet Luther had written: "Whatever is without the word of God is by that very fact against God"; see his Briefe, ed. DeWette, II:292; J. G. Walch, De Fide in Utero. There was great discordance between Luther as reformer, and Luther as conservative churchman. His Catholicism, only half overcome, broke into all his views of faith. In his early years, he stood for reason and Scripture; in his later years he fought reason and Scripture in the supposed interest of the church.

Mat. 18:10—"See that ye despise not one of these little ones"—which refers not to little children but to childlike believers, Luther adduces as a proof of infant baptism, holding that the child is said to believe—"little ones that believe on me" (verse 6)—because it has been circumcised and received into the number of the elect. "And so, through baptism, children become believers. How else could the children of Turks and Jews be distinguished from those of Christians?" Does this involve the notion that infants dying unbaptized are lost? To find the very apostle of justification by faith saying that a little child becomes a believer by being baptized, is humiliating and disheartening (so Broadus. Com. on Matthew, page 384, note).

Pfleiderer, Philos. Religion, 2:342-345, quotes from Lang as follows: "By mistaking and casting down the Protestant spirit which put forth its demands on the time in Carlstadt, Zwingle, and others, Luther made Protestantism lose its salt; he inflicted wounds upon it from which it has not yet recovered to-day; and the ecclesiastical struggle of the present is just a struggle of spiritual freedom against Lutherism." E. G. Robinson: "Infant baptism is a rag of Romanism. Since regeneration is always through the truth, baptismal regeneration is an absurdity." See Christian Review, Jan. 1851; Neander, Church History, 1:311, 313; Coleman, Christian Antiquities, 258-260; Arnold, in Bap. Quarterly, 1869:32; Hovey, in Bap. Quarterly, 1871:75.

(d) The reasoning by which it is supported is unscriptural, unsound, and dangerous in its tendency.

First,—in assuming the power of the church to modify or abrogate a command of Christ. This has been sufficiently answered above. Secondly,—in maintaining that infant baptism takes the place of circumcision under the Abrahamic covenant. To this we reply that the view contradicts the New Testament idea of the church, by making it a hereditary body, in which fleshly birth, and not the new birth, qualifies for membership. "As the national Israel typified the spiritual Israel, so the circumcision which immediately followed, not preceded, natural birth, bids us baptize children, not before, but after spiritual birth." Thirdly,—in declaring that baptism belongs to the infant because of an organic connection of the child with the parent, which permits the latter to stand for the former and to make profession of faith for it,—faith already existing germinally in the child by virtue of this organic union, and certain for the same reason to be developed as the child grows to maturity. "A law of organic connection as regards character subsisting between the parent and the child,—such a connection as induces the conviction that the character of the one is actually included in the character of the other, as the seed is formed in the capsule." We object to this view that it unwarrantably confounds the personality of the child with that of the parent; practically ignores the necessity of the Holy Spirit's regenerating influences in the case of children of Christian parents; and presumes in such children a gracious state which facts conclusively show not to exist.

What takes the place of circumcision is not baptism but regeneration. Paul defeated the attempt to fasten circumcision on the church, when he refused to have that rite performed on Titus. But later Judaizers succeeded in perpetuating circumcision under the form of infant baptism, and afterward of infant sprinkling (McGarvey, Com. on Acts). E. G. Robinson: "Circumcision is not a type of baptism: 1. It is purely a gratuitous assumption that it is so. There is not a word in Scripture to authorize it; 2. Circumcision was a national, a theocratic, and not a personal, religious rite; 3. If circumcision be a type, why did Paul circumcise Timothy? Why did he not explain, on an occasion so naturally calling for it, that circumcision was replaced by baptism?"

On the theory that baptism takes the place of circumcision, see Pepper, Baptist Quarterly, April, 1857; Palmer, in Baptist Quarterly, 1871:314. The Christian Church is either a natural, hereditary body, or it was merely typified by the Jewish people. In the former case, baptism belongs to all children of Christian parents, and the church is indistinguishable from the world. In the latter case, it belongs only to spiritual descendants, and therefore only to true believers. "That Jewish Christians, who of course had been circumcised, were also baptized, and that a large number of them insisted that Gentiles who had been baptized should also be circumcised, shows conclusively that baptism did not take the place of circumcision.... The notion that the family is the unit of society is a relic of barbarism. This appears in the Roman law, which was good for property but not for persons. It left none but a servile station to wife or son, thus degrading society at the fountain of family life. To gain freedom, the Roman wife had to accept a form of marriage which opened the way for unlimited liberty of divorce."

Hereditary church-membership is of the same piece with hereditary priesthood, and both are relics of Judaism. J. J. Murphy, Nat. Selection and Spir. Freedom, 81—"The institution of hereditary priesthood, which was so deeply rooted in the religions of antiquity and was adopted into Judaism, has found no place in Christianity; there is not, I believe, any church whatever calling itself by the name of Christ, in which the ministry is hereditary." Yet there is a growing disposition to find in infant baptism the guarantee of hereditary church membership. Washington Gladden, What is Left? 252-254—"Solidarity of the generations finds expression in infant baptism. Families ought to be Christian and not individuals only. In the Society of Friends every one born of parents belonging to the Society is a birthright member. Children of Christian parents are heirs of the kingdom. The State recognizes that our children are organically connected with it. When parents are members of the State, children are not aliens. They are not called to perform duties of citizenship until a certain age, but the rights and privileges of citizenship are theirs from the moment of their birth. The State is the mother of her children; shall the church be less motherly than the State?... Baptism does not make the child God's child; it simply recognizes and declares the fact."

Another illustration of what we regard as a radically false view is found in the sermon of Bishop Grafton of Fond du Lac, at the consecration of Bishop Nicholson in Philadelphia: "Baptism is not like a function in the natural order, like the coronation of a king, an acknowledgment of what the child already is. The child, truly God's loved offspring by way of creation, is in baptism translated into the new creation and incorporated into the Incarnate One, and made his child." Yet, as the great majority of the inmates of our prisons and the denizens of the slums have received this "baptism," it appears that this "loved offspring" very early lost its "new creation" and got "translated" in the wrong direction. We regard infant baptism as only an ancient example of the effort to bring in the kingdom of God by externals, the protest against which brought Jesus to the cross. Our modern methods of salvation by sociology and education and legislation are under the same indictment, as crucifying the Son of God afresh and putting him to open shame.

Prof. Moses Stuart urged that the form of baptism was immaterial, but that the temper of heart was the thing of moment. Francis Wayland, then a student of his, asked: "If such is the case, with what propriety can baptism be administered to those who cannot be supposed to exercise any temper of heart at all, and with whom the form must be everything?"—The third theory of organic connection of the child with its parents is elaborated by Bushnell, in his Christian Nurture, 90-223. Per contra, see Bunsen, Hippolytus and his Times, 179, 211; Curtis, Progress of Baptist Principles, 262. Hezekiah's son Manasseh was not godly; and it would be rash to say that all the drunkard's children are presumptively drunkards.

(e) The lack of agreement among pedobaptists.

The lack of agreement among pedobaptists as to the warrant for infant baptism and as to the relation of baptized infants to the church, together with the manifest decline of the practice itself, are arguments against it.

The propriety of infant baptism is variously argued, says Dr. Bushnell, upon the ground of "natural innocence, inherited depravity, and federal holiness; because of the infant's own character, the parent's piety, and the church's faith; for the reason that the child is an heir of salvation already, and in order to make it such.... No settled opinion on infant baptism and on Christian nurture has ever been attained to."

Quot homines, tot sententiæ. The belated traveler in a thunderstorm prayed for a little more light and less noise. Bushnell, Christian Nurture, 9-89, denies original sin, denies that hereditary connection can make a child guilty. But he seems to teach transmitted righteousness, or that hereditary connection can make a child holy. He disparages "sensible experiences" and calls them "explosive conversions."

But because we do not know the time of conversion, shall we say that there never was a time when the child experienced God's grace? See Bib. Sac., 1872:665. Bushnell said: "I don't know what right we have to say that a child can't be born again before he is born the first time." Did not John the Baptist preach Christ before he was born? (Luke 1:15, 41, 44). The answer to Bushnell is simply this, that regeneration is through the truth, and an unborn child cannot know the truth. To disjoin regeneration from the truth, is to make it a matter of external manipulation in which the soul is merely passive and the whole process irrational. There is a secret work of God in the soul, but it is always accompanied by an awakening of the soul to perceive the truth and to accept Christ.

Are baptized infants members of the Presbyterian Church? We answer by citing the following standards: 1. The Confession of Faith, 25:2—"The visible church ... consists of all those throughout the world, that profess the true religion, together with their children." 2. The Larger Catechism, 62—"The visible church is a society made up of all such as in all ages and places of the world do profess the true religion, and of their children." 166—"Baptism is not to be administered to any that are not of the visible church ... till they profess their faith in Christ and obedience to him: but infants descending from parents either both or but one of them professing faith in Christ and obedience to him are in that respect within the covenant and are to be baptized." 3. The Shorter Catechism, 96—"Baptism is not to be administered to any that are out of the visible church, till they profess their faith in Christ and obedience to him: but the infants of such as are members of the visible church are to be baptized." 4. Form of Government, 3—"A particular church consists of a number of professing Christians, with their offspring." 5. Directory for Worship, 1—"Children born within the pale of the visible church and dedicated to God in baptism are under the inspection and government of the church.... When they come to years of discretion, if they be free from scandal, appear sober and steady, and to have sufficient knowledge to discern the Lord's body, they ought to be informed it is their duty and their privilege to come to the Lord's Supper."

The Maplewood Congregational Church of Malden, Mass., enrolls as members all children baptized by the church. The relation continues until they indicate a desire either to continue it or to dissolve it. The list of such members is kept distinct from that of the adults, but they are considered as members under the care of the church. Dr. W. G. T. Shedd: "The infant of a believer is born into the church as the infant of a citizen is born into the State. A baptized child in adult years may renounce his baptism, become an infidel, and join the synagogue of Satan, but until he does this, he must be regarded as a member of the church of Christ."

On the Decline of Infant Baptism, see Vedder, in Baptist Review, April, 1882:173-189, who shows that in fifty years past the proportion of infant baptisms to communicants in general has decreased from one in seven to one in eleven; among the Reformed, from one in twelve to one in twenty; among the Presbyterians, from one in fifteen to one in thirty-three; among the Methodists, from one in twenty-two to one in twenty-nine; among the Congregationalists, from one in fifty to one in seventy-seven.

(f) The evil effects of infant baptism.

First,—in forestalling the voluntary act of the child baptized, and thus practically preventing his personal obedience to Christ's commands.

The person baptized in infancy has never performed any act with intent to obey Christ's command to be baptized, never has put forth a single volition looking toward obedience to that command; see Wilkinson, The Baptist Principle, 40-46. Every man has the right to choose his own wife. So every man has the right to choose his own Savior.

Secondly,—in inducing superstitious confidence in an outward rite as possessed of regenerating efficacy.

French parents still regard infants before baptism as only animals (Stanley). The haste with which the minister is summoned to baptize the dying child shows that superstition still lingers in many an otherwise evangelical family in our own country. The English Prayerbook declares that in baptism the infant is "made a child of God and an inheritor of the kingdom of heaven." Even the Westminster Assembly's Catechism, 28:6, holds that grace is actually conferred in baptism, though the efficacy of it is delayed till riper years. Mercersburg Review: "The objective medium or instrumental cause of regeneration is baptism. Men are not regenerated outside the church and then brought into it for preservation, but they are regenerated by being incorporated with or engrafted into the church through the sacrament of baptism." Catholic Review: "Unbaptized, these little ones go into darkness; but baptized, they rejoice in the presence of God forever."

Dr. Beebe of Hamilton went after a minister to baptize his sick child, but before he returned the child died. Reflection made him a Baptist, and the Editor of The Examiner. Baptists unhesitatingly permit converts to die unbaptized, showing plainly that they do not regard baptism as essential to salvation. Baptism no more makes one a Christian, than putting a crown on one's head makes him a king. Zwingle held to a symbolic interpretation of the Lord's Supper, but he clung to the sacramental conception of Baptism. E. H. Johnson, Uses and Abuses of Ordinances, 33, claims that, while baptism is not a justifying or regenerating ordinance, it is a sanctifying ordinance,—sanctifying, in the sense of setting apart. Yes, we reply, but only as church going and prayer are sanctifying; the efficacy is not in the outward act but in the spirit which accompanies it. To make it signify more is to admit the sacramental principle.

In the Roman Catholic Church the baptism of bells and of rosaries shows how infant baptism has induced the belief that grace can be communicated to irrational and even material things. In Mexico people bring caged birds, cats, rabbits, donkeys, and pigs, for baptism. The priest kneels before the altar in prayer, reads a few words in Latin, then sprinkles the creature with holy water. The sprinkling is supposed to drive out any evil spirit that may have vexed the bird or beast. In Key West, Florida, a town of 22,000 inhabitants, infant baptism has a stronger hold than anywhere else at the South. Baptist parents had sometimes gone to the Methodist preachers to have their children baptized. To prevent this, the Baptist pastors established the custom of laying their hands upon the heads of infants in the congregation, and "blessing" them, i. e., asking God's blessing to rest upon them. But this custom came to be confounded with christening, and was called such. Now the Baptist pastors are having a hard struggle to explain and limit the custom which they themselves have introduced. Perverse human nature will take advantage of even the slightest additions to N. T. prescriptions, and will bring out of the germs of false doctrine a fearful harvest of evil. Obsta principiis—"Resist beginnings."

Thirdly,—in obscuring and corrupting Christian truth with regard to the sufficiency of Scripture, the connection of the ordinances, and the inconsistency of an impenitent life with church-membership.

Infant baptism in England is followed by confirmation, as a matter of course, whether there has been any conscious abandonment of sin or not. In Germany, a man is always understood to be a Christian unless he expressly states to the contrary—in fact, he feels insulted if his Christianity is questioned. At the funerals even of infidels and debauchees the pall used may be inscribed with the words: "Blessed are the dead that die in the Lord." Confidence in one's Christianity and hopes of heaven based only on the fact of baptism in infancy, are a great obstacle to evangelical preaching and to the progress of true religion.

Wordsworth, The Excursion, 596, 602 (book 5)—"At the baptismal font. And when the pure And consecrating element hath cleansed The original stain, the child is thus received Into the second ark, Christ's church, with trust That he, from wrath redeemed therein shall float Over the billows of this troublesome world To the fair land of everlasting life.... The holy rite That lovingly consigns the babe to the arms Of Jesus and his everlasting care." Infant baptism arose in the superstitious belief that there lay in the water itself a magical efficacy for the washing away of sin, and that apart from baptism there could be no salvation. This was and still remains the Roman Catholic position. Father Doyle, in Anno Domini, 2:182—"Baptism regenerates. By means of it the child is born again into the newness of the supernatural life." Theodore Parker was baptized, but not till he was four years old, when his "Oh, don't!"—in which his biographers have found prophetic intimation of his mature dislike for all conventional forms—was clearly the small boy's dislike of water on his face; see Chadwick, Theodore Parker, 6, 7. "How do you know, my dear, that you have been christened?" "Please, mum, 'cos I've got the marks on my arm now, mum!"

Fourthly,—in destroying the church as a spiritual body, by merging it in the nation and the world.

Ladd, Principles of Church Polity: "Unitarianism entered the Congregational churches of New England through the breach in one of their own avowed and most important tenets, namely, that of a regenerate church-membership. Formalism, indifferentism, neglect of moral reforms, and, as both cause and results of these, an abundance of unrenewed men and women, were the causes of their seeming disasters in that sad epoch." But we would add, that the serious and alarming decline of religion which culminated in the Unitarian movement in New England had its origin in infant baptism. This introduced into the Church a multitude of unregenerate persons and permitted them to determine its doctrinal position.

W. B. Matteson: "No one practice of the church has done so much to lower the tone of its life and to debase its standards. The first New England churches were established by godly and regenerated men. They received into their churches, through infant baptism, children presumptively, but alas not actually, regenerated. The result is well known—swift, startling, seemingly irresistible decline. 'The body of the rising generation,' writes Increase Mother, 'is a poor perishing, inconverted, and, except the Lord pour out his Spirit, an undone generation.' The 'Halfway Covenant' was at once a token of preceding, and a cause of further, decline. If God had not indeed poured out his Spirit in the great awakening under Edwards, New England might well, as some feared, 'be lost even to New England and buried in its own ruins.' It was the new emphasis on personal religion—an emphasis which the Baptists of that day largely contributed—that gave to the New England churches a larger life and a larger usefulness. Infant baptism has never since held quite the same place in the polity of those churches. It has very generally declined. But it is still far from extinct, even among evangelical Protestants. The work of Baptists is not yet done. Baptists have always stood, but they need still to stand, for a believing and regenerated church-membership."

Fifthly,—in putting into the place of Christ's command a commandment of men, and so admitting the essential principle of all heresy, schism, and false religion.

There is therefore no logical halting-place between the Baptist and the Romanist positions. The Roman Catholic Archbishop Hughes of New York, said well to a Presbyterian minister: "We have no controversy with you. Our controversy is with the Baptists." Lange of Jena: "Would the Protestant church fulfil and attain to its final destiny, the baptism of infants must of necessity be abolished." The English Judge asked the witness what his religious belief was. Reply: "I haven't any." "Where do you attend church?" "Nowhere." "Put him down as belonging to the Church of England." The small child was asked where her mother was. Reply: "She has gone to a Christian and devil meeting." The child meant a Christian Endeavor meeting. Some systems of doctrine and ritual, however, answer her description, for they are a mixture of paganism and Christianity. The greatest work favoring the doctrine which we here condemn is Wall's History of Infant Baptism. For the Baptist side of the controversy see Arnold, in Madison Avenue Lectures, 160-182; Curtis, Progress of Baptist Principles, 274, 275; Dagg, Church Order, 144-202.

II. The Lord's Supper

The Lord's Supper is that outward rite in which the assembled church eats bread broken and drinks wine poured forth by its appointed representative, in token of its constant dependence on the once crucified, now risen Savior, as source of its spiritual life; or, in other words, in token of that abiding communion of Christ's death and resurrection through which the life begun in regeneration is sustained and perfected.

Norman Fox, Christ in the Daily Meal, 31, 33, says that the Scripture nowhere speaks of the wine as "poured forth"; and in 1 Cor. 11:24—"my body which is broken for you," the Revised Version omits the word "broken"; while on the other hand the Gospel according to John (19:36) calls especial attention to the fact that Christ's body was not broken. We reply that Jesus, in giving his disciples the cup, did speak of his blood as "poured out" (Mark 14:24); and it was not the body, but "a bone of him," which was not to be broken. Many ancient manuscripts add the word "broken" in 1 Cor. 11:24. On the Lord's Supper in general, see Weston, in Madison Avenue Lectures, 183-195; Dagg, Church Order, 203-214.

1. The Lord's Supper an ordinance instituted by Christ.

(a) Christ appointed an outward rite to be observed by his disciples in remembrance of his death. It was to be observed after his death; only after his death could it completely fulfil its purpose as a feast of commemoration.

Luke 22:19—"And be took bread, and when he had given thanks, he brake it, and gave to them, saying, This is my body which is given for you: this do in remembrance of me. And the cup in like manner after supper, saying, This cup is the new covenant in my blood, even that which is poured out for you"; 1 Cor. 11:23-25—"For I received of the Lord that which also I delivered unto you, that the Lord Jesus in the night in which he was betrayed took bread; and when he had given thanks, he brake it, and said, This is my body, which is for you: this do in remembrance of me. In like manner also the cup, after supper, saying, This cup is the new covenant in my blood: this do, as often as ye drink it, in remembrance of me." Observe that this communion was Christian communion before Christ's death, just as John's baptism was Christian baptism before Christ's death.

(b) From the apostolic injunction with regard to its celebration in the church until Christ's second coming, we infer that it was the original intention of our Lord to institute a rite of perpetual and universal obligation.

1 Cor. 11:26—"For as often as ye eat this bread, and drink the cup, ye proclaim the Lord's death till he come"; cf. Mat. 26:29—"But I say unto you, I shall not drink henceforth of this fruit of the vine, until that day when I drink it new with you in my Father's kingdom"; Mark 14:25—"Verily I say unto you, I will no more drink of the fruit of the vine, until that day when I drink it new in the kingdom of God." As the paschal supper continued until Christ came the first time in the flesh, so the Lord's Supper is to continue until he comes the second time with all the power and glory of God.

(c) The uniform practice of the N. T. churches, and the celebration of such a rite in subsequent ages by almost all churches professing to be Christian, is best explained upon the supposition that the Lord's Supper is an ordinance established by Christ himself.

Acts 2:42—"And they continued stedfastly in the apostles' teaching and fellowship, in the breaking of bread and the prayers"; 46—"And day by day, continuing stedfastly with one accord in the temple, and breaking bread at home, they took their food with gladness and singleness of heart"—on the words here translated "at home" (κατ' οἶκον), but meaning, as Jacob maintains, "from one worship-room to another," see page 961. Acts 20:7—"And upon the first day of the week, when we were gathered together to break bread, Paul discoursed with them"; 1 Cor. 10:16—"The cup of blessing which we bless, is it not a communion of the blood of Christ? The bread which we break, is it not a communion of the body of Christ? seeing that we, who art many, are one bread, one body: for we all partake of the one bread."

2. The Mode of administering the Lord's Supper.

(a) The elements are bread and wine.

Although the bread which Jesus broke at the institution of the ordinance was doubtless the unleavened bread of the Passover, there is nothing in the symbolism of the Lord's Supper which necessitates the Romanist use of the wafer. Although the wine which Jesus poured out was doubtless the ordinary fermented juice of the grape, there is nothing in the symbolism of the ordinance which forbids the use of unfermented juice of the grape,—obedience to the command "This do in remembrance of me" (Luke 22:19) requires only that we should use the "fruit of the vine" (Mat. 26:29).

Huguenots and Roman Catholics, among Parkman's Pioneers of France in the New World, disputed whether the sacramental bread could be made of the meal of Indian corn. But it is only as food, that the bread is symbolic. Dried fish is used in Greenland. The bread only symbolizes Christ's life and the wine only symbolizes his death. Any food or drink may do the same. It therefore seems a very conscientious but unnecessary literalism, when Adoniram Judson (Life by his Son, 352) writes from Burma: "No wine to be procured in this place, on which account we are unable to meet with the other churches this day in partaking of the Lord's Supper." For proof that Bible wines, like all other wines, are fermented, see Presb. Rev., 1881:80-114; 1882:78-108, 394-399, 586; Hovey, in Bap. Quar. Rev., April, 1887:152-180. Per contra, see Samson, Bible Wines. On the Scripture Law of Temperance, see Presb. Rev., 1882:287-324.

(b) The communion is of both kinds,—that is, communicants are to partake both of the bread and of the wine.

The Roman Catholic Church withholds the wine from the laity, although it considers the whole Christ to be present under each of the forms. Christ, however, says: "Drink ye all of it" (Mat. 26:27). To withhold the wine from any believer is disobedience to Christ, and is too easily understood as teaching that the laity have only a portion of the benefits of Christ's death. Calvin: "As to the bread, he simply said 'Take, eat.' Why does he expressly bid them all drink? And why does Mark explicitly say that 'they all drank of it' (Mark 14:23)?" Bengel: Does not this suggest that, if communion in "one kind alone were sufficient, it is the cup which should be used? The Scripture thus speaks, foreseeing what Rome would do." See Expositor's Greek Testament on 1 Cor. 11:27. In the Greek Church the bread and wine are mingled and are administered to communicants, not to infants only but also to adults, with a spoon.

(c) The partaking of these elements is of a festal nature.

The Passover was festal in its nature. Gloom and sadness are foreign to the spirit of the Lord's Supper. The wine is the symbol of the death of Christ, but of that death by which we live. It reminds us that he drank the cup of suffering in order that we might drink the wine of joy. As the bread is broken to sustain our physical life, so Christ's body was broken by thorns and nails and spear to nourish our spiritual life.

1 Cor. 11:29—"For he that eateth and drinketh, eateth and drinketh judgment onto himself, if he discern not the body." Here the Authorized Version wrongly had "damnation" instead of "judgment." Not eternal condemnation, but penal judgment in general, is meant. He who partakes "in an unworthy manner" (verse 27), i. e., in hypocrisy, or merely to satisfy bodily appetites, and not discerning the body of Christ of which the bread is the symbol (verse 29), draws down upon him God's judicial sentence. Of this judgment, the frequent sickness and death in the church at Corinth was a token. See verses 30-34, and Meyer's Com.; also Gould, in Am. Com. on 1 Cor. 11:27—"unworthily"—"This is not to be understood as referring to the unworthiness of the person himself to partake, but to the unworthy manner of partaking.... The failure to recognize practically the symbolism of the elements, and hence the treatment of the Supper as a common meal, is just what the apostle has pointed out as the fault of the Corinthians, and it is what he characterizes as an unworthy eating and drinking." The Christian therefore should not be deterred from participation in the Lord's Supper by any feeling of his personal unworthiness, so long as he trusts Christ and aims to obey him, for "All the fitness he requireth Is to feel our need of him."

(d) The communion is a festival of commemoration,—not simply bringing Christ to our remembrance, but making proclamation of his death to the world.

1 Cor. 11:24, 26—"this do in remembrance of me.... For as often as ye eat this bread and drink this cup, ye proclaim the Lord's death till he come." As the Passover commemorated the deliverance of Israel from Egypt, and as the Fourth of July commemorates our birth as a nation, so the Lord's Supper commemorates the birth of the church in Christ's death and resurrection. As a mother might bid her children meet over her grave and commemorate her, so Christ bids his people meet and remember him. But subjective remembrance is not its only aim. It is public proclamation also. Whether it brings perceptible blessing to us or not, it is to be observed as a means of confessing Christ, testifying our faith, and publishing the fact of his death to others.

(e) It is to be celebrated by the assembled church. It is not a solitary observance on the part of individuals. No "showing forth" is possible except in company.

Acts 20:7—"gathered together to break bread"; 1 Cor. 11:18, 20, 22, 33, 34—"when ye come together in the church ... assemble yourselves together ... have ye not houses to eat and to drink in? or despise ye the church of God, and put them to shame that have not? ... when ye come together to eat.... If any man is hungry, let him eat at home; that your coming together be not unto judgment."

Jacob, Eccl. Polity of N. T., 191-194, claims that in Acts 2:46—"breaking bread at home"—where we have οἶκος, not οἰκία, οἶκος is not a private house, but a "worship-room," and that the phrase should be translated "breaking bread from one worship-room to another," or "in various worship-rooms." This meaning seems very apt in Acts 5:42—"And every day, in the temple and at home [rather, 'in various worship-rooms'], they ceased not to teach and to preach Jesus as the Christ"; 8:3—"But Saul laid waste the church, entering into every house [rather, 'every worship-room'] and dragging men and women committed them to prison"; Rom. 16:5—"salute the church that is in their house [rather, 'in their worship-room']"; Titus 1:11—"men who overthrow whole houses [rather, 'whole worship-rooms'], teaching things which they ought not, for filthy lucre's sake." Per contra, however, see 1 Cor. 11:34—"let him eat at home," where οἶκος is contrasted with the place of meeting; so also 1 Cor. 14:35 and Acts 20:20, where οἶκος seems to mean a private house.

The celebration of the Lord's Supper in each family by itself is not recognized in the New Testament. Stanley, in Nineteenth Century, May, 1878, tells us that as infant communion is forbidden in the Western Church, and evening communion is forbidden by the Roman Church, so solitary communion is forbidden by the English Church, and death-bed communion by the Scottish Church. E. G. Robinson: "No single individual in the New Testament ever celebrates the Lord's Supper by himself." Mrs. Browning recognized the essentially social nature of the ordinance, when she said that truth was like the bread at the Sacrament—to be passed on. In this the Supper gives us a type of the proper treatment of all the goods of life, both temporal and spiritual.

Dr. Norman Fox, Christ in the Daily Meal, claims that the Lord's Supper is no more an exclusively church ordinance than is singing or prayer; that the command to observe it was addressed, not to an organized church, but only to individuals; that every meal in the home was to be a Lord's Supper, because Christ was remembered in it. But we reply that Paul's letter with regard to the abuses of the Lord's Supper was addressed, not to individuals, but to "the church of God which is at Corinth." (1 Cor. 1:2). Paul reproves the Corinthians because in the Lord's Supper each ate without thought of others: "What, have ye not houses to eat and to drink in? or despise ye the church of God, and put them to shame that have not?" (11:22). Each member having appeased his hunger at home, the members of the church "come together to eat" (11:30), as the spiritual body of Christ. All this shows that the celebration of the Lord's Supper was not an appendage to every ordinary meal.

In Acts 20:7—"upon the first day of the week, when we were gathered together to break bread, Paul discoursed with them"—the natural inference is that the Lord's Supper was a sacred rite, observed apart from any ordinary meal, and accompanied by religious instruction. Dr. Fox would go back of these later observances to the original command of our Lord. He would eliminate all that we do not find in Mark, the earliest gospel. But this would deprive us of the Sermon on the Mount, the parable of the Prodigal Son, and the discourses of the fourth gospel. McGiffert gives A. D. 52, as the date of Paul's first letter to the Corinthians, and this ante-dates Mark's gospel by at least thirteen years. Paul's account of the Lord's Supper at Corinth is therefore an earlier authority than Mark.

(f) The responsibility of seeing that the ordinance is properly administered rests with the church as a body; and the pastor is, in this matter, the proper representative and organ of the church. In cases of extreme exigency, however, as where the church has no pastor and no ordained minister can be secured, it is competent for the church to appoint one from its own number to administer the ordinance.

1 Cor. 11:2, 23—"Now I praise you that ye remember me in all things, and hold fast the traditions, even as I delivered them to you.... For I received of the Lord that which also I delivered unto you, that the Lord Jesus in the night in which he was betrayed took bread." Here the responsibility of administering the Lord's Supper is laid upon the body of believers.

(g) The frequency with which the Lord's Supper is to be administered is not indicated either by the N. T. precept or by uniform N. T. example. We have instances both of its daily and of its weekly observance. With respect to this, as well as with respect to the accessories of the ordinance, the church is to exercise a sound discretion.

Acts 2:46—"And day by day, continuing stedfastly with one accord in the temple, and breaking bread at home [or perhaps, 'in various worship-rooms']"; 20:7—"And upon the first day of the week, when we were gathered together to break bread." In 1878, thirty-nine churches of the Establishment in London held daily communion; in two churches it was held twice each day. A few churches of the Baptist faith in England and America celebrate the Lord's Supper on each Lord's day. Carlstadt would celebrate the Lord's Supper only in companies of twelve, and held also that every bishop must marry. Reclining on couches, and meeting in the evening, are not commanded; and both, by their inconvenience, might in modern times counteract the design of the ordinance.

3. The Symbolism of the Lord's Supper.

The Lord's Supper sets forth, in general, the death of Christ as the sustaining power of the believer's life.

A. Expansion of this statement.

(a) It symbolizes the death of Christ for our sins.

1 Cor. 11:26—"For as often as ye eat this bread, and drink the cup, ye proclaim the Lord's death till he come"; cf. Mark 14:24—"This is my blood of the covenant, which is poured out for many"—the blood upon which the covenant between God and Christ, and so between God and us who are one with Christ, from eternity past was based. The Lord's Supper reminds us of the covenant which ensures our salvation, and of the atonement upon which the covenant was based; cf. Heb. 13:20—"blood of an eternal covenant."

Alex. McLaren: "The suggestion of a violent death, implied in the doubling of the symbols, by which the body is separated from that of the blood, and still further implied in the breaking of the bread, is made prominent in the words in reference to the cup. It symbolizes the blood of Jesus which is 'shed.' That shed blood is covenant blood. By it the New Covenant, of which Jeremiah had prophesied, one article of which was, 'Their sins and iniquities I will remember no more,' is sealed and ratified, not for Israel only but for an indefinite 'many,' which is really equivalent to all. Could words more plainly declare that Christ's death was a sacrifice? Can we understand it, according to his own interpretation of it, unless we see in his words here a reference to his previous words (Mat. 20:28) and recognize that in shedding his blood 'for many,' he 'gave his life a ransom for many'? The Lord's Supper is the standing witness, voiced by Jesus himself, that he regarded his death as the very centre of his work, and that he regarded it not merely as a martyrdom, but as a sacrifice by which he put away sins forever. Those who reject that view of that death are sorely puzzled what to make of the Lord's Supper."

(b) It symbolizes our personal appropriation of the benefits of that death.

1 Cor. 11:24—"This is my body, which is for you"; cf. 1 Cor. 5:7—"Christ our passover is sacrificed for us"; or R. V.—"our passover also hath been sacrificed, even Christ"; here it is evident not only that the showing forth of the Lord's death is the primary meaning of the ordinance, but that our partaking of the benefits of that death is as clearly taught as the Israelites' deliverance was symbolized in the paschal supper.

(c) It symbolizes the method of this appropriation, through union with Christ himself.

1 Cor. 10:16—"The cup of blessing which we bless, is it not a communion of [marg.: 'participation in'] the blood of Christ? The bread which we break, is it not a communion of [marg.: 'participation in'] the body of Christ?" Here "is it not a participation" = "does it not symbolize the participation?" So Mat. 26:26—"this is my body" = "this symbolizes my body."

(d) It symbolizes the continuous dependence of the believer for all spiritual life upon the once crucified, now living, Savior, to whom he is thus united.

Cf. John 6:53—"Verily, verily, I say unto you, except ye eat the flesh of the Son of man and drink his blood, ye have not life in yourselves"—here is a statement, not with regard to the Lord's Supper, but with regard to spiritual union with Christ, which the Lord's Supper only symbolizes; see page 965, (a). Like Baptism, the Lord's Supper presupposes and implies evangelical faith, especially faith in the Deity of Christ; not that all who partake of it realize its full meaning, but that this participation logically implies the five great truths of Christ's preëxistence, his supernatural birth, his vicarious atonement, his literal resurrection, and his living presence with his followers. Because Ralph Waldo Emerson perceived that the Lord's Supper implied Christ's omnipresence and deity, he would no longer celebrate it, and so broke with his church and with the ministry.

(e) It symbolizes the sanctification of the Christian through a spiritual reproduction in him of the death and resurrection of the Lord.

Rom. 8:10—"And if Christ is in you, the body is dead because of sin; but the spirit is life because of righteousness"; Phil. 3:10—"that I may know him, and the power of his resurrection, and the fellowship of his sufferings, becoming conformed unto his death; if by any means I may attain unto the resurrection from the dead." The bread of life nourishes; but it transforms me, not I it.

(f) It symbolizes the consequent union of Christians in Christ, their head.

1 Cor. 10:17—"seeing that we, who are many, are one bread, one body: for we all partake of the one bread." The Roman Catholic says that bread is the unity of many kernels, the wine the unity of many berries, and all are changed into the body of Christ. We can adopt the former part of the statement, without taking the latter. By being united to Christ, we become united to one another; and the Lord's Supper, as it symbolizes our common partaking of Christ, symbolizes also the consequent oneness of all in whom Christ dwells. Teaching of the Twelve Apostles, IX—"As this broken bread was scattered upon the mountains, and being gathered together became one, so may thy church be gathered together from the ends of the earth into thy kingdom."

(g) It symbolizes the coming joy and perfection of the kingdom of God.

Luke 22:18—"for I say unto you, I shall not drink from henceforth of the fruit of the vine, until the kingdom of God shall come"; Mark 14:25—"Verily I say unto you, I will no more drink of the fruit of the vine, until that day when I drink it new in the kingdom of God"; Mat. 26:29—"But I say unto you, I shall not drink henceforth of this fruit of the vine, until that day when I drink it new with you in my Father's kingdom."

Like Baptism, which points forward to the resurrection, the Lord's Supper is anticipatory also. It brings before us, not simply death, but life; not simply past sacrifice, but future glory. It points forward to the great festival, "the marriage supper of the Lamb" (Rev. 19:9). Dorner: "Then Christ will keep the Supper anew with us, and the hours of highest solemnity in this life are but a weak foretaste of the powers of the world to come." See Madison Avenue Lectures, 176-216; The Lord's Supper, a Clerical Symposium, by Pressensé, Luthardt, and English Divines.

B. Inferences from this statement.

(a) The connection between the Lord's Supper and Baptism consists in this, that they both and equally are symbols of the death of Christ. In Baptism, we show forth the death of Christ as the procuring cause of our new birth into the kingdom of God. In the Lord's Supper, we show forth the death of Christ as the sustaining power of our spiritual life after it has once begun. In the one, we honor the sanctifying power of the death of Christ, as in the other we honor its regenerating power. Thus both are parts of one whole,—setting before us Christ's death for men in its two great purposes and results.

If baptism symbolized purification only, there would be no point of connection between the two ordinances. Their common reference to the death of Christ binds the two together.

(b) The Lord's Supper is to be often repeated,—as symbolizing Christ's constant nourishment of the soul, whose new birth was signified in Baptism.

Yet too frequent repetition may induce superstitious confidence in the value of communion as a mere outward form.

(c) The Lord's Supper, like Baptism, is the symbol of a previous state of grace. It has in itself no regenerating and no sanctifying power, but is the symbol by which the relation of the believer to Christ, his sanctifier, is vividly expressed and strongly confirmed.

We derive more help from the Lord's Supper than from private prayer, simply because it is an external rite, impressing the sense as well as the intellect, celebrated in company with other believers whose faith and devotion help our own, and bringing before us the profoundest truths of Christianity—the death of Christ, and our union with Christ in that death.

(d) The blessing received from participation is therefore dependent upon, and proportioned to, the faith of the communicant.

In observing the Lord's Supper, we need to discern the body of the Lord (1 Cor. 11:29)—that is, to recognize the spiritual meaning of the ordinance, and the presence of Christ, who through his deputed representatives gives to us the emblems, and who nourishes and quickens our souls as these material things nourish and quicken the body. The faith which thus discerns Christ is the gift of the Holy Spirit.

(e) The Lord's Supper expresses primarily the fellowship of the believer, not with his brethren, but with Christ, his Lord.

The Lord's Supper, like Baptism, symbolizes fellowship with the brethren only as consequent upon, and incidental to, fellowship with Christ. Just as we are all baptized "into one body" (1 Cor. 12:13) only by being "baptized into Christ" (Rom. 6:3), so we commune with other believers in the Lord's Supper, only as we commune with Christ. Christ's words: "this do in remembrance of me" (1 Cor. 11:24), bid us think, not of our brethren, but of the Lord. Baptism is not a test of personal worthiness. Nor is the Lord's Supper a test of personal worthiness, either our own or that of others. It is not primarily an expression of Christian fellowship. Nowhere in the New Testament is it called a communion of Christians with one another. But it is called a communion of the body and blood of Christ (1 Cor. 10:16)—or, in other words, a participation in him. Hence there is not a single cup, but many: "divide it among yourselves" (Luke 22:17). Here is warrant for the individual communion-cup. Most churches use more than one cup: if more than one, why not many?

1 Cor. 11:26—"as often as ye eat ... ye proclaim the Lord's death"—the Lord's Supper is a teaching ordinance, and is to be observed, not simply for the good that comes to the communicant and to his brethren, but for the sake of the witness which it gives to the world that the Christ who died for its sins now lives for its salvation. A. H. Ballard, in The Standard, Aug. 18, 1900, on 1 Cor. 11:29—"eateth and drinketh judgment unto himself, if he discern not the body"—"He who eats and drinks, and does not discern that he is redeemed by the offering of the body of Jesus Christ once for all, eats and drinks a double condemnation, because he does not discern the redemption which is symbolized by the things which he eats and drinks. To turn his thought away from that sacrificial body to the company of disciples assembled is a grievous error—the error of all those who exalt the idea of fellowship or communion in the celebration of the ordinance."

The offence of a Christian brother, therefore, even if committed against myself, should not prevent me from remembering Christ and communing with the Savior. I could not commune at all, if I had to vouch for the Christian character of all who sat with me. This does not excuse the church from effort to purge its membership from unworthy participants; it simply declares that the church's failure to do this does not absolve any single member of it from his obligation to observe the Lord's Supper. See Jacob, Eccl. Polity of N. T., 285.

4. Erroneous views of the Lord's Supper.

A. The Romanist view.

The Romanist view,—that the bread and wine are changed by priestly consecration into the very body and blood of Christ; that this consecration is a new offering of Christ's sacrifice; and that, by a physical partaking of the elements, the communicant receives saving grace from God. To this doctrine of "transubstantiation" we reply:

(a) It rests upon a false interpretation of Scripture. In Mat. 26:26, "this is my body" means: "this is a symbol of my body." Since Christ was with the disciples in visible form at the institution of the Supper, he could not have intended them to recognize the bread as being his literal body. "The body of Christ is present in the bread, just as it had been in the passover lamb, of which the bread took the place" (John 6:53 contains no reference to the Lord's Supper, although it describes that spiritual union with Christ which the Supper symbolizes; cf. 63. In 1 Cor. 10:16, 17, κοινωίαν τοῦ σώματος τοῦ Χριστοῦ is a figurative expression for the spiritual partaking of Christ. In Mark 8:33, we are not to infer that Peter was actually "Satan," nor does 1 Cor. 12:12 prove that we are all Christs. Cf. Gen. 41:26; 1 Cor. 10:4).

Mat. 26:28—"This is my blood ... which is poured out," cannot be meant to be taken literally, since Christ's blood was not yet shed. Hence the Douay version (Roman Catholic), without warrant, changes the tense and reads, "which shall be shed." At the institution of the Supper, it is not conceivable that Christ should hold his body in his own hands, and then break it to the disciples. There were not two bodies there. Zwingle: "The words of institution are not the mandatory 'become': they are only an explanation of the sign." When I point to a picture and say: "This is George Washington," I do not mean that the veritable body and blood of George Washington are before me. So when a teacher points to a map and says: "This is New York," or when Jesus refers to John the Baptist, and says: "this is Elijah, that is to come" (Mat. 11:14). Jacob, The Lord's Supper, Historically Considered—"It originally marked, not a real presence, but a real absence, of Christ as the Son of God made man"—that is, a real absence of his body. Therefore the Supper, reminding us of his body, is to be observed in the church "till he come" (1 Cor. 11:26).

John 6:53—"Except ye eat the flesh of the Son of man and drink his blood, ye have not life in yourselves" must be interpreted by verse 63—"It is the spirit that giveth life; the flesh profiteth nothing: the words that I have spoken unto you are spirit, and are life." 1 Cor. 10:16—"The cup of blessing which we bless, is it not a communion of [marg.: 'participation in'] the blood of Christ? The bread which we break, is it not a communion of [marg. 'participation in'] the body of Christ?"—see Expositor's Greek Testament, in loco; Mark 8:33—"But he turning about, and seeing his disciples, rebuked Peter, and saith, Get thee behind me, Satan"; 1 Cor. 12:12—"For the body is one, and hath many members, and all the members of the body, being many, are one body; so also is Christ." cf. Gen. 41:26—"The seven good kine are seven years; and the seven good ears are seven years: the dream is one;" 1 Cor. 10:4—"they drank of a spiritual rock that followed them: and the rock was Christ."

Queen Elizabeth: "Christ was the Word that spake it: He took the bread and brake it; And what that Word did make it, That I believe and take it." Yes, we say; but what does the Lord make it? Not his body, but only a symbol of his body. Sir Thomas More went back to the doctrine of transubstantiation which the wisdom of his age was almost unanimous in rejecting. In his Utopia, written to earlier years, he had made deism the ideal religion. Extreme Romanism was his reaction from this former extreme. Bread and wine are mere remembrancers, as were the lamb and bitter herbs at the Passover. The partaker is spiritually affected by the bread and wine, only as was the pious Israelite in receiving the paschal symbols; see Norman Fox, Christ in the Daily Meal, 25, 42.

E. G. Robinson: "The greatest power in Romanism is its power of visible representation. Ritualism is only elaborate symbolism. It is interesting to remember that this prostration of the priest before the consecrated wafer is no part of even original Roman Catholicism." Stanley, Life and Letters, 2:213—"The pope, when he celebrates the communion, always stands in exactly the opposite direction [to that of modern ritualists], not with his back but with his face to the people, no doubt following the primitive usage." So in Raphael's picture of the Miracle of Bolsina, the priest is at the north end of the table, in the very attitude of a Protestant clergyman. Pfleiderer, Philos. Religion, 2:211—"The unity of the bread, of which each enjoys a part, represents the unity of the body of Christ, which consists in the community of believers. If we are to speak of a presence of the body of Christ in the Lord's Supper, that can only be thought of, in the sense of Paul, as pertaining to the mystical body, i. e., the Christian Community. Augustine and Zwingle, who have expressed most clearly this meaning of the Supper, have therefore caught quite correctly the sense of the Apostle."

Norman Fox, Christ in the Daily Meal, 40-53—"The phrase 'consecration of the elements' is unwarranted. The leaven and the mustard seed were in no way consecrated when Jesus pronounced them symbols of divine things. The bread and wine are not arbitrarily appointed remembrancers, they are remembrancers in their very nature. There is no change in them. So every other loaf is a symbol, as well as that used in the Supper. When St. Patrick held up the shamrock as the symbol of the Trinity, he meant that every such sprig was the same. Only the bread of the daily meal is Christ's body. Only the washing of dirty feet is the fulfilment of Christ's command. The loaf not eaten to satisfy hunger is not Christ's symbolic body at all." Here we must part company with Dr. Fox. We grant the natural fitness of the elements for which he contends. But we hold also to a divine appointment of the bread and wine for a special and sacred use, even as the "bow in the cloud" (Gen. 9:13), because it was a natural emblem, was consecrated to a special religious use.

(b) It contradicts the evidence of the senses, as well as of all scientific tests that can be applied. If we cannot trust our senses as to the unchanged material qualities of bread and wine, we cannot trust them when they report to us the words of Christ.

Gibbon was rejoiced at the discovery that, while the real presence is attested by only a single sense—our sight [as employed in reading the words of Christ]—the real presence is disproved by three of our senses, sight, touch, and taste. It is not well to purchase faith in this dogma at the price of absolute scepticism. Stanley, on Baptism, in his Christian Institutions, tells us that, in the third and fourth centuries, the belief that the water of baptism was changed into the blood of Christ was nearly as firmly and widely fixed as the belief that the bread and wine of the communion were changed into his flesh and blood. Döllinger: "When I am told that I must swear to the truth of these doctrines [of papal infallibility and apostolic succession], my feeling is just as if I were asked to swear that two and two make five, and not four." Teacher: "Why did Henry VIII quarrel with the pope?" Scholar: "Because the pope had commanded him to put away his wife on pain of transubstantiation." The transubstantiation of Henry VIII is quite as rational as the transubstantiation of the bread and wine in the Eucharist.

(c) It involves the denial of the completeness of Christ's past sacrifice, and the assumption that a human priest can repeat or add to the atonement made by Christ once for all (Heb. 9:28—ἅπαξ προσενεχθείς). The Lord's Supper is never called a sacrifice, nor are altars, priests, or consecrations ever spoken of, in the New Testament. The priests of the old dispensation are expressly contrasted with the ministers of the new. The former "ministered about sacred things," i. e., performed sacred rites and waited at the altar; but the latter "preach the gospel" (1 Cor. 9:13, 14).

Heb. 9:28—"so Christ also, having been once offered"—here ἅπαξ means "once for all," as in Jude 3—"the faith which was once for all delivered unto the saints"; 1 Cor. 9:13, 14—"Know ye not that they that minister about sacred things eat of the things of the temple, and they that wait upon the altar have their portion with the altar? Even so did the Lord ordain that they that proclaim the gospel should live of the gospel." Romanism introduces a mediator between the soul and Christ, namely, bread and wine,—and the priest besides.

Dorner, Glaubenslehre, 2:680-687 (Syst. Doct., 4: 146-163)—"Christ is thought of as at a distance, and as represented only by the priest who offers anew his sacrifice. But Protestant doctrine holds to a perfect Christ, applying the benefits of the work which he long ago and once for all completed upon the cross." Chillingworth: "Romanists hold that the validity of every sacrament but baptism depends upon its administration by a priest; and without priestly absolution there is no assurance of forgiveness. But the intention of the priest is essential in pronouncing absolution, and the intention of the bishop is essential in consecrating the priest. How can any human being know that these conditions are fulfilled?" In the New Testament, on the other hand, Christ appears as the only priest, and each human soul has direct access to him.

Norman Fox, Christ in the Daily Meal, 22—"The adherence of the first Christians to the Mosaic law makes it plain that they did not hold the doctrine of the modern Church of Rome that the bread of the Supper is a sacrifice, the table an altar, and the minister a priest. For the old altar, the old sacrifice, and the old priesthood still remained, and were still in their view appointed media of atonement with God. Of course they could not have believed in two altars, two priesthoods and two contemporaneous sets of sacrifices." Christ is the only priest. A. A. Hodge, Popular Lectures, 257—"The three central dangerous errors of Romanism and Ritualism are: 1. the perpetuity of the apostolate; 2. the priestly character and offices of Christian ministers; 3. the sacramental principle, or the depending upon sacraments, as the essential, initial, and ordinary channels of grace." "Hierarchy," says another, "is an infraction of the divine order; it imposes the weight of an outworn symbolism on the true vitalities of the gospel; it is a remnant rent from the shroud of the dead past, to enwrap the limbs of the living present."

(d) It destroys Christianity by externalizing it. Romanists make all other service a mere appendage to the communion. Physical and magical salvation is not Christianity, but is essential paganism.

Council of Trent, Session VII, On Sacraments in General, Canon IV: "If any one saith that the sacraments of the New Testament are not necessary to salvation, but are superfluous, and that without them, and without the desire thereof, men attain of God, through faith alone, the grace of justification; though all [the sacraments] are not indeed necessary for every individual: let him be anathema." On Baptism, Canon IV: "If any one saith that the baptism which is even given by heretics in the name of the Father, Son and Holy Ghost, with the intention of doing what the church doth, is not true baptism, let him be anathema." Baptism, in the Romanist system, is necessary to salvation: and baptism, even though administered by heretics, is an admission to the church. All baptized persons who, through no fault of their own, but from lack of knowledge or opportunity, are not connected outwardly with the true church, though they are apparently attached to some sect, yet in reality belong to the soul of the true church. Many belong merely to the body of the Catholic church, and are counted as its members, but do not belong to its soul. So says Archbishop Lynch, of Toronto; and Pius IX extended the doctrine of invincible ignorance, so as to cover the case of every dissentient from the church whose life shows faith working by love.

Adoration of the Host (Latin hostia, victim) is a regular part of the service of the Mass. If the Romanist view were correct that the bread and wine were actually changed into the body and blood of Christ, we could not call this worship idolatry. Christ's body in the sepulchre could not have been a proper object of worship, but it was so after his resurrection, when it became animated with a new and divine life. The Romanist error is that of holding that the priest has power to transform the elements; the worship of them follows as a natural consequence, and is none the less idolatrous for being based upon the false assumption that the bread and wine are really Christ's body and blood.

The Roman Catholic system involves many absurdities, but the central absurdity is that of making religion a matter of machinery and outward manipulation. Dr. R. S. MacArthur calls sacramentalism "the pipe-line conception of grace." There is no patent Romanist plumbing. Dean Stanley said that John Henry Newman "made immortality the consequence of frequent participation of the Holy Communion." Even Faber made game of the notion, and declared that it "degraded celebrations to be so many breadfruit trees." It is this transformation of the Lord's Supper into the Mass that turns the church into "the Church of the Intonement." "Cardinal Gibbons," it was once said, "makes his own God—the wafer." His error is at the root of the super-sanctity and celibacy of the Romanist clergy, and President Garrett forgot this when he made out the pass on his railway for "Cardinal Gibbons and wife." Dr. C. H. Parkhurst: "There is no more place for an altar in a Christian church than there is for a golden calf." On the word "priest" in the N. T., see Gardiner, in O. T. Student, Nov. 1889:285-291; also Bowen, in Theol. Monthly, Nov. 1889:316-329. For the Romanist view, see Council of Trent, session XIII, canon III: per contra, see Calvin, Institutes, 2:585-602; C. Hebert, The Lord's Supper: History of Uninspired Teaching.

B. The Lutheran and High Church view.

The Lutheran and High Church view,—that the communicant, in partaking of the consecrated elements, eats the veritable body and drinks the veritable blood of Christ in and with the bread and wine, although the elements themselves do not cease to be material. To this doctrine of "consubstantiation" we object:

(a) That the view is not required by Scripture.—All the passages cited in its support may be better interpreted as referring to a partaking of the elements as symbols. If Christ's body be ubiquitous, as this theory holds, we partake of it at every meal, as really as at the Lord's Supper.

(b) That the view is inseparable from the general sacramental system of which it forms a part.—In imposing physical and material conditions of receiving Christ, it contradicts the doctrine of justification only by faith; changes the ordinance from a sign, into a means, of salvation; involves the necessity of a sacerdotal order for the sake of properly consecrating the elements; and logically tends to the Romanist conclusions of ritualism and idolatry.

(c) That it holds each communicant to be a partaker of Christ's veritable body and blood, whether he be a believer or not,—the result, in the absence of faith, being condemnation instead of salvation. Thus the whole character of the ordinance is changed from a festival occasion to one of mystery and fear, and the whole gospel method of salvation is obscured.

Encyc. Britannica, art.: Luther, 15:81—"Before the peasants' war, Luther regarded the sacrament as a secondary matter, compared with the right view of faith. In alarm at this war and at Carlstadt's mysticism, he determined to abide by the tradition of the church, and to alter as little as possible. He could not accept transubstantiation, and he sought a via media. Occam gave it to him. According to Occam, matter can be present in two ways, first, when it occupies a distinct place by itself, excluding every other body, as two stones mutually exclude each other; and, secondly, when it occupies the same space as another body at the same time. Everything which is omnipresent must occupy the same space as other things, else it could not be ubiquitous. Hence consubstantiation involved no miracle. Christ's body was in the bread and wine naturally, and was not brought into the elements by the priest. It brought a blessing, not because of Christ's presence, but because of God's promise that this particular presence of the body of Christ should bring blessings to the faithful partaker." Broadus, Am. Com. on

Mat., 529—"Luther does not say how Christ is in the bread and wine, but his followers have compared his presence to that of heat or magnetism in iron. But how then could this presence be in the bread and wine separately?"

For the view here combated, see Gerhard, x: 352—"The bread, apart from the sacrament instituted by Christ, is not the body of Christ, and therefore it is ἀρτολατρία (bread-worship) to adore the bread in these solemn processions" (of the Roman Catholic church). 397—"Faith does not belong to the substance of the Eucharist; hence it is not the faith of him who partakes that makes the bread a communication of the body of Christ; nor on account of unbelief in him who partakes does the bread cease to be a communication of the body of Christ." See also Sadler, Church Doctrine, 124-199; Pusey, Tract No. 90, of the Tractarian Series; Wilberforce, New Birth; Nevins, Mystical Presence.

Per contra, see Calvin, Institutes, 2:525-584; G. P. Fisher, in Independent, May 1, 1884—"Calvin differed from Luther, in holding that Christ is received only by the believer. He differed from Zwingle, in holding that Christ is truly, though spiritually, received." See also E. G. Robinson, in Baptist Quarterly, 1869:85-109; Rogers, Priests and Sacraments. Consubstantiation accounts for the doctrine of apostolic succession and for the universal ritualism of the Lutheran Church. Bowing at the name of Jesus, however, is not, as has been sometimes maintained, a relic of the papal worship of the Real Presence, but is rather a reminiscence of the fourth century, when controversies about the person of Christ rendered orthodox Christians peculiarly anxious to recognize Christ's deity.

"There is no 'corner' in divine grace" (C. H. Parkhurst). "All notions of a needed 'priesthood,' to bring us into connection with Christ, must yield to the truth that Christ is ever with us" (E. G. Robinson). "The priest was the conservative, the prophet the progressive. Hence the conflict between them. Episcopalians like the idea of a priesthood, but do not know what to do with that of prophet." Dr. A. J. Gordon: "Ritualism, like eczema in the human body, is generally a symptom of a low state of the blood. As a rule, when the church becomes secularized, it becomes ritualized, while great revivals, pouring through the church, have almost always burst the liturgical bands and have restored it to the freedom of the Spirit."

Puseyism, as defined by Pusey himself, means: "1. high thoughts of the two sacraments; 2. high estimate of Episcopacy as God's ordinance; 3. high estimate of the visible church as the body wherein we are made and continue to be members of Christ; 4. regard for ordinances as directing our devotions and disciplining us, such as daily public prayers, fasts and feasts; 5. regard for the visible part of devotion, such as the decoration of the house of God, which acts insensibly on the mind; 6. reverence for and deference to the ancient church, instead of the reformers, as the ultimate expounder of the meaning of our church." Pusey declared that he and Maurice worshiped different Gods.

5. Prerequisites to Participation in the Lord's Supper.

A. There are prerequisites.

This we argue from the fact:

(a) That Christ enjoined the celebration of the Supper, not upon the world at large, but only upon his disciples; (b) that the apostolic injunctions to Christians, to separate themselves from certain of their number, imply a limitation of the Lord's Supper to a narrower body, even among professed believers; (c) that the analogy of Baptism, as belonging only to a specified class of persons, leads us to believe that the same is true of the Lord's Supper.

The analogy of Baptism to the Lord's Supper suggests a general survey of the connections between the two ordinances: 1. Both ordinances symbolize primarily the death of Christ; then secondarily our spiritual death to sin because we are one with him; it being absurd, where there is no such union, to make our Baptism the symbol of his death. 2. We are merged in Christ first in Baptism; then in the Supper Christ is more and more taken into us; Baptism = we in Christ, the Supper = Christ in us. 3. As regeneration is instantaneous and sanctification continues in time, so Baptism should be for once, the Lord's Supper often; the first single, the second frequent. 4. If one ordinance, the Supper, requires discernment of the Lord's body, so does the other, the ordinance of Baptism; the subject of Baptism should know the meaning of his act. 5. The order of the ordinances teaches Christian doctrine, as the ordinances do; to partake of the Lord's Supper before being baptized is to say in symbol that one can be sanctified without being regenerated. 6. Both ordinances should be public, as both "show forth" the Lord's death and are teaching ordinances; no celebration of either one is to be permitted in private. 7. In both the administrator does not act at his own option, but is the organ of the church; Philip acts as organ of the church at Jerusalem when he baptizes the eunuch. 8. The ordinances stand by themselves, and are not to be made appendages of other meetings or celebrations; they belong, not to associations or conventions, but to the local church. 9. The Lord's Supper needs scrutiny of the communicant's qualifications as much as Baptism; and only the local church is the proper judge of these qualifications. 10. We may deny the Lord's Supper to one whom we know to be a Christian, when he walks disorderly or disseminates false doctrine, just as we may deny Baptism to such a person. 11. Fencing the tables, or warning the unqualified not to partake of the Supper, may, like instruction with regard to Baptism, best take place before the actual administration of the ordinance; and the pastor is not a special policeman or detective to ferret out offences. See Expositor's Greek Testament on 1 Cor. 10:1-6.

B. The prerequisites are those only which are expressly or implicitly laid down by Christ and his apostles.

(a) The church, as possessing executive but not legislative power, is charged with the duty, not of framing rules for the administering and guarding of the ordinance, but of discovering and applying the rules given it in the New Testament. No church has a right to establish any terms of communion; it is responsible only for making known the terms established by Christ and his apostles. (b) These terms, however, are to be ascertained not only from the injunctions, but also from the precedents, of the New Testament. Since the apostles were inspired, New Testament precedent is the "common law" of the church.

English law consists mainly of precedent, that is, past decisions of the courts. Immemorial customs may be as binding as are the formal enactments of a legislature. It is New Testament precedent that makes obligatory the observance of the first day, instead of the seventh day, of the week. The common law of the church consists, however, not of any and all customs, but only of the customs of the apostolic church interpreted in the light of its principles, or the customs universally binding because sanctioned by inspired apostles. Has New Testament precedent the authority of a divine command? Only so far, we reply, as it is an adequate, complete and final expression of the divine life in Christ. This we claim for the ordinances of Baptism and of the Lord's Supper, and for the order of these ordinances. See Proceedings of the Baptist Congress, 1896:23.

The Mennonites, thinking to reproduce even the incidental phases of N. T. action, have adopted: 1. the washing of feet; 2. the marriage only of members of the same faith; 3. non-resistance to violence; 4. the use of the ban, and the shunning of expelled persons; 5. refusal to take oaths; 6. the kiss of peace; 7. formal examination of the spiritual condition of each communicant before his participation in the Lord's Supper; 8. the choice of officials by lot. And they naturally break up into twelve sects, dividing upon such points as holding all things in common; plainness of dress, one sect repudiating buttons and using only hooks upon their clothing, whence their nickname of Hookers; the holding of services in private houses only; the asserted possession of the gift of prophecy (A. S. Carman).

C. On examining the New Testament, we find that the prerequisites to participation in the Lord's Supper are four.

First,—Regeneration.

The Lord's Supper is the outward expression of a life in the believer, nourished and sustained by the life of Christ. It cannot therefore be partaken of by one who is "dead through ... trespasses and sins." We give no food to a corpse. The Lord's Supper was never offered by the apostles to unbelievers. On the contrary, the injunction that each communicant "examine himself" implies that faith which will enable the communicant to "discern the Lord's body" is a prerequisite to participation.

1 Cor. 11:27-29—"Wherefore whosoever shall eat the bread or drink the cup of the Lord in an unworthy manner, shall be guilty of the body and the blood of the Lord. But let a man prove himself, and so let him eat of the bread, and drink of the cup. For he that eateth and drinketh, eateth and drinketh judgment unto himself, if he discern not the Lord's body." Schaff, in his Church History, 2:517, tells us that in the Greek Church, in the seventh and eighth centuries, the bread was dipped in the wine, and both elements were delivered in a spoon. See Edwards, on Qualifications for Full Communion, in Works, 1:81.

Secondly,—Baptism.

In proof that baptism is a prerequisite to the Lord's Supper, we urge the following considerations:

(a) The ordinance of baptism was instituted and administered long before the Supper.

Mat. 21:25—"The baptism of John, whence was it? from heaven or from men?"—Christ here intimates that John's baptism had been instituted by God before his own.

(b) The apostles who first celebrated it had, in all probability, been baptized.

Acts 1:21, 22—"Of the men therefore that have companied with us all the time that the Lord Jesus went in and went out among us, beginning from the baptism of John ... of these must one become a witness with us of his resurrection"; 19:4—"John baptized with the baptism of repentance, saying unto the people that they should believe on him that should come after him, that is, on Jesus."

Several of the apostles were certainly disciples of John. If Christ was baptized, much more his disciples. Jesus recognized John's baptism as obligatory, and it is not probable that he would take his apostles from among those who had not submitted to it. John the Baptist himself, the first administrator of baptism, must have been himself unbaptized. But the twelve could fitly administer it, because they had themselves received it at John's hands. See Arnold, Terms of Communion, 17.

(c) The command of Christ fixes the place of baptism as first in order after discipleship.

Mat. 28:19, 20—"Go ye therefore, and make disciples of all the nations, baptizing them into the name of the Father and of the Son and of the Holy Spirit: teaching them to observe all things whatsoever I commanded you"—here the first duty is to make disciples, the second to baptize, the third to instruct in right Christian living. Is it said that there is no formal command to admit only baptized persons to the Lord's Supper? We reply that there is no formal command to admit only regenerate persons to baptism. In both cases, the practice of the apostles and the general connections of Christian doctrine are sufficient to determine our duty.

(d) All the recorded cases show this to have been the order observed by the first Christians and sanctioned by the apostles.

Acts 2:41, 46—"They then that received his word were baptized.... And day by day, continuing stedfastly with one accord in the temple, and breaking bread at home [rather, 'in various worship-rooms'] they took their food with gladness and singleness of heart"; 8:12—"But when they believed Philip ... they were baptized"; 10:47, 48—"Can any man forbid the water, that these should not be baptized, who have received the Holy Spirit as well as we? And he commanded them to be baptized in the name of Jesus Christ"; 22:16—"And now why tarriest thou? arise, and be baptized, and wash away thy sins, calling on his name."

(e) The symbolism of the ordinances requires that baptism should precede the Lord's Supper. The order of the facts signified must be expressed in the order of the ordinances which signify them; else the world is taught that sanctification may take place without regeneration. Birth must come before sustenance—"nascimur, pascimur." To enjoy ceremonial privileges, there must be ceremonial qualifications. As none but the circumcised could eat the passover, so before eating with the Christian family must come adoption into the Christian family.

As one must be "born of the Spirit" before he can experience the sustaining influence of Christ, so he must be "born of water" before he can properly be nourished by the Lord's Supper. Neither the unborn nor the dead can eat bread or drink wine. Only when Christ had raised the daughter of the Jewish ruler to life, did he say: "Give her to eat." The ordinance which symbolizes regeneration, or the impartation of new life, must precede the ordinance which symbolizes the strengthening and perfecting of the life already begun. The Teaching of the Twelve Apostles, dating back to the second half of the second century, distinctly declares (9:5, 10)—"Let no one eat or drink of your Eucharist except those baptized into the name of the Lord; for as regards this also the Lord has said: 'Give not that which is holy unto the dogs'.... The Eucharist shall be given only to the baptized."

(f) The standards of all evangelical denominations, with unimportant exceptions, confirm the view that this is the natural interpretation of the Scripture requirements respecting the order of the ordinances.

"The only protest of note has been made by a portion of the English Baptists." To these should be added the comparatively small body of the Free Will Baptists in America. Pedobaptist churches in general refuse full membership, office-holding, and the ministry, to unbaptized persons. The Presbyterian church does not admit to the communion members of the Society of Friends. Not one of the great evangelical denominations accepts Robert Hall's maxim that the only terms of communion are terms of salvation. If individual ministers announce this principle and conform their practice to it, it is only because they transgress the standards of the churches to which they belong.

See Tyerman's Oxford Methodists, preface, page vi—"Even in Georgia, Wesley excluded dissenters from the Holy Communion, on the ground that they had not been properly baptized; and he would himself baptize only by immersion, unless the child or person was in a weak state of health." Baptist Noel gave it as his reason for submitting to baptism, that to approach the Lord's Supper conscious of not being baptized would be to act contrary to all the precedents of Scripture. See Curtis, Progress of Baptist Principles, 304.

The dismission of Jonathan Edwards from his church at Northampton was due to his opposing the Halfway Covenant, which admitted unregenerate persons to the Lord's Supper as a step on the road to spiritual life. He objected to the doctrine that the Lord's Supper was "a converting ordinance." But these very unregenerated persons had been baptized, and he himself had baptized many of them. He should have objected to infant baptism, as well as to the Lord's Supper, in the case of the unregenerate.

(g) The practical results of the opposite view are convincing proof that the order here insisted on is the order of nature as well as of Scripture. The admission of unbaptized persons to the communion tends always to, and has frequently resulted in, the disuse of baptism itself, the obscuring of the truth which it symbolizes, the transformation of Scripturally constituted churches into bodies organized after methods of human invention, and the complete destruction of both church and ordinances as Christ originally constituted them.

Arnold, Terms of Communion, 76—The steps of departure from Scriptural precedent have not unfrequently been the following: (1) administration of baptism on a weekday evening, to avoid giving offence; (2) reception, without baptism, of persons renouncing belief in the baptism of their infancy; (3) giving up of the Lord's Supper as non-essential,—to be observed or not observed by each individual, according as he finds it useful; (4) choice of a pastor who will not advocate Baptist views; (5) adoption of Congregational articles of faith; (6) discipline and exclusion of members for propagating Baptist doctrine. John Bunyan's church, once either an open communion church or a mixed church both of baptized and unbaptized believers, is now a regular Congregational body. Armitage, History of the Baptists, 482 sq., claims that it was originally a Baptist church. Vedder, however, in Bap. Quar. Rev., 1886:289, says that "The church at Bedford is proved by indisputable documentary evidence never to have been a Baptist church in any strict sense." The results of the principle of open communion are certainly seen in the Regent's Park church in London, where some of the deacons have never been baptized. The doctrine that baptism is not essential to church membership is simply the logical result of the previous practice of admitting unbaptized persons to the communion table. If they are admitted to the Lord's Supper, then there is no bar to their admission to the church. See Proceedings of the Baptist Congress, Boston, November, 1902; Curtis, Progress of Baptist Principles, 296-298.

Thirdly,—Church membership.

(a) The Lord's Supper is a church ordinance, observed by churches of Christ as such. For this reason, membership in the church naturally precedes communion. Since communion is a family rite, the participant should first be a member of the family.

Acts 2:46 47—"breaking bread at home [rather, 'in various worship-rooms']" (see Com. of Meyer); 20:7—"upon the first day of the week, when we were gathered together to break bread"; 1 Cor. 11:18, 22—"when ye come together in the church ... have ye not houses to eat and to drink in? or despise ye the church of God, and put them to shame that have not?"

(b) The Lord's Supper is a symbol of church fellowship. Excommunication implies nothing, if it does not imply exclusion from the communion. If the Supper is simply communion of the individual with Christ, then the church has no right to exclude any from it.

1 Cor. 10:17—"we, who are many, are one bread, one body: for we all partake of the one bread." Though the Lord's Supper primarily symbolizes fellowship with Christ, it symbolizes secondarily fellowship with the church of Christ. Not all believers in Christ were present at the first celebration of the Supper, but only those organized into a body—the apostles. I can invite proper persons to my tea-table, but that does not give them the right to come uninvited. Each church, therefore, should invite visiting members of sister churches to partake with it. The Lord's Supper is an ordinance by itself, and should not be celebrated at conventions and associations, simply to lend dignity to something else.

The Panpresbyterian Council at Philadelphia, in 1880, refused to observe the Lord's Supper together, upon the ground that the Supper is a church ordinance, to be observed only by those who are amenable to the discipline of the body, and therefore not to be observed by separate church organizations acting together. Substantially upon this ground, the Old School General Assembly long before, being invited to unite at the Lord's table with the New School body with whom they had dissolved ecclesiastical relations, declined to do so. See Curtis, Progress of Baptist Principles, 304; Arnold, Terms of Communion, 36.

Fourthly,—An orderly walk.

Disorderly walking designates a course of life in a church member which is contrary to the precepts of the gospel. It is a bar to participation in the Lord's Supper, the sign of church fellowship. With Arnold, we may class disorderly walking under four heads:—

(a) Immoral conduct.

1 Cor. 5:1-13—Paul commands the Corinthian church to exclude the incestuous person: "I wrote unto you in my epistle to have no company with fornicators;... but now I write unto you not to keep company, if any man that is named a brother be a fornicator, or covetous, or an idolater, or a reviler, or a drunkard, or

an extortioner; with such a one no, not to eat.... Put away the wicked man from among yourselves."—Here it is evident that the most serious forms of disorderly walking require exclusion not only from church fellowship but from Christian fellowship as well.

(b) Disobedience to the commands of Christ.

1 Cor. 14:37—"If any man thinketh himself to be a prophet, or spiritual, let him take knowledge of the things which I write unto you, that they are the commandments of the Lord"; 2 Thess. 3:6, 11, 15—"Now we command you, brethren,... that ye withdraw yourselves from every brother that walketh disorderly, and not after the tradition which they received of us... For we hear of some that walk among you disorderly, that work not at all, but are busybodies.... And if any man obeyeth not our word by this epistle, note that man, that ye have no company with him, to the end that he may be ashamed. And yet count him not as an enemy, but admonish him as a brother."—Here is exclusion from church fellowship, and from the Lord's Supper its sign, while yet the offender is not excluded from Christian fellowship, but is still counted "a brother." Versus G. B. Stevens, in N. Englander, 1887:40-47.

In these passages Paul intimates that "not to walk after the tradition received from him, not to obey the word contained in his epistles, is the same as disobedience to the commands of Christ, and as such involves the forfeiture of church fellowship and its privileged tokens" (Arnold, Prerequisites to Communion, 68). Since Baptism is a command of Christ, it follows that we cannot properly commune with the unbaptized. To admit such to the Lord's Supper is to give the symbol of church fellowship to those who, in spite of the fact that they are Christian brethren, are, though perhaps unconsciously, violating the fundamental law of the church. To withhold protest against plain disobedience to Christ's commands is to that extent to countenance such disobedience. The same disobedience which in the church member we should denominate disorderly walking must a fortiori destroy all right to the Lord's Supper on the part of those who are not members of the church.

(c) Heresy, or the holding and teaching of false doctrine.

Titus 3:10—"A man that is heretical [Am. Revisers: 'a factious man'] after a first and second admonition refuse"; see Ellicott, Com., in loco: "αἱρετικὸς ἄνθρωπος = one who gives rise to divisions by erroneous teaching, not necessarily of a fundamentally heterodox nature, but of the kind just described in verse 9." Cf. Acts 20:30—"from among your own selves shall men arise, speaking perverse things, to draw away the disciples after them"; 1 John 4:2, 3—"Hereby know ye the Spirit of God: every spirit that confesseth that Jesus Christ is come in the flesh is of God: and every spirit that confesseth not Jesus is not of God: and this is the spirit of the antichrist." B. B. Bosworth: "Heresy, in the N. T., does not necessarily mean the holding of erroneous opinions,—it may also mean the holding of correct opinions in an unbrotherly or divisive spirit." We grant that the word "heretical" may also mean "factious"; but we claim that false doctrine is the chief source of division, and is therefore in itself a disqualification for participation in the Lord's Supper. Factiousness is an additional bar, and we treat it under the next head of Schism.

The Panpresbyterian Council, mentioned above, refused to admit to their body the Cumberland Presbyterians, because, though the latter adhere to the Presbyterian form of church government, they are Arminian in their views of the doctrines of grace. As we have seen, on pages 940-942, that Baptism is a confession of evangelical faith, so here we see that the Lord's Supper also is a confession of evangelical faith, and that no one can properly participate in it who denies the doctrines of sin, of the deity, incarnation and atonement of Christ, and of justification by faith, which the Lord's Supper symbolizes. Such denial should exclude from all Christian fellowship as well.

There is heresy which involves exclusion only from church fellowship. Since pedobaptists hold and propagate false doctrine with regard to the church and its ordinances—doctrines which endanger the spirituality of the church, the sufficiency of the Scriptures, and the lordship of Christ—we cannot properly admit them to the Lord's Supper. To admit them or to partake with them, would be to treat falsehood as if it were truth. Arnold, Prerequisites to Communion, 72—"Pedobaptists are guilty of teaching that the baptized are not members of the church, or that membership in the church is not voluntary; that there are two sorts of baptism, one of which is a profession of faith of the person baptized, and the other is profession of faith of another person; that regeneration is given in and by baptism, or that the church is composed in great part of persons who do not give, and were never supposed to give, any evidence of regeneration; that the church has a right to change essentially one of Christ's institutions, or that it is unessential whether it be observed as he ordained it or in some other manner; that baptism may be rightfully administered in a way which makes much of the language in which it is described in the Scriptures wholly unsuitable and inapplicable, and which does not at all represent the facts and doctrines which baptism is declared in the Scriptures to represent; that the Scriptures are not in all religious matters the sufficient and only binding rule of faith and practice."

(d) Schism, or the promotion of division and dissension in the church.—This also requires exclusion from church fellowship, and from the Lord's Supper which is its appointed sign.

Rom. 16:17—"Now I beseech you, brethren, mark them that are causing the divisions and occasions of stumbling contrary to the doctrine which ye learned: and turn away from them." Since pedobaptists, by their teaching and practice, draw many away from Scripturally constituted churches,—thus dividing true believers from each other and weakening the bodies organized after the model of the New Testament,—it is imperative upon us to separate ourselves from them, so far as regards that communion at the Lord's table which is the sign of church fellowship. Mr. Spurgeon admits pedobaptists to commune with his church "for two or three months." Then they are kindly asked whether they are pleased with the church, its preaching, doctrine, form of government, etc. If they say they are pleased, they are asked if they are not disposed to be baptized and become members? If so inclined, all is well; but if not, they are kindly told that it is not desirable for them to commune longer. Thus baptism is held to precede church membership and permanent communion, although temporary communion is permitted without it.

Arnold, Prerequisites to Communion, 80—"It may perhaps be objected that the passages cited under the four preceding subdivisions refer to church fellowship in a general way, without any specific reference to the Lord's Supper. In reply to this objection, I would answer, in the first place, that having endeavored previously to establish the position that the Lord's Supper is an ordinance to be celebrated in the church, and expressive of church fellowship, I felt at liberty to use the passages that enjoin the withdrawal of that fellowship as constructively enjoining exclusion from the Communion, which is its chief token. I answer, secondly, that the principle here assumed seems to me to pervade the Scriptural teachings so thoroughly that it is next to impossible to lay down any Scriptural terms of communion at the Lord's table, except upon the admission that the ordinance is inseparably connected with church fellowship. To treat the subject otherwise, would be, as it appears to me, a violent putting asunder of what the Lord has joined together. The objection suggests an additional argument in favor of our position that the Lord's Supper is a church ordinance." "Who Christ's body doth divide, Wounds afresh the Crucified; Who Christ's people doth perplex, Weakens faith and comfort wrecks; Who Christ's order doth not see, Works in vain for unity; Who Christ's word doth take for guide, With the Bridegroom loves the Bride."

D. The local church is the judge whether these prerequisites are fulfilled.

The local church is the judge whether these prerequisites are fulfilled in the case of persons desiring to partake of the Lord's Supper.—This is evident from the following considerations:

(a) The command to observe the ordinance was given, not to individuals, but to a company.

(b) Obedience to this command is not an individual act, but is the joint act of many.

(c) The regular observance of the Lord's Supper cannot be secured, nor the qualifications of persons desiring to participate in it be scrutinized, unless some distinct organized body is charged with this responsibility.

(d) The only organized body known to the New Testament is the local church, and this is the only body, of any sort, competent to have charge of the ordinances. The invisible church has no officers.

(e) The New Testament accounts indicate that the Lord's Supper was observed only at regular appointed meetings of local churches, and was observed by these churches as regularly organized bodies.

(f) Since the duty of examining the qualifications of candidates for baptism and for membership is vested in the local church and is essential to its distinct existence, the analogy of the ordinances would lead us to believe that the scrutiny of qualifications for participation in the Lord's Supper rests with the same body.

(g) This care that only proper persons are admitted to the ordinances should be shown, not by open or forcible debarring of the unworthy at the time of the celebration, but by previous public instruction of the congregation, and, if needful in the case of persistent offenders, by subsequent private and friendly admonition.

"What is everybody's business is nobody's business." If there be any power of effective scrutiny, it must be lodged in the local church. The minister is not to administer the ordinance of the Lord's Supper at his own option, any more than the ordinance of Baptism. He is simply the organ of the church. He is to follow the rules of the church as to invitations and as to the mode of celebrating the ordinance, of course instructing the church as to the order of the New Testament. In the case of sick members who desire to communicate, brethren may be deputed to hold a special meeting of the church at the private house or sick room, and then only may the pastor officiate. If an invitation to the Communion is given, it may well be in the following form: "Members in good standing of other churches of like faith and practice are cordially invited to partake with us." But since the comity of Baptist churches is universally acknowledged, and since Baptist views with regard to the ordinances are so generally understood, it should be taken for granted that all proper persons will be welcome even if no invitation of any sort is given.

Mr. Spurgeon, as we have seen, permitted unbaptized persons temporarily to partake of the Lord's Supper unchallenged, but if there appeared a disposition to make participation habitual, one of the deacons in a private interview explained Baptist doctrine and urged the duty of baptism. If this advice was not taken, participation in the Lord's Supper naturally ceased. Dr. P. S. Henson proposes a middle path between open and close communion, as follows: "Preach and urge faith in Jesus and obedience to him. Leave choice with participants themselves. It is not wise to set up a judgment-seat at the Lord's table. Always preach the Scriptural order—1. Faith in Jesus; 2. Obedience in Baptism; 2. Observance of the Lord's Supper." J. B. Thomas: "Objections to strict communion come with an ill grace from pedobaptists who withhold communion from their own baptized, whom they have forcibly made quasi-members in spite of the only protest they are capable of offering, and whom they have retained as subjects of discipline without their consent."

A. H. Strong, Cleveland Sermon on Our Denominational Outlook, May 19, 1904—"If I am asked whether Baptists still hold to restricted communion, I answer that our principle has not changed, but that many of us apply the principle in a different manner from that of our fathers. We believe that Baptism logically precedes the Lord's Supper, as birth precedes the taking of nourishment, and regeneration precedes sanctification. We believe that the order of the ordinances is an important point of Christian doctrine, and itself teaches Christian doctrine. Hence we proclaim it and adhere to it, in our preaching and our practice. But we do not turn the Lord's Supper into a judgment-seat, or turn the officers of the church into detectives. We teach the truth, and expect that the truth will win its way. We are courteous to all who come among us; and expect that they in turn will have the courtesy to respect our convictions and to act accordingly. But there is danger here that we may break from our moorings and drift into indifferentism with regard to the ordinances. The recent advocacy of open church- membership is but the logical consequence of a previous concession of open communion. I am persuaded that this new doctrine is confined to very few among us. The remedy for this false liberalism is to be found in that same Christ who solves for us all other problems. It is this Christ who sets the solitary in families, and who makes of one every nation that dwells on the face of the earth. Christian denominations are at least temporarily his appointment. Loyalty to the body which seems to us best to represent his truth is also loyalty to him. Love for Christ does not involve the surrender of the ties of family, or nation, or denomination, but only consecrates and ennobles them.

"Yet Christ is King in Zion. There is but one army of the living God, even though there are many divisions. We can emphasize our unity with other Christian bodies, rather than the differences between us. We can regard them as churches of the Lord Jesus, even though they are irregularly constituted. As a marriage ceremony may be valid, even though performed without a license and by an unqualified administrator; and as an ordination may be valid, even though the ordinary laying-on of hands be omitted; so the ordinance of the Lord's Supper as administered in pedobaptist churches may be valid, though irregular in its accompaniments and antecedents. Though we still protest against the modern perversions of the New Testament doctrine as to the subjects and mode of Baptism, we hold with regard to the Lord's Supper that irregularity is not invalidity, and that we may recognize as churches even those bodies which celebrate the Lord's Supper without having been baptized. Our faith in the larger Christ is bringing us out from our denominational isolation into an inspiring recognition of our oneness with the universal church of God throughout the world." On the whole subject, see Madison Avenue Lectures, 217-260; and A. H. Strong, on Christian Truth and its Keepers, in Philosophy and Religion, 238-244.

E. Special objections to open communion.

The advocates of this view claim that baptism, as not being an indispensable term of salvation, cannot properly be made an indispensable term of communion.

Robert Hall, Works, 1:285, held that there can be no proper terms of communion which are not also terms of salvation. He claims that "we are expressly commanded to tolerate in the church all those diversities of opinion which are not inconsistent with salvation." For the open communion view, see also John M. Mason, Works, 1:369; Princeton Review, Oct. 1850; Bib. Sac., 21:449; 24:482; 25:401; Spirit of the Pilgrims, 6:103, 142. But, as Curtis remarks, in his Progress of Baptist Principles, 292, this principle would utterly frustrate the very objects for which visible churches were founded—to be "the pillar and ground of the truth" (1 Tim. 3:15); for truth is set forth as forcibly in ordinances as in doctrine.

In addition to what has already been said, we reply:

(a) This view is contrary to the belief and practice of all but an insignificant fragment of organized Christendom.

A portion of the English Baptists, and the Free Will Baptists in America, are the only bodies which in their standards of faith accept and maintain the principles of open communion. As to the belief and practice of the Methodist Episcopal denomination, the New York Christian Advocate states the terms of communion as being: 1. Discipleship; 2. Baptism; 3. Consistent church life, as required in the "Discipline"; and F. G. Hibbard, Christian Baptism, 174, remarks that, "in one principle the Baptist and pedobaptist churches agree. They both agree in rejecting from the communion at the table of the Lord, and denying the rights of church fellowship to all who have not been baptized. Valid baptism, they consider, is essential to constitute visible church membership. This also we [Methodists] hold.... The charge of close communion is no more applicable to the Baptists than to us."

The Interior states the Presbyterian position as follows: "The difference between our Baptist brethren and ourselves is an important difference. We agree with them, however, in saying that unbaptized persons should not partake of the Lord's Supper. Close communion, in our judgment, is a more defensible position than open communion." Dr. John Hall: "If I believed, with the Baptists, that none are baptized but those who are immersed on profession of faith, I should, with them, refuse to commune with any others."

As to the views of Congregationalists, we quote from Dwight, Systematic Theology, sermon 160—"It is an indispensable qualification for this ordinance that the candidate for communion be a member of the visible church of Christ, in full standing. By this I intend that he should be a man of piety; that he should have made a public profession of religion; and that he should have been baptized." The Independent: "We have never been disposed to charge the Baptist church with any special narrowness or bigotry in their rule of admission to the Lord's table. We do not see how it differs from that commonly admitted and established among Presbyterian churches."

The Episcopal standards and authorities are equally plain. The Book of Common Prayer, Order of Confirmation, declares: "There shall none be admitted to the holy communion, until such time as he be confirmed, or be ready and desirous to be confirmed"—confirmation always coming after baptism. Wall, History of Infant Baptism, part 2, chapter 9—"No church ever gave the communion to any persons before they were baptized. Among all the absurdities that ever were held, none ever maintained that any person should partake of the communion before he was baptized."

(b) It assumes an unscriptural inequality between the two ordinances. The Lord's Supper holds no higher rank in Scripture than does Baptism. The obligation to commune is no more binding than the obligation to profess faith by being baptized. Open communion, however, treats baptism as if it were optional, while it insists upon communion as indispensable.

Robert Hall should rather have said: "No church has a right to establish terms of baptism which are not also terms of salvation," for baptism is most frequently in Scripture connected with the things that accompany salvation. We believe faith to be one prerequisite, but not the only one. We may hold a person to be a Christian, without thinking him entitled to commune unless he has been also baptized.

Ezra's reform in abolishing mixed marriages with the surrounding heathen was not narrow nor bigoted nor intolerant. Miss Willard said well that from the Gerizim of holy beatitudes there comes a voice: "Blessed are the inclusive, for they shall be included," and from Mount Ebal a voice, saying: "Sad are the exclusive, for they shall be excluded." True liberality is both Christian and wise. We should be just as liberal as Christ himself, and no more so. Even Miss Willard would not include rum-sellers in the Christian Temperance Union, nor think that town blessed that did not say to saloon keepers: "Repent, or go." The choir is not narrow because it does not include those who can only make discords, nor is the sheepfold intolerant that refuses to include wolves, nor the medical society that excludes quacks, nor the church that does not invite the disobedient and schismatic to its communion.

(c) It tends to do away with baptism altogether. If the highest privilege of church membership may be enjoyed without baptism, baptism loses its place and importance as the initiatory ordinance of the church.

Robert Hall would admit to the Lord's Supper those who deny Baptism to be perpetually binding on the church. A foreigner may love this country, but he cannot vote at our elections unless he has been naturalized. Ceremonial rites imply ceremonial qualifications. Dr. Meredith in Brooklyn said to his great Bible Class that a man, though not a Christian, but who felt himself a sinner and needing Christ, could worthily partake of the Lord's Supper. This is the logic of open communion. The Supper is not limited to baptized persons, nor to church members, nor even to converted people, but belongs also to the unconverted world. This is not only to do away with Baptism, but to make the Lord's Supper a converting ordinance.

(d) It tends to do away with all discipline. When Christians offend, the church must withdraw its fellowship from them. But upon the principle of open communion, such withdrawal is impossible, since the Lord's Supper, the highest expression of church fellowship, is open to every person who regards himself as a Christian.

H. F. Colby: "Ought we to acknowledge that evangelical pedobaptists are qualified to partake of the Lord's Supper? We are ready to admit them on precisely the same terms on which we admit ourselves. Our communion bars come to be a protest, but from no plan of ours. They become a protest merely as every act of loyalty to truth becomes a protest against error." Constitutions of the Holy Apostles, book 2, section 7 (about 250 A. D.)—"But if they [those who have been convicted of wickedness] afterwards repent and turn from their error, then we receive them as we receive the heathen, when they wish to repent, into the church indeed to hear the word, but do not receive them to communion until they have received the seal of baptism and are made complete Christians."

(e) It tends to do away with the visible church altogether. For no visible church is possible, unless some sign of membership be required, in addition to the signs of membership in the invisible church. Open communion logically leads to open church membership, and a church membership open to all, without reference to the qualifications required in Scripture, or without examination on the part of the church as to the existence of these qualifications in those who unite with it, is virtually an identification of the church with the world, and, without protest from Scripturally constituted bodies, would finally result in its actual extinction.

Dr. Walcott Calkins, in Andover Review: "It has never been denied that the Puritan way of maintaining the purity and doctrinal soundness of the churches is to secure a soundly converted membership. There is one denomination of Puritans which has never deviated a hair's breadth from this way. The Baptists have always insisted that regenerate persons only ought to receive the sacraments of the church. And they have depended absolutely upon this provision for the purity and doctrinal soundness of their churches."

At the Free Will Baptist Convention at Providence, Oct., 1874, the question came up of admitting pedobaptists to membership. This was disposed of by resolving that "Christian baptism is a personal act of public consecration to Christ, and that believers' baptism and immersion alone, as baptism, are fundamental principles of the denomination." In other words, unimmersed believers would not be admitted to membership. But is it not the Lord's church? Have we a right to exclude? Is this not bigotry? The Free Will Baptist answers: "No, it is only loyalty to truth."

We claim that, upon the same principle, he should go further, and refuse to admit to the communion those whom he refuses to admit to church membership. The reasons assigned for acting upon the opposite principle are sentimental rather than rational. See John Stuart Mill's definition of sentimentality, quoted in Martineau's Essays, 1:94—"Sentimentality consists in setting the sympathetic aspect of things, or their loveableness, above their æsthetic aspect, their beauty; or above the moral aspect of them, their right or wrong."

OBJECTIONS TO STRICT COMMUNION, AND ANSWERS TO THEM (condensed from Arnold, Terms of Communion, 82):

"1st. Primitive rules are not applicable now. Reply: (1) The laws of Christ are unchangeable. (2) The primitive order ought to be restored.

"2d. Baptism, as an external rite, is of less importance than love. Reply: (1) It is not inconsistent with love, but the mark of love, to keep Christ's commandments. (2) Love for our brethren requires protest against their errors.

"3d. Pedobaptists think themselves baptized. Reply: (1) This is a reason why they should act as if they believed it, not a reason why we should act as if it were so. (2) We cannot submit our consciences to their views of truth without harming ourselves and them.

"4th. Strict communion is a hindrance to union among Christians. Reply: (1) Christ desires only union in the truth. (2) Baptists are not responsible for the separation. (3) Mixed communion is not a cure but a cause of disunion.

"5th. The rule excludes from the communion baptized members of pedobaptist churches. Reply: (1) These persons are walking disorderly, in promoting error. (2) The Lord's Supper is a symbol of church fellowship, not of fellowship for individuals, apart from their church relations.

"6th. A plea for dispensing with the rule exists in extreme cases where persons must commune with us or not at all. Reply: (1) It is hard to fix limits to these exceptions: they would be likely to encroach more and more, till the rule became merely nominal. (2) It is a greater privilege and means of grace, in such circumstances, to abstain from communing, than contrary to principle to participate. (3) It is not right to participate with others, where we cannot invite them reciprocally.

"7. Alleged inconsistency of our practice.—(a) Since we expect to commune in heaven. Reply: This confounds Christian fellowship with church fellowship. We do commune with pedobaptists spiritually, here as hereafter. We do not expect to partake of the Lord's Supper with them, or with others, in heaven. (b) Since we reject the better and receive the worse. Reply: We are not at liberty to refuse to apply Christ's outward rule, because we cannot equally apply his inward spiritual rule of character. Pedobaptists withhold communion from those they regard as unbaptized, though they may be more spiritual than some in the church. (c) Since we recognize pedobaptists as brethren in union meetings, exchange of pulpits, etc. Reply: None of these acts of fraternal fellowship imply the church communion which admission to the Lord's table would imply. This last would recognize them as baptized: the former do not.

"8th. Alleged impolicy of our practice. Reply: (1) This consideration would be pertinent, only if we were at liberty to change our practice when it was expedient, or was thought to be so. (2) Any particular truth will inspire respect in others in proportion as its advocates show that they respect it. In England our numbers have diminished, compared with the population, in the ratio of 33 per cent; here we have increased 50 per cent. in proportion to the ratio of population.

"Summary. Open communion must be justified, if at all, on one of four grounds: First, that baptism is not prerequisite to communion. But this is opposed to the belief and practice of all churches. Secondly, that immersion on profession of faith is not essential to baptism. But this is renouncing Baptist principles altogether. Thirdly, that the individual, and not the church, is to be the judge of his qualifications for admission to the communion. But this is contrary to sound reason, and fatal to the ends for which the church is instituted. For, if the conscience of the individual is to be the rule of the action of the church in regard to his admission to the Lord's Supper, why not also with regard to his regeneration, his doctrinal belief, and his obedience to Christ's commands generally? Fourthly, that the church has no responsibility in regard to the qualifications of those who come to her communion. But this is abandoning the principle of the independence of the churches, and their accountableness to Christ, and it overthrows all church discipline."

See also Hovey, in Bib. Sac., 1862:133; Pepper, in Bap. Quar., 1867:216; Curtis on Communion, 292; Howell, Terms of Communion; Williams, The Lord's Supper; Theodosia Ernest, pub. by Am. Bap. Pub. Soc.; Wilkinson, The Baptist Principle. In concluding our treatment of Ecclesiology, we desire to call attention to the fact that Jacob, the English Churchman, in his Ecclesiastical Polity of the N. T., and Cunningham, the Scotch Presbyterian, in his Croall Lectures for 1886, have furnished Baptists with much valuable material for the defence of the New Testament doctrine of the Church and its Ordinances. In fact, a complete statement of the Baptist positions might easily be constructed from the concessions of their various opponents. See A. H. Strong, on Unconscious Assumptions of Communion Polemics, in Philosophy and Religion, 245-249.

PART VIII - ESCHATOLOGY, OR THE DOCTRINE OF FINAL THINGS

Neither the individual Christian character, nor the Christian church as a whole, attains its destined perfection in this life (Rom. 8:24). This perfection is reached in the world to come (1 Cor. 13:10). As preparing the way for the kingdom of God in its completeness, certain events are to take place, such as death, Christ's second coming, the resurrection of the body, the general judgment. As stages in the future condition of men, there is to be an intermediate and an ultimate state, both for the righteous and for the wicked. We discuss these events and states in what appears from Scripture to be the order of their occurrence.

Rom. 8:24—"in hope were we saved: but hope that is seen is not hope: for who hopeth for that which he seeth?" 1 Cor. 13:10—"when that which is perfect is come, that which is in part will be done away." Original sin is not wholly eradicated from the Christian, and the Holy Spirit is not yet sole ruler. So, too, the church is still in a state of conflict, and victory is hereafter. But as the Christian life attains its completeness only in the future, so with the life of sin. Death begins here, but culminates hereafter. James 1:15—"the sin, when it is full grown, bringeth forth death." The wicked man here has only a foretaste of "the wrath to come" (Mat. 3:7). We may "lay up ... treasures in heaven" (Mat. 6:20), but we may also "treasure up for ourselves wrath" (Rom. 2:5), i. e., lay up treasures in hell.

Dorner: "To the actuality of the consummation of the church belongs a cessation of reproduction through which there is constantly renewed a world which the church must subdue.... The mutually external existence of spirit and nature must give way to a perfect internal existence. Their externality to each other is the ground of the mortality of the natural side, and of its being a means of temptation to the spiritual side. For in this externality the natural side has still too great independence and exerts a determining power over the personality.... Art, the beautiful, receives in the future state its special place; for it is the way of art to delight in visible presentation, to achieve the classical and perfect with unfettered play of its powers. Every one morally perfect will thus wed the good to the beautiful. In the rest, there will be no inactivity; and in the activity also, no unrest."

Schleiermacher: "Eschatology is essentially prophetic; and is therefore vague and indefinite, like all unfulfilled prophecy." Schiller's Thekla: "Every thought of beautiful, trustful seeming Stands fulfilled in Heaven's eternal day; Shrink not then from erring and from dreaming,—Lofty sense lies oft in childish play." Frances Power Cobbe, Peak of Darien, 265—"Human nature is a ship with the tide out; when the tide of eternity comes in, we shall see the purpose of the ship." Eschatology deals with the precursors of Christ's second coming, as well as with the second coming itself. We are to labor for the coming of the kingdom of God in society as well as in the individual and in the church, in the present life as well as in the life to come.

Kidd, in his Principles of Western Civilization, says that survives which helps the greatest number. But the greatest number is always in the future. The theatre has become too wide for the drama. Through the roof the eternal stars appear. The image of God in man implies the equality of all men. Political equality implies universal suffrage; economic equality implies universal profit. Society has already transcended, first, city isolation, and secondly, state isolation. The United States presents thus far the largest free trade area in history. The next step is the unity of the English speaking peoples. The days of separate nationalities are numbered. Laissez faire = surviving barbarism. There are signs of larger ideas in art, ethics, literature, philosophy, science, politics, economics, religion. Competition must be moralized, and must take into account the future as well as the present. See also Walter Rauschenbusch, Christianity and the Social Crisis.

George B. Stevens, in Am. Jour. Theology, Oct. 1902: 666-684, asks: "Is there a self-constituted New Testament Eschatology?" He answers, for substance, that only three things are sure: 1. The certain triumph of the kingdom—this being the kernel of truth in the doctrine of Christ's second coming; 2. the victory of life over death—the truth in the doctrine of the resurrection; 3. the principle of judgment—the truth at the basis of the belief in rewards and punishments in the world to come. This meagre and abstract residuum argues denial both of the unity and the sufficiency of Scripture. Our view of inspiration, while it does not assure us of minute details, does notwithstanding give us a broad general outline of the future consummation, and guarantees its trustworthiness by the word of Christ and his apostles.

Faith in that consummation is the main incitement to poetic utterance and to lofty achievement. Shairp, Province of Poetry, 28—"If poetry be not a river fed from the clear wells that spring on the highest summits of humanity, but only a canal to drain off stagnant ditches from the flats, it may be a very useful sanitary contrivance, but has not, in Bacon's words, any 'participation of divineness.'" Shakespeare uses prose for ideas detached from emotion, such as the merrymaking of clowns or the maundering of fools. But lofty thought with him puts on poetry as its singing robe. Savage, Life beyond Death, 1-5—"When Henry D. Thoreau lay dying at Concord, his friend Parker Pillsbury sat by his bedside. He leaned over, took him by the hand, and said: 'Henry, you are so near to the border now, can you see anything on the other side?' And Thoreau answered: 'One world at a time, Parker!' But I cannot help asking about that other world, and if I belong to a future world as well as to this, my life will be a very different one." Jesus knew our need of certain information about the future, and therefore he said: "In my Father's house are many mansions; if it were not so, I would have told you; for I go to prepare a place for you" (John 14:2).

Hutton, Essays, 2:211—"Imagination may be powerful without being fertile; it may summon up past scenes and live in them without being able to create new ones. National unity and supernatural guidance were beliefs which kept Hebrew poetry from being fertile or original in its dealings with human story; for national pride is conservative, not inventive, and believers in actual providence do not care to live in a world of invention. The Jew saw in history only the illustration of these two truths. He was never thoroughly stirred by mere individual emotion. The modern poet is a student of beauty; the O. T. poet a student of God. To the latter all creation is a mere shadow; the essence of its beauty and the sustaining power of its life are in the spiritual world. Go beyond the spiritual nature of man, and the sympathy of the Hebrew poet is dried up at once. His poetry was true and divine, but at the expense of variousness of insight and breadth of sympathy. It was heliocentric rather than geocentric. Only Job, the latest, is a conscious effort of the imagination." Apocalyptic poetry for these reasons was most natural to the Hebrew mind.

Balfour, Foundations of Belief, 66—"Somewhere and for some Being, there shines an unchanging splendor of beauty, of which in nature and in art we see, each of us from his own standpoint, only passing gleams and stray reflections, whose different aspects we cannot now coördinate, whose import we cannot fully comprehend, but which at least is something other than the chance play of subjective sensibility or the far-off echo of ancestral lusts." Dewey, Psychology, 200—"All products of the creative imagination are unconscious testimonials to the unity of spirit which binds man to man, and man to nature, in one organic whole." Tennyson, Idylls of the King: "As from beyond the limit of the world, Like the last echo born of a great cry, Sounds, as if some fair city were one voice Around a king returning from his wars." See, on the whole subject of Eschatology, Luthardt, Lehre von den letzten Dingen, and Saving Truths of Christianity; Hodge, Systematic Theology, 3:713-880; Hovey, Biblical Eschatology; Heagle, That Blessed Hope.

I. Physical Death

Physical death is the separation of the soul from the body. We distinguish it from spiritual death, or the separation of the soul from God; and from the second death, or the banishment from God and final misery of the reünited soul and body of the wicked.

Spiritual death: Is. 59:2—"but your iniquities have separated between you and your God, and your sins have hid his face from you, so that he will not hear"; Rom. 7:24—"Wretched man that I am! who shall deliver me out of the body of this death?" Eph. 2:1—"dead through your trespasses and sins." The second death: Rev. 2:11—"He that overcometh shall not be hurt of the second death"; 20:14—"And death and Hades were cast into the lake of fire. This is the second death, even the lake of fire"; 21:8—"But for the fearful, and unbelieving, and abominable, and murderers, and fornicators, and sorcerers, and idolaters, and all liars, their part shall be in the lake that burneth with fire and brimstone; which is the second death."

Julius Müller, Doctrine of Sin, 2:303—"Spiritual death, the inner discord and enslavement of the soul, and the misery resulting therefrom, to which belongs that other death, the second death, an outward condition corresponding to that inner slavery." Trench, Epistles to the Seven Churches, 151—"This phrase ['second death'] is itself a solemn protest against the Sadduceeism and Epicureanism which would make natural death the be-all and the end-all of existence. As there is a life beyond the present life for the faithful, so there is death beyond that which falls under our eyes for the wicked." E. G. Robinson: "The second death is the continuance of spiritual death in another and timeless existence." Hudson, Scientific Demonstration of a Future Life, 222—"If a man has a power that transcends the senses, it is at least presumptive evidence that it does not perish when the senses are extinguished.... The activity of the subjective mind is in inverse proportion to that of the body, though the objective mind weakens with the body and perishes with the brain."

Prof. H. H. Bawden: "Consciousness is simply the growing of an organism, while the organism is just that which grows. Consciousness is a function, not a thing, not an order of existence at all. It is the universe coming to a focus, flowering so to speak in a finite centre. Society is an organism in the same sense that the human being is an organism. The spatial separation of the elements of the social organism is relatively no greater than the separation of the unit factors of the body. As the neurone cannot deny the consciousness which is the function of the body, so the individual member of society has no reason for denying the existence of a cosmic life of the organism which we call society."

Emma M. Caillard, on Man in the Light of Evolution, in Contemp. Rev., Dec. 1893:878—"Man is nature risen into the consciousness of its relationship to the divine. There is no receding from this point. When 'that which drew from out the boundless deep turns again home,' the persistence of each personal life is necessitated. Human life, as it is, includes, though it transcends the lower forms through which it has developed. Human life, as it will be, must include though it may transcend its present manifestation, viz., personality." "Sometime, when all life's lessons have been learned, And suns and stars forevermore have set, And things which our weak judgments here have spurned, The things o'er which we grieved with lashes wet, Will flash before us through our life's dark night, As stars shine most in deepest tints of blue: And we shall see how all God's plans were right, And most that seemed reproof was love most true: And if sometimes commingled with life's wine We find the wormwood and rebel and shrink, Be sure a wiser hand than yours or mine Pours out this portion for our lips to drink. And if some friend we love is lying low, Where human kisses cannot reach his face, O do not blame the loving Father so, But wear your sorrow with obedient grace; And you shall shortly know that lengthened breath Is not the sweetest gift God sends his friend, And that sometimes the sable pall of death Conceals the fairest boon his love can send. If we could push ajar the gates of life, And stand within, and all God's working see, We could interpret all this doubt and strife, And for each mystery find a key."

Although physical death falls upon the unbeliever as the original penalty of sin, to all who are united in Christ it loses its aspect of penalty, and becomes a means of discipline and of entrance into eternal life.

To the Christian, physical death is not a penalty: see Ps. 116:15—"Precious in the sight of Jehovah Is the death of his saints"; Rom. 8:10—"And if Christ is in you, the body is dead because of sin; but the spirit is life because of righteousness"; 14:8—"For whether we live, we live unto the Lord; or whether we die, we die unto the Lord: whether we live therefore, or die, we are the Lord's"; 1 Cor. 3:22—"whether Paul, or Apollos, or Cephas, or the world, or life, or death, or things present, or things to come; all are yours"; 15:55—"O death, where is thy victory? O death, where is thy sting?" 1 Pet. 4:6—"For unto this end was the gospel preached even to the dead, that they might be judged indeed according to men in the flesh, but live according to God in the spirit"; cf. Rom. 1:18—"For the wrath of God is revealed from heaven against all ungodliness and unrighteousness of men, who hinder the truth in unrighteousness"; 8:1, 2—"There is therefore now no condemnation to them that are in Christ Jesus. For the law of the Spirit of life in Christ Jesus made me free from the law of sin and of death"; Heb. 12:6—"For whom the Lord loveth he chasteneth."

Dr. Hovey says that "the present sufferings of believers are in the nature of discipline, with an aspect of retribution; while the present sufferings of unbelievers are retributive, with a glance toward reformation." We prefer to say that all penalty has been borne by Christ, and that, for him who is justified in Christ, suffering of whatever kind is of the nature of fatherly chastening, never of judicial retribution; see our discussion of the Penalty of Sin, pages 652-660.

"We see but dimly through the mists and vapors Amid these earthly damps; What are to us but sad funereal tapers May be Heaven's distant lamps. There is no death,—what seems so is transition; This life of mortal breath Is but a suburb of the life Elysian Whose portal men call death." "'Tis meet that we should pause awhile, Ere we put off this mortal coil, And in the stillness of old age, Muse on our earthly pilgrimage." Shakespeare, Romeo and Juliet, 4:5—"Heaven and yourself Had part in this fair maid; now Heaven hath all, And all the better is it for the maid: Your part in her you could not keep from death, But Heaven keeps his part in eternal life. The most you sought was her promotion, For 't was your heaven she should be advanced; And weep ye now, seeing she is advanced Above the clouds, as high as Heaven itself?" Phœbe Cary's Answered: "I thought to find some healing clime For her I loved; she found that shore, That city whose inhabitants Are sick and sorrowful no more. I asked for human love for her; The Loving knew how best to still The infinite yearning of a heart Which but infinity could fill. Such sweet communion had been ours, I prayed that it might never end; My prayer is more than answered; now I have an angel for my friend. I wished for perfect peace to soothe The troubled anguish of her breast; And numbered with the loved and called She entered on untroubled rest. Life was so fair a thing to her, I wept and pleaded for its stay; My wish was granted me, for lo! She hath eternal life to-day!"

Victor Hugo: "The tomb is not a blind alley; it is a thoroughfare. It closes with the twilight, to open with the dawn.... I feel that I have not said the thousandth part of what is in me.... The thirst for infinity proves infinity." Shakespeare: "Nothing is here for tears; nothing to wail, Or knock the breast; no weakness, no contempt, Dispraise or blame; nothing but well and fair." O. W. Holmes: "Build thee more stately mansions, O my soul, As the swift seasons roll! Leave thy low-vaulted past! Let each new temple, nobler than the last Shut thee from heaven with a dome more vast, Till thou at length art free, Leaving thine outgrown shell by life's unresting sea!" J. G. Whittier: "So when Time's veil shall fall asunder, The soul may know No fearful change or sudden wonder, Nor sink the weight of mystery under, But with the upward rise, and with the vastness grow."

To neither saint nor sinner is death a cessation of being. This we maintain, against the advocates of annihilation:

1. Upon rational grounds.

(a) The metaphysical argument.—The soul is simple, not compounded. Death, in matter, is the separation of parts. But in the soul there are no parts to be separated. The dissolution of the body, therefore, does not necessarily work a dissolution of the soul. But, since there is an immaterial principle in the brute, and this argument taken by itself might seem to prove the immortality of the animal creation equally with that of man, we pass to consider the next argument.

The Gnostics and the Manichæans held that beasts had knowledge and might pray. The immateriality of the brute mind was probably the consideration which led Leibnitz, Bishop Butler, Coleridge, John Wesley, Lord Shaftesbury, Mary Somerville, James Hogg, Toplady, Lamartine, and Louis Agassiz to encourage the belief in animal immortality. See Bp. Butler, Analogy, part i, chap. i (Bohn's ed., 81-91); Agassiz, Essay on Classification, 99—"Most of the arguments for the immortality of man apply equally to the permanency of this principle in other living beings." Elsewhere Agassiz says of animals: "I cannot doubt of their immortality any more than I doubt of my own." Lord Shaftesbury in 1881 remarked: "I have ever believed in a happy future for animals; I cannot say or conjecture how or where; but sure I am that the love, so manifested by dogs especially, is an emanation from the divine essence, and as such it can, or rather, it will, never be extinguished." St. Francis of Assisi preached to birds, and called sun, moon, earth, fire, water, stones, flowers, crickets, and death, his brothers and sisters. "He knew not if the brotherhood His homily had understood; He only knew that to one ear The meaning of his words was clear" (Longfellow, The Sermon of St. Francis—to the birds). "If death dissipates the sagacity of the elephant, why not that of his captor?" See Buckner, Immortality of Animals; William Adams Brown, Christian Theology in Outline, 240.

Mansel, Metaphysics, 371, maintains that all this argument proves is that the objector cannot show the soul to be compound, and so cannot show that it is destructible. Calderwood, Moral Philosophy, 259—"The facts which point toward the termination of our present state of existence are connected with our physical nature, not with our mental." John Fiske, Destiny of the Creature, 110—"With his illegitimate hypothesis of annihilation, the materialist transgresses the bounds of experience quite as widely as the poet who sings of the New Jerusalem, with its river of life and its streets of gold. Scientifically speaking, there is not a particle of evidence for either view." John Fiske, Life Everlasting, 80-85—"How could immortal man have been produced through heredity from an ephemeral brute? We do not know. Nature's habit is to make prodigious leaps, but only after long preparation. Slowly rises the water in the tank, inch by inch through many a weary hour, until at length it overflows, and straightway vast systems of machinery are awakened into rumbling life. Slowly the ellipse becomes eccentric, until suddenly the finite ellipse becomes an infinite paraboloid."

Ladd, Philosophy of Mind, 206—"The ideas of dividing up or splitting off are not applicable to mind. The argument for the indestructibility of mind as growing out of its indiscerptibility, and the argument by which Kant confuted it, are alike absurd within the realm of mental phenomena." Adeney, Christianity and Evolution, 127—"Nature, this argument shows, has nothing to say against the immortality of that which is above the range of physical structure." Lotze: "Everything which has once originated will endure forever so soon as it possesses an unalterable value for the coherent system of the world; but it will, as a matter of course, in turn cease to be, if this is not the case." Bowne, Int. to Psych. Theory, 315-318—"Of what use would brutes be hereafter? We may reply: Of what use are they here?... Those things which have perennial significance for the universe will abide." Bixby, Crisis in Morals, 203—"In living beings there is always a pressure toward larger and higher existence.... The plant must grow, must bloom, must sow its seeds, or it withers away.... The aim is to bring forth consciousness, and in greatest fulness.... Beasts of prey and other enemies to the ascending path of life are to be swept out of the way."

But is not the brute a part of that Nature which has been subjected to vanity, which groans and travails in pain, and which waits to be redeemed? The answer seems to be that the brute is a mere appendage to man, has no independent value in the creation, is incapable of ethical life or of communion with God the source of life, and so has no guarantee of continuance. Man on the other hand is of independent value. But this is to anticipate the argument which follows. It is sufficient here to point out that there is no proof that consciousness is dependent upon the soul's connection with a physical organism. McLane, Evolution in Religion, 261—"As the body may preserve its form and be to a degree made to act after the psychic element is lost by removal of the brain, so this psychic element may exist, and act according to its nature after the physical element ceases to exist." Hovey, Bib. Eschatology, 19—"If I am in a house, I can look upon surrounding objects only through its windows; but open the door and let me go out of the house, and the windows are no longer of any use to me." Shaler, Interpretation of Nature, 295—"To perpetuate mind after death is less surprising than to perpetuate or transmit mind here by inheritance." See also Martineau, Study, 2:332-337, 363-365.

William James, in his Essay on Human Immortality, argues that thought is not necessarily a productive function of the brain; it may rather be a permissive or transmissive function. Thought is not made in the brain, so that when the brain perishes the soul dies. The brain is only the organ for the transmission of thought, just as the lens transmits the light which it does not produce. There is a spiritual world behind and above the material world. Our brains are thin and half transparent places in the veil, through which knowledge comes in. Savage, Life after Death, 289—"You may attach a dynamo for a time to some particular machine. When you have removed the machine, you have not destroyed the dynamo. You may attach it to some other machine and find that you have the old time power. So the soul may not be confined to one body." These analogies seem to us to come short of proving personal immortality. They belong to "psychology without a soul," and while they illustrate the persistence of some sort of life, they do not render more probable the continuance of my individual consciousness beyond the bounds of death. They are entirely consistent with the pantheistic theory of a remerging of the personal existence in the great whole of which it forms a part. Tennyson, In Memoriam: "That each, who seems a separate whole, Should move his rounds and, fusing all The skirts of self again, should fall Remerging in the general Soul, Is faith as vague as all unsweet." See Pfleiderer, Die Ritschl'sche Theologie, 12; Howison, Limits of Evolution, 279-312.

Seth, Hegelianism: "For Hegel, immortality is only the permanence of the Absolute, the abstract process. This is no more consoling than the continued existence of the chemical elements of our bodies in new transformations. Human self-consciousness is a spark struck in the dark, to die away on the darkness whence it has arisen." This is the only immortality of which George Eliot conceived in her poem, The Immortal Choir: "O may I join the choir invisible Of those immortal dead who live again In minds made better by their presence; live In pulses stirred to generosity, In deeds of daring rectitude, in scorn For miserable aims that end in self, In thoughts sublime that pierce the night like stars, And with their mild persistence urge man's search To vaster issues." Those who hold to this unconscious immortality concede that death is not a separation of parts, but rather a cessation of consciousness; and that therefore, while the substance of human nature may endure, mankind may ever develop into new forms, without individual immortality. To this we reply, that man's self- consciousness and self-determination are different in kind from the consciousness and determination of the brute. As man can direct his self-consciousness and self-determination to immortal ends, we have the right to believe this self-consciousness and self-determination to be immortal. This leads us to the next argument.

(b) The teleological argument.—Man, as an intellectual, moral, and religious being, does not attain the end of his existence on earth. His development is imperfect here. Divine wisdom will not leave its work incomplete. There must be a hereafter for the full growth of man's powers, and for the satisfaction of his aspirations. Created, unlike the brute, with infinite capacities for moral progress, there must be an immortal existence in which those capacities shall be brought into exercise. Though the wicked forfeit all claim to this future, we have here an argument from God's love and wisdom to the immortality of the righteous.

In reply to this argument, it has been said that many right wishes are vain. Mill, Essays on Religion, 294—"Desire for food implies enough to eat, now and forever? hence an eternal supply of cabbage?" But our argument proceeds upon three presuppositions: (1) that a holy and benevolent God exists; (2) that he has made man in his image; (3) that man's true end is holiness and likeness to God. Therefore, what will answer the true end of man will be furnished; but that is not cabbage—it is holiness and love, i. e., God himself. See Martineau, Study, 2:370-381.

The argument, however, is valuable only in its application to the righteous. God will not treat the righteous as the tyrant of Florence treated Michael Angelo, when he bade him carve out of ice a statue, which would melt under the first rays of the sun. In the case of the wicked, the other law of retribution comes in—the taking away of "even that which he hath" (Mat. 25:29). Since we are all wicked, the argument is not satisfactory, unless we take into account the further facts of atonement and justification—facts of which we learn from revelation alone.

But while, taken by itself, this rational argument might be called defective, and could never prove that man may not attain his end in the continued existence of the race, rather than in that of the individual, the argument appears more valuable as a rational supplement to the facts already mentioned, and seems to render certain at least the immortality of those upon whom God has set his love, and in whom he has wrought the beginnings of righteousness.

Lord Erskine: "Inferior animals have no instincts or faculties which are not subservient to the ends and purposes of their being. Man's reason, and faculties endowed with power to reach the most distant worlds, would be useless if his existence were to terminate in the grave." There would be wastefulness in the extinction of great minds; see Jackson, James Martineau, 439. As water is implied by the organization of the fish, and air by that of the bird, so "the existence of spiritual power within us is likewise presumption that some fitting environment awaits the spirit when it shall be set free and perfected, and sex and death can be dispensed with" (Newman Smyth, Place of Death in Evolution, 106). Nägeli, the German botanist, says that Nature tends to perfection. Yet the mind hardly begins to awake, ere the bodily powers decline (George, Progress and Poverty, 505). "Character grows firmer and solider as the body ages and grows weaker. Can character be vitally implicated in the act of physical dissolution?" (Upton, Hibbert Lectures, 353). If a rational and moral Deity has caused the gradual evolution in humanity of the ideas of right and wrong, and has added to it the faculty of creating ethical ideals, must he not have provided some satisfaction for the ethical needs which this development has thus called into existence? (Balfour, Foundations of Belief, 351).

Royce, Conception of God, 50, quotes Le Conte as follows: "Nature is the womb in which, and evolution the process by which, are generated sons of God. Without immortality this whole process is balked—the whole process of cosmic evolution is futile. Shall God be so long and at so great pains to achieve a spirit, capable of communing with himself, and then allow it to lapse again into nothingness?" John Fiske, Destiny of Man, 116, accepts the immortality of the soul by "a supreme act of faith in the reasonableness of God's work." If man is the end of the creative process and the object of God's care, then the soul's career cannot be completed with its present life upon the earth (Newman Smyth, Place of Death in Evolution, 92, 93). Bowne, Philosophy of Theism, 254—"Neither God nor the future life is needed to pay us for present virtue, but rather as the condition without which our nature falls into irreconcilable discord with itself, and passes on to pessimism and despair. High and continual effort is impossible without correspondingly high and abiding hopes.... It is no more selfish to desire to live hereafter than it is to desire to live to-morrow." Dr. M. B. Anderson used to say that there must be a heaven for canal horses, washerwomen, and college presidents, because they do not get their deserts in this life.

Life is a series of commencements rather than of accomplished ends. Longfellow, on Charles Sumner: "Death takes us by surprise, And stays our hurrying feet; The great design unfinished lies, Our lives are incomplete. But in the dark unknown Perfect their circles seem, Even as a bridge's arch of stone Is rounded in the stream." Robert Browning, Abt Vogler: "There never shall be one lost good"; Prospice: "No work begun shall ever pause for death"; "Pleasure must succeed to pleasure, else past pleasure turns to pain; And this first life claims a second, else I count its good no gain"; Old Pictures in Florence: "We are faulty—why not? We have time in store"; Grammarian's Funeral: "What's time? Leave Now for dogs and apes,—Man has Forever." Robert Browning wrote in his wife's Testament the following testimony of Dante: "Thus I believe, thus I affirm, thus I am certain it is, that from this life I shall pass to another better, there where that lady lives, of whom my soul was enamored." And Browning says in a letter: "It is a great thing—the greatest—that a human being should have passed the probation of life, and sum up its experience in a witness to the power and love of God.... I see even more reason to hold by the same hope."

(c) The ethical argument.—Man is not, in this world, adequately punished for his evil deeds. Our sense of justice leads us to believe that God's moral administration will be vindicated in a life to come. Mere extinction of being would not be a sufficient penalty, nor would it permit degrees of punishment corresponding to degrees of guilt. This is therefore an argument from God's justice to the immortality of the wicked. The guilty conscience demands a state after death for punishment.

This is an argument from God's justice to the immortality of the wicked, as the preceding was an argument from God's love to the immortality of the righteous. "History defies our moral sense by giving a peaceful end to Sulla." Louis XV and Madame Pompadour died in their beds, after a life of extreme luxury. Louis XVI and his queen, though far more just and pure, perished by an appalling tragedy. The fates of these four cannot be explained by the wickedness of the latter pair and the virtue of the former. Alexander the Sixth, the worst of the popes, was apparently prosperous and happy in his iniquities. Though guilty of the most shameful crimes, he was serenely impenitent, and to the last of his days he defied both God and man. Since there is not an execution of justice here, we feel that there must be a "judgment to come," such as that which terrified Felix (Acts 24:25). Martineau, Study, 2:383-388. Stopford A. Brooke, Justice: "Three men went out one summer night, No care had they or aim, And dined and drank. 'Ere we go home We'll have,' they said, 'a game.' Three girls began that summer night A life of endless shame, And went through drink, disease, and death As swift as racing flame. Lawless and homeless, foul, they died; Rich, loved and praised, the men: But when they all shall meet with God, And Justice speaks,—what then?" See John Caird, Fund. Ideas of Christianity, 2:255-297. G. F. Wilkin, Control in Evolution: "Belief in immortality is a practical necessity of evolution. If the decisions of to-day are to determine our eternal destiny, then it is vastly more important to choose and act aright, than it is to preserve our earthly life. The martyrs were right. Conscience is vindicated. We can live for the ideal of manhood. Immortality is a powerful reformatory instrument." Martineau, Study of Religion, 2:388—"If Death gives a final discharge to the sinner and the saint alike, Conscience has told us more lies than it has ever called to their account." Shakespeare, Henry V, 4:2—"If [transgressors] have defeated the law and outrun native punishment, though they can outstrip men, they have no wings to fly from God"; Henry VI, 2d part, 5:2—"Can we outrun the heavens?" Addison, Cato: "It must be so,—Plato, thou reasonest well.—Else whence this pleasing hope, this fond desire, This longing after immortality? Or whence this secret dread and inward horror Of falling into naught? Why shrinks the soul Back on herself and startles at destruction? 'Tis the divinity that stirs within us, 'Tis Heaven itself that points out a hereafter, And intimates eternity to man."

Gildersleeve, in The Independent, March 30, 1899—"Plato in the Phædo argues for immortality from the alternation of opposites: life must follow death as death follows life. But alternation of opposites is not generation of opposites. He argues from reminiscence. But this involves pre-existence and a cycle of incarnations, not the immortality which we crave. The soul abides, as the idea abides, but there is no guarantee that it abides forever. He argues from the uncompounded nature of the soul. But we do not know the soul's nature, and at most this is an analogy: as soul is like God, invisible, it must like God abide. But this is analogy, and nothing more." William James, Will to Believe, 87—"That our whole physical life may lie soaking in a spiritual atmosphere, a dimension of being which we at present have no organ for apprehending, is vividly suggested to us by the analogy of the life of our domestic animals. Our dogs, for example, are in our human life, but are not of it. They bite, but do not know what it means; they submit to vivisection, and do not know the meaning of that."

George Eliot, walking with Frederic Myers in the Fellows' Garden at Trinity, Cambridge, "stirred somewhat beyond her wont, and taking as her text the three words which have been used so often as the inspiring trumpet-calls of men—the words God, Immortality, Duty—pronounced with terrible earnestness how inconceivable was the first, how unbelievable the second, and yet how peremptory and absolute the third." But this idea of the infinite nature of Duty is the creation of Christianity—the last infinite would never have attained its present range and intensity, had it not been indissolubly connected with the other two (Forrest, Christ of History and Experience, 16).

This ethical argument has probably more power over the minds of men than any other. Men believe in Minos and Rhadamanthus, if not in the Elysian Fields. But even here it may be replied that the judgment which conscience threatens may be, not immortality, but extinction of being. We shall see, however, in our discussion of the endlessness of future punishment, that mere annihilation cannot satisfy the moral instinct which lies at the basis of this argument. That demands a punishment proportioned in each case to the guilt incurred by transgression. Extinction of being would be the same to all. As it would not admit of degrees, so it would not, in any case, sufficiently vindicate God's righteousness. F. W. Newman: "If man be not immortal, God is not just."

But while this argument proves life and punishment for the wicked after death, it leaves us dependent on revelation for our knowledge how long that life and punishment will be. Kant's argument is that man strives equally for morality and for well- being; but morality often requires the sacrifice of well-being; hence there must be a future reconciliation of the two in the well-being or reward of virtue. To all of which it might be answered, first, that there is no virtue so perfect as to merit reward; and secondly, that virtue is its own reward, and so is well-being.

(d) The historical argument.—The popular belief of all nations and ages shows that the idea of immortality is natural to the human mind. It is not sufficient to say that this indicates only such desire for continued earthly existence as is necessary to self-preservation; for multitudes expect a life beyond death without desiring it, and multitudes desire a heavenly life without caring for the earthly. This testimony of man's nature to immortality may be regarded as the testimony of the God who made the nature.

Testimonies to this popular belief are given in Bartlett, Life and Death Eternal, preface: The arrow-heads and earthen vessels laid by the side of the dead Indian; the silver obolus put in the mouth of the dead Greek to pay Charon's passage money; the furnishing of the Egyptian corpse with the Book of the Dead, the papyrus-roll containing the prayer he is to offer and the chart of his journey through the unseen world. The Gauls did not hesitate to lend money, on the sole condition that he to whom they lent it would return it to them in the other life,—so sure were they that they should get it again (Valerius Maximus, quoted in Boissier, La Religion Romaine, 1:264). The Laplanders bury flint and tinder with the dead, to furnish light for the dark journey. The Norsemen buried the horse and armor for the dead hero's triumphant ride. The Chinese scatter paper images of sedan porters over the grave, to help along in the sombre pilgrimage. The Greenlanders bury with the child a dog to guide him (George Dana Boardman, Sermon on Immortality).

Savage, Life after Death, 1-18—"Candles at the head of the casket are the modern representatives of the primitive man's fire which was to light the way of the soul on its dark journey.... Ulysses talks in the underworld with the shade of Hercules though the real Hercules, a demigod, had been transferred to Olympus, and was there living in companionship with the gods.... The Brahman desired to escape being reborn. Socrates: 'To die and be released is better for me.' Here I am walking on a plank. It reaches out into the fog, and I have got to keep walking. I can see only ten feet ahead of me. I know that pretty soon

I must walk over the end of that plank,—I haven't the slightest idea into what, and I don't believe anybody else knows. And I don't like it." Matthew Arnold: "Is there no other life? Pitch this one high." But without positive revelation most men will say: "Let us eat and drink, for to-morrow we die" (1 Cor. 15:32).

"By passionately loving life, we make Loved life unlovely, hugging her to death." Theodore Parker: "The intuition of mortality is written in the heart of man by a Hand that writes no falsehoods.... There is evidence of a summer yet to be, in the buds which lie folded through our northern winter—efflorescences in human nature unaccountable if the end of man is in the grave." But it may be replied that many universal popular impressions have proved false, such as belief in ghosts, and in the moving of the sun round the earth. While the mass of men have believed in immortality, some of the wisest have been doubters. Cyrus said: "I cannot imagine that the soul lives only while it remains in this mortal body." But the dying words of Socrates were: "We part; I am going to die, and you to live; which of us goes the better way is known to God alone." Cicero declared: "Upon this subject I entertain no more than conjectures;" and said that, when he was reading Plato's argument for immortality, he seemed to himself convinced, but when he laid down the book he found that all his doubts returned. Farrar, Darkness and Dawn, 134—"Though Cicero wrote his Tusculan Disputations to prove the doctrine of immortality, he spoke of that doctrine in his letters and speeches as a mere pleasing speculation, which might be discussed with interest, but which no one practically held."

Aristotle, Nic. Ethics, 3:9, calls death "the most to be feared of all things ... for it appears to be the end of everything; and for the deceased there appears to be no longer either any good or any evil." Æschylus: "Of one once dead there is no resurrection." Catullus: "When once our brief day has set, we must sleep one everlasting night." Tacitus: "If there is a place for the spirits of the pious; if, as the wise suppose, great souls do not become extinct with their bodies." "In that if," says Uhlhorn, "lies the whole torturing uncertainty of heathenism." Seneca, Ep. liv.—"Mors est non esse"—"Death is not to be"; Troades, V, 393—"Post mortem nihil est, ipsaque mors nihil"—"There is nothing after death, and death itself is nothing." Marcus Aurelius: "What springs from earth dissolves to earth again, and heavenborn things fly to their native seat." The Emperor Hadrian to his soul: "Animula, vagula, blandula, Hospes comesque corporis, Quæ nunc abibis in loca? Pallidula, rigida, nudula." Classic writers might have said of the soul at death: "We know not where is that Promethean torch That can its light relume."

Chadwick, 184—"With the growth of all that is best in man of intelligence and affection, there goes the development of the hope of an immortal life. If the hope thus developed is not a valid one, then we have a radical contradiction in our moral nature. The survival of the fittest points in the same direction." Andrew Marvell (1621-1678)—"At my back I always hear Time's winged chariot hurrying near; And yonder all before us lie Deserts of vast Eternity." Goethe in his last days came to be a profound believer in immortality. "You ask me what are my grounds for this belief? The weightiest is this, that we cannot do without it." Huxley wrote in a letter to Morley: "It is a curious thing that I find my dislike to the thought of extinction increasing as I get older and nearer the goal. It flashes across me at all sorts of time that in 1900 I shall probably know no more of what is going on than I did in 1800. I had sooner be in hell, a great deal,—at any rate in one of the upper circles, where climate and the company are not too trying."

The book of Job shows how impossible it is for man to work out the problem of personal immortality from the point of view of merely natural religion. Shakespeare, in Measure for Measure, represents Claudio as saying to his sister Isabella: "Aye, but to die, and go we know not where; To lie in cold obstruction and to rot; This sensible warm motion to become A kneaded clod." Strauss, Glaubenslehre, 2:739—"The other world is in all men the one enemy, in its aspect of a future world, however, the last enemy, which speculative criticism has to fight, and if possible to overcome." Omar Khayyám, Rubáiyát, Stanzas 28-35—"I came like Water, and like Wind I go.... Up from Earth's Centre through the seventh gate I rose, and on the throne of Saturn sate, And many a knot unravelled by the Road, But not the master-knot of human fate. There was the Door to which I found no Key; There was the Veil through which I might not see: Some little talk awhile of Me and Thee There was,—And then no more of Thee and Me. Earth could not answer, nor the Seas that mourn, In flowing purple, of their Lord forlorn; Nor rolling Heaven, with all his signs revealed, And hidden by the sleeve of Night and Morn. Then of the Thee in Me, who works behind The veil, I lifted up my hands to find A Lamp, amid the darkness; and I heard As from without—'The Me within Thee blind.' Then to the lip of this poor earthen Urn I leaned, the secret of my life to learn; And Lip to Lip it murmur'd—'While you live, Drink!—for, once dead, you never shall return!' " So "The Phantom Caravan has reached The Nothing it set out from." It is a demonstration of the hopelessness and blindness and sensuality of man, when left without the revelation of God and of the life to come.

The most that can be claimed for this fourth argument from popular belief is that it indicates a general appentency for continued existence after death, and that the idea is congruous with our nature. W. E. Forster said to Harriet Martineau that he would rather be damned than annihilated; see F. P. Cobbe, Peak of Darien, 44. But it may be replied that there is reason enough for this desire for life in the fact that it ensures the earthly existence of the race, which might commit universal suicide without it. There is reason enough in the present life for its existence, and we are not necessitated to infer a future life therefrom. This objection cannot be fully answered from reason alone. But if we take our argument in connection with the Scriptural revelation concerning God's making of man in his image, we may regard the testimony of man's nature as the testimony of the God who made it.

We conclude our statement of these rational proofs with the acknowledgment that they rest upon the presupposition that there exists a God of truth, wisdom, justice, and love, who has made man in his image, and who desires to commune with his creatures. We acknowledge, moreover, that these proofs give us, not an absolute demonstration, but only a balance of probability, in favor of man's immortality. We turn therefore to Scripture for the clear revelation of a fact of which reason furnishes us little more than a presumption.

Everett, Essays, 76, 77—"In his Träume eines Geistersehers, Kant foreshadows the Method of his Kritik. He gives us a scheme of disembodied spirits, and calls it a bit of mystic (geheimen) philosophy; then the opposite view, which he calls a bit of vulgar (gemeimen) philosophy. Then he says the scales of the understanding are not quite impartial, and the one that has the inscription 'Hope for the future' has a mechanical advantage. He says he cannot rid himself of this unfairness. He suffers feeling to determine the result. This is intellectual agnosticism supplemented by religious faith." The following lines have been engraved upon the tomb of Professor Huxley: "And if there be no meeting past the grave, If all is darkness, silence, yet 'tis rest. Be not afraid, ye waiting hearts that weep, For God still giveth his beloved sleep, And if an endless sleep he wills, so best." Contrast this consolation with: "Let not your heart be troubled: ye believe in God, believe also in me. In my Father's house are many mansions: if it were not so, I would have told you. I go to prepare a place for you. And if I go and prepare a place for you, I will come again, and receive you unto myself, that where I am, there ye may be also" (John 14:1-3).

Dorner: "There is no rational evidence which compels belief in immortality. Immortality has its pledge in God's making man in his image, and in God's will of love for communion with men." Luthardt, Compendium, 289—"The truth in these proofs from reason is the idea of human personality and its relation to God. Belief in God is the universal presupposition and foundation of the universal belief in immortality." When Strauss declared that this belief in immortality is the last enemy which is to be destroyed, he forgot that belief in God is more ineradicable still. Frances Power Cobbe, Life, 92—"The doctrine of immortality is to me the indispensable corollary of that of the goodness of God."

Hadley, Essays, Philological and Critical, 392-397—"The claim of immortality may be based on one or the other of two assumptions: (1) The same organism will be reproduced hereafter, and the same functions, or part of them, again manifested in connection with it, and accompanied with consciousness of continued identity; or, (2) The same functions may be exercised and accompanied with consciousness of identity, though not connected with the same organism as before; may in fact go on without interruption, without being even suspended by death, though no longer manifested to us." The conclusion is: "The light of nature, when all directed to this question, does furnish a presumption in favor of immortality, but not so strong a presumption as to exclude great and reasonable doubts upon the subject."

For an excellent synopsis of arguments and objections, see Hase, Hutterus Redivivus, 276. See also Bowen, Metaph. and Ethics, 417-441; A. M. Fairbairn, on Idea of Immortality, in Studies in Philos. of Religion and of History; Wordsworth, Intimations of Immortality; Tennyson, Two Voices; Alger, Critical History of Doctrine of Future Life, with Appendix by Ezra Abbott, containing a Catalogue of Works relating to the Nature, Origin, and Destiny of the Soul; Ingersoll Lectures on Immortality, by George A. Gordon, Josiah Royce, William James, Dr. Osler, John Fiske, B. I. Wheeler, Hyslop, Münsterberg, Crothars.

2. Upon scriptural grounds.

(a) The account of man's creation, and the subsequent allusions to it in Scripture, show that, while the body was made corruptible and subject to death, the soul was made in the image of God, incorruptible and immortal.

Gen. 1:26, 27—"Let us make man in our image"; 2:7—"And Jehovah God formed man of the dust of the ground, and breathed into his nostrils the breath of life; and man became a living soul"—here, as was shown in our treatment of Man's Original State, page 523, it is not the divine image, but the body, that is formed of dust; and into this body the soul that possesses the divine image is breathed. In the Hebrew records, the animating soul is everywhere distinguished from the earthly body. Gen. 3:22, 23—"Behold, the man is become as one of us, to know good and evil; and now, lest he put forth his hand, and take also of the tree of life, and eat, and live for ever: therefore Jehovah God sent him forth from the garden of Eden"—man had immortality of soul, and now, lest to this he add immortality of body, he is expelled from the tree of life. Eccl. 12:7—"the dust returneth to the earth as it was, and the spirit returneth unto God who gave it"; Zech. 12:1—"Jehovah, who stretcheth forth the heavens, and layeth the foundation of the earth, and formeth the spirit of man within him."

Mat. 10:28—"And be not afraid of them that kill the body, but are not able to kill the soul: but rather fear him who is able to destroy both soul and body in hell"; Acts 7:59—"And they stoned Stephen, calling upon the Lord, and saying, Lord Jesus, receive my spirit": 2 Cor. 12:2—"I know a man in Christ, fourteen years ago (whether in the body, I know not; or whether out of the body, I know not; God knoweth), such a one caught up even to the third heaven"; 1 Cor. 15:45, 46—"The first man Adam became a living soul. The last Adam became a life-giving spirit. Howbeit that is not first which is spiritual, but that which is natural; then that which is spiritual"—the first Adam was made a being whose body was psychical and mortal—a body of flesh and blood, that could not inherit the kingdom of God. So Paul says the spiritual is not first, but the psychical; but there is no intimation that the soul also was created mortal, and needed external appliances, like the tree of life, before it could enter upon immortality.

But it may be asked: Is not all this, in 1 Cor. 15, spoken of the regenerate—those to whom a new principle of life has been communicated? We answer, yes; but that does not prevent us from learning from the passage the natural immortality of the soul; for in regeneration the essence is not changed, no new substance is imparted, no new faculty or constitutive element is added, and no new principle of holiness is infused. The truth is simply that the spirit is morally readjusted. For substance of the above remarks, see Hovey, State of Impenitent Dead, 1-27.

Savage, Life after Death, 46, 53—"The word translated 'soul', in Gen. 2:7, is the same word which in other parts of the O. T. is used to denote the life-principle of animals. It does not follow that soul implies immortality, for then all animals would be immortal.... The firmament of the Hebrews was the cover of a dinner-platter, solid, but with little windows to let the rain through. Above this firmament was heaven where God and angels abode, but no people went there. All went below. But growing moral sense held that the good could not be imprisoned in Hades. So came the idea of resurrection.... If a force, a universe with God left out, can do all that has been done, I do not see why it cannot also continue my existence through what is called death."

Dr. H. Heath Bawden: "It is only the creature that is born that will die. Monera and Amœbæ are immortal, as Weismann tells us. They do not die, because they never are born. The death of the individual as a somatic individual is for the sake of the larger future life of the individual in its germinal immortality. So we live ourselves spiritually into our children, as well as physically. An organism is nothing but a centre or focus through which the world surges. What matter if the irrelevant somatic portion is lost in what we call death! The only immortality possible is the immortality of function. My body has changed completely since I was a boy, but I have become a larger self thereby. Birth and death simply mark steps or stages in the growth of such an individual, which in its very nature does not exclude but rather includes within it the lives of all other individuals. The individual is more than a passive member, he is an active organ of a biological whole. The laws of his life are the social organism functioning in one of its organs. He lives and moves and has his being in the great spirit of the whole, which comes to a focus or flowers out in his conscious life."

(b) The account of the curse in Genesis, and the subsequent allusions to it in Scripture, show that, while the death then incurred includes the dissolution of the body, it does not include cessation of being on the part of the soul, but only designates that state of the soul which is the opposite of true life, viz., a state of banishment from God, of unholiness, and of misery.

Gen. 2:17—"in the day that thou eatest thereof thou shalt surely die"; cf. 3:8—"the man and his wife hid themselves from the presence of Jehovah God"; 16-19—the curse of pain and toil: 22-24—banishment from the garden of Eden and from the tree of life. Mat. 8:22—"Follow me; and leave the dead to bury their own dead"; 25:41, 46—"Depart from me, ye cursed, into the eternal fire.... These shall go away into eternal punishment"; Luke 15:32—"this thy brother was dead, and is alive again; and was lost, and is found"; John 5:24—"He that heareth my word, and believeth him that sent me, hath eternal life, and cometh not into judgment, but hath passed out of death into life"; 6:47, 53, 63—"He that believeth hath eternal life.... Except ye eat the flesh of the Son of man and drink his blood, ye have not life in yourselves.... the words that I have spoken unto you are spirit, and are life": 8:51—"If a man keep my word, he shall never see death."

Rom. 5:21—"that, as sin reigned in death, even so might grace reign through righteousness unto eternal life"; 8:13—"if ye live after the flesh, ye must die; but if by the Spirit ye put to death the deeds of the body, ye shall live"; Eph. 2:1—"dead through your trespasses and sins"; 5:14—"Awake, thou that sleepest, and arise from the dead, and Christ shall shine upon thee"; James 5:20—"he who converteth a sinner from the error of his way shall save a soul from death, and shall cover a multitude of sins"; 1 John 3:14—"We know that we have passed out of death into life, because we love the brethren"; Rev. 3:1—"I know thy works, that thou hast a name that thou livest, and thou art dead."

We are to interpret O. T. terms by the N. T. meaning put into them. We are to interpret the Hebrew by the Greek, not the Greek by the Hebrew. It never would do to interpret our missionaries' use of the Chinese words for "God", "spirit", "holiness", by the use of those words among the Chinese before the missionaries came. By the later usage of the N. T., the Holy Spirit shows us what he meant by the usage of the O. T.

(c) The Scriptural expressions, held by annihilationists to imply cessation of being on the part of the wicked, are used not only in connections where they cannot bear this meaning (Esther 4:16), but in connections where they imply the opposite.

Esther 4:16—"if I perish, I perish"; Gen. 6:11—"And the earth was corrupt before God"—here, in the LXX, the word ἐφθάρη, translated "was corrupt," is the same word which in other places is interpreted by annihilationists as meaning extinction of being. In Ps. 119:176, "I have gone astray like a lost sheep" cannot mean "I have gone astray like an annihilated sheep." Is. 49:17—"thy destroyers [annihilators?] and they that made thee waste shall go forth from thee"; 57:1, 2—"The righteous perisheth [is annihilated?] and no man layeth it to heart; and merciful men are taken away, none considering that the righteous is taken away from the evil to come. He entereth into peace; they rest in their beds, each one that walketh in his uprightness"; Dan. 9:26—"And after the three score and two weeks shall the anointed one be cut off [annihilated?]."

Mat. 10:6, 39, 42—"the lost sheep of the house of Israel ... he that loseth his life for my sake shall find it ... he shall in no wise lose his reward"—in these verses we cannot substitute "annihilate" for "lose"; Acts 13:41—"Behold, ye despisers, and wonder, and perish"; cf. Mat. 6:16—"for they disfigure their faces"—where the same word ἀφανίζω is used. 1 Cor. 3:17—"If any man destroyeth [annihilates?] the temple of God, him shall God destroy"; 2 Cor. 7:2—"we corrupted no man"—where the same word φθείρω is used. 2 Thess. 1:9—"who shall suffer punishment, even eternal destruction from the face of the Lord and from the glory of his might" = the wicked shall be driven out from the presence of Christ. Destruction is not annihilation. "Destruction from" = separation; (per contra, see Prof. W. A. Stevens, Com. in loco: "from" = the source from which the "destruction" proceeds). "A ship engulfed in quicksands is destroyed; a temple broken down and deserted is destroyed"; see Lillie, Com. in loco. 2 Pet. 3:7—"day of judgment and destruction of ungodly men"—here the word "destruction" (ἀπωλείας) is the same with that used of the end of the present order of things, and translated "perished" (ἀπώλετο) in verse 6. "We cannot accordingly infer from it that the ungodly will cease to exist, but only that there will be a great and penal change in their condition" (Plumptre, Com. in loco).

(d) The passages held to prove the annihilation of the wicked at death cannot have this meaning, since the Scriptures foretell a resurrection of the unjust as well as of the just; and a second death, or a misery of the reunited soul and body, in the case of the wicked.

Acts 24:15—"there shall be a resurrection both of the just and unjust"; Rev. 2:11—"He that overcometh shall not be hurt of the second death"; 20:14, 15—"And death and Hades were cast into the lake of fire. This is the second death, even the lake of fire. And if any was not found written in the book of life, he was cast into the lake of fire"; 21:8—"their part shall be in the lake that burneth with fire and brimstone; which is the second death." The "second death" is the first death intensified. Having one's "part in the lake of fire" is not annihilation.

In a similar manner the word "life" is to be interpreted not as meaning continuance of being, but as meaning perfection of being. As death is the loss not of life, but of all that makes life desirable, so life is the possession of the highest good. 1 Tim. 5:6—"She that giveth herself to pleasure is dead while she liveth"—here the death is spiritual death, and it is implied that true life is spiritual life. John 10:10—"I came that they may have life, and may have it abundantly"—implies that "life" is not: 1. mere existence, for they had this before Christ came; nor 2. mere motion, as squirrels go in a wheel, without making progress; nor 3. mere possessions, "for a man's life consisteth not in the abundance of things which he possesseth" (Luke 12:15). But life is: 1. right relation of our powers, or holiness; 2. right use of our powers, or love; 3. right number of our powers, or completeness; 4. right intensity of our powers, or energy of will; 5. right environment of our powers, or society; 6. right source of our powers, or God.

(e) The words used in Scripture to denote the place of departed spirits have in them no implication of annihilation, and the allusions to the condition of the departed show that death, to the writers of the Old and the New Testaments, although it was the termination of man's earthly existence, was not an extinction of his being or his consciousness.

On לואש Sheol, Gesenius, Lexicon, 10th ed., says that, though לואש is commonly explained as infinitive of לאש, to demand, it is undoubtedly allied to לעש (root לש), to be sunk, and = "sinking," "depth," or "the sunken, deep, place." Ἁιδης, Hades, = not "hell," but the "unseen world," conceived by the Greeks as a shadowy, but not as an unconscious, state of being. Genung, Epic of the Inner Life, on Job 7:9—"Sheol, the Hebrew word designating the unseen abode of the dead; a neutral word, presupposing neither misery nor happiness, and not infrequently used much as we use the word 'the grave', to denote the final undefined resting-place of all."

Gen. 25:8, 9—Abraham "was gathered to his people. And Isaac and Ishmael his sons buried him in the cave of Machpelah." "Yet Abraham's father was buried in Haran, and his more remote ancestors in Ur of the Chaldees. So Joshua's generation is said to be 'gathered to their fathers' though the generation that preceded them perished in the wilderness, and previous generations died in Egypt" (W.

H. Green, in S. S. Times). So of Isaac in Gen. 35:29, and of Jacob in 19:29, 33,—all of whom were gathered to their fathers before they were buried. Num. 20:24—"Aaron shall be gathered unto his people"—here it is very plain that being "gathered unto his people" was something different from burial. Deut. 10:6—"There Aaron died, and there he was buried." Job 3:13, 18—"For now should I have lain down and been quiet; I should have slept; then had I been at rest.... There the prisoners are at ease together; They hear not the voice of the taskmaster"; 7:9—"As the cloud is consumed and vanisheth away, So he that goeth down to Sheol shall come up no more"; 14:22—"But his flesh upon him hath pain, And his soul within him mourneth."

Ez. 32:21—"The strong among the mighty shall speak to him out of the midst of Sheol"; Luke 16:23—"And in Hades he lifted up his eyes, being in torments, and seeth Abraham afar off, and Lazarus in his bosom"; 23:43—"To-day shalt thou be with me in Paradise"; cf. 1 Sam. 28:19—Samuel said to Saul in the cave of Endor: "to-morrow shalt thou and thy sons be with me"—evidently not in an unconscious state. Many of these passages intimate a continuity of consciousness after death. Though Sheol is unknown to man, it is naked and open to God (Job 26:6); he can find men there to redeem them from thence (Ps. 49:15)—proof that death is not annihilation. See Girdlestone, O. T. Synonyms, 447.

(f) The terms and phrases which have been held to declare absolute cessation of existence at death are frequently metaphorical, and an examination of them in connection with the context and with other Scriptures is sufficient to show the untenableness of the literal interpretation put upon them by the annihilationists, and to prove that the language is merely the language of appearance.

Death is often designated as a "sleeping" or a "falling asleep"; see John 11:11, 14—"Our friend Lazarus is fallen asleep; but I go, that I may awake him out of sleep.... Then Jesus therefore said unto them plainly, Lazarus is dead." Here the language of appearance is used; yet this language could not have been used, if the soul had not been conceived of as alive, though sundered from the body; see Meyer on 1 Cor. 1:18. So the language of appearance is used in Eccl. 9:10—"there is no work, nor device, nor knowledge, nor wisdom, in Sheol whither thou goest"—and in Ps. 146:4—"His breath goeth forth; he returneth to his earth; In that very day his thoughts perish."

See Mozley, Essays, 2:171—"These passages often describe the phenomena of death as it presents itself to our eyes, and so do not enter into the reality which takes place beneath it." Bartlett, Life and Death Eternal, 189-358—"Because the same Hebrew word is used for 'spirit' and 'breath,' shall we say that the spirit is only breath? 'Heart' in English might in like manner be made to mean only the material organ; and David's heart, panting, thirsting, melting within him, would have to be interpreted literally. So a man may be 'eaten up with avarice,' while yet his being is not only not extinct, but is in a state of frightful activity."

(g) The Jewish belief in a conscious existence after death is proof that the theory of annihilation rests upon a misinterpretation of Scripture. That such a belief in the immortality of the soul existed among the Jews is abundantly evident: from the knowledge of a future state possessed by the Egyptians (Acts 7:22); from the accounts of the translation of Enoch and of Elijah (Gen. 5:24; cf. Heb. 11:5; 2 K. 2:11); from the invocation of the dead which was practised, although forbidden by the law (1 Sam. 28:7-14; cf. Lev. 20:28; Deut. 18:10, 11); from allusions in the O. T. to resurrection, future retribution, and life beyond the grave (Job 19:25-27; Ps. 16:9-11; Is. 26:19; Ez. 37:1-14; Dan. 12:2, 3, 13); and from distinct declarations of such faith by Philo and Josephus, as well as by the writers of the N. T. (Mat. 22:31, 32; Acts 23:6; 26:6-8; Heb. 11:13-16).

The Egyptian coffin was called "the chest of the living." The Egyptians called their houses "hostelries," while their tombs they called their "eternal homes" (Butcher, Aspects of Greek Genius, 30). See the Book of the Dead, translated by Birch, in Bunsen's Egypt's Place, 123-333: The principal ideas of the first part of the Book of the Dead are "living again after death, and being born again as the sun," which typified the Egyptian resurrection (138). "The deceased lived again after death" (134). "The Osiris lives after he dies, like the sun daily; for as the sun died and was born yesterday, so the Osiris is born" (164). Yet the immortal part, in its continued existence, was dependent for its blessedness upon the preservation of the body; and for this reason the body was embalmed. Immortality of the body is as important as the passage of the soul to the upper regions. Growth or natural reparation of the body is invoked as earnestly as the passage of the soul. "There is not a limb of him without a god; Thoth is vivifying his limbs" (197).

Maspero, Recueil de Travaux, gives the following readings from the inner walls of pyramids twelve miles south of Cairo: "O Unas, thou hast gone away dead, but living"; "Teti is the living dead"; "Arise, O Teti, to die no more"; "O Pepi, thou diest no more";—these inscriptions show that to the Egyptians there was life beyond death. "The life of Unas is duration; his period is eternity"; "They render thee happy throughout all eternity"; "He who has given thee life and eternity is Ra";—here we see that the life beyond death was eternal. "Rising at his pleasure, gathering his members that are in the tomb, Unas goes forth"; "Unas has his heart, his legs, his arms"; this asserts reunion with the body. "Reunited to thy soul, thou takest thy place among the stars of heaven"; "the soul is thine within thee";—there was reunion with the soul. "A god is born, it is Unas"; "O Ra, thy son comes to thee, this

Unas comes to thee"; "O Father of Unas, grant that he may be included in the number of the perfect and wise gods"; here it is taught that the reunited soul and body becomes a god and dwells with the gods.

Howard Osgood: "Osiris, the son of gods, came to live on earth. His life was a pattern for others. He was put to death by the god of evil, but regained his body, lived again, and became, in the other world, the judge of all men." Tiele, Egyptian Religion, 280—"To become like god Osiris, a benefactor, a good being, persecuted but justified, judged but pronounced innocent, was looked upon as the ideal of every pious man, and as the condition on which alone eternal life could be obtained, and as the means by which it could be continued." Ebers, Études Archéologiques, 21—"The texts in the pyramids show us that under the Pharaohs of the 5th dynasty (before 2500 B. C.) the doctrine that the deceased became god was not only extant, but was developed more thoroughly and with far higher flight of imagination than we could expect from the simple statements concerning the other world hitherto known to us as from that early time." Revillout, on Egyptian Ethics, in Bib. Sac., July, 1890:304—"An almost absolute sinlessness was for the Egyptian the condition of becoming another Osiris and enjoying eternal happiness. Of the penitential side, so highly developed in the ancient Babylonians and Hebrews, which gave rise to so many admirable penitential psalms, we find only a trace among the Egyptians. Sinlessness is the rule,—the deceased vaunts himself as a hero of virtue." See Uarda, by Ebers; Dr. Howard Osgood, on Resurrection among the Egyptians, in Hebrew Student, Feb. 1885. The Egyptians, however, recognized no transmigration of souls; see Renouf, Hibbert Lectures, 181-184.

It is morally impossible that Moses should not have known the Egyptian doctrine of immortality: Acts 7:22—"And Moses was instructed in all the wisdom of the Egyptians." That Moses did not make the doctrine more prominent in his teachings, may be for the reason that it was so connected with Egyptian superstitions with regard to Osiris. Yet the Jews believed in immortality: Gen. 5:24—"and Enoch walked with God: and he was not; for God took him"; cf. Heb. 11:5—"By faith Enoch was translated that he should not see death"; 2 Kings 2:11—"Elijah went up by a whirlwind into heaven"; 1 Sam. 28:7-14—the invocation of Samuel by the woman of Endor; cf. Lev. 20:27—"A man also or a woman that hath a familiar spirit, or that is a wizard, shall surely be put to death"; Deut. 18:10, 11—"There shall not be found with thee ... a consulter with a familiar spirit, or a wizard, or a necromancer."

Job 19:25-27—"I know that my Redeemer liveth, And at last he will stand up upon the earth: And after my skin, even this body, is destroyed, Then without my flesh shall I see God; Whom I, even I, shall see, on my side, And mine eyes shall behold, and not as a stranger. My heart is consumed within me"; Ps. 16:9-11—"Therefore my heart is glad, and my glory rejoiceth: My flesh also shall dwell in safety. For thou wilt not leave my soul to Sheol; Neither wilt thou suffer thy holy one to see corruption. Thou wilt show me the path of life: In thy presence is fulness of joy; In thy right hand there are pleasures for evermore"; Is. 26:19—"Thy dead shalt live; my dead bodies shall arise. Awake and sing, ye that dwell in the dust; for thy dew is as the dew of herbs, and the earth shall cast forth the dead"; Ez. 37:1-14—the valley of dry bones—"I will open your graves, and cause you to come up out of your graves, O my people"—a prophecy of restoration based upon the idea of immortality and resurrection; Dan. 12:2, 3, 13—"And many of them that sleep in the dust of the earth shall awake, some to everlasting life, and some to shame and everlasting contempt. And they that are wise shall shine as the brightness of the firmament; and they that turn many to righteousness as the stars for ever and ever.... But go thou thy way till the end be: for thou shalt rest, and shalt stand in thy lot, at the end of the days."

Josephus, on the doctrine of the Pharisees, in Antiquities, XVIII:1:3, and Wars of the Jews, II:8:10-14—"Souls have an immortal vigor. Under the earth are rewards and punishments. The wicked are detained in an everlasting prison. The righteous shall have power to revive and live again. Bodies are indeed corruptible, but souls remain exempt from death forever. But the doctrine of the Sadducees is that souls die with their bodies." Mat. 22:31, 32—"But as touching the resurrection of the dead, have ye not read that which was spoken unto you by God, saying, I am the God of Abraham, and the God of Isaac, and the God of Jacob? God is not the God of the dead, but of the living."

Christ's argument, in the passage last quoted, rests upon the two implied assumptions: first, that love will never suffer the object of its affection to die; beings who have ever been the objects of God's love will be so forever; secondly, that body and soul belong normally together; if body and soul are temporarily separated, they shall be united; Abraham, Isaac, and Jacob are living, and therefore they shall rise again. It was only an application of the same principle, when Robert Hall gave up his early materialism as he looked down into his father's grave: he felt that this could not be the end; cf. Ps. 22:26—"Your heart shall live forever." Acts 23:6—"I am a Pharisee, a son of Pharisees: touching the hope and resurrection of the dead I am called in question"; 26:7, 8—"And concerning this hope I am accused by the Jews, O king! Why is it judged incredible with you, if God doth raise the dead?" Heb. 11:13-16—the present life was reckoned as a pilgrimage; the patriarchs sought "a better country, that is, a heavenly"; cf. Gen. 47:9. On Jesus' argument for the resurrection, see A. H. Strong, Christ in Creation, 406-421.

The argument for immortality itself presupposes, not only the existence of a God, but the existence of a truthful, wise, and benevolent God. We might almost say that God and immortality must be proved together,—like two pieces of a broken crock, when put together there is proof of both. And yet logically it is only the existence of God that is intuitively certain. Immortality is an inference therefrom. Henry More: "But souls that of his own good life partake He loves as his own self; dear as his eye They are to him: he'll never them forsake; When they shall die, then God himself shall die; They live, they live in blest eternity." God could not let Christ die, and he cannot let us die. Southey: "They sin who tell us love can die. With life all other passions fly; All others are but vanity. In heaven ambition cannot dwell, Nor avarice in the vaults of hell; They perish where they had their birth; But love is indestructible."

Emerson, Threnody on the death of his beloved and gifted child: "What is excellent, As God lives, is permanent: Hearts are dust, hearts' loves remain; Heart's love will meet thee again." Whittier, Snowbound, 200 sq.—"Yet Love will dream, and Faith will trust (Since He who knows our need is just), That somehow, somewhere, meet we must. Alas for him who never sees The stars shine through his cypress trees! Who hopeless lays his dead away, Nor looks to see the breaking day Across his mournful marbles play! Who hath not learned, in hours of faith, The truth to flesh and sense unknown, That Life is ever lord of death, And Love can never lose its own." Robert Browning, Evelyn Hope: "For God above Is great to grant as mighty to make, And creates the love to reward the love; I claim you still for my own love's sake! Delayed it may be for more lives yet, Through worlds I shall traverse not a few; Much is to learn and much to forget, Ere the time be come for taking you."

The river St. John in New Brunswick descends seventeen feet between the city and the sea, and ships cannot overcome the obstacle, but when the tide comes in, it turns the current the other way and bears vessels on mightily to the city. So the laws of nature bring death, but the tides of Christ's life counteract them, and bring life and immortality (Dr. J. W. A. Stewart). Mozley, Lectures, 26-59, and Essays, 2:169—"True religion among the Jews had an evidence of immortality in its possession of God. Paganism was hopeless in its loss of friends, because affection never advanced beyond its earthly object, and therefore, in losing it, lost all. But religious love, which loves the creature in the Creator, has that on which to fall back, when its earthly object is removed."

(h) The most impressive and conclusive of all proofs of immortality, however, is afforded in the resurrection of Jesus Christ,—a work accomplished by his own power, and demonstrating that the spirit lived after its separation from the body (John 2:19, 21; 10:17, 18). By coming back from the tomb, he proves that death is not annihilation (2 Tim. 1:10).

John 2:19, 21—"Jesus answered and said unto them, Destroy this temple, and in three days I will raise it up.... But he spake of the temple of his body"; 10:17, 18—"Therefore doth the Father love me, because I lay down my life, that I may take it again.... I have power to lay it down, and I have power to take it again"; 2 Tim. 1:10—"our Savior Christ Jesus, who abolished death, and brought life and immortality to light through the gospel"—that is, immortality had been a truth dimly recognized, suspected, longed for, before Christ came; but it was he who first brought it out from obscurity and uncertainty into clear daylight and convincing power. Christ's resurrection, moreover, carries with it the resurrection of his people: "We two are so joined, He'll not be in glory and leave me behind."

Christ taught immortality: (1) By exhibiting himself the perfect conception of a human life. Who could believe that Christ could become forever extinct? (2) By actually coming back from beyond the grave. There were many speculations about a trans-Atlantic continent before 1492, but these were of little worth compared with the actual word which Columbus brought of a new world beyond the sea. (3) By providing a way through which his own spiritual life and victory may be ours; so that, though we pass through the valley of the shadow of death, we may fear no evil. (4) By thus gaining authority to teach us of the resurrection of the righteous and of the wicked, as he actually does. Christ's resurrection is not only the best proof of immortality, but we have no certain evidence of immortality without it. Hume held that the same logic which proved immortality from reason alone, would also prove preëxistence. "In reality," he said, "it is the Gospel, and the Gospel alone, that has brought immortality to light." It was truth, though possibly spoken in jest.

There was need of this revelation. The fear of death, even after Christ has come, shows how hopeless humanity is by nature. Krupp, the great German maker of cannon, would not have death mentioned in his establishment. He ran away from his own dying relatives. Yet he died. But to the Christian, death is an exodus, an unmooring, a home-coming. Here we are as ships on the stocks; at death we are launched into our true element. Before Christ's resurrection, it was twilight; it is sunrise now. Balfour: "Death is the fall of the curtain, not at the end of the piece, but at the end of the act." George Dana Boardman: "Christ is the resurrection and the life. Being himself the Son of man—the archetypal man, the representative of human nature, the head and epitome of mankind—mankind ideally, potentially, virtually rose, when the Son of man rose. He is the resurrection, because he is the life. The body does not give life to itself, but life takes on body and uses it."

George Adam Smith, Yale Lectures: "Some of the Psalmists have only a hope of corporate immortality. But this was found wanting. It did not satisfy Israel. It cannot satisfy men to-day. The O. T. is of use in reminding us that the hope of immortality is a secondary, subordinate, and dispensable element of religious experience. Men had better begin and work for God's sake, and not for future reward. The O. T. development of immortality is of use most of all because it deduces all immortality from God." Athanasius: "Man is, according to nature, mortal, as a being who has been made of things that are perishable. But on account of his likeness to God he can by piety ward off and escape from his natural mortality and remain indestructible if he retain the knowledge of God, or lose his incorruptibility if he lose his life in God" (quoted in McConnell, Evolution of Immortality, viii, 46-48). Justin Martyr, 1 Apol., 17, expects resurrection of both just and unjust; but in Dial. Tryph., 5, he expressly denounces and dismisses the Platonic doctrine that the soul is immortal. Athenagoras and Tertullian hold to native immortality, and from it argue to bodily resurrection. So Augustine. But Theophilus, Irenæus, Clemens Alexandrinus, with Athanasius, counted it a pagan error. For the annihilation theory, see Hudson, Debt and Grace, and Christ our Life; also Dobney, Future Punishment. Per contra, see Hovey, State of the Impenitent Dead, 1-27, and Manual of Theology and Ethics, 153-168; Luthardt, Compendium, 289-292; Delitzsch, Bib. Psych., 397-407; Herzog, Encyclop., art.: Tod; Splittgerber, Schlaf und Tod; Estes, Christian Doctrine of the Soul; Baptist Review, 1879:411-439; Presb. Rev., Jan. 1882:203.

II. The Intermediate State

The Scriptures affirm the conscious existence of both the righteous and the wicked, after death, and prior to the resurrection. In the intermediate state the soul is without a body, yet this state is for the righteous a state of conscious joy, and for the wicked a state of conscious suffering.

That the righteous do not receive the spiritual body at death, is plain from 1 Thess. 4:16,17 and 1 Cor. 15:52, where an interval is intimated between Paul's time and the rising of those who slept. The rising was to occur in the future, "at the last trump." So the resurrection of the wicked had not yet occurred in any single case (2 Tim. 2:18—it was an error to say that the resurrection was "past already"); it was yet future (John 5:28-30—"the hour cometh"—ἔρχεται ὥρα, not καὶ νῦν ἐστίν—"now is," as in verse 25; Acts 24:15—"there shall be a resurrection"—ἀνάστασιν μέλλειν ἔσεσθαι). Christ was the firstfruits (1 Cor. 15:20, 23). If the saints had received the spiritual body at death, the patriarchs would have been raised before Christ.

1. Of the righteous.

Of the righteous, it is declared:

(a) That the soul of the believer, at its separation from the body, enters the presence of Christ.

2 Cor. 5:1-8—"if the earthly house of our tabernacle be dissolved, we have a building from God, a house not made with hands, eternal in the heavens. For verily in this we groan, longing to be clothed upon with our habitation which is from heaven: if so be that being clothed we shall not be found naked. For indeed we that are in this tabernacle do groan, being burdened; not for that we would be unclothed, but that we would be clothed upon, that what is mortal may be swallowed up of life ... willing rather to be absent from the body, and to be at home with the Lord"—Paul hopes to escape the violent separation of soul and body—the being "unclothed"—by living till the coming of the Lord, and then putting on the heavenly body, as it were, over the present one (ἐπενδύσασθαι); yet whether he lived till Christ's coming or not, he knew that the soul, when it left the body, would be at home with the Lord.

Luke 23:43—"To-day shalt thou be with me in Paradise"; John 14:3—"And if I go and prepare a place for you, I come again, and will receive you unto myself; that where I am, there ye may be also"; 2 Tim. 4:18—"The Lord will deliver me from every evil work, and will save me unto [or, 'into'] his heavenly kingdom" = will save me and put me into his heavenly kingdom (Ellicott), the characteristic of which is the visible presence of the King with his subjects. It is our privilege to be with Christ here and now. And nothing shall separate us from Christ and his love, "neither death, nor life ... nor things present, nor things to come" (Rom. 8:38); for he himself has said: "Lo, I am with you always, even unto the consummation of the age" (Mat. 28:20).

(b) That the spirits of departed believers are with God.

Heb. 12:23—Ye are come "to the general assembly and church of the firstborn who are enrolled in heaven, and to God the Judge of all"; cf. Eccl. 12:7—"the dust returneth to the earth as it was, and the spirit returneth unto God who gave it"; John 20:17—"Touch me not; for I am not yet ascended unto the Father"—probably means: "my body has not yet ascended." The soul had gone to God during the interval between death and the resurrection, as is evident from Luke 23:43, 46—"with me in Paradise ... Father, into thy hands I commend my spirit."

(c) That believers at death enter paradise.

Luke 23:42, 43—"And he said, Jesus, remember me when thou comest in thy kingdom. And he said unto him, Verily I say unto thee, To-day shalt thou be with me in paradise"; cf. 2 Cor. 12:4—"caught up into Paradise, and heard unspeakable words, which it is not lawful for a man to utter"; Rev. 2:7—"To him that overcometh, to him will I give to eat of the tree of life, which is in the Paradise of God"; Gen. 2:8—"And Jehovah God planted a garden eastward, in Eden; and there he put the man whom he had formed." Paradise is none other than the abode of God and the blessed, of which the primeval Eden was the type. If the penitent thief went to Purgatory, it was a Purgatory with Christ, which was better than a Heaven without Christ. Paradise is a place which Christ has gone to prepare, perhaps by taking our friends there before us.

(d) That their state, immediately after death, is greatly to be preferred to that of faithful and successful laborers for Christ here.

Phil. 1:23—"I am in a strait betwixt the two, having the desire to depart and be with Christ; for it is very far better"—here Hackett says: "ἀναλῦσαι = departing, cutting loose, as if to put to sea, followed by σὺν Χριστῷ εἶναι, as if Paul regarded one event as immediately subsequent to the other." Paul, with his burning desire to preach Christ, would certainly have preferred to live and labor, even amid great suffering, rather than to die, if death to him had been a state of unconsciousness and inaction. See Edwards the younger, Works, 2:530, 531; Hovey, Impenitent Dead, 61.

(e) That departed saints are truly alive and conscious.

Mat. 22:32—"God is not the God of the dead, but of the living"; Luke 16:22—"carried away by the angels into Abraham's bosom"; 23:43—"To-day shalt thou be with me in Paradise"—"with me" = in the same state,—unless Christ slept in unconsciousness, we cannot think that the penitent thief did; John 11:26—"whosoever liveth and believeth on me shall never die"; 1 Thess. 5:10—"who died for us, that, whether we wake or sleep, we should live together with him"; Rom. 8:10—"And if Christ is in you, the body is dead because of sin; but the spirit is life because of righteousness." Life and consciousness clearly belong to the "souls under the altar" mentioned under the next head, for they cry: "How long?" Phil. 1:6—"he who began a good work in you will perfect it until the day of Jesus Christ"—seems to imply a progressive sanctification, through the Intermediate State, up to the time of Christ's second coming. This state is: 1. a conscious state ("God of the living"); 2. a fixed state (no "passing from thence"); 3. an incomplete state ("not to be unclothed").

(f) That they are at rest and blessed.

Rev. 6:9-11—"I saw underneath the altar the souls of them that had been slain for the word of God, and for the testimony which they held: and they cried with a great voice, saying, How long, O Master, the holy and true, dost thou not judge and avenge our blood on them that dwell on the earth? And there was given them to each one a white robe; and it was said unto them, that they should rest yet for a little time, until their fellow-servants also and their brethren, who should be killed even as they were, should have fulfilled their course"; 14:13—"Blessed are the dead who die in the Lord from henceforth: yea, saith the Spirit, that they may rest from their labors; for their works follow with them"; 20:14—"And death and Hades were cast into the lake of fire"—see Evans, in Presb. Rev., 1883:303—"The shadow of death lying upon Hades is the penumbra of Hell. Hence Hades is associated with death in the final doom."

2. Of the wicked.

Of the wicked, it is declared:

(a) That they are in prison,—that is, are under constraint and guard (1 Peter 3:19—φυλακή).

1 Pet. 3:19—"In which [spirit] also he went and preached unto the spirits in prison"—there is no need of putting unconscious spirits under guard. Hovey: "Restraint implies power of action, and suffering implies consciousness."

(b) That they are in torment, or conscious suffering (Luke 16:23—ἐν βασάνοις).

Luke 16:23—"And in Hades he lifted up his eyes, being in torments, and seeth Abraham afar off, and Lazarus in his bosom. And he cried and said, Father Abraham, have mercy on me, and send Lazarus, that he may dip the tip of his finger in water, and cool my tongue; for I am in anguish in this flame."

Here many unanswerable questions may be asked: Had the rich man a body before the resurrection, or is this representation of a body only figurative? Did the soul still feel the body from which it was temporarily separated, or have souls in the intermediate state temporary bodies? However we may answer these questions, it is certain that the rich man suffers, while probation still lasts for his brethren on earth. Fire is here the source of suffering, but not of annihilation. Even though this be a parable, it proves conscious existence after death to have been the common view of the Jews, and to have been a view sanctioned by Christ.

(c) That they are under punishment (2 Pet. 2:9—κολαζομένους).

2 Pet. 2:9—"the Lord knoweth how to deliver the godly out of temptation, and to keep the unrighteous under punishment unto the day of judgment"—here "the unrighteous" = not only evil angels, but ungodly men; cf. verse 4—"For if God spared not angels when they sinned, but cast them down to hell, and committed them to pits of darkness, to be reserved unto judgment."

In the parable of the rich man and Lazarus, the body is buried, yet still the torments of the soul are described as physical. Jesus here accommodates his teaching to the conceptions of his time, or, better still, uses material figures to express spiritual realities. Surely he does not mean to say that the Rabbinic notion of Abraham's bosom is ultimate truth. "Parables," for this reason among others, "may not be made primary sources and seats of doctrine." Luckock, Intermediate State, 20—"May the parable of the rich man and Lazarus be an anticipatory picture of the final state? But the rich man seems to assume that the judgment has not yet come, for he speaks of his brethren as still undergoing their earthly probation, and as capable of receiving a warning to avoid a fate similar to his own."

The passages cited enable us properly to estimate two opposite errors.

A. They refute, on the one hand, the view that the souls of both righteous and wicked sleep between death and the resurrection.

This view is based upon the assumption that the possession of a physical organism is indispensable to activity and consciousness—an assumption which the existence of a God who is pure spirit (John 4:24), and the existence of angels who are probably pure spirits (Heb. 1:14), show to be erroneous. Although the departed are characterized as "spirits" (Eccl. 12:7; Acts 7:59; Heb. 12:23; 1 Pet. 3:19), there is nothing in this 'absence from the body' (2 Cor. 5:8) inconsistent with the activity and consciousness ascribed to them in the Scriptures above referred to. When the dead are spoken of as "sleeping" (Dan. 12:2; Mat. 9:24; John 11:11; 1 Cor. 11:30; 15:51; 1 Thess. 4:14; 5:10), we are to regard this as simply the language of appearance, and as literally applicable only to the body.

John 4:24—"God is a Spirit [or rather, as margin, 'God is spirit']"; Heb. 1:14—"Are they [angels] not all ministering spirits?" Eccl. 12:7—"the dust returneth to the earth as it was, and the spirit returneth unto God who gave it"; Acts 7:59—"And they stoned Stephen, calling upon the Lord, and saying, Lord Jesus, receive my spirit"; Heb. 12:23—"to God the Judge of all, and to the spirits of just men made perfect"; 1 Pet. 3:19—"in which also he went and preached unto the spirits in prison"; 2 Cor. 5:8—"we are of good courage, I say, and are willing rather to be absent from the body, and to be at home with the Lord"; Dan. 12:2—"many of them that sleep in the dust of the earth shall awake"; Mat. 9:24—"the damsel is not dead, but sleepeth"; John 11:11—"Our friend Lazarus is fallen asleep; but I go, that I may awake him out of sleep"; 1 Cor. 11:30—"For this cause many among you are weak and sickly, and not a few sleep"; 1 Thess. 4:14—"For if we believe that Jesus died and rose again, even so them also that are fallen asleep in Jesus will God bring with him"; 5:10—"who died for us, that, whether we wake or sleep, we should live together with him."

B. The passages first cited refute, on the other hand, the view that the suffering of the intermediate state is purgatorial.

According to the doctrine of the Roman Catholic church, "all who die at peace with the church, but are not perfect, pass into purgatory." Here they make satisfaction for the sins committed after baptism by suffering a longer or shorter time, according to the degree of their guilt. The church on earth, however, has power, by prayers and the sacrifice of the Mass, to shorten these sufferings or to remit them altogether. But we urge, in reply, that the passages referring to suffering in the intermediate state give no indication that any true believer is subject to this suffering, or that the church has any power to relieve from the consequences of sin, either in this world or in the world to come. Only God can forgive, and the church is simply empowered to declare that, upon the fulfilment of the appointed conditions of repentance and faith, he does actually forgive. This theory, moreover, is inconsistent with any proper view of the completeness of Christ's satisfaction (Gal. 2:21; Heb. 9:28); of justification through faith alone (Rom. 3:28); and of the condition after death, of both righteous and wicked, as determined in this life (Eccl. 11:3; Mat. 25:10; Luke 16:26; Heb. 9:27; Rev.22:11).

Against this doctrine we quote the following texts: Gal 2:21—"I do not make void the grace of God: for if righteousness is through the law, then Christ died for nought"; Heb. 9:28—"so Christ also, having been once [or, 'once for all'] offered to bear the sins of many, shall appear a second time, apart from sin, to them that wait for him, unto salvation"; Rom. 3:28—"We reckon therefore that a man is justified by faith apart from the works of the law"; Eccl. 11:3—"if a tree fall toward the south or toward the north, in the place where the tree falleth there shall it be"; Mat. 25:10—"And while they went away to buy, the bridegroom came; and they that were ready went in with him to the marriage feast: and the door was shut"; Luke 16:26—"And besides all this, between us and you there is a great gulf fixed, that they that would pass from hence to you may not be able, and that none may cross over from thence to us"; Heb. 9:27—"it is appointed unto men once to die, and after this cometh judgment"; Rev. 22:11—"He that is unrighteous, let him do unrighteousness still: and he that is filthy, let him be made filthy still: and he that is righteous, let him do righteousness still: and he that is holy, let him be made holy still."

Rome teaches that the agonies of purgatory are intolerable. They differ from the pains of the damned only in this, that there is a limit to the one, not the other. Bellarmine, De Purgatorio, 2:14—"The pains of purgatory are very severe, surpassing any endured in this life." Since none but actual saints escape the pains of purgatory, this doctrine gives to the death and the funeral of the Roman Catholic a dreadful and repellent aspect. Death is not the coming of Christ to take his disciples home, but is rather the ushering of the shrinking soul into a place of unspeakable suffering. This suffering makes satisfaction for guilt. Having paid their allotted penalty, the souls of the purified pass into Heaven without awaiting the day of judgment. The doctrine of purgatory gives hope that men may be saved after death; prayer for the dead has influence; the priest is authorized to offer this prayer; so the church sells salvation for money. Amory H. Bradford, Ascent of the Soul, 267-287, argues in favor of prayers for the dead. Such prayers, he says, help us to keep in mind the fact that they are living still. If the dead are free beings, they may still choose good or evil, and our prayers may help them to choose the good. We should be thankful, he believes, to the Roman Catholic Church, for keeping up such prayers. We reply that no doctrine of Rome has done so much to pervert the gospel and to enslave the world.

For the Romanist doctrine, see Perrone, Prælectiones Theologicæ, 2:391-420. Per contra, see Hodge, Systematic Theology, 3:743-770; Barrows, Purgatory. Augustine, Encheiridion, 69, suggests the possibility of purgatorial fire in the future for some believers. Whiton, Is Eternal Punishment Endless? page 69, says that Tertullian held to a delay of resurrection in the case of faulty Christians; Cyprian first stated the notion of a middle state of purification; Augustine thought it "not incredible"; Gregory the Great called it "worthy of belief"; it is now one of the most potent doctrines of the Roman Catholic Church; that church has been, from the third century, for all souls who accept her last consolations, practically restorationist. Gore, Incarnation, 18—"In the Church of Rome, the 'peradventure' of an Augustine as to purgatory for the imperfect after death—'non redarguo', he says, 'quia forsitan verum est,'—has become a positive teaching about purgatory, full of exact information."

Elliott, Horæ Apocalypticæ, 1:410, adopts Hume's simile, and says that purgatory gave the Roman Catholic Church what Archimedes wanted, another world on which to fix its lever, that so fixed, the church might with it move this world. We must remember, however, that the Roman church teaches no radical change of character in purgatory,—purgatory is only a purifying process for believers. The true purgatory is only in this world,—for only here are sins purged away by God's sanctifying Spirit; and in this process of purification, though God chastises, there is no element of penalty. On Dante's Purgatory, see A. H. Strong, Philosophy and Religion, 515-518.

Luckock, After Death, is an argument, based upon the Fathers, against the Romanist doctrine. Yet he holds to progress in sanctification in the intermediate state, though the work done in that state will not affect the final judgment, which will be for the deeds done in the body. He urges prayer for the departed righteous. In his book entitled The Intermediate State, Luckock holds to mental and spiritual development in that state, to active ministry, mutual recognition, and renewed companionship. He does not believe in a second probation, but in a first real probation for those who have had no proper opportunities in this life. In their reaction against purgatory, the Westminister divines obliterated the Intermediate State. In that state there is gradual purification, and must be, since not all impurity and sinfulness are removed at death. The purging of the will requires time. White robes were given to them while they were waiting (Rev. 6:11). But there is no second probation for those who have thrown away their opportunities in this life. Robert Browning, The Ring and the Book, 232 (Pope, 2129), makes the Pope speak of following Guido "Into that sad, obscure, sequestered state Where God unmakes but to remake the soul He else made first in vain; which must not be." But the idea of hell as permitting essential change of character is foreign to Roman Catholic doctrine.

We close our discussion of this subject with a single, but an important, remark,—this, namely, that while the Scriptures represent the intermediate state to be one of conscious joy to the righteous, and of conscious pain to the wicked, they also represent this state to be one of incompleteness. The perfect joy of the saints, and the utter misery of the wicked, begin only with the resurrection and general judgment.

That the intermediate state is one of incompleteness, appears from the following passages: Mat. 8:29—"What have we to do with thee, thou Son of God? art thou come hither to torment us before the time?" 2 Cor. 5:3, 4—"if so be that being clothed we shall not be found naked. For indeed we that are in this tabernacle do groan, being burdened; not for that we would be unclothed, but that we would be clothed upon, that what is mortal may be swallowed up of life"; cf. Rom. 8:23—"And not only so, but ourselves also, who have the first-fruits of the Spirit, even we ourselves groan within ourselves, waiting for our adoption, to wit, the redemption of our body"; Phil. 3:11—"if by any means I may attain unto the resurrection from the dead"; 2 Pet. 2:9—"the Lord knoweth how to deliver the godly out of temptation, and to keep the unrighteous under punishment unto the day of judgment"; Rev. 6:10—"and they [the souls underneath the altar] cried with a great voice, saying, How long, O Master, the holy and true, dost thou not judge and avenge our blood on them that dwell on the earth?"

In opposition to Locke, Human Understanding, 2:1:10, who said that "the soul thinks not always"; and to Turner, Wish and Will, 48, who declares that "the soul need not always think, any more than the body always move; the essence of the soul is potentiality for activity"; Descartes, Kant, Jouffroy, Sir William Hamilton, all maintain that it belongs to mental existence continuously to think. Upon this view, the intermediate state would be necessarily a state of thought. As to the nature of that thought, Dorner remarks in his Eschatology that "in this relatively bodiless state, a still life begins, a sinking of the soul into itself and into the ground of its being,—what Steffens calls 'involution,' and Martensen 'self-brooding.' In this state, spiritual things are the only realities. In the unbelieving, their impurity, discord, alienation from God, are laid bare. If they still prefer sin, its form becomes more spiritual, more demoniacal, and so ripens for the judgment."

Even here, Dorner deals in speculation rather than in Scripture. But he goes further, and regards the intermediate state as one, not only of moral progress, but of elimination of evil; and holds the end of probation to be, not at death, but at the judgment, at least in the case of all non-believers who are not incorrigible. We must regard this as a practical revival of the Romanist theory of purgatory, and as contradicted not only by all the considerations already urged, but also by the general tenor of Scriptural representation that the decisions of this life are final, and that character is fixed here for eternity. This is the solemnity of preaching, that the gospel is "a savor from life unto life," or "a savor from death unto death" (2 Cor. 2:16).

Descartes: "As the light always shines and the heat always warms, so the soul always thinks." James, Psychology, 1:164-175, argues against unconscious mental states. The states were conscious at the time we had them; but they have been forgotten. In the Unitarian Review, Sept. 1884, Prof. James denies that eternity is given at a stroke to omniscience. Lotze, in his Metaphysics, 268, in opposition to Kant, contends for the transcendental validity of time. Green, on the contrary, in Prolegomena to Ethics, book 1, says that every act of knowledge in the case of man is a timeless act. In comparing the different aspects of the stream of successive phenomena, the mind must, he says, be itself out of time. Upton, Hibbert Lectures, 306, denies this timeless consciousness even to God, and apparently agrees with Martineau in maintaining that God does not foreknow free human acts.

De Quincey called the human brain a palimpsest. Each new writing seems to blot out all that went before. Yet in reality not one letter has ever been effaced. Loeb, Physiology of the Brain, 213, tells us that associative memory is imitated by machines like the phonograph. Traces left by speech can be reproduced in speech. Loeb calls memory a matter of physical chemistry. Stout, Manual of Psychology, 8—"Consciousness includes not only awareness of our own states, but these states themselves whether we are aware of them or not. If a man is angry, that is a state of consciousness, even though he does not know that he is angry. If he does know that he is angry, that is another modification of consciousness, and not the same." On unconscious mental action, see Ladd, Philosophy of Mind, 378-382—"Cerebration cannot be identified with psychical processes. If it could be, materialism would triumph. If the brain can do these things, why not do all the phenomena of consciousness? Consciousness becomes a mere epiphenomenon. Unconscious cerebration = wooden iron or unconscious consciousness. What then becomes of the soul in its intervals of unconsciousness? Answer: Unconscious finite minds exist only in the World-ground in which all minds and things have their existence."

On the whole subject, see Hovey, State of Man after Death; Savage, Souls of the Righteous; Julius Müller, Doct. Sin, 2:304-446; Neander, Planting and Training, 482-484; Delitzsch, Bib. Psychologie, 407-448; Bib. Sac., 13:153; Methodist Rev., 34:240; Christian Rev., 20:381; Herzog, Encyclop., art.: Hades; Stuart, Essays on Future Punishment; Whately, Future State; Hovey, Biblical Eschatology, 79-144.

III. The Second Coming of Christ

While the Scriptures represent great events in the history of the individual Christian, like death, and great events in the history of the church, like the outpouring of the Spirit at Pentecost and the destruction of Jerusalem, as comings of Christ for deliverance or judgment, they also declare that these partial and typical comings shall be concluded by a final, triumphant return of Christ, to punish the wicked and to complete the salvation of his people.

Temporal comings of Christ are indicated in: Mat. 24:23, 27, 34—"Then if any man shall say unto you, Lo, here is the Christ, or, Here; believe it not.... For as the lightning cometh forth from the east, and is seen even unto the west; so shall be the coming of the Son of man.... Verily I say unto you, This generation shall not pass away, till all these things be accomplished"; 16:28—"Verily I say unto you, There are some of them that stand here, who shall in no wise taste of death, till they see the Son of man coming in his kingdom"; John 14:3, 18—"And if I go and prepare a place for you, I come again, and will receive you unto myself; that where I am, there ye may be also.... I will not leave you desolate: I come unto you"; Rev. 3:20—"Behold, I stand at the door and knock: if any man hear my voice and open the door, I will come in to him, and will sup with him, and he with me." So the Protestant Reformation, the modern missionary enterprise, the battle against papacy in Europe and against slavery in this country, the great revivals under Whitefield in England and under Edwards in America, were all preliminary and typical comings of Christ. It was a sceptical spirit which indited the words: "God's new Messiah, some great Cause"; yet it is true that in every great movement of civilization we are to recognize a new coming of the one and only Messiah, "Jesus Christ, the same yesterday and to-day and forever" (Heb. 13:8). Schaff, Hist. Christ. Church, 1:840—"The coming began with his ascension to heaven (cf. Mat. 26:64—'henceforth ἀπ' ἄρτι [from now] ye shall see the Son of man sitting at the right hand of Power, and coming on the clouds of heaven')." Matheson, Spir. Devel. of St. Paul, 286—"To Paul, in his later letters, this world is already the scene of the second advent. The secular is not to vanish away, but to be permanent, transfigured, pervaded by the divine life. Paul began with the Christ of the resurrection; he ends with the Christ who already makes all things new." See Metcalf, Parousia vs. Second Advent, in Bib. Sac., Jan. 1907:61-65.

The final coming of Christ is referred to in: Mat. 24:30—"they shall see the Son of man coming on the clouds of heaven with power and great glory. And he shall send forth his angels with a great sound of a trumpet, and they shall gather together his elect from the four winds, from one end of heaven to the other"; 25:31—"But when the Son of man shall come in his glory, and all the angels with him, then shall he sit on the throne of his glory"; Acts 1:11—"Ye men of Galilee, why stand ye looking into heaven? this Jesus, who was received up from you into heaven, shall so come in like manner as ye beheld him going into heaven"; 1 Thess. 4:16—"For the Lord himself shall descend from heaven, with a shout, with the voice of the archangel, and with the trump of God"; 2 Thess. 1:7, 10—"the revelation of the Lord Jesus from heaven with the angels of his power ... when he shall come to be glorified in his saints, and to be marvelled at in all them that believed"; Heb. 9:28—"so Christ also, having been once offered to bear the sins of many, shall appear a second time, apart from sin, to them that wait for him, unto salvation"; Rev. 1:7—"Behold, he cometh with the clouds; and every eye shall see him, and they that pierced him; and all the tribes of the earth shall mourn over him." Dr. A. C. Kendrick, Com. on Heb. 1:6—"And when he shall conduct back again into the inhabited world the First-born, he saith, And let all the angels of God worship him"—in the glory of the second coming Christ's superiority to angels will be signally displayed—a contrast to the humiliation of his first coming.

The tendency of our day is to interpret this second class of passages in a purely metaphorical and spiritual way. But prophecy can have more than one fulfilment. Jesus' words are pregnant words. The present spiritual coming does not exhaust their meaning. His coming in the great movements of history does not preclude a final and literal coming, in which "every eye shall see him" (Rev. 1:7). With this proviso, we may assent to much of the following quotation from Gould, Bib. Theol. N. T., 44-58—"The last things of which Jesus speaks are not the end of the world, but of the age—the end of the Jewish period in connection with the destruction of Jerusalem.... After the entire statement is in, including both the destruction of Jerusalem and the coming of the Lord which is to follow it, it is distinctly said that that generation was not to pass away until all these things are accomplished. According to this, the coming of the Son of man must be something other than a visible coming. In O. T. prophecy any divine interference in human affairs is represented under the figure of God coming in the clouds of heaven. Mat. 26:64 says: 'From this time ye shall see the Son of man seated ... and coming in the clouds of heaven.' Coming and judgment are both continuous. The slow growth in the parables of the leaven and the mustard seed contradicts the idea of Christ's early coming. 'After a long time the Lord of these servants cometh' (Mat. 25:19). Christ came in one sense at the destruction of Jerusalem; in another sense all great crises in the history of the world are comings of the Son of man. These judgments of the nations are a part of the process for the final setting up of the kingdom. But this final act will not be a judgment process, but the final entire submission of the will of man to the will of God. The end is to be, not judgment, but salvation." We add to this statement the declaration that the final act here spoken of will not be purely subjective and spiritual, but will constitute an external manifestation of Christ comparable to that of his first coming in its appeal to the senses, but unspeakably more glorious than was the coming to the manger and the cross. The proof of this we now proceed to give.

1. The nature of this coming.

Although without doubt accompanied, in the case of the regenerate, by inward and invisible influences of the Holy Spirit, the second advent is to be outward and visible. This we argue:

(a) From the objects to be secured by Christ's return. These are partly external (Rom. 8:21, 23). Nature and the body are both to be glorified. These external changes may well be accompanied by a visible manifestation of him who "makes all things new" (Rev. 21:5).

Rom. 8:10-23—"in hope that the creation also shall be delivered from the bondage of corruption into the liberty of the glory of the children of God ... waiting for our adoption, to wit, the redemption of our body"; Rev. 21:5—"Behold, I make all things new." A. J. Gordon, Ministry of the Spirit, 49—"We must not confound the Paraclete and the Parousia. It has been argued that, because Christ came in the person of the Spirit, the Redeemer's advent in glory has already taken place. But in the Paraclete Christ comes spiritually and invisibly; in the Parousia he comes bodily and gloriously."

(b) From the Scriptural comparison of the manner of Christ's return with the manner of his departure (Acts 1:11)—see Commentary of Hackett, in loco:—"ὃν τρόπον = visibly, and in the air. The expression is never employed to affirm merely the certainty of one event as compared with another. The assertion that the meaning is simply that, as Christ had departed, so also he would return, is contradicted by every passage in which the phrase occurs."

Acts 1:11—"this Jesus, who was received up from you into heaven, shall so come in like manner as ye beheld him going into heaven"; cf. Acts 7:28—"wouldest thou kill me, as ὃν τρόπον thou killedst the Egyptian yesterday?" Mat. 23:37—"how often would I have gathered thy children together, even as ὃν τρόπον a hen gathereth her chickens under her wings"; 2 Tim. 3:8—"as ὃν τρόπον Jannes and

Jambres withstood Moses, so do these also withstand the truth." Lyman Abbott refers to Mat. 23:37, and Luke 13:35, as showing that, in Acts 1:11, "in like manner" means only "in like reality." So, he says, the Jews expected Elijah to return in form, according to Mal. 4:5, whereas he returned only in spirit. Jesus similarly returned at Pentecost in spirit, and has been coming again ever since. The remark of Dr. Hackett, quoted in the text above, is sufficient proof that this interpretation is wholly unexegetical.

(c) From the analogy of Christ's first coming. If this was a literal and visible coming, we may expect the second coming to be literal and visible also.

1 Thess. 4:16—"For the Lord himself [= in his own person] shall descend from heaven, with a shout [something heard], with the voice of the archangel, and with the trump of God"—see Com. of Prof. W. A. Stevens: "So different from Luke 17:20, where 'the kingdom of God cometh not with observation.' The 'shout' is not necessarily the voice of Christ himself (lit. 'in a shout,' or 'in shouting'). 'Voice of the archangel' and 'trump of God' are appositional, not additional." Rev. 1:7—"every eye shall see him"; as every ear shall hear him: John 5:28, 29—"all that are in the tombs shall hear his voice"; 2 Thess. 2:2—"to the end that ye be not quickly shaken from your mind, nor yet be troubled ... as that the day of the Lord is now present"—they may have "thought that the first gathering of the saints to Christ was a quiet, invisible one—a stealthy advent, like a thief in the night" (Lillie). 2 John 7—"For many deceivers are gone forth into the world, even they that confess not that Jesus Christ cometh in the flesh"—here denial of a future second coming of Christ is declared to be the mark of a deceiver.

Alford and Alexander, in their Commentaries on Acts 1:11, agree with the view of Hackett quoted above. Warren, Parousia, 61-65, 106-114, controverts this view and says that "an omnipresent divine being can come, only in the sense of manifestation." He regards the parousia, or coming of Christ, as nothing but Christ's spiritual presence. A writer in the Presb. Review, 1883:221, replies that Warren's view is contradicted "by the fact that the apostles often spoke of the parousia as an event yet future, long after the promise of the Redeemer's spiritual presence with his church had begun to be fulfilled, and by the fact that Paul expressly cautions the Thessalonians against the belief that the parousia was just at hand." We do not know how all men at one time can see a bodily Christ; but we also do not know the nature of Christ's body. The day exists undivided in many places at the same time. The telephone has made it possible for men widely separated to hear the same voice,—it is equally possible that all men may see the same Christ coming in the clouds.

2. The time of Christ's coming.

(a) Although Christ's prophecy of this event, in the twenty-fourth chapter of Matthew, so connects it with the destruction of Jerusalem that the apostles and the early Christians seem to have hoped for its occurrence during their life-time, yet neither Christ nor the apostles definitely taught when the end should be, but rather declared the knowledge of it to be reserved in the counsels of God, that men might ever recognize it as possibly at hand, and so might live in the attitude of constant expectation.

1 Cor. 15:51—"We shall not all sleep, but we shall all be changed"; 1 Thess. 4:17—"then we that are alive, that are left, shall together with them be caught up in the clouds, to meet the Lord in the air; and so shall we ever be with the Lord"; 2 Tim. 4:8—"henceforth there is laid up for me the crown of righteousness, which the Lord, the righteous judge, shall give to me at that day: and not only to me, but also to all them that have loved his appearing"; James

5:7—"Be patient therefore, brethren, until the coming of the Lord"; 1 Pet. 4:7—"But the end of all things is at hand: be ye therefore of sound mind, and be sober unto prayer"; 1 John 2:18—"Little children, it is the last hour: and as ye heard that antichrist cometh, even now have there risen many antichrists; whereby we know that it is the last hour."

Phil. 4:5—"The Lord is at hand (ἐγγύς). In nothing be anxious"—may mean "the Lord is near" (in space), without any reference to the second coming. The passages quoted above, expressing as they do the surmises of the apostles that Christ's coming was near, while yet abstaining from all definite fixing of the time, are at least sufficient proof that Christ's advent may not be near to our time. We should be no more warranted than they were, in inferring from these passages alone the immediate coming of the Lord.

Wendt, Teaching of Jesus, 2:349-350, maintains that Jesus expected his own speedy second coming and the end of the world. There was no mention of the death of his disciples, or the importance of readiness for it. No hard and fast organization of his disciples into a church was contemplated by him,—Mat. 16:18 and 18:17 are not authentic. No separation of his disciples from the fellowship of the Jewish religion was thought of. He thought of the destruction of Jerusalem as the final judgment. Yet his doctrine would spread through the earth, like leaven and mustard seed, though accompanied by suffering on the part of his disciples. This view of Wendt can be maintained only by an arbitrary throwing out of the testimony of the evangelist, upon the ground that Jesus' mention of a church does not befit so early a stage in the evolution of Christianity. Wendt's whole treatment is vitiated by the presupposition that there can be nothing in Jesus' words which is inexplicable upon the theory of natural development. That Jesus did not expect speedily to return to earth is shown in Mat. 25:19—"After a long time the Lord of those servants cometh"; and Paul, in 2 Thess., had to correct the mistake of those who interpreted him as having in his first Epistle declared an immediate coming of the Lord.

A. H. Strong, Cleveland Sermon, 1904:27—"The faith in a second coming of Christ has lost its hold upon many Christians in our day. But it still serves to stimulate and admonish the great body, and we can never dispense with its solemn and mighty influence. Christ comes, it is true, in Pentecostal revivals and in destructions of Jerusalem, in Reformation movements and in political upheavals. But these are only precursors of another and literal and final return of Christ, to punish the wicked and to complete the salvation of his people. That day for which all other days are made will be a joyful day for those who have fought a good fight and have kept the faith. Let us look for and hasten the coming of the day of God. The Jacobites of Scotland never ceased their labors and sacrifices for their king's return. They never tasted wine, without pledging their absent prince; they never joined in song, without renewing their oaths of allegiance. In many a prison cell and on many a battlefield they rang out the strain: 'Follow thee, follow thee, wha wadna follow thee? Long hast thou lo'ed and trusted us fairly: Chairlie, Chairlie, wha wadna follow thee? King o' the Highland hearts, bonnie Prince Chairlie!' So they sang, so they invited him, until at last he came. But that longing for the day when Charles should come to his own again was faint and weak compared with the longing of true Christian hearts for the coming of their King. Charles came, only to suffer defeat, and to bring shame to his country. But Christ will come, to put an end to the world's long sorrow, to give triumph to the cause of truth, to bestow everlasting reward upon the faithful. 'Even so, Lord Jesus, come! Hope of all our hopes the sum, Take thy waiting people home! Long, so long, the groaning earth, Cursed with war and flood and dearth, Sighs for its redemption birth. Therefore come, we daily pray; Bring the resurrection-day; Wipe creation's curse away!' "

(b) Hence we find, in immediate connection with many of these predictions of the end, a reference to intervening events and to the eternity of God, which shows that the prophecies themselves are expressed in a large way which befits the greatness of the divine plans.

Mat. 24:36—"But of that day and hour knoweth no one, not even the angels of heaven, neither the Son, but the Father only"; Mark 13:32—"But of that day or that hour knoweth no one, not even the angels in heaven, neither the Son, but the Father. Take ye heed, watch and pray: for ye know not when the time is"; Acts 1:7—"And he said unto them, It is not for you to know times or seasons, which the Father hath set within his own authority"; 1 Cor. 10:11—"Now these things happened unto them by way of example; and they were written for our admonition, upon whom the ends of the ages are come"; 16:22—"Marana tha [marg.: that is, O Lord, come!]"; 2 Thess. 2:1-3—"Now we beseech you, brethren, touching the coming of our Lord Jesus Christ, and our gathering together unto him; to the end that ye be not quickly shaken from your mind, nor yet be troubled ... as that the day of the Lord is now present [Am. Rev.: 'is just at hand']; let no man beguile you in any wise: for it will not be, except the falling away come first, and the man of sin be revealed, the son of perdition."

James 5:8, 9—"Be ye also patient; establish your hearts: for the coming of the Lord is at hand. Murmur not, brethren, one against another, that ye be not judged: behold, the judge standeth before the doors"; 2 Pet. 3:3-12—"in the last days mockers shall come ... saying, Where is the promise of his coming? for, from the day that the fathers fell asleep, all things continue as they were from the beginning of the creation. For this they wilfully forget, that there were heavens from of old.... But forget not this one thing, beloved, that one day is with the Lord as a thousand years, and a thousand years as one day. The Lord is not slack concerning his promise.... But the day of the Lord will come as a thief ... what manner of persons ought ye to be in all holy living and godliness, looking for and earnestly desiring [marg.: 'hastening'] the coming of the day of God"—awaiting it, and hastening its coming by your prayer and labor.

Rev. 1:3—"Blessed is he that readeth, and they that hear the words of the prophecy, and keep the things that are written therein: for the time is at hand": 22:12, 20—"Behold, I come quickly; and my reward is with me, to render to each man according as his work is.... He who testifieth these things saith, Yea: I come quickly. Amen: come, Lord Jesus." From these passages it is evident that the apostles did not know the time of the end, and that it was hidden from Christ himself while here in the flesh. He, therefore, who assumes to know, assumes to know more than Christ or his apostles—assumes to know the very thing which Christ declared it was not for us to know!

Gould, Bib. Theol. N.T., 152—"The expectation of our Lord's coming was one of the elements and motifs of that generation, and the delay of the event caused some questioning. But there is never any indication that it may be indefinitely postponed. The early church never had to face the difficulty forced upon the church to-day, of belief in his second coming, founded upon a prophecy of his coming during the lifetime of a generation long since dead. And until this Epistle [2 Peter], we do not find any traces of this exegetical legerdemain as such a situation would require. But here we have it full-grown; just such a specimen of harmonistic device as orthodox interpretation familiarizes us with. The definite statement that the advent is to be within that generation is met with the general principle that 'one day is with the Lord as a thousand years, and a thousand years as one day' (2 Pet. 3:8)." We must regard this comment of Dr. Gould as an unconscious fulfilment of the prediction that "in the last days mockers shall come with mockery" (2 Pet. 3:3). A better understanding of prophecy, as divinely pregnant utterance, would have enabled the critic to believe that the words of Christ might be partially fulfilled in the days of the apostles, but fully accomplished only at the end of the world.

(c) In this we discern a striking parallel between the predictions of Christ's first, and the predictions of his second, advent. In both cases the event was more distant and more grand than those imagined to whom the prophecies first came. Under both dispensations, patient waiting for Christ was intended to discipline the faith, and to enlarge the conceptions, of God's true servants. The fact that every age since Christ ascended has had its Chiliasts and Second Adventists should turn our thoughts away from curious and fruitless prying into the time of Christ's coming, and set us at immediate and constant endeavor to be ready, at whatsoever hour he may appear.

Gen. 4:1—"And the man knew Eve his wife; and she conceived, and bare Cain, and said, I have gotten a man with the help of Jehovah [lit.: 'I have gotten a man, even Jehovah']"—an intimation that Eve fancied her first-born to be already the promised seed, the coming deliverer; see MacWhorter, Jahveh Christ. Deut. 18:15—"Jehovah thy God will raise up unto thee a prophet from the midst of thee, of thy brethren, like unto me; unto him ye shall hearken"—here is a prophecy which Moses may have expected to be fulfilled in Joshua, but which God designed to be fulfilled only in Christ. Is. 7:14, 16—"Therefore the Lord himself will give you a sign: behold, a virgin shall conceive, and bear a son, and shall call his name Immanuel.... For before the child shall know to refuse the evil, and choose the good, the land whose two kings thou abhorrest shall be forsaken"—a prophecy which the prophet may have expected to be fulfilled in his own time, and which was partly so fulfilled, but which God intended to be fulfilled ages thereafter.

Luke 2:25—"Simeon; and this man was righteous and devout, looking for the consolation of Israel"—Simeon was the type of holy men, in every age of Jewish history, who were waiting for the fulfilment of God's promise, and for the coming of the deliverer. So under the Christian dispensation. Augustine held that Christ's reign of a thousand years, which occupies the last epoch of the world's history, did not still lie in the future, but began with the founding of the church (Ritschl, Just. and Reconc., 286). Luther, near the time of his death, said: "God forbid that the world should last fifty years longer! Let him cut matters short with his last judgment!" Melanchthon put the end less than two hundred years from his time. Calvin's motto was: "Domine, quousque?"—"O Lord, how long?" Jonathan Edwards, before and during the great Awakening, indulged high expectations as to the probable extension of the movement until it should bring the world, even in his own lifetime, into the love and obedience of Christ (Life, by Allen, 234). Better than any one of these is the utterance of Dr. Broadus: "If I am always ready, I shall be ready when Jesus comes." On the whole subject, see Hovey, in Baptist Quarterly, Oct. 1877:416-432; Shedd, Dogm. Theol., 2:641-646; Stevens, in Am. Com. on Thessalonians, Excursus on The Parousia, and notes on 1 Thess. 4:13, 16; 5:11; 2 Thess. 2:3, 12; Goodspeed, Messiah's Second Advent; Heagle, That Blessed Hope.

3. The precursors of Christ's coming.

(a) Through the preaching of the gospel in all the world, the kingdom of Christ is steadily to enlarge its boundaries, until Jews and Gentiles alike become possessed of its blessings, and a millennial period is introduced in which Christianity generally prevails throughout the earth.

Dan. 2:44, 45—"And in the days of those kings shall the God of heaven set up a kingdom which shall never be destroyed, nor shall the sovereignty thereof be left to another people; but it shall break in pieces and consume all these kingdoms, and it shall stand forever. Forasmuch as thou sawest that a stone was cut out of the mountain without hands, and that it brake in pieces the iron, the brass, the clay, the silver, and the gold; the great God hath made known to the king what shall come to pass hereafter: and the dream is certain, and the interpretation thereof sure."

Mat. 13:31, 32—"The kingdom of heaven is like unto a grain of mustard seed ... which indeed is less than all seeds; but when it is grown, it is greater than the herbs, and becometh a tree, so that the birds of heaven come and lodge in the branches thereof"—the parable of the leaven, which follows, apparently illustrates the intensive, as that of the mustard seed illustrates the extensive, development of the kingdom of God; and it is as impossible to confine the reference of the leaven to the spread of evil as it is impossible to confine the reference of the mustard seed to the spread of good.

Mat. 24:14—"And this gospel of the kingdom shall be preached in the whole world for a testimony unto all the nations; and then shall the end come"; Rom. 11:25, 26—"a hardening in part hath befallen Israel, until the fulness of the Gentiles be come in; and so all Israel shall be saved"; Rev. 20:4-6—"And I saw thrones, and they sat upon them, and judgment was given unto them: and I saw the souls of them that had been beheaded for the testimony of Jesus, and for the word of God, and such as worshipped not the beast, neither his image, and received not the mark upon their forehead and upon their hand; and they lived, and reigned with Christ a thousand years."

Col. 1:23—"the gospel which ye heard, which was preached in all creation under heaven"—Paul's phrase here and the apparent reference in Mat. 24:14 to A. D. 70 as the time of the end, should restrain theorizers from insisting that the second coming of Christ cannot occur until this text has been fulfilled with literal completeness (Broadus).

(b) There will be a corresponding development of evil, either extensive or intensive, whose true character shall be manifest not only in deceiving many professed followers of Christ and in persecuting true believers, but in constituting a personal Antichrist as its representative and object of worship. This rapid growth shall continue until the millennium, during which evil, in the person of its chief, shall be temporarily restrained.

Mat. 13:30, 38—"Let both grow together until the harvest: and in the time of the harvest I will say to the reapers, Gather up first the tares, and bind them in bundles to burn them: but gather the wheat into my barn ... the field is the world; and the good seed, these are the sons of the kingdom; and the tares are the sons of the evil one"; 24:5, 11, 12, 24—"For many shall come in my name, saying, I am the Christ; and shall lead many astray.... And many false prophets shall arise, and shall lead many astray. And because iniquity shall be multiplied, the love of the many shall wax cold.... For there shall arise false Christs, and false prophets, and shall show great signs and wonders; so as to lead astray, if possible, even the elect."

Luke 21:12—"But before all these things, they shall lay their hands on you, and shall persecute you, delivering you up to the synagogues and prisons, bringing you before kings and governors for my name's sake"; 2 Thess. 2:3, 4, 7, 8,—"it will not be, except the falling away come first, and the man of sin be revealed, the son of perdition, he that opposeth and exalteth himself against all that is called God or that is worshipped; so that he sitteth in the temple of God, setting himself forth as God.... For the mystery of lawlessness doth already work: only there is one that restraineth now, until he be taken out of the way. And then shall be revealed the lawless one, whom the Lord Jesus shall slay with the breath of his mouth, and bring to nought by the manifestation of his coming."

Elliott, Horæ Apocalypticæ, 1:65, holds that "Antichrist means another Christ, a pro-Christ, a vice-Christ, a pretender to the name of Christ, and in that character, an usurper and adversary. The principle of Antichrist was already sown in the time of Paul. But a certain hindrance, i. e., the Roman Empire as then constituted, needed first to be removed out of the way, before room could be made for Antichrist's development." Antichrist, according to this view, is the hierarchical spirit, which found its final and most complete expression in the Papacy. Dante, Hell, 19:106-117, speaks of the Papacy, or rather the temporal power of the Popes, as Antichrist: "To you St. John referred, O shepherds vile, When she who sits on many waters, had Been seen with kings her person to defile"; see A. H. Strong, Philosophy and Religion, 507.

It has been objected that a simultaneous growth both of evil and of good is inconceivable, and that the progress of the divine kingdom implies a diminution in the power of the adversary. Only a slight reflection however convinces us that, as the population of the world is always increasing, evil men may increase in numbers, even though there is increase in the numbers of the good. But we must also consider that evil grows in intensity just in proportion to the light which good throws upon it. "Wherever God erects a house of prayer, The devil always builds a chapel there." Every revival of religion stirs up the forces of wickedness to opposition. As Christ's first advent occasioned an unusual outburst of demoniac malignity, so Christ's second advent will be resisted by a final desperate effort of the evil one to overcome the forces of good. The great awakening in New England under Jonathan Edwards caused on the one hand a most remarkable increase in the number of Baptist believers, but also on the other hand the rise of modern Unitarianism. The optimistic Presbyterian pastor at Auburn argued with the pessimistic chaplain of the State's Prison that the world was certainly growing better, because his congregation was increasing; whereupon the chaplain replied that his own congregation was increasing also.

(c) At the close of this millennial period, evil will again be permitted to exert its utmost power in a final conflict with righteousness. This spiritual struggle, moreover, will be accompanied and symbolized by political convulsions, and by fearful indications of desolation in the natural world.

Mat. 24:29, 30—"But immediately after the tribulation of those days the sun shall be darkened, and the moon shall not give her light, and the stars shall fall from heaven, and the powers of the heavens shall be shaken: and then shall appear the sign of the Son of man in heaven"; Luke 21:8-28—false prophets; wars and tumults; earthquakes; pestilences; persecutions; signs in the sun, moon, and stars; "And then shall they see the Son of man coming in a cloud with power and great glory. But when these things begin to come to pass, look up, and lift up your heads; because your redemption draweth nigh."

Interpretations of the book of Revelation are divided into three classes: (1) the Præterist (held by Grotius, Moses Stuart, and Warren), which regards the prophecy as mainly fulfilled in the age immediately succeeding the time of the apostles (666 = Neron Kaisar); (2) the Continuous (held by Isaac Newton, Vitringa, Bengel, Elliott, Kelly, and Cumming), which regards the whole as a continuous prophetical history, extending from the first age until the end of all things (666 = Lateinos); Hengstenberg and Alford hold substantially this view, though they regard the seven seals, trumpets, and vials as synchronological, each succeeding set going over the same ground and exhibiting it in some special aspect; (3) the Futurist (held by Maitland and Todd), which considers the book as describing events yet to occur, during the times immediately preceding and following the coming of the Lord.

Of all these interpretations, the most learned and exhaustive is that of Elliott, in his four volumes entitled Horæ Apocalypticæ. The basis of his interpretation is the "time and times and half a time" of Dan. 7:25, which according to the year-day theory means 1260 years—the year, according to ancient reckoning, containing 360 days, and the "time" being therefore 360 years [360 + (2 X 360) + 180 = 1260]. This phrase we find recurring with regard to the woman nourished in the wilderness (Rev. 12:14). The blasphemy of the beast for forty and two months (Rev. 13:5) seems to refer to the same period [42 X 30 = 1260, as before]. The two witnesses prophecy 1260 days (Rev. 11:3); and the woman's time in the wilderness is stated (Rev. 12:6) as 1260 days. This period of 1260 years is regarded by Elliott as the time of the temporal power of the Papacy.

There is a twofold terminus a quo, and correspondingly a twofold terminus ad quem. The first commencement is A. D. 531, when in the edict of Justinian the dragon of the Roman Empire gives its power to the beast of the Papacy, and resigns its throne to the rising Antichrist, giving opportunity for the rise of the ten horns as European kings (Rev. 13:1-3). The second commencement, adding the seventy-five supplementary years of Daniel 12:12 [1335 - 1260 = 75], is A. D. 606, when the Emperor Phocas acknowledges the primacy of Rome, and the ten horns, or kings, now diademed, submit to the Papacy (Rev. 17:12, 13). The first ending-point is A. D. 1791, when the French Revolution struck the first blow at the independence of the Pope [531 + 1260 = 1791]. The second ending-point is A. D. 1866, when the temporal power of the Pope was abolished at the unification of the kingdom of Italy [606 + 1260 = 1866]. Elliott regards the two-horned beast (Rev. 13:11) as representing the Papal Clergy, and the image of the beast (Rev. 13:14, 15) as representing the Papal Councils.

Unlike Hengstenberg and Alford, who consider the seals, trumpets, and vials as synchronological, Elliott makes the seven trumpets to be an unfolding of the seventh seal, and the seven vials to be an unfolding of the seventh trumpet. Like other advocates of the premillennial advent of Christ, Elliott regards the four chief signs of Christ's near approach as being: (1) the decay of the Turkish Empire (the drying up of the river Euphrates—Rev. 16:12); (2) the Pope's loss of temporal power (the destruction of Babylon—Rev. 17:19); (3) the conversion of the Jews and their return to their own land (Ez. 37; Rom. 11:12-15, 25-27—but on this last, see Meyer); (4) the pouring out of the Holy Spirit and the conversion of the Gentiles (the way of the kings of the East—Rev. 16:12; the fulness of the Gentiles—Rom. 11:25).

Elliott's whole scheme, however, is vitiated by the fact that he wrongly assumes the book of Revelation to have been written under Domitian (94 or 96), instead of under Nero (67 or 68). His terminus a quo is therefore incorrect, and his interpretation of chapters 5-9 is rendered very precarious. The year 1866, moreover, should have been the time of the end, and so the terminus ad quem seems to be clearly misunderstood—unless indeed the seventy- five supplementary years of Daniel are to be added to 1866. We regard the failure of this most ingenious scheme of Apocalyptic interpretation as a practical demonstration that a clear understanding of the meaning of prophecy is, before the event, impossible, and we are confirmed in this view by the utterly untenable nature of the theory of the millennium which is commonly held by so-called Second Adventists, a theory which we now proceed to examine.

A long preparation may be followed by a sudden consummation. Drilling the rock for the blast is a slow process; firing the charge takes but a moment. The woodwork of the Windsor Hotel in New York was in a charred and superheated state before the electric wires that threaded it wore out their insulation,—then a slight increase of voltage turned heat into flame. The Outlook, March 30, 1895—"An evolutionary conception of the Second Coming, as a progressive manifestation of the spiritual power and glory of Christ, may issue in a dénouement as unique as the first advent was which closed the preparatory ages."

Joseph Cook, on A. J. Gordon: "There is a wide distinction between the flash-light theory and the burning-glass theory of missions. The latter was Dr. Gordon's view. When a burning-glass is held over inflammable material, the concentrated rays of the sun rapidly produce in it discoloration, smoke, and sparks. At a certain instant, after the sparks have been sufficiently diffused, the whole material suddenly bursts into flame. There is then no longer any need of the burning-glass, for fire has itself fallen from on high and is able to do its own work. So the world is to be regarded as inflammable material to be set on fire from on high. Our Lord's life on earth is a burning-glass, concentrating rays of light and heat upon the souls of men. When the heating has gone on far enough, and the sparks of incipient conflagration have been sufficiently diffused, suddenly spiritual flame will burst up everywhere and will fill the earth. This is the second advent of him who kindled humanity to new life by his first advent. As I understand the premillenarian view of history, the date when the sparks shall kindle into flame is not known, but it is known that the duty of the church is to spread the sparks and to expect at any instant, after their wide diffusion, the victorious descent of millennial flame, that is, the beginning of our Lord's personal and visible reign over the whole earth." See article on Millenarianism, by G. P. Fisher, in McClintock and Strong's Cyclopædia; also by Semisch, in Schaff-Herzog, Cyclopædia; cf. Schaff, History of the Christian Church, 1:840.

4. Relation of Christ's second coming to the millennium.

The Scripture foretells a period, called in the language of prophecy "a thousand years," when Satan shall be restrained and the saints shall reign with Christ on the earth. A comparison of the passages bearing on this subject leads us to the conclusion that this millennial blessedness and dominion is prior to the second advent. One passage only seems at first sight to teach the contrary, viz.: Rev. 20:4-10. But this supports the theory of a premillennial advent only when the passage is interpreted with the barest literalness. A better view of its meaning will be gained by considering:

(a) That it constitutes a part, and confessedly an obscure part, of one of the most figurative books of Scripture, and therefore ought to be interpreted by the plainer statements of the other Scriptures.

We quote here the passage alluded to: Rev. 20:4-10—"And I saw thrones, and they sat upon them, and judgment was given unto them: and I saw the souls of them that had been beheaded for the testimony of Jesus, and for the word of God, and such as worshipped not the beast, neither his image, and received not the mark upon their forehead and upon their hand; and they lived, and reigned with Christ a thousand years. The rest of the dead lived not until the thousand years should be finished. This is the first resurrection. Blessed and holy is he that hath part in the first resurrection: over these the second death hath no power; but they shall be priests of God and of Christ, and shall reign with him a thousand years."

Emerson and Parker met a Second Adventist who warned them that the end of the world was near. Parker replied: "My friend, that does not concern me; I live in Boston." Emerson said: "Well, I think I can get along without it." A similarly cheerful view is taken by Denney, Studies in Theology, 232—"Christ certainly comes, according to the picture in Revelation, before the millennium; but the question of importance is, whether the conception of the millennium itself, related as it is to Ezekiel, is essential to faith. I cannot think that it is. The religious content of the passages—what they offer for faith to grasp—is, I should say, simply this: that until the end the conflict between the kingdom of God and the kingdom of the world must go on; that as the end approaches it becomes ever more intense, progress in humanity not being a progress in goodness merely or in badness only, but in the antagonism between the two; and that the necessity for conflict is sure to emerge even after the kingdom of God has won its greatest triumphs. I frankly confess that to seek more than this in such Scriptural indications seems to me trifling."

(b) That the other Scriptures contain nothing with regard to a resurrection of the righteous which is widely separated in time from that of the wicked, but rather declare distinctly that the second coming of Christ is immediately connected both with the resurrection of the just and the unjust and with the general judgment.

Mat. 16:27—"For the Son of man shall come in the glory of his Father with his angels; and then shall he render unto every man according to his deeds"; 25:31-33—"But when the Son of man shall come in his glory, and all the angels with him, then shall he sit on the throne of his glory: and before him shall be gathered all the nations: and he shall separate them one from another, as the shepherd separateth the sheep from the goats"; John 5:28, 29—"Marvel not at this: for the hour cometh, in which all that are in the tombs shall hear his voice, and shall some forth; they that have done good, unto the resurrection of life; and they that have done evil, unto the resurrection of judgment"; 2 Cor. 5:10—"For we must all be made manifest before the judgment seat of Christ; that each one may receive the things done in the body, according to what he hath done, whether it be good or bad"; 2 Thess. 1:6-10—"if so be that it is a righteous thing with God to recompense affliction to them that afflict you, and to you that are afflicted rest with us, at the revelation of the Lord Jesus from heaven with the angels of his power in flaming fire, rendering vengeance to them that know not God, and to them that obey not the gospel of our Lord Jesus: who shall suffer punishment, even eternal destruction from the face of the Lord and from the glory of his might, when he shall come to be glorified in his saints, and to be marvelled at in all them that believed."

2 Pet. 3:7, 10—"the day of judgment and destruction of ungodly men.... But the day of the Lord will come as a thief; in the which the heavens shall pass away with a great noise, and the elements shall be dissolved with fervent heat, and the earth and the works that are therein shall be burned up"; Rev. 20:11-15—"And I saw a great white throne, and him that sat upon it, from whose face the earth and the heaven fled away; and there was found no place for them. And I saw the dead, the great and the small, standing before the throne; and books were opened: and another book was opened, which is the book of life: and the dead were judged out of the things that were written in the books, according to their works. And the sea gave up the dead that were in it; and death and Hades gave up the dead that were in them: and they were judged every man according to their works. And death and Hades were cast into the lake

of fire. This is the second death, even the lake of fire. And if any was not found written in the book of life, he was cast into the lake of fire."

Here is abundant evidence that there is no interval of a thousand years between the second coming of Christ and the resurrection, general judgment, and end of all things. All these events come together. The only answer of the premillennialists to this objection to their theory is, that the day of judgment and the millennium may be contemporaneous,—in other words, the day of judgment may be a thousand years long. Elliott holds to a conflagration, partial at the beginning of this period, complete at its close,—Peter's prophecy treating the two conflagrations as one, while the book of Revelation separates them; so a nearer view resolves binary stars into two. But we reply that, if the judgment occupies the whole period of a thousand years, then the coming of Christ, the resurrection, and the final conflagration should all be a thousand years also. It is indeed possible that, in this case, as Peter says in connection with his prophecy of judgment, "one day is with the Lord as a thousand years, and a thousand years as one day" (2 Pet. 3:8). But if we make the word "day" so indefinite in connection with the judgment, why should we regard it as so definite, when we come to interpret the 1260 days?

(c) That the literal interpretation of the passage—holding, as it does, to a resurrection of bodies of flesh and blood, and to a reign of the risen saints in the flesh, and in the world as at present constituted—is inconsistent with other Scriptural declarations with regard to the spiritual nature of the resurrection-body and of the coming reign of Christ.

1 Cor. 15:44, 50—"it is sown a natural body; it is raised a spiritual body.... Now this I say, brethren, that flesh and blood cannot inherit the kingdom of God; neither doth corruption inherit incorruption." These passages are inconsistent with the view that the resurrection is a physical resurrection at the beginning of the thousand years—a resurrection to be followed by a second life of the saints in bodies of flesh and blood. They are not, however, inconsistent with the true view, soon to be mentioned, that "the first resurrection" is simply the raising of the church to a new life and zeal. Westcott, Bib. Com. on John 14:18, 19—"I will not leave you desolate [marg.: 'orphans']: I come unto you. Yet a little while, and the world beholdeth me no more; but ye behold me":—"The words exclude the error of those who suppose that Christ will 'come' under the same conditions of earthly existence as those to which he submitted at his first coming." See Hovey, Bib. Eschatology, 66-78.

(d) That the literal interpretation is generally and naturally connected with the expectation of a gradual and necessary decline of Christ's kingdom upon earth, until Christ comes to bind Satan and to introduce the millennium. This view not only contradicts such passages as Dan. 2:34, 35, and Mat. 13:31, 32, but it begets a passive and hopeless endurance of evil, whereas the Scriptures enjoin a constant and aggressive warfare against it, upon the very ground that God's power shall assure to the church a gradual but constant progress in the face of it, even to the time of the end.

Dan. 2:34, 35—"Thou sawest till that a stone was cut out without hands, which smote the image upon its feet that were of iron and clay, and brake them in pieces. Then was the iron, the clay, the brass, the silver, and the gold, broken in pieces together, and became like the chaff of the summer threshing-floors; and the wind carried them away, so that no place was found for them: and the stone that smote the image became a great mountain, and filled the whole earth"; Mat. 13:31, 32—"The kingdom of heaven is like unto a grain of mustard seed, which a man took, and sowed in his field: which indeed is less than all seeds; but when it is grown, it is greater than the herbs, and becometh a tree, so that the birds of the heaven come and lodge in the branches thereof." In both these figures there is no sign of cessation or of backward movement, but rather every indication of continuous advance to complete victory and dominion. The premillennial theory supposes that for the principle of development under the dispensation of the Holy Spirit, God will substitute a reign of mere power and violence. J. B. Thomas: "The kingdom of heaven is like a grain of mustard seed, not like a can of nitro-glycerine." Leighton Williams: "The kingdom of God is to be realized on earth, not by a cataclysm, apart from effort and will, but through the universal dissemination of the gospel all but lost to the world." E. G. Robinson: "Second Adventism stultifies the system and scheme of Christianity." Dr. A. J. Gordon could not deny that the early disciples were mistaken in expecting the end of the world in their day. So we may be. Scripture does not declare that the end should come in the lifetime of the apostles, and no definite date is set. "After a long time" (Mat. 25:19) and "the falling away come first" (2 Thess. 2:3) are expressions which postpone indefinitely. Yet a just view of Christ's coming as ever possible in the immediate future may make us as faithful as were the original disciples.

The theory also divests Christ of all kingly power until the millennium, or, rather, maintains that the kingdom has not yet been given to him; see Elliott, Horæ Apocalypticæ, 1:94—where Luke 19:12—"A certain nobleman went into a far country, to receive for himself a kingdom, and to return"—is interpreted as follows: "Subordinate kings went to Rome to receive the investiture to their kingdoms from the Roman Emperor, and then returned to occupy them and reign. So Christ received from his Father, after his ascension, the investiture to his kingdom; but with the intention not to occupy it, till his return at his second coming. In token of this investiture he takes his seat as the Lamb on the divine throne" (Rev. 5:6-8). But this interpretation contradicts Mat. 28:18, 20—"All authority hath been given unto me in heaven and on earth ... lo, I am with you always, even unto the end of the world." See Presb. Rev., 1882:228. On the effects of the premillennial view in weakening Christian endeavor, see J. H. Seelye, Christian Missions, 94-127; per contra, see A. J. Gordon, in Independent, Feb. 1886.

(e) We may therefore best interpret Rev. 20:4-10 as teaching in highly figurative language, not a preliminary resurrection of the body, in the case of departed saints, but a period in the later days of the church militant when, under special influence of the Holy Ghost, the spirit of the martyrs shall appear again, true religion be greatly quickened and revived, and the members of Christ's churches become so conscious of their strength in Christ that they shall, to an extent unknown before, triumph over the powers of evil both within and without. So the spirit of Elijah appeared again in John the Baptist (Mal. 4:5; cf. Mat. 11:13, 14). The fact that only the spirit of sacrifice and faith is to be revived is figuratively indicated in the phrase: "The rest of the dead lived not again until the thousand years should be finished" = the spirit of persecution and unbelief shall be, as it were, laid to sleep. Since resurrection, like the coming of Christ and the judgment, is twofold, first, spiritual (the raising of the soul to spiritual life), and secondly, physical (the raising of the body from the grave), the words in Rev. 20:5—"this is the first resurrection"—seem intended distinctly to preclude the literal interpretation we are combating. In short, we hold that Rev. 20:4-10 does not describe the events commonly called the second advent and resurrection, but rather describes great spiritual changes in the later history of the church, which are typical of, and preliminary to, the second advent and resurrection, and therefore, after the prophetic method, are foretold in language literally applicable only to those final events themselves (cf. Ez. 37:1-14; Luke 15:32).

Mal. 4:5—"Behold, I will send you Elijah the prophet before the great and terrible day of Jehovah come"; cf. Mat. 11:13, 14—"For all the prophets and the law prophesied until John. And if ye are willing to receive it, this is Elijah, that is to come"; Ez. 37:1-14—the vision of the valley of dry bones = either the political or the religious resuscitation of the Jews; Luke 15:32—"this thy brother was dead, and is alive again"—of the prodigal son. It will help us in our interpretation of Rev. 20:4-10 to notice that death, judgment, the coming of Christ, and the resurrection, are all of two kinds, the first spiritual, and the second literal:

(1) First, a spiritual death (Eph. 2:1—"dead through your trespasses and sins"); and secondly, a physical and literal death, whose culmination is found in the second death (Rev. 20:14—"And death and Hades were cast into the lake of fire. This is the second death, even the lake of fire").

(2) First, a spiritual judgment (Is. 26:9—"when thy judgments are in the earth"; John 12:31—"Now is the judgment of this world: now shall the prince of this world be cast out"; 3:18—"he that believeth not hath been judged already"); and secondly, an outward and literal judgment (Acts 17:31—"hath appointed a day in which he will judge the world in righteousness by the man whom he hath ordained").

(3) First, the spiritual and invisible coming of Christ (Mat. 16:28—"shall in no wise taste of death, till they see the Son of man coming in his kingdom"—at the destruction of Jerusalem; John 14:16, 18—"another Comforter ... I come unto you"—at Pentecost; 14:3—"And if I go and prepare a place for you, I come again, and will receive you unto myself"—at death); and secondly, a visible literal coming (Mat. 25:31—"the Son of man shall come in his glory, and all the angels with him").

(4) First, a spiritual resurrection (John 5:25—"The hour cometh, and now is, when the dead shall hear the voice of the Son of God; and they that hear shall live"); and secondly, a physical and literal resurrection (John 5:28, 29—"the hour cometh, in which all that are in the tombs shall hear his voice, and shall come forth; they that have done good, unto the resurrection of life; and they that have done evil, unto the resurrection of judgment"). The spiritual resurrection foreshadows the bodily resurrection.

This twofoldness of each of the four terms, death, judgment, coming of Christ, resurrection, is so obvious a teaching of Scripture, that the apostle's remark in Rev. 20:5—"This is the first resurrection"—seems distinctly intended to warn the reader against drawing the premillenarian inference, and to make clear the fact that the resurrection spoken of is the first or spiritual resurrection,—an interpretation which is made indubitable by his proceeding, further on, to describe the outward and literal resurrection in verse 13—"And the sea gave up the dead that were in it: and death and Hades gave up the dead that were in them." This physical resurrection takes place when "the thousand years" are "finished" (verse 5).

This interpretation suggests a possible way of reconciling the premillenarian and postmillenarian theories, without sacrificing any of the truth in either of them. Christ may come again, at the beginning of the millennium, in a spiritual way, and his saints may reign with him spiritually, in the wonderful advances of his kingdom; while the visible, literal coming may take place at the end of the thousand years. Dorner's view is postmillennial, in this sense, that the visible coming of Christ will be after the thousand years. Hengstenberg curiously regards the millennium as having begun in the Middle Ages (800-1800 A. D.). This strange view of an able interpreter, as well as the extraordinary diversity of explanations given by others, convinces us that no exegete has yet found the key to the mysteries of the Apocalypse. Until we know whether the preaching of the gospel in the whole world (Mat. 24:14) is to be a preaching to nations as a whole, or to each individual in each nation, we cannot determine whether the millennium has already begun, or whether it is yet far in the future.

The millennium then is to be the culmination of the work of the Holy Spirit, a universal revival of religion, a nation born in a day, the kings of the earth bringing their glory and honor into the city of God. A. J. Gordon, Ministry of the Spirit, 211—"After the present elective work of the Spirit has been completed, there will come a time of universal blessing, when the Spirit shall literally be poured out upon all flesh, when that which is perfect shall come and that which is in part shall be done away.... The early rain of the Spirit was at Pentecost; the latter rain will be at the Parousia."

A. H. Strong, Sermon before the Baptist World Congress, London, July 12, 1905—"Let us expect the speedy spiritual coming of the Lord. I believe in an ultimate literal and visible coming of Christ in the clouds of heaven to raise the dead, to summon all men to the judgment, and to wind up the present dispensation. But I believe that this visible and literal coming of Christ must be preceded, and prepared for, by his invisible and spiritual coming and by a resurrection of faith and love in the hearts of his people. 'This is the first resurrection' (Rev. 20:5). I read in Scripture of a spiritual second coming that precedes the literal, an inward revelation of Christ to his people, a restraining of the powers of darkness, a mighty augmentation of the forces of righteousness, a turning to the Lord of men and nations, such as the world has not yet seen. I believe in a long reign of Christ on earth, in which his saints shall in spirit be caught up with him, and shall sit with him upon his throne, even though this muddy vesture of decay compasses them about, and the time of their complete glorification has not yet come. Let us hasten the coming of the day of God by our faith and prayer. 'When the Son of man cometh, shall he find faith on the earth?' (Luke 18:8). Let him find faith, at least in us. Our faith can certainly secure the coming of the Lord into our hearts. Let us expect that Christ will be revealed in us, as of old he was revealed in the Apostle Paul."

Our own interpretation of Rev. 20:1-10, was first given, for substance, by Whitby. He was followed by Vitringa and Faber. For a fuller elaboration of it, see Brown, Second Advent, 206-259; Hodge, Outlines of Theology, 447-453. For the postmillennial view generally, see Kendrick, in Bap. Quar., Jan. 1870; New Englander, 1874:356; 1879:47-49, 114-147; Pepper, in Bap. Rev., 1880:15; Princeton Review, March, 1879:415-434; Presb. Rev., 1883:221-252; Bib. Sac., 15:381, 625; 17:111; Harris, Kingdom of Christ, 220-237; Waldegrave, Bampton Lectures for 1854, on the Millennium; Neander, Planting and Training, 526, 527; Cowles, Dissertation on Premillennial Advent, in Com. on Jeremiah and Ezekiel; Weiss, Premillennial Advent; Crosby, Second Advent; Fairbairn on Prophecy, 432-480; Woods, Works, 3:267; Abp. Whately, Essays on Future State. For the premillennial view, see Elliott, Horæ Apocalypticæ, 4:140-196; William Kelly, Advent of Christ Premillennial; Taylor, Voice of the Church on the Coming and Kingdom of the Redeemer; Litch, Christ Yet to Come.

IV. The Resurrection

While the Scriptures describe the impartation of new life to the soul in regeneration as a spiritual resurrection, they also declare that, at the second coming of Christ, there shall be a resurrection of the body, and a reunion of the body to the soul from which, during the intermediate state, it has been separated. Both the just and the unjust shall have part in the resurrection. To the just, it shall be a resurrection unto life; and the body shall be a body like Christ's—a body fitted for the uses of the sanctified spirit. To the unjust, it shall be a resurrection unto condemnation; and analogy would seem to indicate that, here also, the outward form will fitly represent the inward state of the soul—being corrupt and deformed as is the soul which inhabits it. Those who are living at Christ's coming shall receive spiritual bodies without passing through death. As the body after corruption and dissolution, so the outward world after destruction by fire, shall be rehabilitated and fitted for the abode of the saints.

Passages describing a spiritual resurrection are: John 5:24-27, especially 25—"The hour cometh, and now is, when the dead shall hear the voice of the Son of God; and they that hear shall live"; Rom. 6:4, 5—"as Christ was raised from the dead through the glory of the Father, so we also might walk in newness of life. For if we have become united with him by the likeness of his death, we shall be also by the likeness of his resurrection"; Eph. 2:1, 5, 6—"And you did he make alive, when ye were dead through your trespasses and sins ... even when we were dead through our trespasses, made us alive together with Christ ... and raised us up with him, and made us to sit with him in the heavenly places, in Christ Jesus"; 5:14—"Awake, thou that sleepest, and arise from the dead, and Christ shall shine upon thee." Phil. 3:10—"that I may know him, and the power of his resurrection"; Col. 2:12, 13—"having been buried with him in baptism, wherein ye were also raised with him through faith in the working of God, who raised him from the dead. And you, being dead through your trespasses and the uncircumcision of your flesh, you, I say, did he make alive together with him"; cf. Is. 26:19—"Thy dead shall live; my dead bodies shall arise. Awake and sing, ye that dwell in the dust; for thy dew is as the dew of herbs, and the earth shall cast forth the dead"; Ez. 37:1-14—the valley of dry bones: "I will open your graves, and cause you to come up out of your graves, O my people; and I will bring you into the land of Israel."

Passages describing a literal and physical resurrection are: Job 14:12-15—"So man lieth down and riseth not: Till the heavens be no more, they shall not awake, Nor be raised out of their sleep. Oh that thou wouldest hide me in Sheol, That thou wouldest keep me secret, until thy wrath be past, That thou wouldest appoint me a set time, and remember me! If a man die, shall he live again? All the days of my warfare would I wait, Till my release should come. Thou wouldest call, and I would answer thee: Thou wouldest have a desire to the work of thy hands"; John 5:28, 29—"the hour cometh, in which all that are in the tombs shall hear his voice, and shalt come forth: they that have done good, unto the resurrection of life; and they that have done evil, unto the resurrection of judgment."

Acts 24:15—"having hope toward God ... that there shall be a resurrection both of the just and unjust"; 1 Cor. 15:13, 17, 22, 42, 51, 52—"if there is no resurrection of the dead, neither hath Christ been raised ... and if Christ hath not been raised, your faith is vain; ye are yet in your sins ... as in Adam all die, so also in Christ shall all be made alive ... it is sown in corruption: it is raised in incorruption.... We shall not all sleep, but we shall all be changed, in a moment, in the twinkling of an eye, at the last trump: for the trumpet shall sound, and the dead shall be raised incorruptible"; Phil. 3:21—"who shall fashion anew the body of our humiliation, that it may be conformed to the body of his glory, according to the working whereby he is able even to subject all things unto himself"; 1 Thess. 4:14-16—"For if we believe that Jesus died and rose again, even so them also that are fallen asleep in Jesus will God bring with him. For this we say unto you by the word of the Lord, that we that are alive, that are left unto the coming of the Lord, shall in no wise precede them that are fallen asleep. For the Lord himself shall descend from heaven, with a shout, with the voice of the archangel, and with the trump of God: and the dead in Christ shall rise first."

2 Pet. 3:7, 10, 13—"the heavens that now are, and the earth, by the same word have been stored up for fire, being reserved against the day of judgment and destruction of ungodly men.... But the day of the Lord will come as a thief in the night, which the heavens shall pass away with a great noise, and the elements shall be dissolved with fervent heat, and the earth and the works that are therein shall be burned up.... But, according to his promise, we look for new heavens and a new earth, wherein dwelleth righteousness"; Rev. 20:13—"And the sea gave up the dead that were in it; and death and Hades gave up the dead that were in them"; 21:1, 5—"And I saw a new heaven and a new earth: for the first heaven and the first earth are passed away; and the sea is no more.... And he that sitteth on the throne said, Behold, I make all things new."

The smooth face of death with the lost youth restored, and the pure white glow of the marble statue with all passion gone and the lofty and heroic only visible, are indications of what is to be. Art, in its representations alike of the human form, and of an ideal earth and society in landscape and poem, is prophetic of the future,—it suggests the glorious possibilities of the resurrection-morning. Nicoll, Life of Christ: "The river runs through the lake and pursues its way beyond. So the life of faith passes through death and is only purified thereby. As to the body, all that is worth saving will be saved. Other resurrections [such as that of Lazarus] were resurrections to the old conditions of earthly life; the resurrection of Christ was the revelation of new life."

Stevens, Pauline Theology, 357 note—"If we could assume with confidence that the report of Paul's speech before Felix accurately reproduced his language in detail, the apostle's belief in a 'resurrection both of the just and of the unjust' (Acts 24:15) would be securely established: but, in view of the silence of his epistles, this assumption becomes a precarious one. Paul speaks afterwards of 'attaining to the resurrection from the dead' (Phil. 3:11), as if this did not belong to all." The scepticism of Prof. Stevens seems to us entirely needless and unjustified. It is the blessed resurrection to which Paul would "attain," and which he has in mind in Philippians, as in 1 Cor. 15—a fact perfectly consistent with a resurrection of the wicked to "shame and everlasting contempt" (Daniel 12:2; John 5:29).

A. J. Gordon, Ministry of the Spirit, 205, 206—"The rapture of the saints (1 Thess. 4:17) is the earthly Christ rising to meet the heavenly Christ; the elect church, gathered in the Spirit and named ὁ Χριστός (1 Cor. 12:12), taken up to be united in glory with Christ the head of the church, 'himself the Savior of the body' (Eph. 5:23). It is not by acting upon the body of Christ from without, but by energizing it from within, that the Holy Ghost will effect its glorification. In a word, the Comforter, who on the day of Pentecost came down to form a body out of flesh, will at the Parousia return to heaven in that body, having fashioned it like unto the body of Christ (Phil. 3:31).... Here then is where the lines of Christ's ministry terminate,—in sanctification, the perfection of the spirit's holiness; and in resurrection, the perfection of the body's health."

E. G. Robinson: "Personality is the indestructible principle—not intelligence, else deny that infants have souls. Personality takes to itself a material organization. It is a divinely empowered second cause. This refutes materialism and annihilationism. No one pretends that the individual elements of the body will be raised. The individuality only, the personal identity, will be preserved. The soul is the organific power. Medical practice teaches that merely animal life is a mechanical process, but this is used by a personal power. Materialism, on the contrary, would make the soul the product of the body.

Every man, in becoming a Christian, begins the process of resurrection. We do not know but resurrection begins at the moment of dissolution, yet we do not know that it does. But if Christ arose with identically the same body unchanged, how can his resurrection be a type of ours? Answer: The nature of Christ's resurrection body is an open question."

Upon the subject of the resurrection, our positive information is derived wholly from the word of God. Further discussion of it may be most naturally arranged in a series of answers to objections. The objections commonly urged against the doctrine, as above propounded, may be reduced to two:

1. The exegetical objection.

The exegetical objection,—that it rests upon a literalizing of metaphorical language, and has no sufficient support in Scripture. To this we answer:

(a) That, though the phrase "resurrection of the body" does not occur in the New Testament, the passages which describe the event indicate a physical, as distinguished from a spiritual, change (John 5:28, 29; Phil. 3:21; 1 Thess. 4:13-17). The phrase "spiritual body" (1 Cor. 15:44) is a contradiction in terms, if it be understood as signifying "a body which is simple spirit." It can only be interpreted as meaning a material organism, perfectly adapted to be the outward expression and vehicle of the purified soul. The purely spiritual interpretation is, moreover, expressly excluded by the apostolic denial that "the resurrection is past already" (2 Tim. 2:18), and by the fact that there is a resurrection of the unjust, as well as of the just (Acts 24:15).

John 5:28, 29—"all that are in the tombs shall hear his voice, and shall come forth"; Phil. 3:21—"who shall fashion anew the body of our humiliation"; 1 Thess. 4:16, 17—"For the Lord himself shall descend from heaven, with a shout, with the voice of the archangel, and with the trump of God; and the dead in Christ shall rise first"; 1 Cor. 15:44—"it is sown a natural [marg.: 'psychical'] body; it is raised a spiritual body"; 2 Tim. 2:17, 18—"Hymenæus and Philetus; men who concerning the truth have erred, saying that the resurrection is past already, and overthrow the faith of some"; Acts 24:15—"Having hope toward God ... that there shall be a resurrection both of the just and the unjust."

In 1 Cor. 15:44, the word ψυχικόν, translated "natural" or "psychical," is derived from the Greek word ψυχή, soul, just as the word πνευματικόν, translated "spiritual," is derived from the Greek word πνεῦμα, spirit. And as Paul could not mean to say that this earthly body is composed of soul, neither does he say that the resurrection body is composed of spirit. In other words, these adjectives "psychical" and "spiritual" do not define the material of the respective bodies, but describe those bodies in their relations and adaptations, in their powers and uses. The present body is adapted and designed for the use of the soul; the resurrection body will be adapted and designed for the use of the spirit.

2 Tim. 2:18—"saying that the resurrection is past already" = undue contempt for the body came to regard the resurrection as a purely spiritual thing (Ellicott). Dr. A. J. Gordon said that the "spiritual body" means "the body spiritualized." E. H. Johnson: "The phrase 'spiritual body' describes not so much the nature of the body itself, as its relations to the spirit." Savage, Life after Death, 80—"Resurrection does not mean the raising up of the body, and it does not mean the mere rising of the soul in the moment of death, but a rising again from the prison house of the dead, after going down at the moment of death." D. R. Goodwin, Journ. Soc. Bib. Exegesis, 1881:84—"The spiritual body is body, and not spirit, and therefore must come under the definition of body. If it were to be mere spirit, then every man in the future state would have two spirits—the spirit that he has here and another spirit received at the resurrection."

(b) That the redemption of Christ is declared to include the body as well as the soul (Rom. 8:23; 1 Cor. 6:13-20). The indwelling of the Holy Spirit has put such honor upon the frail mortal tenement which he has made his temple, that God would not permit even this wholly to perish (Rom. 8:11—διὰ τὸ ἐνοικοῦν αὐτοῦ πνεῦμα ἐν ὑμῖν, i. e., because of his indwelling Spirit, God will raise up the mortal body). It is this belief which forms the basis of Christian care for the dead (Phil. 3:21; cf. Mat. 22:32).

Rom. 8:23—"waiting for our adoption, to wit, the redemption of our body"; 1 Cor. 6:13-20—"Meats for the belly and the belly for meats: but God shall bring to nought both it and them. But the body is not for fornication, but for the Lord; and the Lord for the body: and God both raised the Lord, and will raise up us through his power.... But he that is joined unto the Lord is one spirit.... Or know ye not that your body is a temple of the Holy Spirit which is in you, which ye have from God?... glorify God therefore in your body"; Rom. 8:11—"But if the Spirit of him that raised up Jesus from the dead dwelleth in you, he that raised up Christ Jesus from the dead shall give life also to your mortal bodies through his Spirit that dwelleth in you"—here the Revised Version follows Tisch., 8th ed., and Westcott and Hort's reading of διὰ τοῦ ἐνοικοῦντος αὐτοῦ πνεύματος. Tregelles, Tisch., 7th ed., and Meyer, have διὰ τὸ ἐνοικοῦν αὐτοῦ πνεῦμα, and this reading we regard as, on the whole, the best supported. Phil. 3:21—"shall fashion anew the body of our humiliation."

Dr. R. D. Hitchcock, in South Church Lectures, 338, says that "there is no Scripture declaration of the resurrection of the flesh, nor even of the resurrection of the body." While this is literally true, it conveys a false idea. The passages just cited foretell a quickening of our mortal bodies, a raising of them up, a changing of them into the likeness of Christ's body. Dorner, Eschatology: "The New Testament is not contented with a bodiless immortality. It is opposed to a naked spiritualism, and accords completely with a deeper philosophy which discerns in the body, not merely the sheath or garment of the soul, but a side of the person belonging to his full idea, his mirror and organ, of the greatest importance for his activity and history."

Christ's proof of the resurrection in Mat. 22:32—"God is not the God of the dead, but of the living"—has for its basis this very assumption that soul and body belong normally together, and that, since they are temporally separated in the case of the saints who live with God, Abraham, Isaac, and Jacob shall rise again. The idealistic philosophy of thirty years ago led to a contempt of the body; the recent materialism has done at least this service, that it has reasserted the claims of the body to be a proper part of man.

(c) That the nature of Christ's resurrection, as literal and physical, determines the nature of the resurrection in the case of believers (Luke 24:36; John 20:27). As, in the case of Christ, the same body that was laid in the tomb was raised again, although possessed of new and surprising powers, so the Scriptures intimate, not simply that the saints shall have bodies, but that these bodies shall be in some proper sense an outgrowth or transformation of the very bodies that slept in the dust (Dan. 12:2; 1 Cor. 15:53, 54). The denial of the resurrection of the body, in the case of believers, leads naturally to a denial of the reality of Christ's resurrection (1 Cor. 15:13).

Luke 24:39—"See my hands and my feet, that it is I myself: handle me, and see; for a spirit hath not flesh and bones, as ye behold me having"; John 20:27—"Then saith he to Thomas, Reach hither thy finger, and see my hands; and reach hither thy hand, and put it into my side: and be not faithless, but believing"; Dan. 12:2—"And many of them that sleep in the dust of the earth shall awake, some to everlasting life, and some to shame and everlasting contempt"; 1 Cor. 15:53, 54—"For this corruptible must put on incorruption, and this mortal must put on immortality. But when this corruption shall have put on incorruption, and this mortal shall have put on immortality, then shall come to pass the saying that is written, Death is swallowed up in victory"; 13—"But if there is no resurrection of the dead, neither hath Christ been raised."

Sadducean materialism and Gnostic dualism, which last held matter to be evil, both denied the resurrection. Paul shows that to deny it is to deny that Christ rose; since, if it were impossible in the case of his followers, it must have been impossible in his own case. As believers, we are vitally connected with him; and his resurrection could not have taken place without drawing in its train the resurrection of all of us. Having denied that Christ rose, where is the proof that he is not still under the bond and curse of death? Surely then our preaching is vain. Paul's epistle to the Corinthians was written before the Gospels; and is therefore, as Hanna says, the earliest written account of the resurrection. Christ's transfiguration was a prophecy of his resurrection.

S. S. Times, March 22, 1902:161—"The resurrection of Jesus was not a mere rising again, like that of Lazarus and the son of the widow of Nain. He came forth from the tomb so changed that he was not at once or easily recognized, and was possessed of such new and surprising powers that he seemed to be pure spirit, no longer subject to the conditions of his natural body. So he was the 'first-fruits' of the resurrection-harvest (1 Cor. 15:20). Our resurrection, in like manner, is to involve a change from a corruptible body to an incorruptible, from a psychical to a spiritual."

(d) That the accompanying events, as the second coming and the judgment, since they are themselves literal, imply that the resurrection is also literal.

Rom. 8:19-23—"For the earnest expectation of the creation waiteth for the revealing of the sons of God ... the whole creation groaneth and travaileth in pain together until now ... even we ourselves groan within ourselves, waiting for our adoption, to wit, the redemption of our body"—here man's body is regarded as a part of nature, or the "creation," and as partaking in Christ of its deliverance from the curse; Rev. 21:4, 5—"he shall wipe away every tear from their eyes; and death shall be no more.... And he that sitteth on the throne said, Behold, I make all things new"—a declaration applicable to the body, the seat of pain and the avenue of temptation, as well as to outward nature. See Hanna, The Resurrection, 28; Fuller, Works, 3:291; Boston, Fourfold State, in Works, 8:271-289. On Olshausen's view of immortality as inseparable from body, see Aids to the Study of German Theology, 63. On resurrection of the flesh, see Jahrbuch f. d. Theol., 1:289-317.

2. The scientific object.

This is threefold:

(a) That a resurrection of the particles which compose the body at death is impossible, since they enter into new combinations, and not unfrequently become parts of other bodies which the doctrine holds to be raised at the same time.

We reply that the Scripture not only does not compel us to hold, but it distinctly denies, that all the particles which exist in the body at death are present in the resurrection-body (1 Cor. 15:37—οὐ τὸ σῶμα τὸ γενησόμενον; 50). The Scripture seems only to indicate a certain physical connection between the new and the old, although the nature of this connection is not revealed. So long as the physical connection is maintained, it is not necessary to suppose that even a germ or particle that belonged to the old body exists in the new.

1 Cor. 15:37, 38—"that which thou sowest, thou sowest not the body that shall be, but a bare grain, it may chance of wheat, or of some other kind; but God giveth it a body even as it pleased him, and to each seed a body of its own." Jerome tells us that the risen saints "habent dentes, ventrem, genitalia, et tamen nec cibis nec uxoribus indigent." This view of the resurrection is exposed to the objection mentioned above. Pollok's Course of Time represented the day of resurrection as a day on which the limbs that had been torn asunder on earth hurtled through the air to join one another once more. The amputated arm that has been buried in China must traverse thousands of miles to meet the body of its former owner, as it rose from the place of its burial in England.

There are serious difficulties attending this view. The bodies of the dead fertilized the field of Waterloo. The wheat grown there has been ground and made into bread, and eaten by thousands of living men. Particles of one human body have become incorporated with the bodies of many others. "The Avon to the Severn runs, The Severn to the sea, And Wycliffe's dust shall spread abroad, Wide as the waters be." Through the clouds and the rain, particles of Wycliffe's body may have entered into the water which other men have drunk from their wells and fountains. There is a propagation of disease by contagion, or the transmission of infinitesimal germs from one body to another, sometimes by infection of the living from contact with the body of a friend just dead. In these various ways, the same particle might, in the course of history, enter into the constitution of a hundred living men. How can this one particle, at the resurrection, be in a hundred places at the same time? "Like the woman who had seven husbands, the same matter may belong in succession to many bodies, for 'they all had it' " (Smyth). The cannibal and his victim cannot both possess the same body at the resurrection. The Providence Journal had an article entitled: "Who ate Roger Williams?" When his remains were exhumed, it was found that one large root of an apple tree followed the spine, divided at the thighs, and turned up at the toes of Roger Williams. More than one person had eaten its apples. This root may be seen to-day in the cabinet of Brown University.

These considerations have led some, like Origen, to call the doctrine of a literal resurrection of the flesh "the foolishness of beggarly minds," and to say that resurrection may be only "the gathering round the spirit of new materials, and the vitalizing them into a new body by the spirit's God-given power"; see Newman Smyth, Old Faiths in a New Light, 349-391; Porter, Human Intellect, 39. But this view seems as great an extreme as that from which it was a reaction. It gives up all idea of unity between the new and the old. If my body were this instant annihilated, and if then, an hour hence, God should create a second body, precisely like the present, I could not call it the same with the present body, even though it were animated by the same informing soul, and that soul had maintained an uninterrupted existence between the time of the annihilation of the first body and the creation of the second. So, if the body laid in the tomb were wholly dissipated among the elements, and God created at the end of the world a wholly new body, it would be impossible for Paul to say: "this corruptible must put on incorruption" (1 Cor. 15:53), or: "it is sown in dishonor; it it raised in glory" (verse 43). In short, there is a physical connection between the old and the new, which is intimated by Scripture, but which this theory denies.

Paul himself gives us an illustration which shows that his view was midway between the two extremes: "that which thou sowest, thou sowest not the body that shall be" (1 Cor. 15:37). On the one hand, the wheat that springs up does not contain the precise particles, perhaps does not contain any particles, that were in the seed. On the other hand, there has been a continuous physical connection between the seed sown and the ripened grain at the harvest. If the seed had been annihilated, and then ripe grain created, we could not speak of identity between the one and the other. But, because there has been a constant flux, the old particles pressed out by new, and these new in their turn succeeded by others that take their places, we can say: "the wheat has come up." We bury grain in order to increase it. The resurrection-body will be the same with the body laid away in the earth, in the same sense as the living stalk of grain is identical with the seed from which it germinated. "This mortal must put on immortality"—not the immortal spirit put on an immortal body, but the mortal body put on immortality, the corruptible body put on incorruption (1 Cor. 15:53). "Ye know not the Scriptures, nor the power of God" (Mark 12:24), says our Lord; and Paul asks: "Why is it judged incredible with you, if God doth raise the dead?" (Acts 26:8).

Or, to use another illustration nearer to the thing we desire to illustrate: My body is the same that it was ten years ago, although physiologists declare that every particle of the body is changed, not simply once in seven years, but once in a single year. Life is preserved only by the constant throwing off of dead matter and the introduction of new. There is indeed a unity of consciousness and personality, without which I should not be able to say at intervals of years: "this body is the same; this body is mine." But a physical connection between the old and the new is necessary in addition.

The nails of the hands are renewed in less than four months, or about twenty-one times in seven years. They grow to full length, an average of seven twelfths of an inch, in from 121 to 138 days. Young people grow them more rapidly, old people more slowly. In a man of 21, it took 126 days; in a man of 67, it took 244; but the average was a third of a year. A Baptist pastor attempted to prove that he was a native of South Carolina though born in another state, upon the ground that the body he brought with him from Tennessee had exchanged its physical particles for matter taken from South Carolina. Two dentists, however, maintained that he still had the same teeth which he owned in Tennessee seven years before, there being no circulation in the enamel. Should we then say: Every particle of the body has changed, except the enamel of the teeth?

Pope's Martinus Scriblerus: "Sir John Cutler had a pair of black worsted stockings which his maid darned so often with silk that they became at last a pair of silk stockings." Adeney, in Christianity and Evolution, 122, 123—"Herod's temple was treated as identical with the temple that Haggai knew, because the rebuilding was gradual, and was carried on side by side with the demolition of the several parts of the old structure." The ocean wave travels around the world and is the same wave; but it is never in two consecutive seconds composed of the same particles of water.

The North River is the same to-day that it was when Hendrick Hudson first discovered it; yet not a particle of its current, nor the surface of the banks which that current touches now, is the same that it was then. Two things make the present river identical with the river of the past. The first is, that the same formative principle is at work,—the trend of the banks is the same, and there is the same general effect in the flow and direction of the waters drained from a large area of country. The second is, the fact that, ever since Hendrick Hudson's time, there has been a physical connection, old particles in continuous succession having been replaced by new.

So there are two things requisite to make our future bodies one with the bodies we now inhabit: first, that the same formative principle be at work in them; and secondly, that there be some sort of physical connection between the body that now is and the body that shall be. What that physical connection is, it is vain to speculate. We only teach that, though there may not be a single material particle in the new that was present in the old, there yet will be such a physical connection that it can be said: "the new has grown out of the old"; "that which was in the grave has come forth"; "this mortal has put on immortality."

(b) That a resurrection-body, having such a remote physical connection with the present body, cannot be recognized by the inhabiting soul or by other witnessing spirits as the same with that which was laid in the grave.

To this we reply that bodily identity does not consist in absolute sameness of particles during the whole history of the body, but in the organizing force, which, even in the flux and displacement of physical particles, makes the old the basis of the new, and binds both together in the unity of a single consciousness. In our recognition of friends, moreover, we are not wholly dependent, even in this world, upon our perception of bodily form; and we have reason to believe that in the future state there may be methods of communication far more direct and intuitive than those with which we are familiar here.

Cf. Mat. 17:3, 4—"And behold, there appeared unto them Moses and Elijah talking with him. And Peter answered, and said unto Jesus, Lord, it is good for us to be here: if thou wilt, I will make here three tabernacles; one for thee, and one for Moses, and one for Elijah"—here there is no mention of information given to Peter as to the names of the celestial visitants; it would seem that, in his state of exalted sensibility, he at once knew them. The recent proceedings of the English Society for Psychical Research seem to indicate the possibility of communication between two minds without physical intermediaries. Hudson, Scientific Demonstration of a Future Life, 294, 295, holds that telepathy is the means of communication in the future state.

G. S. Fullerton, Sameness and Identity, 6, 32, 67—"Heracleitus of Ephesus declared it impossible to enter the same river twice. Cratylus replied that the same river could not be entered once.... The kinds of sameness are: 1. Thing same with itself at any one instant; 2. Same pain to-day I felt yesterday = a like pain; 3. I See the same tree at different times = two or more percepts represent the same object; 4. Two plants belonging to the same class are called the same; 5. Memory gives us the same object that we formerly perceived; but the object is not the past, it is the memory-image which represents it; 6. Two men perceive the same object = they have like percepts, while both percepts are only representative of the same object; 7. External thing same with its representative in consciousness, or with the substance or noumenon supposed to underlie it."

Ladd, Philosophy of Mind, 153, 255—"What is called 'remaining the same,' in the case of all organic beings is just this,—remaining faithful to some immanent idea, while undergoing a great variety of changes in the pursuit, as it were, of the idea.... Self- consciousness and memory are themselves processes of becoming. The mind that does not change, in the way of growth, has no claim to be called mind. One cannot be conscious of changes without also being conscious of being the very being that is changed. When he loses this consciousness, we say that 'he has lost his mind.' Amid changes of its ideas the ego remains permanent because it is held within limits by the power of some immanent idea.... Our bodies as such have only a formal existence. They are a stream in constant flow and are ever changing. My body is only a temporary loan from Nature, to be repaid at death."

With regard to the meaning of the term "identity," as applied to material things, see Porter, Human Intellect, 631—"Here the substance is called the same, by a loose analogy taken from living agents and their gradual accretion and growth." The Euphrates is the same stream that flowed, "When high in Paradise By the four rivers the first roses blew," even though after that time the flood, or deluge, stopped its flow and obliterated all the natural features of the landscape. So this flowing organism which we call the body may be the same, after the deluge of death has passed away.

A different and less satisfactory view is presented in Dorner's Eschatology: "Identity involves: 1. Plastic form, which for the earthly body had its moulding principle in the soul. That principle could effect nothing permanent in the intermediate state; but with the spiritual consummation of the soul, it attains the full power which can appropriate to itself the heavenly body, accompanied by a cosmical process, made like Christ. 2. Appropriation, from the world of elements, of what it needs. The elements into which everything bodily of earth is dissolved, are an essentially uniform mass, like an ocean; and it is indifferent what parts of this are assigned to each individual man. The whole world of substance, which makes the constant change of substance possible, is made over to humanity as a common possession (Acts 4:32—'not one of them said that aught of the things which he possessed was his own; but they had all things common')."

(c) That a material organism can only be regarded as a hindrance to the free activity of the spirit, and that the assumption of such an organism by the soul, which, during the intermediate state, had been separated from the body, would indicate a decline in dignity and power rather than a progress.

We reply that we cannot estimate the powers and capacities of matter, when brought by God into complete subjection to the spirit. The bodies of the saints may be more ethereal than the air, and capable of swifter motion than the light, and yet be material in their substance. That the soul, clothed with its spiritual body, will have more exalted powers and enjoy a more complete felicity than would be possible while it maintained a purely spiritual existence, is evident from the fact that Paul represents the culmination of the soul's blessedness as occurring, not at death, but at the resurrection of the body.

Rom. 8:23—"waiting for our adoption, to wit, the redemption of our body"; 2 Cor. 5:4—"not for that we would be unclothed; but that we would be clothed upon, that what is mortal may be swallowed up of life"; Phil. 3:11—"if by any means I may attain unto the resurrection from the dead." Even Ps. 86:11—"Unite my heart to fear thy name"—may mean the collecting of all the powers of the body as well as soul. In this respect for the body, as a normal part of man's being, Scripture is based upon the truest philosophy. Plotinus gave thanks that he was not tied to an immortal body, and refused to have his portrait taken, because the body was too contemptible a thing to have its image perpetuated. But this is not natural, nor is it probably anything more than a whim or affectation. Eph. 5:29—"no man ever hated his own flesh; but nourisheth and cherisheth it." What we desire is not the annihilation of the body, but its perfection.

Renouf, Hibbert Lectures, 188—"In the Egyptian Book of the Dead, the soul reunites itself to the body, with the assurance that they shall never again be separated." McCosh, Intuitions, 213—"The essential thing about the resurrection is the development, out of the dead body, of an organ for the communion and activity of the spiritual life." Ebrard, Dogmatik, 2:226-234, has interesting remarks upon the relation of the resurrection-body to the present body. The essential difference he considers to be this, that whereas, in the present body, matter is master of the spirit, in the resurrection-body spirit will be the master of matter, needing no reparation by food, and having control of material laws. Ebrard adds striking speculations with regard to the glorified body of Christ.

A. J. Gordon, Ministry of the Spirit, 126—"Now the body bears the spirit, a slow chariot whose wheels are often disabled, and whose swiftest motion is but labored and tardy. Then the spirit will bear the body, carrying it as on wings of thought whithersoever it will. The Holy Ghost, by his divine inworking will, has completed in us the divine likeness, and perfected over us the divine dominion. The human body will now be in sovereign subjection to the human spirit, and the human spirit to the divine Spirit, and God will be all in all." Newman Smyth, Place of Death in Evolution, 112—"Weismann maintains that the living germ not only persists and is potentially immortal, but also that under favorable conditions it seems capable of surrounding itself with a new body. If a vital germ can do this, why not a spiritual germ?" Two martyrs were led to the stake. One was blind, the other lame. As the fires kindled, the latter exclaimed: "Courage, brother! this fire will cure us both!"

We may sum up our answers to objections, and may at the same time throw light upon the doctrine of the resurrection, by suggesting four principles which should govern our thinking with regard to the subject,—these namely: 1. Body is in continual flux; 2. Since matter is but the manifestation of God's mind and will, body is plastic in God's hands; 3. The soul in complete union with God may be endowed with the power of God; 4. Soul determines body, and not body soul, as the materialist imagines.

Ice, the flowing stream, the waterfall with the rainbow upon it, steam with its power to draw the railway train or to burst the boiler of the locomotive, are all the same element in varied forms, and they are all material. Wundt regards physical development, not as the cause, but as the effect, of psychical development. Aristotle defines the soul as "the prime entelechy of the living body." Swedenborg regarded each soul here as fashioning its own spiritual body, either hideous or lovely. Spenser, A Hymne to Beautie: "For of the soul the body form doth take, For soul is form, and doth the body make." Wordsworth, Sonnet 36, Afterthought: "Far backward, Duddon, as I cast my eyes, I see what was, and is, and will abide; Still glides the stream, and shall not cease to glide; The Form remains, the Function never dies"; The Primrose of the Rock: "Sin-blighted as we are, we too, The reasoning sons of men, From one oblivious winter called, Shall rise and breathe again, And in eternal summer lose Our three-score years and ten. To humbleness of heart descends This prescience from on high. The faith that elevates the just Before and when they die, And makes each soul a separate heaven, A court for Deity." Robert Browning, Asolando: "One who never turned his back, but marched breastforward; Never doubted clouds would break; Never dreamed, though right were worsted, Wrong would triumph; Held we fall to rise, are baffled to fight better, Sleep to wake." Mrs. Browning: "God keeps a niche In heaven to hold our idols, and albeit He broke them to our faces and denied That our close kisses should impair their white, I know we shall behold them raised, complete, The dust shook off, their beauty glorified."

On the spiritual body as possibly evolved by will, see Harris, Philos. Basis of Theism, 386. On the nature of the resurrection- body, see Burnet, State of the Departed, chaps. 3 and 8; Cudworth, Intell. System, 3:310 sq.; Splittgerber, Tod, Fortleben and Auferstehung. On the doctrine of the Resurrection among the Egyptians, see Dr. Howard Osgood, in Hebrew Student, Feb. 1885; among the Jews, see Gröbler, in Studien und Kritiken, 1879: Heft 4; DeWünsche, in Jahrbuch f. prot. Theol., 1880: Heft 2 and 4; Revue Théologique, 1881:1-17. For the view that the resurrection is wholly spiritual and takes place at death, see Willmarth, in Bap. Quar., October, 1868, and April, 1870; Ladd, in New Englander, April, 1874; Crosby, Second Advent.

On the whole subject, see Hase, Hutterus Redivivus, 280; Herzog, Encyclop., art.; Auferstehung; Goulburn, Bampton Lectures for 1850, on the Resurrection; Cox, The Resurrection; Neander, Planting and Training, 479-487, 524-526; Naville, La Vie Éternelle, 253, 254; Delitzsch, Bib. Psychologie, 453-463; Moorhouse, Nature and Revelation, 87-112; Unseen Universe, 33; Hovey, in Baptist Quarterly, Oct. 1867; Westcott, Revelation of the Risen Lord, and in Contemporary Review, vol. 30; R. W. Macan, Resurrection of Christ; Cremer, Beyond the Grave.

V. The Last Judgment

While the Scriptures represent all punishment of individual transgressors and all manifestations of God's vindicatory justice in the history of nations as acts or processes of judgment, they also intimate that these temporal judgments are only partial and imperfect, and that they are therefore to be concluded with a final and complete vindication of God's righteousness. This will be accomplished by making known to the universe the characters of all men, and by awarding to them corresponding destinies.

Passages describing temporal or spiritual judgment are: Ps. 9:7—"He hath prepared his throne for judgment"; Is. 26:9—"when thy judgments are in the earth, the inhabitants of the world learn righteousness"; Mat. 16:27, 28—"For the Son of man shall come in the glory of his Father with his angels; and then shall he render unto every man according to his deeds. Verily I say unto you, There be some of them that stand here, who shall in no wise taste of death, till they see the Son of man coming in his kingdom"; John 3:18, 19—"he that believeth not hath been judged already, because he hath not believed on the name of the only begotten Son of God. And this is the judgment, that the light is come into the world, and men loved the darkness rather than the light; for their works were evil"; 9:39—"For judgment came I into this world, that they that see not may see; and that they that see may become blind"; 12:31—"Now is the judgment of this world: now shall the prince of this world be cast out."

Passages describing the final judgment are: Mat. 25:31-46—"But when the Son of man shall come in his glory, and all the angels with him, then shall he sit on the throne of his glory: and before him shall be gathered all the nations: and he shall separate them one from another, as the shepherd separateth the sheep from the goats...." Acts 17:31—"he hath appointed a day, in which he will judge the world in righteousness by the man whom he hath ordained; whereof he hath given assurance unto all men, in that he hath raised him from the dead"; Rom. 2:16—"in the day when God shall judge the secrets of men, according to my gospel, by Jesus Christ"; 2 Cor. 5:10—"For we must all be made manifest before the judgment-seat of Christ; that each one may receive the things done in the body, according to what he hath done, whether it be good or bad"; Heb. 9:27, 28—"And inasmuch as it is appointed unto men once to die, and after this cometh judgment; so Christ also, having been once offered to bear the sins of many, shall appear a second time, apart from sin, to them that wait for him, unto salvation"; Rev. 20:12—"And I saw the dead, the great and the small, standing before the throne; and books were opened: and another book was opened, which is the book of life: and the dead were judged out of the things which were written in the books, according to their works."

Delitzsch: "The fall of Jerusalem was the day of the Lord, the bloody and fiery dawn of the last great day—the day of days, the ending-day of all days, the settling day of all days, the day of the promotion of time into eternity, the day which for the church breaks through and breaks off the night of this present world." E. G. Robinson: "Judgment begins here. The callousing of conscience in this life is a penal infliction. Punishment begins in this life and is carried on in the next. We have no right to assert that there are no positive inflictions, but, if there are none, still every word of Scripture threatening would stand. There is no day of judgment or of resurrection all at one time. Judgment is an eternal process. The angels in 2 Pet. 2:4—'cast ... down to hell'—suffer the self-perpetuating consequences of transgression..... Man is being judged every day. Every man honest with himself knows where he is going to. Those who are not honest with themselves are playing a trick, and, if they are not careful, they will get a trick played on them."

1. The nature of the final judgment.

The final judgment is not a spiritual, invisible, endless process, identical with God's providence in history, but is an outward and visible event, occurring at a definite period in the future. This we argue from the following considerations:

(a) The judgment is something for which the evil are "reserved " (2 Peter 2:4, 9); something to be expected in the future (Acts 24:25; Heb. 10:27); something after death (Heb. 9:27); something for which the resurrection is a preparation (John 5:29).

2 Pet. 2:4, 9—"God spared not angels when they sinned, but cast them down to hell ... reserved unto judgment ... the lord knoweth how ... to keep the unrighteous unto punishment unto the day of judgment"; Acts 24:25—"as he reasoned of righteousness, and self-control, and the judgment to come, Felix was terrified"; Heb. 10:27—"a certain fearful expectation of judgment"; 9:27—"it is appointed unto men once to die, and after this cometh judgment"; John 5:29—"the resurrection of judgment."

(b) The accompaniments of the judgment, such as the second coming of Christ, the resurrection, and the outward changes of the earth, are events which have an outward and visible, as well as an inward and spiritual, aspect. We are compelled to interpret the predictions of the last judgment upon the same principle.

John 5:28, 29—"Marvel not at this: for the hour cometh, in which all that are in the tombs shall hear his voice, and shall come forth; they that have done good, unto the resurrection of life; and they that have done evil, unto the resurrection of judgment"; 2 Pet. 3:7, 10—"the day of judgment ... the day of the Lord ... in the which the heavens shall pass away with a great noise, and the elements shall be dissolved with fervent heat"; 2 Thess. 1:7, 8, 2:10—"the revelation of the Lord Jesus from heaven with the angels of his power in flaming fire, rendering vengeance to them that know not God ... when he shall come ... in that day."

(c) God's justice, in the historical and imperfect work of judgment, needs a final outward judgment as its vindication. "A perfect justice must judge, not only moral units, but moral aggregates; not only the particulars of life, but the life as a whole." The crime that is hidden and triumphant here, and the goodness that is here maligned and oppressed, must be brought to light and fitly recompensed. "Otherwise man is a Tantalus—longing but never satisfied"; and God's justice, of which his outward administration is the expression, can only be regarded as approximate.

Renouf, Hibbert Lectures, 194—"The Egyptian Book of the Dead represents the deceased person as standing in the presence of the goddess Maāt , who is distinguished by the ostrich-feather on her head; she holds the sceptre in one hand and the symbol of life in the other. The man's heart, which represents his entire moral nature, is being weighed in the balance in the presence of Osiris, seated upon his throne as judge of the dead." Rationalism believes in only present and temporal judgment; and this it regards as but the reaction of natural law: "Die Weltgeschichte ist das Weltgericht,—the world's history is the world's judgment" (Schiller, Resignation). But there is an inner connection between present, temporal, spiritual judgments, and the final, outward, complete judgment of God. Nero's murder of his mother was not the only penalty of his murder of Germanicus.

Dorner: "With Christ's appearance, faith sees that the beginning of the judgment and of the end has come. Christians are a prophetic race. Without judgment, Christianity would involve a sort of dualism: evil and good would be of equal might and worth. Christianity cannot always remain a historic principle alongside of the contrary principle of evil. It is the only reality." God will show or make known his righteousness with regard to: (1) the disparity of lots among men; (2) the prosperity of the wicked; (3) the permission of moral evil in general; (4) the consistency of atonement with justice. "The συντέλεια τοῦ αἰῶνος ('end of the world,' Mat. 13:39) = stripping hostile powers of their usurped might, revelation of their falsity and impotence, consigning them to the past. Evil shall be utterly cut off, given over to its own nothingness, or made a subordinate element."

A great statesman said that what he dreaded for his country was not the day of judgment, but the day of no judgment. "Jove strikes the Titans down, Not when they first begin their mountain-piling, But when another rock would crown their work." R. W. Emerson: "God said: I am tired of kings, I suffer them no more; Up to my ears the morning brings The outrage of the poor." Royce, The World and the Individual, 2:384 sq.—"If God's life is given to free individual souls, then God's life can be given also to free nations and to a free race of men. There may be an apostasy of a family, nation, race, and a judgment of each according to their deeds."

The Expositor, March, 1898—"It is claimed that we are being judged now, that laws execute themselves, that the system of the universe is automatic, that there is no need for future retribution. But all ages have agreed that there is not here and now any sufficient vindication of the principle of eternal justice. The mills of the gods grind slowly. Physical immorality is not proportionately punished. Deterioration is not an adequate penalty. Telling a second lie does not recompense the first. Punishment includes pain, and here is no pain. That there is not punishment here is due, not to law, but to grace."

Denney, Studies in Theology, 240, 241—"The dualistic conception of an endless suspense, in which good and evil permanently balance each other and contest with each other the right to inherit the earth, is virtually atheistic, and the whole Bible is a protest against it.... It is impossible to overestimate the power of the final judgment, as a motive, in the primitive church. On almost every page of St. Paul, for instance, we see that he lives in the presence of it; he lets the awe of it descend into his heart to keep his conscience quick."

2. The object of the final judgment.

The object of the final judgment is not the ascertainment, but the manifestation, of character, and the assignment of outward condition corresponding to it.

(a) To the omniscient Judge, the condition of all moral creatures is already and fully known. The last day will be only "the revelation of the righteous judgment of God."

They are inwardly judged when they die, and before they die; they are outwardly judged at the last day: Rom. 2:5, 6—"treasurest up for thyself wrath in the day of wrath and revelation of the righteous judgment of God; who will render to every man according to his works"—see Meyer on this passage; not "against the day of wrath," but "in the day of wrath"—wrath existing beforehand, but breaking out on that day. 1 Tim. 5:24, 25—"Some men's sins are evident, going before unto judgment; and some men also they follow after. In like manner also there are good works that are evident; and such as are otherwise cannot be hid"; Rev. 14:13—"for their works follow with them"—as close companions, into God's presence and judgment (Ann. Par. Bible).

Epitaph: "Hic jacet in expectatione diei supremi.... Qualis erat, dies iste indicabit"—"Here lies, in expectation of the last day.... Of what sort he was, that day will show." Shakespeare, Hamlet, 3:3—"In the corrupted currents of this world Offence's glided hand may shove by justice. But 'tis not so above. There is no shuffling, there the action lies In his true nature; and we ourselves compelled, Even to the teeth and forehead of our faults. To give in evidence"; King John, 4:2—"Oh, when the last account 'twixt heaven and earth Is to be made, then shall this hand and seal [the warrant for the murder of Prince Arthur] Witness against us to damnation." "Not all your piety nor wit Can lure it [justice] back to cancel half a line, Nor all your tears wash out one word of it."

(b) In the nature of man, there are evidences and preparations for this final disclosure. Among these may be mentioned the law of memory, by which the soul preserves the records of its acts, both good and evil (Luke 16:25); the law of conscience, by which men involuntarily anticipate punishment for their own sins (Rom. 2:15, 16; Heb. 10:27); the law of character, by which every thought and deed makes indelible impress upon the moral nature (Heb. 3:8, 15).

The law of memory.—Luke 16:25—"Son, remember!" See Maclaren, Sermons, 1:109-122—Memory (1) will embrace all the events of the past life; (2) will embrace them all at the same moment; (3) will embrace them continuously and continually. Memory is a process of self-registry. As every business house keeps a copy of all letters sent or orders issued, so every man retains in memory the record of his sins. The mind is a palimpsest; though the original writing has been erased, the ink has penetrated the whole thickness of the parchment, and God's chemistry is able to revive it. Hudson, Dem. of Future Life, 212, 213—"Subjective memory is the retention of all ideas, however superficially they may have been impressed upon the objective mind, and it admits of no variation in different individuals. Recollection is the power of recalling ideas to the mind. This varies greatly. Sir William Hamilton calls the former 'mental latency.' "

The law of conscience.—Rom. 2:15, 16—"they show the work of the law written in their hearts, their conscience bearing witness therewith, and their thoughts one with another accusing or else excusing them; in the day when God shall judge the secrets of men, according to my gospel, by Jesus Christ"; Heb. 10:27—"a certain fearful expectation of judgment, and a fierceness of fire which shall devour the adversaries." Goethe said that his writings, taken together, constituted a great confession. Wordsworth, Excursion, III:579—"For, like a plague will memory break out. And, in the blank and solitude of things, Upon his spirit, with a fever's strength, Will conscience prey." A man who afterwards became a Methodist preacher was converted in Whitefield's time by a vision of the judgment, in which he saw all men gathered before the throne, and each one coming up to the book of God's law, tearing open his heart before it "as one would tear open the bosom of his shirt," comparing his heart with the things written in the book, and, according as they agreed or disagreed with that standard, either passing triumphant to the company of the blest, or going with howling to the company of the damned. No word was spoken; the Judge sat silent; the judgment was one of self-revelation and self-condemnation. See Autobiography of John Nelson (quoted in the Diary of Mrs. Kitty Trevylyan, 207, by Mrs. E. Charles, the author of The Schönberg-Cotta Family).

The law of character.—Heb. 3:8, 15—"Harden not your hearts, as in the provocation, Like as in the day of the trial in the wilderness.... Today, if ye shall hear his voice, Harden not your hearts, as in the provocation." Sin leaves its marks upon the soul; men become "past feeling" (Eph. 4:19). In England, churchmen claim to tell a dissenter by his walk—not a bad sign by which to know a man. God needs only to hold up our characters to show what have been our lives. Sin leaves its scars upon the soul, as truly as lust and hatred leave their marks upon the body. So with the manifestation of the good—"the chivalry that does the right, and disregards The yea and nay of the world.... Expect nor question nor reply At what we figure as God's judgment-bar" (Robert Browning, Ring and Book, 178, 202). Mr. Edison says: "In a few years the world will be just like one big ear; it will be unsafe to speak in a house till one has examined the walls and the furniture for concealed phonographs." But the world even now is "one big ear", and we ourselves in our characters are writing the books of the judgment. Brooks, Foundations of Zoölogy, 134, 135—"Every part of the material universe contains a permanent record of every change that has taken place therein, and there is also no limit to the power of minds like ours to read and interpret the record."

Draper, Conflict of Science and Religion: "If on a cold polished metal, as a new razor, any object, such as a wafer, be laid, and the metal breathed upon, and when the moisture has had time to disappear, the wafer be thrown off, though now the most critical inspection of the polished surface can discern no trace of any form, if we breathe once more upon it, a spectral image of the wafer comes plainly into view; and this may be done again and again. Nay, more; if the polished metal be carefully put aside where nothing can injure its surface, and be kept so for many months, on breathing upon it again, the shadowy form emerges. A shadow never falls upon a wall without leaving thereon a permanent trace, a trace which might be made visible by resorting to proper processes. Upon the walls of our most private apartments, where we think the eye of intrusion is altogether shut out, and our retirement can never be profaned, there exist the vestiges of all our acts."

Babbage, Ninth Bridgewater Treatise, 113-115—"If we had power to follow and detect the minutest effects of any disturbance, each particle of existing matter would furnish a register of all that has happened. The track of every canoe, of every vessel that has yet disturbed the surface of the ocean, whether impelled by manual force or elemental power, remains forever registered in the future movement of all succeeding particles which may occupy its place. The furrow which it left is indeed filled up by the closing waters, but they draw after them other and larger portions of the surrounding element, and these again, once moved, communicate motion to others in endless succession. The air itself is one vast library, in whose pages are forever written all that man has said or even whispered. There, in their mutable but unerring characters, mixed with the earliest as well as the latest sighs of mortality, stand forever recorded vows unredeemed, promises unfulfilled, perpetuating in the united movements of each particle the testimony of man's changeful will."

(c) Single acts and words, therefore, are to be brought into the judgment only as indications of the moral condition of the soul. This manifestation of all hearts will vindicate not only God's past dealings, but his determination of future destinies.

Mat. 12:36—"And I say unto you, that every idle word that man shall speak, they shall give account thereof in the day of judgment"; Luke 12:2, 8, 9—"there is nothing covered up, that shall not be revealed; and hid, that shall not be known.... Every one who shall confess me before men, him shall the Son of man also confess before the angels of God: but he that denieth me in the presence of men shall be denied in the presence of the angels of God"; John 3:18—"He that believeth on him is not judged: he that believeth not hath been judged already, because he hath not believed on the name of the only begotten Son of God"; 2 Cor. 5:10—"For we must all be made manifest [not: 'must all appear,' as in A. Vers.] before the judgment-seat of Christ."

Even the human judge, in passing sentence, commonly endeavors so to set forth the guilt of the criminal that he shall see his doom to be just. So God will awaken the consciences of the lost, and lead them to pass judgment on themselves. Each lost soul can say as Byron's Manfred said to the fiend that tortured his closing hour: "I have not been thy dupe, nor am thy prey, But was my own destroyer." Thus God's final judgment will be only the culmination of a process of natural selection, by which the unfit are eliminated, and the fit are caused to survive.

O. J. Smith, The Essential Verity of Religion: "Belief in the immortality of the soul and belief in the accountability of the soul are fundamental beliefs in all religion. The origin of the belief in immortality is found in the fact that justice can be established in human affairs only upon the theory that the soul of man is immortal, and the belief that man is accountable for his actions eternally is based upon the conviction that justice should and will be enforced. The central verity in religion therefore is eternal justice. The sense of justice makes us men. Religion has no miraculous origin,—it is born with the awakening of man's moral sense. Friendship and love are based on reciprocity, which is justice.

'Universal justice,' says Aristotle, 'includes all virtues.' " If by justice here is meant the divine justice, implied in the awakening of man's moral sense, we can agree with the above. As we have previously intimated, we regard the belief in immortality as an inference from the intuition of God's existence, and every new proof that God is just strengthens our conviction of immortality.

3. The Judge in the final judgment.

God, in the person of Jesus Christ, is to be the judge. Though God is the judge of all (Heb. 12:23), yet this judicial activity is exercised through Christ, at the last day, as well as in the present state (John 5:22, 27).

Heb. 12:23—"to God the judge of all"; John 5:22, 27—"For neither doth the Father judge any man, but he hath given all judgment unto the Son ... and he gave him authority to execute judgment, because he is a son of man." Stevens, Johannine Theology, 349—"Jesus says that he judges no man (John 8:15). He does not personally judge men. His attitude toward men is solely that of Savior. It is rather his work, his word, his truth, which pronounces condemnation against them both here and hereafter. The judgment is that light is come; men's attitude toward the light involves their judgment; the light judges them, or, they judge themselves.... The Savior does not come to judge but to save them; but, by their rejection of salvation, they turn the saving message itself into a judgment."

This, for three reasons:

(a) Christ's human nature enables men to understand both the law and the love of God, and so makes intelligible the grounds on which judgment is passed.

Whoever says that God is too distant and great to be understood may be pointed to Christ, in whose human life the divine "law appears, drawn out in living characters," and the divine love is manifest, as suffering upon the cross to save men from their sins.

(b) The perfect human nature of Christ, united as it is to the divine, ensures all that is needful in true judgment, viz.: that it be both merciful and just.

Acts 17:31—"he will judge the world in righteousness by the man whom he hath ordained; whereof he hath given assurance unto all men, in that he hath raised him from the dead."

As F. W. Robertson has shown in his sermon on "The Sympathy of Christ" (vol. 1: sermon vii), it is not sin that most sympathizes with sin. Sin blinds and hardens. Only the pure can appreciate the needs of the impure, and feel for them.

(c) Human nature, sitting upon the throne of judgment, will afford convincing proof that Christ has received the reward of his sufferings, and that humanity has been perfectly redeemed. The saints shall "judge the world" only as they are one with Christ.

The lowly Son of man shall sit upon the throne of judgment. And with himself he will join all believers. Mat. 19:28—"ye who have followed me, in the regeneration when the Son of man shall sit on the throne of his glory, ye also shall sit upon twelve thrones, judging the twelve tribes of Israel"; Luke 22:28-30—"But ye are they that have continued with me in my temptations; and I appoint unto you a kingdom, even as my Father appointed unto me, that ye may eat and drink at my table in my kingdom; and ye shall sit on thrones judging the twelve tribes of Israel"; 1 Cor. 6:2, 3—"know ye not that the saints shall judge the world?... Know ye not that we shall judge angels?" Rev. 3:21—"He that overcometh, I will give to him to sit down with me in my throne, as I also overcame, and sat down with my Father in his throne."

4. The subjects of the final judgment.

The persons upon whose characters and conduct this judgment shall be passed are of two great classes:

(a) All men—each possessed of body as well as soul,—the dead having been raised, and the living having been changed.

1 Cor. 15:51, 52—"We all shall not sleep, but we shall all be changed, in a moment, in the twinkling of an eye, at the last trump: for the trumpet shall sound, and the dead shall be raised incorruptible, and we shall be changed"; 1 Thess. 4:16, 17—"For the Lord himself shall descend from heaven, with a shout, with the voice of an archangel, and with the trump of God: and the dead in Christ shall rise first; then we that are alive, that are left, shall together with them be caught up in the clouds, to meet the Lord in the air: and so shall we ever be with the Lord."

(b) All evil angels,—good angels appearing only as attendants and ministers of the Judge.

Evil angels: 2 Pet. 2:4—"For if God spared not angels when they sinned, but cast them down to hell, and committed them to pits of darkness, to be reserved unto judgment"; Jude 6—"And angels that kept not their own principality, but left their proper habitation, he hath kept in everlasting bonds under darkness unto the judgment of the great day"; Good angels: Mat. 13:41, 42—"The Son of man shall send forth his angels, and they shall gather out of his kingdom all things that cause stumbling, and them that do iniquity, and shall cast them into the furnace of fire: there shall be the weeping and the gnashing of teeth"; 25:31—"But when the Son of man shall come in his glory, and all the angels with him, then shall he sit on the throne of his glory: and before him shall be gathered all the nations."

5. The grounds of the final judgment.

These will be two in number:

(a) The law of God,—as made known in conscience and in Scripture.

John 12:48—"He that rejecteth me, and receiveth not my sayings, hath one that judgeth him: the word that I spake, the same shall judge him in the last day"; Rom. 2:12—"For as many as have sinned without the law shall also perish without the law: and as many as have sinned under the law shall be judged by the law." On the self-registry and disclosure of sin, see F. A. Noble, Our Redemption, 59-76. Dr. Noble quotes Daniel Webster in the Knapp case at Salem: "There is no refuge from confession but suicide, and suicide is confession." Thomas Carlyle said to Lord Houghton: "Richard Milnes! in the day of judgment, when the Lord asks you why you did not get that pension for Alfred Tennyson, it will not do to lay the blame on your constituents,—it is you that will be damned."

(b) The grace of Christ (Rev. 20:12),—those whose names are found "written in the book of life" being approved, simply because of their union with Christ and participation in his righteousness. Their good works shall be brought into judgment only as proofs of this relation to the Redeemer. Those not found "written in the book of life" will be judged by the law of God, as God has made it known to each individual.

Rev. 20:12—"And I saw the dead, the great and the small, standing before the throne; and books were opened: and another book was opened, which is the book of life: and the dead were judged out of the things which were written in the books, according to their works." The "book of life" = the book of justification, in which are written the names of those who are united to Christ by faith; as the "book of death" would = the book of condemnation, in which are written the names of those who stand in their sins, as unrepentant and unforgiven transgressors of God's law.

Ferries, in Hastings' Bible Dictionary, 2:821—"The judgment, in one aspect or stage of it, is a present act. For judgment Christ is come into this world (John 9:39). There is an actual separation of men in progress here and now.... This judgment which is in progress now, is destined to be perfected.... In the last assize, Christ will be the Judge as before.... It may be said that men will hereafter judge themselves. Those who are unlike Christ will find themselves as such to be separate from him. The two classes of people are parted because they have acquired distinct natures like the sheep and the goat.... The character of each person is a 'book' or record, preserving, in moral and spiritual effects, all that he has been and done and loved, and in the judgment these books will be 'opened,' or each man's character will be manifested as the light of Christ's character falls upon it.... The people of Christ themselves receive different rewards, according as their life has been."

Dr. H. E. Robins, in his Restatement, holds that only under the grace-system can the deeds done in the body be the ground of judgment. These deeds will be repentance and faith, not words of external morality. They will be fruits of the Spirit, such as spring from the broken and contrite heart. Christ, as head of the mediatorial kingdom, will fitly be the Judge. So Judgment will be an unmixed blessing to the righteous. To them the words "prepare to meet thy God" (Amos 4:12) should have no terror; for to meet God is to meet their deliverance and their reward. "Teach me to live that I may dread The grave as little as my bed: Teach me to die, that so I may Rise glorious at the judgment day." On the whole subject, see Hodge, Outlines of Theology, 456, 457; Martensen, Christian Dogmatics, 465, 466; Neander, Planting and Training, 524-526; Jonathan Edwards, Works, 2:499, 500; 4:202-225; Fox, in Lutheran Rev., 1887:206-226.

VI. The Final States of the Righteous and of the Wicked

1. Of the righteous.

The final state of the righteous is described as eternal life (Mat. 25:46), glory (2 Cor. 4:17), rest (Heb. 4:9), knowledge (1 Cor. 13:8-10), holiness (Rev. 21:27), service (Rev. 22:3), worship (Rev. 19:1), society (Heb. 12:23), communion with God (Rev. 21:3).

Mat. 25:46—"And these shall go away into eternal punishment: but the righteous into eternal life"; 2 Cor. 4:17—"For our light affliction, which is for the moment, worketh for us more and more exceedingly an eternal weight of glory"; Heb. 4:9—"There remaineth therefore a sabbath rest for the people of God"; 1 Cor. 13:8-10—"Love never faileth: but whether there be prophecies, they shall be done away; whether there be tongues, they shall cease; whether there be knowledge, it shall be done away. For we know in part, and we prophesy in part: but when that which is perfect is come, that which is in part shall be done away"; Rev. 21:27—"and there shall in no wise enter into it anything unclean, or he that maketh an abomination and a lie: but only they that are written in the Lamb's book of life"; 22:3—"and his servants shall serve him"; 19:1, 2—"After these things I heard as it were a great voice of a great multitude in heaven, saying, Hallelujah; Salvation, and glory, and power, belong to our God; for true and righteous are his judgments"; Heb. 12:23—"to the general assembly and church of the firstborn who are enrolled in heaven"; Rev. 21:3—"And I heard a great voice out of the throne saying, Behold, the tabernacle of God is with men, and he shall dwell with them, and they shall be his peoples, and God himself shall be with them, and be their God."

Is. 35:7—"The mirage shall become a pool" = aspiration shall become reality; Hos. 2:15—"I will give her ... the valley of Achor [that is, Troubling] for a door of hope." Victor Hugo: "If you persuade Lazarus that there is no Abraham's bosom awaiting him, he will not lie at Dives' door, to be fed with his crumbs,—he will make his way into the house and fling Dives out of the window." It was the preaching of the Methodists that saved England from the general crash of the French Revolution. It brought the common people to look for the redress of the inequalities and injustices of this life in a future life—a world of less friction than this (S. S. Times). In the Alps one has no idea of the upper valleys until he enters them. He may long to ascend, but only actual ascending can show him their beauty. And then, "beyond the Alps lies Italy," and the revelation of heaven will be like the outburst of the sunny landscape after going through the darkness of the St. Gothard tunnel.

Robert Hall, who for years had suffered acute bodily pain, said to Wilberforce: "My chief conception of heaven is rest." "Mine," replied Wilberforce, "is love—love to God and to every bright inhabitant of that glorious place." Wilberforce enjoyed society. Heaven is not all rest. On the door is inscribed: "No admission except on business." "His servants shall serve him" (Rev. 21:3). Butler, Things Old and New, 143—"We know not; but if life be there The outcome and the crown of this: What else can make their perfect bliss Than in their Master's work to share? Resting, but not in slumberous ease, Working, but not in wild unrest, Still ever blessing, ever blest, They see us as the Father sees." Tennyson, Crossing the Bar: "Sunset and evening star, And one clear call for me; And may there be no moaning of the bar When I put out to sea! But such a tide as moving seems asleep, Too full for sound and foam, When that which drew from out the boundless deep Turns again home. Twilight and evening bell, And after that the dark; And may there be no sadness of farewell, When I embark. For though from out our bourne of time and place The flood may bear me far, I hope to see my Pilot face to face, When I have crossed the bar."

Mat. 6:20—"lay up for yourselves treasures in heaven" = there are no permanent investments except in heaven. A man at death is worth only what he has sent on before him. Christ prepares a place for us (John 14:3) by gathering our friends to himself. Louise Chandler Moulton: "Some day or other I shall surely come Where true hearts wait for me; Then let me learn the language of that home, While here on earth I be; Lest my poor lips for want of words be dumb In that high company." Bronson Alcott: "Heaven will be to me a place where I can get a little conversation." Some of his friends thought it would be a place where he could hear himself talk. A pious Scotchman, when asked whether he ever expected to reach heaven, replied: "Why, mon, I live there noo!"

Summing up all these, we may say that it is the fulness and perfection of holy life, in communion with God and with sanctified spirits. Although there will be degrees of blessedness and honor, proportioned to the capacity and fidelity of each soul (Luke 19:17, 19; 1 Cor. 3:14, 15), each will receive as great a measure of reward as it can contain (1 Cor. 2:9), and this final state, once entered upon, will be unchanging in kind and endless in duration (Rev. 3:12; 22:15).

Luke 19:17, 19—"Well done, thou good servant: because thou wast found faithful in a very little, have thou authority over ten cities.... Be thou also over five cities"; 1 Cor. 3:14, 15—"If any man's work shall abide which he built thereon, he shall receive a reward. If any man's work shall be burned, he shall suffer loss: but he himself shall be saved; yet so as through fire"; 2:9—"Things which eye saw not, and ear heard not, And which entered not into the heart of man, Whatsoever things God prepared for them that love him"; Rev. 3:12—"He that overcometh, I will make

him a pillar in the temple of my God, and he shall go out thence no more"; 22:15—"Without are the dogs, and the sorcerers, and the fornicators, and the murderers, and the idolaters, and every one that loveth and maketh a lie."

In the parable of the laborers (Mat. 20:1-16), each receives a penny. Rewards in heaven will be equal, in the sense that each saved soul will be filled with good. But rewards will vary, in the sense that the capacity of one will be greater than that of another; and this capacity will be in part the result of our improvement of God's gifts in the present life. The relative value of the penny may in this way vary from a single unit to a number indefinitely great, according to the work and spirit of the recipient. The penny is good only for what it will buy. For the eleventh hour man, who has done but little work, it will not buy so sweet rest as it buys for him who has "borne the burden of the day and the scorching heat." It will not buy appetite, nor will it buy joy of conscience.

E. G. Robinson: "Heaven is not to be compared to a grasshopper on a shingle floating down stream. Heaven is a place where men are taken up, as they leave this world, and are carried forward. No sinners will be there, though there may be incompleteness of character. There is no intimation in Scripture of that sudden transformation in the hour of dissolution which is often supposed." Ps. 84:7—"They go from strength to strength; Every one of them appeareth before God in Zion"—it is not possible that progress should cease with our entrance into heaven; rather is it true that uninterrupted progress will then begin. 1 Cor. 13:12—"now we see in a mirror, darkly; but then face to face." There, progress is not towards, but within, the sphere of the infinite. In this world we are like men living in a cave, and priding themselves on the rushlights with which they explore it, unwilling to believe that there is a region of sunlight where rushlights are needless.

Heaven will involve deliverance from defective physical organization and surroundings, as well as from the remains of evil in our hearts. Rest, in heaven, will be consistent with service, an activity without weariness, a service which is perfect freedom. We shall be perfect when we enter heaven, in the sense of being free from sin; but we shall grow to greater perfection thereafter, in the sense of a larger and completer being. The fruit tree shows perfection at each stage of its growth—the perfect bud, the perfect blossom, and finally the perfect fruit; yet the bud and the blossom are preparatory and prophetic; neither one is a finality. So "when that which is perfect is come, that which is in part shall be done away" (1 Cor. 13:10). A broadshouldered convert at the Rescue Mission said: "I'm the happiest man in the room to-night. I couldn't be any happier unless I were larger." A little pail can be as full of water as is a big tub, but the tub will hold much more than the pail. To be "filled unto all the fulness of God" (Eph. 3:19) will mean much more in heaven than it means here, because we shall then "be strong to apprehend with all the saints what is the breadth and length and height and depth, and to know the love of Christ which passeth knowledge." In the book of Revelation, John seems to have mistaken an angel for the Lord himself, and to have fallen down to worship (Rev. 22:8). The time may come in eternity when we shall be equal to what we now conceive God to be (1 Cor. 2:9).

Plato's Republic and More's Utopia are only earthly adumbrations of St. John's City of God. The representation of heaven as a city seems intended to suggest security from every foe, provision for every want, intensity of life, variety of occupation, and closeness of relation to others; or, as Hastings' Bible Dictionary, 1:446, puts it: "Safety, Security, Service." Here, the greatest degradation and sin are found in the great cities. There, the life of the city will help holiness, as the life of the city here helps wickedness. Brotherly love in the next world implies knowing those we love, and loving those we know. We certainly shall not know less there than here. If we know our friends here, we shall know them there. And, as love to Christ here draws us nearer to each other, so there we shall love friends, not less but more, because of our greater nearness to Christ.

Zech. 8:5—"And the streets of the city shall be full of boys and girls playing in the streets thereof." Newman Smyth, Through Science to Faith, 125—"As of the higher animals, so even more of men and women it may be true, that those who play best may succeed best and thrive best." Horace Bushnell, in his essay, Work and Play, holds that ideal work is work performed so heartily and joyfully, and with such a surplus of energy, that it becomes play. This is the activity of heaven: John 10:10—"I came that they may have life, and may have it abundantly." We enter into the life of God: John 5:17—"My Father worketh even until now, and I work." A nurse who had been ill for sixteen years, said: "If I were well, I would be at the small-pox hospital. I'm not going to heaven to do nothing." Savage, Life after Death, 129, 292—"In Dante's universe, the only reason for any one's wanting to get to heaven is for the sake of getting out of the other place. There is nothing in heaven for him to do, nothing human for him to engage in.... A good deacon in his depression thought he was going to hell; but when asked what he would do there, he replied that he would try to start a prayer meeting."

With regard to heaven, two questions present themselves, namely:

(a) Is heaven a place, as well as a state?

We answer that this is probable, for the reason that the presence of Christ's human body is essential to heaven, and that this body must be confined to place. Since deity and humanity are indissolubly united in Christ's single person, we cannot regard Christ's human soul as limited to place without vacating his person of its divinity. But we cannot conceive of his human body as thus omnipresent. As the new bodies of the saints are confined to place, so, it would seem, must be the body of their Lord. But, though heaven be the place where Christ manifests his glory through the human body which he assumed in the incarnation, our ruling conception of heaven must be something higher even than this, namely, that of a state of holy communion with God.

John 14:2, 3—"In my Father's house are many mansions; if it were not so, I would have told you; for I go to prepare a place for you. And if I go and prepare a place for you, I come again, and will receive you unto myself; that where I am, there ye may be also"; Heb. 12:14—"follow after peace with all men, and the sanctification without which no man shall see the Lord."

Although heaven is probably a place, we are by no means to allow this conception to become the preponderant one in our minds. Milton: "The mind is its own place, and in itself Can make a heaven of hell, a hell of heaven." As he goes through the gates of death, every Christian can say, as Cæsar said when he crossed the Rubicon: "Omnia mea mecum porto." The hymn "O sing to me of heaven, when I am called to die" is not true to Christian experience. In that hour the soul sings, not of heaven, but of Jesus and his cross. As houses on river-flats, accessible in time of flood by boats, keep safe only goods in the upper story, so only the treasure laid up above escapes the destroying floods of the last day. Dorner: "The soul will possess true freedom, in that it can no more become unfree; and that through the indestructible love-energy springing from union with God."

Milton: "What if earth be But the shadow of heaven, and things therein Each to the other like, more than on earth is thought?" Omar Khayyám, Rubáiyát, stanzas 66, 67—"I sent my soul through the Invisible, Some letter of that After-life to spell: And by and by my soul returned to me, And answered 'I myself am Heaven and Hell' ... Heaven but the vision of fulfilled desire, And Hell the shadow of a soul on fire." In other words, not the kind of place, but the kind of people in it, makes Heaven or Hell. Crane, Religion of To- morrow, 341—"The earth is but a breeding-ground from which God intends to populate the whole universe. After death, the soul goes to that place which God has prepared as its home. In the resurrection they 'neither marry nor are given in marriage' (Mat. 22:30) = ours is the only generative planet. There is no reproduction hereafter. To incorporate himself into the race, the Father must come to the reproductive planet."

Dean Stanley: "Till death us part! So speaks the heart When each repeats to each the words of doom; Through blessing and through curse, For better and for worse, We will be one till that dread hour shall come. Life, with its myriad grasp, Our yearning souls shall clasp, By ceaseless love and still expectant wonder, In bonds that shall endure, Indissolubly sure, Till God in death shall part our paths asunder. Till death us join! O voice yet more divine, That to the broken heart breathes hope sublime; Through lonely hours and shattered powers, We still are one despite of change or time. Death, with his healing hand, Shall once more knit the band, Which needs but that one link which none may sever; Till through the only Good, Heard, felt and understood, Our life in God shall make us one forever."

(b) Is this earth to be the heaven of the saints?

We answer:

First,—that the earth is to be purified by fire, and perhaps prepared to be the abode of the saints,—although this last is not rendered certain by the Scriptures.

Rom. 8:19-23—"For the earnest expectation of the creation waiteth for the revealing of the sons of God. For the creation was subjected to vanity, not of its own will, but by reason of him who subjected it, in hope that the creation itself also shall be delivered from the bondage of corruption into the liberty of the glory of the children of God. For we know that the whole creation groaneth and travaileth in pain together until now. And not only so, but ourselves also, who have the first-fruits of the Spirit, even we ourselves groan within ourselves, waiting for our adoption, to wit, the redemption of our body"; 2 Pet. 3:12, 13—"looking for and earnestly desiring the coming of the day of God, by reason of which the heavens being on fire shall be dissolved, and the elements shall melt with fervent heat. But, according to his promise, we look for new heavens and a new earth, wherein dwelleth righteousness"; Rev. 21:1—"And I saw a new heaven and a new earth: for the first heaven and the first earth are passed away; and the sea is no more." Dorner: "Without loss of substantiality, matter will have exchanged its darkness, hardness, heaviness, inertia, and impenetrableness, for clearness, radiance, elasticity, and transparency. A new stadium will begin—God's advance to new creations, with the coöperation of perfected mankind."

Is the earth a molten mass, with a thin solid crust? Lord Kelvin says no,—it is more rigid and solid than steel. The interior may be intensely hot, yet pressure may render it solid to the very centre. The wrinkling of the surface may be due to contraction, or "solid flow," like the wrinkling in the skin of a baked apple that has cooled. See article on The Interior of the Earth, by G. F. Becker, in N. American Rev., April, 1893. Edward S. Holden, Director of the Lick Observatory, in The Forum, Oct. 1893:211-220, tells us that "the star Nova Aurigæ, which doubtless resembled our sun, within two days increased in brilliancy sixteen fold. Three months after its discovery it had become invisible. After four months again it reappeared and was comparatively bright. But it was no longer a star but a nebula. In other words it had developed changes of light and heat which, if repeated in the case of our own sun, would mean a quick end of the human race, and the utter annihilation of every vestige of animal and other life upon this earth.... This catastrophe occured in December, 1891, or was announced to us by light which reached us then. But this light must have left the star twenty, perhaps fifty, years earlier."

Secondly,—that this fitting-up of the earth for man's abode, even if it were declared in Scripture, would not render it certain that the saints are to be confined to these narrow limits (John 14:2). It seems rather to be intimated that the effect of Christ's work will be to bring the redeemed into union and intercourse with other orders of intelligence, from communion with whom they are now shut out by sin (Eph. 1:20; Col. 1:20).

John 14:2—"In my Father's house are many mansions"; Eph. 1:10—"unto a dispensation of the fulness of the times, to sum up all things in Christ, the things in the heavens, and the things upon the earth"; Col. 1:20—"through him to reconcile all things unto himself, having made peace through the blood of his cross; through him, I say, whether things upon the earth, or things in the heavens."

See Dr. A. C. Kendrick, in Bap. Quarterly, Jan. 1870. Dr. Kendrick thinks we need local associations. Earth may be our home, yet from this home we may set out on excursions through the universe, after a time returning again to our earthly abodes. So Chalmers, interpreting literally 2 Pet. 3. We certainly are in a prison here, and look out through the bars, as the Prisoner of Chillon looked over the lake to the green isle and the singing birds. Why are we shut out from intercourse with other worlds and other orders of intelligence? Apparently it is the effect of sin. We are in an abnormal state of durance and probation. Earth is out of harmony with God. The great harp of the universe has one of its strings out of tune, and that one discordant string makes a jar through the whole. All things in heaven and earth shall be reconciled when this one jarring string is keyed right and set in tune by the hand of love and mercy. See Leitch, God's Glory in the Heavens, 327-330.

2. Of the wicked.

The final state of the wicked is described under the figures of eternal fire (Mat. 25:41); the pit of the abyss (Rev. 9:2, 11); outer darkness (Mat. 8:12); torment (Rev. 14:10, 11); eternal punishment (Mat. 25:46); wrath of God (Rom. 2:5); second death (Rev. 21:8); eternal destruction from the face of the Lord (2 Thess. 1:9); eternal sin (Mark 3:29).

Mat. 25:41—"Depart from me, ye cursed, into the eternal fire which is prepared for the devil and his angels"; Rev. 9:2, 11—"And he opened the pit of the abyss; and there went up a smoke out of the pit, as the smoke of a great furnace.... They have over them as king the angel of the abyss: his name in Hebrew is Abaddon, and in the Greek tongue he hath the name Apollyon"; Mat. 8:12—"but the sons of the kingdom shall be cast forth into the outer darkness: there shall be the weeping and the gnashing of teeth"; Rev. 14:10, 11—"he also shall drink of the wine of the wrath of God, which is prepared unmixed in the cup of his anger; and he shall be tormented with fire and brimstone in the presence of the holy angels, and in the presence of the Lamb: and the smoke of their torment goeth up for ever and ever"; Mat. 25:46—"And these shall go away into eternal punishment."

Rom. 2:5—"after thy hardness and impenitent heart treasurest up for thyself wrath in the day of wrath and revelation of the righteous judgment of God"; Rev. 21:8—"But for the fearful, and unbelieving, and abominable, and murderers, and fornicators, and sorcerers, and idolaters, and all liars, their part shall be in the lake that burneth with fire and brimstone; which is the second death": 2 Thess. 1:9—"who shall suffer punishment, even eternal destruction from the face of the Lord and from the glory of his might"—here ἀπό, from, = not separation, but "proceeding from," and indicates that the everlasting presence of Christ, once realized, ensures everlasting destruction; Mark 3:29—"whosoever shall blaspheme against the Holy Spirit hath never forgiveness, but is guilty of an eternal sin"—a text which implies that (1) some will never cease to sin; (2) this eternal sinning will involve eternal misery; (3) this eternal misery, as the appointed vindication of the law, will be eternal punishment. As Uzziah, when smitten with leprosy, did not need to be thrust out of the temple, but "himself hasted also to go out" (2 Chron. 26:20), so Judas is said to go "to his own place" (Acts 1:25; cf. 4:23—where Peter and John, "being let go, they came to their own company"). Cf. John 8:35—"the bondservant abideth not in the house forever" = whatever be his outward connection with God, it can be only for a time; 15:2—"Every branch in me that beareth not fruit, he taketh it away"—at death; the history of Abraham showed that one might have outward connection with God that was only temporary: Ishmael was cast out; the promise belonged only to Isaac.

Wrightnour: "Gehenna was the place into which all the offal of the city of Jerusalem was swept. So hell is the penitentiary of the moral universe. The profligate is not happy in the prayer meeting, but in the saloon; the swine is not at home in the parlor, but in the sty. Hell is the sinner's own place; he had rather be there than in heaven; he will not come to the house of God, the nearest thing to heaven; why should we expect him to enter heaven itself?"

Summing up all, we may say that it is the loss of all good, whether physical or spiritual, and the misery of an evil conscience banished from God and from the society of the holy, and dwelling under God's positive curse forever. Here we are to remember, as in the case of the final state of the righteous, that the decisive and controlling element is not the outward, but the inward. If hell be a place, it is only that the outward may correspond to the inward. If there be outward torments, it is only because these will be fit, though subordinate, accompaniments of the inward state of the soul.

Every living creature will have an environment suited to its character—"its own place." "I know of the future judgment, How dreadful so e'er it be, That to sit alone with my conscience Will be judgment enough for me." Calvin: "The wicked have the seeds of hell in their own hearts." Chrysostom, commenting on the words "Depart, ye cursed," says: "Their own works brought the punishment on them; the fire was not prepared for them, but for Satan; yet, since they cast themselves into it, 'Impute it to yourselves,' he says, 'that you are there.' " Milton, Par. Lost, 4:75—Satan: "Which way I fly is hell; myself am hell." Byron: "There is no power in holy men, Nor charm in prayer, nor purifying form Of penitence, nor outward look, nor fast, Nor agony, nor, greater than all these, The innate torture of that deep despair Would make a hell of heaven, can exorcise From out the unbounded spirit the quick sense Of its own sins."

Phelps, English Style, 228, speaks of "a law of the divine government, by which the body symbolizes, in its experience, the moral condition of its spiritual inhabitant. The drift of sin is to physical suffering. Moral depravity tends always to a corrupt and tortured body. Certain diseases are the product of certain crimes. The whole catalogue of human pains, from a toothache to the angina pectoris, is but a witness to a state of sin expressed by an experience of suffering. Carry this law into the experience of eternal sin. The bodies of the wicked live again as well as those of the righteous. You have therefore a spiritual body, inhabited and used, and therefore tortured, by a guilty soul,—a body, perfected in its sensibilities, inclosing and expressing a soul matured in its depravity." Augustine, Confessions, 25—"Each man's sin is the instrument of his punishment, and his iniquity is turned into his torment." Lord Bacon: "Being, without well-being, is a curse, and the greater the being, the greater the curse."

In our treatment of the subject of eternal punishment we must remember that false doctrine is often a reaction from the unscriptural and repulsive over-statements of Christian apologists. We freely concede: 1. that future punishment does not necessarily consist of physical torments,—it may be wholly internal and spiritual; 2. that the pain and suffering of the future are not necessarily due to positive inflictions of God,—they may result entirely from the soul's sense of loss, and from the accusations of conscience; and 3. that eternal punishment does not necessarily involve endless successions of suffering,—as God's eternity is not mere endlessness, so we may not be forever subject to the law of time.

An over-literal interpretation of the Scripture symbols has had much to do with such utterances as that of Savage, Life after Death, 101—"If the doctrine of eternal punishment was clearly and unmistakably taught in every leaf of the Bible, and on every leaf of all the Bibles of all the world, I could not believe a word of it. I should appeal from these misconceptions of even the seers and the great men to the infinite and eternal Good, who only is God, and who only on such terms could be worshiped."

The figurative language of Scripture is a miniature representation of what cannot be fully described in words. The symbol is a symbol; yet it is less, not greater, than the thing symbolized. It is sometimes fancied that Jonathan Edwards, when, in his sermon on "Sinners in the Hands of an Angry God," he represented the sinner as a worm shriveling in the eternal fire, supposed that hell consists mainly of such physical torments. But this is a misinterpretation of Edwards. As he did not fancy heaven essentially to consist in streets of gold or pearly gates, but rather in holiness and communion with Christ, of which these are the symbols, so he did not regard hell as consisting in fire and brimstone, but rather in the unholiness and separation from God of a guilty and accusing conscience, of which the fire and brimstone are symbols. He used the material imagery, because he thought that this best answered to the methods of Scripture. He probably went beyond the simplicity of the Scripture statements, and did not sufficiently explain the spiritual meaning of the symbols he used; but we are persuaded that he neither understood them literally himself, nor meant them to be so understood by others.

Sin is self-isolating, unsocial, selfish. By virtue of natural laws the sinner reaps as he has sown, and sooner or later is repaid by desertion or contempt. Then the selfishness of one sinner is punished by the selfishness of another, the ambition of one by the ambition of another, the cruelty of one by the cruelty of another. The misery of the wicked hereafter will doubtless be due in part to the spirit of their companions. They dislike the good, whose presence and example is a continual reproof and reminder of the height from which they have fallen, and they shut themselves out of their company. The judgment will bring about a complete cessation of intercourse between the good and the bad. Julius Müller, Doctrine of Sin, 1:239—"Beings whose relations to God are diametrically opposite, and persistently so, differ so greatly from each other that other ties of relationship became as nothing in comparison."

In order, however, to meet opposing views, and to forestall the common objections, we proceed to state the doctrine of future punishment in greater detail:

A. The future punishment of the wicked is not annihilation.

In our discussion of Physical Death, we have shown that, by virtue of its original creation in the image of God, the human soul is naturally immortal; that neither for the righteous nor the wicked is death a cessation of being; that on the contrary, the wicked enter at death upon a state of conscious suffering which the resurrection and the judgment only augment and render permanent. It is plain, moreover, that if annihilation took place at death, there could be no degrees in future punishment,—a conclusion itself at variance with express statements of Scripture.

The old annihilationism is represented by Hudson, Debt and Grace, and Christ our Life; also by Dobney, Future Punishment. It maintains that κόλασις, "punishment" (in Mat. 25:46—"eternal punishment"), means etymologically an everlasting "cutting-off." But we reply that the word had to a great degree lost its etymological significance, as is evident from the only other passage where it occurs in the New Testament, namely, 1 John 4:18—"fear hath punishment" (A. V.: "fear hath torment"). For full answer to the old statements of the annihilation-theory, see under Physical Death, pages 991-998.

That there are degrees of punishment in God's administration is evident from Luke 12:47, 48—"And that servant, who knew his Lord's will, and made not ready, nor did according to his will, shall be beaten with many stripes; but he that knew not, and did things worthy of stripes, shall be beaten with few stripes"; Rom. 2:5, 6—"after thy hardness and impenitent heart treasurest up for thyself wrath in the day of wrath and revelation of the righteous judgment of God; who will render to every man according to his works"; 2 Cor. 5:10—"For we must all be made manifest before the judgment-seat of Christ; that each one may receive the things done in the body, according to what he hath done, whether it be good or bad"; 11:15—"whose end shall be according to their works"; 2 Tim. 4:14—"Alexander the coppersmith did me much evil: the Lord will render to him according to his works"; Rev. 2:23—"I will give unto each one of you according to your works"; 18:5, 6—"her sins have reached even unto heaven, and God hath remembered her iniquities. Render unto her even as she rendered, and double unto her the double according to her works: in the cup which she mingled, mingle unto her double."

A French Christian replied to the argument of his deistical friend: "Probably you are right; probably you are not immortal; but I am." This was the doctrine of conditional immortality, the doctrine that only the good survive. We grant that the measure of our faith in immortality is the measure of our fitness for its blessings; but it is not the measure of our possession of immortality. We are immortal beings, whether we believe it or not. The acorn is potentially an oak, but it may never come to its full development. There is a saltless salt, which, though it does not cease to exist, is cast out and trodden under foot of men. Denney, Studies in Theology, 256—"Conditional immortality denies that man can exist after death without being united to Christ by faith. But the immortality of man cannot be something accidental, something appended to his nature, after he believes in Christ. It must be something, at the very lowest, for which his nature is constituted, even if apart from Christ it can never realize itself as it ought."

Broadus, Com. on Mat. 25:46 (page 514)—"He who caused to exist could keep in existence. Mark 9:49—'Every one shall be salted with fire'—has probably this meaning. Fire is usually destructive; but this unquenchable fire will act like salt, preserving instead of destroying. So Keble, Christian Year, 5th Sunday in Lent, says of the Jews in their present condition: 'Salted with fire, they seem to show How spirits lost in endless woe May undecaying live. Oh, sickening thought! Yet hold it fast Long as this glittering world shall last, Or sin at heart survive.' "

There are two forms of the annihilation theory which are more plausible, and which in recent times find a larger number of advocates, namely:

(a) That the powers of the wicked are gradually weakened, as the natural result of sin, so that they finally cease to be.—We reply, first, that moral evil does not, in this present life, seem to be incompatible with a constant growth of the intellectual powers, at least in certain directions, and we have no reason to believe the fact to be different in the world to come; secondly, that if this theory were true, the greater the sin, the speedier would be the relief from punishment.

This form of the annihilation theory is suggested by Bushnell, in his Forgiveness and Law, 146, 147, and by Martineau, Study, 2:107-8. Dorner also, in his Eschatology, seems to favor it as one of the possible methods of future punishment. He says: "To the ethical also pertains ontological significance. The 'second death' may be the dissolving of the soul itself into nothing. Estrangement from God, the source of life, ends in extinction of life. The orthodox talk about demented beings, raging in impotent fury, amounts to the same—annihilation of their human character. Evil is never the substance of the soul,—this remains metaphysically good." It is argued that even for saved sinners there is a loss. The prodigal regained his father's favor, but he could not regain his lost patrimony. We cannot get back the lost time, nor the lost growth. Much more, then, in the case of the wicked, will there be perpetual loss. Draper: "At every return to the sun, comets lose a portion of their size and brightness, stretching out until the nucleus loses control, the mass breaks up, and the greater portion navigates the sky, in the shape of disconnected meteorites."

To this argument it is often replied that certain minds grow in their powers, at least in certain directions, in spite of their sin. Napoleon's military genius, during all his early years, grew with experience. Sloane, in his Life of Napoleon, however, seems to show that the Emperor lost his grip as he went on. Success unbalanced his judgment; he gave way to physical indulgence; his body was not equal to the strain he put upon it; at Waterloo he lost precious moments of opportunity by vacillation and inability to keep awake. There was physical, mental, and moral deterioration. But may this not be the result of the soul's connection with a body? Satan's cunning and daring seem to be on the increase from the first mention of him in Scripture to its end. See Princeton Review, 1882:673-694. Will not this very cunning and daring, however, work its own ruin, and lead Satan to his final and complete destruction? Does not sin blunt the intellect, unsettle one's sober standards of decision, lead one to prefer a trifling present triumph or pleasure to a permanent good?

Gladden, What is Left? 104, 105—"Evil is benumbing and deadening. Selfishness weakens a man's mental grasp, and narrows his range of vision. The schemer becomes less astute as he grows older; he is morally sure, before he dies, to make some stupendous blunder which even a tyro would have avoided.... The devil, who has sinned longest, must be the greatest fool in the universe, and we need not be at all afraid of him." To the view that this weakening of powers leads to absolute extinction of being, we oppose the consideration that its award of retribution is glaringly unjust in making the greatest sinner the least sufferer; since to him relief, in the way of annihilation, comes the soonest.

(b) That there is for the wicked, certainly after death, and possibly between death and the judgment, a positive punishment proportioned to their deeds, but that this punishment issues in, or is followed by, annihilation.—We reply first, that upon this view, as upon any theory of annihilation, future punishment is a matter of grace as well as of justice—a notion for which Scripture affords no warrant; secondly, that Scripture not only gives no hint of the cessation of this punishment, but declares in the strongest terms its endlessness.

The second form of the annihilation theory seems to have been held by Justin Martyr (Trypho, Edinb. transl.)—"Some, who have appeared worthy of God, never die; but others are punished so long as God wills them to exist and be punished." The soul exists because God wills, and no longer than he wills. "Whenever it is necessary that the soul should cease to exist, the spirit of life is removed from it, and there is no more soul, but it goes back to the place from which it was taken."

Schaff, Hist. Christ. Church, 2:608, 609—"Justin Martyr teaches that the wicked or hopelessly impenitent will be raised at the judgment to receive an eternal punishment. He speaks of it in twelve passages: 'We believe that all who live wickedly and do not repent will be punished in eternal fire.' Such language is inconsistent with the annihilation theory for which Justin Martyr has been claimed. He does indeed reject the idea of the independent immortality of the soul, and hints at the possible final destruction of the wicked; but he puts that possibility countless ages beyond the final judgment, so that it loses all practical significance."

A modern advocate of this view is White, in his Life in Christ. He favors a conditional immortality, belonging only to those who are joined to Christ by faith; but he makes a retributive punishment and pain fall upon the godless, before their annihilation. The roots of this view lie in a false conception of holiness as a form or manifestation of benevolence, and of punishment as deterrent and preventive instead of vindicative of righteousness. To the minds of its advocates, extinction of being is a comparative blessing; and they, for this reason, prefer it to the common view. See Whiton, Is Eternal Punishment Endless?

A view similar to that which we are opposing is found in Henry Drummond, Natural Law in the Spiritual World. Evil is punished by its own increase. Drummond, however, leaves no room for future life or for future judgment in the case of the unregenerate. See reviews of Drummond, in Watts, New Apologetic, 332; and in Murphy, Nat. Selection and Spir. Freedom, 19-21, 77-124. While Drummond is an annihilationist, Murphy is a restorationist. More rational and Scriptural than either of these is the saying of Tower: "Sin is God's foe. He does not annihilate it, but he makes it the means of displaying his holiness; as the Romans did not slay their captured enemies, but made them their servants." The terms αἰών and αἰώνιος, which we have still to consider, afford additional Scripture testimony against annihilation. See also the argument from the divine justice, pages 1046-1051; article on the Doctrine of Extinction, in New Englander, March, 1879:201-224; Hovey, Manual of Theology and Ethics, 153-168; J. S. Barlow, Endless Being; W. H. Robinson, on Conditional Immortality, in Report of Baptist Congress for 1886.

Since neither one of these two forms of the annihilation theory is Scriptural or rational, we avail ourselves of the evolutionary hypothesis as throwing light upon the problem. Death is not degeneracy ending in extinction, nor punishment ending in extinction,—it is atavism that returns, or tends to return, to the animal type. As moral development is from the brute to man, so abnormal development is from man to the brute.

Lord Byron: "All suffering doth destroy, or is destroyed." This is true, not of man's being, but of his well being. Ribot, Diseases of the Will, 115—"Dissolution pursues a regressive course from the more voluntary and more complex to the less voluntary and more simple, that is to say, toward the automatic. One of the first signs of mental impairment is incapacity for sustained attention. Unity, stability, power, have ceased, and the end is extinction of the will." We prefer to say, loss of the freedom of the will. On the principle of evolution, abuse of freedom may result in reversion to the brute, annihilation not of existence but of higher manhood, punishment from within rather than from without, eternal penalty in the shape of eternal loss. Mat. 24:13—"he that endureth to the end, the same shall be saved"—has for its parallel passage Luke 21:19—"In your patience ye shall win your souls," i. e., shall by free will get possession of your own being. Losing one's soul is just the opposite, namely, losing one's free will, by disuse renouncing freedom, becoming a victim of habit, nature, circumstance, and this is the cutting off and annihilation of true manhood. "To be in hell is to drift; to be in heaven is to steer" (Bernard Shaw).

In John 15:2 Christ says of all men—the natural branches of the vine—"Every branch in me that beareth not fruit, he taketh it away"; Ps. 49:20—"Man that is in honor, and understandeth not, Is like the beasts that perish"; Rev. 22:15—"Without are the dogs." In heathen fable men were turned into beasts, and even into trees. The story of Circe is a parable of human fate,—men may become apes, tigers, or swine. They may lose their higher powers of consciousness and will. By perpetual degradation they may suffer eternal punishment. All life that is worthy of the name may cease, while still existence of a low animal type is prolonged. We see precisely these results of sin in this world. We have reason to believe that the same laws of development will operate in the world to come.

McConnell, Evolution of Immortality, 85-95, 99, 124, 180—"Immortality, or survival after death, depends upon man's freeing himself from the law which sweeps away the many, and becoming an individual (indivisible) that is fit to survive. The individual must become stronger than the species. By using will aright, he lays hold of the infinite Life, and becomes one who, like Christ, has 'life in himself' (John 5:26). Gravitation and chemical affinity had their way in the universe until they were arrested and turned about in the interest of life. Overproduction, death, and the survival of the fittest, had their ruthless sway until they were reversed in the interest of affection. The supremacy of the race at the expense of the individual we may expect to continue until something in the individual comes to be of more importance than that law, and no longer.... Goodness can arrest and turn back for nations the primal law of growth, vigor, and decline. Is it too much to believe that it may do the same for an individual man?... Life is a thing to be achieved. At every step there are a thousand candidates who fail, for one that attains.... Until moral sensibility becomes self-conscious, all question of personal immortality becomes irrelevant, because there is, accurately speaking, no personality to be immortal. Up to that point the individual living creature, whether in human form or not, falls short of that essential personality for which eternal life can have any meaning." But how about children who never come to moral consciousness? McConnell appeals to heredity. The child of one who has himself achieved immortality may also prove to be immortal. But is there no chance for the children of sinners? The doctrine of McConnell leans toward the true solution, but it is vitiated by the belief that individuality is a transient gift which only goodness can make permanent. We hold on the other hand that this gift of God is "without repentance" (Rom. 11:29), and that no human being can lose life, except in the sense of losing all that makes life desirable.

B. Punishment after death excludes new probation and ultimate restoration of the wicked.

Some have maintained the ultimate restoration of all human beings, by appeal to such passages as the following: Mat. 19:28; Acts 3:21; Eph. 1:9, 10.

Mat. 19:28—"in the regeneration when the Son of man shall sit on the throne of his glory"; Acts 3:21—Jesus, "whom the heaven must receive until the times of restoration of all things"; 1 Cor. 15:26—"The last enemy that shall be abolished is death"; Eph. 1:9, 10—"according to his good pleasure which he purposed in him unto a dispensation of the fulness of the times, to sum up all things in Christ, the things in the heavens, and the things upon the earth"; Phil. 2:10, 11—"that in the name of Jesus every knee should bow, of things in heaven and things on earth and things under the earth, and that every tongue should confess that Jesus Christ is Lord, to the glory of God the Father"; 2 Pet. 3:9, 13—"not wishing that any should perish, but that all should come to repentance ... But, according to his promise, we look for new heavens and a new earth, wherein dwelleth righteousness."

Robert Browning: "That God, by God's own ways occult, May—doth, I will believe—bring back All wanderers to a single track." B. W. Lockhart: "I must believe that evil is essentially transient and mortal, or alter my predicates of God. And I must believe in the ultimate extinction of that personality whom the power of God cannot sometime win to goodness. The only alternative is the termination of a wicked life either through redemption or through extinction." Mulford, Republic of God, claims that the soul's state cannot be fixed by any event, such as death, outside of itself. If it could, the soul would exist, not under a moral government, but under fate, and God himself would be only another name for fate. The soul carries its fate, under God, in its power of choice; and who dares to say that this power to choose the good ceases at death?

For advocacy of a second probation for those who have not consciously rejected Christ in this life, see Newman Smyth's edition of Dorner's Eschatology. For the theory of restoration, see Farrar, Eternal Hope; Birks, Victory of Divine Goodness; Jukes, Restitution of All Things; Delitzsch, Bib. Psychologie, 469-476; Robert Browning, Apparent Failure; Tennyson, In Memoriam, § liv. Per contra, see Hovey, Bib. Eschatology, 95-144. See also, Griffith-Jones, Ascent through Christ, 406-440.

(a) These passages, as obscure, are to be interpreted in the light of those plainer ones which we have already cited. Thus interpreted, they foretell only the absolute triumph of the divine kingdom, and the subjection of all evil to God.

The true interpretation of the passages above mentioned is indicated in Meyer's note on Eph. 1:9, 10—this namely, that "the allusion is not to the restoration of fallen individuals, but to the restoration of universal harmony, implying that the wicked are to be excluded from the kingdom of God." That there is no allusion to a probation after this life, is clear from Luke 16:19-31—the parable of the rich man and Lazarus. Here penalty is inflicted for the sins done "in thy lifetime" (v. 25); this penalty is unchangeable—"there is a great gulf fixed" (v. 26); the rich man asks favors for his brethren who still live on the earth, but none for himself (v. 27, 28). John 5:25-29—"The hour cometh, and now is, when the dead shall hear the voice of the Son of God; and they that hear shall live. For as the Father hath life in himself, even so gave he to the Son also to have life in himself: and he gave him authority to execute judgment, because he is a son of man. Marvel not at this: for the hour cometh, in which all that are in the tombs shall hear his voice, and shall come forth; they that have done good, unto the resurrection of life; and they that have done evil, until the resurrection of judgment"—here it is declared that, while for those who have done good there is a resurrection of life, there is for those who have done ill only a resurrection of judgment. John 8:21, 24—"shall die in your sin: whither I go, ye cannot come ... except ye believe that I am he, ye shall die in your sins"—sayings which indicate finality in the decisions of this life.

Orr, Christian View of God and the World, 243—"Scripture invariably represents the judgment as proceeding on the data of this life, and it concentrates every ray of appeal into the present." John 9:4—"We must work the works of him that sent me, while it is day: the night cometh

when no man can work"—intimates that there is no opportunity to secure salvation after death. The Christian hymn writer has caught the meaning of Scripture, when he says of those who have passed through the gate of death: "Fixed in an eternal state, They have done with all below; We a little longer wait; But how little, none can know."

(b) A second probation is not needed to vindicate the justice or the love of God, since Christ, the immanent God, is already in this world present with every human soul, quickening the conscience, giving to each man his opportunity, and making every decision between right and wrong a true probation. In choosing evil against their better judgment even the heathen unconsciously reject Christ. Infants and idiots, as they have not consciously sinned, are, as we may believe, saved at death by having Christ revealed to them and by the regenerating influence of his Spirit.

Rom. 1:18-28—there is probation under the light of nature as well as under the gospel, and under the law of nature as well as under the gospel men may be given up "unto a reprobate mind"; 2:6-16—Gentiles shall be judged, not by the gospel, but by the law of nature, and shall "perish without the law ... in the day when God shall judge the secrets of men." 2 Cor. 5:10—"For we must all be made manifest before the judgment-seat of Christ; [not that each may have a new opportunity to secure salvation, but] that each one may receive the things done in the body, according to what he hath done, whether it be good or bad"; Heb. 6:8—"whose end is to be burned"—not to be quickened again; 9:27—"And inasmuch as it is appointed unto men once to die, and after this cometh [not a second probation, but] judgment." Luckock, Intermediate State, 22—"In Heb. 9:27, the word 'judgment' has no article. The judgment alluded to is not the final or general judgment, but only that by which the place of the soul is determined in the Intermediate State."

Denney, Studies in Theology, 243—"In Mat. 25, our Lord gives a pictorial representation of the judgment of the heathen. All nations—all the Gentiles—are gathered before the King; and their destiny is determined, not by their conscious acceptance or rejection of the historical Savior, but by their unconscious acceptance or rejection of him in the persons of those who needed services of love.... This does not square with the idea of a future probation. It rather tells us plainly that men may do things of final and decisive import in this life, even if Christ is unknown to them.... The real argument against future probation is that it depreciates the present life, and denies the infinite significance that, under all conditions, essentially and inevitably belongs to the actions of a self-conscious moral being. A type of will may be in process of formation, even in a heathen man, on which eternal issues depend.... Second probation lowers the moral tone of the spirit. The present life acquires a relative unimportance. I dare not say that if I forfeit the opportunity the present life gives me I shall ever have another, and therefore I dare not say so to another man."

For an able review of the Scripture testimony against a second probation, see G. F. Wright, Relation of Death to Probation, iv. Emerson, the most recent advocate of restorationism, in his Doctrine of Probation Examined, 42, is able to evade these latter passages only by assuming that they are to be spiritually interpreted, and that there is to be no literal outward day of judgment—an error which we have previously discussed and refuted,—see pages 1024, 1025.

(c) The advocates of universal restoration are commonly the most strenuous defenders of the inalienable freedom of the human will to make choices contrary to its past character and to all the motives which are or can be brought to bear upon it. As a matter of fact, we find in this world that men choose sin in spite of infinite motives to the contrary. Upon the theory of human freedom just mentioned, no motives which God can use will certainly accomplish the salvation of all moral creatures. The soul which resists Christ here may resist him forever.

Emerson, in the book just referred to, says: "The truth that sin is in its permanent essence a free choice, however for a time it may be held in mechanical combination with the notion of moral opportunity arbitrarily closed, can never mingle with it, and must in the logical outcome permanently cast it off. Scripture presumes and teaches the constant capability of souls to obey as well as to be disobedient." Emerson is correct. If the doctrine of the unlimited ability of the human will be a true one, then restoration in the future world is possible. Clement and Origen founded on this theory of will their denial of future punishment. If will be essentially the power of contrary choice, and if will may act independently of all character and motive, there can be no objective certainty that the lost will remain sinful. In short, there can be no finality, even to God's allotments, nor is any last judgment possible.

Upon this view, regeneration and conversion are as possible at any time in the future as they are to-day.

But those who hold to this defective philosophy of the will should remember that unlimited freedom is unlimited freedom to sin, as well as unlimited freedom to turn to God. If restoration is possible, endless persistence in evil is possible also; and this last the Scripture predicts. Whittier: "What if thine eye refuse to see, Thine ear of heaven's free welcome fail, And thou a willing captive be, Thyself thine own dark jail?" Swedenborg says that the man who obstinately refuses the inheritance of the sons of God is allowed the pleasures of the beast, and enjoys in his own low way the hell to which he has confined himself. Every occupant of hell prefers it to heaven. Dante, Hell, iv—"All here together come from every clime, And to o'erpass the river are not loth, For so heaven's justice goads them on, that fear Is turned into desire. Hence never passed good spirit." The lost are Heautoutimoroumenoi, or self-tormentors, to adopt the title of Terence's play. See Whedon, in Meth. Quar. Rev., Jan. 1884; Robbins, in Bib. Sac., 1881:460-507.

Denney, Studies in Theology, 255—"The very conception of human freedom involves the possibility of its permanent misuse, or of what our Lord himself calls 'eternal sin' (Mark 3:29)." Shedd, Dogm. Theology, 2:699—"Origen's restorationism grew naturally out of his view of human liberty"—the liberty of indifference—"endless alternations of falls and recoveries, of hells and heavens; so that practically he taught nothing but a hell." J. C. Adams, The Leisure of God: "It is lame logic to maintain the inviolable freedom of the will, and at the same time insist that God can, through his ample power, through protracted punishment, bring the soul into a disposition which it does not wish to feel. There is no compulsory holiness possible. In our Civil War there was some talk of 'compelling men to volunteer,' but the idea was soon seen to involve a self-contradiction."

(d) Upon the more correct view of the will which we have advocated, the case is more hopeless still. Upon this view, the sinful soul, in its very sinning, gives to itself a sinful bent of intellect, affection, and will; in other words, makes for itself a character, which, though it does not render necessary, yet does render certain, apart from divine grace, the continuance of sinful action. In itself it finds a self-formed motive to evil strong enough to prevail over all inducements to holiness which God sees it wise to bring to bear. It is in the next world, indeed, subjected to suffering. But suffering has in itself no reforming power. Unless accompanied by special renewing influences of the Holy Spirit, it only hardens and embitters the soul. We have no Scripture evidence that such influences of the Spirit are exerted, after death, upon the still impenitent; but abundant evidence, on the contrary, that the moral condition in which death finds men is their condition forever.

See Bushnell's "One Trial Better than Many," in Sermons on Living Subjects; also see his Forgiveness and Law, 146, 147. Bushnell argues that God would give us fifty trials, if that would do us good. But there is no possibility of such result. The first decision adverse to God renders it more difficult to make a right decision upon the next opportunity. Character tends to fixity, and each new opportunity may only harden the heart and increase its guilt and condemnation. We should have no better chance of salvation if our lives were lengthened to the term of the sinners before the flood. Mere suffering does not convert the soul; see Martineau, Study, 2:100. A life of pain did not make Blanco White a believer; see Mozley, Hist. and Theol. Essays, vol. 2, essay 1.

Edward A. Lawrence, Does Everlasting Punishment Last Forever?—"If the deeds of the law do not justify here, how can the penalties of the law hereafter? The pain from a broken limb does nothing to mend the break, and the suffering from disease does nothing to cure it. Penalty pays no debts,—it only shows the outstanding and unsettled accounts." If the will does not act without motive, then it is certain that without motives men will never repent. To an impenitent and rebellious sinner the motive must come, not from within, but from without. Such motives God presents by his Spirit in this life; but when this life ends and God's Spirit is withdrawn, no motives to repentance will be presented. The soul's dislike for God will issue only in complaint and resistance. Shakespeare, Hamlet, 3:4—"Try what repentance can? what can it not? Yet what can it, when one cannot repent?" Marlowe, Faustus: "Hell hath no limits, nor is circumscribed In one self place; for where we are is hell, And where hell is, there we must ever be."

The pressure of the atmosphere without is counteracted by the resistance of the atmosphere within the body. So God's life within is the only thing that can enable us to bear God's afflictive dispensations without. Without God's Spirit to inspire repentance the wicked man in this world never feels sorrow for his deeds, except as he realizes their evil consequences. Physical anguish and punishment inspire hatred, not of sin, but of the effects of sin. The remorse of Judas induced confession, but not true repentance. So in the next world punishment will secure recognition of God and of his justice, on the part of the transgressor, but it will not regenerate or save. The penalties of the future life will be no more effectual to reform the sinner than were the invitations of Christ and the strivings of the Holy Spirit in the present life. The transientness of good resolves which are forced out of us by suffering is illustrated by the old couplet: "The devil was sick,—the devil a monk would be; The devil got well,—the devil a monk was he."

Charles G. Sewall: "Paul Lester Ford, the novelist, was murdered by his brother Malcolm, because the father of the two brothers had disinherited the one who committed the crime. Has God the right to disinherit any one of his children? We answer that God disinherits no one. Each man decides for himself whether he will accept the inheritance. It is a matter of character. A father cannot give his son an education. The son may play truant and throw away his opportunity. The prodigal son disinherited himself. Heaven is not a place,—it is a way of living, a condition of being. If you have a musical ear, I will admit you to a lovely concert. If you have not a musical ear, I may give you a reserved seat and you will hear no melody. Some men fail of salvation because they have no taste for it and will not have it."

The laws of God's universe are closing in upon the impenitent sinner, as the iron walls of the mediæval prison closed in night by night upon the victim,—each morning there was one window less, and the dungeon came to be a coffin. In Jean Ingelow's poem "Divided," two friends, parted by a little rivulet across which they could clasp hands, walk on in the direction in which the stream is flowing, till the rivulet becomes a brook, and the brook a river, and the river an arm of the sea across which no voice can be heard and there is no passing. By constant neglect to use our opportunity, we lose the power to cross from sin to righteousness, until between the soul and God "there is a great gulf fixed" (Luke 16:26).

John G. Whittier wrote within a twelvemonth of his death: "I do believe that we take with us into the next world the same freedom of will we have here, and that there, as here, he that turns to the Lord will find mercy; that God never ceases to follow his creatures with love, and is always ready to hear the prayer of the penitent. But I also believe that now is the accepted time, and that he who dallies with sin may find the chains of evil habit too strong to break in this world or the other." And the following is the Quaker poet's verse: "Though God be good and free be heaven, Not force divine can love compel; And though the song of sins forgiven Might sound through lowest hell, The sweet persuasion of his voice Respects the sanctity of will. He giveth day; thou hast thy choice To walk in darkness still."

Longfellow, Masque of Pandora: "Never by lapse of time The soul defaced by crime Into its former self returns again; For every guilty deed Holds in itself the seed Of retribution and undying pain. Never shall be the loss Restored, till Helios Hath purified them with his heavenly fires; Then what was lost is won, And the new life begun, Kindled with nobler passions and desires." Seth, Freedom as Ethical Postulate, 42—"Faust's selling his soul to Mephistopheles, and signing the contract with his life's blood, is no single transaction, done deliberately, on one occasion; rather, that is the lurid meaning of a life which consists of innumerable individual acts,—the life of evil means that." See John Caird, Fundamental Ideas of Christianity, 2:88; Crane, Religion of To- morrow, 315.

(e) The declaration as to Judas, in Mat. 26:24, could not be true upon the hypothesis of a final restoration. If at any time, even after the lapse of ages, Judas be redeemed, his subsequent infinite duration of blessedness must outweigh all the finite suffering through which he has passed. The Scripture statement that "good were it for that man if he had not been born" must be regarded as a refutation of the theory of universal restoration.

Mat. 26:24—"The Son of man goeth, even as it is written of him: but woe unto that man through whom the Son of man is betrayed! good were it for that man if he had not been born." G. F. Wright, Relation of Death to Probation: "As Christ of old healed only those who came or were brought to him, so now he waits for the coöperation of human agency. God has limited himself to an orderly method in human salvation. The consuming missionary zeal of the apostles and the early church shows that they believed the decisions of this life to be final decisions. The early church not only thought the heathen world would perish without the gospel, but they found a conscience in the heathen answering to this belief. The solicitude drawn out by this responsibility for our fellows may be one means of securing the moral stability of the future. What is bound on earth is bound in heaven; else why not pray for the wicked dead?" It is certainly a remarkable fact, if this theory be true, that we have in Scripture not a single instance of prayer for the dead.

The apocryphal 2 Maccabees 12:39 sq. gives an instance of Jewish prayer for the dead. Certain who were slain had concealed under their coats things consecrated to idols. Judas and his host therefore prayed that this sin might be forgiven to the slain, and they contributed 2,000 drachmas of silver to send a sin offering for them to Jerusalem. So modern Jews pray for the dead; see Luckock, After Death, 54-66—an argument for such prayer. John Wesley, Works, 9:55, maintains the legality of prayer for the dead. Still it is true that we have no instance of such prayer in canonical Scriptures. Ps. 132:1—"Jehovah, remember for David All his affliction"—is not a prayer for the dead, but signifies: "Remember for David", so as to fulfil thy promise to him, "all his anxious cares"—with regard to the building of the temple; the psalm having been composed, in all probability, for the temple dedication. Paul prays that God will "grant mercy to the house of Onesiphorus" (2 Tim. 1:16), from which it has been unwarrantably inferred that Onesiphorus was dead at the time of the apostle's writing; but Paul's further prayer in verse 18—"the Lord grant unto him to find mercy of the Lord in that day"—seems rather to point to the death of Onesiphorus as yet in the future.

Shedd, Dogm. Theology, 2:715 note—"Many of the arguments constructed against the doctrine of endless punishment proceed upon the supposition that original sin, or man's evil inclination, is the work of God: that because man is born in sin (Ps. 51:5), he was created in sin. All the strength and plausibility of John Foster's celebrated letter lies in the assumption that the moral corruption and impotence of the sinner, whereby it is impossible to save himself from eternal death, is not self- originated and self-determined, but infused by his Maker. 'If,' says he, 'the very nature of man, as created by the Sovereign Power, be in such desperate disorder that there is no possibility of conversion or salvation except in instances where that Power interposes with a special and redeeming efficacy, how can we conceive that the main portion of the race, thus morally impotent (that is, really and absolutely impotent), will be eternally punished for the inevitable result of this moral impotence?' If this assumption of concreated depravity and impotence is correct, Foster's objection to eternal retribution is conclusive and fatal.... Endless punishment supposes the freedom of the human will, and is impossible without it. Self-determination runs parallel with hell."

The theory of a second probation, as recently advocated, is not only a logical result of that defective view of the will already mentioned, but it is also in part a consequence of denying the old orthodox and Pauline doctrine of the organic unity of the race in Adam's first transgression. New School Theology has been inclined to deride the notion of a fair probation of humanity in our first father, and of a common sin and guilt of mankind in him. It cannot find what it regards as a fair probation for each individual since that first sin; and the conclusion is easy that there must be such a fair probation for each individual in the world to come. But we may advise those who take this view to return to the old theology. Grant a fair probation for the whole race already passed, and the condition of mankind is no longer that of mere unfortunates unjustly circumstanced, but rather that of beings guilty and condemned, to whom present opportunity, and even present existence, is a matter of pure grace,—much more the general provision of a salvation, and the offer of it to any human soul. This world is already a place of second probation; and since the second probation is due wholly to God's mercy, no probation after death is needed to vindicate either the justice or the goodness of God. See Kellogg, in Presb. Rev., April, 1885:226-256; Cremer, Beyond the Grave, preface by A. A. Hodge, xxxvi sq.; E. D. Morris, Is There Salvation After Death? A. H. Strong, on The New Theology, in Bap. Quar. Rev., Jan. 1888,—reprinted in Philosophy and Religion, 164-179.

C. Scripture declares this future punishment of the wicked to be eternal.

It does this by its use of the terms αἰών, αἰώνιος.—Some, however, maintain that these terms do not necessarily imply eternal duration. We reply:

(a) It must be conceded that these words do not etymologically necessitate the idea of eternity; and that, as expressing the idea of "age-long," they are sometimes used in a limited or rhetorical sense.

2 Tim. 1:9—"his own purpose and grace, which was given us in Christ Jesus before times eternal"—but the past duration of the world is limited; Heb. 9:26—"now once at the end of the ages hath he been manifested"—here the αἰῶνες have an end; Tit. 1:2—"eternal life ... promised before times eternal"; but here there may be a reference to the eternal covenant of the Father with the Son; Jer. 31:3—"I have loved thee with an everlasting love" = a love which antedated time; Rom. 16:25, 26—"the mystery which hath been kept in silence through times eternal ... according to the commandment of the eternal God"—here "eternal" is used in the same verse in two senses. It is argued that in Mat. 25:46—"these shall go away into eternal punishment"—the word "eternal" may be used in the narrower sense.

Arthur Chambers, Our Life after Death, 222-236—"In Mat. 13:39—'the harvest is the end of the αἰών,' and in 2 Tim. 4:10—'Demas forsook me, having loved this present αἰών'—the word αἰών clearly implies limitation of time. Why not take the word αἰών in this sense in Mark 3:29—'hath never forgiveness, but is guilty of an eternal sin'? We must not translate αἰών by 'world,' and so express limitation, while we translate αἰώνιος by 'eternal,' and so express endlessness which excludes limitation; cf. Gen. 13:15—'all the land which thou seest, to thee will I give it, and to thy seed forever'; Num. 25:13—'it shall be unto him [Phinehas], and to his seed after him, the covenant of an everlasting priesthood'; Josh. 24:2—'your fathers dwelt of old time [from eternity] beyond the River'; Deut. 23:3—'An Ammonite or a Moabite shall not enter ... into the assembly of Jehovah for ever'; Ps. 24:7, 8—'be ye lifted up, ye everlasting doors.' "

(b) They do, however, express the longest possible duration of which the subject to which they are attributed is capable; so that, if the soul is immortal, its punishment must be without end.

Gen. 49:26—"the everlasting hills"; 17:8, 13—"I will give unto thee ... all the land of Canaan, for an everlasting possession ... my covenant [of circumcision] shall be in your flesh for an everlasting covenant"; Ex. 21:6—"he [the slave] shall serve him [his master] for ever"; 2 Chron. 6:2—"But I have built thee an house of habitation, and a place for thee to dwell in for ever"—of the temple at Jerusalem; Jude 6, 7—"angels ... he hath kept in everlasting bonds under darkness unto the judgment of the great day. Even as Sodom and Gomorrah ... are set forth as an example, suffering the punishment of eternal fire"—here in Jude 6, bonds which endure only to the judgment day are called ἀΐδίοις (the same word which is used in Rom. 1:20—"his everlasting power and divinity"), and fire which lasts only till Sodom and Gomorrah are consumed is called αἰωνίου. Shedd, Dogm. Theology, 2:687—"To hold land forever is to hold it as long as grass grows and water runs, i. e., as long as this world or æon endures."

In all the passages cited above, the condition denoted by αἰώνιος lasts as long as the object endures of which it is predicated. But we have seen (pages 982-998) that physical death is not the end of man's existence, and that the soul, made in the image of God, is immortal. A punishment, therefore, that lasts as long as the soul, must be an everlasting punishment. Another interpretation of the passages in Jude is, however, entirely possible. It is maintained by many that the "everlasting bonds" of the fallen angels do not cease at the judgment, and that Sodom and Gomorrah suffer "the punishment of eternal fire" in the sense that their condemnation at the judgment will be a continuation of that begun in the time of Lot (see Mat. 10:15—"It shall be more tolerable for the land of Sodom and Gomorrah in the day of judgment, than for that city").

(c) If, when used to describe the future punishment of the wicked, they do not declare the endlessness of that punishment, there are no words in the Greek language which could express that meaning.

C. F. Wright, Relation of Death to Probation: "The Bible writers speak of eternity in terms of time, and make the impression more vivid by reduplicating the longest time-words they had [e. g., εἰς τοὺς αἰῶνας τῶν αἰώνων = 'unto the ages of the ages']. Plato contrasts χρόνος and αἰών, as we do time and eternity, and Aristotle says that eternity [αἰών] belongs to God.... The Scriptures have taught the doctrine of eternal punishment as clearly as their general style allows." The destiny of lost men is bound up with the destiny of evil angels in Mat. 25:41—"Depart from me, ye cursed, into the eternal fire which is prepared for the devil and his angels." If the latter are hopelessly lost, then the former are hopelessly lost also.

(d) In the great majority of Scripture passages where they occur, they have unmistakably the signification "everlasting." They are used to express the eternal duration of God, the Father, Son, and Holy Spirit (Rom. 16:26; 1 Tim. 1:17; Heb. 9:14; Rev. 1:18); the abiding presence of the Holy Spirit with all true believers (John 14:17); and the endlessness of the future happiness of the saints (Mat. 19:29; John 6:54, 58; 2 Cor. 9:9).

Rom. 16:26—"the commandment of the eternal God"; 1 Tim. 1:17—"Now unto the King eternal, incorruptible, invisible, the only God, be honor and glory for ever and ever"; Heb. 9:14—"the eternal Spirit"; Rev. 1:17, 18—"I am the first and the last, and the Living one; and I was dead, and behold, I am alive for evermore"; John 14:16, 17—"And I will pray the Father, and he shall give you another Comforter, that he may be with you for ever, even the Spirit of truth"; Mat. 19:29—"every one that hath left houses, or brethren, or sisters ... for my name's sake, shall receive a hundredfold, and shall inherit eternal life"; John 6:54, 58—"He that eateth my flesh and drinketh my blood hath eternal life.... he that eateth this bread shall live for ever"; 2 Cor. 9:9—"His righteousness abideth for ever"; cf. Dan. 7:18—"But the saints of the Most High shall receive the kingdom, and possess the kingdom for ever, even for ever and ever."

Everlasting punishment is sometimes said to be the punishment which takes place in, and belongs to, an αἰών, with no reference to duration. But President Woolsey declares, on the other hand, that "αἰώνιος cannot denote 'pertaining to an αἰών, or world period.' " The punishment of the wicked cannot cease, any more than Christ can cease to live, or the Holy Spirit to abide with believers; for all these are described in the same terms; "αἰώνιος is used in the N. T. 66 times,—51 times of the happiness of the righteous, 2 times of the duration of God and his glory, 6 times where there is no doubt as to its meaning 'eternal,' 7 times of the punishment of the wicked; αἰών is used 95 times,—55 times of unlimited duration, 31 times of duration that has limits, 9 times to denote the duration of future punishment." See Joseph Angus, in Expositor, Oct. 1887:274-286.

(e) The fact that the same word is used in Mat. 25:46 to describe both the sufferings of the wicked and the happiness of the righteous shows that the misery of the lost is eternal, in the same sense as the life of God or the blessedness of the saved.

Mat. 25:46—"And these shall go away into eternal punishment: but the righteous into eternal life." On this passage see Meyer: "The absolute idea of eternity, in respect to the punishments of hell, is not to be set aside, either by an appeal to the popular use of αἰώνιος, or by an appeal to the figurative term 'fire'; to the incompatibility of the idea of the eternal with that of moral evil and its punishment, or to the warning design of the representation; but it stands fast exegetically, by means of the contrasted ζωὴν αἰώνιον, which signifies the endless Messianic life."

(f) Other descriptions of the condemnation and suffering of the lost, excluding, as they do, all hope of repentance or forgiveness, render it certain that αἰών and αἰώνιος, in the passages referred to, describe a punishment that is without end.

Mat. 12:31, 32—"Every sin and blasphemy shall be forgiven unto men; but the blasphemy against the Spirit shall not be forgiven.... it shall not be forgiven him, neither in this world, nor in that which is to come"; 25:10—"and the door was shut"; Mark 3:29—"whosoever shall blaspheme against the Holy Spirit hath never forgiveness, but is guilty of an eternal sin"; 9:43, 48—"to go into hell, into the unquenchable fire ... where their worm dieth not, and the fire is not quenched"—not the dying worm but the undying worm; not the fire that is quenched, but the fire that is unquenchable; Luke 3:17—"the chaff he will burn up with unquenchable fire"; 16:26—"between us and you there is a great gulf fixed, that they that would pass from hence to you may not be able, and that none may cross over from thence to us"; John 3:36—"he that obeyeth not the Son shall not see life, but the wrath of God abideth on him."

Review of Farrar's Eternal Hope, in Bib. Sac., Oct. 1878:782—"The original meaning of the English word 'hell' and 'damn' was precisely that of the Greek words for which they stand. Their present meaning is widely different, but from what did it arise? It arose from the connotation imposed upon these words by the impression the Scriptures made on the popular mind. The present meaning of these words is involved in the Scripture, and cannot be removed by any mechanical process. Change the words, and in a few years 'judge' will have in the Bible the same force that 'damn' has at present. In fact, the words were not mistranslated, but the connotation of which Dr. Farrar complains has come upon them since, and that through the Scriptures. This proves what the general impression of Scripture upon the mind is, and shows how far Dr. Farrar has gone astray."

(g) While, therefore, we grant that we do not know the nature of eternity, or its relation to time, we maintain that the Scripture representations of future punishment forbid both the hypothesis of annihilation, and the hypothesis that suffering will end in restoration. Whatever eternity may be, Scripture renders it certain that after death there is no forgiveness.

We regard the argument against endless punishment drawn from αἰών and αἰώνιος as a purely verbal one which does not touch the heart of the question at issue. We append several utterances of its advocates. The Christian Union: "Eternal punishment is punishment in eternity, not throughout eternity; as temporal punishment is punishment in time, not throughout time." Westcott: "Eternal life is not an endless duration of being in time, but being of which time is not a measure. We have indeed no powers to grasp the idea except through forms and images of sense. These must be used, but we must not transfer them to realities of another order."

Farrar holds that ἀΐδιος, "everlasting", which occurs but twice in the N. T. (Rom. 1:20 and Jude 6), is not a synonym of αἰώνιος, "eternal", but the direct antithesis of it; the former being the unrealizable conception of endless time, and the latter referring to a state from which our imperfect human conception of time is absolutely excluded. Whiton, Gloria Patri, 145, claims that the perpetual immanence of God in conscience makes recovery possible after death; yet he speaks of the possibility that in the incorrigible sinner conscience may become extinct. To all these views we may reply with Schaff, Ch. History, 2:66—"After the general judgment we have nothing revealed but the boundless prospect of æonian life and æonian death.... Everlasting punishment of the wicked always was and always will be the orthodox theory."

For the view that αἰών and αἰώνιος are used in a limited sense, see De Quincey, Theological Essays, 1:126-146; Maurice, Essays, 436; Stanley, Life and Letters, 1:485-488; Farrar, Eternal Hope, 200; Smyth, Orthodox Theology of To-day, 118-123; Chambers, Life after Death; Whiton, Is Eternal Punishment Endless? For the common orthodox view, see Fisher and Tyler, in New Englander, March, 1878; Gould, in Bib. Sac., 1880:212-248; Princeton Review, 1873:620; Shedd, Doctrine of Endless Punishment, 12-117; Broadus, Com. on Mat. 25:45.

D. This everlasting punishment of the wicked is not inconsistent with God's justice, but is rather a revelation of that justice.

(a) We have seen in our discussion of Penalty (pages 652-656) that its object is neither reformatory nor deterrent, but simply vindicatory; in other words, that it primarily aims, not at the good of the offender, nor at the welfare of society, but at the vindication of law. We have also seen (pages 269, 291) that justice is not a form of benevolence, but is the expression and manifestation of God's holiness. Punishment, therefore, as the inevitable and constant reaction of that holiness against its moral opposite, cannot come to an end until guilt and sin come to an end.

The fundamental error of Universalism is its denial that penalty is vindicatory, and that justice is distinct from benevolence. See article on Universalism, in Johnson's Cyclopædia: "The punishment of the wicked, however severe or terrible it may be, is but a means to a beneficent end; not revengeful, but remedial; not for its own sake, but for the good of those who suffer its infliction." With this agrees Rev. H. W. Beecher: "I believe that punishment exists, both here and hereafter; but it will not continue after it ceases to do good. With a God who could give pain for pain's sake, this world would go out like a candle." But we reply that the doctrine of eternal punishment is not a doctrine of "pain for pain's sake," but of pain for holiness' sake. Punishment could have no beneficial effect upon the universe, or even upon the offender, unless it were just and right in itself. And if just and right in itself, then the reason for its continuance lies, not in any benefit to the universe, or to the sufferer, to accrue therefrom.

F. L. Patton, in Brit. and For. Ev. Rev., Jan. 1878:126-139, on the Philosophy of Punishment—"If the Universalist's position were true, we should expect to find some manifestations of love and pity and sympathy in the infliction of the dreadful punishments of the future. We look in vain for this, however. We read of God's anger, of his judgments, of his fury, of his taking vengeance; but we get no hint, in any passage which describes the sufferings of the next world, that they are designed to work the redemption and recovery of the soul. If the punishments of the wicked were chastisements, we should expect to see some bright outlook in the Bible-picture of the place of doom. A gleam of light, one might suppose, might make its way from the celestial city to this dark abode. The sufferers would catch some sweet refrain of heavenly music which would be a promise and prophecy of a far-off but coming glory. But there is a finality about the Scripture statements as to the condition of the lost, which is simply terrible."

The reason for punishment lies not in the benevolence, but in the holiness, of God. That holiness reveals itself in the moral constitution of the universe. It makes itself felt in conscience—imperfectly here, fully hereafter. The wrong merits punishment. The right binds, not because it is the expedient, but because it is the very nature of God. "But the great ethical significance of this word right will not be known," (we quote again from Dr. Patton,) "its imperative claims, its sovereign behests, its holy and imperious sway over the moral creation will not be understood, until we witness, during the lapse of the judgment hours, the terrible retribution which measures the ill- desert of wrong." When Dr. Johnson seemed overfearful as to his future, Boswell said to him: "Think of the mercy of your Savior." "Sir," replied Johnson, "my Savior has said that he will place some on his right hand, and some on his left."

A Universalist during our Civil War announced his conversion to Calvinism, upon the ground that hell was a military necessity. "In Rom. 12:19, 'vengeance,' ἐκδίκησις, means primarily 'vindication.' God will show to the sinner and to the universe that the apparent prosperity of evil was a delusion and a snare" (Crane, Religion of To-morrow, 319 note). That strange book, Letters from Hell, shows how memory may increase our knowledge of past evil deeds, but may lose the knowledge of God's promises. Since we retain most perfectly that which has been the subject of most constant thought, retribution may come to us through the operation of the laws of our own nature.

Jackson, James Martineau, 193-195—"Plato holds that the wise transgressor will seek, not shun, his punishment. James Martineau painted a fearful picture of the possible lashing of conscience. He regarded suffering for sin, though dreadful, yet as altogether desirable, not to be asked reprieve from, but to be prayed for: 'Smite, Lord; for thy mercy's sake, spare not!' The soul denied such suffering is not favored, but defrauded. It learns the truth of its condition, and the truth and the right of the universe are vindicated." The Connecticut preacher said: "My friends, some believe that all will be saved; but we hope for better things. Chaff and wheat are not to be together always. One goes to the garner, and the other to the furnace."

Shedd, Dogm. Theology, 2:755—"Luxurious ages and luxurious men recalcitrate at hell, and 'kick against the goad' (Acts 26:14). No theological doctrine is more important than eternal retribution to those modern nations which, like England, Germany and the United States, are growing rapidly in riches, luxury and earthly power. Without it, they will infallibly go down in that vortex of sensuality and wickedness that swallowed up Babylon and Rome. The bestial and shameless vice of the dissolute rich that has recently been uncovered in the commercial metropolis of the world is a powerful argument for the necessity and reality of 'the lake that burneth with fire and brimstone' (Rev. 21:8)." The conviction that after death there must be punishment for sin has greatly modified the older Universalism. There is little modern talk of all men, righteous and wicked alike, entering heaven the moment this life is ended. A purgatorial state must intervene. E. G. Robinson: "Universalism results from an exaggerated idea of the atonement. There is no genuine Universalism in our day. Restorationism has taken its place."

(b) But guilt, or ill-desert, is endless. However long the sinner may be punished, he never ceases to be ill-deserving. Justice, therefore, which gives to all according to their deserts, cannot cease to punish. Since the reason for punishment is endless, the punishment itself must be endless. Even past sins involve an endless guilt, to which endless punishment is simply the inevitable correlate.

For full statement of this argument that guilt, as never coming to an end, demands endless punishment, see Shedd, Doctrine of Endless Punishment, 118-163—"Suffering that is penal can never come to an end, because guilt is the reason for its infliction, and guilt once incurred, never ceases to be.... One sin makes guilt, and guilt makes hell." Man does not punish endlessly, because he does not take account of God. "Human punishment is only approximate and imperfect, not absolute and perfect like the divine. It is not adjusted exactly and precisely to the whole guilt of the offence, but is more or less modified, first, by not considering its relation to God's honor and majesty; secondly, by human ignorance of inward motives; and thirdly, by social expediency." But "hell is not a penitentiary.... The Lamb of God is also Lion of the tribe of Judah.... The human penalty that approaches nearest to the divine is capital punishment. This punishment has a kind of endlessness. Death is a finality. It forever separates the murderer from earthly society, even as future punishment separates forever from the society of God and heaven." See Martineau, Types, 2:65-69.

The lapse of time does not convert guilt into innocence. The verdict "Guilty for ten days" was Hibernian. Guilt is indivisible and untransferable. The whole of it rests upon the criminal at every moment. Richelieu: "All places are temples, and all seasons summer, for justice." George Eliot: "Conscience is harder than our enemies, knows more, accuses with more nicety." Shedd: "Sin is the only perpetual motion that has ever been discovered. A slip in youth, committed in a moment, entails lifelong suffering. The punishment nature inflicts is infinitely longer than the time consumed in the violation of law, yet the punishment is the legitimate outgrowth of the offence."

(c) Not only eternal guilt, but eternal sin, demands eternal punishment. So long as moral creatures are opposed to God, they deserve punishment. Since we cannot measure the power of the depraved will to resist God, we cannot deny the possibility of endless sinning. Sin tends evermore to reproduce itself. The Scriptures speak of an "eternal sin" (Mark 3:29). But it is just in God to visit endless sinning with endless punishment. Sin, moreover, is not only an act, but also a condition or state, of the soul; this state is impure and abnormal, involves misery; this misery, as appointed by God to vindicate law and holiness, is punishment; this punishment is the necessary manifestation of God's justice. Not the punishing, but the not-punishing, would impugn his justice; for if it is just to punish sin at all, it is just to punish it as long as it exists.

Mark 3:29—"whosoever shall blaspheme against the Holy Spirit hath never forgiveness, but is guilty of an eternal sin"; Rev. 22:11—"He that is unrighteous, let him do unrighteousness still; and he that is filthy, let him be made filthy still." Calvin: "God has the best reason for punishing everlasting sin everlastingly." President Dwight: "Every sinner is condemned for his first sin, and for every sin that follows, though they continue forever." What Martineau (Study, 2:106) says of this life, we may apply to the next: "Sin being there, it would be simply monstrous that there should be no suffering."

But we must remember that men are finally condemned, not merely for sins, but for sin; they are punished, not simply for acts of disobedience, but for evil character. The judgment is essentially a remanding of men to their "own place" (Acts 1:25). The soul that is permanently unlike God cannot dwell with God. The consciences of the wicked will justify their doom, and they will themselves prefer hell to heaven. He who does not love God is at war with himself, as well as with God, and cannot be at peace. Even though there were no positive inflictions from God's hand, the impure soul that has banished itself from the presence of God and from the society of the holy has in its own evil conscience a source of torment.

And conscience gives us a pledge of the eternity of this suffering. Remorse has no tendency to exhaust itself. The memory of an evil deed grows not less but more keen with time, and self- reproach grows not less but more bitter. Ever renewed affirmation of its evil decision presents to the soul forever new occasion for conviction and shame. F. W. Robertson speaks of "the infinite maddening of remorse." And Dr. Shedd, in the book above quoted, remarks: "Though the will to resist sin may die out of a man, the conscience to condemn it never can. This remains eternally. And when the process is complete; when the responsible creature, in the abuse of free agency, has perfected his ruin; when his will to good is all gone; there remain these two in his immortal spirit—sin and conscience, 'brimstone and fire' (Rev. 21:8)."

E. G. Robinson: "The fundamental argument for eternal punishment is the reproductive power of evil. In the divine law penalty enforces itself. Rom. 6:19—'ye presented your members as servants ... to iniquity unto iniquity.' Wherever sin occurs, penalty is inevitable. No man of sense would now hold to eternal punishment as an objective judicial infliction, and the sooner we give this up the better. It can be defended only on the ground of the reactionary power of elective preference, the reduplicating power of moral evil. We have no right to say that there are no other consequences of sin but natural ones; but, were this so, every word of threatening in Scripture would still stand. We shall never be as complete as if we never had sinned. We shall bear the scars of our sins forever. The eternal law of wrong-doing is that the wrong-doer is cursed thereby, and harpies and furies follow him into eternity. God does not need to send a policeman after the sinner; the sinner carries the policeman inside. God does not need to set up a whipping post to punish the sinner; the sinner finds a whipping post wherever he goes, and his own conscience applies the lash."

(d) The actual facts of human life and the tendencies of modern science show that this principle of retributive justice is inwrought into the elements and forces of the physical and moral universe. On the one hand, habit begets fixity of character, and in the spiritual world sinful acts, often repeated, produce a permanent state of sin, which the soul, unaided, cannot change. On the other hand, organism and environment are correlated to each other; and in the spiritual world, the selfish and impure find surroundings corresponding to their nature, while the surroundings react upon them and confirm their evil character. These principles, if they act in the next life as they do in this, will ensure increasing and unending punishment.

Gal. 6:7, 8—"Be not deceived; God is not mocked: for whatsoever a man soweth, that shall he also reap. For he that soweth unto his own flesh shall of the flesh reap corruption"; Rev. 21:11—"He that is unrighteous, let him do unrighteousness still: and he that is filthy, let him be made filthy still." Dr. Heman Lincoln, in an article on Future Retribution (Examiner, April 2, 1885)—speaks of two great laws of nature which confirm the Scripture doctrine of retribution. The first is that "the tendency of habit is towards a permanent state. The occasional drinker becomes a confirmed drunkard. One who indulges in oaths passes into a reckless blasphemer. The gambler who has wasted a fortune, and ruined his family, is a slave to the card-table. The Scripture doctrine of retribution is only an extension of this well-known law to the future life." The second of these laws is that "organism and environment must be in harmony. Through the vast domain of nature, every plant and tree and reptile and bird and mammal has organs and functions fitted to the climate and atmosphere of its habitat. If a sudden change occur in climate, from torrid to temperate, or from temperate to arctic; if the atmosphere change from dry to humid, or from carbonic vapors to pure oxygen, sudden death is certain to overtake the entire fauna and flora of the region affected, unless plastic nature changes the organism to conform to the new environment. The interpreters of the Bible find the same law ordained for the world to come. Surroundings must correspond to character. A soul in love with sin can find no place in a holy heaven. If the environment be holy, the character of the beings assigned to it must be holy also. Nature and Revelation are in perfect accord." See Drummond, Natural Law in the Spiritual World, chapters: Environment, Persistence of Type, and Degradation.

Hosea 13:9—"It is thy destruction, O Israel, that thou art against me, against thy help"—if men are destroyed, it is because they destroy themselves. Not God, but man himself, makes hell. Schurman: "External punishment is unthinkable of human sins." Jackson, James Martineau, 152—"Our light, such as we have, we carry with us; and he who in his soul knows not God is still in darkness though, like the angel in the Apocalypse, he were standing in the sun." Crane, Religion of To-morrow, 313—"To insure perpetual hunger deprive a man of nutritious food, and so long as he lives he will suffer; so pain will last so long as the soul is deprived of God, after the artificial stimulants of sin's pleasures have lost their effect. Death has nothing to do with it; for as long as the soul lives apart from God, whether on this or on another planet, it will be wretched. If the unrepentant sinner is immortal, his sufferings will be immortal." "Magnas inter opes, inops"—poverty-stricken amid great riches—his very nature compels him to suffer. Nor can he change his nature; for character, once set and hardened in this world, cannot be cast into the melting- pot and remoulded in the world to come. The hell of Robert G. Ingersoll is far more terrible than the orthodox hell. He declares that there is no forgiveness and no renewal. Natural law must have its way. Man is a Mazeppa bound to the wild horse of his passions; a Prometheus, into whose vitals remorse, like a vulture, is ever gnawing.

(e) As there are degrees of human guilt, so future punishment may admit of degrees, and yet in all those degrees be infinite in duration. The doctrine of everlasting punishment does not imply that, at each instant of the future existence of the lost, there is infinite pain. A line is infinite in length, but it is far from being infinite in breadth or thickness. "An infinite series may make only a finite sum; and infinite series may differ infinitely in their total amount." The Scriptures recognize such degrees in future punishment, while at the same time they declare it to be endless (Luke 12:47, 48; Rev. 20:12, 13).

Luke 12:47, 48—"And that servant who knew his Lord's will, and made not ready, nor did according to his will shall be beaten with many stripes; but he that knew not, and did things worthy of stripes, shall be beaten with few stripes"; Rev. 20:12, 13—"And I saw the dead, the great and the small, standing before the throne; and books were opened: and another book was opened, which is the book of life: and the dead were judged out of the things which were written in the books, according to their works ... judged every man according to their works."

(f) We know the enormity of sin only by God's own declarations with regard to it, and by the sacrifice which he has made to redeem us from it. As committed against an infinite God, and as having in itself infinite possibilities of evil, it may itself be infinite, and may deserve infinite punishment. Hell, as well as the Cross, indicates God's estimate of sin.

Cf. Ez. 14:23—"ye shall know that I have not done without cause all that I have done in it, saith the Lord Jehovah." Valuable as the vine is for its fruit, it is fit only for fuel when it is barren. Every single sin, apart from the action of divine grace, is the sign of pervading and permanent apostasy. But there is no single sin. Sin is a germ of infinite expansion. The single sin, left to itself, would never cease in its effects of evil,—it would dethrone God. "The idea of disproportion between sin and its punishment grows out of a belittling of sin and its guilt. One who regards murder as a slight offence will think hanging an outrageous injustice. Theodore Parker hated the doctrine of eternal punishment, because he considered sin as only a provocation to virtue, a step toward triumph, a fall upwards, good in the making." But it is only when we regard its relation to God that we can estimate sin's ill desert. See Edwards the younger, Works, 1:1-294.

Dr. Shedd maintains that the guilt of sin is infinite, because it is measured, not by the powers of the offender, but by the majesty of the God against whom it is committed; see his Dogm. Theology, 2:740, 749—"Crime depends upon the object against whom it is committed, as well as upon the subject who commits it.... To strike is a voluntary act, but to strike a post or a stone is not a culpable act.... Killing a dog is as bad as killing a man, if merely the subject who kills and not the object killed is considered.... As God is infinite, offence against him is infinite in its culpability.... Any man who, in penitent faith, avails himself of the vicarious method of setting himself right with the eternal Nemesis, will find that it succeeds; but he who rejects it must through endless cycles grapple with the dread problem of human guilt in his own person, and alone."

Quite another view is taken by others, as for example E. G. Robinson, Christian Theology, 292—

"The notion that the qualities of a finite act can be infinite—that its qualities can be derived from the person to whom the act is directed rather than from the motives that prompt it, needs no refutation. The notion itself, one of the bastard thoughts of mediæval metaphysical theology, has maintained its position in respectable society solely by the services it has been regarded as capable of rendering." Simon, Reconciliation, 123—"To represent sins as infinite, because God against whom they are committed is infinite, logically requires us to say that trust or reverence or love towards God are infinite, because God is infinite." We therefore regard it as more correct to say, that sin as a finite act demands finite punishment, but as endlessly persisted in demands an endless, and in that sense an infinite, punishment.

E. This everlasting punishment of the wicked is not inconsistent with God's benevolence.

It is maintained, however, by many who object to eternal retribution, that benevolence requires God not to inflict punishment upon his creatures except as a means of attaining some higher good. We reply:

(a) God is not only benevolent but holy, and holiness is his ruling attribute. The vindication of God's holiness is the primary and sufficient object of punishment. This constitutes a good which fully justifies the infliction.

Even love has dignity, and rejected love may turn blessing into cursing. Love for holiness involves hatred of unholiness. The love of God is not a love without character. Dorner: "Love may not throw itself away.... We have no right to say that punishment is just only when it is the means of amendment." We must remember that holiness conditions love (see pages 296-298). Robert Buchanan forgot God's holiness when he wrote: "If there is doom for one, Thou, Maker, art undone!" Shakespeare, King John, 4:3—"Beyond the infinite and boundless reach Of mercy, if thou didst this deed of death, Art thou damned, Hubert!" Tennyson: "He that shuts Love out, in turn shall be Shut out from Love, and on the threshold lie Howling in utter darkness." Theodore Parker once tried to make peace between Wendell Phillips and Horace Mann, whom Phillips had criticized with his accustomed severity. Mann wrote to Parker: "What a good man you are! I am sure nobody would be damned if you were at the head of the universe. But," he continued, "I will never treat a man with respect whom I do not respect, be the consequences what they may—so help me—Horace Mann!" (Chadwick, Theodore Parker, 330). The spirit which animated Horace Mann may not have been the spirit of love, but we can imagine a case in which his words might be the utterance of love as well as of righteousness. For love is under law to righteousness, and only righteous love is true love.

(b) In this life, God's justice does involve certain of his creatures in sufferings which are of no advantage to the individuals who suffer; as in the case of penalties which do not reform, and of afflictions which only harden and embitter. If this be a fact here, it may be a fact hereafter.

There are many sufferers on earth, in prisons and on sick-beds, whose suffering results in hardness of heart and enmity to God. The question is not a question of quantity, but of quality. It is a question whether any punishment at all is consistent with God's benevolence,—any punishment, that is to say, which does not result in good to the punished. This we maintain; and claim that God is bound to punish moral impurity, whether any good comes therefrom to the impure or not. Archbishop Whately says it is as difficult to change one atom of lead to silver as it is to change a whole mountain. If the punishment of many incorrigibly impenitent persons is consistent with God's benevolence, so is the punishment of one incorrigibly impenitent person; if the punishment of incorrigibly impenitent persons for eternity is inconsistent with God's benevolence, so is the punishment of such persons for a limited time, or for any time at all.

In one of his early stories William Black represents a sour- tempered Scotchman as protesting against the idea that a sinner he has in mind should be allowed to escape the consequences of his acts: "What's the good of being good," he asks, "if things are to turn out that way?" The instinct of retribution is the strongest instinct of the human heart. It is bound up with our very intuition of God's existence, so that to deny its rightfulness is to deny that there is a God. There is "a certain fearful expectation of judgment" (Heb. 10:27) for ourselves and for others, in case of persistent transgression, without which the very love of God would cease to inspire respect. Since neither annihilation nor second probation is Scriptural, our only relief in contemplating the doctrine of eternal punishment must come from: 1. the fact that eternity is not endless time, but a state inconceivable to us; and 2. the fact that evolution suggests reversion to the brute as the necessary consequence of abusing freedom.

(c) The benevolence of God, as concerned for the general good of the universe, requires the execution of the full penalty of the law upon all who reject Christ's salvation. The Scriptures intimate that God's treatment of human sin is matter of instruction to all moral beings. The self-chosen ruin of the few may be the salvation of the many.

Dr. Joel Parker, Lectures on Universalism, speaks of the security of free creatures as attained through a gratitude for deliverance "kept alive by a constant example of some who are suffering the vengeance of eternal fire." Our own race may be the only race (of course the angels are not a "race") that has fallen away from God. As through the church the manifold wisdom of God is made manifest "to principalities and powers in the heavenly places" (Eph. 3:10); so, through the punishment of the lost,

God's holiness may be made known to a universe that without it might have no proof so striking, that sin is moral suicide and ruin, and that God's holiness is its irreconcilable antagonist.

With regard to the extent and scope of hell, we quote the words of Dr. Shedd, in the book already mentioned: "Hell is only a spot in the universe of God. Compared with heaven, hell is narrow and limited. The kingdom of Satan is insignificant, in contrast with the kingdom of Christ. In the immense range of God's dominion, good is the rule and evil is the exception. Sin is a speck upon the infinite azure of eternity; a spot on the sun. Hell is only a corner of the universe. The Gothic etymon denotes a covered-up hole. In Scripture, hell is a 'pit,' a 'lake'; not an ocean. It is 'bottomless,' not boundless. The Gnostic and Dualistic theories which make God, and Satan or the Demiurge, nearly equal in power and dominion, find no support in Revelation. The Bible teaches that there will always be some sin and death in the universe. Some angels and men will forever be the enemies of God. But their number, compared with that of unfallen angels and redeemed men, is small. They are not described in the glowing language and metaphors by which the immensity of the holy and blessed is delineated (Ps. 68:17; Deut. 32:2; Ps. 103:21; Mat. 6:13; 1 Cor. 15:25; Rev. 14:1; 21:16, 24, 25.) The number of the lost spirits is never thus emphasized and enlarged upon. The brief, stern statement is, that 'the fearful and unbelieving ... their part shall be in the lake that burneth with fire and brimstone' (Rev. 21:8). No metaphors and amplifications are added to make the impression of an immense 'multitude which no man can number.' " Dr. Hodge: "We have reason to believe that the lost will bear to the saved no greater proportion than the inmates of a prison do to the mass of a community."

The North American Review engaged Dr. Shedd to write an article vindicating eternal punishment, and also engaged Henry Ward Beecher to answer it. The proof sheets of Dr. Shedd's article were sent to Mr. Beecher, whereupon he telegraphed from Denver to the Review: "Cancel engagement, Shedd is too much for me. I half believe in eternal punishment now myself. Get somebody else." The article in reply was never written, and Dr. Shedd remained unanswered.

(d) The present existence of sin and punishment is commonly admitted to be in some way consistent with God's benevolence, in that it is made the means of revealing God's justice and mercy. If the temporary existence of sin and punishment lead to good, it is entirely possible that their eternal existence may lead to yet greater good.

A priori, we should have thought it impossible for God to permit moral evil,—heathenism, prostitution, the saloon, the African slave-trade. But sin is a fact. Who can say how long it will be a fact? Why not forever? The benevolence that permits it now may permit it through eternity. And yet, if permitted through eternity, it can be made harmless only by visiting it with eternal punishment. Lillie on Thessalonians, 457—"If the temporary existence of sin and punishment lead to good, how can we prove that their eternal existence may not lead to greater good?" We need not deny that it causes God real sorrow to banish the lost. Christ's weeping over Jerusalem expresses the feelings of God's heart: Mat. 23:37, 38—"O Jerusalem, Jerusalem, that killeth the prophets, and stoneth them that are sent unto her! how often would I have gathered thy children together, even as a hen gathered her chickens under her wings, and ye would not! Behold, your house is left unto you desolate"; cf. Hosea 11:8—"How shall I give thee up, Ephraim? how shall I cast thee off, Israel? how shall I make thee as Admah? how shall I set thee as Zeboiim? my heart is turned within me, my compassions are kindled together." Dante, Hell, iii—the inscription over the gate of Hell: "Justice the founder of my fabric moved; To rear me was the task of power divine, Supremest wisdom and primeval love."

A. H. Bradford, Age of Faith, 254, 267—"If one thinks of the Deity as an austere monarch, having a care for his own honor but none for those to whom he has given being, optimism is impossible. For what shall we say of our loved ones who have committed sins? That splendid boy who yielded to an inherited tendency—what has become of him? Those millions who with little light and mighty passions have gone wrong—what of them? Those countless myriads who peopled the earth in ages past and had no clear motive to righteousness, since their perception of God was dim—is this all that can be said of them: In torment they are exhibiting the glorious holiness of the Almighty in his hatred of sin? Some may believe that, but, thank God, the number is not large.... No, penalty, remorse, despair, are only signs of the deep remedial force in the nature of things, which has always been at work and always will be, and which, unless counteracted, will result sometime in universal and immortal harmony.... Retribution is a natural law; it is universal in its sweep; it is at the same time a manifestation of the beneficence that pervades the universe. This law must continue its operation so long as one free agent violates the moral order. Neither justice nor love would be honored if one soul were allowed to escape the action of that law. But the sting in retribution is ordained to be remedial and restorative rather than punitive and vengeful.... Will any forever resist that discipline? We know not; but it is difficult to understand how any can be willing to do so, when the fulness of the divine glory is revealed."

(e) As benevolence in God seems in the beginning to have permitted moral evil, not because sin was desirable in itself, but only because it was incident to a system which provided for the highest possible freedom and holiness in the creature; so benevolence in God may to the end permit the existence of sin and may continue to punish the sinner, undesirable as these things are in themselves, because they are incidents of a system which provides for the highest possible freedom and holiness in the creature through eternity.

But the condition of the lost is only made more hopeless by the difficulty with which God brings himself to this, his "strange work" of punishment (Is. 28:21). The sentence which the judge pronounces with tears is indicative of a tender and suffering heart, but it also indicates that there can be no recall. By the very exhibition of "eternal judgment" (Heb. 6:2), not only may a greater number be kept true to God, but a higher degree of holiness among that number be forever assured. The Endless Future, published by South. Meth. Pub. House, supposes the universe yet in its infancy, an eternal liability to rebellion, an ever-growing creation kept from sin by one example of punishment. Mat. 7:13, 14—"few there be that find it"—"seems to have been intended to describe the conduct of men then living, rather than to foreshadow the two opposite currents of human life to the end of time"; see Hovey, Bib. Eschatology, 167. See Goulburn, Everlasting Punishment; Haley, The Hereafter of Sin.

A. H. Bradford, Age of Faith, 239, mentions as causes for the modification of view as to everlasting punishment: 1. Increased freedom in expression of convictions; 2. Interpretation of the word "eternal"; 3. The doctrine of the immanence of God,—if God is in every man, then he cannot everlastingly hate himself, even in the poor manifestation of himself in a human creature; 4. The influence of the poets, Burns, Browning, Tennyson, and Whittier. Whittier, Eternal Goodness: "The wrong that pains my soul below, I dare not throne above: I know not of his hate,—I know His goodness and his love." We regard Dr. Bradford as the most plausible advocate of restoration. But his view is vitiated by certain untenable theological presuppositions: 1. that righteousness is only a form of love; 2. that righteousness, apart from love, is passionate and vengeful; 3. that man's freedom is incapable of endless abuse; 4. that not all men here have a fair probation; 5. that the amount of light against which they sin is not taken into consideration by God; 6. that the immanence of God does not leave room for free human action; 7. that God's object in his administration is, not to reveal his whole character, and chiefly his holiness, but solely to reveal his love; 8. that the declarations of Scripture with regard to "an eternal sin" (Mark 3:29), "eternal punishment" (Mat. 25:46), "eternal destruction" (2 Thess. 1:9), still permit us to believe in the restoration of all men to holiness and likeness to God.

We regard as more Scriptural and more rational the view of Max Müller, the distinguished Oxford philologist: "I have always held that this would be a miserable universe without eternal punishment. Every act, good or evil, must carry its consequences, and the fact that our punishment will go on forever seems to me a proof of the everlasting love of God. For an evil deed to go unpunished would be to destroy the moral order of the universe." Max Müller simply expresses the ineradicable conviction of mankind that retribution must follow sin; that God must show his disapproval of sin by punishment; that the very laws of man's nature express in this way God's righteousness; that the abolition of this order would be the dethronement of God and the destruction of the universe.

F. The proper preaching of the doctrine of everlasting punishment is not a hindrance to the success of the gospel.

The proper preaching of the doctrine of everlasting punishment is not a hindrance to the success of the gospel, but is one of its chief and indispensable auxiliaries.—It is maintained by some, however, that, because men are naturally repelled by it, it cannot be a part of the preacher's message. We reply:

(a) If the doctrine be true, and clearly taught in Scripture, no fear of consequences to ourselves or to others can absolve us from the duty of preaching it. The minister of Christ is under obligation to preach the whole truth of God; if he does this, God will care for the results.

Ez. 2:7—"And thou shalt speak my words unto them, whether they will hear, or whether they will forbear"; 3:10, 11, 18, 19—"Moreover he said unto me, Son of man, all my words that I shall speak unto thee receive in thine heart, and hear with thine ears. And go, get thee to them of the captivity, unto the children of thy people, and speak unto them, and tell them, Thus saith the Lord Jehovah; whether they will hear, or whether they will forbear.... When I say unto the wicked, Thou shalt surely die; and thou givest him not warning, nor speakest to warn the wicked from his wicked way, to save his life; the same wicked man shall die in his iniquity; but his blood will I require at thy hand. Yet if thou warn the wicked, and he turn not from his wickedness, nor from his wicked way, he shall die in his iniquity; but thou hast delivered thy soul."

The old French Protestant church had as a coat of arms the device of an anvil, around which were many broken hammers, with this motto: "Hammer away, ye hostile bands; Your hammers break, God's anvil stands." St. Jerome: "If an offence come out of the truth, better is it that the offence come, than that the truth be concealed." Shedd, Dogm. Theology, 2:680—"Jesus Christ is the Person responsible for the doctrine of eternal perdition." The most fearful utterances with regard to future punishment are those of Jesus himself, as for example, Mat. 23:33—"Ye serpents, ye offspring of vipers, how shall ye escape the judgment of hell?" Mark 3:29—"whosoever shall blaspheme against the Holy Spirit hath never forgiveness, but is guilty of an eternal sin"; Mat. 10:28—"be not afraid of them that kill the body, but are not able to kill the soul: but rather fear him who is able to destroy both soul and body in hell"; 25:46—"these shall go away into eternal punishment."

(b) All preaching which ignores the doctrine of eternal punishment just so far lowers the holiness of God, of which eternal punishment is an expression, and degrades the work of Christ, which was needful to save us from it. The success of such preaching can be but temporary, and must be followed by a disastrous reaction toward rationalism and immorality.

Much apostasy from the faith begins with refusal to accept the doctrine of eternal punishment. Theodore Parker, while he acknowledged that the doctrine was taught in the New Testament, rejected it, and came at last to say of the whole theology which includes this idea of endless punishment, that it "sneers at common sense, spits upon reason, and makes God a devil."

But, if there be no eternal punishment, then man's danger was not great enough to require an infinite sacrifice; and we are compelled to give up the doctrine of atonement. If there were no atonement, there was no need that man's Savior should himself be more than man; and we are compelled to give up the doctrine of the deity of Christ, and with this that of the Trinity. If punishment be not eternal, then God's holiness is but another name for benevolence; all proper foundation for morality is gone, and God's law ceases to inspire reverence and awe. If punishment be not eternal, then the Scripture writers who believed and taught this were fallible men who were not above the prejudices and errors of their times; and we lose all evidence of the divine inspiration of the Bible. With this goes the doctrine of miracles; God is identified with nature, and becomes the impersonal God of pantheism.

Theodore Parker passed through this process, and so did Francis W. Newman. Logically, every one who denies the everlasting punishment of the wicked ought to reach a like result; and we need only a superficial observation of countries like India, where pantheism is rife, to see how deplorable is the result in the decline of public and of private virtue. Emory Storrs: "When hell drops out of religion, justice drops out of politics." The preacher who talks lightly of sin and punishment does a work strikingly analogous to that of Satan, when he told Eve: "Ye shall not surely die" (Gen. 3:4). Such a preacher lets men go on what Shakespeare calls "the primrose way to the everlasting bonfire" (Macbeth, 2:3).

Shedd, Dogm. Theology, 2:671—"Vicarious atonement is incompatible with universal salvation. The latter doctrine implies that suffering for sin is remedial only, while the former implies that it is retribution.... If the sinner himself is not obliged by justice to suffer in order to satisfy the law he has violated, then certainly no one needs suffer for him for this purpose." Sonnet by Michael Angelo: "Now hath my life across a stormy sea Like a frail bark reached that wide port where all Are bidden, ere the final reckoning fall Of good and evil for eternity. Now know I well how that fond fantasy, Which made my soul the worshiper and thrall Of earthly art, is vain; how criminal Is that which all men seek unwillingly. Those amorous thoughts that were so lightly dressed—What are they when the double death is nigh? The one I know for sure, the other dread. Painting nor sculpture now can lull to rest My soul that turns to his great Love on high, Whose arms, to clasp us, on the Cross were spread."

(c) The fear of future punishment, though not the highest motive, is yet a proper motive, for the renunciation of sin and the turning to Christ. It must therefore be appealed to, in the hope that the seeking of salvation which begins in fear of God's anger may end in the service of faith and love.

Luke 12:4, 5—"And I say unto you my friends, Be not afraid of them that kill the body, and after that have no more that they can do. But I will warn you whom ye shall fear: Fear him, who after he hath killed hath power to cast into hell; yea, I say unto you, Fear him"; Jude 23—"and some save, snatching them out of the fire." It is noteworthy that the Old Testament, which is sometimes regarded, though incorrectly, as a teacher of fear, has no such revelations of hell as are found in the New. Only when God's mercy was displayed in the Cross were there opened to men's view the depths of the abyss from which the Cross was to save them. And, as we have already seen, it is not Peter or Paul, but our Lord himself, who gives the most fearful descriptions of the suffering of the lost, and the clearest assertions of its eternal duration.

Michael Angelo's picture of the Last Judgment is needed to prepare us for Raphael's picture of the Transfiguration. Shedd, Dogm. Theology, 2:752—"What the human race needs is to go to the divine Confessional.... Confession is the only way to light and peace.... The denial of moral evil is the secret of the murmuring and melancholy with which so much of modern letters is filled." Matthew Arnold said to his critics: "Non me tua fervida terrent dicta; Dii me terrent et Jupiter hostis"—"I am not afraid of your violent judgments; I fear only God and his anger." Heb. 10:31—"It is a fearful thing to fall into the hands of the living God." Daniel Webster said: "I want a minister to drive me into a corner of the pew, and make me feel that the devil is after me."

(d) In preaching this doctrine, while we grant that the material images used in Scripture to set forth the sufferings of the lost are to be spiritually and not literally interpreted, we should still insist that the misery of the soul which eternally hates God is greater than the physical pains which are used to symbolize it. Although a hard and mechanical statement of the truth may only awaken opposition, a solemn and feeling presentation of it upon proper occasions, and in its due relation to the work of Christ and the offers of the gospel, cannot fail to accomplish God's purpose in preaching, and to be the means of saving some who hear.

Acts 20:31—"Wherefore watch ye, remembering that by the space of three years I ceased not to admonish every one night and day with tears"; 2 Cor. 2:14-17—"But thanks be unto God, who always leadeth us in triumph in Christ, and maketh manifest through us the savor of his knowledge in every place. For we are a sweet savor of Christ unto God, in them that are being saved, and in them that are perishing; to the one a savor from death unto death; to the other a savor from life unto life. And who is sufficient for these things? For we are not as the many, corrupting the word of God: but as of sincerity, but as of God, in the sight of God, speak we in Christ"; 5:11—"Knowing therefore the fear of the Lord, we persuade men, but we are made manifest unto God; and I hope that we are made manifest also in your consciences"; 1 Tim. 4:16—"Take heed to thyself and to thy teaching. Continue in these things; for in doing this thou shalt save both thyself and them that hear thee."

"Omne simile claudicat" as well as "volat"—"Every simile halts as well as flies." No symbol expresses all the truth. Yet we need to use symbols, and the Holy Spirit honors our use of them. It is "God's good pleasure through the foolishness of the preaching to save them that believe" (1 Cor. 1:21). It was a deep sense of his responsibility for men's souls that moved Paul to say: "woe is unto me, if I preach not the gospel" (1 Cor. 9:16). And it was a deep sense of duty fulfilled that enabled George Fox, when he was dying, to say: "I am clear! I am clear!"

So Richard Baxter wrote: "I preached as never sure to preach again. And as a dying man to dying men." It was Robert McCheyne who said that the preacher ought never to speak of everlasting punishment without tears. McCheyne's tearful preaching of it prevailed upon many to break from their sins and to accept the pardon and renewal that are offered in Christ. Such preaching of judgment and punishment were never needed more than now, when lax and unscriptural views with regard to law and sin break the force of the preacher's appeals. Let there be such preaching, and then many a hearer will utter the thought, if not the words, of the Dies Iræ, 8-10—"Rex tremendæ majestatis, Qui salvandos salvas gratis, Salva me, fons pietatis. Recordare, Jesu pie, Quod sum causa tuæ viæ: Ne me perdas ilia die. Quærens me sedisti lassus, Redemisti crucem passus: Tautus labor non sit cassus." See Edwards, Works, 4:226-321; Hodge, Outlines of Theology, 459-468; Murphy, Scientific Bases of Faith, 310, 319, 464; Dexter, Verdict of Reason; George, Universalism not of the Bible; Angus, Future Punishment; Jackson, Bampton Lectures for 1875, on the Doctrine of Retribution; Shedd, Doctrine of Endless Punishment, preface, and Dogm. Theol., 2:667-754.

www.ingramcontent.com/pod-product-compliance
Lightning Source LLC
LaVergne TN
LVHW010936100826
845153LV00001B/54

* 9 7 8 1 7 7 3 5 6 0 4 1 0 *